Donald Haagen

Frontispiece (overleaf):
American Commissioners at the Preliminary Peace Negotiations with Great Britain, Paris, 1782, unfinished painting by Benjamin West (1782). Representing the United States at the negotiations for a treaty concluding the Revolutionary War were, left to right, John Jay, John Adams, Benjamin Franklin, Henry Laurens, and William Temple Franklin. The first four signed the preliminary articles on November 20, 1782, but only Jay, Adams, and Franklin signed the definitive Peace of Paris of September 3, 1783.

Courtesy, Henry Francis du Pont Winterthur Museum.

SCOTT, FORESMAN AND COMPANY

THE DEMOCRATIC EXPERIENCE

A SHORT AMERICAN HISTORY

Louis B. Wright
The Folger Shakespeare Library

Clarence L. Ver Steeg
Northwestern University

Russel B. Nye
Michigan State University

Holman Hamilton
University of Kentucky

David M. Potter
Stanford University

Vincent P. De Santis
University of Notre Dame

William H. Harbaugh
Bucknell University

Arthur S. Link
Princeton University

Thomas C. Cochran
University of Pennsylvania

Carl N. Degler
Vassar College

CHICAGO   ATLANTA   DALLAS   PALO ALTO   FAIR LAWN, N.J.

ACKNOWLEDGMENTS: Frontispiece, Courtesy, Henry Francis du Pont Winterthur Museum; Page 3, State of Maryland; Page 4, The Pennsylvania Academy of the Fine Arts; Page 5 (left), Courtesy, Museum of Fine Arts, Boston; Page 5 (right), Courtesy, Historical Society of Pennsylvania; Page 63, Courtesy, New York Historical Society; Page 64, Courtesy, New York Historical Society; Page 65, In the Collection of the Corcoran Gallery of Art; Page 121, Mellon Collection, National Gallery of Art, Washington, D.C.; Page 122, Gift of Mrs. Huttleston Rogers, National Gallery of Art, Washington, D.C.; Page 123, Collection, City Art Museum of St. Louis; Page 175, The Newberry Library, Chicago; Page 176, The Metropolitan Museum of Art, Gift of Mrs. Frank B. Porter, 1922; Page 177 (left), Yale University Art Gallery, Mable Brady Garvan Collection; Page 177 (right), Courtesy, Chicago Historical Society; Page 235, Courtesy, University of Chicago; Page 236 (left), The Metropolitan Museum of Art, Gift of Lyman G. Bloomingdale, 1901; Page 236 (right), Courtesy, University of Pennsylvania; Page 237, Collection of the Detroit Institute of Arts; Page 287, Courtesy National Park Service, Washington, D.C.; Page 288, Collection of the Whitney Museum of American Art, New York; Page 289 (left), Courtesy, U.S. Naval Academy Museum; Page 289 (right), The Los Angeles County Museum of Art; Page 349, Courtesy, Franklin D. Roosevelt Library; Page 350, Courtesy of Armand G. Erpf, New York; Page 351 (left), Gift of Edith and Milton Lowenthal in memory of Juliana Force, Collection of the Whitney Museum of American Art, New York; Page 351 (right), Courtesy, The Art Institute of Chicago; Page 407, Courtesy, The Eisenhower Museum; Page 408 (left), Courtesy, The Art Institute of Chicago; Page 408 (right), Courtesy, The Art Institute of Chicago; Page 409 (left), Collection of the Whitney Museum of American Art, New York; Page 409 (right), Collection, The Museum of Modern Art, New York.

Library of Congress Catalog No. 63-17123

Copyright © 1963 by SCOTT, FORESMAN AND COMPANY

Printed in the United States of America

PREFACE

■ In recent years there has been a growing need in colleges and universities for a concise yet scholarly textbook of American history. Not only has the number of short introductory courses continued to increase, but many instructors of longer courses have come to prefer a brief text that will permit generous assignments of "outside readings" in documentary materials, historical monographs, anthologies, and library collections. In the judgment of the authors and publishers of *The Democratic Experience,* none of the texts previously available have been wholly satisfactory in meeting the requirements of such courses.

The writing of a succinct yet scholarly history of the United States presents special problems. Because the amount of historical detail that can be included in a short text is necessarily limited, a careful decision must be made as to which facts are essential to the understanding of a particular topic, which ones can be safely omitted. To balance this selective approach to detail, expert knowledge and authority must be applied to the interpretation and analysis of each historical period and event. Only thus can a brief text satisfy both the needs of students and the demands of instructors.

The publishers of *The Democratic Experience* believe they have found a solution to these problems in the collaboration of a number of historians, each writing about the particular period or aspect of American history in which he is a specialist. In preparing the manuscript, the individual authors determined the material and approach they would use in their own sections of the text, while drawing on the advice and critical suggestions of their colleagues to make sure that every section would be well integrated with the whole. Important decisions regarding division of subject matter, historical approach, and the inclusion or exclusion of historical detail were reached through discussion and agreement among the various contributors. (Although many chapters were assigned beginning and ending dates for convenience's sake, the authors reached beyond these dates when it was generally agreed that certain subjects could be better handled in one part than in another.) Thus, the book as a whole reflects the collective judgment of the various scholars who have participated in its planning and writing, while each part displays its author's own intellectual and literary individuality.

The contributors have been encouraged to apply their interpretive powers in recounting the American chronicle. Within the framework of facts basic to a sound knowledge of American history, they have focused on the evolution of our nation's institutions and ideas. In the view of both authors and publishers, knowledge of the mere *existence* of certain institutions and ideas in the past is far less important to the student than an understanding of the *processes* by which these institutions developed and changed. It is such understanding that will help the student to take an intelligent and responsible approach to the problems of his present world.

To facilitate the telling of the American story, each of the eight parts of *The Democratic Experience* has been organized into three chapters. The first two chapters of each part cover the basic political and economic history of the period under consideration; the third (Chapters 3, 6, 9, 12, 15, 18, 21, and 24) focuses on its intellectual and cultural history—the "spirit of the times." For example, the student is introduced to Puritanism, Romanticism, and social Darwinism, as they developed in American intellectual and cultural life and as they were related to political and economic events of the period. But although the "third chapters" will enrich the student's understanding of American history, they are not essential to the continuity of the narrative and may be left unassigned by the instructor who, in offering a short course, prefers to concentrate on political and economic history.

THE PUBLISHERS

CONTENTS

PART 1   **THE FOUNDING OF AMERICA: Louis B. Wright and Clarence L. Ver Steeg**

	INTRODUCTION	2
Chapter 1	EVOLUTION OF THE AMERICAN COLONIES	6
Chapter 2	REVOLUTION AND INDEPENDENCE, 1763–1783	26
Chapter 3	PATTERNS OF COLONIAL CULTURE	46
	Bibliography	59

PART 2   **THE YOUNG REPUBLIC: Russel B. Nye**

	INTRODUCTION	62
Chapter 4	THE CONSTITUTION AND THE FEDERALISTS, 1783–1800	66
Chapter 5	THE JEFFERSONIAN ERA, 1800–1824	88
Chapter 6	THE EMERGENCE OF A NATIONAL CULTURE	107
	Bibliography	119

PART 3   **DEMOCRACY AND MANIFEST DESTINY: Holman Hamilton**

	INTRODUCTION	120
Chapter 7	GROWTH OF DEMOCRATIC GOVERNMENT, 1824–1848	124
Chapter 8	WESTWARD EXPANSION AND ECONOMIC GROWTH, 1824–1848	141
Chapter 9	THE AMERICAN RENAISSANCE	162
	Bibliography	173

PART 4   **A HOUSE DIVIDED: David M. Potter**

	INTRODUCTION	174
Chapter 10	THE SECTIONAL CRISIS, 1848–1861	178
Chapter 11	CIVIL WAR AND RECONSTRUCTION, 1861–1877	199
Chapter 12	THE CHANGING NATION	222
	Bibliography	231

PART 5   **THE AGE OF INDUSTRIALISM: Vincent P. De Santis**

	INTRODUCTION	234
Chapter 13	INDUSTRIALISM AND URBANIZATION, 1865–1900	238
Chapter 14	THE POLITICS OF CONSERVATISM AND DISSENT, 1877–1900	256
Chapter 15	INDUSTRIALISM AND AMERICAN CULTURE	274
	Bibliography	285

PART 6   **THE EMERGENCE OF A MODERN NATION: William H. Harbaugh and Arthur S. Link**

	INTRODUCTION	286
Chapter 16	THE FORGING OF MODERN GOVERNMENT, 1900–1917	290
Chapter 17	THE RISE OF AMERICA AS A WORLD POWER, 1898–1919	310
Chapter 18	CULTURE AND THOUGHT IN THE PROGRESSIVE ERA	331
	Bibliography	346

PART 7   **BETWEEN TWO WARS: Thomas C. Cochran**

	INTRODUCTION	348
Chapter 19	PROSPERITY IN ISOLATION, 1919–1929	352
Chapter 20	THE GREAT DEPRESSION AND THE NEW DEAL, 1930–1941	371
Chapter 21	THE AGE OF ANALYSIS	393
	Bibliography	405

PART 8   **THE GLOBAL CONFLICT: Carl N. Degler**

	INTRODUCTION	406
Chapter 22	THE PRICE OF POWER, 1941–1948	410
Chapter 23	THE AGE OF COLD WAR, 1948–	431
Chapter 24	TOWARD 2000: THEMES OF CONCERN	453
	Bibliography	465

APPENDICES

THE DECLARATION OF INDEPENDENCE	x
THE CONSTITUTION OF THE UNITED STATES OF AMERICA	xii
PRESIDENTS, VICE-PRESIDENTS, AND CABINET MEMBERS	xxii
PARTY DISTRIBUTION IN CONGRESS	xxvi
JUSTICES OF THE UNITED STATES SUPREME COURT	xxviii
SOVEREIGNS OF ENGLAND AND GREAT BRITAIN, 1485–1820: Some Historical Notes	xxix
PRESIDENTIAL ELECTIONS: ELECTORAL AND POPULAR VOTE	xxx
POPULATION OF THE UNITED STATES, 1790–1960	xxxiv

INDEX xxxvi

MAPS AND CHARTS

ENGLISH COLONIES	15
MAJOR REVOLUTIONARY CAMPAIGNS	39
STATE CLAIMS TO WESTERN LANDS, 1780	43
NORTHWEST TERRITORY	69
LOUISIANA PURCHASE	89
MISSOURI COMPROMISE, 1820	103
ELECTION OF 1824	125
ELECTION OF 1828	127
ELECTION OF 1840	137
WESTERN EXPLORATIONS	143
WESTERN TRAILS	144
OREGON BOUNDARY DISPUTE	148
MEXICAN WAR	152
TERRITORIAL GROWTH OF THE UNITED STATES, 1783–1853	155
COMPROMISE OF 1850	185
KANSAS-NEBRASKA ACT, 1854	188
ELECTION OF 1860	195
THE UNITED STATES ON THE EVE OF CIVIL WAR	196
NORTHERN ADVANCES IN THE CIVIL WAR, 1861–1865	201
THE CIVIL WAR IN VIRGINIA	203
THE CIVIL WAR IN THE WEST	204
ELECTION OF 1876	221
ELECTION OF 1896	271
ELECTION OF 1912	307
THE CONTINENTAL UNITED STATES AND PRINCIPAL OVERSEAS STATES AND TERRITORIES	315
LATIN AMERICA, 1914	320
EUROPEAN IMMIGRATION TO THE UNITED STATES, 1870–1900	332
EUROPEAN IMMIGRATION TO THE UNITED STATES, 1901–1920	333
ELECTION OF 1928	361
INDEX OF COMMON STOCK PRICES, 1920–1962	373
ELECTION OF 1932	375
ANNUAL AVERAGE OF EMPLOYMENT, UNEMPLOYMENT, AND UNION MEMBERSHIP, 1920–1960	384
THE MAIN AXIS CAMPAIGNS, 1942	415
ALLIED ADVANCES IN EUROPE IN WORLD WAR II	420
ALLIED ADVANCES IN THE PACIFIC IN WORLD WAR II	421
THE COLONIAL WORLD, 1939	432
THE NEWLY INDEPENDENT NATIONS, 1964	434
ELECTION OF 1948	435
THE KOREAN WAR	437
ELECTION OF 1952	441
ELECTION OF 1960	449

THE DEMOCRATIC EXPERIENCE

PART 1: INTRODUCTION

THE FOUNDING OF AMERICA

■ At the end of the fifteenth century Europe was stirring with new interests and a fresh vitality. In Italy a zeal for the literature and culture of ancient Greece and Rome had stimulated a renewed interest in classical learning. Clerics and scholars who a few generations earlier might have concentrated their attention upon discussions of the Seven Deadly Sins now talked of Plato, Aristotle, Terence, and Plautus. Painters who a little earlier might have found their themes in the lives of the Christian saints now painted scenes from the loves and lives of Greek and Roman gods and goddesses. The world of late fifteenth-century Italy had become strikingly secularized, and the spirit of Italy would soon spread to the rest of Europe.

The new spirit of secularism focused attention upon the goodness of the world that man had inherited. No longer could the priest insist that this vale of tears was but a brief abiding place where one seasoned his soul for bliss in the world to come. Men wanted comforts and pleasures here below in a greater quantity and variety than they had known before. The Venetians and the Genoese, enterprising Italian traders that they were, had long brought luxury goods from the Near East and the Orient to please the wealthy of Europe. Now the demand was greater. More money was available. Silver mines in the Tyrol and elsewhere in eastern Europe were producing more precious metal, and the circulation of money was increasing. With more money in more hands than earlier generations had known, the demand for goods and commodities multiplied, especially for those goods that came from the East.

The trade routes that for centuries had supplied Europe with silks from China and spices and pepper from the East Indies had recently been subject to harassment from the Ottoman Turks. Overland caravans had always been slow and expensive; now they were more hazardous and uncertain than ever. If a quicker and easier sea route to the Indies could be discovered, European trades would profit enormously from it.

The Portuguese had made some promising forays into unknown oceans. Bartholomew Diaz in 1486 had rounded the Cape of Good Hope and come back to tell tales of a wondrous land and to suggest the possibility of a passage to India. A few years later, a Genoese in the service of Spain, one Christopher Columbus, persuaded Queen

Washington, Lafayette, and Aide-de-Camp Tilghman at Yorktown, painting by Charles Willson Peale (1781). American and French flags, flanking defeated Britons with colors furled, background the victory portrait of Washington and his comrades at Yorktown.

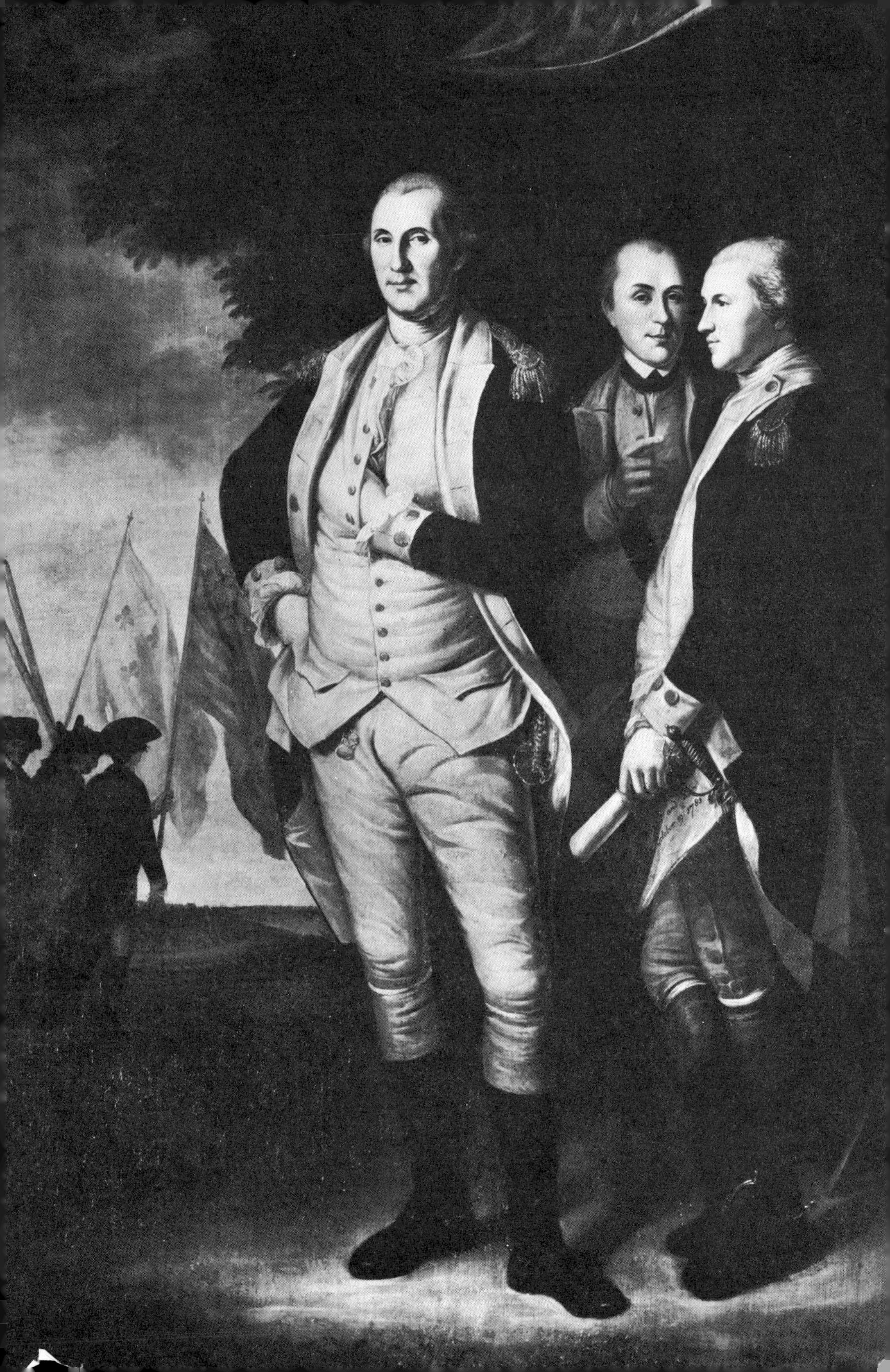

Penn's Treaty with the Indians, painting by Benjamin West (c. 1781). The signing of a single "Great Treaty" at Kensington is an idealized portrayal of Penn's negotiations for peace and land purchase; actually William Penn signed several treaties with the Indians.

Isabella of Castile to help finance a western voyage that he promised would lead to Asia and riches. When Columbus sailed from Palos on August 3, 1492, he believed that he could open a new trade route that would enable Spain to tap the wealth of Asia. When on October 12 he made a landfall in the Caribbean (perhaps Watling Island), he thought he had reached the outskirts of China; and a bit later, when he landed on Cuba, he sent messengers in search of the Great Khan. After four voyages across the Atlantic, Columbus died still believing that he had discovered a sea route to Asia.

Columbus' exaggerated accounts of the wealth of Cathay sent a stream of voyagers across the Atlantic and roused the greed of other European nations. Soon it was known that a new continent lay athwart the route to the East. A Florentine by the name of Amerigo Vespucci, who claimed to have made three voyages to the New World between 1497 and 1502, wrote so persuasively about his "explorations" that a German geographer and map maker, Martin Waldeseemüller, declared that the land should be named after him. So it happened that the New World came to be called America.

In the meantime, Pope Alexander VI, who claimed the right to dispose of lands seized from unbelievers, with a stroke of his pen in 1493 divided the world, giving to Spain all new lands one hundred leagues west of the Azores and Cape Verde Islands and to Portugal the lands east of the line. By the Treaty of Tordesillas in 1494 the line of demarcation was made three hundred and seventy leagues west of the Cape Verde Islands, which gave Portugal the hump of South America known later as Brazil. France was displeased at being left out. Francis I sent Jacques Cartier to explore the Gulf of St. Lawrence and lay French claim to a portion of the New World, naming the area New France. Henry VII of England was also not content to accept the Pope's geographical wisdom as infallible. He took John Cabot, a Genoese naturalized in Venice,

(Left) *Samuel Adams*, portrait by John Singleton Copley (c. 1770). "I doubt whether there is a greater incendiary in the King's dominion," said Gov. Hutchinson of Adams. (Above) *Congress Voting Independence*, painting by Robert Edge Pine (1785), completed by Edward Savage.

into his service and in 1497 dispatched him on a voyage of discovery along the North Atlantic seaboard. Upon Cabot's voyage, England based its claims to territory in North America.

Within a generation after Columbus' discovery of America, Europe witnessed other events that would in time profoundly influence not only the Old World but the development of the New. On October 31, 1517, Martin Luther nailed to the door of the castle church in Wittenberg his famous ninety-five theses challenging debate on alleged corruptions in the Catholic Church, then the only recognized church in western and central Europe. No one in Wittenberg could have foreseen that this gesture would begin a cataclysmic movement known to history as the Protestant Revolt, which gave birth to the various Protestant sects and split Christendom into rival, often warring, Protestant and Catholic nations. Nor was it foreseen that this movement would determine the nature of many of the settlements in North America. In England a few years later the dark eyes of Anne Boleyn attracted the attention of King Henry VIII, whose conscience presently began to hurt because he had married the Catholic Catherine of Aragon, the betrothed of his dead brother. To obtain a divorce (in order to marry Anne), Henry renounced the Pope of Rome and in a "Protestant" move in 1531 had himself declared supreme head of the Church of England. No one in England could have foreseen that this event would also affect the history of the New World. But from the union of Henry and Anne was born Elizabeth, whose circumstances of birth forced her to maintain the Protestant position in England when she became queen. Under Elizabeth (reigned 1558-1603) Englishmen began a long contest with Catholic Spain, the great colonial power in the New World. Out of that contest came the determination to establish English colonies in America. Under Elizabeth's Protestant successor, James I, Englishmen in 1607 finally gained a permanent foothold on the Atlantic seaboard at Jamestown.

CHAPTER 1

EVOLUTION OF THE AMERICAN COLONIES

BACKGROUND TO COLONIZATION

The Reasons Why Europe Was Prepared to Expand. America had been discovered as early as A.D. 1000, when the Vikings dominated northern Europe and the northern Atlantic, yet their adventures did not stimulate European expansion into the New World. Obviously, influential historical factors brought a significant change in western Europe by the time of Columbus' voyage in 1492, not only making European expansion possible but also instilling an adventurous spirit among the peoples of Europe, causing them to be eager to explore new lands and new opportunities.

Essentially, it was a change from the feudal mind and practices of the Middle Ages to the inquiring mind and changed conditions characteristic of early modern Europe. In the Middle Ages, western Europe had been dominated by the feudal and manorial system in which each man's place in society—ranging from the peasantry to the nobility—was determined by his relationship to the land. The commodities produced were consumed by the inhabitants of the manor. But the rise of early modern capitalism brought a revival of trade, the rise of the city, the emergence of a merchant class, production for an outside market, and the growth of banking; and as a result, men were no longer dependent exclusively upon their relationship to the land. Business transactions brought an accumulation of money, and money could be employed to finance new enterprises.

The mind of Europe also was awakened. The Crusades beginning in the eleventh century introduced western Europe to the ways of the Near East and to such exotic commodities as spices and silks. Journeys of Italian merchants —most notably, Marco Polo—to China and Japan aroused the interest of western Europe. The fear of the unknown and of new experiences which gripped many people in the Middle Ages was matched later by the spirit of innovators, men whose minds were stimulated by a curiosity of the unknown, men who wished to explore the riches of the East.

Portugal was the first nation bordering the Atlantic to engage in wide-scale exploration, especially along the western coast of Africa. This primacy was not accidental. Portugal was the first of the Atlantic nations to be unified, giving its leaders an opportunity to look outward rather than to be preoccupied with internal disorder. Among the most forward looking of its leaders was Prince Henry the Navigator (1394-1460), who established a center for the study of cartography and astronomy and for the improvement of ships and seamanship. Portugal was eventually rewarded when Bartholomew Diaz rounded Africa's southernmost Cape of Good Hope in 1486 and when Vasco da Gama reached India by way of the Cape of Good Hope in 1498.

The significance of national unity was underscored when Columbus' voyage in 1492 coincided with the expulsion of the Moors from Spain by the capture of Granada. Columbus' voyage, sailing west to reach the fabulous riches of the East, marked the great historical divide which eventually made the Atlantic rather than the Mediterranean a principal artery of trade and communication.

The efforts of Portugal and Spain to find new routes to the East were prompted in large part by their desire to avoid the commercial monopoly of the Italian cities, which, because of their dominating geographical position in the Mediterranean, lay astride this rich source of trade with the East. When the expedition of Ferdinand Magellan sailed around the world in 1519-1522, losing all but one ship and most of the men including Magellan, the voyage still showed a substantial profit, proving once again that the Italian cities were becoming rich at the expense of the nations of western Europe.

In following up the voyage of Columbus by establishing an American empire, Spain set an example which the nations of western Europe attempted to imitate. Spain not only extended its hold on the New World by conquering Mexico and Peru but also constructed a tightly knit, closely supervised colonial system whose object was to make its American colonies a source of wealth for the mother country and to prevent any encroachment by other nations. In 1574, long before the English had established a successful colony in the New World, the Spanish population in Mexico City alone exceeded 15,000; throughout the New World it exceeded 160,000. More than two hundred Spanish cities and towns had been founded, and Mexico City boasted a university. The principal agency used by Spain to transplant the culture of the Old World to the New was the Catholic Church, the only church in existence in the western world at the time the Spanish colonial system was founded. The Spanish, in contrast to the colonial policy followed later by the English, considered the native population as subjects of the sovereign, resulting in a fusion of cultures which is still characteristic of Latin America today.

The Expansion of England. Although John Cabot, representing the English crown, explored the eastern coast of North America within a decade of Columbus' voyage, successful English settlement was delayed for a century; as a consequence, economic, religious, and political factors affecting the English colonies were entirely different from those that had influenced the Spanish colonies.

The two outstanding economic changes were in trade and agriculture. Whereas no trading companies flourished in 1500, over two hundred English trading companies operated aggressively by 1600, including the Muscovy Company (1553), the Levant Company (1592), and the famous East India Company (1600). Moreover, in 1500 German and Italian merchants dominated English trade; by 1600 this domination had been eliminated and a strong merchant group of native Englishmen had emerged. In 1500 most of the raw wool raised in England was shipped to Flanders, a vigorous textile center, to be made into cloth; by 1600 an indigenous English textile industry absorbed much of the wool produced in England.

These economic changes had a direct effect upon the development of the English colonies. The first three successful English colonies in America—Plymouth, Virginia, and Massachusetts Bay—were planted by cooperatively owned "joint-stock companies," precur-

Evolution of the American Colonies 7

sors of modern corporations, in which a number of investors had pooled their capital. Many of the men engaged in the American enterprises had gained their experience in trading companies elsewhere, and they continued to participate in trading enterprises throughout the world. As Charles M. Andrews, a prominent historian of the colonial period, has written: "English America would hardly have been settled at this time had not the period of occupation coincided with the era of capitalism in the first flush of its power."

The experience in trade influenced mercantilist thought in England. Mercantilism embodied a set of economic ideas held throughout western Europe from 1500 to 1800, though the precise measures taken differed from country to country. The mercantilist advocated that the economic affairs of the nation should be regulated to encourage the development of a strong state. Within this broad objective, a number of propositions customarily were made: a nation could become stronger by exporting more than it imported, resulting in a "favorable balance of trade"; national self-sufficiency should be encouraged by subsidizing domestic manufactures; a nation's wealth was to be measured by the amount of precious metals it could obtain (thus the emphasis on the accumulation of bullion); labor should be regulated for the well-being and benefit of the state; and colonies should be established to provide the nation with raw materials that it was unable to produce.

Although this does not exhaust the list of desirable attributes advocated by mercantilist thinkers, it does show that trade was considered one of the most important measures of a nation's wealth and that colonies contributed to that wealth. In England the mercantile emphasis between 1500 and 1600 was upon internal regulation, while after 1600 the emphasis was on external regulation, particularly the commercial relationship of England to its colonies. The phenomenal increase in English mercantile activity, therefore, not only provided an agency to plant colonies in the world but also provided a national purpose for founding colonies.

A second significant economic change took place in agriculture. Between 1500 and 1600 an "enclosure" movement gained strength in Britain. Essentially, "enclosures" meant that smaller landholdings in certain areas of England were incorporated into larger holdings, forcing certain Englishmen off the land. The result was a dislocation of population which caused many political thinkers to conclude that England was overpopulated. As a result, English colonization operated on the theory that almost anyone should be permitted to go to the New World to reduce "overpopulation," whereas Spain had restricted immigration to selected individuals favored by the crown.

In the sixteenth century a religious revolution, the Protestant Reformation, swept through Europe and profoundly affected the religious and political development of England which, in turn, placed an enduring stamp upon the English colonies in America. In 1500 England (and Europe) was within the folds of the Catholic Church. By 1600 not only had England broken away from the Catholic Church and established the national Anglican Church, but the religious rupture had also encouraged the rise of splinter religious groups. This diversity of faiths was carried directly to the New World: of the first four settlements, Virginia was Anglican, Plymouth was Separatist, Massachusetts Bay was Puritan, and Maryland was Catholic.

The story of this religious rupture in England is too involved for extended treatment in this text, but what is particularly important is that in the process of waging his contest with the Roman Catholic Church, King Henry VIII, beginning in 1529, enlisted the aid of Parliament. Parliament passed a series of enactments creating a national church, culminating in the Act of Supremacy (1534), which made King Henry VIII, instead of the Pope of Rome, the ecclesiastical sovereign of England. Eventually, by means of parliamentary acts, the church lands were taken over by the king, greatly enhancing his wealth.

The ramifications of these actions invaded almost every sphere of English life, but the two major effects on the English colonies were the following: (1) the king, by utilizing the support of Parliament, demonstrated that in practice the authority of the crown was limited—a concept carried to the English colonies in America and a concept in direct contrast to Spanish doctrine which held the power of the sovereign to be without restriction; (2) the break with the Catholic Church, as has been previously mentioned, produced a wide diversity of religious groups.

Some Englishmen believed that separation from the Catholic Church should never have taken place and, therefore, they held to their original Catholic belief and position. Others felt that the monarchs—Henry VIII and, later, Elizabeth I—had not gone far enough. The Puritans, an impassioned and vocal minority, believed that the Reformation in England had stopped short of its goal, that ritual should be further simplified, and that the authority of crown-appointed bishops should be lessened; however, they resolved to stay within the Church of England and attempt to achieve their goals—that is, "purify" the church—without a division. The Separatists, a small minority, believed that each congregation should become its own judge of religious orthodoxy. They were no more willing to give allegiance to the crown than they had been to the Pope. This religious fractionalism was transferred to the American colonies.

Early in the seventeenth century, then, a number of English "dissenters" —men and women who were dissatisfied with political, economic, or religious conditions in England—were ready to migrate to the New World; English trading companies provided an agency for settlement.

THE ENGLISH SETTLEMENTS

Thus, for one hundred and fifteen years after the discovery of America, the English had not established a single permanent foothold in the Western Hemisphere. Although they had made several voyages and two attempts at settlement, as late as 1600 they had not one colony to show for their efforts. By 1700 some twenty colonies, composed of 350,000 inhabitants, a multitude in terms of the New World wilderness, stretched all the way from Newfoundland on the North Atlantic to the island of Barbados in the southern Caribbean. Heavy losses originally deterred growth, but promoters and settlers learned to adjust to the new environment. By the end of the century their settlements had taken root, had attained prosperity, and had entered upon a stage of steady growth. The English dream of expansion overseas had become a reality, and Britain could look with pride upon her empire in the West Indies and along the Atlantic coast from Maine to Carolina.

Founding Virginia. The first permanent English colony in America was Virginia. In the year 1606 King James I granted a group of London merchants the privilege of establishing colonies in "the part of America commonly called Virginia." Securing a charter, this Virginia Company of London raised sufficient funds by the sale of shares to fit out three ships and send them to Virginia, where on May 24, 1607, 120 men established a settlement, Jamestown, on the banks of the James River.

The early Jamestown settlers had no experience in colonization; many of them had come for adventure rather than from any desire to become permanent residents in the wilderness. They knew nothing of subsistence farming and displayed little ingenuity. Although the James River teemed with fish, they nearly perished for want of food. Of the first five thousand people who migrated to Virginia, less than a thousand survived. Much of the credit for the survival of even this number must be given to Captain John Smith, who emerged as a vigorous leader during the "starving time" of 1609.

Gradually, however, the Jamestown colonists devised ways of making a livelihood. Some traded with the Indians and began a traffic that would grow in importance with the years. Others planted foodstuffs and learned to raise Indian corn. John Rolfe, who married the Indian princess Pocahontas, developed the skill of growing tobacco profitably. Rolfe's contribution ensured Virginia's prosperity, for tobacco was a commodity much in demand in Europe.

In governing the colony, the Virginia Company at first adopted a policy of severe laws administered by a strong-armed governor, but after this failed, it made the momentous decision to let the settlers share in their own government. When Governor George Yeardley arrived in Virginia in 1619, he carried instructions to call annually an assembly to consist of two members or burgesses from the various local units in the colony, these burgesses to be elected by residents who qualified on a basis of almost complete manhood suffrage. This assembly, which met in the church at Jamestown in the summer of 1619, was the first representative lawmaking body in English America and as such was the forerunner of representative government in the United States. Even when the Virginia Company at last succumbed to bankruptcy in 1624 and lost its charter, with the result that Virginia became a royal colony, the company's greatest contribution was preserved intact: the Virginia House of Burgesses continued to meet. It was ironical that this transfer took place under King James I, for it meant that the very monarch who was the most severe enemy of Parliament in England was also, unwittingly, the one who permitted representative government in America to become a regular part of the system of colonial government under the crown.

The Pilgrims in Plymouth. The first permanent settlement in New England was made by a small band of religious zealots who arrived off Cape Cod in the *Mayflower* in November 1620. They were a congregation of Separatists or Pilgrims who had fled to Holland in 1608 under the leadership of William Brewster, William Bradford, and their minister, John Robinson. After a decade in Holland, Robinson's congregation grew restless and decided to emigrate to the New World. Thirty members of the congregation sailed to England, where they crowded aboard the *Mayflower,* a ship financed by an English joint-stock company. The *Mayflower,* carrying 101 passengers, the majority non-Pilgrims, set out for Virginia but was blown off course and landed at Plymouth, where the settlers went ashore and began work on their first house on December 25, 1620.

The story of the Pilgrims has become a part of the American legend. The hardships of the first winter, the friendship of two Indians, Samoset and Squanto, who taught the settlers to plant corn, and the first harvest and thanksgiving festival have given the little colony at Plymouth a significant place in the American imagination.

The "Great Migration" to Massachusetts Bay. Although the Pilgrims' character and heroism bequeathed a poetic heritage to the American people, the more populous colony of Massachusetts Bay contributed more to New

England's civilization. Sporadic efforts had been made during the first two decades of the seventeenth century to establish settlements in New England, and a few fishermen and other adventurous folk were scattered along the coast from Plymouth to Maine when the main body of settlers under the leadership of John Winthrop arrived in the summer of 1630 in the *Arbella.* This was one of four ships that carried the first wave of the "Great Migration," which between 1630 and 1640 brought some 20,000 arrivals into Massachusetts.

The Winthrop group—most of them Puritans—had managed to obtain a royal charter for the Massachusetts Bay Company. Unlike other colonial enterprises, this company vested control, not in a board of governors in England, but in the members of the company who themselves were emigrating to New England. They came bringing their charter with them and were self-governing, subject only to the English crown. Over the years the prerogative of self-government guaranteed by the charter gave Massachusetts Bay a quality of independence that was important for the future of the nation.

During the ten years after the landing of the *Arbella,* Massachusetts Bay became the most populous English colony in the New World. From towns established at Boston, Cambridge, Dorchester, Salem, and elsewhere, groups from time to time broke away and moved into fresh territory. In the summer of 1636, for example, the Reverend Thomas Hooker, with about one hundred of his followers, set out on foot from Cambridge and settled a new township at Hartford, in what became Connecticut. Other towns proliferated in similar fashion.

The Spreading Colonies of New England. Occasionally colonists left Massachusetts Bay because they had offended the ruling authorities or because they were discontented with a thoroughgoing Puritan commonwealth that punished dissenters severely and tried to impose its religious tenets upon all comers. Freedom of conscience or religion was not a virtue of Massachusetts Bay. Roger Williams, pastor of the church at Salem, was banished from the colony in 1635 because he had complained publicly that interference of the clergy in politics threatened the freedom of individual congregations, and because he questioned the right of the settlers to take land from the Indians. Williams fled in the dead of winter to the Narragansett Indians, and in January 1636 he arranged to purchase from the Indians land for a little settlement which he called Providence. Before long, other fugitives from the persecution of the Puritan clergy in Massachusetts Bay found their way to Williams' colony.

The Providence settlers made a compact which guaranteed liberty of conscience to all men regardless of faith and which provided for the separation of church and state. Other groups came to Rhode Island and settled at Portsmouth, Newport, and Warwick, and in 1644 Parliament granted a charter which united the various groups in Rhode Island into one civil government. A royal charter in 1663 once more reiterated the liberties earlier established; this charter was so democratic that it remained the basis of Rhode Island's laws until 1842. Rhode Island was far ahead of its time in its legal provisions: as early as 1647, for example, it outlawed trials for witchcraft and imprisonment for debt.

Massachusetts Bay emigrants settled a colony at New Haven under the leadership of John Davenport and Theophilus Eaton, both conservative and strict Puritans. As in Massachusetts, only church members were permitted to vote, a policy which in effect gave the church political control over the affairs of the colony. Since the Scriptures made no mention of jury trials, New Haven—in contrast to other

New England colonies—forbade jury trials and left the dispensation of justice in the hands of the magistrates. In 1662 Connecticut received a royal charter which confirmed the rights of self-government and provided for the Fundamental Orders, a platform of government extending the franchise to non-church members. To the distress of New Haven, that colony was absorbed into Connecticut and the guarantees of Connecticut's charter extended to its citizens.

Other Massachusetts Bay residents moved into New Hampshire and Maine, where they found other settlers who had already established themselves in small fishing villages. Massachusetts laid claim to both regions; after many disputes, New Hampshire in 1679 gained a royal charter and freed itself from the domination of Massachusetts, but Maine was not separated until 1820.

Catholic Maryland. While Virginia was gradually gaining vitality, a neighboring colony developed on its northern flank. In 1632 Sir George Calvert, First Lord Baltimore, received from Charles I a charter for the tract of land extending from the fortieth degree of north latitude to the south bank of the Potomac River. Calvert, a Roman Catholic, intended to make Maryland a refuge for oppressed Catholics. He died before he could settle his grant, but his son Cecilius became lord proprietor and sent his brother Leonard to take possession of Maryland, where the first group of Catholic settlers landed on March 25, 1634.

A "proprietary colony" such as the Calverts obtained was a return to a feudal and baronial system which in the seventeenth century was becoming outmoded. The manorial system of land tenure, which made the inhabitants of Maryland tenants of the Calverts instead of landowners, was the source of much unrest and would never have lasted at all had the Calverts not made tenancy approximate ownership.

In order to attract settlers and make the colony pay, the Calverts from the outset encouraged Protestants as well as Catholics to go to Maryland, and Catholics never constituted a majority of the population, though most of the manorial families were Catholic. Catholics and Anglicans held separate worship, and Lord Baltimore would not allow the Jesuits in the colony to place any restrictions upon Protestants. In 1649 he sponsored the famous Maryland Toleration Act, which guaranteed freedom of worship to all Christians. This was not yet full liberty of conscience, for there was a death penalty for non-Christians, but the act marked an advance in the direction of ultimate religious freedom.

Proprietary Colonies. Except for Maryland, the original colonies were established by joint-stock companies, but after 1660 almost all the newly founded colonies were proprietaries. Joint-stock companies as a whole did not make a profit, and business enterprisers became less interested in investing in colonial establishments. King Charles II after 1660 began to grant large segments of American land to those who supported the Stuart claim to the throne during the period of Puritan control in England (1642-1660). Moreover, once the original beachheads of settlements had been established, proprietors could make a success of colonies. Proprietors had been unsuccessful in the late sixteenth century because they could neither command sufficient capital nor sustain a colonizing effort over an extended period of time. With the successful founding of Virginia, Maryland, Plymouth, and Massachusetts Bay, the risk of founding proprietary colonies was greatly reduced. As a result, Pennsylvania was founded in 1682; the territory of the Carolinas was given to a number of proprietors in 1663, although as late as 1670 the number of settlers was severely limited. New Jersey began as a proprietorship but eventually was made a crown or royal colony, in which affairs were directed by crown officials. New York also began as a proprietary colony under the Duke of York after its capture from the Dutch, and it became a crown colony when the Duke of York became James II, the English king.

Dutch on the Hudson. In 1609 Henry Hudson, an Englishman in the employ of the Dutch East India Company, sailed the Hudson River as far as the present town of Albany. Five years later a private Dutch corporation, the New Netherland Company, received from the Dutch government a concession of exclusive rights in the region extending from New France (as Canada was called) to Virginia on the south.

The monopoly of the New Netherland Company ended in 1618, and five years later the Dutch West India Company was formed to develop trade in the region along the river that Hudson had discovered. Between 1624 and 1626 little settlements were established at Fort Amsterdam on Manhattan, at Fort Orange (later Albany), and at Fort Nassau on the Delaware River.

Because Holland was a prosperous and tolerant country, its citizens were not eager to emigrate to a wilderness, and the Dutch West India Company had trouble finding colonists. Included among the early settlers were French Protestant refugees and citizens of other nationalities resident in Holland. From the earliest times, New Netherland (later New York) was a polyglot region. But despite incompetent governors, quarreling inhabitants, and frequent wars with the Indians, the colony made progress and New Amsterdam (New York City) became an important shipping point for furs and farm products.

Peter Stuyvesant, the last Dutch governor of New Netherland, was an irascible man with the disposition of a dictator, but under him the country prospered. Dutch farmers made the back country produce abundant food crops. The fur trade was profitable. New Amsterdam, with a population of about 2500, was second only to Boston as a trading port. The population of the colony as a whole amounted to about 8000, of whom many were English.

The English Capture of New York. The English had never admitted the right of the Dutch to the territory they had occupied. In 1664 Charles II named his brother James, Duke of York, proprietor over lands occupied by the Dutch in the New World. The Duke sent out an expedition under Colonel Richard Nicolls to take over New Netherland; since England and the Netherlands were not at war, the English claimed that this was not an act of war but merely an action to regain from the Dutch West India Company territory that was rightfully English. With an English fleet in the harbor of New Amsterdam, Stuyvesant had no choice but to surrender, which he did on September 8, 1664. The town and territory were both rechristened New York in honor of the royal proprietor. Though the Dutch reoccupied New York temporarily from July 30, 1673, to November 10, 1674, the English had come to stay.

The Dutch occupation of the Hudson valley had benefited the English far more than the new overlords cared to admit. Had the Dutch not been in possession in the first half of the seventeenth century, when English settlements on the Atlantic seaboard were too sparse and weak to prevent the French from moving down the Hudson from Canada, the thin line of English colonies along the coast might have been divided by England's traditional enemy, France.

The Jerseys. Soon after the Duke of York took over New Netherland in

1664, he granted the land between the Hudson and the Delaware to two courtiers, John Lord Berkeley and Sir George Carteret, royalists who had defended the island of Jersey against the Parliamentarians during the Puritan Revolution in England. Berkeley sold his proprietary right to two Quakers, and in 1676 the province was divided into East Jersey (belonging to Carteret) and West Jersey (which became a Quaker colony). The later division of the two portions of New Jersey among many heirs of the proprietors bequeathed a land problem so complex that it vexes holders of real estate in that state to the present day.

Penn's Experiment. In 1681 King Charles II granted to William Penn, a Quaker, a charter to the land between New Jersey and Maryland, naming him and his heirs forever owners of the soil of Pennsylvania, as the domain was called. Penn set about establishing a colony that would serve as a refuge for persecuted Christians from all lands. He drew up his celebrated first Frame of Government and made various concessions and laws to govern the colony, which already had a conglomerate group of English, Dutch, Swedish, and Finnish settlers scattered here and there. In April 1681 Penn sent his cousin, William Markham, to serve as deputy governor, and a year later he himself came to Pennsylvania. He provided for the calling of a popular assembly on December 4, 1682, which passed the "Great Law," guaranteeing, among other things, the rights of all Christians to liberty of conscience.

Penn determined to keep peace with the Indians and was careful to purchase the land which his settlers occupied. The tradition of a single "Great Treaty" signed under an ancient elm at Kensington is probably a myth, but Penn held many powwows with the Indians and negotiated treaties of peace and amity after purchasing needed land. To the credit of Penn and the Quakers these agreements with the Indians were, for the most part, conscientiously kept.

Pennsylvania's growth from the first was phenomenal. Penn's success was largely due to his own skill as a promoter, for he wrote enticing tracts and on preaching journeys described the opportunities offered by his colony. Mennonites from Switzerland and Germany—especially Pietists from the Rhineland, which had so often been overrun by invading armies—soon were coming to Pennsylvania in large numbers. Dutch sectarians, French Huguenots, Presbyterian Scots from Ulster, Baptists from Wales, and distressed English Quakers also came. Somewhat after the Mennonites, Lutheran emigrants from Germany swarmed into Pennsylvania's back country, where they cleared the forests and developed fertile farms. From the beginning Pennsylvania was prosperous.

Settlement of the Carolinas. Among the later colonies to be settled was Carolina, which also began as a proprietorship awarded to eight courtiers who received from Charles II on March 23, 1663, a grant of the territory between the southern border of Virginia and Spanish Florida. The eight proprietors drew up an instrument of government called the Fundamental Constitutions (probably the handiwork of the English political philosopher John Locke), which provided for a hierarchy of colonial nobility and set up a platform of government with a curious mixture of feudal and liberal elements. The Fundamental Constitutions eventually had to be abandoned in favor of a more workable plan of government.

The division of Carolina into two distinct colonies came about gradually. English settlers were already occupying land around Albemarle Sound when the proprietors received their charter, and Albemarle continued to attract a scattering of settlers. It was geographically remote from the other settlement declared a royal province, and eight years later North Carolina also became a crown colony.

Georgia. Georgia, founded in 1733, was administered for two decades by 20 trustees in England. Georgia was established to serve many purposes: as an extension of the southern provincial frontier; as a buffer or a first line of defense between the Spanish colony of Florida and the English settlements; as a planned Utopia where the trustees hoped to establish a model society; as a refuge for persecuted Protestants from Europe; as a new opportunity for men who had been released from debtor's prisons in England; and as a model "colony" that would produce commodities that England wanted, notably silk and citrus fruits. Because of these multiple objectives, no single one was carried out with success. In fact, by 1740 many of its colonists had left; equally important, new migration from England and Europe failed to materialize. Not until the crown took over the colony in the 1750's was Georgia rescued, and even then the colony did not flourish until after the American Revolution.

COLONIAL ADMINISTRATION AND POLITICS

Administration of the English Colonies. In London, administrative agencies to govern the colonies were slow in evolving. Originally a standing committee of the Privy Council, the "Lord Commissioners for Plantations," directly supervised the colonies. Variations of this committee operated until 1675, when the Lords of Trade was created—an agency whose vigorous actions set a new standard in colonial policy. It opposed the disposition on the part of the crown to issue proprietary grants, and it advocated the revocation of proprietary grants, bringing such colonies under direct royal control.

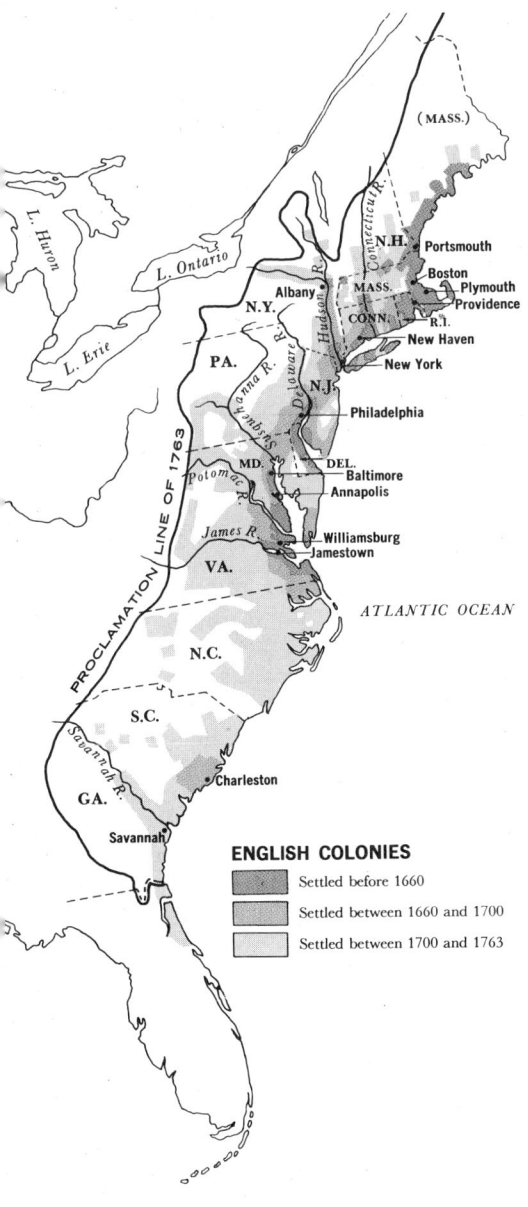

on the Ashley and Cooper rivers to the south. As the two separate sections gained population, they set up separate legislative assemblies, approved by the proprietors. In 1710 the proprietors appointed a governor of North Carolina, "independent of the governor of Carolina," thus recognizing the complete separation of North from South Carolina. In 1721 South Carolina was

Evolution of the American Colonies 15

The most important effort of the Lords of Trade was made in 1686, when it established the Dominion of New England. The charter of Massachusetts Bay had been annulled in 1684, and the Dominion represented an attempt to centralize the authority of the crown by creating a "super-colony," including Massachusetts, New Hampshire, Connecticut, Rhode Island, New York, and New Jersey. It was expected that eventually Pennsylvania would also be incorporated within the framework of the Dominion. The crown, acting upon the recommendation of the Lords of Trade, appointed Edmond Andros as governor, to reside in Boston, with Francis Nicholson as his deputy, to reside in New York. No provision was made for an assembly, although there was to be a council of advisers. Andros, unfortunately, was of limited mind and of a petty spirit; he was scarcely the man to carry out such a dramatic, far-reaching colonial experiment. Resentment among the colonies included within the Dominion was intense, not only because their original charters had been arbitrarily set aside, not only because the crown had appointed the arbitrary Andros, but because they lacked a representative assembly.

A twist of fate—England's Glorious Revolution of 1688, which deposed the despotic James II and firmly championed Parliament, and thus representative government, in England—provided an opportunity for the colonials to overthrow the Dominion. Acting on the premise that Governor Andros now represented a discarded royal regime, the colonials imprisoned him as a signal of their allegiance to the new government in England set up under William and Mary. Each colony that had been included within the Dominion hastily returned to its previous path of colonial self-government; the Glorious Revolution, therefore, marked the end of an experiment to consolidate the colonies within a larger framework to be administered more directly by home authorities.

In many respects, the experiment of the Dominion of New England was a turning point in colonial political affairs. At this time the colonials were not yet strong enough to defeat the royal will. If the experiment had been a success, individual self-government within the colonies would have been eliminated and the entire course of American history might have been changed. With the fall of the Dominion, the individual colonies received a new lease, and they used it to gain strength politically and economically.

In 1696 the Lords of Trade were replaced by the Board of Trade, an administrative agency which survived into the period of the American Revolution. However, during the eighteenth century Parliament was overwhelmed with its own problems—namely, the internal political transition to parliamentary supremacy in England and the turmoil of foreign policy; thus, the leaders of Parliament could not spare the time to formulate new policies for the empire. As a result, the general policies formulated very early in the eighteenth century were followed throughout the period regardless of changing circumstances. An instruction issued to a governor in 1750 was little changed from the instructions given in 1700. The American provinces were changing, England was changing, the world was changing, but British imperial policy remained, for the most part, unchanged.

The Political Structure. English colonies in America experienced a vigorous political life, in contrast to the colonies of other western European countries. The concept of self-government was transferred to the English colonies almost from the outset in most settlements, but of course the political structure throughout the colonies generally had taken more definitive shape early in the eighteenth century.

The political structures that evolved in royal, proprietary, and charter colonies were remarkably similar. Each colony had a governor who executed colonial laws, served as commander in chief of the militia, presided over the colony's highest court of appeals, and enforced relevant British enactments. In a proprietary colony like Pennsylvania the governor looked after the interests of the proprietor, most notably in the disposition of land, but he was also expected to enforce the imperial policies laid down by the home authorities. Usually the governor was appointed by the crown, although in proprietary colonies the proprietor held this prerogative and in Rhode Island and Connecticut the governor was elected by the legislature.

Most colonies had a council whose members served as advisers to the governor, comprised the upper house of the legislature, and sat as the highest court of appeal in the colony. Generally these council members were appointed by the crown upon the recommendation of the governor, but exceptions were made. Members of the council were customarily the more affluent colonials, many of whom had powerful friends in England. In a number of colonies the council, although acting in self-interest, was the spokesman for the people against the prerogative of the governor. The council wished to control office patronage, the distribution of lands, and the like.

A colonial assembly, which served as the lower house of the legislature, was elected by the freemen. By the eighteenth century every colony had instituted property requirements as a requisite for freemanship, but recent research has demonstrated that these requirements did not seriously restrict the number of eligible voters. Property requirements for officeholding, however, were frequently much higher than the requirements for suffrage, so that a member of the assembly had to be a person of some means. "Professional politicians" who had no other means of a livelihood were rare in the American provinces.

During the eighteenth century the assemblies of every colony gained power. Among the specific powers obtained by most assemblies were the rights to initiate legislation, to judge the qualifications of their own members, and to elect their speakers. The assemblies were somewhat less successful in determining when elections should be held and in extending the membership of the assembly.

Whereas the basic constitutional position of the home authorities was that the power of the assemblies and the grant of self-government itself were merely an extension of "the royal grace and favor," to be offered, modified, or even eliminated as the crown determined, the constitutional position held by the assemblies was that their power and authority derived from the consent of the governed. The assemblies conceived of themselves as replicas of the British House of Commons, and they attempted to imitate the House of Commons in waging their contest for power against the prerogative of the governor, representing the crown or the proprietor.

Conflicts were inevitable between constitutional positions that differed so markedly. The principal expression of this conflict arose between the assemblies and the governor. The assemblies attempted to restrict the scope of the governor's operations by controlling the disbursement of funds appropriated by the legislature, by failing to appropriate monies for projects asked for by the governor, and occasionally by refusing to pay the governor's salary until he accepted the legislation passed by the assembly.

Local Government. The structure of English local government at the time the colonies were founded was transplanted, for the most part, to the New

World. Among the more important officials were the county sheriffs and the justices of the peace. Although other positions that were important in England, such as lord lieutenant, did not for a variety of reasons flourish in the New World, nevertheless local government in the United States of the present day descends directly from the colonial period.

Local disputes over land titles and other matters were settled by the county courts. Colonial legislation was enforced by the justices of the peace in cooperation with the sheriff, and taxes were collected by the sheriff. In practice, therefore, local government served as a major link between the colonial government and the people of the New World colonies.

Politics in Operation. In every colony, at some time or another, domestic disputes developed which were fought out in the political arena. The issues of land, currency, proportionate representation, defense, and the Indian trade were among those that arose most frequently. In a colony such as Virginia, where tobacco was the principal staple, tobacco inspection acts aroused lively political disputes. Seldom did political parties develop. Generally, a coalition of forces, drawn in most cases from various parts of a province, united to support or defeat a measure. Once the issue was decided, the coalition disintegrated. Whereas a political split between the eastern and western parts of a province was characteristic of a colony like Pennsylvania, which was growing at a swifter pace than most of its sister colonies, the major political division in New York was between influential families whose wealth was based on land and influential families whose wealth was based on commerce. These political issues and the conflicts they aroused were evidence not of internal disorder but of political maturity—of vigorous, healthy self-government in action.

COLONIAL ECONOMY

New England. The rise of capitalism throughout western Europe, which coincided with the founding of the English colonies, determined that the American provincial economy would be capitalistic in orientation with an emphasis on trade, production for market, and eventual regional specialization. Each colony's economy at the outset was rather primitive—merely an economic appendage of England—but shortly after the mid-eighteenth century an indigenous, well-developed capitalism had emerged.

The economic development of New England was strongly influenced by the systems of land distribution and of trade. In the seventeenth century land was granted by the legislature to groups —usually church congregations—who in turn distributed the land among themselves. The result was the encouragement of the famous New England township system, whose principal aim was to maintain an effective social-religious community. Each family was customarily granted a town lot after provision for the church, sometimes a school, and a village green had been made. Plots of land outside the town were then distributed among members of the group, with common land retained for grazing purposes and a specified number of acres reserved for latecomers. Distributing the land in this fashion, of course, meant that all members of the group would be in close proximity to the church, the heart of the Puritan community; that sending youngsters to school would raise no serious problems; that towns would become the basis for representative government; and that town meetings would provide the political structure to resolve local issues.

In the eighteenth century, the New England land system changed. With the central purpose of a concerted social-religious community declining in importance, settlement along western frontier lands seldom was made by church groups. Instead, men of influence and means began to purchase large blocs of land for speculative purposes, selling off smaller parcels to the small farmer or prospective farmer. Even in the older towns conditions changed. Original settlers or descendants of original settlers moved, often selling their land to a third party. Absentee ownership of town lots and township lands was common. Whereas in the seventeenth century town proprietors were nearly always residents of the town, in the eighteenth century this was not so.

Although farming was the predominant occupation in New England up to 1640, trade gained increasing importance thereafter. From 1640 to 1660 the English were preoccupied with civil war and political upheaval at home, and colonials began to replace the English merchant as the trading enterpriser. It was at this time that the developing resources of New England fisheries helped open up trade between the Puritans of New England and the Puritans who had settled in the West Indies.

New England merchants gradually gained a position of economic and political primacy. By the end of the seventeenth century they had already begun to replace the Puritan magistrates as the source of economic and political power, and by the 1760's they constituted the single strongest voice in New England. It is important to remember that merchants were not alone in their dependence on trade for prosperity. The artisans who repaired canvas and built vessels, the farmers who exported meat products—in fact, the entire population in one way or another—were partly dependent upon prosperous commercial relations. Meat, fish, and lumber, the principal articles of export, found their major market in the West Indies. New England was also dependent on its role as a carrier of exports from other provinces and of imports from England.

In New England, the labor force was composed largely of free family labor, although servants were hired and indentured servants were imported. New England, in contrast to some of the other regions, was attractive to skilled workers because they could find a ready market for their talent in an area dominated by a town system. Each town needed a carpenter or a blacksmith.

The Southern Colonies. Three significant factors affected the economic development of the Southern colonies: the distribution of land, the evolution of the plantation system, and the tremendous production of staples for market. In the seventeenth-century Chesapeake colonies (Virginia and Maryland) land was distributed directly to individuals, in contrast to the practice in early New England. Moreover, the colonials, instead of settling in groups, scattered up and down the rivers of the Chesapeake area. Each planter tried to have his own landing where an ocean-going vessel could readily load the tobacco he produced and unload the goods he had ordered from England. This method of settlement made the county the basis of local government, discouraged the establishment of a school system because of the distances involved, and markedly influenced the transplantation of the Anglican Church (see Chapter 3).

In the seventeenth century the average landholding was relatively small, since the man power was lacking to cultivate extensive landholdings. The headright system, whereby a planter could obtain 50 acres of land for each dependent or servant he brought to the colonies, allowed the first accumulations of land to occur; but it was not until the eighteenth century, when American provincials obtained control of the machinery to distribute land, that large grants became fairly common.

Though slaves were imported into the Chesapeake colonies and into South Carolina in the seventeenth century, the principal labor force was composed of indentured servants, that is, adult whites who bound themselves to labor for a definite period, usually three to five years, in order to secure passage to America. Convicts and paupers who were sentenced to labor in America comprised another class of indentured servants. Over 1500 indentures were imported annually into Virginia alone in the 1670's and the 1680's. But as the plantation system became larger, as the Negro slave became a relatively less expensive source of labor in comparison with the indentured servant, as the middle colonies expanded to attract the indentured servant, and as the supply of English indentures decreased because the demand for labor in England increased, the institution of slavery became fastened upon the eighteenth-century Southern colonies. A society that had been made up largely of yeomen now became dominated by a planter elite.

Tobacco continued to be the main staple in the Chesapeake colonies, but rice and indigo became prominent in South Carolina. Naval stores became a major export of North Carolina. Deer skins were the principal article of commerce with the Indians.

In the seventeenth century no merchant group developed in the Southern colonies because planters corresponded directly with English merchants. However, in the eighteenth century an important merchant group developed in strategically located Charleston, South Carolina, entrepôt for a vast hinterland. A group of planter-merchants became important in the Chesapeake colonies early in the eighteenth century, but a true merchant class did not develop until after the mid-eighteenth century. Obviously, these circumstances affected the social structure in the Southern colonies, where the large planter was unchallenged by a mercantile interest centered in the cities.

The Middle Colonies. During the eighteenth century English migration decreased because demand for laborers and opportunities for advancement greatly increased at home as Britain expanded its trade and manufactures. However, a tremendous influx of non-English peoples—Germans, Scotch-Irish, Irish, Swiss, and French Huguenots—into the middle colonies resulted in expansion of that region at a rate exceeding that of New England or the South.

The reasons for the migration of non-English peoples were fundamentally economic, although religious intolerance and fear of destructive wars at home sometimes played a part. Opportunities for the Scotch-Irish in Ireland were limited, whereas opportunities in the New World appeared much more attractive. German Pietists came to Pennsylvania in large numbers because that colony offered an attractive land policy as well as religious toleration.

Land policies in Pennsylvania, the Jerseys, and New York varied greatly. In New York land was granted to favorites who established extensive manors; a settler was often confronted with the unhappy circumstance of obtaining a leasehold and becoming a renter rather than obtaining a clear title to the land. The distribution of lands in Pennsylvania was much more favorable. Small grants could be obtained by outright purchase; in fact, Scotch-Irish settlers on the frontier of Pennsylvania frequently assumed title to the land by right of settlement and refused to pay the proprietors.

New York and Philadelphia developed into major ports in the eighteenth century; Philadelphia, in fact, became the second largest city within the British empire. Both cities developed a strong mercantile class and attracted skilled artisans—cabinetmakers, silversmiths, gunsmiths, and the like. Both ports exported the principal commodity of the middle colonies, grain; the middle provinces became the "bread basket" of the American colonies.

Pennsylvania's rapid growth and early economic maturity reflected the astonishing general growth of the colonies. The handful of English settlers had become two hundred thousand strong by 1700; by 1760, the English colonies in America provided a good livelihood for a population of approximately two million—almost one half the population of England. No wonder, then, that trade quadrupled, that banking and currency became important issues, that tradesmen and merchants carried on sophisticated economic practices, that a stable society was formed, and finally, that the American economic system was sufficiently developed to sustain the shock of political separation from the mother country and to finance a War for Independence. All the ingredients of a well-developed commercial capitalism were present.

English Regulatory Acts. As the economy of the American provinces matured, imperial regulations were enlarged to prevent foreign commercial competition and the competition of colonial manufactures with those of the mother country. As early as the 1620's restrictions were placed on the tobacco trade, but a series of enactments passed from 1651 to 1700 laid the actual framework for the English imperial system.

The Navigation Act of 1651 was designed primarily to reduce competition from non-British carriers. It provided that products manufactured or grown in Asia, Africa, or America and brought to England or its possessions could be transported only in ships of which the proprietor, master, and majority of mariners were English (including colonials). Foreign produce and manufactures could be brought into England or its possessions only in vessels belonging to the country that had produced the goods.

From the English mercantile point of view the Navigation Act of 1651 contained certain shortcomings: it did not prevent American colonists from exporting goods directly to Europe, nor did it prevent them from acquiring manufactured goods on the Continent and transporting these goods directly to the colonies for market. Moreover, with the restoration of the Stuart monarchy in 1660 the question arose as to whether the Navigation Act of 1651 was legal, because it had been passed during the period of England's Puritan Commonwealth (1649-1660), when the English throne was without an occupant.

Therefore, a second Navigation Act (often called the Enumeration Act) passed in 1660 closed the loophole which had permitted colonials to import directly from Europe. It provided that all goods, regardless of origin, could be imported into or exported from any English colony only in English-built vessels of which the owner, master, and three fourths of the crews were English. "Enumerated" goods—including sugar, cotton, indigo, dye goods, and tobacco—of colonial origin were to be shipped only to England or its colonies; they could not be exported directly to other European countries.

The Enumeration Act was particularly hard on Virginia and Maryland, for it meant that colonial tobacco—which the English market could not absorb—had to be shipped to England and then reëxported to France, Germany, the Netherlands, or any other nation serving as a market for colonial tobacco. Reëxportation costs—including handling charges, storage charges, and the costs of frequent loss of tobacco stored in English warehouses—were extremely high. Historians have suggested that the enumeration of tobacco produced an economic depression in Virginia and Maryland in the late seventeenth century and led eventually to the concentration of land ownership, since only the large-scale producer could meet the disadvantages of the market.

In 1663 a third Navigation Act—the Staple Act—required that most commodities (excluding salt, servants, and wine) imported into the colonies from Europe had to be shipped from England in English-built ships. A fourth Navigation Act in 1673 was passed to close a loophole which was exploited by colonials when they shipped enumerated commodities from one colony to another without unloading the cargo at the point of destination and then transported the cargo directly to the European market. The Act of 1673 provided that whenever the vessel carried enumerated commodities, a plantation duty, that is, a bond, had to be paid before a ship could clear a colonial port.

A final enactment in 1696 provided for the creation of vice-admiralty courts in America, to place the enforcement of the navigation laws in the hands of men appointed directly by the crown. This act provided for writs of assistance, which gave the vice-admiralty courts legal permission to search warehouses to check for possible evasion of the Navigation Acts.

It is mistakenly assumed that the Navigation Acts were ineffective because the American colonials evaded them. The most reliable statistics by a recent historian, Lawrence Harper, indicate that the burden of the Navigation Acts was greater at the end of the seventeenth century than at any other time during the colonial period. Moreover, Harper has proved that the acts were seldom evaded. Evasion was to come later with the Molasses Act of 1733.

Whereas in the seventeenth century the English regulations were principally directed at commerce, in the eighteenth century, with the maturing of the American economy, the regulations were principally directed at manufactures. The Woolen Act of 1699, which forbade colonial export of wool products, had little impact upon the continental provinces because the colonial exportation of textiles was limited. However, the Hat Act of 1732—which prohibited exportation of hats from one colony to another and severely restricted the colonial hat industry—adversely affected New York and New England, because they had exploited a vital European market for colonially made hats. The act eliminated this colonial enterprise and, at the same time, greatly benefited London hatters, who had exerted pressure in Parliament to pass the bill.

The Molasses Act of 1733—which showed that Britain in the eighteenth century was not unconcerned with commercial regulation—placed a heavy duty upon sugar, rum, molasses, and other commodities imported from the non-British West Indies. This enactment seriously hampered the trade of the continental provinces, because these commodities—molasses in particular—were imported in quantity from Spanish and French colonies at a price cheaper than could be obtained in the British West Indies. Because the act seriously encroached upon this customary channel of trade, the Molasses Act was evaded by extensive smuggling.

The Iron Act of 1750 encouraged the colonial production of pig and bar iron for use by the English iron and steel industry; however, it prohibited the erection of slitting mills, forges, and other iron-finishing equipment. Certain colonies, notably Pennsylvania, defied the Iron Act by subsidizing the erection of slitting mills. When war broke out between France and England soon after the act was passed, the home authorities were unable to enforce the act with vigor. After 1763, of course, the continual crises between the mother country and the colonies interfered with normal channels of trade and prevented effective enforcement.

BRITAIN WINS SUPREMACY IN NORTH AMERICA

Early Conflicts with the French. The shifting balance of power in eighteenth-century Europe, brought about in part by the emergence of France and Britain as the major nations of the western world, produced a ceaseless contest for position in both the Old World and the New. To the English colonials, the strength of New France was a particular danger: French fur traders in the wilderness were capable of stirring up the Indians to hostility against English traders and settlers who began to penetrate the transmontane region, and French control over the interior regions threatened to curb the westward expansion of the English colonies in America.

The War of the Spanish Succession (1702-1713), or Queen Anne's War, as it is known in America, saw a conflict of the colonists with both Spanish and French forces, but the colonies won few advantages from the struggle. By the Treaty of Utrecht in 1713, which ended the war, Great Britain received Acadia (now Nova Scotia), some vaguely defined land in the region of Hudson Bay, Gibraltar on the Spanish coast, Minorca, and the right to sell slaves to Spanish colonies in America for the next thirty years—perhaps useful perquisites from London's point of view, but not very helpful to the colonists. France was left in possession of the St. Lawrence valley, the Great Lakes region, Louisiana, and Cape Breton Island.

In 1739 Great Britain attacked Spain in a conflict which soon merged into the War of Austrian Succession or King George's War (1740-1748). Believing that the time was ripe to neutralize French power in Canada, Governor William Shirley of Massachusetts took the lead in organizing a force of militia and on June 17, 1744, the Americans, in one of the most audacious—and lucky—episodes in the colonial wars, captured Louisbourg (a fort on Cape Breton Island). But once more they lost the advantage of the conquest when the British, by the Treaty of Aachen in 1748, returned the fortress to the French in exchange for Madras in India.

Preliminaries to the "Great War for Empire." The French now showed a greater determination than ever to hold Canada and the Ohio and Mississippi valleys. In 1749 Celoron de Bienville explored the Ohio River system and at strategic points sank lead plates claiming the land for France. Six years later the French erected blockhouses to fortify the Ohio and Allegheny River valleys against the British.

In the meantime, planters from Virginia and Maryland had organized the Ohio Company to exploit virgin lands as far west as the present site of Louisville, Kentucky. To prevent these western lands from falling into possession of the French, Governor Dinwiddie of Virginia in 1753 sent George Washington into the Ohio valley to remonstrate with the French commander. In a skirmish on the frontier at Great Meadows, Washington's troops fired upon a French detachment, killing the commanding officer and twenty men. The French, however, quickly recovered and forced Washington to retreat to Fort Necessity, which he surrendered to the French on July 4, 1754. These were the first shots in a conflict that was to develop into the French and Indian War, known in Europe as the Seven Years' War (1755-1763), which allied England and Prussia against France and Austria.

With the danger of an Indian war threatening the whole frontier, the colonies were more concerned than ever about the stability of the Indians who had formerly been friendly. Thus, for the purpose of conciliating the Iroquois and securing their aid against the French, the British government called a conference in Albany of commissioners from seven northern and middle colonies. This "Albany Congress," however, was more important for its political proposals than for its few accomplishments in dealing with the disaffected Iroquois. Because the delegates realized that a closer union of the colonies was needed to provide better collective defense and control of Indian affairs, they listened attentively to Benjamin Franklin's "Plan of Union," which would have brought all of the colonies under "one general government" with an executive and legislature, but with each colony retaining its separate existence and government. No colony gave the plan serious consideration, however, and the British government disregarded it altogether.

To provide protection to the colonies, the British government ordered two regiments of regulars sent to America and instructed a British fleet to cruise off Canada to prevent the landing of French troops. Most of the French troopships, however, evaded the patrol and landed fresh soldiers. The French also occupied a strong position at Fort Duquesne, at the present site of Pittsburgh and in control of the upper reaches of the Ohio valley. In an attempt to dislodge the French from this strategic position, a detachment of regulars and colonial militia under the command of the British General Edward Braddock went on the march but were ambushed and routed by French and Indian forces just a few miles from the fort. Braddock himself was killed. After Braddock's defeat, Governor Dinwiddie entrusted to George Washington the responsibility of protecting more than three hundred miles of the Virginia frontier against incursions of Indians and French marauders, who were now more active than ever.

The year 1755 was a period of almost unrelieved misfortune for the British, and for the next two or three years the war raged intermittently and disastrously along the whole frontier. In 1756 the New French commander, the Marquis de Montcalm, a man of genuine ability, captured Fort Oswego on Lake Ontario to keep the British from using it as a staging area for a counterattack on Canada. In 1757 Montcalm followed this victory with the destruction of Fort William Henry on Lake George near the headwaters of the Hudson River, where Indian allies of the French slaughtered their prisoners despite Montcalm's effort to prevent a massacre.

Another stinging defeat awaited the British. With the best-equipped army yet put into the field, totaling fifteen thousand men, Major General James Abercromby, like Braddock a professional soldier of experience in the European theater, marched against Fort Ticonderoga on Lake Champlain, which Montcalm held with less than a fourth of Abercromby's attackers. When the British commander on July 5, 1758, ordered his men to attack without any artillery preparation, the French slaughtered them from behind log barricades. Abercromby withdrew in disgrace, leaving two thousand dead before the fort.

A New Policy Brings British Victory. William Pitt, who had become Secretary of State for War in 1757, realized that part of the trouble in America lay in the incompetence of Britain's officers. To remedy this, he ordered to America fresh troops under the command of Lord Jeffrey Amherst, with General James Wolfe as his second-in-command. He also enlisted more wholehearted cooperation from the American provincials when he promised that Britain would reimburse the individual colonies for their war expenditures.

The campaign against the French soon began to show favorable results. In July 1758 the British captured and destroyed Fort Louisbourg on Cape

Breton Island. They also took Fort Frontenac, which controlled Lake Ontario, and Fort Duquesne. The tide of war on the frontier turned in favor of the British.

A victory which finally decided the issue in Canada came on September 13, 1759, when General Wolfe led a successful attack on Quebec, which had been under siege since late June. The capture of Quebec sealed the fate of France in North America. Elsewhere—in Europe and India—British arms were also victorious, and France could do nothing but capitulate. In 1762 France ceded Louisiana to Spain in recompense for aid in the war and a year later, by the Treaty of Paris, ceded to Great Britain all of Canada except the tiny islands of St. Pierre and Miquelon.

With the close of the war, the British colonies in North America no longer felt the need to contribute to their common defense or to unite against a common enemy. The very magnitude of the British victory paved the way for the disintegration of the British Empire in America.

CHAPTER 2

REVOLUTION AND INDEPENDENCE, 1763-1783

BACKGROUND OF THE REVOLUTION

The Character of the Revolution. The American Revolution was one of the great epochs in human history, not only because it brought a separation between Great Britain and its colonies in America but also because it was the first revolution of modern times founded on the principles of self-government and the protection of individual liberty. In this context, the American Revolution became a beacon to light the way for peoples the world over.

The American Revolution was, in fact, many-sided. It was a War for Independence, in which the colonies fought to be separated from the strongest nation in the world, Great Britain; it was a civil war, in which Englishmen fought Englishmen and occasionally colonials fought colonials; it was part of a world war which affected the course of the conflict; it involved a struggle for power within each colony; and it was a nationalist movement in which the colonies, after separating from Britain, formed a lasting union—an important decision that Americans today take for granted but which was not necessarily predestined. Although the purpose of the Revolution was not to establish democracy any more than it was to establish a union, one of the results of the struggle within certain states was to give the average American a greater voice in government.

Finally, it should be remembered that the first revolt by colonials against the homeland in modern times—the English colonies against Britain—occurred under the most enlightened and least burdensome imperial system of contemporary Europe. The colonials in the English colonies enjoyed far more privileges in every sphere of life than did their counterparts in the French and Spanish colonial systems. Why were the least restricted colonials the first to revolt? The American colonials had enjoyed what they conceived of as their liberties for a century or more, and they had no intention of seeing these liberties restricted, even if, comparatively, they were better off than colonials elsewhere. The Revolution was not inevitable, but any action to limit existing privileges would automatically produce friction. How deep the friction was to become depended upon the course of events and the response to these events by American provincials and by the authorities in Britain.

The Need for Adjustment in the English Imperial System. The crises within the empire from 1763 to 1776 were provoked by a series of specific enactments—the Sugar Act of 1764, the Stamp Act of 1765, the Townshend Duties initiated in 1767, and the Coercive Acts of 1774—but to review the prelude to revolution in such narrow terms is to misconstrue the essential issues that were in dispute. An adjustment in the relationship between Britain and its colonies was inevitable because of the sweeping changes that occurred during the eighteenth century. The colonial and commercial systems of Britain had been established in the seventeenth century; the theory which underlay the system was several centuries old. When the system was inaugurated, England possessed only a few colonies. After the Peace of 1763, Britain possessed more than thirty colonies, scattered throughout the world, each colony endowed with individual characteristics. Did the policies initiated in the 1660's suit conditions as they existed in the colonies in the 1760's? Should the same system apply to India and Massachusetts, despite the great variance in their products, their population, and their experience in self-government?

Even without the specific crises that occurred between 1763 and 1776, the British-colonial relationships required adjustment to meet the realities of the late eighteenth century. Three major changes were clearly evident: the American colonies had matured; the political transition in England required a redefinition of the relationship between the colonies within the empire; and the European colonies in America had become a critical factor within the balance of power in Europe.

By 1760 the British colonies in America were no longer infants dependent solely upon the protection of the mother country. From limited self-government to mature self-government, from inexperience with authority to experience, from a primitive to a complex, well-developed indigenous economy—this had been the course of the American colonies. Any imperial system that failed to recognize these realities was doomed. As it existed, the imperial system had become, in some of its parts, an anachronism. The American provinces had become an insatiable market for British goods; the British system failed to adjust to this fact. The American colonies required a more enlightened money and banking policy; the British system tried to apply outworn theories. The American colonies produced statesmen, and even geniuses, but most American talent was unacknowledged.

The political transition in England by which Parliament steadily gained power at the expense of the crown required a rethinking of the constitutional structure of the empire. The colonies had been established under the auspices of royal charters; they had been administered through the king, the executive authority. As Parliament assumed greater authority, fundamental questions arose: Did Parliament have unlimited legislative supremacy over the colonies? Did Parliament gain the executive power previously exercised by the crown? The home authorities said yes; American colonials said no. Moreover, the Industrial Revolution of the eighteenth century in England introduced new problems with regard to mercantile theories, notably the importance of colonies as markets, which were never resolved.

During the eighteenth century the Spanish, French, and British colonies in the New World had become increasingly critical factors in the European balance of power. Beginning particularly with the Peace of Utrecht in 1713, the European powers attempted to establish an equilibrium in that balance. The balance was clearly tipped in England's favor by the Peace of Paris in 1763, when it acquired New France in North America as well as French possessions elsewhere in the world. These British acquisitions created uneasiness and uncertainty throughout western Europe. France began to explore avenues to redress the balance. Soon after 1763 the French recognized the possibility of redressing the European balance of power, not by recapturing its lost colonies nor by capturing British colonies, but by encouraging a separation between Britain and its colonies in America. This reasoning was responsible for French intervention in 1778 on behalf of the Americans. Any one of these major changes in the eighteenth century—the maturation of the colonies, the political and economic transition in Britain, and the diplomatic evolution—was destined to produce problems. Together, they helped to produce a revolution.

The Constitutional Issue. As mentioned in the previous chapter, the British and the American provincials had differing concepts of the constitutional structure of the empire. The British assumed that the self-government practiced by the separate provinces was a favor granted by the mother country—a favor that could be enlarged, curtailed, or even eliminated. The ultimate authority rested in Britain; the provinces possessed no power except that granted by the home authorities. The provincials, on the other hand, construed self-government to rest upon the consent of the governed (the colonial electorate), not upon the royal grace and favor. The Americans believed they possessed rights (at first called the Rights of Englishmen, later called American Rights) which Britain could in no way curtail. Each provincial assembly viewed itself as struggling against a royal governor (and thus against the king) in much the same fashion as the House of Commons was gaining power at the king's expense.

The rising power of Parliament posed an additional question: What were the limits to the legislative power of Parliament as it applied to the colonies? Conflict on this point was inevitable, and it became a critical issue in the revolutionary crisis that developed.

Early Provincial Grievances. During the Great War for Empire (1755-1763) certain British policies annoyed the American provincials. In 1759 the Privy Council instructed the governor of Virginia to refuse to sign any bill which failed to include a "suspending clause"—that is, a clause which prevented the act from becoming effective until first approved by the home authorities. In 1761 general writs of assistance empowering officers of the British customs service to break into and search homes and stores for smuggled goods provoked strong opposition from the provincials, who claimed that the writs were contrary to law and to the natural rights of men. In that same year the Privy Council prohibited the issuance in New York and New Jersey of judicial commissions with unlimited tenure, specifying that such commissions must always be subject to revocation by the king, even though in England judges no longer held their posts at the king's pleasure. In 1764 the Currency Act extended to all colonies the restrictions upon the issuance of paper money which previously had applied only to Massachusetts.

Defense, Western Lands, and Revenue. The Peace of Paris of 1763 eliminated the French threat to English expansion on the North American continent and made available to English colonials opportunities in the West that had been denied them for a quarter of a century. However, the Peace of Paris raised problems with regard to the administration and distribution of this land. It also raised the issue of revenue to pay the costs of administering the empire. Most important, the Peace of Paris, by eliminating the French threat, made the American provincials bolder in stating their views and, once having adopted a position, to cling to it tenaciously.

Among the principal problems faced by the British was the settlement of the territory west of the Alleghenies. The issue was complicated by the revolt in 1763 of the western Indians under the leadership of Pontiac, chief of the Ottawa tribe. Farms and villages along the whole of the colonial frontier from Canada to Virginia were laid waste. The uprising was put down largely by British troops, but the problem of future defense assumed great importance. This incident, together with a previous policy of appointing a commander in chief for America, produced a major decision on the part of the British: to quarter ten thousand British regulars in the American colonies, including the West Indies.

However well-intentioned, this action met with stern provincial opposition. Americans who had faced the French competition at close quarters for a century could not understand why British troops were needed now that the French menace had been eliminated. Ill will between the British Redcoats and the American provincials increased the tension in the period before the outbreak of the Revolution, especially in New York (after 1765) and in Boston (after 1768), where the troops were stationed. Moreover, the colonials were not accustomed to the accepted British practice of expecting the people who were to be "defended" to quarter the troops. The Quartering Act of 1765, which required New York colonials to house the soldiers and to make available supplies, was bitterly resented.

The solution to the problem of western lands beyond the Appalachians was equally irritating. If the colonies in immediate proximity to the western land, like Pennsylvania, New York, Virginia, and the Carolinas, were permitted to extend their boundaries westward, colonies without a hinterland—Connecticut, Rhode Island, New Jersey, and Maryland, to name the most obvious—would be placed at a disadvantage. Should new colonies, therefore, be formed in the territory beyond the Appalachians?

The solution formulated by the British government was the Royal Proclamation Line of 1763, which established a line along the crest of the Alleghenies west of which white men could not take up land. This policy of delay seemed sensible in London, but the provincials were impatient to take advantage of the new territory. Virginians had fought in the Great War for Empire specifically to open this area to settlement. Not only were frontiersmen eager to exploit these opportunities, but land companies in Pennsylvania, Virginia, and New England, whose membership included affluent provincials and Englishmen, wished to act. For these men the Proclamation Line was a disappointment—an unexpected barrier to enterprise and opportunity.

The Proclamation Line, intended originally as a temporary measure to gain time for a permanent policy, was not revoked before the Revolution. Moreover, the Quebec Act of 1774, often mistakenly included among the Coercive Acts of that year, further annoyed the provincials by annexing the western lands north of the Ohio River to the Province of Quebec. The former French colony, viewed from the perspective of the provincials as the enemy, was to be rewarded while the faithful provincials who had fought to free that territory from French control were denied the fruits of their sacrifices.

The problems of western land and defense did not bring on the Revolution, but they were a grievance which, when added to other irritations, decreased the probability of compatibility and increased the chances of open hostility. If they had been the only grievance, the final result no doubt would have been different; when added to the cumulative resentment they weighed in the balance toward revolt.

Grenville's Program to Obtain Revenue. George Grenville, who became Prime Minister in 1763, though neither an imaginative nor clever man, was a determined one. Coming into office just at the close of the French and Indian War and feeling, as most of his countrymen did, that the American colonists were the greatest beneficiaries of the vast territory of the Ohio and Mississippi valley won from the French, he was determined that the colonists should pay at least part of the costs of defending and pacifying this territory. Currently no revenue was coming from the colonists to aid in imperial defense; the duties imposed by the Navigation Acts were being evaded by smugglers, and, in fact, the American customs service was costing more to operate than it was collecting in fees. Thus, in 1764 Grenville pushed through the Sugar Act, an act intended to produce revenue—a purpose clearly stated in its preface—by means of effective enforcement of certain customs duties on sugar, wine, coffee, silk, and other goods. Although it reduced the duty on molasses bought from non-British sources from 6 pence to 4 pence per gallon—on the surface, an attractive reduction—provincials actually had been smuggling in molasses for no more than a pence and a half per gallon as a bribe to customs officials. Now Grenville intended to enforce the trade laws by stricter administrative procedures. The crux of the issue, however, was the British intention to tax the colonists for purposes of revenue. Before this, duties had been imposed merely as a means of regulating the trade of the empire.

The issue of taxation, raised by the Sugar Act, was brought to a crisis in the Stamp Act of 1765, which provoked spontaneous opposition throughout the colonies. The Stamp Act placed a stamp fee on all legal documents, deeds and diplomas, custom papers, and newspapers, to name the most obvious articles. It directly affected every articulate element in the community, including lawyers, merchants, preachers, and printers. Moreover, the act raised not only the question of who had the right to tax but also the more significant questions: Who had what power? Could Parliament legislate for the colonials in all matters? Was Parliament's authority without limit or were there bounds beyond which it could not reach—bounds based upon certain rights inherent in all Englishmen?

The conflict was contested on two levels, that of specific action and that of constitutional debate. In every colony the men appointed as Stamp Act collectors were forced to resign, sometimes under the threat of force. Sons of Liberty were organized in key colonies to enforce the colonially imposed prohibition on the use of stamps; occasionally mob spirit carried opposition to extremes, as it did in Massachusetts when a band of provincials ransacked the home of Lieutenant Governor Thomas Hutchinson. The courts and the ports which could not, in a strictly legal sense, operate without using the stamps continued after a momentary lull to carry out their regular functions in defiance of the act.

Each colonial legislature met to decide on a course of action, the most famous incident occurring in the Virginia House of Burgesses, where Patrick Henry introduced resolutions declaring that the "General Assembly of this Colony have the only and *sole exclusive* Right and Power to lay Taxes and Impositions upon the Inhabitants of This Colony." Any other course, said Henry, would tend "to destroy British as well as American Freedom." At the invitation of Massachusetts, nine colonies sent delegates to New York in October 1765 to form the Stamp Act Congress, in which a set of resolutions was adopted denying the authority of Parliament to tax the colonials. A boycott of British goods—the use of economic coercion to achieve political ends—was introduced on the theory that the colonial market was so necessary to Britain that it would abandon the act to regain the market.

On the second level, that of defining constitutional theory, the respective arguments of the colonials and the authorities in England developed differently. Colonials argued that they could not be free without being secure in their property and that they could not be secure in their property if, without their consent, others could take it away by taxes. This argument, of course, revealed the close tie between property and liberty in the mind of the eighteenth century Anglo-Americans.

The British responded by saying that the Americans were not being taxed without their consent because they were "virtually," if not directly, represented in Parliament. British exponents argued that many areas in Britain —notably Manchester and other substantial communities—were not directly represented in Parliament, but that no one denied that an act of Parliament had authority over those communities. The same concept of "virtual representation," so asserted British leaders, applied to the colonies.

The colonies vigorously opposed this interpretation of representation. Most of the colonial legislatures echoed Maryland's argument "that it cannot, with any Truth or Propriety, be said, That the Freemen of this Province of Maryland are Represented in the British Parliament." Daniel Dulany, a Maryland attorney, in his *Considerations on the Propriety of Imposing Taxes in the British Colonies,* argued that even those people in Britain who did not have the right to vote were allied in interest with their contemporaries. "But who," he asked, "are the Representatives of the Colonies?" Who could speak for them?

The Right of Exemption from all Taxes without their Consent, the Colonies claim as *British* Subjects. They derive this Right from the Common Law, which their Charters have declared and confirmed. . . . A Right to impose an internal Tax on the Colonies, without their Consent *for the single Purpose of Revenue,* is denied; a Right to regulate their Trade without their Consent is admitted.

In brief, the provincials argued, Parliament had power, but not unlimited power. It could *legislate* and thus impose external duties to regulate trade, but it could not levy a *tax* for revenue. In time, as the revolutionary crisis deepened, the provincial position was modified to deny Parliament's authority to legislate for or tax the colonists for any purpose whatsoever.

A view much closer to the eventual stand taken by the provincials was expressed by George Mason of Virginia, who implicitly denied the infinite subordination of the colonies. "We rarely see anything from your [the English] side of the water free from the authoritative style of a master to a school boy: 'We have with infinite difficulty and fatigue got you excused this one time; pray be a good boy for the future, do what your papa and mama bid you.'" He warned the British that "such another experiment as the stamp-act would produce a general revolt in America."

Parliament backed down—not on the principle at issue, but on the act itself. The Stamp Act was repealed in 1766; at the same time, however, the Declaratory Act was passed stating that Parliament possessed the authority to make laws binding the American colonists. The Americans mistakenly believed not only that their arguments were pursuasive but that the economic pressure brought on by the boycott of English goods had been effective. The boycott, in fact, delayed action rather than hastened it, but the Americans, unaware of their failure, were to employ the boycott as a standard weapon against the British at each time of crisis.

The Townshend Duties. The next major crisis arose in 1767. Misled by Benjamin Franklin, who in February 1766 had told the House of Commons that the provincials objected only to internal taxes, not to taxes on trade, the British Parliament in 1767 enacted the Townshend Duties on glass, lead, paper, paints, and tea. These import or "external" taxes were designed to exploit the distinction between internal taxes and external duties which Parliament mistakenly supposed the Americans were making. At the same time, Parliament reorganized the customs service by appointing a Board of Customs Commissioners to be located at Boston. The following year, 1768, troops were sent to Boston, in part at least because of the urging of the Customs Commissioners. The Townshend Duties failed to awaken the spontaneous reaction of the Stamp Act, but they tested once again colonial versus British theory of the empire and posed anew the question: What were the limits to the power of Parliament?

Again the American provincials resorted to a boycott, although no intercolonial Congress was called. John Dickinson, in his *Letters from a Farmer in Pennsylvania*, reaffirmed the position of the colonials that duties, even "external" duties, could not be levied primarily to obtain revenue, though measures enacted to regulate trade were admitted as a proper prerogative of Parliament. Dickinson's essays were not revolutionary in tone or in spirit; neither, however, did they back away from the fundamental position taken by the provincials, that they alone could levy a tax upon themselves.

As for the British, the Board of Customs Commissioners who came to enforce the Navigation Acts, the Sugar Act of 1764, and the Townshend Duties carried out their responsibility in such a perfidious way that they were properly accused of customs racketeering. One of the Commissioners' favorite devices was to relax enforcement of the laws for a period and then suddenly clamp down. Since one third of the value of the cargo and offending vessel became the property of the official responsible for its seizure, such tactics were financially profitable for the commissioners. At times, enforcement of the technical aspects of the law was so meticulous as to militate against the intended spirit of the law. At any rate, the customs racketeers became leeches, hated particularly by New England merchants. The role of the Board of Customs Commissioners, significant as it was for specific locales, can be overdrawn, because the important fact was not merely that Americans most vulnerable to their activity were disposed to stand against the British; but a consensus of opposition pervaded all the colonies, many of which experienced no serious problem with customs officials. This consensus was made possible because of a more profound issue: Where did the regulatory power of Parliament end and that of the colonials begin?

The Townshend Duties disappointed their British advocates, for they did not produce the revenue expected. In 1770, therefore, the British repealed the Townshend Duties (except the duty on tea, which was retained as a symbol of Parliament's right to tax); the Americans relaxed their opposition and reopened their ports to British goods, though they condemned tea drinking as unpatriotic. Despite the "Boston Massacre" of 1770, when, egged on by provincials hurling snowballs and rocks, British Redcoats opened fire on Americans, killing three persons and wounding eight, the prosperous period from 1770 to 1773 was remarkably free from disturbance.

'TIS TIME TO PART

The Boston Tea Party and the Coercive Acts. Beginning in 1772, provoked by a British decision to pay the salary of Lieutenant Governor Hutchinson out of customs revenues and thus free him from dependence on the colonial assembly, a Committee of Correspondence was established in Massachusetts at the urging of Sam Adams. Many other colonies followed the Massachusetts pattern and formed such committees in order to keep one another informed of possible British action. In 1772 the *Gaspee,* a customs vessel in pursuit of colonial shipping, was boarded and burned off Providence, Rhode Island. These isolated incidents indicated that Americans had not abandoned their position but that, unless new provocations occurred, the situation probably would remain static. In 1773 and 1774, with the Boston Tea Party and the passage of the Coercive Acts, the conflict between Great Britain and its colonies entered a new and conclusive phase.

By the Tea Act of May 1773 the British government permitted the British East India Company, which had built up an excess stock of tea in England, to market—"dump" would perhaps be a more accurate term—it in America. The company was also authorized to employ its own agents in this transaction, and thus, in effect, to seize monopolistic control of the American market. With this act the British reawakened the latent hostility of the American provincials. When the ships carrying the tea arrived in American ports, they were met with unbroken opposition. In some provinces, the ships were forced to return to England without unloading; in other cases the tea was placed in a warehouse to prevent its distribution; in Boston a band of men, haphazardly disguised as Indians, dumped the tea into the harbor.

The reaction in England upon hearing the news was prompt and decisive: punitive legislation must be passed to teach those property-destroying Massachusetts provincials a lesson. This position was endorsed by members of Parliament previously well disposed to the Americans. In quick succession, three Coercive or "Intolerable" Acts were passed: the Boston Port Act (March 31, 1774), which closed that port to commerce; the Massachusetts Government Act (May 30, 1774), which altered the manner of choosing the Governor's Council, but more significantly indicated to the Americans that parliamentary power knew no limits; and finally, the Administration of Justice Act (May 30, 1774), which removed certain cases involving crown officials from the jurisdiction of Massachusetts. The American provincials immediately rallied to the support of Massachusetts in opposing these "Intolerable Acts"— much to the surprise of the British authorities, who had anticipated the support rather than the condemnation of the colonies outside Massachusetts. After all, had not property been destroyed? No action on the part of the Americans revealed the basic issue so clearly. Essentially, the issue was not customs racketeering, or the presence of Redcoats, or the problem of western lands, or even taxes. The issue was: Who had what power?

The Coercive Acts set in motion a series of actions and counteractions which led directly to separation. If there was any one point at which the Revolution seemed to become inevitable it was 1774, with the passage of the Coercive Acts and the provincial response to those acts. What would Parliament do next, the provincials asked themselves. Change the administration of justice in Virginia? Eliminate self-government in New York? Close the port of Philadelphia? Once the supremacy of Parliament in all areas was conceded, self-government would live merely on sufferance.

The colonials at this stage were not calling for independence; such a step was too frightening. The Americans had lived within the British Empire for more than a century; it was the most enlightened government of its time, where liberty was a word that meant something. To separate from Britain in the 1770's was somewhat similar to an abrupt change in the current form of government under which Americans have lived since 1789. It was not a step to be taken, as the revolutionary fathers later declared in the Declaration of Independence, for light and transient causes.

The Provincials Act. Events proceeded once again on two levels—that of action and that of theory. The First Continental Congress was called to meet in Philadelphia in September 1774. A number of important decisions made early in the deliberations set the tone of the meeting. Carpenters Hall, instead of the legislative chambers of Pennsylvania, was selected as the meeting hall, a victory for Sam Adams of Massachusetts and those who wished to take firm action against Britain. A more important show of strength came when resolutions proposing a union of colonies and regarded as conciliatory were offered by Joseph Galloway. His resolutions were tabled by a close vote, and the Suffolk Resolves were adopted, asserting that the colonies should make no concessions until Britain first repealed the Coercive Acts, thus placing the burden of conciliation upon the home authorities. In addition, the First Continental Congress adopted a series of resolutions embodying their position and sent them off to the king. At the same time a Continental Association was established to cut off trade with the British. Although Congress avowed its "allegiance to his majesty" and its "affection for our fellow subjects" in Great Britain, the stand taken placed the British on notice.

When the First Continental Congress adjourned, its members agreed to meet again in the spring of 1775 if no action was forthcoming from Britain. Conditions failed to improve; in fact, they became worse. In Massachusetts "minutemen" were training to guard against possible actions by British Redcoats stationed in Boston; guns, powder, and other military stores were being collected at Concord. When on April 18, 1775, the British military governor sent out from Boston about 700 British regulars to destroy the stores at Concord, they were met by minutemen companies in Lexington and Concord. With minutemen swarming in from the countryside, the Redcoats faced unexpected hazards on their return to Boston. Before the day was spent, they suffered nearly 300 casualties and escaped total destruction only because reinforcements came from Boston. Dogging the regulars all the way back to Boston, the minutemen encamped on its land approaches, thus beginning the seige of Boston. Meanwhile, on May 10, New England forces led by Benedict Arnold and Ethan Allen captured Fort Ticonderoga on Lake Champlain and subsequently moved northward to seize points along the Canadian border.

Therefore, when the Second Continental Congress met in May 1775, the thin line between peace and war was in danger of vanishing. Congress appointed a Virginian, George Washington, commander in chief of the provincial forces surrounding Boston. His nomination by John Adams, a Massachusetts man, revealed the determined effort of the provincials to present a united front. Congress tried to win Canada to its cause, but failed. On July 6, 1775, Congress adopted the "Declaration of the Causes and Necessity of taking up Arms" in an attempt to assure fellow Britons that dissolution of the union was not intended but neither would Americans back away from their convictions. "Our cause is just. Our union is perfect. Our internal resources are great, and, if necessary, foreign assistance is undoubtedly attainable." In August 1775 the king declared his subjects were already in rebellion and he began to recruit foreign mercenaries and to prepare the British regulars.

During the remainder of 1775 the Americans attempted the conquest of Canada, chiefly in order to deprive Britain of a base of attack on the revolutionary colonies. A force commanded by Richard Montgomery crossed the Canadian border from Lake Champlain, captured Montreal, and moved toward Quebec via the St. Lawrence River. Another group of volunteers under Benedict Arnold set out across the wilderness of Maine. A combined assault on Quebec by the two forces ended in defeat; Montgomery was killed and Arnold wounded.

Beginning in January 1776 the movement for independence gained ground. Thomas Paine published his *Common Sense,* asserting "'tis time to part." Appreciatively read by thousands upon thousands, *Common Sense* helped to crystallize opinion. By late spring, a number of colonies instructed their delegates to advocate independence. On June 7, 1776, Richard Henry Lee of Virginia, once again reflecting the unity of colonials regardless of region, introduced a resolution calling for independence. It was adopted on July 2 by such a close vote that the deliberate absence of several Pennsylvania delegates who were not convinced that independence was the best policy provided the winning margin.

The Constitutional Issue Refined. Action and theory were moving together. James Wilson, later a Supreme Court justice, published *Considerations on the Authority of Parliament* in August 1774, which posed a series of questions: "And have those, whom we have hitherto been accustomed to consider as our fellow-subjects, an absolute and unlimited power over us? Have they a natural right to make laws, by which we may be deprived of our properties, of our liberties, of our lives? By what title do they claim to be our masters? . . . Do those, who embark freemen in Great Britain, disembark slaves in America?" Wilson answered by affirming, without qualification, that Parliament had no authority over the colonies. Their dependence upon Britain was exclusively through the crown; the colonies were "different members of the British Empire . . . , independent of each other, but connected together under the same sovereign."

The Declaration of Independence. Wilson's assumption underlay the philosophy of the Declaration of Independence. The entire document is directed against the king; nowhere is Parliament mentioned.

The Continental Congress could have separated from Britain by means of a simple declarative resolution; an elaborate document to explain the reason for revolution was unnecessary. That such a document was written is in itself an insight into the nature of the Revolution, for it was not of tattered flags, of starved and desperate people, or of lawlessness. Its leadership included some of the most substantial and prominent men in America—John Hancock, John Brown, Thomas Willing, George Washington, and a host of others. Because of their influential position and their regard for law, these men and their associates felt a deep need to explain to a "candid world" why they took such a drastic step.

Five delegates of the Continental Congress, among them John Adams and Benjamin Franklin, were assigned the task of writing the Declaration, but the draft was composed by Thomas Jefferson. Modest changes were made in Jefferson's draft by the members of the committee, and the document was then debated in Congress, where additional alterations were made.

The philosophy upon which the Declaration was based was that which underlay treatises written by John Locke on the occasion of the English Glorious Revolution of 1688; the similarity between the ideas and even the phraseology of Locke and the Declaration is striking. The Declaration appealed to the highest authority within the intellectual structure of the eighteenth century, "the Laws of Nature and Nature's God." The king had violated his compact with the people, and so it was the "right of the people to alter or to abolish it, and to institute new government, laying its foundation on such principles and organizing its power in such form, as to them [the governed] shall seem most likely to effect their safety and happiness." To prove the "absolute tyranny" of the king over these states, a list of grievances—in a sense an indictment—was appended. With the Declaration, the issue that provincial governments derived their power from the consent of the governed and did not exist on sufferance of the royal grace and favor reached its consummation.

The Declaration operated as a divisive as well as a unifying force. Provincials were finally required to choose the side they wished to support—to remain loyal to Britain or to select the path of Revolution. It was not an easy choice by any means. Men like Daniel Dulany and Joseph Galloway, who had firmly supported the colonial position throughout the crises, became Loyalists. In fact, more people proportionately left the colonies because of the consequences of the Declaration than were to flee France at the time of the French Revolution.

With the Declaration, the character of the conflict changed. Whereas the colonials had been secretly soliciting aid from France since 1775, the Continental Congress, representing an independent people, now established ministries throughout Europe to obtain recognition and help for the United States. Washington, who had been leading a militia force to obtain recognition of the rights of the provincials, now headed an army fighting for American independence. Thirteen colonies became thirteen states with the problem of working out appropriate constitutions. Facing the experience of union, the Americans had to work out an acceptable constitutional structure for the national government. With the Declaration, the Continental Congress was no longer an extra-legal body of rebels but the symbol of a sovereign nation.

The Internal Revolution. Emphasis has been placed on the principal issue— what were the limits of the power of Parliament?—but historians have investigated a second question: Within each colony, who was to possess authority? The point of view of historians has ranged widely on this question. Some have insisted that the issue of who was going to rule at home was preëminent, that the break with Britain was brought about by a radical group within each colony who were so anxious to overthrow the existing structure of power within their colony that they worked for revolution to accomplish this purpose. Other historians contend that those who held power in the late colonial period wished to preserve it and that they were willing to fight to maintain it.

The present consensus among historians is perhaps best expressed as follows: Internal conflicts within a colony contributed to the coming of the Revolution because men hoped to correct grievances under the new regime. However, this internal struggle for control was not the decisive or preëminent force. The principal issue was the conflict over the constitutional framework of the empire. Even without an internal struggle, the Revolution would have occurred. The internal grievances are related, however, to later developments in the revolutionary and post-revolutionary periods as Americans set about to resolve their own problems.

PROSECUTING THE WAR

Continental Congress. To make independence a reality, the war had to be won. The Continental Congress became the central agency for the prosecution of the longest war in the history of the United States (1776-1783). Though Congress had neither a specific grant of authority nor a fixed constitutional basis until 1781, it resolved the financial, military, diplomatic, and constitutional questions during this critical period. Occasionally, action lagged and arguments centered upon trivialities, but Congress should be remembered for its major achievements rather than for its minor failures. Congress unified the American war effort and fashioned an instrument of national government without violating individual liberty and without producing dissension so divisive as to splinter the Revolution. Most of America's greatest leaders served at one time or another in the Congress, gaining their first political experience at the national rather than at the colony-state level.

Revolutionary Finance. One of the early problems facing Congress was to finance the war. Four major methods were quickly employed: issuing Loan Office Certificates, the equivalent of present-day government bonds; requisitions, that is, requests for money and later supplies from individual states to fight the war; foreign loans, which were insignificant until 1781; and finally, paper currency.

The first issues of paper money were made by Congress before the Declaration of Independence. This avenue of revenue was one that had been used by many colonies during the colonial period. At first the paper money circulated at its face value, but as more money was issued its value declined (although intermittently the value of the currency increased when successful military operations revived hopes for a quick victory). By the spring of 1781, however, the value of paper currency had declined so precipitously that it cost more to print than it was worth as money once it was printed. Up to this point, however, paper money paid for no less than 75 per cent of the cost of the war. After 1781 foreign loans became especially important, because these loans provided capital for the establishment of a national bank, the Bank of North America, from which the government borrowed money in excess of the bank's capitalization. After 1781, Morris Notes—a form of paper currency backed by the word of Robert Morris, appointed Superintendent of Finance in 1781—helped to restore the public credit. At the conclusion of the war the national government as well as the various states had incurred a substantial debt that was to figure in the movement to write the federal Constitution of 1787.

Military Strategy. The British did not take advantage of their most promising military strategy until 1782, when, too late, they managed to blockade all the American ports. An intensive blockade, if it had been coordinated with swift, devastating land campaigns to lay waste the resources of the Americans, might have brought success, for the British, in order to win, had to demand unconditional surrender. The Americans, to be successful, needed an army in the field as a symbol of resistance. Any negotiations automatically recognized the United States as an independent nation because a sovereign power does not negotiate with rebels.

The first military operations of the British were concentrated in the middle states, with an eye to dividing the United States physically, crippling their unity, and exploiting the possibility of support from American Loyalists. When this failed, the emphasis shifted to the southern theater of operations beginning in 1780.

The War in the North. Washington forced the British under General Sir William Howe to abandon Boston by capturing Dorchester Heights in March 1776. Howe loaded his troops on transports and sailed to Nova Scotia to prepare for an attack on New York. He took with him more than a thousand Loyalists who preferred residence in

Canada to independence from Great Britain. In an effort to prevent Howe's taking New York, Washington moved south and occupied Brooklyn Heights on Long Island. There on August 27, 1776, Howe with an army of thirty-three thousand attacked and defeated Washington, who withdrew to Manhattan Island. After Howe's brother, Lord Richard Howe, in command of a naval force, had occupied New York, Washington retreated to New Jersey. The British troops continued to occupy the city of New York for the duration of the Revolution.

With an army that seemed destined to disappear entirely at times, Washington could not hope to recapture New York or to prevent the British from making further advances. Only the stupidity or laziness of General Howe prevented the annihilation of Washington's army. Even though at one time his troops numbered only three thousand men, Washington managed to keep the semblance of an army together. Indeed, on two occasions he won startling victories over British units. On Christmas night, 1776, Washington crossed the Delaware, fell on a garrison of Hessian troops at Trenton, and captured or killed most of them. Again, on January 3, he won a small battle at Princeton and marched with his army to Morristown, where he established winter quarters.

In 1777 Howe bestirred himself sufficiently to send an army by sea against Philadelphia. Washington proceeded overland south of Philadelphia and met units of Howe's army at Brandywine Creek on September 11, 1777, suffering defeat after being badly outmaneuvered. Howe entered Philadelphia with ease, but British units were severely tested when Washington launched an unexpected counterattack at Germantown on October 4. Though the American army was defeated, its offensive spirit aided the cause of independence at home and in France.

In the meantime the British had planned a three-pronged attack to capture the Hudson valley and thus isolate New England from the colonies to the south. From Canada, General Sir John Burgoyne was to push southward down Lake Champlain and the upper Hudson with the expectation of joining Howe moving up the Hudson from New York City; Burgoyne would then join Howe in an attack on Philadelphia and the occupation of other rebel territory to the south. Why Howe did not attempt to cooperate with Burgoyne, nobody knows, except that Howe received conflicting orders and decided that the immediate capture of Philadelphia was more urgent. Burgoyne had also expected to converge with a third British force (mostly Loyalists and Indians) moving eastward from Lake Ontario along the Mohawk valley, but this force was beaten back by American forces at the Battle of Oriskany. Nevertheless, throughout the summer of 1777 Burgoyne pressed southward toward Albany. At last, in two battles fought near Saratoga, Burgoyne, failing to receive aid from either Howe or the force from Lake Ontario, suffered complete defeat, and on October 17, 1777, he surrendered his entire force of 5800 men to the American General Horatio Gates. Thus ended the British hope of isolating New England by occupying the Hudson valley.

European Aid to the Americans. The victory over Burgoyne and the Battle of Germantown had significant political results. They indicated to European politicians that the Americans could win independence and that British power could be crippled by loss of its continental colonies. France, of course, was anxious for revenge upon its ancient enemy, and the efforts of American diplomats in Paris now began to bear fruit. Benjamin Franklin proved a most effective ambassador to France. Wearing a fur cap as the symbol of republican and frontier simplic-

MAJOR REVOLUTIONARY CAMPAIGNS

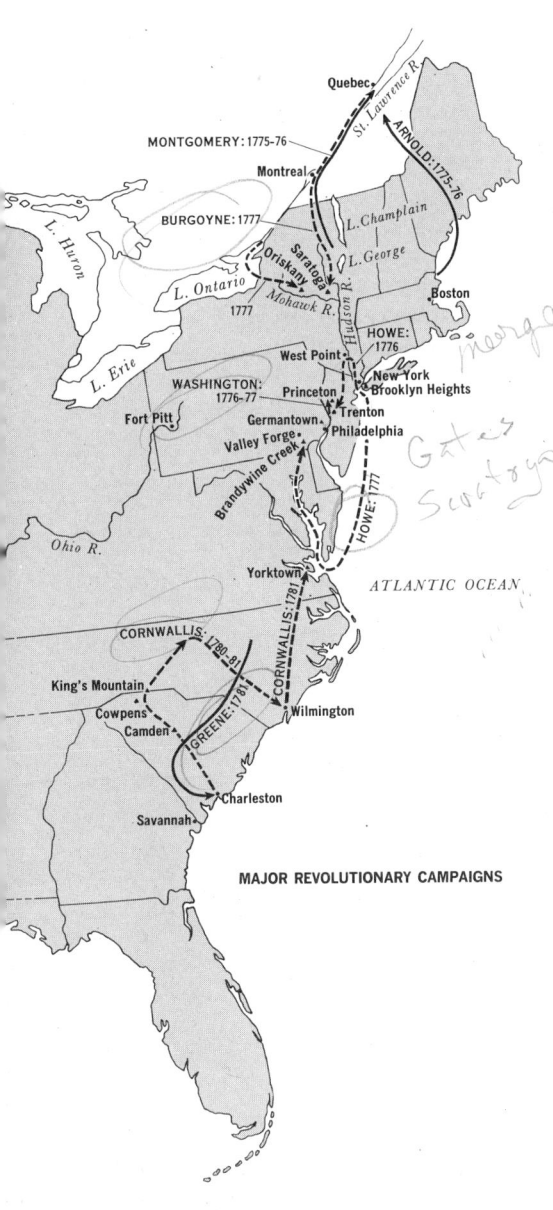

ity, he soon became the toast of Paris and made friends with those politicians best able to help the American cause. On February 6, 1778, he consummated an alliance with France. Since Spain was at this time closely allied with France, America expected aid from Spain, though these hopes were never fulfilled. Because Holland was eager to gain access to American markets, from which Great Britain had long tried to exclude her, she also provided aid, largely in the form of loans underwritten by the French. France immediately supplied limited funds to aid the American cause and in 1780 dispatched troops and ships. French ports were now opened to such war vessels as the Americans had and privateers could attack British vessels and stand a better chance of getting away to a safe haven. The French navy provided sea power that the colonies had previously lacked. European aid, prompted by self-interest, contributed to the American victory.

New Campaigns in the North. The winter of 1778 was a bitter one for Washington. His army went into winter quarters at Valley Forge, not far from Philadelphia, where Howe and the British were quartered. Because the British could pay in gold, farmers kept them supplied with everything they could want, while Washington's troops nearly starved and went barefoot in the snow, not because of the unavailability of supplies but because of the maladministration in their distribution.

Howe, notorious for his dilatoriness, was relieved by Sir Henry Clinton, who evacuated Philadelphia and returned to New York for a new campaign in the North. Washington, without the power to inflict defeat, could only hang on the flanks of the British army. He established a base at White Plains, New York, and saw to it that West Point on the Hudson was fortified. The arrival off New York of a French naval force under Count d'Estaing did little to help the American cause, for D'Estaing showed little audacity and soon sailed away to the West Indies. Only from the western frontier in 1778 was the news encouraging. George Rogers Clark, leading a group of frontiersmen, captured Kaskaskia, on the Mississippi; in February 1779 he seized Vincennes, in what is now Indiana. Clark helped to hold the West against the British.

Revolution and Independence, 1763–1783

Benedict Arnold, who had fought ably for the Americans in several significant engagements, was frustrated and bitter because he was not given a higher command. Ironically, Washington appointed Arnold to a post of exceptional responsibility—commanding the fortress of West Point—just at the time Arnold was plotting to betray his country. In September 1780, Washington discovered a plan that Arnold had made with the British to deliver West Point into their hands. Major John André, the British go-between, was arrested with incriminating evidence and hanged. Arnold escaped, fled to the British army, and eventually fought against the Americans in the Virginia Campaign of 1781. If Arnold's treachery had succeeded, Washington's position would have been imperiled.

The War in the South. When they proved largely ineffective in the middle region, the British turned to the southern theater of operations. They captured Savannah (1778) and Charleston (1780) and hoped to collaborate with the Loyalists in the interior and gain control of Georgia and the Carolinas.

Despite the efforts of American guerrilla bands the fate of the South remained in doubt. On August 16, 1780, the British under Cornwallis inflicted a disastrous defeat upon American forces at Camden, South Carolina, but this defeat was redeemed on October 7, 1780, by the destruction of a Loyalist force at the Battle of King's Mountain near the North Carolina border. This victory, coupled with the brilliant victory of Daniel Morgan and his farmer-cavalrymen at the Battle of Cowpens, South Carolina, on January 17, 1781, turned the tide in the Carolinas. Through the winter, spring, and summer of 1781, General Nathanael Greene, commander of the American army in the South, skillfully threw militia, cavalry, and guerrilla forces against the British armies. By autumn those British forces that had not moved north to Virginia were pocketed in a small area about Charleston, South Carolina.

Battle of Yorktown. At the beginning of 1781, the British were still active in the Carolinas; Clinton was holding New York, and though Washington's troops could hamper his movements by land, Clinton still could operate by sea. Utilizing this opportunity, he sent an army under Cornwallis to Virginia in April 1781 to occupy the coastal region and unite with British forces supposedly marching north from South Carolina.

Meanwhile, in 1780 the French dispatched an army of 5500 men under an able soldier, the Count Rochambeau, to aid Washington. These troops encamped at Newport, while Rochambeau and Washington waited to see what success collaborative effort would bring.

The Count de Grasse, a brilliant French naval commander with a well-equipped squadron, had arrived in the West Indies. After an exchange of correspondence, De Grasse decided that his squadron could attack more successfully in the Chesapeake than in the harbor of New York, so a decision was made for a coordinated land and sea attack in Virginia. Washington and Rochambeau began to move their armies southward, a maneuver which the British believed was a feint to catch them off guard in New York, where they expected the main attack to take place. With De Grasse controlling the Chesapeake Bay area and with a French and American force of fifteen thousand men surrounding Cornwallis' camp on the York peninsula, Cornwallis was doomed. He surrendered on October 19, 1781. As his men marched out to lay down their arms, a band from Washington's army played "The World Turned Upside Down." When the news of Yorktown reached Britain, the King's ministers agreed that peace must be made with the rebellious colonies.

The War in Retrospect. The war had been a strange, and at times a hopeless, one for the Americans. But Washington had emerged as a persistent, determined leader. He may have lacked brilliance as a military tactician, but he had the courage, integrity, and character essential to successful command. Despite the demoralization of his forces by lack of supplies, by desertions, and occasionally by mutinies, he held on until the Americans, with French help, achieved victory.

British incompetence played a part in the eventual outcome of the war. Without the assistance that British commanders—Howe and Clinton, particularly—unwittingly gave the patriots, the end might have been different. It was the good fortune of America that Great Britain had been engaged in a world war, and that some of her best troops and more competent commanders were in India, Africa, the West Indies, and elsewhere.

Although a few young Frenchmen like Lafayette came to America to fight for the patriots out of sheer idealism, the alliance of the Bourbon powers, France and Spain, against Great Britain was not motivated by love of liberty or of the republican principles so nobly stated in the Declaration of Independence. By a trick of fate, these very principles of liberty would exercise an enormous influence in France within a few years and would overturn the French monarchy. But in the conflict between the colonies and Great Britain, France was merely playing the game of power politics. It hoped to wreak revenge on an ancient enemy and perhaps to regain some of the American territory it had lost.

Spain also had an interest in territory west of the British possessions in North America. To weaken Great Britain's strength in the New World would provide possible opportunities for later aggrandizement there for France and Spain. A weak and struggling republic without money and friends would be easy to dominate and perhaps to devour.

France had promised its satellite, Spain, that it would help wrest Gibraltar from the British, but France and Spain had attacked Gibraltar in vain. Now France proposed to appease Spain by obtaining for Spain territory west of the Appalachians that Great Britain or Spanish colonies claimed. In the peace negotiations, which had begun even before Yorktown, the disposition of western territories was a critical consideration.

The Peace of Paris, 1783. To negotiate a peace with England, Congress appointed five commissioners: Benjamin Franklin, envoy in France; John Jay, American agent in Spain; John Adams, envoy in Holland; Henry Laurens; and Thomas Jefferson. Only the first three, assembled at Paris, took active part in the discussions. From the first, Jay was suspicious of the motives of the Count de Vergennes, the French foreign minister, and of the British agent Richard Oswald. Oswald came with instructions to treat with the commissioners as if they represented rebellious colonies. Jay insisted that Oswald go back and obtain new instructions to treat with the representatives of the "Thirteen United States," which would be tantamount to recognizing at the outset the independence of the new republic. This Oswald did.

Although the commissioners had received from Congress full power to negotiate the best treaty possible, Congress had specifically instructed them to take no steps that France would not approve. Since Jay was convinced that France was determined to sacrifice American interest to satisfy Spain, he persuaded Adams and Franklin to deal secretly with England and to make a preliminary treaty that promised favorable terms. The news leaked out and Vergennes was incensed, but Franklin, a great favorite of the French, managed to placate him by admitting that their action was merely an "indiscretion." Nevertheless, the preliminary treaty had established the pattern for the final treaty which was signed on September 3, 1783.

Great Britain, partly to sow dissension among the Bourbon allies and partly to win the friendship of the late colonies and to keep them from becoming satellites of France, offered such favorable terms that Vergennes in anger declared that the English were ready to "buy peace rather than make it." Instead of Spain obtaining the trans-Appalachian region, Great Britain agreed that the Mississippi should be the western boundary of the United States. Although Franklin had tried to obtain all of Canada "to insure peace," Great Britain agreed that the Great Lakes should determine the northern border. Since the ultimate disposition of East and West Florida was in doubt, it was agreed that if Great Britain gave the Floridas back to Spain, the border of the United States would run along the thirty-first degree of north latitude. If Great Britain retained the Floridas, the boundary would be approximately a degree and a half farther north. In the end Spain regained the Floridas, which it in time sold to the United States. The provisions of the treaty sounded clear, but in some areas the boundary lines were not definitely stated, as for example in Maine, where the border remained in dispute for years.

The treaty also provided that American citizens were to enjoy the same fishing rights as British subjects in Canadian waters, and that they might dry their fish and nets in any uninhabited spots that they chose. The two countries agreed that the Mississippi River would be forever open to navigation by both American and British shipping. The British demanded restitution of Loyalist property confiscated during the war, but all Congress could do was to recommend that this be done. The payment of debts owed to British subjects was also demanded. The commissioners pointed out that Congress had no authority over the states, but the treaty agreed that suits might be brought by British subjects in the state courts for the recovery of debts. The Treaty of Paris was ratified by Congress on January 14, 1784.

EFFECTS OF THE WAR

Unrestricted Trade. Wars traditionally result in social and financial upheavals, and the American Revolution was no exception. Within the space of twenty years of controversy and war, old and settled traditions were altered and the patterns of a new society emerged.

No longer were the American colonies the source of raw materials supplied exclusively to Great Britain, as had been the case in colonial times. Dutch, French, Spanish, and Portuguese ships could slip into American ports and load tobacco, wheat, corn, meat, rice, and other products needed in Europe. Despite the war—even as a result of it—some American merchants made more money than ever before, and some European commodities, received in exchange for produce, were more abundant during the war than previously.

A few fortunes were made by war profiteers, but more important, a network of colonial merchants experienced the challenges and problems of unrestricted trade on an international scale. Patriotism did not keep dealers from charging 200 or 300 per cent profit for clothing and supplies needed by the Continental soldiers. New industries, particularly war industries, developed. Iron foundries multiplied. Gunsmiths flourished, and factories for the manufacture of muskets, gunpowder, and cannon developed, particularly in New

STATE CLAIMS TO WESTERN LANDS, 1780

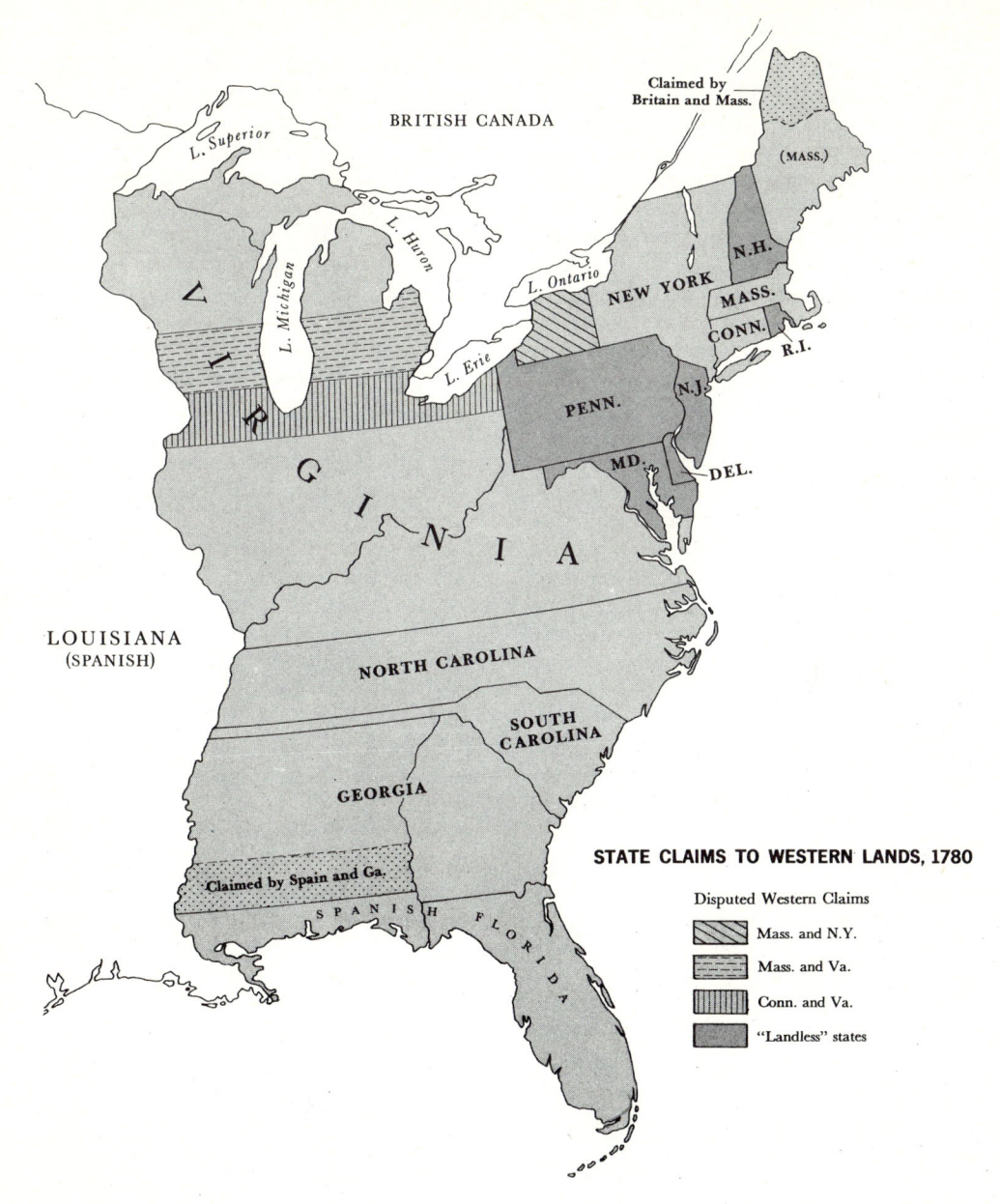

Disputed Western Claims
- Mass. and N.Y.
- Mass. and Va.
- Conn. and Va.
- "Landless" states

England and in Pennsylvania. Since the usual trade in English woolens and other fabrics was cut off, cloth making was encouraged.

The Westward Movement. With the elimination of the prohibition against movement into the trans-Appalachian region that the British had tried to enforce after 1763, fresh migrations began. Frontiersmen were soon filtering into valleys and clearings beyond the mountains. In 1776 Virginia had organized into a county a portion of what later became the state of Kentucky. Before the Revolution, frontiersmen from Virginia under the leadership of John Sevier had settled on the Watauga River in what became Tennessee. After the Revolution, uprooted citizens and restless souls all along the frontier began a trek west that would continue until one day the whole of the American continent would be occupied. Land companies were organized, and within a few years speculation in western lands would become an obsession.

Modifications of American Society. Socially, the Revolution brought changes. The most immediate result was the elimination of royal governors, other British officials, and the cliques of socially elite who gathered about them. Even in colonies having no royal officials, those who were subservient to the mother country were swept out and new men took their places.

Yet as important as these changes were, the United States nowhere experienced the kind of social revolution that swept France a few years later. The structure of American society was modified rather than radically altered. In Virginia, for example, the influence of the tidewater aristocrats diminished somewhat and back-country politicians of the type represented by Patrick Henry gained power; but the families that had produced leaders before the Revolution still continued to supply many of the leaders in the new nation.

One reason the new republic moved with relative ease from the status of a colony to that of a self-governing nation was the tradition of local responsibility established in all of the colonies early in the development of the British settlements. This was an inheritance from the British tradition of local self-government, and it ensured a reservoir of leadership from which individuals could be drawn for any level of responsibility required.

Soon after the Declaration of Independence, a committee was appointed, with John Dickinson as chairman, to draw up Articles of Confederation to bind the thirteen states together into a union. It took more than a year to draft the Articles, and they then had to be submitted to the states for ratification. Not until the spring of 1781 were the Articles ratified. Among the most important contributions of the Articles were their preservation of the union and their definition of powers to be granted to the central government as opposed to the state governments. The operation of the Articles, together with the formation and operation of state governments, is more properly the subject of Chapter 4 on the postwar period.

During almost the entire war—that is, until 1781—the rebel colonies operated under the authority of the extra-legal Continental Congress; the delay in ratification of the Articles of Confederation setting up a formal central government was due chiefly to a conflict of economic interests. Seven states —under the terms of colonial charters, royal grants, Indian treaties, or proprietary claims—asserted ownership of tremendous grants of lands in the West; these states were Massachusetts, Connecticut, New York, Virginia, Georgia, and the Carolinas. To be able to retain these western lands would be a great economic boon, for the sale of these back regions would provide the governments of these landed states with a steady income without taxing their citizens at all. Naturally the advantage that would come to states with western land claims was resented by the states with fixed boundaries. They protested that the War for Independence was being fought for the benefit of all and that every state should share in the rewards to be found in western territory. Thus these landless states were reluctant to sign the Articles of Confederation until the westward limits of the existing states were set and until Congress, the central government, was given authority to grant lands and to create new states beyond these limits.

The debate was not motivated entirely by the question of the equality of the states. Land speculators had formed companies in Maryland and Pennsylvania, for example, and had made purchases from the Indians in the Ohio valley. Now they wished governmental validation of their titles, but how could they secure clear title to land claimed by Virginia and New York when such states were inclined not to recognize the Indian purchases made by out-of-state residents?

Eventually, after considerable political maneuvering and propagandizing, both sides gave in. Between 1777 and 1781 the land companies vacated their claims to western territory purchased from the Indians, and upon recommendation of a congressional committee in 1780, the landed states, led by Virginia, New York, and Connecticut, gave up claim to most of the trans-Appalachian country, thus making the western lands the territory of the union. In February 1781 the last of the landless states, Maryland, ratified the Articles, and on March 1 the Confederation was formally proclaimed. The problem of western lands was now placed squarely before the new central government (see Chapter 4).

When the war was over, many thoughtful citizens throughout the country feared that the loose provisions of the Articles of Confederation would not permit the evolution of a nation strong enough to survive. For example, in the realm of foreign policy much depended upon the power of a centralized authority. Furthermore, a central authority was required to establish the financial stability of the nation and to deal with problems of credit, the issuance of money, and the maintenance of national defense—functions beyond the capacity of individual states. These problems and their solution would form an important chapter in Constitution making.

CHAPTER 3

PATTERNS OF COLONIAL CULTURE

COLONIAL SOCIAL STRUCTURE

Influences on Cultural Development. In intellectual and social life, as in political and economic life, the first English settlers carried with them the attitudes, habits of thought, and ambitions characteristic of their seventeenth-century contemporaries in England. During the colonial period, however, these characteristics were modified—in part because of the changing intellectual life of England, which affected the colonies in a variety of ways, and in part because of the fact that men and women born and educated in America knew at first hand only the ways of their colonial countrymen. They experienced English culture and English intellectual currents second-hand. Furthermore, the transplanting of non-English peoples to the English colonies in America brought added diversity and dimension to the provincial social and intellectual scene. An evaluation of the degree of distinctiveness of American culture depends on the relative weight placed upon those elements—English, American, and non-English. Because individual historians have placed different emphasis upon these factors, their judgments have differed; all agree, however, that conditions in the New World influenced social and intellectual development.

English Society. In Elizabethan England, the top level within the structure of society consisted of noble families, whose position depended upon extensive land holdings and the favors which accrued to a privileged segment of society. Some members of the nobility served the nation in important capacities at the court of the king or in Parliament; others served their communities, frequently as lord lieutenants in their shires. The nobility acquired the characteristics of extravagance and arrogance, and their lives were often troubled by debts, dissipation, boredom, and a lack of purpose. The nobility was not quite a closed circle, because younger sons who did not inherit a substantial estate or title generally sought their fortunes along other routes—through the life of the gentry, through commercial connections, or through the professions, particularly the church and the military. Moreover, it was possible for a highly successful entrepreneur to penetrate the magic circle, though full-fledged acceptance as a member of the elite was often delayed for several generations.

Below the nobility ranked the gentry, the country gentlemen. Land was the basis of their position, although their estates were much less extensive than those of the nobility. The life of the gentry centered around the land; the country gentleman knew his tenants and their problems, and he experienced at first hand the vicissitudes, as well as the blessings, of farming. The

46 The Founding of America

gentry served as the backbone of governing authority, in part because the sovereign encouraged their participation as a shield against ambitious nobles. The gentry formed the largest group in Parliament; they held those local offices which were mainly responsible for enforcing the statutes of the state. Marriage alliances between gentry and commercial families were fairly frequent, and gentry families contributed younger sons to trade, to adventure, to the military, to the church, and sometimes to the universities as well as to the secretarial retinue of the nobility. A hunter and a man of the outdoors, the country gentleman also enjoyed a leisurely intellectual life, pondering over select books, collecting a few manuscripts, and exchanging original compositions with his friends for general enjoyment and edification.

Below the gentry ranked the yeomen. A yeoman by definition supposedly held a freehold producing a value of forty shillings annually, but variations from this norm were so common that it is more accurate to state that a yeoman could be a leaseholder, a renter, or a man who owned a small estate. A yeoman was the dirt farmer of Elizabethan days, a man attached to the soil, who lived a simple life and farmed with frugality. If the gentry represented the backbone of the political system, the stalwart yeomanry represented the tradition of English strength, resourcefulness, and nationhood. The greatest scientist of the seventeenth century, Sir Isaac Newton, was born the son of an English yeoman.

The laborers and servant classes of Elizabethan England ranked below the yeomen. A laborer might be an apprentice who in time would enter a trade and make a good living, or he might be a man who worked for daily wages and whose chances of rising to a better social and economic position were remote. In the same fashion, to be a servant could mean to serve with a gentry family in the expectation that by means of a good marriage or hard work an elevation of status could be secured, or to be a servant could involve the meanest kind of position from which no escalation of status seemed possible.

The Transplanted Social Structure. The English social structure was not transplanted intact to America. Members of the English aristocracy did not come to America; because they were relatively content and well off at home, they had no incentive to migrate to a primitive New World wilderness. Members of noble families occasionally received grants of land in the New World, usually as payment for favors given the king, but they seldom migrated. Occasionally, younger sons of noble families came to America to try their fortune, but even this element was rare.

For the other end of the social structure—day laborers and servants—migration to the New World was restricted, since the impoverished were unable to pay transportation costs. But servants were transported by the gentry class, and as the system of indentured servitude became widespread after the mid-seventeenth century, laborers sometimes took advantage of the system and migrated.

Therefore, the first settlers were principally drawn from the yeomanry and the gentry, the latter bringing with them servants. At the outset, these class divisions were scrupulously maintained. In early Massachusetts, to cite an illustration, a laborer's wife who appeared at church wearing a frock or hat of a quality that, in the eyes of the elders, exceeded the social station of laborer was severely admonished.

Influence of the American Environment. Modifications in this structure of society which were made during the colonial period gave rise to a social structure indigenous to English America. The gradual growth of a system of indentured servitude enabled people without money to emigrate to America. These indentured servants usually became yeoman farmers or free laborers. Furthermore, men who arrived as hired servants or as yeomen sometimes acquired substantial estates through industry or good fortune. Ships' captains who brought immigrants to certain colonies claimed headrights—an allotment of 50 acres of land for each person transported—and these grants formed the nucleus around which some of the landed estates were formed. Labor was so scarce that a skilled workman not only could make a good living but also could become an employer. Men of modest means who engaged in trade built up strong mercantile firms, and wealth brought an elevation of social status and often political power.

Among the most important determinants of social position in America was the possession of land, and its very abundance helped to encourage a more mobile society. Nowhere is this more clearly demonstrated than in the Chesapeake colonies. In the first century of settlement the vast majority of the settlers in Virginia and Maryland were yeomen or indentured servants who were able to rise to the status of yeomen after completing their term of servitude. During various crises of the seventeenth century, especially during the Puritan ascendency in England of the 1640's and 1650's and immediately after the restoration of the Stuart monarchy in 1660, members of gentry families or, more rarely, younger sons of noble families migrated to Virginia, but they acted as no more than leaven to the loaf. A Virginia gentry class gradually emerged, but it was made up primarily of men who had risen to this status in America. It was not a gentry group transplanted to America.

By the late seventeenth and early eighteenth centuries, the Virginia gentry were imitating their English counterparts by participating in gaming, riding, and sports; by encouraging leisurely learning, an indulgence in books, and an amateur interest in science and writing; by serving as the leading political group; by opening their doors to travelers, in part because the stranger brought news and thus was welcome, and in part because offering such hospitality was the mark of a gentleman; and by belonging to the established Anglican church and serving as vestrymen.

The colonial elite which evolved in each colony was composed of families who had over several generations achieved this level by gaining wealth in America—through the acquisition of land, through trade, or through business operations. The pinnacle of Virginia society—except for the governor and a limited number of crown appointees—comprised the gentry; in contrast, the gentry in England, important as they were, did not make up the top level of English society.

In summary, the structure of colonial society differed from that of English society in three important respects. First, the top level of English society—the nobility—was shorn off by the process of transplantation. Second, although some of the structure of American society had its counterpart in England—the gentry and the yeomanry, for example—the composition of American classes was not the result of direct transplants from England. Third, the structure of society in America reflected somewhat different contours from that in England. In America there were more slaves who were condemned to perpetual servitude and who had little if any mobility; but there were fewer servants, because the opportunities to acquired land and other forms of wealth were so abundant. American society ranged, therefore, from the colonial elite—the important merchants in Massachusetts and Rhode Island, the planters along the Chesapeake and in the Carolinas, and the large landholders in New York and Pennsylvania—to the small farmers and skilled workmen, to the unskilled workmen and servants, and finally, at the base, to the slaves.

The special contours of American society also reflected a modification of professional opportunities. A man in England could always advance professionally through the church, the military, or the law. In America, the church in New England offered an avenue for advancement for a time, but by the eighteenth century a man looking for advancement generally sought out land and commerce, not the church. Moreover, Americans, accustomed to their special militia forces, could not advance professionally through the naval or military service. In America, a man who had already achieved status as a merchant or landholder was placed in command of a colonial expedition.

Not until the 1730's and 1740's did the practice of law acquire sufficient status to serve as an avenue for advancement. In earlier periods, merchants and landholders frequently served as their own lawyers. Only as provincial society became more sophisticated did the practice of law become a profession. A number of colonials, some of whom were already in a substantial social position—James Otis and John Adams in New England, John Dickinson in the middle colonies, and Patrick Henry and Charles Pinckney in the southern colonies—improved their status by becoming expert in the practice of law.

The seed of American society was English, but the American environment dramatically affected its growth. Its evolution, as a result, was distinctive, not a replica.

THE AGE OF FAITH

In America's intellectual and religious life, as in its social structure, English ideas and practices transplanted to the New World were modified by the unique American environment.

The late sixteenth and early seventeenth centuries in England were an Age of Faith, and the characteristics of this age were indelibly stamped upon the English colonies in America. The Protestant Reformation in Europe had unleashed a flood of ideas concerning the role of the church, the qualifications for church membership, and the concept of man's relationship to God—particularly with regard to the degree of man's freedom of will. Were individual men elected by God and thus saved from eternal damnation? Or were men able to win salvation through individual faith and the exercise of free will? Sermons, essays, and the life-long devotion to minor points of doctrine which appear quarrelsome in a modern context were for the early seventeenth-century Englishman the difference between salvation and damnation.

Puritanism in England. When Henry VIII broke with the Catholic Church and established the Church of England of which he, as king, served as the head, specific church practice and doctrine were little altered. But within the Anglican Church, opposition groups began to appear late in the sixteenth century, and they had grown stronger by the early seventeenth century. These opposition groups became known as Puritans.

Various groups of Puritans protested to different extents against practices of the Church of England. All Puritans agreed that to become a member of God's elect an individual must undergo a "conversion experience," in which he sensed a spiritual rebirth; and most agreed that certain rituals within the church service should be changed (for example, inspired, extemporaneous prayers should replace the traditional formal prayers). Puritans definitely disagreed, however, on the question of church government.

One group, the Presbyterian Puritans, followed the precepts of John Calvin. They believed in a close church-state relationship in which policies would be established by the ruling hierarchy and, once adopted, would be enforced among the individual congregations. In addition, the Presbyterian Puritans believed that the church should include the nonelect as well as the elect, since mortal man was not capable of knowing with certainty whom God had elected for salvation.

A second group of Puritans were the Non-Conforming Congregationalists. They believed, first of all, that a church should be composed only of the elect and that such men and women could be identified. In their view the invisible church, God's elect, and the visible church, the church in daily operation, were one. The Non-Conforming Congregational Puritans held that individual congregations should rule themselves and that church doctrine and practice should be enforced by the individual congregation, not by a superior church hierarchy. Both of these groups of Puritans—the Presbyterians and the Congregationalists—were willing to remain within the Church of England and to carry out their reforms, their "religious revolution," within the structure of the established church.

A group closely related to the Puritans—though less influential—were the Non-Conforming Congregational Separatists. As their name indicates, these people held many of the same views as the Non-Conforming Congregational Puritans; they agreed that the invisible and visible church were one and that individual congregations should enforce church doctrine and practice. But they differed on one vital matter. The Separatists believed that reforming the Church of England was an impossible task so they wished to separate from the church. In the eyes of the king, their views were particularly dangerous, because by following their religious inclinations they were in effect repudiating the king as head of the church; their religious-intellectual position, therefore, carried with it strong political implications.

It would be a mistake to assume that in England Puritans and Anglicans were directly opposed. Actually, they shared many of the same convictions: Anglicans as well as Puritans believed that man was sinful, to be liberated only by God's grace, and saved by faith rather than by deeds; that a learned ministry was required to find Biblical truth; and that God conversed with man through His revealed word, the Bible.

Puritanism in America. The people who settled in New England were the Non-Conforming Separatists, a small, uninfluential group who founded Plymouth, and the Non-Conforming Congregational Puritans, who founded Massachusetts Bay and spread throughout New England. That the Puritans settling New England were of the nonconforming sect is an important factor, because these New England Puritans for more than a half century fought savagely against any evidence of Puritan Presbyterianism; although they did not disagree with the Presbyterian beliefs about church government, they did oppose the Presbyterians on the question of church membership. Unlike the Presbyterians, the New England Puritans were convinced that the church should not include the unregenerate as well as the regenerate, the nonelect as well as the elect. Moreover, although Puritanism was to have a dramatic career in England, where the Presbyterian Puritans, at least for a time, gained strength, in America Puritan ideas were transmitted into a distinct social organization only in New England.

The Puritans of New England conceived of themselves as a covenanted people. In essence, the "covenant theology" held that God made a contract with man setting down the terms of salvation. God pledged himself to abide by these terms. This covenant in no way changed the doctrine that God elected the saints, but it explained why certain people were elected and others were not. How did a person know that he was numbered among the elect? By experiencing God's grace and reflecting this regeneration before his peers.

The terms of the covenant were to be found in the Bible; therefore, the Bible became the rule of conduct and was constantly searched for meaning and interpretation. Each law, each act, each policy, because of the covenant, demanded literal Biblical support.

The Puritan mind emphasized the vigorous use of reason; as a result, the Puritans supported the idea of a highly trained clergy and a literate laity. Although several leaders conceded that laymen might find the fine theological points difficult to follow, they agreed that all churchmen should attempt to master the contours of theological inquiry. The Puritans firmly opposed all religious enthusiasms or any evidence of self-revelation (the doctrine that God revealed himself directly to an individual). For this reason, both the Puritans and the Anglicans abhorred the Quakers. The "inner light" which the Quakers claimed involved a mystical force and a direct communication between God and man, was, to the New England Puritans, offensive, as they demonstrated when they hanged several Quakers who refused to leave Massachusetts Bay.

The New England Puritans turned to congregationalism as a form of church government, but they attempted informally to retain close ties between the individual congregations by means of synods, or assemblies of delegates which discussed and decided ecclesiastical affairs. Theoretically, each congregation could select its own course, but in practice a consensus of the Puritan leaders usually marked the course of action. It would be a mistake to think that the Puritan clergy were all-powerful; indeed, conformity to Puritan beliefs was enforced by civil authority. Lay leaders like John Winthrop, not the leading ministers, were primarily responsible for the banishment of colonials who protested against the Puritan doctrines.

The premises of New England Puritanism affected every sphere of life—political, economic, cultural, social, and intellectual. For example, land was distributed to church congregations so that a social-religious community could be created and sustained. Settlement by towns enabled the Puritans to center their lives and activities around the church, and designated practice could easily be enforced. With the Puritans in political control and thus able to determine those groups who were to receive land grants, the objective of creating a Bible Commonwealth could be achieved.

Equally important, of course, was the impact of Puritanism upon education and literature. Because the Puritans firmly believed in a rational religion, they soon began to think about establishing a center of higher learning to continue the tradition of a learned ministry untainted by divergent strains of theology. The upshot was the founding of Harvard College in 1636. At first a Harvard education consisted of two years of relatively rigorous training, but the program was eventually expanded to four years. Harvard's principal aim was to produce a trained ministry, but because its curriculum was based upon a broad training in the humanities, with emphasis on the classics, it served in addition to light the lamp of learning in the New World. There were no other institutions of higher learning in the colonies until the College of William and Mary was founded in 1693; furthermore, this college failed to provide an active program until the eighteenth century.

The premise of a reasoned religion also called for a literate laity, and the New England Puritans responded by enacting legislation for the establishment of a school system. Town settlements made schools practical; in 1642, an act was passed which required every town of fifty or more householders to establish an "elementary school" to teach the fundamentals of reading and writing. An enactment of 1647 required each community of one hundred householders or more to provide a "grammar school," a school to prepare students for college by means of vigorous instruction in the Greek and Latin classics. Historians have vigorously debated the nature of these schools, some asserting that they marked the beginning of a public school system in America, and others arguing with equal vigor that the schools were, in fact, no more than appendages of the established church. The source of funds for the schools was public, but the schools reflected the consensus of the religious community.

New England Puritans expressed themselves in prose and poetry; sometimes their tone was harsh, but it was always unmistakably clear. Sermons were cultivated as an art form, and they were published by the press founded in Massachusetts Bay in 1639. Originally, the press was expected to be the voice of Puritans in Old as well as New England, because Archbishop Laud of the Church of England vigorously opposed the expression of Puritan views at home. This expectation never materialized, however, for the Puritans in England, as they gained ascendancy, secured their own press outlets. The press in Massachusetts Bay, therefore, became almost exclusively the voice of Puritanism in America. Its productivity was fabulous; its output exceeded that of the presses of Cambridge and Oxford in England.

In addition to sermons, the press published prose and poetry. The best seller was Michael Wigglesworth's *Day of Doom*, a 224-verse epic describing the Day of Judgment. It has been estimated that *Day of Doom*, with its harsh, unrelieved cadences, was read by half the New England population.

A more attractive and enduring contribution to literature was made by Anne Bradstreet, mother of eight children, whose sensitive verse was published in England and New England:

Some time now past in the Autumnal tide,
When Phoebus wanted but one hour to bed,
The trees all richly clad, yet void of pride,
Were gilded o'er by his rich golden head....
I heard the merry grasshopper then sing
The black-clad cricket bear a second part,
They kept one tune and played on the same string,
Seeming to glory in their little Art....

Books were constant companions of the Puritan fathers; most of the books were on religious subjects, although a smattering of Latin grammars, a few histories, and some English literature were in evidence. Some of the best works of New England colonials in the seventeenth century—William Bradford's *Of Plymouth Plantation* and John Winthrop's *Journals*—were not published until modern times.

Influence of the New World Environment. During the seventeenth century, Puritanism in America was gradually modified by New World conditions. This modification took numerous forms: in theology, in church practice, and in the everyday life in shops, ships, and farms. The course of this change has been brilliantly analyzed in exacting detail by historian Perry Miller, but for purposes of this text, a single example—the adoption of the Half-Way Covenant in 1662—will suffice.

The church, you will recall, was presumably made up exclusively of the elect, the covenanted people. Children of the elect, however, sometimes failed to evidence "conversion" and thereby to demonstrate their election, which would qualify them for full membership within the church. As the body of church members became smaller in proportion to the total population, the clergy feared that the influence of the church in the community at large would be seriously undermined. By the terms of the Half-Way Covenant, therefore, the children of the elect who had not entered full membership in the church were permitted in turn to have their children baptized. Baptism enabled the children to participate in some, though not all, of the sacraments of the church. This opening wedge, which made an association with the church possible without proof of "election," was gradually widened until a number of prominent ministers advocated opening the church to those who tried to live according to the precepts of the church even though they could not prove regeneration.

The New World environment affected other areas of Puritan intellectual life as well. The intellectual vigor of Harvard College declined; its historian, Samuel Eliot Morison, marks the low point as the 1670's; its intellectual direction became, at least to old-line Puritans, "radical," which meant that it diverted from early Puritan precepts and intellectual rigor. The enforcement of the school acts lagged, and few intellectuals of late seventeenth-century New England could match the intellectual creativity of the first-line Puritans —John Cotton, Thomas Hooker, Roger Williams, and their like.

Making the terms of church membership easier was also important outside intellectual life. During most of the seventeenth century only church members could vote in the colony-wide elections of Massachusetts Bay, and, therefore, a substantial majority of the population failed to qualify for the franchise. Broadened church membership, therefore, had direct political effects. The Puritans lost outright control of Massachusetts in 1691 when a new charter made property ownership the basis for franchise, but the church as a social-religious institution was a powerful influence in New England well into the nineteenth century.

The Transplanted Anglicans. In the Age of Faith, the Anglican Church was transplanted to Virginia; it later expanded into the Carolinas and Maryland, and in the eighteenth century to the middle colonies and New England. In contrast to Puritanism in America, Anglicanism in America did not center around theological disquisitions and dogmas. The theological structure of Anglicanism was exclusively the product and concern of the clerical hierarchy within England. A highly learned Anglican ministry did not migrate to America.

As a result, the influence of the New World environment cannot be measured in terms of its modification of doctrine but in terms of its modifications of church practice and of church ceremonials. For example, the Anglican Church was highly centralized and carefully supervised by its hierarchy in England, but it became in America a decentralized church ruled by laymen. In America the Anglican vestries became so powerful that for all intents and purposes church government in practice resembled congregationalism. The clergy who migrated to America were almost impotent before the vestry, a dramatic departure from conditions in England.

The Anglican parishes in seventeenth-century America were much too large and this, too, affected church practices. A clergyman could not readily serve his congregation because its membership was widely scattered. Laymen, therefore, began to read the services on the Sabbath, and laymen soon exercised a role in religious functions which violated the canons of the church. Because people found it difficult to travel ten or twelve miles to church on horseback or by boat, they did not appear at services. Moreover, because of the distances, weddings took place on a plantation rather than in church, and the dead were buried on the plantation in an unconsecrated family plot rather than in consecrated church ground— again a violation of church ordinances.

The absence of a guiding intellectual premise in the Chesapeake colonies dramatically affected education and literature. The scattered nature of the settlement made a community school impractical; by the time the children arrived at the schoolhouse by horseback or boat, it would be time for them to return home. Consequently, responsibility for education was placed upon the family, not upon the community, and the finances and intellectual values of an individual family determined its response.

Obviously, in comparison with the lesser folk, the Virginia gentry had a decided advantage in a plantation system which made public schools well-nigh impossible. Occasionally, when a sufficient number of plantations were proximate, Old Field Schools were founded in which the children were taught by a clergyman or by the wife of a planter. More often a family or a group of families hired an indentured servant to teach the children. With no way of obtaining an advanced education in the colony, those planters who wished their children to receive a college education sent them to England. William Byrd II, born in 1674, was educated at Felstead Grammar School in Essex, England, whose headmaster, Christopher Glasscock, had tutored the sons of Oliver Cromwell. Byrd later was associated with mercantile firms in Holland and in London before being trained in law at the English Inns of Court. He returned to America to take his place as one of the most prominent Virginians of the seventeenth and early eighteenth centuries.

The literature read in the Chesapeake colonies was more like than unlike that read in New England, but the literary productivity was different in quantity and character. In the Chesapeake colonies, as in New England, religious books and the Bible occupied a prominent place on the reading tables. In addition, the classics, Homer's *Iliad*, certain Roman historians, books on law and on medical treatment were included in many libraries. Whereas the published writings of New Englanders were profuse and almost exclusively religious in character, those of the Chesapeake region were limited and nonreligious. Robert Beverley's *History and Present State of Virginia*, originally published in 1705, consummated the literary output of the Chesapeake colonies in the seventeenth century. Beverley did not have the training—or interest—to write a learned work of history on some past civilization. His subject matter, therefore, involved his own habitat, and his *History* represents an amalgam of investigating, recording, and interpreting past events as well as making observations on the contemporary scene. The direct style and illuminating observation of the *History* make it an important source for historians today.

THE EIGHTEENTH-CENTURY MIND

The Enlightenment in England. During the seventeenth century, English intellectual life underwent a transformation which was triggered by the momentous advance of science and the application of the theoretical framework of science to all phases of human experience. The writings of the father of scientific reasoning, Francis Bacon, marked the beginning of a movement which was consummated by the great scientific discoveries of Sir Isaac Newton, whose *Mathematical Principles of Natural Philosophy* (published in 1697) set forth, by precise demonstration, the laws of motion and gravitation. Newton was to the eighteenth century what Einstein is to the twentieth.

As Newton had discovered laws in the physical universe, reasoned many men, so laws must operate in the relationship between man and the universe.

In summary, eighteenth-century Enlightenment thought held that God as the Prime Mover had created the universe with a perfectly operating, harmonious system of immutable laws—the laws of nature. Once the universe was created, God was inconsequential; only the immutable laws of nature were important, and they were the highest authority to which man could appeal. Belief in God as merely the Prime Mover was called deism. The laws of nature could be discovered only by reason, and therefore a premium was placed on learning and on books. Once a law was discovered, men should adjust their lives and the institutions they had created—for example, their political and educational systems—to conform with these laws. The closer the alignment between man and the laws of nature, the closer human institutions would be to perfection. In this view, man was perfectible and progress was inevitable.

It should be emphasized that the ideas of the Enlightenment in England and America affected only a few people, since most persons went about their daily lives unaware of recent intellectual trends. Moreover, Enlightenment ideas did not gain strong advocates in America until the mid-eighteenth century, and even then the Enlightenment was influential only in select areas of American experience. In England, for example, Enlightenment ideas permeated literature as well as political thought; in America, Enlightenment ideas found expression in political thought but not in literature. The Declaration of Independence, you will recall, appeals to the "laws of nature and nature's God."

Although the Enlightenment dominated intellectual life in England, it constituted only one rivulet in the mainstream of intellectual life in eighteenth-century America. The widespread immigration of non-English groups brought a diversity of cultures. Coming as they did from the rank and file, the non-English immigrants were usually much more interested in opportunities than ideas. Moreover, the large migration of German Pietists reinforced the influence of an evangelical religious faith which was reflected in the Great Awakening of the 1720's to 1750's (see p. 57). Whereas the impetus of the Age of Faith in the late sixteenth and much of the seventeenth century dominated seventeenth-century colonial America, the eighteenth-century American provinces reflected what was to become a characteristic of the American mind—a wide diversity of intellectual streams. To understand this multiple mind, this discussion will center upon the growth of toleration and the emergence of secularization, the religious awakening of the eighteenth century, and the Enlightenment in America.

The Growth of Toleration. The basis for the rise of religious toleration in England and America was laid in the seventeenth century. In England the political-religious upheaval of the mid-seventeenth century and the subsequent restoration of the Stuart monarchy placed a premium on religious toleration which was consummated in the Toleration Act of 1689, after the Glorious Revolution of 1688 had won for Parliament a more balanced role in relationship to the authority of the crown. The Toleration Act gave sufferance to all Protestant sects in England, but it specifically excluded Catholics, who were presumed to owe allegiance to the Pope. The act was made necessary not only by the tragic experiences of the church during the seventeenth century but also by the new science that encouraged a thorough reëxamination of religious doctrine and beliefs.

In America, the background for toleration had been laid as early as 1636, when Roger Williams founded Rhode Island. In a sense, Williams backed into the principle of religious toleration. He had found the Puritans of Massachusetts Bay imperfect in their religious fervor, and he consequently vowed to pray only with those he knew to be regenerate. Because he was unsure of other men, he finally was forced to pray only with his wife. From this restricted, impractical position, Williams took the long step to religious toleration on the premise that since he could not determine decisively which persons were regenerate, he had no alternative but to extend toleration to everyone with religious convictions. Williams' ultimate attitude of toleration was well in advance of the mainstream in England and in America.

The Maryland Toleration Act of 1649 lent impetus to the growth of toleration, but it should be emphasized that the act arose not from broad humanitarian principles but from the reality of immediate circumstances. Maryland, established originally as a Catholic refuge, was being heavily populated by Protestants. Not only were the Catholics in a minority but, because of the Puritan domination in England, they were seriously threatened by persecution. The Toleration Act, advocated by Lord Baltimore, was intended to protect the Catholic minority and to forestall action against Baltimore's proprietorship.

Toleration flourished in the eighteenth century, in part because of seventeenth-century precedents but, more important, because of the realities of the eighteenth century which made intolerance an anachronism. The migration of dissenter sects from Germany, the emergence of an intercolonial Presbyterian church increasingly fortified by newly arrived Scots and Scotch-Irish, the spread of Anglicanism throughout the colonies, the intercolonial migrations from Pennsylvania south along the eastern edge of the Appalachians to Georgia, the application of the English Toleration Act in America—these developments made toleration a necessity. The diversity of religious faiths made any other course impossible.

Toleration for provincial America did not mean disruption of church-state establishments. Men of all faiths were taxed, for example, to maintain the Anglican church in Virginia and the Congregational church in Massachusetts, although in each colony men of differing faith could practice it without undue molestation. The separation of church and state became a question of principle during and after the American Revolution, when it was apparent that no single church was sufficiently strong to be elevated to the status of a national church.

The Rise of Secularism. The emergence of secularism is related to the growth of toleration, for restraint is seldom achieved when religious zeal is white hot. The people who migrated to America in the eighteenth century were primarily seeking opportunity, not religious toleration. If toleration had been their principal desire, the German Pietists could easily have migrated to Rhode Island—and at an earlier date. But choice Pennsylvania land in combination with religious toleration proved to be a superior attraction. Moreover, the new generations of Americans who were native born turned with avidity to enrichment and advancement; they were less concerned than their seventeenth-century forebears with the saving of souls.

Perhaps the best index of the rise of secularism is the production of the provincial press. In the eighteenth century, newspapers flourished. The first newspaper was published in Boston in 1704, and by the 1750's almost every colony had one newspaper and a number of colonies had several newspapers. In contrast to Michael Wigglesworth's *Day of Doom* of the seventeenth century, almanacs became the best sellers of the eighteenth century. *Poor Richard's Almanac*, which Benjamin Franklin edited in Philadelphia from 1732 to 1758, sold 10,000 copies a year and became the most popular reading matter—except for the Bible—in the colonies. The emergence of secularism can also be detected in the appearance of a significant, if slim, theater fare in provincial America.

The Great Awakening. The growth of toleration and the emergence of secularism should not obscure a third significant and persistent theme of eighteenth-century intellectual and social life, the Great Awakening, an evangelical religious movement—a series of revivals preached by stirring evangelists and causing the greatest emotional excitement—that swept through provincial America. The Great Awakening began in the middle colonies, in part because the German migration carried along the Pietist movement from Europe; in part because the rapid expansion characteristic of the middle colonies tended to overtax traditional religious institutions and thus to encourage the creation of new organizations and new forms for religious expression; and in part because a church-state relationship did not exist to thwart an evangelical movement. In the 1730's the Great Awakening extended into New England, and its fire-and-brimstone preachers drew large revivalistic crowds in cities and towns. In the 1740's and 1750's, the movement reached into the southern colonies, carried along in part by the migration of the Scotch-Irish and Germans southward along the eastern edge of the Appalachians. The absence of towns and the presence of the Anglican establishment in the southern colonies had precluded early manifestations of the Awakening in that section of the country.

Among the noted preachers associated with the Great Awakening was Jonathan Edwards of the Northampton Church in Massachusetts. Because of his remarkable intellectual and philosophical gifts, Edwards is often called the greatest theologian America has produced. Edwards used Enlightenment reasoning to construct a theological paradox to Enlightenment ideas. Beginning in the 1720's, many New England ministers were influenced by a theology basing salvation on human moral effort as well as divine grace. Edwards opposed this tendency and reasserted the absolute justice of God's power to elect or to condemn as He chose. Conversion and redemption Edwards further described as a supernatural illumination of the soul, an effusion of God's beauty in the mind, an intuitive vision of the holiness that is in God and Christ; thus, Edwards' test of conversion was in some respects less mild than formerly. Overall, he defended with exceptional skill the basic Calvinistic position that God was omnipotent and that, before God, man was impotent. Edwards was scarcely representative of most Awakening preachers, whose intellectual gifts were limited and who appealed to the emotions rather than to the mind.

The Great Awakening caused divisions within existing church organizations. Those church members who followed the attractions of the evangelical group were called "new lights," and they attempted to wrest control of the church from the conservative members who held power, the "old lights." The Awakening fervor also was responsible for the founding of four colleges by separate religious denominations: Dartmouth (Congregationalist), Princeton (Presbyterian), Brown (Baptist), and Rutgers (Dutch Reformed). The premise in each case was that the existing institutions of higher learning—Yale for instance, which had been founded in 1701—were unsuitable for training acceptable "new light" ministers. The Awakening, because it was an intercolonial movement, also strengthened intercolonial ties. Many historians have advanced the idea that the Awakening, by emphasizing the individual and his relationship to God, aroused a democratic spirit which influenced the revolutionary generation. This generalization cannot be proved or disproved, but it seems fair to suggest that the Awakening in reviewing traditional institutions—which in this case happened to be ecclesiastical institutions—encouraged a climate of freedom.

The Enlightenment in America. The greatest influence of the Enlightenment in America was the encouragement it gave to scientific inquiry. Cotton Mather, the most prominent New England clergyman in the late seventeenth and early eighteenth centuries, was attracted to scientific investigation; Mather was an advocate of smallpox inoculations when others greeted this medical advance with uncertainty or fear. James Logan, a Pennsylvania founder who made a fortune in the fur trade and in land speculation, actively promoted the dissemination of scientific information. William Byrd II of Virginia, along with other provincials, belonged to England's Royal Society and frequently sent observations of New World phenomena to his friends in England.

The contribution of most provincials was to that aspect of science called "natural history." Almost every botanical specimen collected in America constituted a contribution to knowledge because it added to the storehouse of scientific information. John Bartram, who collected specimens throughout the provinces and cultivated rare species in his garden at Philadelphia, was called the finest contemporary "natural botanist" by Carolus Linnaeus of Sweden, the foremost botanist in Europe. Another celebrated work was Mark Catesby's extraordinary *Natural History of Carolina*.

Only Benjamin Franklin contributed to theoretical science, although many of his provincial contemporaries pursued allied investigations with vigor and persistence. Fortunately for Franklin, he entered a field of physics in which relatively little work had been done and thus he was not handicapped by his lack of background, particularly his limited knowledge of mathematics. His identification of lightning as electricity and his observations with regard to the flow of electricity and the equalization that took place between highly charged particles and those less highly charged were contributions which won him a reputation throughout Europe.

Although science became increasingly important within the curricula of the colleges, it was pursued most fervently by men outside the institutions of learning who, like proper eighteenth-century generalists, were interested in politics, science, writing, and other broad-gauged, stimulating activities. Representative of this group was the American Philosophical Society, founded in 1744. Its membership included Dr. John Mitchell of Virginia, a fellow of the Royal Society whose major interest was botany; Cadwallader Colden, whose intellectual interests ranged from electricity to a history of the Iroquois Indians; and David Rittenhouse of Pennsylvania, an astronomer and mathematician.

As the impact of science in provincial America makes clear, the Enlightenment, unlike Puritanism, was peculiarly the possession of the educated and social elite. Whereas Puritanism was imposed upon the community and the individual, the Enlightenment was not. Its expression, therefore, reflected but one sector of the provincial mind.

Yet in several ways Enlightenment ideas encompassed the whole people. First of all, provincial America, because it represented a new, formative society, appeared in the eyes of some European and American observers to be the laboratory of the Enlightenment. American society, free from the incrustations of the centuries, could presumably adjust to the immutable laws of nature more readily than could that of Europe. Indeed, American intellectuals were confident that a perfect society was already being created. For this reason, the French found in Franklin a living inspiration, an image of a new society. In political thought and practice, provincial Americans, regardless of status or location, embraced many Enlightenment ideas. The right of men to challenge a governmental system when it stood athwart the immutable laws of nature, and the right of men to replace such a government with one which conformed with nature's laws, were two assumptions of the Enlightenment which deeply penetrated the American mind.

Cultural Maturity. In some areas of intellectual life, such as painting and music, provincial America lagged. Moreover, a great outpouring of imaginative literature, poetry, fiction, and drama failed to develop. But these manifestations of cultural life could not be expected of a people whose principal energies were devoted to creating a new civilization. Yet, Philadelphia stood as a cosmopolitan city, second in population only to London within the British empire. The American cities in the aggregate, as well as the American countryside, comprised a stimulating atmosphere which bred men of intelligence, indeed of genius, as well as men whose contributions to statesmanship would endure beyond those of most of their cultivated counterparts in England.

The standard criteria for evaluating the level of intellectual life, therefore, do not apply to provincial America. What were important were its zest for learning, its new modes of society, its mobility, its ability to prosper and to set examples that in time would be imitated. The promise of the American "minds" fashioned from the experience of the seventeenth and eighteenth centuries formed the foundation upon which American nationhood and an American culture were to be built.

BIBLIOGRAPHY

The most comprehensive studies of the settlement of the English colonies in America are Charles M. Andrews, *The Colonial Period of American History*, 4 vols. (New Haven: Yale University Press, 1934-1938); Herbert Levi Osgood, *The American Colonies in the Seventeenth Century*, 3 vols. (New York: Macmillan, 1904-1907); and Herbert Levi Osgood, *The American Colonies in the Eighteenth Century*, 4 vols. (New York: Columbia University Press, 1924-1925). Andrews gives a judicial appraisal of controversial questions; Osgood, despite his lack of interpretation, provides important material found nowhere else. An account of the colonies within the framework of the whole empire will be found in Lawrence Henry Gipson, *The British Empire before the American Revolution*, 10 vols. (New York: Alfred A. Knopf, 1936-1961). Thomas J. Wertenbaker in *The Founding of American Civilization*, 3 vols. (New York: Charles Scribner's Sons, 1938-1947) provides both political and social history with a volume devoted to each of the principal regions.

Useful single-volume treatments of the colonial development are Oliver P. Chitwood, *A History of Colonial America* (New York: Harper, 1931); Curtis P. Nettels, *The Roots of American Civilization* (New York: F. S. Crofts, 1938); Louis B. Wright, *The Atlantic Frontier* (New York: Knopf, 1947); and Clarence L. Ver Steeg, *The Formative Years* (New York: Hill and Wang, 1963).

A succinct account of the establishment of all the southern colonies except Georgia is to be found in Wesley Frank Craven, *The Southern Colonies in the Seventeenth Century, 1607-1789* (Baton Rouge: Louisiana State University Press, 1949). The most recent and most detailed history of Virginia in this period is Richard L. Morton, *Colonal Virginia*, 2 vols. (Chapel Hill: University of North Carolina Press, 1960). A discussion of the transit of English social ideas to Virginia will be found in Louis B. Wright, *The First Gentlemen of Virginia* (San Marino, Calif.: The Huntington Library, 1940). The history of South Carolina as a colony is treated in detail in Edward McCrady, *The History of South Carolina under the Proprietary Government, 1719-1720* (New York: Macmillan, 1899). Samuel A. Ashe, *History of North Carolina*, 2 vols. (Greensboro, N. C.: C. L. Van Noppen, 1908-1925) gives considerable space to the colonial period. More recent is Hugh T. Lefler and Albert R. Newsome, *North Carolina; the History of a Southern State* (Chapel Hill: University of North

Carolina Press, 1954). E. Merton Coulter, *Georgia: a Short History* (Chapel Hill: University of North Carolina Press, 1947) gives a good brief account of the colonial period.

Although unsympathetic to the New England clergy, James Truslow Adams, *The Founding of New England* (Boston: Atlantic Monthly Press, 1921) and *Revolutionary New England, 1691-1776* (Boston: Atlantic Monthly Press, 1923) provide much detailed information. Excellent biographical material is to be found in Samuel E. Morison, *Builders of the Bay Colony* (Boston: Houghton Mifflin, 1930). Information about the economic background will be found in William B. Weeden, *Economic and Social History of New England, 1620-1789*, 2 vols. (Boston: Houghton Mifflin, 1890) and E. A. Johnson, *American Economic Thought in the Seventeenth Century* (London: P. S. King & Son, 1932). Perry Miller, *Orthodoxy in Massachusetts, 1630-1650* (Cambridge, Mass.: Harvard University Press, 1933) is a valuable introduction to the religious history of the Puritans. In *The New England Mind: The Seventeenth Century* (New York: Macmillan, 1939) and *The New England Mind: From Colony to Province* (Cambridge, Mass.: Harvard University Press, 1953) Mr. Miller gives a minute account of Puritan theology.

A synthesis of material on the early history of New York will be found in Alexander C. Flick, ed., *History of the State of New York*, 10 vols. (New York: University of the State of New York, 1933-1937). For material on Pennsylvania see Sydney G. Fisher, *The Quaker Colonies* (New Haven: Yale University Press, 1919) and Wayland F. Dunaway, *A History of Pennsylvania* (New York: Prentice-Hall, 1935).

Information about the social and intellectual life of the colonies is supplied by Louis B. Wright, *The Cultural Life of the American Colonies, 1607-1763* (New York: Harper, 1957) and Daniel Boorstin, *Americans; The Colonial Experience* (New York: Random House, 1958).

For a discussion of ideas leading up to independence see Carl L. Becker, *The Declaration of Independence* (New York: Harcourt, Brace, 1922), and Randolph G. Adams, *The Political Ideas of the American Revolution* (Durham, N.C.: Trinity College Press, 1922). For political aspects of the years of controversy see Lawrence H. Gipson, *The Coming of the American Revolution, 1763-1775* (New York: Harper, 1954); Edmund S. and Helen M. Morgan, *The Stamp Act Crisis: Prologue to Revolution* (Chapel Hill: University of North Carolina, 1953); Edmund S. Morgan, *The Birth of the Republic, 1763-1789* (Chicago: University of Chicago Press, 1956); and Allan Nevins, *The American States during and after the Revolution, 1775-1789* (New York: Macmillan, 1924). A useful survey of this period is Evarts B. Greene, *The Revolutionary Generation, 1763-1790* (New York: Macmillan, 1943). A succinct account of the campaigns of the Revolution may be found in John Alden, *The American Revolution* (New York: Harper, 1954). A good single-volume work that provides a sound balance between political and military affairs is John C. Miller, *Triumph of Freedom, 1775-1783* (Boston: Little, Brown, 1948). See also Esmond Wright, *Fabric of Freedom* (New York: Hill and Wang, 1961).

PART 2: INTRODUCTION

THE YOUNG REPUBLIC

■ The first forty years of American life after the Revolution were years in which the work of independence was completed, the republic shaped, the national character determined, a foreign policy developed, and the federal system established. This was a period of crucial decisions and important events, yet we have no good name for it. It is not an easy period to categorize, to label as the Age of This or the Era of That. It was dominated by no single great figure, but by several. It exhibits no internal consistency, for during these years everything that was done was being done for the first time; if it could be characterized at all, it would be perhaps as a period of precedents. Still, it is possible to identify in the pattern of events from 1783 to 1824 four threads which seem to give it coherence: the drift away from the confederation concept of government toward constitutional federalism; the emergence of two-party politics, arising from the tensions of the two Federalist administrations; the construction of a set of distinctive American attitudes in foreign policy, reaching culmination in the Monroe Doctrine; the development of an American cultural "style," deriving from a gradual self-awareness of an American character.

Few periods in history have shown more ebullience and optimism, more hopeful experimentation with life. The postwar generation felt that its revolution was a spark which might well activate an age of revolutions, changing or toppling all other existing forms of government in the western world. It was a domestic revolution, designed for export; Jefferson found it "impossible not to be sensible that we are acting for all mankind." It was heavy responsibility, this sense of destiny, and the generation of men who, after the Revolution, turned from affairs of war to matters of peace, felt it deeply. If the "bold and sublime" American experiment worked, Thomas Paine said in *Common Sense*, "the birthday of a new world is at hand."

Britons and other Europeans who visited the new nation found this faith difficult to understand. The United States was neither England nor Europe, which made it puzzling enough, and its principles and aims, judged in terms of the old order, simply did not make sense. Few could be found who held much hope for it. And as a matter of fact, by contemporary standards there was not much reason to believe that the United States *would* succeed. Poised on the edge of a raw, wild continent, with neither

Thomas Jefferson, portrait by Rembrandt Peale (1805). Living before the age of specialization, Jefferson sought a variety of interests characteristic of a Renaissance man, achieving greatness as statesman, political philosopher, scientist, patron, architect, and scholar.

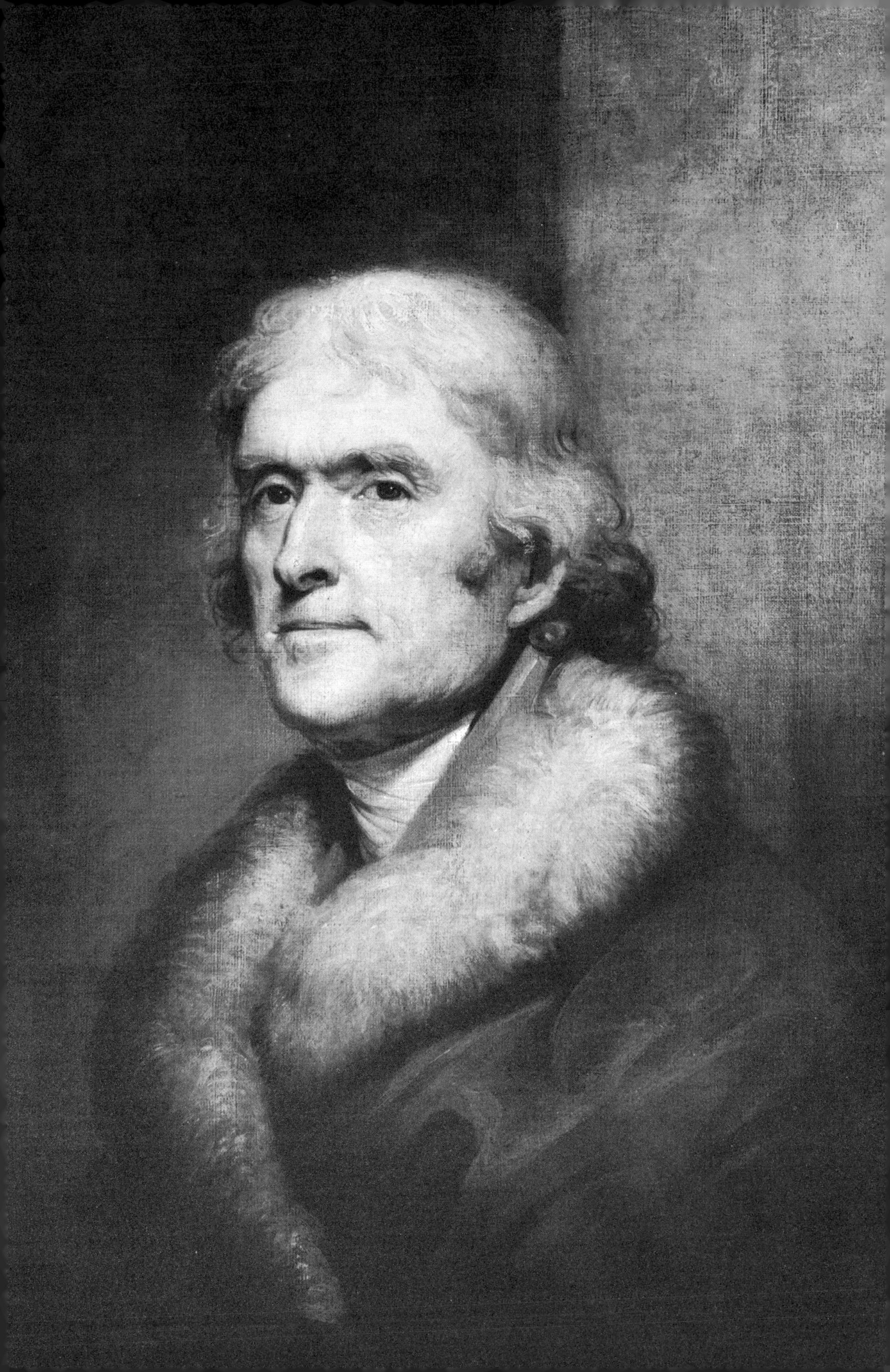

Congress Hall: Old House of Representatives, painting by Samuel F. B. Morse (1821-1822). Depicted at candle-lighting time prior to an evening session, the House displayed democracy in action: congressmen, Supreme Court justices (on rear dias), and gallery visitors, pages, and attendants.

culture nor tradition of its own, and possessed of no more than doubtful unity, this young republic seemed to have little chance of success. Its government was founded on questionable and untested principles. Everything upon which Britain and Europe had been taught to depend for stability and safety—an established church, an army, aristocratic leadership, a monarch, a sound tradition—the United States had largely abandoned in favor of a somewhat dubious trust in the ability and integrity of the individual man.

Fortunately, the majority of American leaders faced the future with vigor and confidence and turned their energies to constructing a government that would be workable and durable. The problem was, as William Miller wrote, "to make liberty a *practical principle,* and to *prove* it." Naturally, there were differences of opinion over how this might be done. But there was clear agreement about certain central concepts which, when combined and adjusted with one another, merged into the pattern called "American." There was no one—however much these men may have differed about the *means* of realizing the principles of the Revolution—who wished to undo it. The present necessity, all agreed, was to strike the proper balance between what was and what ought to be, between desire and reality.

The Founding Fathers did inherit an ideological blueprint from Europe, of course, and they had behind them the whole political tradition of England. But in addition, the United States began to build its new society with certain distinct advantages. The sense of limitless space and opportunity which Americans gained from the land itself in these postrevolutionary years—the sense of "new lands, new power, the full freedom of virgin world," as Woodrow Wilson once phrased it—provided a wholly new environment, impossible in Europe, for the American experiment. The necessity of

Tontine Coffee House, painting by Francis Guy (c. 1797). The Tontine Coffee House at the corner of Wall and Water Streets in New York housed the stock exchange and insurance offices and, as the registry for ship arrivals and clearances, symbolized the booming commerce of America's northeastern ports.

building new settlements, year after year, where none existed before, forced Americans constantly to make new decisions, continuously to reconsider and reaffirm their fundamental social and political principles. For this reason life during these years displayed a dynamism, an adaptability and a practicality that became integral parts of the American style.

It was also true, as the astute French traveler De Tocqueville observed, that the American "arrived at a state of democracy without having to endure a democratic revolution, and that he is born free without having to become so." The Revolution did not have to destroy a feudal society in order to evolve a new one; the United States began its existence with no single established church, no entrenched aristocracy, no monarch or court. The postwar leaders acted and thought within an *American,* non-feudal framework. No other western nation began its modern history under quite such conditions. At the same time the society in which the American operated was much more open, fluid, and available than any other of the era; power and position within it were open to more men in the United States than anywhere else in the world.

The years 1783-1824 in American history are characterized by a steadily developing sense of nationalism; an increasing awareness of America's place in relation to the rest of the world; and a maturing realization of the issues and problems involved in creating a government dedicated to the proposition that all men are created equal. The people of the period were vitally concerned with the search for ways and means of bringing into being that distinctively American society and state which, as Joel Barlow wrote, belonged to "new men in a new world." At the close of the period they believed that they had achieved it.

CHAPTER 4

THE CONSTITUTION AND THE FEDERALISTS, 1783-1800

THE SEARCH FOR STABILITY

The Articles of Confederation. Of prime importance in the political life of the United States throughout its history has been the problem of federalism —the division of power between the states and the federal government—or, more simply, the issue of local control or "states' rights," versus central authority. The origins of this problem are to be found in the British imperial system of the mid-eighteenth century. At the center of this system had stood Great Britain, whose government had directed foreign affairs and intercolonial relations with the view of keeping the machinery and policies of the empire working in harmony. At the extremities of this system had been the colonies themselves, each of which had attained the right to govern its internal affairs.

In practice, however, the dividing line between imperial and local affairs was variously interpreted, and out of the conflict of interpretations arose the American Revolution. With the Declaration of Independence, the American colonies rejected the government in London altogether and, under the pressures of war, united sufficiently to set up a central authority of their own making—the Confederation.

When Richard Henry Lee on June 7, 1776 offered a resolution to Continental Congress declaring American independence, he also proposed that "a plan of confederation be prepared and transmitted to the respective colonies for their consideration and approbation." A committee headed by John Dickinson of Pennsylvania presented such a plan to the Continental Congress on July 12, and on November 15, 1777, after more than a year of debate, the Articles of Confederation were approved and sent to the states for ratification.

The loyalty of Americans was strongly attached to the states, and it was readily agreed that the sovereign powers of government belonged with them. The Articles were designed to create not a strong central government but an assembly of equal states, each of which retained its "sovereignty, freedom, and independence, and every Power, Jurisdiction, and right." The Articles of Confederation therefore created a quasi-federal system with a new Congress almost exactly like the wartime Continental Congress which then existed, in which each state—regardless of size, population, or wealth —had an equal vote. The Articles delegated to Congress the power to declare war, make peace, conclude treaties, raise and maintain armies, maintain a navy, establish a postal system, regulate Indian affairs, borrow money, issue bills of credit, and regulate the value of

66 The Young Republic

coin of the United States and the several states. However, nine of the thirteen states had to give their consent before any legislation of importance could be enacted, and the enforcement of the decisions of Congress depended upon the cooperation of all the states. For example, Congress could make treaties but could not force the states to live up to their stipulations; it could authorize an army but could not fill its ranks without the cooperation of each state; it could borrow money but had to depend on requisitions from the states to repay its debts. The Articles provided no standing agencies of enforcement: Congress could pass laws, but there was no formal executive or judicial branch to execute and adjudicate them. The day-to-day operations of government were handled rather precariously by officials or committees appointed by Congress.

Because of their recent quarrels with Parliament over questions of taxation and commercial regulation, the states also withheld two key powers from their new central government: the power to levy taxes (Congress could merely request contributions from the state legislatures) and the power to regulate commerce. Without these powers the Confederation government could not depend upon a regular and adequate supply of revenue to sustain its own functions, nor could it attempt to foster a national economy, a factor essential to the political unity of America.

The central government, therefore, was what the Articles called it—nothing more than "a firm league of friendship." Sharing a common cause or facing common danger, its members could work together with some measure of effectiveness; any suspicion that Congress would infringe upon their own right of independent action, however, would throw the states on their guard.

The State Governments. The Declaration of Independence in 1776 made necessary the creation of two kinds of government: central and local. While only tentative motions were made toward centralization, the people were quick to make the transition from colonial government to state government. Actually the process was one of revision and adaptation, since each of the former colonies already possessed an existing government with experienced methods of operation. Indeed, two states (Connecticut and Rhode Island) continued to operate under their colonial charters, simply by deleting all references to the British crown. Ten other states completed new constitutions within a year after the Declaration of Independence, and the last (Massachusetts) by 1780. The state constitutions, though varying in detail, reflected both the colonial experience and the current revolutionary controversy.

The framers of the constitution placed the center of political authority in the legislative branch, where it would be especially responsive to popular and local control. As a Massachusetts town meeting bluntly resolved in 1778, "The oftener power Returns to the hands of the people, the Better... Where can the power be lodged so Safe as in the Hands of the people?" Members of the legislature, if they wished to be reëlected, had to keep in mind the feelings of their people "back home." Legislators were held constantly accountable by being restricted to brief terms: in ten states the lower house, which originated tax legislation, was newly elected every year; in Connecticut and Rhode Island every six months; and in South Carolina every two years.

Framers of the constitutions, remembering their recent troubles with royal governors and magistrates, restricted the powers of governors and justices almost to the vanishing point. The average governor, contemporary jokesters claimed, had just about enough authority to collect his salary.

The imbalance of power among the branches of government often severely hampered the states' abilities to meet and solve the political and economic problems which faced them during and after the war. Yet these constitutions, whatever their shortcomings, were the first attempts to translate the generalities of the Declaration into usable instruments of government. They were constructed on the premise, novel to the eighteenth century, that a government should be formed under a *written* document, thus recognizing for the first time in modern political life the difference between fundamental and statute law. The introduction of such precisely formed instruments of governmental law, on such a grand scale, was a major contribution to the science of government.

The state constitutions reaffirmed the powerful colonial tradition of individual freedom in their bills of rights, which guaranteed each citizen freedom of religion, speech, and assembly, trial by jury, the right of habeas corpus, and other natural and civil rights. In addition, property qualifications for voting were reduced everywhere but in Massachusetts. In any case, in a country where land was cheap the vast majority of Americans could probably meet the property qualifications demanded of them.

The popular fear of governmental power tended to render the state governments politically and financially impotent. Afraid to antagonize the voters who could quickly run them out of office, legislators had difficulty, for example, passing effective measures of taxation; and, even then, revenue men were hard put in forcing collections from the people.

THE CRITICAL PERIOD

Such was the political framework within which the new nation entered the "critical period," 1783-1789, from the close of the Revolutionary War to the inauguration of the federal government under the Constitution. Long after the label of "critical period" was first introduced by historian John Fiske in 1889, historians came to acknowledge that the years of the Confederation were more creative and constructive than once was supposed. During these years a peace was won on terms highly favorable to the United States; an orderly policy for Western territorial expansion was established; a postwar recession was overcome and replaced by economic prosperity; the population expanded; and the Constitution was born. Nevertheless, except in regard to the West, the achievements of the period were largely due to the efforts of individuals and groups and to some of the more foresighted state governments. The central government was much too dependent on the conflicting whims of the several states to be consistently effective.

Establishing a Western Policy. Ratification of the Articles of Confederation was slow; it was not until late in 1779 that twelve states gave their approval, and Maryland, the last to ratify, did not do so until 1781. During almost the entire war, therefore, the country operated under the authority of the Continental Congress without a formal central government.

The solution of the Western land problem (see Chapter 2), which kept Maryland from ratifying the Articles, was of paramount importance to the new government. It represented a first step toward nationalization, and made certain that the nation, as it moved west, would gradually evolve as a unit rather than as thirteen colonies with a set of permanently dependent territories. It also meant that since Congress now controlled the entire West, it could determine a central policy for the development of its vast unpopulated territory.

During and after the Revolution a stream of settlers poured west, creating

NORTHWEST TERRITORY

WISCONSIN Admitted 1848
MICHIGAN Admitted 1837
ILLINOIS Admitted 1818
INDIANA Admitted 1816
OHIO Admitted 1803

SEVEN RANGES
First area surveyed under Ordinance of 1785

A TOWNSHIP
A township is 6 miles square and contains 36 square miles or sections.

6	5	4	3	2	1
7	8	9	10	11	12
18	17	16	15	14	13
19	20	21	22	23	24
30	29	28	27	26	25
31	32	33	34	35	36

A SECTION
A section is 1 mile square or 640 acres.

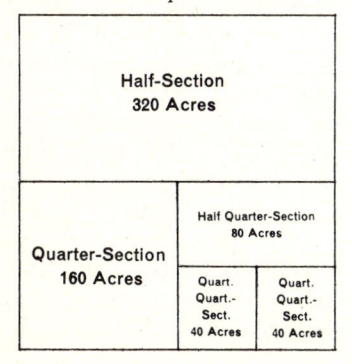

Half-Section 320 Acres

Quarter-Section 160 Acres

Half Quarter-Section 80 Acres

Quart. Quart.-Sect. 40 Acres

Quart. Quart.-Sect. 40 Acres

---

an urgent need for a systematic plan of land sale and territorial government. A Land Ordinance passed by Congress in 1785 provided for a government survey to divide the land of the Northwest Territory (north of the Ohio River, west of Pennsylvania, and east of the Mississippi River) into townships of thirty-six square miles, each township to be split into thirty-six sections of one square mile (640 acres) each and each section into quarter-sections. Four sections in every township were reserved as bounties for soldiers of the Continental army, and another section was set aside for the use of the public schools. The remainder of the land was to be sold at public auction for at least one dollar an acre in minimum lots of 640 acres.

The Ordinance of 1785 proved advantageous to wealthy land speculators, who bought up whole townships and resold them at handsome profits. Sensing even greater returns, a group of speculators (including some congressmen and government officials) pressed for further legislation to provide a form of government for the West; the result was the Northwest Ordinance of 1787, based largely on a similar ordinance drafted by Jefferson in 1784 but never put into effect.

Though it favored the wealthy land speculator over the indigent farmer, the Northwest Ordinance did provide a model for translating the unsettled Northwest, by orderly political procedures, from frontier to statehood. It provided that Congress should appoint from among the landholders of the region a governor, a secretary, and three judges. When the territory reached a population of five thousand free adult males, a bicameral legislature was to be established. When there were sixty thousand free inhabitants (the population of the smallest state at that time) the voters might adopt a constitution, elect their own officers, and enter the Union on equal terms with the original thirteen states. From three to five states were to be formed from the territory. Slavery was forbidden in the area, and freedom of worship and trial by jury were guaranteed.

So successfully did the Northwest Ordinance accomplish its political aims that it set the pattern for the absorption of the entire West (as well as Alaska and Hawaii) into the Union. Settlers flooded into the Northwest Territory as soon as the ordinance went into effect; the great drive to the West had begun, not to cease for another hundred years.

Relations with Europe. Perhaps the greatest problems facing Congress under the Articles arose from its lack of a unified, coherent foreign policy and its lack of authority to evolve one. The core of diplomatic power lay equally among the states, each of which possessed the right to arrange its own foreign affairs, with the national government virtually helpless to operate independently. The United States was in a most delicate position in regard to England, France, and Spain. There was no reason to suppose that Britain intended to allow America to remain independent without interference if Britain's interests dictated otherwise. The United States, for its part, desperately needed trade agreements with Europe, especially with England, its largest market. It was also involved in a border dispute with Spain over Florida, and when the Spanish, who controlled the lower Mississippi and New Orleans, closed them to American trade in 1784, the nation was in trouble. If Congress could not open the Mississippi to trade, a number of Western leaders favored either taking New Orleans by force or joining a British protectorate which might help them do so. Washington felt that the West in 1784 was so near to secession that "the touch of a feather" might divide it from the country. The Spanish, who needed American trade, seemed willing to negotiate, and in 1785 the Spanish minister Diego de Gardoqui discussed terms with Secretary of Foreign Affairs John Jay. Both diplomats were bound by specific instructions which led to a stalemate; eventually Jay was forced to agree to a commercial treaty which simply gave up all claim to United States navigation rights on the Mississippi in exchange for certain trading rights with Spain's colonies, which favored seaboard merchants and shippers, and to Spain's profit. Such a roar of protest went up from the West that Jay let the negotiations lapse, and finally the Spanish in 1788 helped to settle the matter by opening the river under restrictions with which the West could live, though not happily. The Jay-Gardoqui negotiations not only pointed up the impotence of the Articles in foreign affairs, but left behind in the West a lingering suspicion of the East.

The Difficulties of Trade. When the colonies left the imperial system, thus giving up their favored economic position, American merchants and shippers found themselves in cutthroat competition with the British, Dutch, and French for world markets. John Adams tried unsuccessfully for three years to make some kind of trade agreement with England, but as Lord Sheffield commented, putting his finger squarely on the commercial weaknesses of the Articles of Confederation, "America cannot retaliate. It will not be an easy matter to bring the Americans to act as a nation. They are not to be feared by such as us."

Sheffield proved to be correct, for when Congress asked the states in 1784 for exclusive authority to regulate foreign trade over a fifteen-year period, the states immediately refused. Under the Articles of Confederation Congress was powerless to do more than protest.

Domestic commerce as well as foreign trade suffered from confusion and interstate rivalries. The states used their power to levy tariffs, creating barriers between them that seriously hampered domestic commerce and created further dissatisfaction with the central government. At the same time, American industry was struggling to survive. The war and blockade stimulated American manufacturing by cutting off British and continental imports; some of the states, in fact, offered premiums and subsidies for the production of manufactured goods. At the close of the war, much of the artificial stimulation which had encouraged American commerce was withdrawn and the inevitable postwar lag set in. Capital was short, the currency disordered, transportation deficient, and investments risky.

Frenzied Finances. The Articles of Confederation gave the national government no power to tax; if the states refused to pay their levies in full or on time, Congress simply was forced to accumulate ever larger foreign and domestic debts. The states responded erratically to Congress' requests for taxes, so that while Congress occasionally had money, it never had enough at the right time. Although Congress repudiated most of its war debts by simply cancelling out millions of dollars in Continental currency, the country in 1785 still owed about $35 million in domestic debts and a growing foreign debt. The states, meanwhile, had war debts of their own, which they increased after the war by assuming that part of the congressional debt owed their citizens.

In addition to these debts, both national and state governments lacked a uniform, stable, sound currency. There was no trustworthy federal currency, and the states were loaded with badly inflated wartime paper money. The postwar slump which hit the country in 1783, sinking to its lowest point in mid-1786, affected the farmer and the small debtor most of all. In states where they controlled the legislatures, the solution seemed easy: seven state legislatures simply approved the issue of paper money in larger quantities; in addition, to help distressed farmers, they passed "stay laws" to prevent creditors from foreclosing mortgages.

Crisis and Rebellion. At the depth of the depression in 1786 there was a severe hard money shortage; farmers, especially, were in difficulty. Protest meetings in several states won some concessions from the legislatures, but in Massachusetts, when mobs of unruly men closed the courts at Northampton, Worcester, and Springfield, thereby preventing farm foreclosures and prosecutions for debt, Governor James Bowdoin sent militia to scatter them.

In reply to Bowdoin, Daniel Shays, a veteran of the Revolution, organized a band of farmers in 1786 for an attack on the Springfield Arsenal, from which he hoped to get arms. The governor sent a force of militia (paid for by contributions from Boston businessmen) to protect the arsenal, and Shays' poorly mounted attack in January 1787 failed miserably. In a few weeks the leaders of the rebellion had been captured and convicted, and a few sentenced to death. The legislature pardoned them all, however, even Shays, who was released in 1788.

Shays' rebellion had swift effects in Massachusetts: Governor Bowdoin was defeated in the next election by John Hancock, and the legislature prudently decided to grant the farmers some measure of relief. The effect on the country at large was equally swift, and much greater. As Abigail Adams wrote Thomas Jefferson, when "ignorant, restless desperadoes, without conscience or principles" could persuade "a deluded multitude to follow their standards . . ." who could be safe, anywhere in the land? "There are combustibles," wrote Washington, "in every state which a spark might set fire to."

The Drift Toward a New Government. Even the most earnest states' rights advocates were willing to admit the existence of imperfections in the Articles of Confederation, and proposals for conventions to discuss their amendment had already appeared in the New York legislature in 1782 and Massachusetts in 1785. In 1786, under the cloud of Shays' rebellion, Congress agreed that the Articles needed revision, though as James Monroe told Jefferson, "Some gentlemen have inveterate prejudices against all attempts to increase the powers of Congress, others see the necessity but fear the consequences."

It remained for Alexander Hamilton of New York to seize the initiative. When Virginia invited representatives from the states to meet at Annapolis in 1786 for a discussion of problems of interstate commerce, Hamilton called upon the states to appoint delegates to a meeting to be held in March 1787 at Philadelphia, to discuss ways "to render the Constitution of the Federal Government adequate to the exigencies of the Union." Since almost at the same moment Daniel Shays' men were being pursued by Boston militia, Hamilton's report found receptive audiences in the states. Congress adopted the suggestion and authorized a convention "for the sole and express purpose of revising the Articles of Confederation and reporting to Congress and the several legislatures such alterations and provisions therein."

There were those who believed that the Articles could be amended and reworked into an effective and efficient government. However, there were a number of determined political leaders —among them Hamilton, Madison, John Jay, and Henry Knox—who believed that the country's interests demanded a much stronger central government, who believed in executive and judicial control rather than legislative, and who did not fully trust the decentralized, mass-dominated state governments. There was a general belief among the mercantile and financial classes that, as Madison wrote, the United States needed the kind of government which would "support a due supremacy of the national authority, and leave in force the local authorities so far as they can be subordinately useful."

FRAMING A NEW CONSTITUTION

The Question of Federalism. The meetings at Philadelphia began on May 25, 1787. Conspicuously absent were many of the popular leaders of the pre-revolutionary era. These "antifederalists," men like Samuel Adams and Patrick Henry, had involved themselves in the Revolution when it still comprised a scattering of colonial protests and then state revolts, rather loosely guided by the Continental Congress. Deeply devoted to winning independence for their own states, most of these men continued to believe that the states should be governed without the interference of a strong central government. Some antifederalists, like George Clinton of New York, had a vital stake in local state politics, which the enlargement of the powers of a continental government might endanger. Others saw the need to strengthen the Confederation but insisted that the supremacy of the states should not be basically altered. All of the antifederalists were passionately convinced that a republican system could survive only on the local level, under their watchful eyes. A republic on a continental scale was beyond their imagination.

The fifty-five delegates who made their appearance in the Philadelphia State House were men of generally broader views. George Washington (chosen presiding officer of the convention) and Benjamin Franklin were distinguished representatives of an older generation, long experienced in guiding the military or diplomatic affairs of the colonies as a whole. Most of the delegates, however, were men in their thirties or forties whose careers had only begun when the Revolution broke out and whose public reputations had been achieved as a result of their identification with the continental war effort. With the coming of peace, these "nationalists" were disquieted by the ease with which the states slid back into their old provincial ways. In vainly advocating revenue and commercial powers for the Confederation Congress, Robert Morris, James Wilson, Gouverneur Morris, James Madison, Alexander Hamilton, Charles Pinckney, and others began to see the futility of trying to govern a large country with thirteen states following diverse policies.

These federalists distrusted unchecked power in government as much as their opponents did; however, they believed that under the current system power *was* being exercised in one quarter without effective restraints. Jefferson branded it the "legislative tyranny" of the states. There was no way to appeal the decisions of the legislators; the executive and judicial branches, and even the central Confederation, were powerless to overrule the legislative branch. In addition, nations abroad were beginning to look with contempt upon the disunited states, and there were even dangerous signs of territorial encroachments — by Britain in the Northwest and by Spain in the South and Southwest. National survival and prestige, the federalists insisted, demanded that a stronger central government be created.

The Philosophy of the Constitution. The feeling of urgency which permeated the minds of the delegates goes far toward explaining their eagerness to reach compromises on matters in dispute. Whenever the debates became deadlocked, speakers would arise and warn of the consequences should the Convention fail. Said Elbridge Gerry at mid-session: "Something must be done or we shall disappoint not only America, but the whole world. . . . We must make concessions on both sides." And Caleb Strong warned, "It is agreed, on all hands, that Congress are nearly at an end. If no accommodation takes place, the Union itself must soon be dissolved."

Such warnings climaxed a series of heated arguments during the meetings; nevertheless, differences of opinion continued to arise, mostly over matters of detail and method. The Founding Fathers were in essential agreement in regard to the broad outlines of the new government and in regard to political principles, learned through years of experience in dealing with a "tyrannous" Parliament and serving in state legislatures and in Congress.

First, they believed that the central government must be empowered to act without the mediation of the states and to exercise its will directly upon individual citizens. It must have its own administrative agencies, with the ability to enforce its own laws and treaties, to collect its own revenues, and to regulate commerce and other matters of welfare affecting the states generally.

Secondly, they believed that power in government, though imperative, must somehow be held in check. Like most enlightened men of the eighteenth century, they recognized that human nature was not perfect. "Men are ambitious, vindictive, and rapacious," said Alexander Hamilton, and while his language was strong, his appraisal of human nature was generally shared by his colleagues. They agreed with the French political philosopher Montesquieu that "men entrusted with power tend to abuse it." The system advocated by Montesquieu to prevent this evil was to distribute the functions of government among three coequal branches of government, each of which would hold a veto or check on the power of the others. This doctrine of "separation of powers" had earlier been outlined by John Adams:

A legislative, an executive, and a judicial power comprehend the whole of what is meant and understood by government. It is by balancing each of these powers against the other two, that the efforts in human nature toward tyranny can alone be checked and restrained, and any degree of freedom preserved in the constitution.

That such a system had failed in the state governments did not shake the delegates' faith in the *principle* of separation of powers. The states had only gone through the motions of creating three branches; in actuality they had not given the executive and judicial branches sufficient checks on the legislatures, which in some states were running riot in control of government.

Finally, most of the delegates were committed to some form of federalism, the political system which would unite the states under an independently operating central government while permitting them to retain some portion of their former power and identity. Few agreed with George Read of Delaware that the states "must be done away." Even Alexander Hamilton, who formally introduced such a scheme, acknowledged that the Convention might "shock the public opinion by proposing such a measure." It was generally agreed that the states must remain; the argument arose over how, in operating terms, power could be properly distributed between the states and the national government.

The Convention at Work. Four days after the Convention opened, Edmund Randolph of Virginia proposed fifteen resolutions, drafted by his colleague James Madison, which demonstrated immediately that the general intent was to proceed beyond mere revision of the Articles of Confederation in favor of forming a new national government. This "Virginia Plan" proposed a national executive, a national judiciary, and a national legislature consisting of two houses, both representing the states proportionally according to either population or tax contributions, with the lower house popularly elected and the upper house chosen by members of the lower. Although William Paterson proposed a rival "New Jersey Plan," which in substance would merely have enlarged the taxation and commerce powers of the Confederation Congress, it was never seriously considered. The Virginia Plan, after four months of debate, amendment, and considerable enlargement, became the United States Constitution.

Although the delegates agreed upon the main features of the new government, it was in working out the details that discord came almost to the point of breaking up the convention. That a breakup was avoided is attributable in part to the delegates' recognition of the urgent need for compromise and concession. They were pressed to balance special interest against special interest, the large states against the small, section against section, in order to realize a constitution that the majority could accept. No individual could be perfectly satisfied with the result, but each could feel that the half loaf he garnered for his interest was far better than none.

Major opposition to the original Virginia Plan came from the small states; in the existing Congress each of their votes was equal to that of any large state, but under the proposed system of proportional representation in the national legislature they would be consistently outvoted by the larger, more populous states. The large states retorted that government should represent people, not geography. "Is [a government] for *men*," asked James Wilson, "or for the imaginary beings called *States?*" The issue came down to the question of how federal the federal government should be. In acknowledging the permanence of the states, were the delegates obligated to go further and introduce the concept of the states into the very structure and representation of the new central government?

The final answer to this question was yes. In the end, the large states gave in. After the New Jersey Plan was rejected and the principle of a bicameral legislature established, the small states, while hesitating to object to proportional representation in the lower house, persisted in claiming the right of equal representation for states in the Senate, or upper house. And by threatening to walk out of the Convention, they won. In essence, this "Great Compromise," as it came to be called, was hardly a compromise at all. The major issue concerned representation in the Senate, and when the large states conceded on this point they received no concession in return. However, the major crisis of the Convention had been resolved.

In the process of accepting a two-house legislature, the delegates acknowledged not only a balance between large and small states but also a balance between the common people and propertied, supposedly conservative interests. Many delegates had argued against giving the people a direct voice in government; "The people," said Roger Sherman, "should have as little to do as may be about the government. They want information, and are constantly liable to be misled." Elbridge Gerry pointed to the "evils" that "flow from the excess of democracy." Other delegates agreed, however, with James Madison, who stated "that the great fabric to be raised would be more stable and durable, if it should rest on the solid foundation of the people themselves." Thus the basis of representation in the lower house was set at one representative for every forty thousand persons—each representative to be elected by voters eligible to elect "the most numerous branch of [their] State legislature." On the other hand, the senators of the upper house—two from each state—were to be chosen by the state legislatures, putting them at a second remove from popular control. As a result, the Senate was expected to represent the more conservative interests, "to consist," as John Dickinson noted, "of the most distinguished characters, distinguished for their rank in life and their weight of property." In sum, the two houses of Congress were to balance the rights of the lower and higher ranks of society, but with the edge given to the higher.

Another issue arose over the manner of choosing the President, the head of the executive branch of the new government. To have the national legislature appoint him, as the original Virginia Plan proposed, might mean, it was argued, that a candidate to that high office would be "a mere creature of the legislature." A second plan, championed by James Wilson, called for popular election of the President; but the delegates had too great a distrust of unchecked democracy to find this plan fully acceptable. Other proposals sought to bring the states into the elective process by having either the state legislatures or the governors combine to elect the nation's chief executive.

The final compromise embodied elements from all these plans. Each state legislature was to appoint a number of presidential "electors" equal to the total number of senators and representatives to which the state was entitled in Congress. The electors would meet in their own states and vote for two presidential candidates, and the candidate receiving the majority of votes from all the states would become President. It should be noted that the method of choosing the electors was left to the decision of the state legislatures. Thus, the legislatures might decide to keep the power of appointment in their own hands, as most of them did, or they could submit the appointment to popular vote, a method which became widespread only much later. In either case, the electoral system was intended to minimize popular influence in the choice of the President.

Few of the delegates, however, believed that the election would end in the electoral college. It was believed that each state would try to advance a native son, and thus no candidate would receive a majority vote. In that event, the election would be referred to the House of Representatives, where votes would be taken by state delegations, each state having one vote. In effect, this presidential compromise echoed the earlier issue over proportional representation. In the first phase of the election, votes would be drawn on the basis of population; in the second phase, on the basis of statehood.

The conflict between North and South was not so serious in the Convention as it was later to become, but the differing sectional economics did arouse specific issues of governmental structure and powers. Because the South was an agricultural region dependent on a world market for its staple exports like tobacco and rice, it wanted commercial regulation—tariffs and export duties—eliminated or minimized. Southerners were also committed to slavery, not necessarily through moral conviction of its justice but because of their inescapably large investment in slave labor. Finally, the southern states, six in number and comparatively less populous than northern states, were aware that in Congress they would be outnumbered by the North. They thus felt compelled to secure constitutional guarantees for their sectional interests before launching a new government in which they could be consistently outvoted.

In the North, on the other hand, agricultural products like grain and livestock had for the most part a ready domestic market. Many Northerners were more interested in having the government promote shipping and foster manufacturing by means of protective tariffs. Many also roundly condemned slavery and demanded an end to the "nefarious" slave trade. Their attitude, however, was not entirely without self-interest. The Convention had already agreed that direct taxes were to be assessed on the basis of population. The North was quite willing to have Negro slaves counted as part of the population in apportioning such taxes, thus upping the South's assessments, but objected to counting slaves in apportioning representation in the House of Representatives, a plan which would enlarge the Southern delegations.

The Convention resolved these differences by negotiating compromises. In regard to commerce, the South won a ban on export taxes and a provision requiring a two-thirds vote in the Senate for ratification of treaties; in return, the North secured a provision that a simple congressional majority was sufficient to pass all other acts of commercial regulation. The slave trade was not to be prohibited before the year 1808, but a tax of ten dollars might be imposed on each slave imported. The so-called "three-fifths compromise" specified that five slaves would equal three free men for purposes of both taxation and representation.

The influence of the states in the framework of the new constitution was greater than some nationalists would have liked. But one of the most important factors shaping the delegates' decisions was their practical recognition that they had to offer a constitution which the people would approve, and popular loyalty to the respective states was too strong to be ignored.

Results and Accomplishments. By the close of summer the Constitution was slowly taking shape, and on September 17, 1787, twelve state delegations voted approval of the final draft. Edmund Randolph and George Mason of Virginia, along with Elbridge Gerry of Massachusetts, refused to sign it, feeling that it went too far toward consolidation and lacked a bill of rights. (Randolph, however, later decided to support it.) The remaining thirty-nine delegates affixed their signatures and sent the document to Congress with two recommendations: that it be submitted to state ratifying conventions especially called for the purpose, rather than directly to the voters; and that it be declared officially operative when nine (not thirteen) states accepted it, since there was real doubt that any document so evolved could ever get unanimous approval. Some of the delegates feared that they had far exceeded their instructions to *revise* the Articles, for the document they sent to Congress certainly represented much more than revision.

Federalists and Antifederalists. The new Constitution met with great favor and equally great opposition in the states. Its strongest proponents, who adopted the name "Federalists," were drawn from the ranks of bankers, lawyers, businessmen, merchants, planters, and men of property in the urban areas. Hamilton and Jay favored it in New York; Madison, Randolph, and John Marshall argued for it in Virginia; and the fact that Washington and Franklin, the two most honored Americans, supported it was much in its favor. Opposition to its ratification came from the small farmers, laborers, and the debtor, agrarian classes. However, it is misleading to arrange the argument over ratification on lines of economic interest alone, however convenient. Obviously there were businessmen and merchants who voted for the document because they felt it would mean expanded markets, better regulation of commerce, greater credit stability, and less control of economic affairs by the states. Just as obviously there were farmers and debtors who voted against it for equally self-interested reasons. But the lines of demarcation between rich and poor, or mercantile and agrarian interests, were by no means so clear in the voting as one might expect. Claiming that the nation could obtain progress and prosperity under the revised Articles, the Antifederalists accused the Convention of creating a government that eventually, as George Mason of Virginia thought, might "produce either a monarchy or a corrupt aristocracy"; there was "apprehension," Rufus King of New York told Madison, "that the liberties of the people are in danger."

On the other hand, the Federalists, who might more accurately have been called "nationalists," possessed a group of leaders of great drive and organizing skill; it was not easy to outargue or outmaneuver men such as Hamilton, Jay, Madison, James Wilson, or Henry Knox. Furthermore, they had the initiative and kept it, giving their opposition little time to temporize or organize. The Federalists immediately began an energetic campaign for ratification in their own states. In New York, where opposition was strong, the Constitution was brilliantly defended in a series of eighty-five newspaper articles written by Hamilton, Madison, and Jay. The essays later were collected in a single volume called *The Federalist*.

The Antifederalists had only a few such talented leaders; George Clinton, Patrick Henry, Elbridge Gerry, Luther Martin, and James Warren were able men, but none, for example, was capable of producing the brilliant *Federalist* papers or of handling the New York campaigns as Hamilton did. The Antifederalists tried to fight the battle piecemeal, without a positive program, and they showed a curious reluctance to match the aggressive, shrewd campaigning of the Federalists.

It has long been fashionable among historians, particularly in the earlier twentieth century, to consider the struggle over ratification as a contest between "conservatives" and "liberals." If the Declaration of Independence represented "radical" or revolutionary thought, the Constitution, it was assumed, therefore represented a conservative counterrevolution which undid some of the Revolution's work. On reëxamination, however, it becomes less clear as to which side deserves which label. It was the Federalists, after all, who proposed the bold and decisive change, who hoped to carry out to completion the powerful nationalism engendered by the revolutionary effort. There was the daring step, the attempt to do something never before accomplished—to create a single, unified nation out of a bundle of disparate states, bound together by common consent and national pride. The Antifederalists, fearful of any power not under their direct restraint, preferred the status quo; to them, apparently, the great experiment in federalism suggested by the Constitution seemed too new, too dangerous. They could not conceive of a nationalized government which did not threaten republican principles.

The Constitution Ratified. The ratification of the document proceeded smoothly in most of the smaller states, which were generally satisfied with the compromises set up to protect them. By January 1788 five states (Delaware, New Jersey, Georgia, Connecticut, and Pennsylvania) had accepted it, with strong opposition to it recorded only in Pennsylvania. In Massachusetts, the sixth state, the state convention ratified the document after long dispute and a close vote, 187 to 168, and then only after attaching a strong recommendation for a bill of rights. Maryland and South Carolina followed, while the ninth state, New Hampshire, took two conventions (the second by a margin of but nine votes) to accept it on June 21, 1788. Legally the Constitution was now in force, yet it was plain that without the approval of New York and Virginia it could never successfully function.

In Virginia, the Federalists won a narrow victory, 89 to 79, on June 25. Like Massachusetts, Virginia attached proposals for twenty changes and a recommendation for a specific bill of rights. In New York, Hamilton and the Federalists pulled the document through on July 26 by a breathtakingly small margin of 30 to 27. North Carolina refused to ratify until a bill of rights was actually attached to the Constitution, and finally approved it in late 1789. Rhode Island held out until 1790. It was apparent that in each of the contested states the chief issue was the lack of a bill of rights, and the First Congress, when it met, immediately added ten amendments to provide one. In six states the Federalist majority was large, in three decisive, and in the remaining four the margin was close.

In view of the contest over ratification, it is amazing that the Constitution was so swiftly adopted and that within a single generation it came generally to be regarded as a sacred, almost divinely inspired document. The reason is that the ideas expressed in the Constitution were themselves implicit in the Articles, the Declaration of Independence, and the revolutionary argument; the Constitution merely gave those ideas explicit, final form. The idea that government should protect life, liberty, and property was already accepted; the idea that government should be powerful enough to perform its functions was already recognized, even in the Articles (though there were sharp differences of opinion over how powerful that need be). No one at the Convention, and very few people in the states, argued for retention of the Articles without change. The question was, did the Constitution change the direction of government too much? The difference between the Articles and the Constitution lay almost wholly in the amount and quality of the authority granted to that "more perfect union."

LAUNCHING THE GOVERNMENT

Washington and Federalist Rule. After the balloting for President in January 1789, and for Congress under the terms of the new Constitution, the presidential electors met in February to choose George Washington as the first President of the United States. John Adams, who had received the smaller number of electoral ballots, was installed as Vice-President in mid-April, and on April 30 Washington, standing on the balcony of the Federal Building at Broad and Wall Streets in New York, was inaugurated as President.

For the first few months of the new administration, Congress and the President moved carefully. Congress quickly created the three executive departments of State, Treasury, and War, and Washington chose Thomas Jefferson, Alexander Hamilton, and Henry Knox to serve as their Secretaries. Congress then passed a tariff on imports and a tonnage duty on foreign vessels, both intended to raise revenue and to protect American trade. The Judiciary Act of 1789 created the office of Attorney General, a Supreme Court, three circuit courts, and thirteen district courts, filling in the outlines of the federal legal system.

Federalist Finance. Washington left the most critical problem of his first term to Alexander Hamilton, his confident young Secretary of the Treasury. Hamilton, in a series of reports to Congress, quickly described what seemed to him the most urgent task of the new administration: to define the proper relationship between the national government and the national economy. He believed, as most Federalists did, that the government should play an active, even decisive role in economic affairs, so that the nation might achieve a self-sufficient, expanding economy, balanced among agriculture, manufacturing, and trade. To this end he proposed, in his *Report on the Public Credit* (1790), *Second Report on the Public Credit* (1791), and *Report on Manufactures* (1791), a firm, unified policy enforced by a strong federal authority.

Hamilton's economic program also had clear political aims. He was convinced that the new government could not last unless the Constitution were strengthened by interpretation and made responsive to changing needs, and unless the forces of wealth and property supported it. Thus he hoped to win business and financial groups to the support of the federal government, and to bind these groups to the national interest. Hamilton fashioned his program from three basic components.

The first, the *Report on the Public Credit,* laid the foundation for the Hamiltonian system. Under the previous regimes—that is, the Continental and Confederation congresses—the general government had accumulated a foreign debt of about $12 million, owed chiefly to France and Holland, and a domestic debt of about $40 million, owed to American nationals. The separate states owed a total of about $22 million more. Hamilton proposed that the federal government promise full payment of the foreign and domestic debt at par value and take over, or *assume,* the unpaid debts of the states. Since the federal government did not possess the money to pay this debt, totaling about $74 million, Hamilton recommended *funding* the entire debt; that is, in exchange for their old Continental and Confederation bonds creditors would be issued new interest-bearing bonds which would be the direct obligation of the new federal government.

No opposition was voiced against payment of the foreign debt in full. However, full payment of the domestic debt at face value was another matter. On the open market these old domestic bonds had been selling at far below their original face value. Because the previous central governments had failed to meet interest payments or provide for retirement of the debt, the original owners of the bonds had lost faith in them and had sold them for whatever they could get. The purchasers were usually men of means who were willing to buy cheap on the chance that the government would make good.

Hamilton did succeed in getting Congress to make the old bonds good at face value (many congressmen were themselves bond holders), but in so doing he aroused charges from his opponents that the new government was being operated in the interest of the wealthy. Hamilton's intentions, however, were actually both honorable and farsighted: by his plan, he felt that the middle and upper classes would find a strong motive for sustaining the national government; their confidence in the solvency and good faith of the government would stimulate business activity. In addition, the funded debt, in the form of negotiable bonds, could be used by creditors as capital to finance new enterprises.

The assumption of the state debts by the federal government also evoked vehement opposition, particularly from the southern states, which had already paid off most of their debts. Southerners protested the use of national funds to help pay off the obligations of states with large outstanding debts, such as the New England states. Hamilton's assumption program was defeated on its first vote in the House, but he finally won in a bargain with Jefferson: in exchange for locating the new national capital on the Potomac across from Virginia, Jefferson's congressional forces agreed to assume the debts of the states.

The second part of Hamilton's program called for the creation of a central bank, somewhat like the Bank of England, which would serve as a depository for federal funds, issue paper money (which the Treasury by law could not do), provide commercial interests with a steady and dependable credit institution, and serve the government with short-term loans. Some leaders in and out of Congress objected to this proposal on two grounds: four fifths of the bank's funds were to come from private sources, which might then control the bank's (and the nation's) fiscal policies; more important, they considered the scheme unconstitutional. Jefferson and Madison, among others, argued that since the federal government was not specifically authorized by the Constitution to create a national bank, for Congress to do so would be unconstitutional.

Hamilton, aware that the bank bill might set an important precedent, argued that Congress was authorized by the Constitution to do what was "necessary and proper" for the national good. If the proposed bank fell within this definition, as he believed it did, the Constitution gave Congress "implied powers" to act in ways not precisely enumerated in the document. He took the position "that every power vested in a government is in its nature *sovereign* and includes, by *force* of the *term,* a right to employ all the *means* requisite and fairly applicable to the attainment of the *ends* of such power...."

Jefferson, to the contrary, argued that the federal government possessed only those powers explicitly granted to it in the Constitution, and that all others, as the Tenth Amendment determined, were reserved to the states. The language of the Constitution must be strictly construed. "To take a single step beyond the boundaries thus specially drawn around the powers of Congress," he wrote, "is to take possession of a boundless field of power, no longer susceptible of any definition." Neither the "general welfare" nor the "necessary and proper" clauses of the Constitution, he maintained, could be so broadly interpreted as Hamilton wished. Washington and Congress, however, accepted Hamilton's argument and in 1791 created the Bank of the United States with a charter for twenty years.

The Whiskey Rebellion. Third, Hamilton proposed to levy an excise tax on a number of commodities to supply money to the federal Treasury, for, he wrote, ". . . the creation of debt should always be accompanied by the means of its extinguishment." Among the items included in the bill, passed in 1791, was whiskey; in western Pennsylvania and North Carolina, where conversion into whiskey was a cheap and efficient way of getting grain to market, Hamilton's excise tax was therefore a tax on the farmer's most valuable cash crop. Collections fell off in this area in 1792, a few tax collectors were manhandled by irritated Pennsylvania farmers in 1793, and in 1794 a sizeable force of angry whiskey makers vowed to march on Pittsburgh to challenge federal authority at its nearest point.

Memories of Daniel Shays were still fresh in Congress, and President Washington acted quickly. He issued a proclamation ordering the Pennsylvanians to return to their homes, declared western Pennsylvania in a state of rebellion, and sent Hamilton and Henry Lee with a force of fifteen thousand militiamen to Pennsylvania. The farmers promptly scattered, but Hamilton, determined to teach the unruly frontiersmen a lesson in federal authority, saw to it that a score of the ringleaders were arrested, tried, and sentenced to death. Washington wisely pardoned them, but neither Hamilton nor Federalism was ever popular in that region again.

The Indian Frontier. When settlers poured across the frontier settlement line into the open land of the West, Indians barred the way. The British, who had promised in the terms of the Peace of Paris to give up their Northwest posts, held on to them as long as possible and encouraged the Indians to resist the American westward advance. The treaties of Fort Stanwix and Fort McIntosh, negotiated with the Northwestern tribes by the United States in 1784-1785, brought no more than temporary peace, while the Creeks in the South, under the leadership of the half-breed chief Alexander McGilliveray, harassed the frontier settlements until forced to sign a treaty in 1785.

The Indian tribes presented a virtually insoluble problem. It was impossible to divert or delay the American drive westward, and the Indians stood in possession of undeveloped lands of great value. They were difficult to negotiate with and few Americans, for that matter, understood much of Indian psychology, politics, or culture. Because the Indian leaders were unequipped to deal with Western political methods, they became little more than pawns in the hands of British agents and American commissioners. Some, like Jefferson, recognized the Indian's tragic position and hoped that he might somehow be assimilated into Western society; others agreed with those frontiersmen who thought that the only good Indian was a dead one. The national policy toward the Indian vacillated between these two extremes, and no one was ever able to work out a satisfactory solution.

In the Northwest Territory, the tribes ranged through the Ohio, Indiana, and Illinois country almost at will. General Harmar, who mounted an expedition against the Ohio Indians in 1790, was ambushed and his fifteen hundred militia scattered. General Arthur St. Clair, who led a larger force into Indian country a year later, was trapped and his army decimated. In 1793 General "Mad Anthony" Wayne organized a third army of four thousand men and after careful preparation smashed the combined Indian tribes at the Battle of Fallen Timbers, in northwest Ohio, in the summer of 1794. The next year the twelve most powerful tribes ceded most of the Ohio country to the U. S. in the Treaty of Greenville.

THE PERILS OF NEUTRALITY

The French Revolution. The outbreak of the French Revolution forced the Washington administration into the first real test of its foreign policy. A good many Americans in 1789 welcomed the news of the French uprisings as the logical outcome of their own revolution, and "in no part of the world," wrote John Marshall later, "was the Revolution hailed with more joy than in America." The execution of Louis XVI and the Reign of Terror which followed led many, however, to sober second thoughts, while the French declaration of war against England, Holland, and Spain in February 1793 introduced the difficult question of neutrality directly into American foreign policy. One segment of opinion, holding that Britain was still the United States' major enemy, favored the French cause. Others felt that British trade was so essential to American prosperity that the United States, whatever its sympathies with revolution, could not afford to offend the world's greatest naval and economic power. Still others, observing the chaos of Jacobin Paris, saw France as a threat to the security and order of society everywhere, even to Christianity itself.

When he received news of the outbreak of war between France and Britain, Washington immediately issued a proclamation in April 1793 (avoiding the word "neutrality") which guaranteed the belligerents the "friendly and impartial conduct" of the United States. America, he believed, needed peace—the opportunity to build up its strength—more than anything else. "If this country is preserved in tranquillity twenty years longer," he wrote, "it may bid defiance in a just cause to any power whatever. . . ." His proclamation, which was to influence American foreign policy for the next half-century, derived from his firm conviction that the United States should avoid, at all reasonable costs, the brawlings of Europe.

But the path of the neutral in a world at war was not smooth. Many Americans believed that Washington's administration had played its old revolutionary ally false, but the President's view prevailed, and in 1794 Congress passed a Neutrality Act which made Washington's position the official American policy.

Strained Relations with Britain. The British navy was large, the French navy small, and the British blockade of France very effective. When the French, desperate for trade, opened up their West Indian ports to American ships, the British immediately declared that any trade with France was a military act and that ships caught at it were subject to seizure. Not only did British men-of-war confiscate American cargoes, but claiming that some American sailors were really deserters from the British navy (as, indeed, a few were) they forcibly "impressed" a number of American seamen into naval service. Still, though American ships were in danger wherever they went in Atlantic waters, wartime trade was so lucrative that many American merchants felt that the profit was worth the risk, and incidents multiplied.

Jay's Treaty. Hoping to reduce tensions, Congress passed an embargo act in 1794 which forbade British ships to call at American ports and American ships to sail in areas where they might be subject to British seizure. Since this hurt American trade more than it hindered the British navy, the embargo lasted less than two months. However, American protests induced the British to relax some of their rules, and in 1794 Washington requested Chief Justice John Jay to sail for London to discuss a treaty to settle outstanding differences.

Jay's arguments were no doubt good ones, but perhaps more important, French military successes persuaded the British it was unwise to antagonize the United States unduly. Under the terms of Jay's Treaty (the Treaty of London, signed in 1794) the British agreed to evacuate the frontier posts by 1796; to open the British West Indies to American trade under certain conditions; to admit American ships to East Indian ports on a nondiscriminatory basis; and to refer to a joint commission the payment of pre-Revolutionary War debts and the northwest boundary dispute. However, they simply refused to discuss other important points at issue, including impressment and the Indian question, and made far fewer concessions than Jay had been instructed to get. Washington reluctantly submitted the treaty to the Senate, which ratified it by only one vote. Not only was the Washington administration severely criticized for the settlement, but Jay himself was burned in effigy in various cities. Though Jay had been perhaps as successful as anyone had a right to expect, the terms of his treaty returned to haunt him and his party for a long time.

Not all news was bad, however. Spain, badly mauled by France in the land war, signed a separate peace in 1795. Fearful of British retaliation for its defection, Spain needed American friendship. In the Treaty of San Lorenzo, signed on October 27, 1795, Spain recognized the line of 31° latitude as the United States' southern boundary and granted the United States free navigation of the Mississippi with a three-year right of deposit at New Orleans.

THE RISE OF FACTION

The Emergence of Partisan Politics. The dispute over Jay's Treaty revealed a deep division in Washington's administration, as well as growing public opposition to a number of Federalist policies. The French Revolution, the Franco-British War, and subsequent problems in foreign relations created further political differences in Congress. By 1792 opposing factions had begun to coalesce about the two strong men of Washington's cabinet, Hamilton and Jefferson. Though John Adams had written, "There is nothing I dread as much as the division of the Republic into two great parties, each under its leader," such a split seemed inevitable. This political division, first observable in the arguments over Hamilton's fiscal program, widened noticeably throughout Washington's first administration.

The pro-Hamilton, pro-Washington group, using the name adopted by the forces favoring the Constitution during the ratification campaign, called themselves "Federalists." The opposition at first called itself "Antifederalists," a somewhat unsatisfactory label but the best that could be devised at the moment.

The Antifederalists opposed the administration's program chiefly on the grounds of what they felt was its tendency to concentrate wealth and influence in a relatively small class. Certainly neither Jefferson nor his followers objected to sound currency and credit, or to economic stability and prosperity; rather, they opposed the Hamiltonian methods of obtaining them—the Bank, tariffs, excise taxes (but not the assumption of state debts) —because these measures might serve to create a permanently privileged class whose interests could well become inimical to the opportunities and welfare of the greater number of people. Through Washington's first term the rivalry between the two factions increased, but despite these internal tensions the Federalists easily reëlected Washington against token opposition for a second term in 1792, with John Adams as his Vice-President.

The Election of 1796. James Madison gave the anti-administration forces a better name when, in 1792, he spoke of "the Republican party," a designation (sometimes "Democratic-Republican") that shortly displaced "Antifederalist." Into this loosely organized opposition group, formed about the commanding figure of Thomas Jefferson, came such men as Monroe and Madison of Virginia; George Clinton and Aaron Burr of New York; Albert Gallatin and Alexander Dallas from Pennsylvania; Willie Jones, the North Carolina back-country leader; and others from the Middle and southern states. Among the Federalists were Hamilton, Schuyler, and John Jay of New York; Timothy Pickering and John Adams of Massachusetts; Thomas Pinckney of South Carolina; and John Marshall of Virginia; with Washington, of course, at the head of the party.

When Jefferson, convinced that he could no longer work with Hamilton and the administration party, resigned as Secretary of State in 1793, Republican partisan politics began in earnest. Hamilton resigned from the Treasury in 1795, partly because he could not afford to neglect his law and business interests, but he still remained the most powerful Federalist leader, since Washington decided not to run again in 1796.

Washington's achievements as President have been overshadowed by his image as "The Father of His Country" and by the dramatic contest during his second term between Hamilton and Jefferson. More recently, historians have pointed out Washington's real skill as an administrator and the importance of his contributions to the skill and efficiency of the fledgling government. Since almost every act of his first term set a precedent, Washington did more than any other man to establish the tone of the presidential office and to establish the whole set of delicate relationships among the executive, the cabinet, the Congress, and the judiciary.

When Washington decided in September 1796 not to seek a third term as President, he submitted to the press a "Farewell Address" which he had written with the aid of Madison and Hamilton. In his valedictory, published in newspapers throughout the nations, Washington explained his reasons for declining to seek a third term; stressed the necessity of preserving the Union, the "main prop" of individual liberty; pointed out the obligation of all Americans to obey the Constitution and the established government "'till changed by an explicit and authentic act of the whole People"; warned of the dangers of a party system, particularly one based on a division along geographical lines; urged that the public credit be cherished; and admonished Americans to observe "good faith and justice towards all Nations."

The most enduring passages of the Farewell Address, however, are those in which Washington counseled Americans to steer clear of permanent alliances with the foreign world. Washington's admonitions for a foreign policy of neutrality have been quoted consistently by isolationists in the past century and a half to justify the dominant American policy of aloofness from the vicissitudes of Europe and from involvement in international politics.

> ... History and experience prove that foreign influence is one of the most baneful foes of republican Government.... The great rule of conduct for us, in regard to foreign Nations, is, in extending our commercial relations, to have with them as little *Political* connection as possible.... Europe has a set of primary interests, which to us have none, or a very remote relation.—Hence she must be engaged in frequent controversies, the causes of which are essentially foreign to our concerns.—Hence therefore it must be unwise in us to implicate ourselves, by artificial ties in the ordinary vicissitudes of her politics.... Taking care always to keep ourselves ... on a respectably defensive posture, we may safely trust to temporary alliances for extraordinary emergencies.

After eight years in office, Washington left behind a government that was a going concern—one that possessed a reasonably good civil service, a workable committee system, an economic program, a foreign policy, and the seeds of a body of constitutional theory. Unfortunately, he also left behind a party already beginning to divide. The election of 1796 gave clear indication of the mounting strength of the Republican opposition. Thomas Jefferson and Aaron Burr campaigned for the Republicans, John Adams and Thomas Pinckney for the Federalists. The margin of Federalist victory was slim: Adams had 71 electoral votes, and Jefferson had 68. Since Jefferson had more votes than Pinckney, he became Vice-President.

Federalist and Republican. It is too broad a generalization to say that the Federalists represented the conservative, commercial, nationalistic interests of the Northeast and Middle Atlantic states, and the Republicans the more radical, agrarian, debtor, states' rights interests of the South and West. Though there is some truth to the statement, the fact is that both parties drew support from all classes in all parts of the country. It would be more accurate to say that these parties were loose combinations of certain economic, social, and intellectual groupings, held together by a set of common attitudes and convictions.

Fundamentally, they reflected two different opinions about the qualities of human nature. Hamiltonians were acutely aware of the "imperfections, weaknesses, and evils of human nature"; they believed that if men were fit to govern themselves at all it must only be under rigid controls imposed on them by society and government. Jeffersonians, on the other hand, believed that men were by inclination rational and good; that if they were freed from the bonds of ignorance, error, and repression, they might achieve real progress toward an ideal society. Others, of course, took positions between these two extremes.

These contrasting concepts of human fallibility were reflected in contemporary political opinions about the structure and aim of government. The Federalists emphasized the need for political machinery to restrain the majority. They believed in a strong central government and a strong executive, and the active participation of that government in manufacturing, commerce, and finance. They believed that leadership in society belonged to a trained, responsible, and (very likely) wealthy class who could be trusted to protect property as well as human rights.

The Jeffersonian Republicans distrusted centralized authority and a powerful executive, preferring instead a less autonomous, decentralized government modeled more on confederation than on federalism. They believed in the leadership of what Jefferson called "a natural aristocracy," founded on talent and intelligence rather than on birth, wealth, or station. Most Republicans believed that human nature in the aggregate was naturally trustworthy and that it could be improved through freedom and education; therefore the majority of men, under proper conditions, could govern themselves wisely. Their aim was to make America into the ideal agrarian commonwealth, built on the virtues of the sturdy, independent yeoman-farmer.

THE TRIALS OF JOHN ADAMS

The XYZ Affair. John Adams took office at a difficult time, for the Federalist party that elected him was showing strain at the seams. Hamilton still dictated a large share of party policy from private life; he did not like Adams and had maneuvered before the election to defeat him. Adams himself was a stubbornly honest man, a keen student of government and law, but deficient in personal charm, blunt, a trifle arrogant, and often tactless.

Adams' administration promptly found itself in trouble. Within his party there was a violently anti-French group who virtually demanded a declaration of war against France, and the French, angry at Jay's Treaty and at an American neutrality that appeared to favor Britain, seemed willing to oblige. Adams, who did not want war, sent John Marshall, C. C. Pinckney, and Elbridge Gerry to Paris in 1797 to try to find some way out. Tallyrand, the French foreign minister, dealing with the American commission through three mediaries called (for purposes of anonymity) X, Y, and Z, demanded not only a loan to the French government, but also a bribe, which the Americans indignantly refused. When the news of the "XYZ Affair" leaked out, the ringing slogan "Millions for defense, but not one cent for tribute!" (presumably Pinckney's reply) became a rallying point for the anti-French faction in Congress.

The Treaty of 1800. Capitalizing on the war fever, Congress created a Department of the Navy, built a number of new ships, armed American merchantmen, and authorized an army of ten thousand men. Though his own party leaders (Hamilton among them) argued that war with France was inevitable, Adams refused to listen, and as it turned out, the French did not want war either. After nearly a year of undeclared naval war, the French government suggested that if an American mission were to be sent to Paris it would be respectfully received. By the time the American commissioners arrived in France in March 1800, the country was in the hands of Napoleon Bonaparte, who quietly agreed to a settlement of differences. The Treaty of 1800 was not popular with the Federalist party or with Congress, which reluctantly ratified it, but it did avoid a war. John Adams got his peace, but very likely at the expense of his own and his party's victory in the coming elections.

The Alien and Sedition Acts. The popular outcry against France, and the near-war that carried through 1797-1799, gave the Federalists a good chance, they believed, to cripple their Republican political opponents under cover of protecting internal security. The country was honeycombed, so the Federalist press claimed, with French agents and propagandists who were secretly at work undermining the national will and subverting public opinion. Since most immigrants were inclined to vote Republican, the Federalist Congress capitalized on anti-foreign feeling in 1798 by passing a series of Alien Acts which lengthened the naturalization period from five to fourteen years, empowered the President to deport undesirable aliens, and authorized him to imprison such aliens as he chose in time of war. Though he signed the bill, Adams did not like the acts and never tried to enforce them.

Congress passed the Sedition Acts, also in 1798, as the second step in its anti-Republican campaign. Under these acts a citizen could be fined, imprisoned, or both for "writing, printing, uttering, or publishing" false statements or any statements which might bring the President or Congress "into contempt or disrepute." Since this last clause covered almost anything Republicans might say about Federalists, its purpose was quite plainly to muzzle the opposition. Under the Sedition Act twenty-five editors and printers were prosecuted and convicted —though later pardoned and their fines returned by the Jeffersonians.

With the Alien and Sedition laws the Federalists went too far. Public opinion sided with the Republicans. The legislatures of Kentucky and Virginia passed resolutions in 1798 and 1799 (Jefferson drafted Kentucky's, Madison Virginia's) condemning the laws and asking the states to join in nullifying them as violations of civil rights. Actually none did, but the Kentucky and Virginia resolutions furnished the Jeffersonians wth excellent ammunition for the approaching presidential campaign. And although the United States had no strong tradition of civil liberties, the Alien and Sedition laws helped to create one by pointing out how easily those rights of free speech and free press guaranteed by the Bill of Rights could be violated.

The Election of 1800. Washington's death in December 1799 symbolized the passing of the Federalist dynasty. The party that he led was in dire distress, divided into wrangling factions. The Republicans were in an excellent position to capitalize on a long string of political moves which had alienated large blocs of voters—the handling of the Whiskey Rebellion, Hamilton's tax policies, the Jay Treaty and the Jay-Gardoqui negotiations, the Alien and Sedition Acts—as well as conflict and resentment within the Federalist party. As a matter of fact, the Federalists had been unable to maintain a balance between the nationalist business interests which formed the core of their support, and the rapidly growing influence of the middle and lower urban and agrarian classes of the South, West, and Middle Atlantic states. After Washington, who had held the party together by the force of his example, no Federalist leader found a way to absorb and control the elements of society which, after 1796, began to look to Jefferson for leadership. The clash of personalities within the Federalist camp, of course, damaged the party further.

John Adams, who through his entire term had to face the internal opposition of the Hamiltonians as well as the Republicans from without, deserves more credit than he is often given. Except for Adams' stubborn desire to keep the peace, the United States most assuredly would have entered into a disastrous war with France, and without him the Federalist party under Hamilton's control would probably have killed itself ten years sooner than it did. Adams' decision to stay out of war, made against the bitter opposition of his own party, was not only an act of courage but very likely his greatest service to the nation.

Though Hamilton circulated a pamphlet violently attacking Adams, the party had no other satisfactory candidate for the election of 1800 and decided to nominate Adams again, choosing C. C. Pinckney to run with him. The Republicans picked Jefferson and Burr once more, hoping thus to unite the two powerful Virginia and New York wings of the party. The campaign was one of the bitterest and most scurrilous in American history; the Republicans, who won the Middle Atlantic states and the South, held a small edge in total electoral votes. Under the Constitution, however, the candidate with the most votes was President and the next Vice-President, so that when the Republican electors all voted for Jefferson and Burr, they created a tie. This threw the election into the House of Representatives, still controlled by lame-duck Federalists. The Federalist hatred of Jefferson was so intense that many of them preferred Burr; at the same time Burr's own party wanted Jefferson, but Burr refused to step aside. Hamilton, much as he disagreed with Jefferson's principles, considered Burr a political adventurer and deeply distrusted him. Hamilton therefore threw his influence behind Jefferson, who was declared President.

CHAPTER 5

THE JEFFERSONIAN ERA, 1800-1824

JEFFERSON IN POWER

"The Revolution of 1800." Thomas Jefferson usually referred to his presidential election victory as "the revolution of 1800," though it was hardly a "revolution" in any accepted sense. It was, nonetheless, an important election, for it shifted national political authority toward the South and West and introduced a new emphasis on decentralized power and state sovereignty. It marked the first successful alliance of agrarian and urban forces later consolidated by Jackson; and, since it was also the first really violent American political campaign, it set "faction" and partisanship firmly into the political process. In actual practice, however, Jefferson did surprisingly little to erase what his predecessors had done, and there was much greater continuity from the Federalist decade into his own than appeared at first glance.

Settling the Barbary Corsairs. Jefferson's administration had hardly caught its breath before it was plunged into a vortex of swift-moving foreign affairs. The President's first problem involved the depredations of the pirates from the Barbary states of North Africa (Tunis, Algiers, Morocco, and Tripoli), who had preyed on Mediterranean commerce for a quarter century, enslaving seamen and levying tribute on shipping. During their administrations, Washington and Adams paid out more than two million dollars in ransom and bribes to the Barbary potentates, and Jefferson determined to end the affair. Beginning in 1803 the United States sent to the Mediterranean four naval squadrons, which in a series of brilliant actions finally forced some of the pirate states to sue for peace. A final treaty was not established until 1815, but after 1805, for the most part, American rights were respected in the Mediterranean and the shameful practice of ransom and tribute was on its way to extinction.

The Purchase of Louisiana. In 1801 Napoleon Bonaparte recovered the territory of Louisiana, lost by France to Spain in 1763. Jefferson recognized the potential danger to the United States of this sudden shift in ownership of half the American continent from impotent Spain to imperial France. The United States could not afford to have New Orleans, he wrote, possessed by "our natural and habitual enemy," Napoleon; "The day that France takes possession of New Orleans, we must marry ourselves to the British Navy." And of course the United States needed the West if its empire were ever, as Jefferson hoped, to stretch from sea to sea.

The President therefore sent James Monroe to Paris to discuss the possible purchase of Louisiana; it was either buy now, Jefferson said, or fight for it later. Napoleon, for his part, did not want to face a British-American alliance in case of war, and since New Orleans was al-

88 The Young Republic

most indefensible against American attack he would probably lose Louisiana anyway.

Napoleon therefore decided to sell, and after some haggling the United States purchased the Louisiana territory and West Florida in April 1803 for $15 million. Jefferson, though overjoyed at the bargain, was also embarrassed by the fact that nowhere in the Constitution could he find presidential authority to buy it. He finally accepted Madison's view that the purchase could be made under a somewhat elastic interpretation of the treaty-making power. The brilliance of the maneuver obscured the constitutional question involved, but the "strict constructionist" doctrine was never the same again.

Whatever its constitutionality, the Louisiana Purchase was one of the most important presidential decisions in American history. At one stroke the United States became a continental power, master of the continent's navigation system, and owner of vast new resources that held out the prospect of greater (and perhaps final) economic independence from Europe. It also, as Jefferson knew, put an end to the likelihood that the West could ever be split from the East.

The Problems of Political Patronage. In addition to the need for keeping a watchful eye on Europe and the Mediterranean, Jefferson had political problems at home. His cabinet, a particularly able group, included James Madison of Virginia as Secretary of State and the brilliant Swiss from Pennsylvania, Albert Gallatin, as Secretary of the Treasury. Quite aware of the utility of patronage, Jefferson quietly replaced Federalist appointments with his own, so that before the close of his first term he had responsible Republicans in positions where it counted. One of his thorniest problems, however, was that of the so-called "midnight judges" appointed by John Adams under the Judiciary Act of 1801. The act reduced

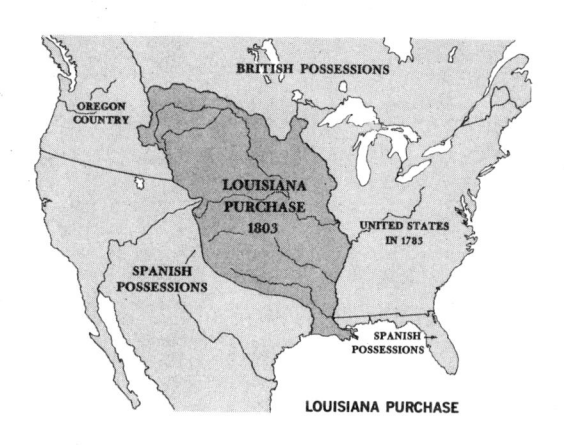

LOUISIANA PURCHASE

the number of Supreme Court justices to five, created sixteen new circuit courts, and added a number of federal marshals and other officials. On the evening of March 3 (a few hours before Jefferson's inauguration) Adams filled these posts with solid Federalist party men, among them his own Secretary of State John Marshall, who was appointed Chief Justice of the Supreme Court.

John Marshall was a stalwart Federalist, but beyond that he was a convinced nationalist who believed that the Constitution was the most sacred of all documents, "framed for ages to come . . . , designed to approach immortality as nearly as human institutions can approach it." He did not trust the Jeffersonians, and he entered the Court determined that none should play fast and loose with the Constitution so long as he could prevent it.

Jefferson v. Marshall. Jefferson was certain that Marshall, that "crafty chief judge," would set as many obstacles as he could in the administration's path and that the "midnight judges" would undoubtedly follow his lead. When Congress repealed the Judiciary Act of 1801, all of Adams' judges were left without salaries or duties. This, the Federalist opposition claimed, was unconstitutional. The judges had been appointed for terms of life or good behavior; therefore, Congress could not in effect cancel these appointments by repealing the act.

As a test to determine the constitutionality of the repeal, William Marbury asked the Supreme Court to issue a writ of mandamus ordering Secretary of State Madison to give Marbury his legal commission as justice of the peace of the District of Columbia. This Madison refused to do. Marshall, in a dextrous opinion, used the case to establish what Jefferson did not want established —the Supreme Court's right of judicial review of legislation, which had been occasionally exercised in practice since 1796 but never firmly accepted.

In *Marbury* v. *Madison* (1803) Marshall made two points: first, that those portions of the Judiciary Act of 1789 which gave the Supreme Court the power to issue writs as Marbury requested were unconstitutional; second, (and Marshall drove this home) that it was the prerogative of the Supreme Court to review an act of Congress, such as the Judiciary Act of 1789, and to declare it constitutional or unconstitutional. The Constitution, wrote Marshall, is "the *supreme* law of the land, superior to any ordinary act of the legislative." "A legislative act contrary to the Constitution is not law," Marshall continued, and "it is the province and duty of the judicial department to say what the law is."

The Jefferson administration then launched an attack directly on the Federalist judiciary itself, using as its tool the constitutional power of impeachment for "high crimes and misdemeanors." The first target was John Pickering of the New Hampshire district court, who was apparently both alcoholic and insane. Pickering was impeached by the House, judged guilty by the Senate, and removed from office. Next, in 1803 the Republicans picked Associate Justice Samuel Chase of the Supreme Court, who had presided over several trials of Jeffersonian editors under the Sedition Act of 1798. In 1805, when the Senate decided it could not quite convict Chase, Jefferson conceded the ineffectiveness of impeachment as a political weapon. Congress instead gradually created a series of new judgeships and filled them with good Republicans, a slower process but one that worked.

Marshall and the Supreme Court. Jefferson's differences with John Marshall were temporarily settled, but Marshall's continued presence on the Court was one of the most important influences on the rapid growth of the power of the federal government over the next three decades. Marshall served on the Court for thirty-five years, from 1801 to 1835, participated in more than a thousand opinions and decisions, and wrote some five hundred of them himself. Whenever the opportunity presented itself, as it frequently did, Marshall never failed to affirm the doctrines of constitutional sanctity and federal supremacy. He stressed the fact that the Constitution was an ordinance of the American people rather than a mere covenant of sovereign states and that the United States was a sovereign nation rather than a mere federation of states.

In *Fletcher* v. *Peck* (1810) Marshall asserted the inviolability of contracts, which even a state could not break. Also in this decision, for the first time a state law was held void because it conflicted with the Constitution. *Martin* v. *Hunter's Lessee* (1816) affirmed the Supreme Court's power to overrule a state court. *McCulloch* v. *Maryland* (1819) embedded the doctrine of Congress' "implied powers" into constitutional law. In *Dartmouth College* v. *Woodward* (1819) Marshall held unconstitutional a New Hampshire law altering the charter of Dartmouth College and placing that institution, against its will, under state control. Marshall established the principle that corporation charters were contracts which could not be impaired. *Gibbons v. Ogden* (1824) affirmed the exclusive right of the federal government to regulate interstate commerce.

In these and other opinions and decisions Marshall consistently emphasized two principles: that the Supreme Court possessed the power to nullify laws in conflict with the Constitution and that the Court alone had the right to interpret the Constitution, especially in regard to such broad grants of authority as might be contained in terms such as "commerce," "general welfare," "necessary and proper," and so on. His opinion did not always become the final version of constitutional issues, but the consistency of his attitudes, carried over a whole generation of legal interpretations, had much to do with the shaping of American constitutional law.

Opening the West. After the Louisiana Purchase there was great anxiety to find out about what the nation had bought, more or less sight unseen. Jefferson, who had already made plans for the exploration of these newly acquired lands, persuaded Congress to finance an expedition up the Missouri River, across the Rocky Mountains, and if possible on to the Pacific. To lead it Jefferson chose his private secretary, a young Virginian named Meriwether Lewis, and William Clark, brother of George Rogers Clark, the frontier soldier.

In the spring of 1804 Lewis and Clark's party of forty-eight, including several scientists, left St. Louis for the West, mapping, gathering specimens of plants and animals, collecting data on soil and weather, observing every pertinent detail of the new country. They wintered in the Dakotas and with the help of a Shoshone Indian woman, Sacajawea, crossed the Rockies and followed the Columbia River to the Pacific, catching their first glimpse of the sea in November 1805. By autumn of 1806 the expedition was back in St. Louis. At almost the same time a party under Lieutenant Zebulon Pike was exploring the upper Mississippi and the mid-Rockies. Other explorations followed, and Louisiana Territory was soon organized on the pattern of the Northwest Ordinance of 1787 (its first state, Louisiana, entered in 1812). The West was no longer a dream but a reality. (See map, page 143.)

The "Essex Junto." The prospect of more states to be carved out of the wide new West greatly disturbed the Federalist party leaders. Ohio entered the Union in 1803, a soundly Republican state, and the probability that all the new states from the Northwest Territory, plus all those to be developed from the Louisiana Purchase, might lean politically to the Jeffersonians was profoundly worrisome. United only in their common hostility to Jefferson, the Federalists had neither issue nor leader to counter his popularity and had little chance of finding either. The gloom was especially thick in New England, so much so that a small number of Federalists (nicknamed the "Essex Junto") explored the possibilities of persuading the five New England states, plus New York and New Jersey, to secede from the Union to form a separate Federalist republic—a "Northern Confederacy," said Senator Timothy Pickering of Massachusetts, "exempt from the corrupt and corrupting influence and oppression of the aristocratic democrats of the South."

Alexander Hamilton of New York showed no inclination to join them, so the New Englanders therefore approached Aaron Burr. Since Burr felt it unlikely that he would be nominated for Vice-President again, he consented to run for the governorship of New York, an office from which, if he won, he might perhaps lead a secession movement. Hamilton disliked Jeffersonians too, but he considered Burr a dangerous man and campaigned against him. After Burr lost he challenged

Hamilton to a duel on the basis of certain slurs on Burr's character reported in the press and killed him in July 1804.

Alexander Hamilton died as he lived, a controversial man who aroused strong feelings. His blunt distrust of "King Mob" and his frank preference for British-style constitutionalism had never endeared him to the public, but the leadership he provided for the country during the crucial postwar years had much to do with its successful transition from a provincial to a federal philosophy. Woodrow Wilson once characterized Hamilton, quite unfairly, as a great man but not a great American; it is more accurate to say perhaps he was not a great man, but an indispensable one.

The duel ruined Burr's reputation and helped to complete the eclipse of the Federalist party. Yet Burr himself was not quite finished, and after the Republicans passed him over as their vice-presidential candidate in 1804 in favor of George Clinton of New York, he apparently entered into a scheme to carve a great empire of his own out of the American West, a conspiracy which ended with his trial for treason in 1807. Burr was acquitted, but everyone drawn into his plan was likewise ruined and Burr himself was forced to flee to England to escape further prosecution for Hamilton's death and additional charges of treason. Meanwhile, the Federalist party approached the election of 1804 with its brilliant leader dead, its reputation tarnished, and neither candidates nor issues of any public value.

The Election of 1804. The election of 1804 was very nearly no contest. The Republican caucus nominated Jefferson for a second time, with George Clinton of New York as his running mate. The Federalists ran the reliable C. C. Pinckney and Rufus King of New York. Jefferson carried every state except Connecticut and Delaware, garnering 162 of the total 176 electoral votes and sweeping an overwhelmingly Republican Congress with him. His first administration ended on a high note of success—as John Randolph said later, the United States was "in the 'full tide of successful experiment.' Taxes repealed; the public debt amply provided for, both principal and interest; sinecures abolished; Louisiana acquired; public confidence unbounded." Unfortunately, it could not last.

AMERICA AND THE WOES OF EUROPE

Neutrality in a World at War. Napoleon Bonaparte loomed large in the future of both Europe and America. Jefferson did not like him but nevertheless Napoleon represented Jefferson's beloved France and what little was left of the legacy of the great French Revolution. Against Napoleon stood England, whose aim Jefferson believed was "the permanent domination of the ocean and the monopoly of the trade of the world." He wanted war with neither, nor did he wish to give aid to either in the great war that flamed up between them in 1803.

It would be an oversimplification, of course, to assume that American foreign policy of the period was governed primarily by a like or dislike of France or England. The objectives of Jefferson's foreign policy, like Washington's and Adams', were first to protect American independence, and second to maintain as much flexibility as possible in American diplomacy without irrevocable commitment to any nation. In the great European power struggle between England and France that developed after 1790, Jefferson saw great advantages to the United States in playing each against the other without being drawn into the orbit of either. An American friendship with France would form a useful counterbalance against the influence of Britain and

Spain, the chief colonial powers in North and South America; a British and Spanish defeat might well mean the end of their American empires. At the same time Jefferson did not want to tie America's future to the fortunes of Napoleon, who might be an even greater threat to American freedom if he won. The wisest policy therefore lay in neutrality to all and trade with any—or, as the British wryly put it, America's best hope was "to gain fortune from Europe's misfortune."

Maintaining neutrality was as difficult for Jefferson as it had been for Washington and Adams before him. The British navy ruled the seas, and Napoleon, particularly after the Battle of Austerlitz in 1805, ruled Europe; the war remained a stalemate while the two countries engaged in a battle of proclamations over wartime naval commerce. Both sides set up blockades of the other's ports, but since neither had sufficient ships to enforce them, American vessels filtered through these "paper blockades" with comparative ease when the risk was warranted.

The British at Sea. From 1804 to 1807 the British and French issued a confusing series of orders and decrees aimed at controlling ocean trade, with the result that American vessels were liable to confiscation by either belligerent if they obeyed the rules of the other. In addition, British men-of-war insolently patrolled the American coast to intercept and inspect American ships for contraband almost as soon as they left port; and, as if this were insufficient provocation, the British claimed the right to search American ships for British deserters.

Conditions in the British navy encouraged desertion, and there were doubtless a number of British sailors who turned up in the American merchant marine; it was also evident that British captains were notoriously careless about matters of citizenship and in many cases simply kidnapped American sailors. Protests from the United States government about these "impressments" were loftily disregarded. Finally, in the summer of 1807 the British *Leopard* stopped the United States navy's *Chesapeake* (a warship, not a merchant vessel), killed or wounded twenty-one men, and took four sailors.

This was by any standard an act of war, and America burst out in a great roar of rage. Had Congress been in session, it almost certainly would have declared war on the spot; but Jefferson held his temper, demanded apologies and reparations, and ordered British ships out of American waters to prevent further incidents. Though the British apologized, they also reaffirmed their right to search American ships and seize deserters. The *Leopard-Chesapeake* affair rankled in American minds for years and had much to do with the drift toward war with Britain in 1812.

The Obnoxious Embargo. Jefferson and Secretary of State Madison bent every effort to avoid provocation that might lead to war. There were only two choices—war or some kind of economic substitute. The easier choice would have been war, for which Jefferson could have obtained public and congressional support; but he chose peace, aware as he was of the troubles he was stirring up for himself and his party. He pinned his hopes on "peaceful coercion," as he called it, by means of a boycott of British goods and a set of nonimportation acts which Congress passed in 1806 and 1807.

Neither was sufficiently effective to do much good. As the situation between the two nations steadily deteriorated, Jefferson asked Congress for a full-scale embargo, a logical move since Britain needed American trade, especially foodstuffs, in increasing quantities as the war progressed. In late 1807 Congress therefore passed the Embargo Act, which forbade American ships to leave the United States for any foreign port or even to engage in the American coastal trade without posting a heavy bond.

Jefferson hoped that the Embargo of 1807 would do two things: first, that it would discourage the British from seizure of American ships and sailors and force them to greater regard for American rights; and, second, that it would encourage the growth of American industry by cutting off British imports.

England suffered shortages, but not enough to matter; France approved of the Embargo since it helped at second hand to enforce Napoleon's own blockade of England. American ships rotted at anchor along the Eastern seaboard; merchants went bankrupt; farm surpluses piled up. In New York, one traveler wrote, "The streets near the waterside were almost deserted; the grass had begun to grow upon the wharves." While the shipping interests suffered, however, New England and the Eastern port states began a transition to manufacturing that was soon to change their economic complexion. With British and European competition removed, capital previously invested in foreign trade was available for new factories and mills, which sprang up in profusion along the seaboard. But the future economic advantages of this were difficult to see in the midst of the paralyzing effects of the Embargo. Jefferson was violently attacked in the taverns and counting houses, and finally Congress repealed the Embargo. Jefferson, on March 1, 1809, three days before his successor Madison took office, reluctantly signed the bill.

The end of Jefferson's second term came during the bitterest disputes over the Embargo, and the President, who had wished for some time to retire to his beloved Monticello, was relieved to accept Washington's two-term precedent and announce his retirement. His eight years of rule, begun in such high confidence, ended on a much more equivocal note. Ironically, Jefferson, the believer in decentralized government, found himself under the Embargo wielding more power over American life than any Federalist would have dreamed of; behind its wall, the architect of the ideal agrarian commonwealth saw the beginnings of the factory system bring industrialism to American shores. Though a "strict constructionist," Jefferson had discovered authority in the Constitution to buy Louisiana; and, though a believer in states' rights, he had coerced the New England states, against their will, into an economic boycott which hurt their commerce badly. In effect, the United States at the close of Jefferson's administration was beginning to resemble Hamilton's vision of an industrialized union rather than the Jeffersonian dream of a commonwealth of agrarian freeholders.

The Election of 1808. Jefferson trusted and admired James Madison and easily secured the Republican nomination for him. The Federalists nominated the tireless C. C. Pinckney again, and in spite of the Embargo and divided Republican sentiment Madison won by 122 to 47 electoral votes.

The Drift to War. James Madison, far from being a mere graceful shadow of Jefferson, was very much his own man. His role in the formation of the Republican party was a decisive one, and the political philosophy of the Jeffersonian group owed much to his thinking. He was an astute practitioner of politics as well as a profound student of it, but when he succeeded Jefferson he inherited from him a large bundle of thorny problems. The Non-Intercourse Act, with which Madison replaced the Embargo in 1809, allowed American ships to trade with any nations except France and England; when this failed to work, Congress replaced it with Macon's Bill No. 2 (named after the chairman of the House Foreign Affairs Committee), which relieved American shipping from all restrictions, while ordering British and French naval vessels from American waters. This failed to influence British policy, but although Madison did not realize it, "peaceable coercion" was beginning to hurt England more than the British admitted. Parliament was preparing to relax some of its restrictions even as Congress moved toward a declaration of war. It simply did not happen soon enough to change the course of events.

The War Hawks. Jefferson's "peaceful coercion" policy was probably the best that could have been pursued under the circumstances, and except for some exceedingly clumsy diplomacy abroad and mounting pressures for war at home, it might have worked. Much of the pressure came from a group of young aggressive congressmen, the first of the postrevolutionary generation of Western politicians—Henry Clay of Kentucky, John C. Calhoun and Langdon Cheves of western South Carolina, Peter B. Porter of western New York, Felix Grundy of Tennessee, and other so-called "buckskin boys." Intensely nationalist and violently anti-British, this group of "War Hawks," as John Randolph of Roanoke called them, clamored loudly for an attack on Britain via Canada and on the seas.

The western states from which these "War Hawks" came believed they had special reasons to dislike England. The West fell on hard times in the years from 1805 to 1809, but instead of the Embargo it blamed the British navy. More serious, however, was the charge that the British, from their Canadian posts, stirred up the Indians and armed them for marauding raids on the American frontier.

When the Shawnee chief Tecumseh conceived the plan of joining all the tribes of the Northwest and South into a single powerful confederacy to oppose the American drive westward, the frontiersmen believed that British influence lay behind it. And when General William Henry Harrison defeated a concentration of Indian forces at the Battle of Tippecanoe in Indiana Territory in November 1811, his men found British-made guns abandoned on the battlefield. A war with England would not only settle the Indian problem, the Westerners felt, but would also open up British Canada to conquest—a company of Kentucky militia, Henry Clay thought, could easily do the job.

"Mr. Madison's War." On June 1, 1812, President Madison asked Congress to declare war on Great Britain, listing the whole catalog of British offenses over the past years, none of major importance in themselves, but adding up to an intolerable total. On June 18 Congress responded with a declaration of war. The vote was close in the Senate—19 to 13—and not overwhelming in the House, 74 to 49, with New England and the Middle Atlantic states against, the South and West for. Ironically, unknown to Madison, Parliament had already on June 16 revoked the orders restricting neutral trade with France—orders which had so stirred American resentment—and there were signs that the British might be willing to negotiate differences further.

The congressional vote reflected the popular attitude toward the war the Westerners wanted; at the news, flags flew at half-mast in New England, and there were minor riots in some of the Eastern cities. The Federalist press dubbed it "Mr. Madison's War," and so it remained. There were some, at least, who regarded it as a stab in Britain's back when she stood alone against Napoleon, who in 1812 was already on his way to Moscow for what seemed to be his last great conquest; as John Randolph told the War Hawks, whether one liked the British or not, the plain fact was that England remained "the only power that holds in check the archenemy of mankind."

The origins of war are never simple, and the War of 1812, especially, derived from a bewildering complexity of causes. It is not enough to say that the United States and Britain "blundered" into war through "inept diplomacy," though there was enough of that. The lingering resentments of two decades of friction, memories of impressed sailors and arrogant British captains, the protection of American maritime rights from men-of-war and frontier settlements from Indian marauders, the land-hunger of the expansionist Westerners—all these were factors.

Yet the chief opposition to the war came from the commercial and maritime interests of New England, whose rights had been most consistently violated; and the largest vote for war came from Georgia, Kentucky, Tennessee, and South Carolina, where sea trade was less important. As much as anything else, it seemed, the United States went to war in 1812 as a matter of national pride. Andrew Jackson of Tennessee said succinctly: "We are going to fight for the reëstablishment of our national character, for the protection of our maritime citizens, to vindicate our right to a free trade, and open market for the productions of our soil because the *mistress of the ocean* has forbid us to carry them to any foreign nations."

THE WAR OF 1812

War on Land: First Phase. The United States was totally unprepared for war. The army, reduced to about seven thousand men, was badly equipped and poorly led. Secretary of War William Eustis, though clearly incompetent, was not replaced until 1813; his successor John Armstrong was hardly better; and not until James Monroe took over in 1814 and not until the quality of American generalship improved did American military affairs seem to have direction and firmness. The utter failure of the army's first move against Canada in the summer of 1812 showed that it would take a good deal more than Clay's militia company to do the job. Meanwhile British forces captured not only Detroit but also Fort Michilimackinac in upper Michigan and Fort Dearborn in Illinois, establishing virtual command of the western Great Lakes.

In the middle of these military failures, Madison was nominated for another term. An Eastern antiwar wing of the Republicans, however, nominated De Witt Clinton of New York against him, and the Federalists added their support for Clinton. Madison won, 128 to 89 electoral votes, but significantly, Clinton carried all of New England and the Middle Atlantic states except Vermont and Pennsylvania. At the same time the Federalists doubled their delegation in Congress.

War on the Land: Second Phase. The army, despite its early disasters, kept trying for Canada. In the winter of 1812-1813 American sailors, commanded by Captain Oliver Hazard Perry, hammered and sawed out a small fleet and in September 1813 met and smashed the British lake squadron at the Battle of Lake Erie, near Sandusky, Ohio. Lake Erie was one of the most savage naval actions of the era (Perry's flagship suffered 80 per cent casualties), but after three hours of fighting Perry dispatched his message to General Harrison commanding the forces near Detroit, "We have met the enemy and they are ours." Without control of Lake Erie, the British evacuated Detroit and fell back toward Niagara, but Harrison's swiftly advancing force caught and defeated them at the Battle of the Thames on October 5, 1813, killing Tecumseh, whose Indians had joined the British after the Battle of Tippecanoe.

By reason of Perry's and Harrison's victories, the United States now commanded the Northwestern frontier. But three American expeditions into Canada failed before a British force struck back at Buffalo, captured and burned it, and then took Fort Niagara in December 1814.

War at Sea. The American navy entered the War of 1812 with sixteen ships; the British had ninety-seven in American waters alone. The outnumbered American navy therefore limited itself to single-ship actions and did surprisingly well against British naval might. The *Constitution* ("Old Ironsides"), a forty-four gun frigate commanded by Yankee Isaac Hull, defeated the British *Guerriere* in one of the most famous sea fights in history. The big frigate *United States*, commanded by Captain Stephen Decatur, captured the British *Macedonian*, a few weeks later, but the American *Chesapeake* lost a bitter fight to the British *Shannon* in 1813.

American privateers, however, contributed most to the success of the war at sea. These swift ships ran circles around the British navy, captured or destroyed thirteen hundred British merchantmen, and even had the impudence to sack British shipping in the English Channel in full sight of the shore. They gave the American public something to crow about now and then, but the overall effect on the outcome of the conflict was negligible. As a matter of fact, the British naval blockade was quite effective, and by 1813 the majority of American ports were tightly bottled up.

War on the Land: Final Phase. Napoleon abdicated in April 1814 and was exiled to the isle of Elba in the Mediterranean. With Bonaparte gone and the French war finished, England turned its huge army of Napoleonic veterans toward American shores. The strategy of the British general staff was to make three coordinated attacks: one from the north, from Canada down Lake Champlain into New York state; a second on the coast, through Chesapeake Bay, at Baltimore, Washington, and Philadelphia; a third up from the south, at New Orleans. The end was in sight, wrote the London *Times*, for this "ill-organized association" of states, and indeed it looked like it.

The northern campaign began in July 1814. Since Lake Champlain was the vital link in the invasion route, British General Sir George Prevost wanted it cleared of American ships. In September 1814 the American lake squadron under Captain Thomas Macdonough decisively defeated the British, and without control of the lake the British drive stalled and eventually dissolved.

The British were more successful at Chesapeake Bay, where in August 1814 General Robert Ross landed a strong force that marched on Washington. The American government fled into Virginia, and after setting fire to the Capitol, the White House, and all government buildings they could ignite, the British moved on the next day toward Baltimore. Here they were stopped at Fort McHenry, whose spirited defense inspired Francis Scott Key to write *The Star Spangled Banner*. Unable to crack the Baltimore defenses, the British took to sea again for the West Indies.

The third British offensive, aimed at New Orleans and commanded by General Edward Pakenham, sailed from Jamaica in November 1814 with 7500 seasoned veterans. To oppose Pakenham, Andrew Jackson took his frontier army on a forced march from Mobile, Ala., arriving at New Orleans in time to meet the British in late December. Though neither Jackson nor Pakenham knew it, American and British representatives were already at work in Belgium on a treaty of peace. Two weeks after the Treaty of Ghent was signed on December 24, 1814, Jackson's Western riflemen almost annihilated Pakenham's army. The British lost two thousand men (including Pakenham), while Jackson's loss totaled eight dead and thirteen wounded in a battle that did not affect the war or the peace.

The Hartford Convention. The New England Federalists never favored the war and gave it only half-hearted support. In 1814, when American prospects seemed darkest, the Federalist Massachusetts legislature called a convention at Hartford, Connecticut, to discuss "public grievances and concerns," that is, the Republican conduct of the war.

The delegates, who came primarily from the Massachusetts, Connecticut, and Rhode Island legislatures, had a great deal to discuss. Some advised amending the Constitution to clip Congress' war-making powers; some proposed a new Constitution which would limit presidential reëligibility and thus get rid of Jefferson; others suggested negotiating a separate peace with England. Curiously enough, the delegates, all Federalists, appealed to the doctrine of states' rights, the same doctrine which the Jeffersonians during Adams' administration had used against Federalist centralization. The delegates argued that since the Republican Congress had violated the Constitution by declaring an unwanted war, those states which did not approve had the right to override Congressional action. At the conclusion of the meeting Massachusetts and Connecticut sent commissioners to Washington to place their protests before Congress—but the commissioners arrived at the same time as the news of Jackson's victory at New Orleans, and whatever they had to say was forgotten.

A Welcome Peace. Early in 1813 Tsar Alexander I of Russia offered to mediate between the United States and England since he wanted the British to be free to concentrate their full force on Napoleon. Madison sent commissioners to Russia, but Lord Castlereagh, the British foreign minister, refused to accept the tsar's suggestion.

Later that same year, however, Castlereagh notified Secretary of State James Monroe that he was willing to discuss differences between the two nations, and in April 1814 American and British representatives met in Ghent, Belgium.

As the meetings dragged on, it became plain that the three-pronged British invasion of the American continent would not succeed. Weary of war, both British and Americans wanted to finish it, and on December 24, 1814, the commissioners signed a peace treaty which did not mention impressment, blockades, seizures at sea, or any of the major disputes over which the war was presumably fought. Most of the critical points at issue, in fact, were left for later commissions to decide.

The Results of the War. The reactions of war-weary Americans to the news of the Treaty of Ghent, which arrived in the United States in February 1815, was swift and spontaneous. Bells rang, parades formed, newspapers broke out in headlines to proclaim the "passage from gloom to glory." Yet "Mr. Madison's War" had accomplished very little in a military or political sense. The treaty realized few if any of the aims for which the war had presumably been fought; the most that can be said is that it opened the way for future settlements, which were worked out over the next decade with Britain, Spain, and France. The war dislocated business and foreign trade, deranged currency values, and exposed glaring cracks in the national political organization. Its record of fumbling, bickering, and unpreparedness remains unmatched by any subsequent American military experience.

But to the American people the outcome, ambiguous as it was, marked a turning point in patriotic self-esteem. If it had been fought as a matter of national pride, in this it had succeeded. It was true that the war might have been avoided by better statesmanship or that it might even have been fought with France on equally reasonable grounds—yet from the American point of view the War of 1812 gave notice to the rest of the world that the United States had arrived as a nation. "Who would not be an American?" crowed *Niles' Register*. "Long live the Republic! All Hail!" When the newspaper talk died down and the orators stilled, old scores were more or less forgotten and British-American relations remained fairly friendly until disturbed by the Civil War.

A Confident Nation. The end of the War of 1812 marked the end of America's lingering colonial complex. It was hardly a "second war of independence," as some called it, but from it there did come a new spirit of national consciousness. "It has renewed," wrote Albert Gallatin, "and reinstated the national feeling and character which the Revolution had given, and which were daily lessening. The people now have more general objects of attachment.... They are more Americans, they feel and act more as a nation."

The war also turned Americans westward. Hitherto they had faced Europe despite their political independence of Britain. Until the War of 1812 America's major trade was foreign trade, its principal problem in foreign affairs that of maintaining neutrality in European struggles, its challenges of statesmanship nearly always those arising from foreign affairs, even its own political campaigns influenced by preferences for France or England. After the Treaty of Ghent the United States turned toward the great hazy West, where half a continent lay empty. America could now concentrate on its domestic problems with less concern for European standards, ideals, and entanglements; indifference to foreign affairs after 1814 was so great that even Napoleon's escape from Elba, his return to France, and his final defeat at Waterloo in June 1815 excited little attention in the American press. The interest of the United States centered on perfecting and expanding the nation it had constructed out of two wars and a generation of experiment; in other words, its chief task lay in developing modern America.

AMERICA MAKES A NEW START

The Aftermath of War. The most persistent postwar problems were economic. Finances during the war were handled almost as ineptly as military affairs, so that by the end of the conflict national credit was at its lowest point since 1786. Banks had multiplied profusely and without proper control; the country was flooded with depreciating paper money; prices were at the most inflated level in America's brief history. Though the shipping industry had been badly hurt by war and blockade, the value of manufacturing had increased tremendously—the total capital investment in American industry in 1816, it was estimated, was somewhat more than $100 million. The West, now producing foodstuffs and raw materials in abundance, balanced on the verge of a tremendous boom. As soon as peace was established the Republican Congress began to consider a three-point program for economic expansion: a tariff to protect infant American industry; a second Bank of the United States, since the charter of Hamilton's original Bank had expired in 1811; and a system of roads, waterways, and canals to provide internal routes of communication and trade.

A Protective Tariff. The protection of America's infant industries was a matter of first priority. New factories, encouraged by the war, had grown in great numbers, especially in the textile industry. As soon as the wartime blockade ended, British-made products streamed toward the United States, and young industries that flourished under conditions of embargo and war found it quite another matter to compete in an open peacetime market. Whereas the total value of United States imports in 1813 had been $13 million, by 1816 the total had leaped to $147 million, while American manufacturers begged for protection. Competition was fierce; some English shippers, in fact, were willing to sell at a loss to clear their clogged warehouses or, as a British trade official said, "to stifle those rising manufacturers in the United States which war had forced into existence."

Congress in 1816 passed a tariff to protect these new factories—the first United States tariff passed not to raise revenue but to encourage and support home industry. The argument over this protective tariff exposed some potentially serious sectional economic conflicts and marked the first appearance of a perennial political issue. Southern producers and New England shippers opposed the tariff, but the growing factory towns of New England supported it, as did some of the younger Southern cotton politicians who hoped to encourage industrial development in the South. The Middle Atlantic states and the West favored it, and the Southwest divided on the issue.

Renewing the Bank of the United States. In 1816 Congress turned its attention to the national Bank. The charter of the first Bank of the United States had been allowed to expire because the Republicans, as Jefferson originally claimed, believed that Hamilton's centralized bank was unconstitutional because banking powers properly belonged to the states. The new contingent of Western congressmen were much less interested in the Bank's constitutionality than in its usefulness. Henry Clay, who had opposed the first Bank in 1811 on constitutional grounds, now supported the second Bank, he explained, because it was necessary for the national (especially Western) interest to have a stable, uniform currency and sound national credit. Therefore, Congress gave the second Bank in 1816 a twenty-year charter, on much the same terms as before except with three and one half times more capital than the first and substantially greater control over state banks.

America Moves West. The Treaty of Ghent released a pent-up flood of migration toward the West. In 1790 a little more than 2 per cent of the population lived west of the Appalachian mountain chain; in 1810, 14 per cent; in 1820, 23 per cent, with the proportion still rising. The stream of migration moved west in two branches following the east-west roads and rivers, one from the South into the Southwest, the other from the northeastern states into the Northwest Territory.

There were a number of reasons for this great westerly movement. One was America's soaring population, which almost doubled in the first two decades of the nineteenth century, from 5.3 million in 1800 to over 9.6 million in 1820. Another was the discharge of war veterans, accompanied by a rush of immigrants from Europe, who moved west to look for new opportunities. Another was improved transportation; there were not many good roads to the West, but the number grew, while the Great Lakes-Ohio River waterway provided an excellent route for settlers to move into the Northwest.

The most compelling force behind the westward migration was land—the rich black bottom lands of the Southwest, the fertile forest and prairie lands of the Northwest. Governor William Henry Harrison of Indiana Territory persuaded Congress in 1800 to reduce the minimum required sale of land to a half-section at two dollars an acre, with four years to pay. In 1804 Congress reduced the minimum to a quarter-section, and in 1820 to eighty acres at $1.25 an acre. This was the great magnet that drew men west.

The Connecting Links: Internal Improvements. The British wartime blockade and the westward movement exposed a critical need for roads, improved waterways, and canals. When coastal shipping was reduced to a trickle by British offshore naval patrols, forcing American goods to move over inland routes, the roads and rivers were soon choked with traffic. The Republican program of improved internal communications was especially popular in the West, but more conservative Easterners, including President Madison, doubted the constitutionality of federal assistance for roads and canals unless an amendment to the Constitution were adopted for the purpose. Calhoun and Clay could see no objections; Calhoun, in fact, proposed using the yearly bonus, paid each year by the national Bank to the Treasury, to finance some of these projects, but Madison vetoed this "Bonus Bill" on his last day in office in 1817. Many of the states, however, started building roads and digging canals themselves. President Monroe later decided that the "general welfare" clause of the Constitution provided the federal government with the necessary authority to participate, inaugurating the great canal and turnpike era of the 1820's.

The Election of 1816. Madison selected James Monroe of Virginia for his successor in the presidential election of 1816, and although some Republicans favored William H. Crawford of Georgia, the party caucus agreed to choose the third Virginian in succession for the presidency. The Federalists, disheartened by the Hartford Convention, failed to nominate an official candidate, though in some states they supported Rufus King of New York. King received only the votes of Massachusetts, Connecticut, and Delaware, and Monroe won easily by 183 to 34 electoral votes.

A tall, distinguished, quiet man, James Monroe had studied law with Jefferson and was the older statesman's close friend and disciple. He drew his advisers impartially from different sections of the country, choosing John Quincy Adams of Massachusetts as Secretary of State, William H. Crawford of Georgia as Secretary of the Treasury, John C. Calhoun of South Carolina as Secretary of War, and William Wirt of Maryland as Attorney General. Henry Clay of Kentucky, Speaker of the House, and others of the Western group dominated Congress, with Daniel Webster of New Hampshire and other New Englanders furnishing the opposition.

The "Era of Good Feelings." The virtually unchallenged Republican control of political life until 1824 gave these years the title of "The Era of Good Feelings." The Federalist party was dead, and it seemed for a time that the two-party system itself was moribund. There were no European wars of consequence during the period to involve the United States, nor any crucial issues in foreign affairs. But, like all titles, this one was true only in part: feelings were "good," true, but as events proceeded they were also mixed, for there were a number of subterranean conflicts which were soon to destroy the political peace.

Sectional interests and aspirations were growing and changing. The new Northwest, as it gained stature and stability, demanded greater influence in national policy. The South, tied more and more to cotton, and New England, changing from an agricultural to a manufacturing economy, were both undergoing inner stresses that took outward political form. Specifically, these sectionalized rivalries were shortly to appear in two issues—tariffs and slavery—which terminated good feelings and produced a good many new bad ones. As if to underline the temporary nature of this tenuous political peace, the

Monroe administration faced immediate dissatisfaction in the West beyond the Alleghenies.

Prosperity and Panic. After 1815 the national economy flourished mightily; the wartime boom continued, industry grew strong behind its tariff wall, and American ships carried goods and raw materials over all the world. Yet much of this prosperity had a hollow ring. Too many small Southern and Western banks had issued far too much paper money in excess of their capital reserves, and in 1818 the second Bank of the United States (which suffered from mismanagement itself) began to close out some of these "wildcat" banks by collecting their notes and demanding payment.

The purpose was fiscally sound—to force stricter control of banking practices—but the effect was disastrous. By early 1819 a number of shaky banks had already collapsed and others were about to follow; in fact, the entire national banking system, none too sound for several years, was nearly ready to topple. In 1819 more and more banks crashed, businesses failed, and a wave of losses and foreclosures swept over the nation, especially through the West. The consequences of the 1819 crisis continued to be felt until 1823; and, for the part it had played in precipitating it, the second Bank of the United States and the financial interests of the East earned the undying resentment of the West.

FIRE BELL IN THE NIGHT

Sectionalism and Slavery. As the tariff issue of 1816 exposed some of the sectional tensions beneath the surface of "good feelings," so the panic of 1819 revealed more. The third great issue, the question of the existence and extension of the institution of slavery, was projected into Congress by Missouri's impending statehood in 1819.

Before this point in American history, few Americans seriously considered slavery as a major issue in national politics. Congress passed a fugitive slave law in 1793 and forbade the further importation of slaves in 1808 without unduly arousing sentiment in North or South; in fact, there were many in both sections who hoped that the 1808 act might lead to the eventual extinction of the entire system. In the North, where slavery was unprofitable and unnecessary, all the states had legally abolished it by 1804 (as the Northwest Ordinance of 1787 already had abolished it from the Northwest Territory), while in the South antislavery societies actively campaigned against it. Still, after 1816 there was noticeable asperity in Northern and Southern discussions of the slavery question.

The most important area of disagreement over slavery concerned its economic relationship to Southern cotton culture. Eli Whitney's invention of the cotton gin, the introduction of new strains of cotton, the expanding postwar textile market at home and abroad, and the opening to production of the rich "Black Belt" lands of the Southwest, all combined to make cotton an extremely profitable cash crop. Cotton was well on the way to becoming "King" in the South.

Cotton required a large, steady supply of cheap, unskilled labor; the Negro slave fitted the need perfectly. At the same time, it was found that the delta lands of Louisiana and Mississippi were ideal for sugar cane, while tobacco culture moved from the East south into Kentucky and Tennessee. All of these economies needed cheap labor. In 1800 there were about 894,000 Negroes in the United States, almost wholly concentrated in the eastern South. In 1808, when the importation of slaves ceased, the figure stood at over one million, and the South's investment in slaves by 1820 was esti-

MISSOURI COMPROMISE, 1820

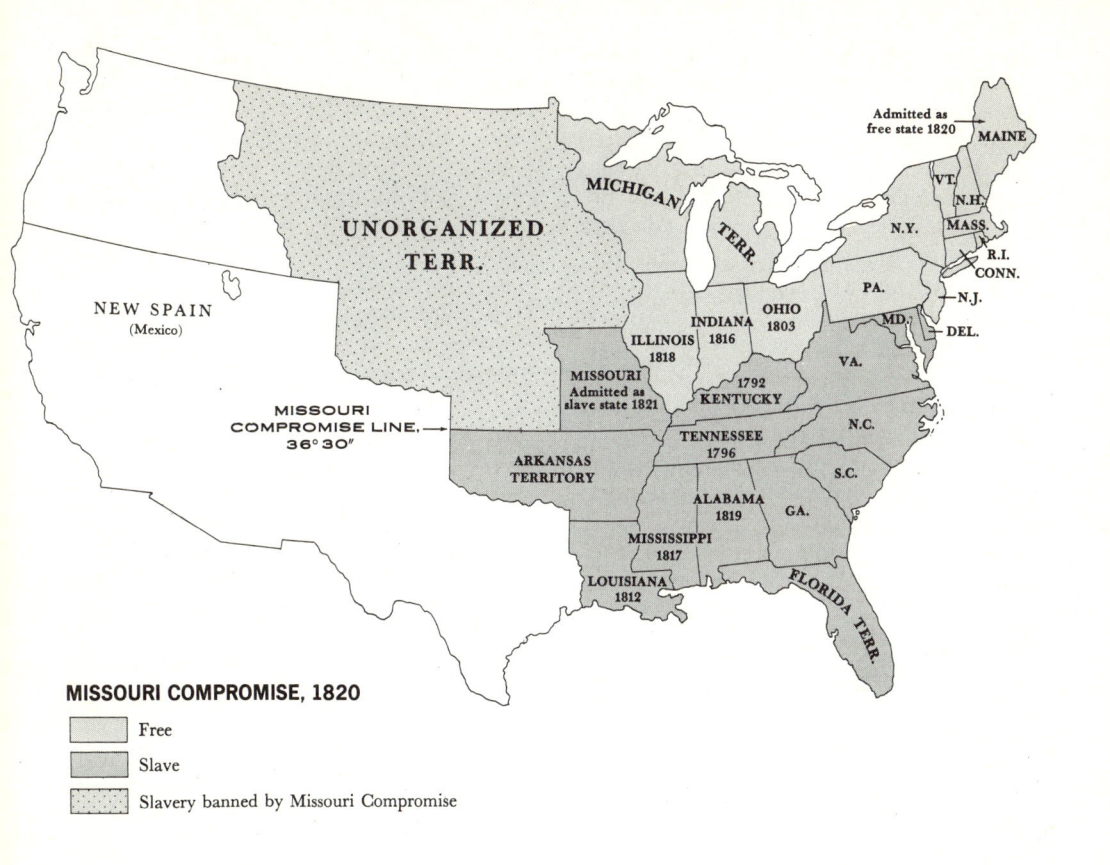

- Free
- Slave
- Slavery banned by Missouri Compromise

mated to be nearly $500 million. It was perfectly clear that slavery and cotton together provided the foundation of Southern society and would continue to do so.

The Missouri Compromise. Missouri, early in 1819, counted sixty thousand persons and applied for entry to the Union as a slave state. No doubt the bill for its admission would have passed without appreciable comment, had not James Tallmadge, Jr., of New York introduced in the House an amendment requiring the gradual abolition of slavery in the new state as a condition of its admission. This amendment immediately exposed the heart of the issue.

The tendency had been, as the nation moved west, to maintain a rough balance of power between slave- and free-state blocs in Washington. The North and Northwest, however, had gained a million more persons than the South and Southwest since the 1790 census, thereby proportionately increasing their congressional representation. The slave states were already outvoted in the House; only in the Senate were the sections equally represented, a situation which might not continue for long.

Of the original thirteen colonies, seven became free states and six slave. Between 1791 and 1819 four more free states were admitted and five slave. When Missouri applied for entrance to the Union in 1819, the balance was even. Therefore Tallmadge's amendment involved far more than Missouri's admission alone. Slavery was already barred from the Northwest Territory, but not from those lands acquired through the Louisiana Purchase.

The Jeffersonian Era, 1800–1824   103

Should Missouri and all other states subsequently admitted from the Louisiana Purchase lands be admitted as slave states, the balance of federal political power would be tipped toward the South and slavery. If they were to be free states, their entry favored the North and emancipation. At stake lay the political control, present and future, of the Union. "It is political power that the northern folk are in pursuit of," Judge Charles Tait of Alabama wrote to a friend concerning the Missouri question, "and if they succeed, the management of the Gen'l Gov't will pass into their hands with all its power and patronage."

Tallmadge's bill finally passed the House in February, after hot and protracted debate. Congress adjourned, however, until December, and during the interval Maine, long attached to Massachusetts, applied for statehood. Sensing compromise, the Senate originated a bill accepting Maine as a free state and Missouri as slave, thereby preserving the balance. The House accepted it, but added a proviso that slavery be banned forever from the Louisiana Purchase lands above the line of 36°30'. The bill was passed and signed in March 1820, but this so-called "Missouri Compromise" merely delayed the ultimate confrontation of the problem of slavery, and everyone knew it. The "momentous question," wrote Jefferson from Monticello, "like a fire-bell in the night, awakened me and filled me with terror."

EVOLVING A FOREIGN POLICY

Catching Up on Old Problems. Following the Treaty of Ghent the United States and Britain gradually worked out their differences one by one. The Rush-Bagot Agreement of 1817 demilitarized the Great Lakes. The Convention of 1818 gave U.S. nationals fishing rights off the coasts of Labrador and Newfoundland, established the northern boundary of the Louisiana Purchase at the 49th parallel, and left the Oregon country, which both claimed, under joint occupation for ten years.

America and Spain, too, settled some old disputes. The United States acquired one section of Florida in 1810 and another in 1816. Secretary of State John Quincy Adams continued negotiations for the rest of the territory, but his diplomacy was disturbed by Florida's Seminole Indians, who kept up raids (with Spanish and British assistance) on the Georgia border. In early 1818 General Andrew Jackson marched into Florida, captured two forts, and hanged two British traders in what has come to be called the First Seminole War. The posts were quickly returned to Spain, but Jackson's action helped precipitate a treaty, signed by Adams and Spanish minister Luis de Onís in February 1819, by which Spain renounced its claims to West Florida and ceded East Florida to the United States. In the Adams-Onís Treaty the Spanish also agreed to a boundary line stretching across the continent to the Pacific, redefining the Louisiana Purchase line, and dividing the old Southwest from Spanish Mexico; and gave up their somewhat vague claims to Oregon in return for a clear title to Texas.

The Monroe Doctrine. Reduced to a third-rate power and racked by internal dissension, Spain was losing her empire in Central and South America. Beginning in 1807, her colonies revolted one after another, and by 1821 nearly all had declared themselves independent republics. Sympathetic to such revolutions and alert to opportunities for new markets, the United States waited until its treaty with Spain was accepted and then recognized these republics early in 1822.

Spain, of course, continued to consider the new Latin American nations simply as Spanish colonies in rebellion. In Europe, meanwhile, Austria, Prussia, Russia, and France had formed an alliance and "congress system" for the purpose of crushing popular revolutions wherever they occurred. The French army had already restored the reactionary Ferdinand VII to the throne of Spain. The United States feared that the alliance would decide to send an army to restore Spain's lost colonies, making royal Catholic Spain once more a power in the New World. Nor was the alliance the only threat to the Americas. Russia had already established trading posts in California, and in 1821 Tsar Alexander's edict claimed part of the Oregon country for Alaska and barred foreign ships from a large area of the northwest Pacific.

The British, who had no desire to see Spain regain its empire or Russia expand its colonial holdings, offered to join with the United States in a declaration against any interference in the Americas on the part of the alliance, but Secretary of State John Quincy Adams convinced President Monroe and the cabinet that the United States should handle the problem alone. For one thing, Adams did not want his country, he said, to "come in as a cockboat in the wake of the British man-of-war." Furthermore, Adams and others recognized the potential value of the new Latin American republics as markets, or perhaps they even visualized a closed hemispheric commercial system with the United States in the dominant position. And lastly, no one wanted to write off the possibility of American expansion southward if one or more of the new republics asked to be annexed to the United States.

President Monroe, in his annual message to Congress on December 2, 1823, therefore stated the official attitude of the United States on the issue. The Monroe Doctrine, as it came to be called, rested on two main principles—noncolonization and nonintervention.

Concerning the first, Monroe stated that any portions of the Americas were "henceforth not to be considered as subjects for future colonization by any European power." In regard to the second, he drew a sharp line of political demarcation between Europe and America. "The political system of the allied powers is essentially different... from that of America," he said. "We should consider any attempt to extend their system to any portion of this hemisphere as dangerous to our peace and safety." These ideas were implicit in all American foreign policy since Washington's Farewell Address, but Monroe's message restated in precise terms the classic American principles of hemispheric separation and avoidance of foreign entanglements that had motivated the diplomacy of his predecessors. His enunciation of American domination over half the globe seemed "arrogant" and "haughty" to European statesmen, nor were the Latin American republics particularly pleased with such doubtful protection. Both knew, whether Monroe or the American public cared to admit it, that it was the British navy and not the Monroe Doctrine that barred European expansion into the Americas.

The Triumph of Isolation. The Monroe Doctrine simply articulated what Americans had believed since the beginnings of their foreign policy—that there were two worlds, old and new, contrasted and separate. The Old World of England and Europe seemed to Americans regressive, corrupted, plagued by wars and ancient hatreds. The New World was thought to be democratic, free, progressive, hopeful. The objective of the United States, reflecting these attitudes, was to keep these worlds apart, lest the "taint" of the old besmirch the "fresh future" of the new.

The first generation of American statesmen, from Washington to Monroe, unanimously insisted that the United States should, whenever possible, avoid entanglements in Old World politics or problems. At the same time it was perfectly clear to them that the United States could not exist without European trade and that, since the major European powers still held territorial possessions in the New World, it would be extremely difficult to avoid some sort of implication in their almost continuous wars. The foreign policy of every President from Washington to John Quincy Adams was shaped by this constant tension between the dream of isolation and the reality of involvement.

Still, there were certain accepted positions on foreign affairs that the United States throughout the period believed it must maintain—freedom of the seas, freedom of trade, neutrality in European disputes, national integrity, and above all others, the promotion of the cause of liberty throughout the world. In practice, American diplomats found it hard to work out solutions within this somewhat rigid framework. Did maintenance of freedom of the seas, for example, justify involvement in a European war? Would American assistance to other nations' revolutions justify entanglement in European affairs, even for the best of motives? Should American policy, when it coincided with that of a European power, be pursued jointly? Ought the United States to assume responsibility for internal affairs of democracy in other American republics?

In attempting to answer these and similar questions, the makers of American foreign policy during the early years of the republic followed rather closely the principles laid down by Washington and the first generation. Fortunately for them, Europe was so preoccupied with its own power conflicts that American diplomacy had time to temporize and room to make a few mistakes. Still, every statement about foreign affairs after 1796 derived from the fundamental American assumption that the United States was detached from Europe and must remain so, always free to pursue its special ends.

CHAPTER 6

THE EMERGENCE OF A NATIONAL CULTURE

THE DEVELOPMENT OF AN AMERICAN CREDO

The Circumstances of Creation. The period between 1783 and 1824 was a time of extraordinary political, economic, and social revolution. This was the age which saw the close of the American Revolution, the ratification of the Constitution, and the development of the two-party system of government. It was the age of George Washington and Thomas Jefferson, of the Louisiana Purchase and the Lewis and Clark expedition, of the War of 1812 and the growth of textile and iron industries, of Henry Clay and John C. Calhoun, of the Missouri Compromise and the Monroe Doctrine. In Europe it was the age of the French Revolution and of the rise and fall of Napoleon, of the Romantic Movement and the Industrial Revolution.

As in all periods of rapid change, Americans in launching a new system of government could look ahead with a strong sense of hope and experiment. They were sanguine about the future, for they had no significant record of failure to disillusion them. They were impatient of "established" institutions or traditions, for they had just established some of their own and disestablished a good many British ones. Though far from possessing the last full measure of democracy, the United States afforded its people considerably more freedom and equality than the world had ever known before.

This glorification of the American destiny, when wedded to the anti-British feeling of the times, made Americans aggressively self-confident. Feeling triumphant in their newly won independence, they became less aware of their commercial, social, religious, and cultural indebtedness to Great Britain; the United States, so Americans felt, had shrugged off all the prejudices, superstitions, and ignorances of the Old World. From the perspective of the twentieth century, however, it is clear that the bonds of Europe were not cut so sharply, and that the old pattern of transplantation and adaption continued with the influx of both immigrants and ideas from across the Atlantic.

American Nationalism. The train of events was propitious for the growth of American nationalism. For one thing, many democratic and humanitarian tendencies were accentuated or set in motion during the Revolution and the early national period. Large Loyalist estates were confiscated and divided; small business and manufacturing were stimulated; church establishments were attacked; slavery, imprisonment for debt, and humiliating punishments were regarded with growing disfavor; the idea of universal education at state expense was voiced. Americans were far from being of one mind about these matters, but they recognized that such tendencies differentiated the United States from the nations of the Old World. They agreed, moreover, in insisting that they were now ready to arrange their own affairs and in being sublimely confident that they could arrange them better than the English had arranged theirs. The Americans were a "new" people, as Crèvecoeur put it. They were ready to teach the rest of the world; they were weary of being taught.

Geographically, American nationalism had its roots in the transatlantic isolation of the American colonies. However, the Napoleonic wars, which disrupted commercial and diplomatic accord with Europe from 1800 to 1815, made American isolation much more complete than it had been before. When the United States was finally drawn into a second war with England —the War of 1812—the nation achieved that economic self-sufficiency which had long been talked about but had never quite been a reality. Industries grew up quickly, and Americans faced the occupation of the West with full assurance that they had the means to fulfill their dreams of greatness.

The West, despite its individualism, was even more nationalistic than the older seaboard states. It looked to the central government for its lands and the means of access to them, and its local ties were new and weak. It was the West which was least respectful of Europe and most certain that the United States, if necessary, could lick the entire Old World.

Indeed, Americans considered the United States to be superior to England and Europe in every way; it was a model of a new kind of New World. And the inevitable corollary was that America's mission was to lead other revolutions, or, as Joel Barlow wrote, "to excite emulation throughout the kingdoms of the earth, and meliorate the conditions of the human race." It was America's responsibility to extend the concepts of liberty, equality, and justice over all the earth; this, said James Wilson at the Constitutional Convention, was "the great design of Providence in regard to this globe."

In order to accomplish its mission, it was considered imperative that Americans cultivate their Americanness, emphasize their differences with Europe, develop their own culture in terms of their own national purpose. "Every engine should be employed to render the people of the country national," wrote Noah Webster, "to call their attachment home to their own country."

Europeans often found this American nationalism bumptious and flamboyant (a British traveler in 1810 thought that "the national vanity of the United States surpasses that of any other country, not excepting France"), but it had a beneficial cultural effect. If the United States were to succeed as an experiment in self-government, the men who governed themselves must have deep faith in it. The patriotic impulse was considered essential to the creation of a national character.

THE FRAMEWORK OF THE AMERICAN MIND

The structure of ideas within which Americans achieved their independence was provided by two great intellectual movements, the Age of Reason and the Age of Romanticism. The United States itself, almost purely a creation of the eighteenth century, emerged at a time when the western world was shifting from one system of thought to another, each involving quite different views of man, the world, and the Deity beyond them.

The Transit of the Enlightenment. The American colonies were children of the Age of Reason, or the "Enlightenment." John Locke, the English political philosopher, wrote a charter for the Carolinas; Rousseau, Franklin, and Montesquieu were friends; Sir Isaac Newton and Cotton Mather were contemporaries; Voltaire was still living when the Continental Congress signed the Declaration of Independence. The Enlightenment, not the Puritanism of New England, provided the first *nationalized* pattern of American thought.

The Age of Reason rested upon three major principles: the perfectibility of men; the inevitability of progress; and the efficacy of reason. It emphasized the scientific method over the theological, reason over faith, skepticism over tradition and authoritarianism. The thinkers of the Enlightenment believed that by subjecting himself, his society, the past, and the universe itself to rational analysis, man could discover certain general laws which would supply him with precise, definitive explanations of human and natural activity. With this knowledge, men could so direct their energies and construct their institutions that their progress would be swift and sure. The Americans who chose the path of revolution, and who, after its successful conclusion, accepted the challenge of making a new nation on new principles, reflected these attitudes.

The Nature of the American Enlightenment. There was an American Enlightenment, but it was late, eclectic, and singularly American. Eighteenth-century America was not merely an extension or a reflection of contemporary Britain or Europe. First of all, there was a culture lag in the transmission of patterns of thinking from one side of the Atlantic to the other. The Founding Fathers worked with ideas fifty to one hundred years old by European standards, in another continent, for different purposes—and mixed with them later borrowings and adaptations. The Romanticists—Goethe, Wordsworth, Coleridge, Schiller, and Kant—it should be remembered, were writing at nearly the same time that Americans were still quoting the men of the Age of Reason—Newton, Locke, and Montesquieu.

Second, Americans chose from British and European thought only those ideas they needed, or those in which they had special interest. They adopted Locke's justification of a century-old English revolution as vindication of their own, for example, and used French "radicalism," aimed at Gallic kings, to overthrow a tyranny that really did not exist. The Americans thus bent the Enlightenment to American uses.

The Arrival of Romanticism. The rise of Romanticism disturbed the orderly patterns of the Age of Reason. Beginning about 1750, European and British philosophers and critics revived interest in a body of ideas which had been relatively neglected in the earlier eighteenth century. These ideas were extended and diffused into a loose philosophical system which spread through Britain, Europe, and America, causing men on both sides of the Atlantic to question some of the attitudes of the Enlightenment and to alter their conceptions of human nature, society, and the world. Many of these "Romantic" ideas were not new, nor were they ever wholly assimilated into a unified system, but the climate of opinion which characterized the intellectual activity of Europe and America from 1750 to 1850 was coherent and consistent enough to warrant calling the period the Age of Romanticism.

The Romantic view of society rested on three general concepts. First, on the idea of organism, that things were conceived as wholes, or units, with their own internal laws of governance and development. This held true both for individual men and for societies. Second, on the idea of dynamism, of motion and growth. Beliefs and institutions were assumed to be fluid, changing, capable of manipulation and adaptation. Third, on the idea of diversity, of the value of differences of opinions, cultures, tastes, societies, characters—as opposed to the uniformitarian norms of the Enlightenment. To the Age of Reason, conformity meant rationalism; diversity meant irrationality, and therefore error. To the Romantic the consensus of the majority seemed much less important than the individual judgment, and diversity seemed "natural" and "right." The Enlightenment viewed man as a mixture of passion and reason, recognizing that passion ought to be controlled by reason if individuals and societies were to move together in harmony.

Much of Romanticism fitted the facts and necessities of American life; some of it did not. As an intellectual movement Romanticism in America turned out to be much more constructive, individualistic, and democratically based than Romanticism in Britain or Europe. Romantic individualism produced rebels (something Americans could understand), but the American Romantic rebel had a much more open and fluid society in which to function and far fewer things he needed to destroy. American Romanticism produced not Byron but Longfellow, not Marx but Thoreau, not Napoleon but Jackson. Americans had too much faith in the individual and too much hereditary Calvinistic intensity of moral feeling, so they put their own distinctive stamp on the Romantic movement as they imported it.

The Professionalization of Science. The clearest manifestation of the intellectual impact of the Enlightenment was observed in the advancement of American science in the later eighteenth century. The colonies had been settled in the scientific age of Galileo and Newton; Americans were never far from the center of the great scientific revolution that marked the European Enlightenment, and, like other men of their times, they lived by contemporary scientific attitudes. They believed that all problems responded to scientific investigation; that the universe was mechanistic, governed by constant natural laws which were discoverable by human reason; that all knowledge was fundamentally scientific; and that the inductive method of thinking was quite possibly the only trustworthy method of arriving at truth. These beliefs, derived from Newtonian science, furnished the most coherent pattern by which the affairs of man and nature might be explained; from science, they believed, they might find solutions to the problems of human society.

The Revolution suspended practically all scientific activity, but immediately after it, as Dr. Amos Eaton wrote, "A thirst for natural science seemed to pervade the United States like the progress of an epidemic." American conditions favored useful research designed for the workaday world, thus emphasizing such branches of practical investigation as cartography, surveying, chemistry, agriculture, metallurgy, medicine, navigational mathematics, astronomy, applied physics, and so on.

The nation was especially fortunate in receiving a number of brilliant immigrants and refugees who came during and after the war. Thomas Cooper, geologist and economist, came from England, as did Joseph Priestley, one of the world's greatest chemists; Pierre du Pont de Nemours, a noted chemist, came from France. Meanwhile, the United States possessed a number of highly competent scientists of its own breeding. President Jefferson, for that matter, was a scientist of repute himself, and the Lewis and Clark expedition which he sent westward in 1804 was one of the most significant scientific projects in American history.

Meanwhile, though long neglected by the colleges and universities, the study of science began to appear in the curriculum, usually as astronomy, chemistry, or physics. Indeed, science itself was becoming a profession rather than a hobby for interested amateurs. Science was narrowing down from broad to confined fields, toward such things as genetics, inorganic and organic chemistry, entomology, paleontology, and others; there was a perceptible drift toward differentiation in research, away from the earlier concept of science as a community of knowledge. The tremendous growth in the amount of scientific knowledge, and the equally great impact of that knowledge on contemporary life, meant that there was no longer a place for the "natural philosopher" who took all scientific knowledge as his province. There was too much to know, too much to investigate. The day of the oldtime jack-of-all-trades like Dr. Mitchill of Columbia (who ranged through chemistry, medicine, mathematics, botany, zoology, and poetry) was nearly over.

Despite the tremendous interest in scientific study and experiment, American scientists readily admitted that they had made no major contributions to scientific theory and that Europe and England still dominated the various fields. Yet their achievements were not negligible, especially in identifying and classifying the flora and fauna of their continent and in exploring the extent of its resources. And Americans were confident that their own great scientific contributions would inevitably come.

Creating American Law. The laws which had governed the American colonies had come from three main sources: decisions of the king; acts of Parliament or boards of trade; and common law, that is, written or unwritten English law embodied in judicial decisions, precedents, and usage. Legal codes and procedures in the colonies had been substantially the same as in the mother country, and colonists had expected and substantially received the same legal rights as Britons at home. The requirements of American environment and experience had naturally made adjustments and modifications necessary—as for example, in laws of land tenure or of navigation—but American law, at the instant of separation in 1776, was English law and the system of courts and justice thoroughly British.

The act of independence theoretically cancelled every law in every state, though in practice, of course, the states took over the existing legal structure and continued to use the laws they had, changing the source of authority. But as these states wrote constitutions and formed governments, they also addressed themselves to the problems of designing for American purposes a legal system of their own out of the mass of materials—English common law, continental law, natural law, colonial acts and precedents, and so on—which they had inherited.

There were two possible approaches: to establish a completely new American code or to remake the colonial legacy into a system of basically English but functionally American law. A very few (like the Kentuckian who "wished to make it a penal offense to bring an English lawbook into the country") favored abandoning British law, but the force of the English tradition and two centuries of history was far too strong for any such drastic revisions. Furthermore, British commercial and common law, hammered out over centuries of experience, met American requirements extremely well.

Though Britain provided form, direction, and detail for the early development of the American legal system, it did not fit every need. The ideals of British law reflected an old, settled, hierarchical society, rather than the fluid, individualistic, open society of a new country. Thus lawyers and courts made a number of changes in translating the British system into American terms. American courts tended to simplify the complexities of British legal machinery, which was largely uncodified, and to organize constitutional and statute law into written codes. Americans also relied much more on juries, in both civil and equity cases, than was true of British practice. The unsettled state of the American courts and the scarcity of experienced judges after the Revolution led to a greater reliance on jury decisions, which appealed to a frontier people who believed in republican equality. Until late in the nineteenth century American juries retained much greater powers at law than those normally granted juries in England.

The revolutionary generation, however, did not wholly trust courts and lawyers. It had fresh memories of royal judges and admiralty courts and of the large number of colonial judges who had remained Loyalist; New Jersey, for example, as a wartime security measure, forced all lawyers to take an oath of loyalty before issuing them licenses to practice. The confusion of postwar economic conditions threw thousands of citizens into the courts, where they popularly believed the poor man always lost. During the years that produced Shays' Rebellion (see page 71) "the mere sight of a lawyer," one of them wrote ruefully, "was enough to call forth an oath or a muttered curse." The Duc de la Rochefoucauld, traveling in the United States during 1795-1797, was astonished to see "how disrespectfully the people carry themselves in regards to the courts of justice."

The people generally placed confidence less in courts than in state legislatures, since legislatures were the lawmaking bodies chosen by the public at large. Early legislatures did not hesitate to act on this assumption. They summoned judges before them for questioning, reversed court decisions, probated wills and handled estates, passed special laws meting out justice, and usurped many of the functions of the courts. But gradually, as time passed, the law gained greater public confidence and lawyers greater responsibilities in the governing of American society. The most distinctive trends in American law from the close of the Revolution until 1830 were the gradual emergence of equality between the judiciary and the legislative branches in American governments and the increasing influence of lawyers in American life.

The excesses of some of the state legislatures during the Confederation disillusioned many sober Americans, and public confidence soon began to shift from state capitals to courts. Because other institutions were weak or unpredictable or slow to develop, citizens turned to the courts for help, providing tremendous opportunities for lawyers in postrevolutionary society. "Scarcely any question arises in the United States," commented De Tocqueville in 1835, "which does not become sooner or later, a subject of juridical debate." In an era when the explication and interpretation of constitutions and statutes furnished the keys to political and economic power, the legal profession possessed great advantages.

Meanwhile, law as a profession was gaining respectability and evolving standards of proficiency and conduct for itself. Instruction was carried out in private schools and in a few colleges and universities; by 1800 all states except Kentucky, North Carolina, and Virginia had fixed standards of legal training. The profession of law, wrote Charles Brockden Brown in 1790, "is withal, in this country, one of the roads to opulence, and the most certain path to political importance and fame."

The "Scottish Philosophy." The necessities of life in the revolutionary and early republican periods demanded men of action rather than speculative philosophers. Americans were too busy shaping a revolution, creating a government, and constructing a society to spend much time in probing or systematizing their assumptions. To them philosophy was often a way of rationalizing the things they intended to do. As a result, the French commentator De Tocqueville remarked in 1835 that nowhere in the world was less attention paid to philosophy than in the United States. Although De Tocqueville exaggerated the case, it was true that American philosophy, as it then existed, was highly derivative of British and French sources, practical rather than speculative and either theologically or politically oriented.

The major strain of American philosophy during the revolutionary era was Lockean empiricism, which based all knowledge on experience and which fitted in admirably with the political and scientific interests of the times. When Locke's popularity faded in the United States (as it did in Britain), Americans found a satisfactory replacement in the philosophy of "common sense" recently developed in Scottish universities by men such as Francis Hutcheson, Thomas Reid, Dugald Stewart, James Beattie, and Adam Ferguson, all well-known in early American intellectual circles.

According to the Scottish school, the human mind possessed the ability to make what Reid called "original and natural judgments" which "served to direct us in the common affairs of life, when our reasoning faculty would leave us in the dark." These judgments, he continued, "make up what is called the *common sense of mankind*," providing men with "first principles" on which they may agree to act and furnishing them a kind of moral and social stability. These ideas met American needs exactly, and the "Scottish philosophy" became the official philosophy of late eighteenth- and early nineteenth-century America, taught in the schools and seminaries and accepted almost unanimously as the way to direct and control one's thinking and acting. Such a mode of thought, wrote the Reverend John Gros of Columbia College, gave "rules for the direction of the will of man in his moral state, such rules to serve for the guidance of the individual, community, and nation."

The Scottish system had particular value in that it fitted current theories of human nature and knowledge. The philosophies of the early eighteenth century had concluded that the mind was distinct from the body, with a pattern and functions of its own, and that it possessed three sets of powers: (1) the reason, by which men reasoned, reflected, remembered, and created ideas out of experience; (2) the passions, by which they comprehended the emotions; and (3) the will, which enabled them to act on motivations provided by the reason and the emotions. Scottish philosophy, with its ideas of innate judgments, was thus easily adapted to contemporary concepts of psychology.

Scottish textbooks were in use in American colleges in the 1790's, and by 1810 the majority of courses in "Moral Science" or "Natural Philosophy" taught in every institution of higher learning were founded on common-sense principles. John Witherspoon, who left Scotland to become president of Princeton in 1768, was one of the earliest emissaries of the Scots school. Others published influential texts which spread Scottish doctrines through the country's colleges. The impact of such ideas, taught by brilliant men to successive generations of college students, was a major influence on the development of American thought throughout the nineteenth century.

The Secularization of Theology. At the time of the Revolution there were approximately three thousand churches in the United States. The majority of these were Calvinist, and belonged to the Presbyterians and Congregationalists, whose differences lay less in creed than in matters of church government. The Anglican Church was seriously divided by the Revolution, supplying, on the one hand, the largest number of Loyalists of any church and, on the other hand, the majority of the signers of the Declaration of Independence. The Methodists, whose first missionaries had arrived only in 1769, were growing rapidly, as were the Baptists, though both were still relatively small and dispersed. Lutheran and Reformed church membership lay chiefly in German- and Dutch-settled areas. The small Catholic population was concentrated primarily in Maryland; in 1782 there were still fewer than twenty-five priests in America.

During the Revolution the states immediately set about to establish proper relationships with the various churches. Since each former colony had its own religious history and since it was plain that no single church could satisfy a diverse, expanding population that already worshipped under seventeen different creeds, the legislatures wisely chose to allow, as New York's did, "free enjoyment of the rights of conscience." The Continental Congress, and later the Constitutional Convention, both reaffirmed the prevailing belief that religion, as Jefferson phrased it, was "a matter which lies solely between man and his God." Most of the state constitutions contained clauses or bills of rights guaranteeing freedom of worship on much the same terms as the federal Constitution.

Also during the war years each legislature, in one way or another, provided for a clear separation of the churches from state authority, with the exception of Massachusetts, Connecticut, and New Hampshire, where the Congregationalists successfully resisted disestablishment for another thirty years. In Virginia, Jefferson saw the successful passage of his Statute for Religious Freedom in 1786, which he counted among his proudest accomplishments. Nevertheless, there was still widespread doubt whether religious freedom and toleration could be fully extended to everyone. A number of states required religious tests or qualifications for full civil and political rights; these tests discriminated against Catholics, Jews, and nonconformist Protestant sects. Most of these, however, had disappeared by 1830.

Ministers of the postwar years generally believed American Protestantism to be in "a low and declining state." The Presbyterian Assembly of 1798 noted "a general dereliction of religious principles and practice among our citizens," and congregations were often restive with authority and impatient of the old doctrines. Churchmen prayed for strength to combat "indifference and irreligion," but the truth was that the Calvinistic churches were fast losing their hold on American society. Even the powerful Congregational and Presbyterian churches in 1800 could count less than 10 per cent of the people of New England and the Middle Atlantic states as church members, while all the major Protestant sects were split by argument and dissension. None of the older Calvinist groups, in fact, had been able to make the necessary adjustments to the great new surge of scientific information sweeping over the era, and none had kept direct touch with the secular, optimistic, republican spirit of the time. The important matters of the day were those of politics, economics, and social advancements; since the facts of contemporary American optimism seemed to have little relationship to a Calvinist theology which argued predestination, many Americans simply ignored it.

Nor was this all. The churches faced another threat in the form of a religio-philosophical movement transported from England and Europe in the latter decades of the eighteenth century under the name of deism. Rooted in the Enlightenment's faith in reason and science and closely in tune with the secular, rationalistic temper of the period, deism had a strong appeal to intellectual and political leaders such as Franklin, Jefferson, Paine, Barlow, Freneau, and others. Cutting away the twisted intricacies of Calvinistic doctrine, the deists proclaimed God's benevolence, man's rationality, goodness, and free will, and nature's order, harmony, and understandability. If men would but live by these beliefs, said Ethan Allen of Vermont, "they would . . . rid themselves of blindness and superstition, gain more exalted ideas of God, and make better members of society."

Against the deists the orthodox theologians put up a sturdy defense, but against the inroads of another "heresy," unitarianism, they had less success. Partly imported from England and partly the legacy of the Great Awakening of the earlier eighteenth century, "liberal" unitarian doctrines, which placed far greater trust in man and his abilities to discern religious truth, interested more and more orthodox Calvinist parishioners and ministers after 1790. Harvard College, the traditional fortress of New England Calvinism, surrendered to the "liberals" in 1805, and under the direction of such men as William Ellery Channing, Andrews Norton, and James Freeman of Cambridge and Boston, they steadily gained ground. The "Conference of Liberal Ministers," called in 1820 to furnish leadership for those dissatisfied with Calvinistic orthodoxy, six years later became the American Unitarian Association, a separate group of 125 churches, among them twenty of the oldest Calvinist churches in New England. "Calvinism," wrote Channing, "is giving place to better views. It has passed its meridian, and is sinking to rise no more."

THE QUEST FOR A NATIONAL CULTURE

A Native Art. Having gained political independence, Americans searched for a culture of their own, for a way of expressing—in literature, drama, and the arts—the fundamentals of their civilization.

Critics, editors, and authors agreed on the need for a native, original, indigenous art; as Noah Webster wrote, "America must be as independent in *literature* as she is in politics," but it was easier to demand great art than to produce it. For one thing, a great deal of creative energy was diverted into business and politics. Politics, Samuel Miller explained in his *Retrospect of the Eighteenth Century* (1802), had a tendency to stifle culture; it was very difficult in his times, remarked John Quincy Adams, "to be a man of business and a man of rime." Furthermore, as Washington Irving pointed out, the United States, lacking "the charms of storied and poetical association . . . , and the accumulated treasures of age," had no usable past to stir the artist's fancy.

Since the United States had no tradition of literary patronage among the wealthy, there were (except for novelist Charles Brockden Brown) no really professional American authors, nor was authorship financially rewarding. For this reason Henry Wadsworth Longfellow's father warned him against being a poet, for "there is not wealth and munificence enough in this country to afford sufficient encouragement and patronage to merely literary men." And last, there was the practical matter of the lack of an adequate copyright law in the United States, which made the market for American-published books thin indeed.

The Literary Discovery of America. The first step toward cultural independence was to declare America's freedom from English and European domination. The second was to define the circumstances and standards by which the United States could produce a distinguished literature of its own. The author must have something

American to write about and a defined, recognizable native manner of writing it. True, Timothy Dwight admitted, the United States lacked "ancient castles, ruined abbeys, and fine pictures." But on the other hand, the American artist possessed a number of things that neither British nor other European artists possessed.

The American artist had the Indian, the frontier, and a brief but eminently usable past. Every author of note made at least one attempt after 1790 to use the American frontier or American history in a major work, though not until James Fenimore Cooper's novel *The Spy* (1821) did any of them find a way to handle the material with success. In addition, American artists possessed ample material for studies of manners, what dramatist James Nelson Barker called "the events, customs, opinions, and characters of American life." The American scene, wrote William Cullen Bryant, displayed "an infinite variety of pursuits and subjects, [an] endless diversity and change of fortunes." All that one needed to exploit it, he concluded, was "sagacity and skill."

The greatest artistic resource was, of course, the land itself—American nature, vast, unspoiled, fascinating in its variety and grandeur. Out of these things, American artists could produce, they believed, something aesthetically valuable, morally true, and uniquely expressive of American life. To create it the artist must, Charles Brockden Brown urged, "examine objects with his own eyes, employ European models merely for the improvement of his taste," and build his art out of "all that is genuine and peculiar in the scene before him." This, then, was the aim of this first generation of American artists.

Patterns in American Prose. The distinguishing characteristic of developments in literature produced during the period from 1783 to 1830 was the growing popularity of the novel, the poem, the essay, and the drama, and the decline of such once-popular forms of writing as the sermon, the journal, the travel narrative, and the autobiography. This reflected in part the increased level of appreciation and sophistication of American society and in part a greater effort by American writers to enter into the main stream of contemporary literary fashions.

The essay, modeled chiefly after the great British essayists, attracted a number of talented Americans, among them Washington Irving, who became famous with the appearance of *The Sketchbook* (1819-1820).

The novel in America still faced public and ecclesiastical suspicion, and the majority of critics did not consider it as an art form worthy of serious effort. Nevertheless, the demand for fiction increased rapidly, the magazines printed novels by the score, and libraries stocked greater numbers of them each year. The most popular ones copied the sentimental novels of the English author Samuel Richardson. William Hill Brown's *Power of Sympathy* (1789); Susannah Rowson's *Charlotte Temple* (1791); and others like them ran through numerous editions, while American readers wept over the predicaments of virtuous young ladies besieged by rascally villains.

A few novelists turned to satire; Royall Tyler's *Algerine Captive* (1797) and Hugh Henry Brackenridge's *Modern Chivalry* (1792-1797) poked fun at politics, fashions, sentimentalism, and almost every other aspect of contemporary life. The Gothic novel of suspense and terror found a gifted American practitioner in Philadelphia's Charles Brockden Brown, the most talented American novelist before Cooper. Brown's *Wieland* (1798), *Ormond* (1799), *Arthur Mervyn* (1799), and *Edgar Huntly* (1799) were uneven in quality but nevertheless indicative of genuine though undisciplined talent.

Most popular of all, however, was the historical romance, patterned on the works of Sir Walter Scott, whose novels enjoyed tremendous vogue in early nineteenth-century America. Dozens of American novelists imitated him, but none successfully fitted the Scott formula to the American scene until James Fenimore Cooper wrote *The Spy* in 1821, *The Pioneers* in 1823, *The Last of the Mohicans* in 1826, and thirty other novels. When Cooper's buckskin hero Natty Bumppo walked into American fiction and leaned on his long rifle, the American novel came of age.

Meanwhile, another American writer, Washington Irving, turned his attention to short fiction in *The Sketchbook* (1820), which was immediately recognized as a major work and acclaimed on both sides of the Atlantic. Stories such as *The Legend of Sleepy Hollow* and *Rip Van Winkle* soon became part of the American cultural heritage and provided a decisive answer to English critic Sidney Smith's sneer, "Who reads an American book?"

Poetic Literature in the New Republic. Poetry found hard going in the period after the Revolutionary War. There were plenty of young men interested in writing verse, but the way of the poet was difficult in a world torn by two wars with England, a near-war with France, bitter political rivalries at home, and a whole new political system a-building. Some young men of talent, like Joel Barlow, tried their hands at "epics" and retreated to politics; John Trumbull, one of the cleverest, went into law; Timothy Dwight, whose poetic gifts were considerable but of doubtful quality, turned to theology and education. Out of the flood of American verse—usually imitating the English classical poetry of Pope, Dryden, Gray, or Goldsmith—that washed over the closing decades of the eighteenth century, very little remained as a lasting contribution to an American poetic tradition.

This was not the case of Philip Freneau, the first authentic poetic voice to be heard in the United States. His poems dealing with nature, beauty, the past, and personal experience, show genuine poetic gifts, and the delicacy and skill of his lyric verse were unmatched by any American poet of his day—and by few British.

American Building: British, Greek, or Roman? There were very few professional architects in the United States at the time of independence, and the majority of existing public buildings were almost wholly copied from designs imported from Britain. The typical colonial style was, therefore, a modification of Georgian, long popular in England. After the Revolution there was an immediate demand for buildings to serve the new state and federal governments and a corresponding need for professional architects. The current vogue for things Greek and Roman, as well as the prevailing English style, created two distinct architectural traditions, a modified British style popular in New England, and a Romanized classical style characteristic of the Middle Atlantic and southern states.

The two greatest practitioners of these architectural styles were Charles Bulfinch of Boston and Thomas Jefferson of Virginia. Deeply impressed by the British style, Bulfinch developed an American version of it, called the Boston (or "Federal") style, rebuilt Faneuil Hall in Boston, designed capitols for Boston, Hartford, and Augusta, built a number of churches, and served for a time as architect in charge of the national Capitol in Washington. His influence may still be seen in the small towns of Ohio, Michigan, and Illinois, or wherever New Englanders migrated in the next fifty years.

Jefferson believed that the United States needed to develop an architectural tradition of its own worthy of a big, new, free nation. Much impressed by Roman remains in France and by French adaptions of the Roman style, he incorporated this inspiration in the new Virginia state capitol at Richmond —the first and perhaps best example of American classical—and in the University of Virginia, his second architectural project. His home at Monticello, on which he worked for forty years, was his crowning achievement and is one of the gems of American architecture.

After Jefferson, the classical tradition was further modified by Benjamin Latrobe, whose source was Greek, not Roman, and who with his followers helped to initiate what soon became the Greek Revival era in American architecture. The Federal, classical, and Greek Revival styles, though they added grace, beauty, and charm to the American scene, still could not yet be called wholly American architecture.

Musicians and Painters. The eighteenth-century colonists were as ardent music-lovers as their English contemporaries. French and German immigrants, too, brought their musical tastes to America, and after 1800 cities such as New York, Philadelphia, Boston, and Charleston supported good orchestras, musical societies, studios, and academies. However, American composers and musicians could hardly hope to match their powerful European contemporaries or to compete with the talented, trained immigrants who came to America from the finest European orchestras and schools. Later in the century, when Stephen Foster published "The Old Folks at Home" and nearly two hundred other songs, something like an American ballad tradition may be said to have begun.

Samuel Miller, in his *Retrospect of the Eighteenth Century* (1803), admitted apologetically that American art had produced as yet no great painters, though he could point with pride to Benjamin West, John Singleton Copley, Charles Willson Peale, Gilbert Stuart, and John Trumbull. These painters, all born into the prerevolutionary generation and rooted in an English and European tradition, looked to Paris, Rome, and especially London for instruction and inspiration. Yet they were men of considerable talent, whose work was admired abroad as well as at home. West, whose forte was historical painting, became court painter to England's King George III and successor to Sir Joshua Reynolds as president of the British Royal Academy. Copley, who developed portrait painting to a high art, finally stayed in London. Peale not only painted well, but founded the first museum in the United States (1786), organized the first public art exhibition in the country (1794), and in 1805 helped establish the Pennsylvania Academy of Fine Arts. Gilbert Stuart, who dominated American portrait art for nearly thirty years (he painted the amazing total of 1150 portraits) was no doubt the best painter of his time in that particular genre. Trumbull, strongly affected by West's grand historical style, became head of the American Academy of Arts in 1817 and exerted considerable influence on American taste and critical standards for many years.

The Course of American Culture. The arts in the United States, during the period from 1787 to 1830, from literature through painting, were in large part derivative, imitative, dependent upon Britain and Europe for standards and inspiration. Literature showed much more of an American disposition than painting, architecture more than music. Artistic production on the whole was increasingly nationalistic in spirit, and the artists were seriously committed to the use of American materials and the expression of American attitudes. Though still suffering from a colonial complex, lacking confidence in their own tastes and ideas, fearful of not conforming to traditional, time-tested artistic norms, they nevertheless hoped to create a new, distinctive, independent culture within the framework of a unified American experience. What the United States wanted was a Golden Age of its own, built out of American materials and ideals, couched in artistic terms and derived from aesthetic theories that could be accepted with confidence and performed with pride. Real cultural independence was yet to come.

BIBLIOGRAPHY

General studies of the early national period include Edmund S. Morgan, *The Birth of the Republic* (Chicago: University of Chicago Press, 1956); Marcus Cunliffe, *The Nation Takes Shape, 1789-1837* (Chicago: University of Chicago Press, 1959); and Charles M. Wiltse, *The New Nation, 1800-1845* (New York: Hill and Wang, 1961). R. R. Palmer, *The Age of Democratic Revolutions* (Princeton: Princeton University Press, 1959) places American events within the larger European context. Thomas D. Clark, *Frontier America* (New York: Charles Scribner's Sons, 1959) and Louis B. Wright, *Culture on the Moving Frontier* (Bloomington: Indiana University Press, 1956) provide insight into frontier life in the later eighteenth and nineteenth centuries. John A. Krout and Dixon Ryan Fox, *The Completion of Independence* (New York: Macmillan, 1944), and Russel B. Nye, *The Cultural Life of the New Nation* (New York: Harper, 1961) treat social and cultural developments.

Carl Becker, *The Declaration of Independence* (New York: Alfred A. Knopf, 1922) remains the classic treatment of the ideological backgrounds of revolutionary philosophy. Merrill Jensen, *The Articles of Confederation* (Madison: University of Wisconsin Press, 1940), and *The New Nation* (New York: Alfred A. Knopf, 1950) have had great influence in reshaping interpretations of the Confederation period. The standard account of the Constitutional Convention is Max Farrand, *The Framing of the Constitution* (New Haven: Yale University Press, 1913); A. T. Prescott, *Drafting the Federal Constitution* (Baton Rouge: Louisiana State University Press, 1941) reorganizes Madison's notes for convenient study and discussion. An important study which has influenced historical thinking for the past half-century is Charles A. Beard, *An Economic Interpretation of the Constitution* (New York: Macmillan, 1913, rev. ed. 1937). The Beardian economic thesis in regard to the framing of the Constitution, however, has recently been challenged by Robert Brown, *Charles Beard and the Constitution* (Princeton: Princeton University Press, 1956), and Forrest McDonald, *We The People: The Economic Origins of the Constitution* (Chicago: University of Chicago Press, 1958). Jackson Turner Main, *The Antifederalists: Critics of the Constitution* (Chapel Hill: University of North Carolina Press, 1961) is a recent study of the opponents of the Constitution.

John C. Miller, *The Federalist Era* (New York: Harper, 1960) is an excellent general survey; Leonard D. White, *The Federalists: A Study in Administrative History* (New York: Macmillan, 1948) and *The Jeffersonians* (New York: Macmillan, 1951) analyze the respective administrations as political operating units. Stephen G. Kurtz, Shaw Livermore, Jr., *The Twilight of Federalism* (Princeton: Princeton University Press, 1962) covers that party's rise and fall. Charles M. Wiltse, *Jeffersonian Tradition in American Democracy* (Chapel Hill: University of North Carolina Press, 1935) is a thoughtful consideration of Jeffersonian ideas. Adrienne Koch, *Jefferson and Madison: The Great Collaboration* (New York: Alfred A. Knopf, 1950) traces the development of political theory and practice through both men's administrations with admirable clarity. Merle E. Cunningham, *The Jeffersonian Republicans* (Chapel Hill: University of North Carolina Press, 1957) and Joseph E. Charles, *The Origins of the American Party System* (New York: Harper, 1956) concern the emergence of partisan politics. Two recent special studies throw new light on the Alien and Sedition Acts and their place in political history: James M. Smith, *Freedom's Fetters* (Ithaca: Cornell University Press, 1956), and John C. Miller, *Crisis in Freedom* (Boston: Little, Brown, 1957).

George Dangerfield, *The Era of Good Feelings* (New York: Harcourt, Brace, 1952) is the best general history of the pre-Jacksonian decades; while Herbert J. Clancy, *The Democratic Party: Jefferson to Jackson* (New York: Fordham University Press, 1962) is concisely considered political history. Bradford Perkins, *Prologue to War: England and the United States 1805-1812* (Boston: Little, Brown, 1962), and Francis F. Beirne, *The War of 1812* (New York: Dutton, 1949) cover events leading up to the war and the war itself. Samuel F. Bemis, *John Quincy Adams and the Foundations of American Foreign Policy* (New York: Alfred A. Knopf, 1949) is a superb treatment of foreign relations.

PART 3: INTRODUCTION

DEMOCRACY AND MANIFEST DESTINY

■ The eighteenth-century British statesman Edmund Burke once partially defined a political party as "a body of men united . . . upon some particular principle in which they all agreed." But whatever validity that definition may have had in eighteenth-century England, it must be used cautiously in reference to the two-party system of a country as economically and regionally diversified as the United States. While rival parties can sometimes be defined in terms of their *tendencies* toward one view or another on major issues, each party draws on a wide spectrum of interests, some of them seriously conflicting with what is considered the dominant philosophy of the party. Thus, a political party might better be defined in terms of purpose—its purpose being to win and exercise power, namely, by gaining control of the government.

The years 1824-1848—often called the "Jacksonian Era" in allusion to its most famous figure—were a time well made for unusual alliances of political forces. The death of the Federalist party in the years after 1815 had virtually left the American political field to the Jeffersonian Republicans, but by 1824 the Republican party itself was breaking up into angry factions, and by the 1830's most men had collected behind one of two rival parties, the Democrats and the Whigs. The main point is that in the regrouping of forces, men sought seemingly strange alliances in their bid for power. The commercial-industrial interests of the Northeast, predominantly Whig, allied with influential planters of the Deep South as well as with leaders in the West. Jackson, a Tennessee plantation owner and a Democrat, drew followers from every source—Western farmers, Northeastern laborers, old Republicans, New York and Pennsylvania businessmen, men from all walks of life. However, more than changing political alignments contributed to the instability of the times. Americans were taken by the fever of progress—material and political—to a degree perhaps unknown in the world before. Industrialism was tasting success in the Northeast. Pioneers were moving westward, many of them hungering with speculative schemes; cities and towns were rising along the Ohio and Mississippi and around the Great Lakes. Cotton culture in the South was steadily expanding to meet the needs of a world market.

Andrew Jackson, portrait by Thomas Sully (1845). "There are no necessary evils in government. Its evils exist only in its abuses. If it would confine itself to equal protection, . . . it would be an unqualified blessing."—Jackson (1832).

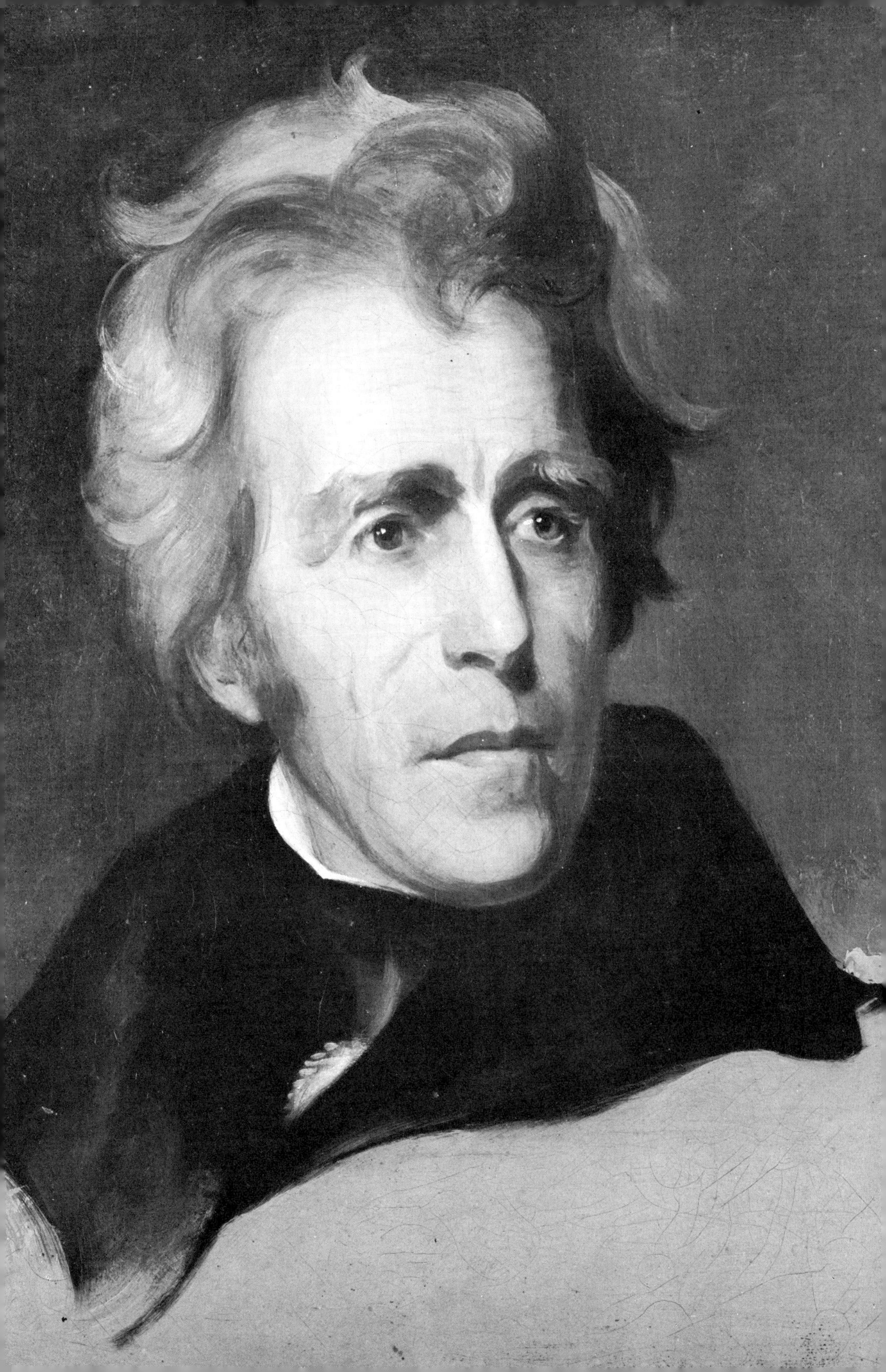

The Lackawanna Valley, painting by George Inness (1855). The achievements of nationhood from Washington to Jackson created new pride in the American frontier. As this painting suggests, however, railroads and industry were already beginning to displace the wilderness.

Political egalitarians were demanding—and securing—an end to restrictions on the franchise so that every man could have his vote in a democratic society.

Thus, to find consistency in the political ideals and actions of the Democrats and Whigs is difficult, merely because change was in the air. "In a rapidly changing America," Vernon L. Parrington said of the Jacksonian period, "with economics in a state of flux, men were no longer free political agents, guiding themselves by the fixed stars of accepted theory; they were borne like corks on the current of the times." Daniel Webster, for example, began his political career as a champion of New England shipping interests in favor of free trade, but after the War of 1812, with the growth of domestic manufactures, Webster caught the spirit of industrial progress and by the late 1820's he had become an aggressive advocate of protective tariffs fostering young American industry. Because the new businessmen were pioneering unknown paths, Webster and like-minded Whigs of the 1830's and 1840's felt they needed all the government aid they could get, including not only a protected market but also a sound banking system which would provide a stable currency and ample, expandable credit.

Henry Clay, too, changed his convictions with the changing times. Reared as a youth in the Virginia environment of Jeffersonian agrarianism, he migrated to Lexington, Kentucky, and was awakened to the new economic ambitions of the West—a West pressing the government for aid in opening roads and canals, expanding markets, and facilitating the flow of immigrants westward. Clay, the spokesman of Western Whigs, believed in a nationalistic program—his so-called "American System"—which, by means of internal improvements, a liberal policy of public-land sales, a central bank, and tariffs, would eliminate America's dependence upon foreign trade and provide a home market for the exchange of the North's manufactures and the West's agricultural products.

The County Election, painting by George Caleb Bingham (1851-1852). From the 1830's on, the rise of Jacksonian democracy inspired a lively growth of popular interest and participation in political affairs.

According to Whiggery, government aid to the business community would ultimately promote the economic progress and well-being of all Americans. However, it should be remembered that the Whig party also embraced prominent Southern planters, whose dependence on cotton exports and low-cost imports in a world market caused them to oppose the nationalistic views of their Northern confreres. The fact that the South, a slaveholding and staple-producing section, was "different" from the rest of the nation prompted its leaders to take anguished turns in their search for adjustment; when that failed, they attempted to break away from the Union. John C. Calhoun of South Carolina, perhaps the South's greatest politician and political philosopher of the period, began as a "War Hawk" nationalist during the days of Jefferson and Madison but later became a defender of states' rights in defiance of federal "authoritarianism"; in the course of an uncertain career he shifted from the Democrats to the Whigs and back to the Democrats.

Andrew Jackson, a former military hero eminently popular with Democrats and most Americans, was a champion of the plain people and the enemy of "privilege" that accorded advantages to one class or one section over others. Often arbitrary in method—once having made a decision, he forced his way to his objective, knocking down any obstacles in his path—Jackson was nevertheless basically temperate and pragmatic in his political and economic principles. He favored only what he called a "judicious" tariff; he approved or opposed internal improvements on the merits of each individual case; and finally, he and his Democratic followers seemed more aware than were the Whigs of the potential dangers of monopolistic institutions like the Bank of the United States. Whether successful or not, Jackson tried to apply salutary restraints on aggressive businessmen, speculative Westerners, and states' rights extremists in an age when America was rushing headlong on an expansionist and industrial course.

CHAPTER 7

GROWTH OF DEMOCRATIC GOVERNMENT, 1824-1848

END OF THE OLD REPUBLICAN PARTY

The Election of 1824. The sands of political allegiance never shifted more swiftly than in the last year and a half of James Monroe's administration. Although the Federalist party continued to exist for awhile in enclaves like Delaware, nearly all men called themselves Republicans, including the four leading candidates for the presidency in 1824. Two, Secretary of State John Quincy Adams and Secretary of the Treasury William H. Crawford, were members of the Monroe cabinet. They were pitted not only against each other but also against House Speaker Henry Clay and the famous hero of New Orleans, "Old Hickory," General Andrew Jackson.

For sixteen years the congressional caucus of the Republican majority had chosen the party's presidential candidates. During Monroe's second administration, however, the caucus system had met with increased opposition. The public looked on the caucus as an undemocratic procedure, dominated by aristocrats and not without its dictatorial aspects. There was growing conviction, also, that it was not in the nation's best interests for the newly elected President to feel that he owed his office to Congress. Politicians, aware of public opposition to the caucus, moved toward dissociating themselves from it; when the Republican caucus was held in February 1824, only 66 of 216 Republican congressmen attended.

The caucus selected Crawford of Georgia for the presidency, but its decision was scorned by Crawford's rivals and their many followers. The partisanship of the days of Jefferson was fast giving way to factional feuds. In a number of states, either the legislature or state conventions nominated their own "favorite sons"; there was a popular vote in only three quarters of the states. New England supported Adams of Massachusetts. Most of Crawford's strength was in the Southeast. Kentucky, Missouri, and Ohio looked to Clay of Kentucky; while Pennsylvania, most of the West, and some of the Southeast rallied behind Jackson of Tennessee. Secretary of War John C. Calhoun of South Carolina had early dropped out of the race, seeking the vice-presidency instead.

The real contest in the presidential election of 1824 was between Jackson and Adams; Jackson received approximately 153,000 popular votes to Adams' 108,000 and 99 electoral votes to Adams' 84. But Crawford and Clay, with 41 and 37 electoral votes respectively, split the total sufficiently so that neither Jackson nor Adams could claim a majority. Constitutional procedure now called for the decision to be referred to the House of Representatives. Here each state had one vote, and the three candidates with the most electoral votes —Jackson, Adams, and Crawford—remained in the running.

House Speaker Clay, no longer a presidential candidate, held the balance of power in the House decision. Although Clay earlier had instigated an anti-Adams campaign in the West, Clay personally disliked Jackson more than Adams and feared Jackson as a future Western rival. Clay therefore decided to support Adams, and as a result the Secretary of State's victory was virtually assured. Adams was elected on the first ballot on February 9, 1825.

The new President promptly appointed Clay his Secretary of State, and just as promptly Jacksonians angrily charged that a "corrupt bargain" accounted for both Adams' election and Clay's appointment. John Randolph of Roanoke called it "the combination, unheard of till then, of the Puritan [Adams] with the blackleg [Clay]." There probably was an implicit—if not explicit—understanding between Adams and Clay, but no evidence exists to demonstrate corruption.

One of the often unseen pivots of history is discernible in the election of 1824. Adams was almost exclusively a New England candidate until the New York General Assembly gave him twenty-six of New York's thirty-six electors. This was the result of tricky maneuvering by Adams' Albany managers, who were able to divert from Clay several of the electoral votes he had counted upon. If Clay instead of Crawford had been the third candidate, it is possible that the popular Speaker of the House of Representatives would have appealed to his fellow representatives more than either Adams or Jackson.

THE J. Q. ADAMS INTERLUDE

Adams in the White House. President Adams projected a bold domestic

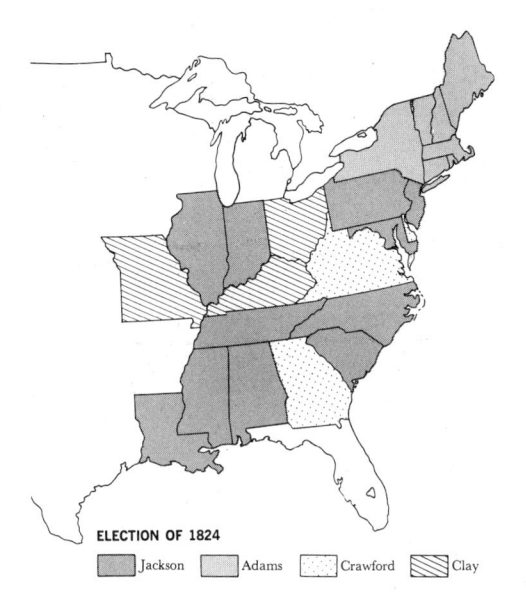

ELECTION OF 1824

Jackson | Adams | Crawford | Clay

program. In his first annual message he called for a national university (first proposed by Washington), a naval academy, a national astronomical observatory, a uniform national militia law, a uniform bankruptcy law, and a federally financed and orderly system of internal improvements. Most of these ideas were highly imaginative, and had his program gone into effect the second Adams might today be considered one of the most constructive Presidents in our history.

Constructive accomplishments of many kinds, however, simply were not forthcoming. From the outset Adams made little effort to push his policies once he enunciated them. A principal cause of this failure was Adams' view that the executive should abstain from what he considered undue interference in the legislative branch. As a consequence, numerous White House proposals, made year after year, were never introduced in Congress as legislative bills or resolutions. In addition, Adams had certain personal defects which prevented his being a natural leader. Aloof and unpleasant toward many associates, Adams disliked public contact and was incapable of appearing to good advantage when little knots of admirers gathered to greet him on his limited travels. Though unquestionably a patriot, he was ungracious and petty in the most minor human relations.

Off to an inauspicious start during the first half of his term, Adams was hopelessly handicapped after 1826 by a congressional coalition which fought him at every turn. Jacksonians would not forget that a "deal" had made Adams President despite the electorate's clear preference for Jackson. Sectional hostilities were increasing, and states' rights adherents opposed Adams' bold plans to increase the federal government's authority. Political idealists might praise Adams for injecting so little partisanship into his conduct of the country's business, but his popularity and effectiveness suffered for this very reason. And his opponents played politics to the hilt, especially after they came to dominate Congress.

It was in the area of tariff debates and tariff votes that sectionalism and partisanship were most rampant. One reason for the passage of the Tariff of 1824, enacted while President Monroe was still in office, had been its inclusion of duties on raw wool and other farm products. These schedules were attractive to the West, but Eastern manufacturers of woolen textiles complained that their profits diminished because raw materials were so expensive. What would have been the Tariff of 1827 provided a "solution" of the wool and woolens controversy, supposedly acceptable to the Northeast and the Northwest; this tariff, however, was defeated in the Senate by Vice-President Calhoun's vote. The Tariff Bill of 1828, concocted in an effort to embarrass Adams and help elect Jackson as his successor, had numerous illogical features from an economic point of view, including higher duties on raw materials than on manufactures. Unexpectedly passed, then signed by Adams and suitably labeled the "Tariff of Abominations," it was offensive to a wide variety of individuals, sections, and interests—and particularly to the Southeast.

Internal Improvements and Foreign Policy. One of Adams' greatest disappointments was Congress' refusal to develop a systematic national public works program. Congressional appropriations followed no logical pattern, and local interests and legislative logrolling left undone some of the most necessary projects. Despite this slapdash approach, however, achievements in the field of internal improvements were significant. Rivers were dredged and harbors made more serviceable; more federal appropriations were voted for these two purposes in Adams' four years than in the previous thirty. Lack of funds had forced a stop to work on the National Road in 1818; congressional appropriations permitted construction to resume in 1825, however, and by mid-century this important highway stretched from Cumberland, Maryland, to Vandalia, Illinois.

It might be supposed that a President with John Quincy Adams' background in diplomacy would leave a memorable record in foreign affairs. He achieved nothing, however, on a par with his success during his last year as Secretary of State in getting Russia to agree to 54°40′ as Alaska's southern boundary. The United States failed to obtain from Great Britain the right of free navigation of the St. Lawrence River. American shippers had to resort to a roundabout trade when the ports of the British West Indies were closed to Yankee merchantmen as tightly as they had ever been. Old claims against France for damages arising out of the wars of the French Revolution were no nearer settlement in 1829 than in 1825.

The United States instructed delegates to attend the Congress of Panama, held in 1826. Although Adams and Clay managed to overcome congressional opposition to the Latin American conference, one delegate died en route to Panama, the other arrived too late, and the mission accomplished nothing. In the entire field of foreign relations, Adams could point with pride only to an unprecedented number of minor treaties and to the renewal in 1827 of the Anglo-American agreement covering joint occupation of Oregon. Aside from these exceptions his administration was a negative interlude in American history.

JACKSONIAN DEMOCRACY TRIUMPHANT

The Election of 1828. Even if Adams' personality had been more attractive, his attitude more gracious, and his leadership stronger, he would have had difficulty in any political contest with the forces arrayed against him. As early as 1825, the general assembly of Tennessee placed Andrew Jackson on the track for the 1828 presidential race. Military glory was Jackson's most obvious asset, but the Tennesseean also was identified in Western minds with frontiersmen's desires for increased recognition by the United States government.

Moreover, Jackson had impressive allies. Vice-President Calhoun, an outstanding South Carolinian who had been Monroe's Secretary of War, did little to conceal his antipathy towards Adams. An important addition to the Jackson high command was Senator Martin Van Buren of New York. Formerly a Crawford lieutenant, the ingratiating Van Buren worked dexterously with Calhoun and others to effect a powerful combination of Southern and Northern Democratic-Republicans opposing Adams and favoring Jackson.

In the 1828 election, backers of both Adams and Jackson indulged in discreditable tactics. Pro-Adams journalists made much of Jackson's reputation for military high-handedness. They dragged the name of Mrs. Jackson through gutters of partisan filth by reminding voters that her divorce from another man had not been final back in the 1790's when she became Jackson's wife. This was a legal technicality which had no proper place in politics; emphasis on it infuriated Jackson and may have had something to do with Mrs. Jackson's death soon after the election.

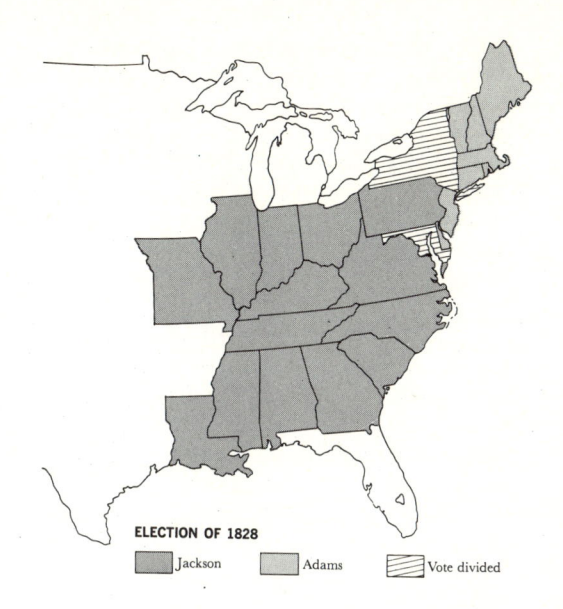

Pro-Jackson editors, however, were no innocent bystanders when the mud was slung. They retaliated with the accusation that Adams, when minister to Russia, had encouraged the sexual seduction by Tsar Alexander I of an American servant girl who worked in Adams' St. Petersburg legation. And, of course, they continued to harp on the "corrupt bargain" that had landed Adams in office four years earlier.

More important issues were not entirely ignored. Since the country had not reached the period of national conventions and platforms, there was no formal enunciation of principles; Jackson's name, however, was bracketed in some minds with proposals for tariff reform, and that of Adams—fairly or unfairly—with the Tariff of Abominations. Critics of the second Bank of the United

ELECTION OF 1828
Jackson | Adams | Vote divided

Growth of Democratic Government, 1824–1848   127

States hoped that Jackson, as President, would oppose it. Some advocates of the construction of roads and canals and the dredging of rivers and harbors seemed to prefer Adams because he had spoken out in favor of federal appropriations for these purposes. Yet there was no unanimity here; other such advocates, chiefly Southerners, believed Jackson would support internal improvements more heartily than did Adams. Old Republicans, of the variety Randolph had led in the Senate, saw danger in Adams' ideas about a national university, observatory, naval academy, and the like. Were these not projections of a trend toward a consolidated national state? If so, they feared, the South might eventually be downtrodden by an aggressive North.

If such opinions were held by some serious citizens, "Hurrah for Jackson!" was the rallying cry that appealed to most Americans. About three times as many people participated directly at the polls in 1828 as four years before, and the results were recorded with somewhat more care. Jackson, the Democratic-Republican candidate, scored a smashing triumph with approximately 647,000 popular votes to 508,000 for Adams. In the electoral college the margin was two to one, with 178 votes for Jackson and 83 for the National Republican.

"King Mob." Jackson's inauguration in March 1829 was accompanied by a demonstration unparalleled in American history. The thousands of people assembled in Washington behaved well enough outside the Capitol while Jackson read his inaugural address. But when the time came for the White House reception, "King Mob" took over. Men, women, and children crashed, trampled, and crushed their way in muddy boots and shoes into and through the mansion. Only when someone thought of placing refreshments on the White House lawn did the crowd move outdoors.

Ex-Federalists and National Republicans were shocked by this public demonstration; they talked darkly of a re-enactment of French Revolution excesses on American soil. Actually, the scene had been more a matter of bad manners and an explosion of pent-up energy than anything else. The base of governmental support had broadened appreciably in the past few years, but no excesses other than social ones upset the evolutionary development of an increasingly democratic state. Nevertheless, when the multitude faded away shortly after inauguration day, the symbol of "King Mob" remained as a counterweight to "King Caucus" of old.

Reorganization of the Cabinet. The Democratic-Republican party of 62-year-old President Jackson charted its administrative course in an atmosphere of confusion. Though Van Buren became Secretary of State, several cabinet members were more closely identified with Vice-President Calhoun than with either Jackson or Van Buren.

Almost at once there erupted one of those odd controversies which occasionally have influenced American political history. Secretary of War John H. Eaton was a Jackson appointee who had long been on intimate terms with the new President. Eaton had recently married Mrs. Peggy O'Neale Timberlake, a young widow whose comeliness was said to have attracted Eaton before her first husband's death. The story goes that Mrs. Calhoun and the wives of Calhoun's cabinet friends took the lead in snubbing Mrs. Eaton. Jackson resented the social chill, associating it with the shameful treatment of his own late wife during the campaign.

Van Buren, who endeared himself to Jackson by siding with the Eatons, offered to resign from his cabinet post, knowing that a cabinet reorganization would enable Jackson to be rid of the problem. Eaton followed Van Buren's example, and in the spring of 1831 Jackson requested resignations from all the remaining cabinet members except one. Calhoun's supporters were excluded from the succeeding cabinet, while Van Buren retained the confidence of Jackson, who promptly named him minister to Britain.

Changing Problems, Changing Arguments. Meanwhile, a more fundamental division between Jackson and Vice-President Calhoun developed over two other issues. First, the President was greatly disturbed by the discovery that, years before, Calhoun had favored Jackson's being court-martialed for his conduct during the Seminole War of 1818. Second and more significant, Jackson hotly disapproved of Calhoun's contention that a state had the right to nullify a federal statute. It was concerning this "nullification" question that the smoldering antipathies of the two ranking officials of the country flared into the open.

The nullification stand of the Vice-President and his fellow South Carolinian, Senator Robert Y. Hayne, resulted from their state's opposition to the tariff tendencies of the United States—especially to the Tariff of Abominations. They believed that while the industrial Northeast benefited, the agricultural South was damaged by the rising customs duties.

Economic conditions in the Southeast were steadily worsening. The extension of cotton planting to the rich bottom lands of Alabama, Mississippi, and Louisiana had expanded production of the staple, and cotton prices consequently dropped. Many Southeastern planters, threatened with ruin by their inability to compete on relatively poor soil, pulled up stakes and took their slaves to the Southwest for a fresh start. The consequent loss of population compounded the Southeast's financial difficulties. There were also political reverberations, since fewer people would mean smaller representation in Congress for South Carolina and similarly affected states.

Calhoun had lately joined Hayne and other South Carolina politicians in the conviction that most of their state's troubles could be traced to the tariff. In 1828, while running for reëlection to the vice-presidency as a Jackson adherent, Calhoun secretly wrote the "South Carolina Exposition." This document, published without his name, declared protective tariffs unconstitutional. It went on to assert the right of any state to "nullify" or prevent the enforcement within its boundaries of an unconstitutional act of Congress. Calhoun's authorship of the "Exposition" was not generally known in 1830, but his new position was becoming clear in some minds, including Jackson's. And the Vice-President carefully coached the less brilliant Hayne when the latter eloquently defended the extreme states' rights position in a dramatic Senate debate with Senator Daniel Webster of Massachusetts. As Massachusetts had become more industrialized and accordingly adopted a high-tariff policy, Webster had abandoned his low-tariff convictions (he opposed the Tariff of 1824), and in 1830 he was a high-tariff advocate. Moreover, Webster identified Massachusetts' changed economic attitude with a political nationalism that contrasted with the growing sectionalism of South Carolina; in so doing, he sought to equate economic interest with patriotic virtue.

The famous Senate debate of 1830 arose as the result of a resolution by Connecticut Senator Samuel A. Foot, which had as one aim a restriction of the sale of public land. The land question was a vital matter to congressmen from the West. Current land laws, in effect since the early 1820's, provided for: (1) a minimum purchase of 80 acres; (2) a minimum price of $1.25 an acre; (3) no credit system; and (4) exceptions which recognized but did not wholly satisfy Western insistence on lower land prices and the preëmption principle that favored squatters rather than speculators. Already in the air were proposals for liberalizing land policies. Eastern laborers joined Western farmers in favoring such liberalization, and Southerners saw an advantage in linking Western land desires to Southern low-tariff hopes; thus the opposition to Foot's restrictive resolution was not limited to any single section.

Senator Thomas H. Benton of Missouri resoundingly assailed the Foot Resolution. Benton saw it as a scheme of New England manufacturers, fearful of losing factory operatives to the lure of the West, to make cheap land inaccessible and so keep their workers in the East. Hayne went to Benton's support but took a different tack. If Foot's proposition were put into effect, he said, future prices of Western land would be high. The income would then constitute "a fund for corruption," adding to the power of the Washington government and endangering the independence of the states. Thereupon Webster launched his first reply to Hayne. Denying that the East was illiberal toward the West, the erstwhile sectionalist from Boston proclaimed his nationalism.

Hayne again spoke, reminding his hearers of New England's anti-Union attitude during the War of 1812. Where, he asked, were New England nationalists then? Had not residents of Webster's section, plotters of the Hartford Convention, favored the same constitutional arguments contained in the "South Carolina Exposition"? The Northeastern sectionalists of old, Hayne insisted, currently avowed theories which they formerly had decried. Their sincerity, he implied, was open to grave doubts. And their past words and tactics hovered as reminders of appalling inconsistencies.

After Hayne spiritedly elaborated on the extreme states' rights point of view, Webster answered him in what is widely regarded as the greatest speech ever delivered in Congress. In New England, he said, what Hayne had discussed was consigned to a bygone time. New Englanders were thinking not of the past but of the present and the future. Vital now was the well-being of America as a whole. Nothing could be more preposterous than the idea that twenty-four states could interpret the Constitution as each of them saw fit. The Union should not be "dissevered, discordant, belligerent." The country should not be "rent with civil feuds, or drenched . . . in fraternal blood." It was delusion and folly to think of "Liberty first, and Union afterwards." Instead, "dear to every true American heart" was that blazing sentiment—"Liberty *and* Union, now and forever, one and inseparable!"

Although generations of young Americans have memorized the peroration of Webster's "Second Reply to Hayne," there was at least as much logic—of the sort premised on the recorded performances of the various sections—on Hayne's side as on his adversary's. Hayne was both consistent and persistent over a period of six years, but Calhoun (who soon overshadowed Hayne as the personification of antinationalist sentiment) was as inconsistent as Webster and as illogical on the basis of his long-established position. Both in the "Exposition" and in subsequent documents Calhoun contributed to his state's cause, the thoughts and theories of a resourceful mind. Still, modern scholarship cannot ignore the circumstances under which Calhoun and Webster made their shifts. Under the pressure of politico-economic necessity, each now occupied the other's previous position.

Calhoun and Jackson succeeded Hayne and Webster in the public spotlight during the spring of the same year, 1830, when a Jefferson birthday banquet was held in Washington's Indian Queen Hotel. Jackson offered fellow Democratic-Republicans a toast: "The Federal Union, it must be preserved!" Calhoun countered with a toast of his own: "The Union, next to our liberty, most dear!" The disparate sentiments were not lost upon the diners. The President had hurled down the gauntlet. The Vice-President had picked it up. After that, their relations became ever more strained, and before Jackson's first term ended, Calhoun had resigned the vice-presidency.

Two Controversial Vetoes. Jackson sternly opposed the Bank of the United States and objected to most proposals to use federal funds for internal improvements. The improvements question bulked large in 1830, when Congress passed a bill authorizing subscription of stock in a private company constructing a road between Maysville and Lexington, Kentucky. Jackson vetoed the proposition on the ground that the Maysville Road lay wholly in one state and therefore was not entitled to financial support from Washington.

Jackson's action was highly controversial. Henry Clay and many other transportation-minded Americans charged Jackson with being an impediment in the march of progress. But the veto was well received by Southern strict-constructionists and by others resentful of what they deemed undue interference by the federal government in purely state affairs. Moreover, Jackson's selection of a western road as a target of his disapproval pleased internal-improvements men in New York and Pennsylvania, who had locally financed their own projects and saw no reason why people in other regions should get the kind of Washington help they themselves had failed to obtain.

Jackson was hostile to the Bank of the United States for at least four reasons. First, he held the Jeffersonian strict-construction view, maintaining that Congress was not empowered by the Constitution to incorporate a bank outside the District of Columbia. Jackson also doubted the expediency of the Bank, accusing it of not having established a sound and uniform currency.

His third objection was that the Bank played politics in election campaigns and influenced congressmen by lending them money or placing them on its payroll. Finally, Old Hickory had an ingrained suspicion of the note issues of all banks—with the Bank of the United States the most notorious offender because it was far and away the most powerful.

Actually, under Nicholas Biddle's leadership the Bank of the United States had made important contributions to American economic stability. Regardless of what Jackson said, it did provide a sound currency. Furthermore, its monetary standards and the financial power it wielded often exerted a salutary effect on the fluctuating currencies of state banks—many of which were dangerously weak. The charge of political activity and legislative influence was, for the most part, warranted. Jackson came to consider the Bank a monopoly, but, although favored by law because government deposits were exclusively entrusted to it, the Bank was not a monopolistic enterprise in the customary sense of the term.

The Bank's charter had four years to run in 1832, but Clay, now a United States senator, was in full accord with Bank President Biddle's desire to see the institution rechartered long in advance of the legal deadline. Clay pushed a Bank Bill through both houses of Congress; then, chosen by the National Republicans as their standard bearer in opposition to Jackson's reëlection, Clay strove to make the Bank the main issue in the campaign. Jackson lost no time in vetoing the rechartering act in July 1832. Thus he and Clay set the stage for a showdown on the subject.

The Election of 1832. It may be argued that Clay was handicapped in his presidential race because of the existence of an Anti-Masonic third party which objected to both Jackson and Clay, each of whom was a Freemason. The Masonic fraternity, its critics claimed, was aristocratic and threatened democratic institutions because of its oaths and secrecy.

The Anti-Masons nominated William Wirt of Maryland, himself ironically a Mason and for twelve years Attorney General under Monroe and Adams. The National Republicans' choice was Clay, while the Democratic-Republicans (now beginning to be called Democrats) of course were for Jackson, with Van Buren as his running mate. In most states the anti-Jackson following was concentrated behind either Clay or Wirt, with the other man staying out of the contest. But even with this tactical advantage neither Clay nor Wirt had a very good chance to oust the well-liked Jackson. Furthermore, the Bank issue did not aid Clay any more than criticism of Masonry helped Wirt.

Not all historians agree on the exact size of the popular vote. It is clear, however, that Jackson won easily; his popular vote was approximately 687,500 against 530,000 for Clay and Wirt combined. Jackson was victorious in nearly the entire South and West, plus the "big" states of New York and Pennsylvania. In the electoral college, Jackson scored 219 to Clay's 49 and Wirt's 7. South Carolina, still voting through its legislature, refused to back any of the regular candidates and cast eleven protest ballots for John Floyd of Virginia.

"KING ANDREW"

Crisis Over Nullification. No sooner was the 1832 election decided than South Carolina brought the nullification controversy to a head. The issue immediately in question was the Tariff of 1832, which lowered customs duties but not enough to satisfy critics in Charleston and Columbia. The newly elected state legislature, composed predominantly of "nullifiers," ordered a special state convention to deal with the problem. The convention met in Columbia in November and took three major steps: it declared the tariffs of 1828 and 1832 null and void within South Carolina; it called on the state legislature to prohibit collection of duties in the state after February 1, 1833; and it warned that South Carolina would secede if the federal government used force to collect duties.

Jackson responded to South Carolina's saber-rattling by dispatching naval and military units to that state and by issuing a stirring Nullification Proclamation which declared in part:

I consider, then, the power to annul a law of the United States, assumed by one State, incompatible with the existence of the Union, contradicted expressly by the letter of the Constitution, unauthorized by its spirit, inconsistent with every principle on which it was founded, and destructive of the great object for which it was formed.

Possible bloodshed was averted when Senator Clay of Kentucky sponsored a compromise tariff bill providing for a gradual reduction of duties year by year until 1842. Though the protectionist New England and Middle Atlantic states bitterly opposed such a tariff reduction, Congress passed the compromise bill and Jackson signed it on March 2, 1833. On the same day, a Force Bill—giving Jackson congressional authority to use arms to enforce collection of customs—became law.

The Compromise Tariff of 1833 was much more reasonable by South Carolina's standards than preceding tariffs had been. The Columbia convention met once again and withdrew its nullification ordinance, but as a face-saving gesture the convention nullified the Jackson's Force Bill. The President regarded this last defiant act of little practical significance. Both sides now considered the issue closed, and both claimed victory.

The United States Bank. Jackson, interpreting his success in the 1832 election as a mandate from the voters to continue action against the Bank of the United States, decided to remove federal deposits from the Bank gradually and deposit them in selected state banks. An order to this effect was issued on September 26, 1833, and by the end of the year twenty-three state banks—dubbed "pet banks" by anti-Jacksonians—had been selected as depositories.

Jackson's move against the Bank met with considerable political opposition. When Secretary of the Treasury William J. Duane refused to carry out the removal order, Jackson replaced him with Roger B. Taney (pronounced "Tawney") of Maryland, until then Jackson's Attorney General. In Congress, Jackson's policy was attacked. In December 1833 Henry Clay introduced Senate resolutions to censure both the Treasury action and the President for having "assumed upon himself authority and power not conferred by the constitution and laws, but in derogation of both."

When those resolutions were adopted, Jackson formally protested that the Senate had charged him with an impeachable offense but denied him an opportunity to defend himself. The Senate, however, rejected Jackson's protest and, as a further measure of defiance, would not approve Taney's nomination as Secretary of the Treasury. Only after a three-year Senate battle did Jackson's supporters succeed in having the resolution of censure expunged from the Senate record.

Hard Money and Land. Jackson's Bank policy contributed to a series of severe nationwide economic reverses. Even though the administration withdrew federal funds from the United States Bank only gradually, using them to meet current expenses while depositing new revenue in "pet banks," the Bank's decline was sharp enough to touch off a nationwide depression in 1833-1834. Nicholas Biddle's actions aggravated the situation: to make up for the lost federal deposits and to force congressional reconsideration of the Bank's charter, Biddle was unnecessarily severe in calling in outstanding loans, thus creating demands for credit from state banks which they could not meet. Only under strong pressure from businessmen and from the governor of Pennsylvania did Biddle at last reverse his policy.

The country pulled out of the economic doldrums and almost immediately headed into a dangerous inflationary spiral. State banks used their newly acquired federal funds for speculative purposes. Then, too, the federal government greatly increased its sale of public land, inadvertently encouraging the most reckless speculators.

Although political leaders were divided in their reaction to the inflationary trend, Jackson agreed with Senator Benton's prediction that "the present bloat in the paper system" could foreshadow another depression. On July 11, 1836, Jackson chose to issue a Specie Circular, which provided that after August 15 all public lands purchased from the federal government were to be paid for in gold or silver, with one exception: until December 15 actual settlers were permitted to use paper money (state bank notes) to purchase parcels of land up to 320 acres. Jackson's sudden policy reversal sharply curtailed western land sales and weakened public confidence in the state banks. It encouraged the hoarding of specie (hard money) and was a factor in bringing on the Panic of 1837.

The western land problem figures repeatedly in congressional debates from Jackson's day to Lincoln's and beyond. Benton and other Westerners favored the policy of "graduation," by which prices for the less desirable portions of the public domain would be reduced from $1.25 an acre to $1.00, 50 cents, or less, depending on the length of time they had been on sale. Westerners also desired a policy of preëmption, by which genuine settlers would have the first chance to buy land at the minimum price.

Although Congress passed no graduation bill until 1854, a temporary Preemption Act in 1830 authorized settlers to buy up to 160 acres of public land at a minimum price of $1.25 an acre. The act was renewed regularly and remained in force until 1842. Not to be confused with preëmption was Henry Clay's advocacy of "distribution." In 1833, the Kentuckian drove through both the House and Senate a bill stipulating that most of the revenue derived from public-land sales be distributed among all the states, with a smaller fraction earmarked for states where the sales took place. That was a typical example of Clay's desire to appeal politically to two sections at once. Jackson, however, pocket-vetoed the bill, thwarting his adversary and identifying himself further with the actual settlers of the Northwest and Southwest.

Jackson's Foreign Policy. Jackson's handling of foreign affairs was at times as forthright and unconventional as one might expect of an old border captain. The only real diplomatic crisis of his two terms concerned spoliation claims against France for depredations on United States commerce during the Napoleonic wars. Adams and preceding Presidents had failed to collect, but at Jackson's urgings France agreed to pay $5 million in a series of indemnity installments. The first $1 million was due in 1833, but when the French made no payment then or the following year, Jackson urged Congress to authorize reprisals on French property unless the money were speedily sent. For a few months there appeared to be danger of war, but French officials finally saw that the President meant business. Payment of the debt began in 1836.

Jackson also faced the problem of whether to recognize the independence of Texas (see p. 150). Because Texas was a potential slave state, Jackson trod carefully in order not to inflame the American people over the slavery issue and possibly jeopardize Van Buren's presidential hopes in the election of 1836. Jackson was fearful also of angering Mexico, which insisted that the United States enforce its neutrality statutes. Though there was no question about Jackson's personal sentiment— his sympathy for the Texan revolutionists was strong—he withheld recognition from the Texas republic until the very day he left office in 1837.

The Supreme Court. Andrew Jackson's most enduring influence on the Supreme Court came indirectly through the justices whom he elevated to the bench. When he retired, five of the sitting judges were his appointees. The number included Rober B. Taney, who succeeded John Marshall as Chief Justice on the latter's death in 1835.

Among the principal early decisions under Taney was *Briscoe* v. *The Bank of Kentucky* (1837), which reduced the application of constitutional limitations on state banking and currency matters. More famous is *Charles River Bridge* v. *Warren Bridge* (1837), which stressed community responsibilities of private property and modified the contract doctrines of Marshall. In *Bank of Augusta* v. *Earle* (1839), the Chief Justice denied that corporations had all legal rights of natural persons. He also held that while corporations could take part in interstate commerce, any state had the right to exclude another state's corporations. In later cases there sometimes was a lack of agreement or consistency regarding the commerce power on one hand and the states' internal police power on the other. This is traceable in part to the Court's changing personnel after Jackson's presidency, and in part to the alterations in Taney's own ideas.

For many years, it was the fashion to be hypercritical of Taney's Supreme Court record. Continuing on the tribunal until he died during the Civil War, he became very unpopular in the North because of his position in favor of states' rights and because of the Dred Scott decision in 1857 (see p. 192). Actually, the word "modify" is the key to Marshall-Taney differences in judicial philosophy and influence. Taney and most of his associates believed that the growing power of corporations needed supervision by states in the public interest. But they were not unsympathetic toward property rights as such, and modern authorities on judicial history see no sharp break between most constitutional interpretations of the two able jurists.

Evaluation of Jackson's Administration. Any President as active and dominant as Jackson is bound to arouse adverse criticism and to inspire praise bordering on idolatry. The Tennesseean's enemies did not hesitate to call him every unpleasant name in the book. They depicted him as "King Andrew," a would-be tyrant with slight regard for the ways of free men and with a ruthless determination to impose his will on the American people. On the other hand, Jackson's friends (and they were a majority) loved him personally and held his governmental talents in the highest esteem.

In the perspective of the years, Jackson's record shows marked differences from issue to issue. Although moderation is not traditionally considered a characteristic of Jackson, he was essentially a moderate on the tariff issue; his attitude toward land policy was generally temperate; and, although he did not block all internal improvements financed with federal funds, he was apt to be conservative or reactionary (depending on one's point of view) on projects in that category.

Most scholars are agreed that Jackson's greatest mistake was his hostility to the Bank of the United States, and his Specie Circular represented a miscalculation in timing if not in principle. On the other hand, Jackson's foreign policy was uniformly successful, and his nationalism was tellingly asserted in opposition to the nullifiers.

Jackson was limited by his educational deficiencies and was especially handicapped in economics. But he had an acute awareness of public preferences and the public interest. He also had an instinct for reaching the "plain" people and for identifying their desires with his own. A simple man with a fighting heart, Jackson was no democratic doctrinaire. He was wedded neither to indigenous abstractions nor to imported systems of dialectics. Jackson judged each issue on its merits—as he understood them—and contributed vigorous leadership to every cause he championed. Scholarly consensus is that as President he was great or near-great.

DEMOCRATS AND WHIGS

The Election of 1836. As Jackson's second term neared its end, Vice-President Martin Van Buren was the Democratic presidential nominee. The opposition, now called the Whig party, tried to throw the contest into the House of Representatives by sponsoring several candidates on a regional basis. Van Buren faced Daniel Webster in the Northeast, Ohio's William Henry Harrison in the Northwest, and Tennessee's Hugh L. White in the South. These three Whigs won 14, 73, and 26 electoral votes respectively; South Carolina gave its 11 votes to the anti-Jacksonian Willie P. Mangum of North Carolina. Their combined total of 124 was well under Van Buren's figure of 170. The Whig popular vote of 739,000 failed to match Van Buren's 765,000. So, while the Whig's made gains, the 1836 regional scheme fell apart, and again the Democrats were victors.

The Panic of 1837. The "Little Magician" or "Red Fox of Kinderhook," as Van Buren was nicknamed, proved to be an unlucky President. A New York lawyer of ability and a politician who up to now had proved himself adroit in difficult situations, Van Buren found himself confronted by an economic disaster beyond his control. In May 1837, only two months after Van Buren's inauguration, a New York bank panic signaled the start of one of America's deep depressions. In part, the trouble stemmed from an English financial crisis during which many British creditors canceled their American investments. Yet Jackson and Van Buren drew much of the blame. Some of Jackson's "pet banks" were among those that went to the wall. And, while the Specie Circular checked speculation in western lands, it curtailed the activities of financiers who had been supplying funds to speculators.

The depression affected the lives and fortunes of people in every part of the country. Widespread unemployment developed in Northeastern seaboard cities, spreading into interior communities and fanning out to the south and west. Bread lines and soup kitchens relieved the hunger of poor families, including thousands of recent immigrants to the United States. Farmers received low prices for their crops. Factories closed. Laborers walked the streets. Canal and railroad projects ground to a halt. In 1839 the worst of the depression seemed to be over, but another decline occurred later that same year, and good times did not return to America as a whole until 1843.

In the meantime, Van Buren's fine display of statesmanship belied his reputation as a crafty politician. Beginning in 1837, he induced Congress to agree to a temporary issue of short-term Treasury notes; these amounted to $47 million in the next six years and enabled the government to meet its obligations. He also advocated an Independent Treasury, where federal funds could be safely retained without running pet-bank risks or resorting to another Bank of the United States. Most Whigs and some Democrats opposed the banking bill on the grounds that removal of federal funds from the state banks where they were deposited would restrict credit at a time when credit was sorely needed. The Independent Treasury Act finally was passed in 1840, but Van Buren's victory was short-lived: the next year, under the Tyler administration, the act was repealed, and for the next five years the Whig majority in Congress defeated Democratic efforts to reëstablish this "subtreasury system."

The *Caroline* Affair. Another problem of the Van Buren regime concerned a spat along the Canadian border. In 1837 Canadian insurgents, dissatisfied with London's rule, fled to an island in the Niagara River, where American Anglophobes reinforced them with recruits and arms. The American steamer *Caroline* was employed in the supply service.

Canadian government soldiers, crossing to the American side of the Niagara, set the *Caroline* afire and turned her adrift. Because of the high state of excitement there was danger of mob invasions in either direction, and the slaying of an American citizen on the night the vessel burned seriously complicated the situation. Three years later a Canadian deputy sheriff named Alexander McLeod was arrested in Lockport, New York, and indicted for murder and arson in connection with the *Caroline* affair. There was loose talk of war, and on both sides of the border additional sums were appropriated for the strengthening of boundary defenses. Even after McLeod was acquitted by a New York court in 1841, the case seemed an unpromising preliminary to the Webster-Ashburton negotiations of the next year.

Tippecanoe and Tyler Too. During Van Buren's presidency, Webster and Clay continued to be prominent in the senatorial spotlight. Webster's oratorical ability was as outstanding as ever, and Clay distinguished himself as a parliamentary leader. The Whigs have logically been equated with mercantile and banking classes, but they possessed substantial rank-and-file support which enabled them to elect so many governors and congressmen.

Northern Whigs favored the creation of a new national bank. They advocated a high tariff and federally financed internal improvements. If their anti-Jackson and anti-Van Buren confreres of the South did not agree about the tariff and the bank, the common bond linking all Whigs was the issue of "executive tyranny." Less domination by the President and more authority vested in Congress were aims which Southern and Northern Whigs shared. They also capitalized on economic distress and were as one in their criticism of Van Buren as the 1840 election approached.

The Whigs played their cards cannily in the 1840 test of skill. In the first place, their standard-bearer was neither Clay nor Webster—able men who had many friends, but also many enemies—but William Henry Harrison of Ohio. Harrison had run well in 1836 and had won a measure of military glory in the dim past at the Indian Battle of Tippecanoe. Second, the Whigs turned to their own advantage a journalist's taunt that Harrison was unfit for the presidency. "Give him a barrel of hard cider, and settle a pension of two thousand a year on him," the newsman sneered, "and [take] my word for it, he will sit the remainder of his days in his log cabin by the side of a 'sea coal' fire, and study moral philosophy."

Yes, the Whigs replied, their nominee was a man of the people who preferred a log cabin and hard cider to the frippery of red-whiskered Van Buren. In reality, Harrison dwelt in a mansion near Cincinnati, and he was an aristocratic Virginian by birth and rearing. But log cabins, barrels of cider, coonskin caps, and even live coons became Harrison symbols.

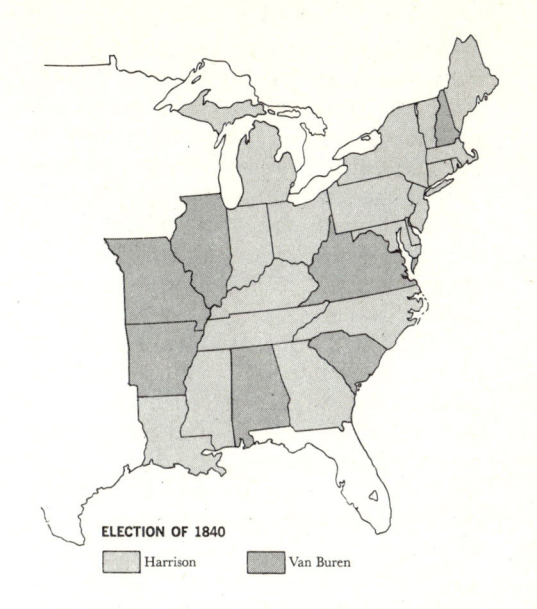

ELECTION OF 1840
Harrison / Van Buren

For the vice-presidency the Whigs had chosen John Tyler of Virginia, a former states' rights Democrat who now was a spokesman for the minority Southern element within the Whig party. The Whigs' most typical campaign verse still remains the best known of all jingles associated with elections:

> What has caused the great commotion, motion, motion,
> Our country through?
> It is the ball a rolling on
> For Tippecanoe and Tyler too—
>   Tippecanoe and Tyler too,
> And with them we'll beat
>   little Van, Van, Van.
> Van is a used up man.

As expected, the Whigs were victorious in 1840. Harrison's electoral showing was impressive (234 to Van Buren's 60), and his popular vote was 1,274,000 to 1,127,000 for the Democrat. Although the Whig margin was not vast in a number of critical states, it was large enough—and Van Buren carried only New Hampshire and Illinois north of the Mason-Dixon line.

Growth of Democratic Government, 1824–1848

President Without a Party. The sweet taste of triumph soon turned bitter in Whig mouths. Inaugurated in March 1841, the 68-year-old Harrison died after a single month in office. Tyler, the first man to reach the presidency through the death of his predecessor, shared few of the ideas of the dominant Whig group in Congress. Twice he vetoed attempts to revive the Bank of the United States. Twice he vetoed Clay-sponsored tariffs. Thrice he defeated distribution to the states of proceeds from public-land sales. All members of Harrison's cabinet, which Tyler inherited, resigned after six months, with the exception of Secretary of State Webster.

Before Webster entered the State Department, the *Caroline* affair was not the only border incident fanning the flames of international misunderstanding. There was also the undeclared Aroostook War, caused by New Brunswick and U.S. claims to the Aroostook River region on the undefined Maine-New Brunswick boundary. Ten thousand Maine troops were committed in 1839 to the defense of a large area subject to dispute. At length, an American general and New Brunswick's lieutenant-governor negotiated a truce.

As the crisis eased, the British government at long last saw the need of diplomats' determining what portions of 12,000 square miles should be acknowledged as belonging respectively to New Brunswick and to the U.S. Secretary Webster met in a series of conferences with England's envoy, Lord Ashburton. In their treaty of 1842, New Brunswick received 5000 square miles out of 12,000. The treaty was resented and Webster's popularity forever damaged in Maine, which felt itself short-changed. Nevertheless, the Webster-Ashburton Treaty did help to achieve order and peace.

John Tyler found himself in the unenviable position of a President without a party. He did agree with Northern Whigs that the Independent Treasury law should be repealed, and this was done in 1841. But his vetoes of Clay's tariff measures made him an apostate in their eyes. The Tariff of 1842, which Congress reluctantly passed and Tyler signed, was but mildly protective. Tyler also approved a General Preëmption Act and cooperated more and more with Democrats, whose nomination he hoped to obtain in 1844. Northern Whigs and border-staters like Clay rued the day when "Tyler too" had been tapped to run with "Tippecanoe."

Return of the Democrats. Fresh issues exerted a vital impact on the election of 1844. Some had to do with the West, others with chattel slavery. Texans had won independence from Mexico in 1836 (see p. 149); now there was considerable sentiment for the annexation of the Republic of Texas by the United States. Southerners particularly favored such a step, while expansion-minded Northerners hoped that Oregon would be wholly occupied by Americans in lieu of its division between the United States and Britain.

Henry Clay's 1844 presidential nomination by the Whigs came as no surprise. But Van Buren was shunted aside by the Democrats because he was thought to be anti-Texas, and little attention was paid to Tyler as a candidate since he was not a reliable party man. Instead, delegates to the Democratic national convention nominated James K. Polk, the first "dark horse" presidential nominee.

A former governor of Tennessee and speaker of the House of Representatives, Polk seemed thoroughly at home on the Democratic platform, which euphoniously but none too accurately described the desired Western policy as "the reannexation of Texas" and "the reoccupation of Oregon." Whigs made light of Polk's qualifications. "Who *is* James K. Polk?" they asked.

But Polk's campaign strategy proved more effective than that of Clay, who tried to straddle the Texas dilemma and was impaled on the horns of equivocation.

Into the close contest came James G. Birney, heading the antislavery Liberty party, who siphoned off Clay votes in New York and caused its electors to go to Polk. This made the difference. Polk received 170 electoral votes, Clay 105. The popular outcome much more narrowly favored the Tennesseean, who appealed to 1,338,000 citizens compared with Clay's 1,300,000.

Features of American Democratic Growth. The years 1824-1848 were characterized by an increase in the number of elected officeholders, by a relative decrease in appointed officials at the state and local levels, and by some reflection of the popular will by the Supreme Court. There was far greater participation in government than had been the case in prior eras. By the time the period was well launched, all states except one chose presidential electors by popular vote. The popular vote itself steadily increased from campaign to campaign, not only because the population was greater but because such barriers as religious and property qualifications were gradually lowered on a state-by-state basis.

The development of democratic government was not without its growing pains. One of the most criticized aspects of the political scene was the "spoils system," by which governmental posts were allotted as "spoils" of victory to members of the party triumphant at the polls. Under Monroe and Adams a small coterie of federal clerks and minor administrators had held offices on what amounted to a lifetime good-conduct basis. Jackson removed a number of these perennials because they had played the partisan game against him, because they were corrupt and inefficient, or because he wanted to make room for partisans of his own. In 1832 Senator William L. Marcy, a Jackson adherent, had remarked, "To the victor belong the spoils of the enemy"; now Jackson's enemies applied the phrase "spoils system" to Jackson's program of rewarding his political supporters with public office.

Jackson removed only one fifth of the 1829 officeholders during his entire presidency, but he did take a decisive step toward perpetuating an undesirable spoils system. Jacksonians defended the policy as the quickest and surest path to reform, but for every Adams man like embezzler Tobias Watkins, Jackson's party contributed a scamp of its own—such as collector Samuel Swartwout of the port of New York, who defaulted for more than a million dollars.

National political conventions, which came into being with an Anti-Masonic assembly held in 1831, were thoroughly established in the political structure by the end of Jackson's second term. Sometimes they have resulted in the choice of second-rate candidates for first-rate posts, but in the main the decisions of conventions have been sound, and they were and are more directly representative and democratic than "King Caucus" ever was. After momentarily striking a pose of aloofness from Jacksonian electioneering tactics, Whigs imitated their rivals by adopting slogans and symbols similar to Democratic ones. And styles of campaigning for over a century were patterned, to an appreciable degree, on the 1840 ballyhoo techniques promoting "Tippecanoe and Tyler Too!"

During Jackson's administration the intimate advisers on whom the President relied came to be known as the "kitchen cabinet"—because they ostensibly conferred with Jackson more intimately than did members of his official cabinet. Later chief executives have followed Jackson's example by surrounding themselves with capable but previously obscure counselors whose advice supplemented—or supplanted—that of department heads. It is doubtful that the "kitchen cabinet" would have originated as and when it did if Jackson had not owed his election in part to Calhounite Deep South support, which at least two cabinet members personified and on which he chose not to rely once his administration was under way.

It would be a mistake to minimize the role of the West in the period 1824-1848. Public lands, the tariff, internal improvements, the United States Bank, and almost all other issues were of interest to Westerners. The West had its own viewpoint or viewpoints of a predominantly sectional variety, yet it also exerted a nationalizing influence. The Southwest had much in common with the Northwest, and Jackson the Southwesterner proved himself a foremost nationalist who was supported as consistently in the Northwest as in any other portion of the country.

It is to the West that the camera of history turns during Tyler's final weeks and all of Polk's White House residence. During Polk's administration the territorial limits of the nation were vastly expanded by settlement of the Oregon controversy with Great Britain (1846), the annexation of Texas (1845), and the Mexican War (1846-1848). These events will be discussed in Chapter 8 within the context of Western expansion.

CHAPTER 8

WESTWARD EXPANSION AND ECONOMIC GROWTH, 1824-1848

THE BACKGROUND OF EXPANSION

Manifest Destiny. New York magazine editor John L. O'Sullivan proclaimed in 1845 that it was "the fulfilment of our manifest destiny to overspread the continent allotted by Providence for the free development of our yearly multiplying millions." O'Sullivan's exuberant words reflected the optimism of fervid nationalists that the American banner soon would wave over all of North America and beyond. For the exponents of Manifest Destiny, even the addition of Texas, New Mexico, California, and the Oregon country to the nation would not be enough; God had destined the people of the United States to extend its sovereignty over Canada, Alaska, Mexico, Cuba, other West Indian islands, and Hawaii.

The dream of Manifest Destiny was less fantastic than it may now appear: it was no less realistic to contemplate the annexation of Canada or Cuba than to dream of extending American sovereignty to Alaska or Hawaii. Furthermore, in the light of America's impressive achievements since 1776, nearly anything seemed possible in the next half century. In 1803 the Louisiana Purchase had doubled the area of the American republic. By 1830 commerce with Europe was flourishing; trade with Asia was burgeoning; adventurers were extracting fortunes from China; and wealthy speculators were willing to invest in almost any feasible enterprise.

Dreams of Manifest Destiny were both an augury of future hemispheric expansion and a concomitant of the westward expansion which was taking place between 1824 and 1848. It was during this period that the Indian barrier was surmounted and the immense areas of the new Southwest and the Far West were added to the United States. It was a period which saw a rapid influx of European immigrants into the United States. Between 1830 and 1850 more than two million Europeans—most of them impoverished farmers or manual workers—crossed the Atlantic. Many were of the new German and Irish wave of immigrants. Between 1830 and 1850 the population of the United States as a whole almost doubled, from about 12.9 million to over 23 million. It was this period of rapid expansion which nourished the dreams of Manifest Destiny.

The Indian Barrier. In 1830 the nation's undisputed land and water area covered more than 1,780,000 square miles. In addition, more than 12,000 square miles in the far Northeast and approximately half a million square miles in the far Northwest were claimed by both Washington and London. Substantial numbers of Americans were living in Texas, which was part of Mexico, on land which the Mexican government had granted to Moses Austin and his son, Stephen F. Austin.

In 1830, however, most pioneers were less concerned with Mexican Texas or with Anglo-American boundary differences than with the nearer Indian barrier. Pressure of frontiersmen and their families on the then American West pushed tens of thousands of Indians west of the Mississippi River. In ninety treaties—some less honorable than others—signed during Jackson's presidency, the Indians reluctantly accepted new western lands in lieu of their old homes.

North of the Ohio River there was relatively little trouble for the white American—or suffering for the red—when what was left of the Shawnees, Wyandots, Delawares, and Miamis submitted to Washington policy and moved to western reservations. The most dramatic example of Northern aborigines' resistance in the century's fourth decade was an exception to the rule. This concerned a resolute but impractical Sauk, Black Hawk by name, who—together with White Cloud, a Winnebago—dreamed Tecumseh-like of an Indian confederation drawing recruits from many tribes and valiantly opposing the white man's encroachment.

A few Potawatomi, Winnebago, and Mascouten encouraged this imaginative man. Black Hawk was convinced that a treaty ceding the Rock River region of southern Wisconsin and northwestern Illinois to the hated whites had been signed by Sauk and Fox chieftains under conditions of trickery. Though Black Hawk reluctantly moved his people to the west bank of the Mississippi, in the spring of 1832 he led them back to southern Wisconsin in search of fertile farm land. Though the Sauks' intentions were peaceful, the whites panicked at the prospect of Indian attack, and plans for war soon rumbled across the fertile quarter-sections of Illinois. Abraham Lincoln and Jefferson Davis were among the volunteers or regulars who fought in the short-lived Black Hawk War.

Black Hawk and his band were no elite fighting corps; the pathetic array of men, women, and children were suffering from both hunger and exposure. But as they tried to flee once again to the Mississippi, more than 850 of Black Hawk's band were mercilessly slaughtered by the whites in the so-called Battle of Bad Axe.

The Black Hawk War marked the end of Indian resistance in the Old Northwest. Westward migration of Sauk, Fox, Winnebago, Potawatomi, Chippewa, and Ottawa tribes increased. Within six years both Wisconsin and Iowa became territories; within sixteen years they became states, as settlers from the East populated the country of red men now dispossessed.

Southern Indians generally were of higher caliber than those being prodded westward north of the Ohio. Sequoyah, inventor of the Cherokee syllabary, enabled thousands of Cherokee adults and children to read and write. And the Cherokees, Chickasaws, Choctaws, Creeks, and Seminoles are known in history as the Five Civilized Tribes. Some of them, notably the Seminoles and Creeks, did not always prove civilized if placidity is a criterion. But there is small wonder that enlightened and virile leaders could not invariably remain placid in light of the white men's tricks and treachery.

The Indian Springs Treaty of 1825, by which Creek agents gave up nearly five million acres of their land between the Flint and Chattahoochee rivers, was so unfair to the Indians that the U.S. Senate refused to ratify it. Often Indian "leaders" were accused of selling out to the whites and of receiving

WESTERN EXPLORATIONS

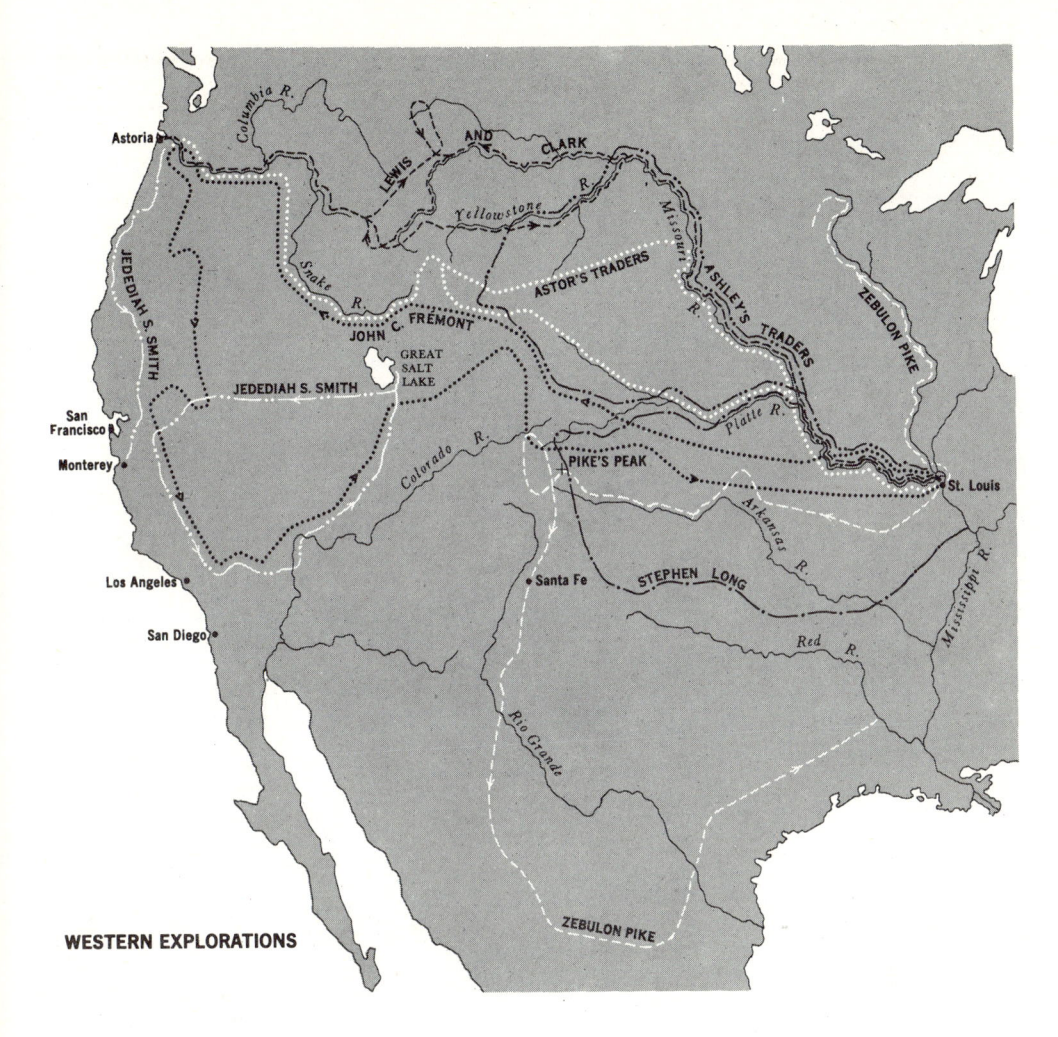

handsome rewards for their "services." Nevertheless, the treaties were effective in securing eastern lands for the white men. The Treaty of Dancing Rabbit (1830) relinquished nearly eight million Choctaw acres in Alabama and Mississippi, and in the next decade other substantial cessions were made.

Not all Southern tribes submitted passively to the whites' intrusions. Osceola, leader of Florida's Seminole tribe, so resented the Treaty of Payne's Landing, which authorized removal of the Seminoles to west of the Mississippi, that he is said to have plunged his knife into the document when he was expected to sign it with his "X."

Osceola's resistance culminated in the Second Seminole War from 1835 to 1842. In 1835, Osceola's band ambushed and massacred 107 of the 110 officers and men of Major Francis L. Dade. Osceola took advantage of Florida's maze of inland rivers and swamps to hide the Seminole women and children. His own forces darted out to harass regimental commands, then rushed back to cover. Osceola was seized and imprisoned when under a flag of truce he came for an interview with an American general. He languished and died in a military prison, but the war he had initiated—the longest, bloodiest, and costliest of all our

WESTERN TRAILS

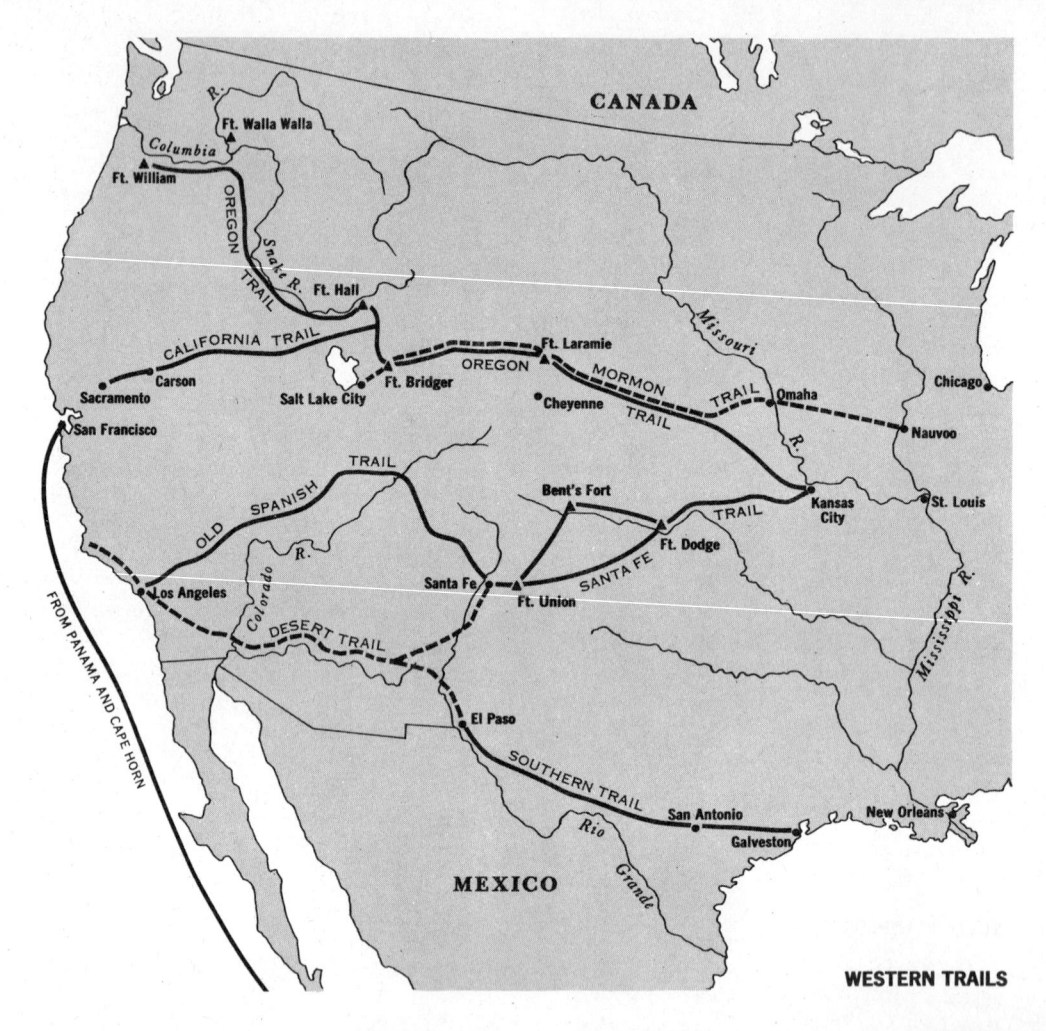

Indian wars—went on for several years. Although there are Seminoles in Florida even today, most of them left at the urgings or threats of white soldiers and Indian agents in the 1840's. Usually they settled in the Indian Territory of present-day Oklahoma.

The Pathfinders. By the 1830's, with the removal of the Indians, the trans-Appalachian West was a great complex of newly admitted states, and already people were moving beyond the Mississippi River (Missouri had been admitted as a state as early as 1821, and Arkansas followed in 1836). The wilderness beyond the Mississippi provided attractive commercial opportunities for aggressive American frontiersmen. The lucrative Northwestern fur trade, for example, had early drawn rugged trappers and traders to that area.

The most successful of the early fur traders was German-born John Jacob Astor, who organized the American Fur Company in 1808 with the intention of establishing a monopoly of the fur trade throughout the West. Astor's acquisitive instincts, ruthlessness, enormous capital, and efficient administration helped him take over Great Lakes and Mississippi valley trading posts which originally had belonged to other companies. In the 1820's he pushed

Democracy and Manifest Destiny

west and northwest, absorbing the Columbia Fur Company in the Oregon country and ruthlessly crushing rival trappers and traders.

Astor's business methods met with severe criticism on the frontier. An army officer had this to say of Astor's operations: "Take the American Fur Company in the aggregate, and they are the greatest scoundrels the world ever knew." But Astor, undaunted by criticism, continued to prosper until he decided in 1834 to withdraw from the fur business and concentrate on New York City real estate.

William Henry Ashley of St. Louis was another who made a fortune from furs in the Northwest. Ashley's Rocky Mountain Fur Company originated the revolutionary "rendezvous" method of fur trading, by which company agents, instead of trading with the Indians, bought furs directly from white trappers at an annual "rendezvous" in the mountains. From 1822 to 1826, Ashley and the rugged trappers on his payroll pushed north and west, penetrated the hostile country of the Blackfeet and Arikara Indians and trapped beaver along the Big Horn, Platte, Wind, Snake, Missouri, and other western rivers.

When Ashley retired he sold his Rocky Mountain Fur Company to Jedediah S. Smith, the "Knight in Buckskin" whose explorations greatly fostered American interest in the Far West. In the autumn of 1826 Smith led the first American overland expedition from Missouri to California. He carved a fabulous career as "mountain man" and plainsman until, when only thirty-two, he was surrounded and killed by wild Comanches.

Smith, Ashley, Jim Bridger, Thomas Fitzpatrick, and the employees of the Astor interests all were experts with the knife, the rifle, and the trap; but, more important, they contributed significantly to frontier expansion and marked the path for others.

Perhaps the most famous explorer among his contemporaries—so famous that he was known as the "Pathfinder" and later won the Republican nomination for President in 1856—was John C. Frémont. Son of a French émigré schoolteacher, Frémont early in life formed a strong taste for meeting and mastering wilderness challenges. It was in 1838-1839, when employed on a survey of the broad plateau between the upper Mississippi and upper Missouri Rivers, that this army officer got his real start as a geological observer, mapmaker, and scientific reporter. In the 1840's he led several expeditions to the West, exploring the Oregon Trail, the Sierra Nevada, California, the Colorado River and the Rio Grande. His well-written reports, avidly read in the East, stimulated further emigration to the West.

The Santa Fe Trail. Santa Fe, in the Mexican territory of New Mexico, also provided attractive commercial opportunities for enterprising Americans. Though the volume of American trade in Santa Fe never was large, it was economically significant because American merchants were able to dispose of goods at handsome profits and because they brought away silver in an era when the specie was at a premium.

William Becknell of Arrow Rock, Missouri, initiated the Santa Fe trade in 1821, when he sold his goods for ten to twenty times what they would have brought on the banks of the Mississippi. Venturesome American merchants and farmers followed Becknell's example, carrying goods along the 800-mile Santa Fe Trail from Independence, Missouri, to the great bend of the Arkansas and into New Mexico. Though the trip was arduous, confronting caravans with the dangers of rattlesnakes, Indian forays, heat, and rain, only eleven whites are reported to have been slain by Indians on the trail before 1843—a figure which illustrates that the Santa Fe Trail was less dangerous than it sometimes has been depicted.

The Oregon Trail. Like the tortuous road to Santa Fe, mention of the Oregon Trail conjures up vistas of caravans moving west, but in this case the caravans carried not merely merchants but farmers and other permanent settlers. Back in Jefferson's time, Lewis and Clark had traversed part of what was to become the celebrated route to the Pacific Northwest. Other hardy spirits followed, adding discoveries of their own.

Two curious characters enter the story. One, Benjamin Louis Eulalie de Bonneville, a native of France and a graduate of West Point, in the 1830's crossed the Continental Divide into Oregon, where he stayed three years. The second was Nathaniel J. Wyeth, a Massachusetts ice merchant who tried without success to exploit the Columbia River country for fish, furs, and timber. The contributions of these men to Oregon developments lay chiefly in their value as propagandists in advertising Oregon in the East.

The Oregon idea was not difficult to sell to land-hungry Americans. Oregon at that time was jointly occupied by the United States and Britain. The Hudson's Bay Company, an English concern, had long been established on the Columbia. Church interest heightened when such American Protestant missionaries as Jason Lee, Samuel Parker, and Dr. Marcus Whitman went out to Oregon. Thus national pride, missionary zeal, the lure of cheap lands, and the favorable reputation of the region all played a part in enticing thousands to Oregon.

As in the case of Santa Fe, Missouri communities like Independence and St. Joseph were takeoff spots for the Oregon-bound. For a couple of days, the two routes coincided. Then, as one went south, the other bent north. Across the Kansas, the Blue, the Platte, the North Platte, and beyond to Fort Laramie, covered wagons and pack trains of the Northwestern homeseekers wound their way in the 1840's. On to Fort Bridger, Soda Springs, Salmon Falls, and across the Snake and Boise Rivers, they proceeded to Dr. Whitman's mission. Eventually they emerged from the Blue Mountains along the Umatilla River to the Columbia. At last they arrived at Fort Vancouver or Astoria or wherever they were going. For two thousand miles the Oregon Trail stretched—over two and a half times the length of the Santa Fe journey.

Western Army Posts. Fortitude evinced by the mountain trappers, the Santa Fe traders, and the Oregon pioneers should not tempt moderns to overlook the tremendous contributions of the professional soldiers. From the 1820's well into the 1840's, the United States army never was large, but the role of the army in aiding the settlement of the West can hardly be exaggerated. Speculators and homesteaders were more likely to bring their families to areas when the military was nearby. Army posts in time became villages, towns, and cities. It was not unusual for a retired officer to become a respected civilian in a new community. Soldiers brought steamboats to western rivers, constructed sawmills, and built their own forts. They farmed adjacent fields, introduced cattle, and gave the lie to the widely credited legend that a "Great American Desert" existed between the Mississippi and the Rockies, where in fact there was no desert at all.

When it came to exploration, the army similarly played its part. So colorful are the reputations of the Jim Bridgers and the Kit Carsons that some of the well-organized infantry and dragoon expeditions into unknown or unfamiliar country seem relatively humdrum despite their significance. There were dozens of occasions when officers like Dodge, Riley, and Bonneville advanced into river valleys or mountain fastnesses about which Washington notions were vague.

WINNING OF THE WEST

A National Question. As long as the westward movement was confined to a few explorers and commercial adventurers, Washington could act indecisively and put off any attempt to reach terms with London and the Mexican empire in regard to territorial disputes in the West. But as American settlers poured into the Far West and the Southwest, setting up communities and then local governments, the United States government could no longer temporize. The dispute with Britain over the boundaries of the Oregon country had to be settled. And the aspirations of fellow Americans living in Texas, claimed by Mexico, had to be heeded. What had been social and economic developments in the West had by the 1840's risen to the level of national political questions.

The Oregon Dispute. The "Oregon country" was a great deal larger than the state we now know by the name. It was bounded roughly by the "Great Stony" Mountains on the east, the Pacific on the west, California on the south, and Alaska (then Russian) on the north. When informed men chatted about Oregon in the era after the War of 1812, they referred to a wondrously varied land with towering pinnacles and fertile valleys, swift-coursing rivers and magnificent forests. Details, however, eluded even the best-posted of commentators; lack of surveys prevented precision in defining its precise area.

Early in the nineteenth century both Russia and Spain laid claim to sections of Oregon. But Spain bowed out of the picture in 1819, and Russia in the next decade acknowledged 54° 40′ as Alaska's southern line. Britain and the United States were left in contention over the Oregon country.

Both countries laid claim to the area between the Columbia River and the line of 49° latitude to the Pacific; it was this area—the northwestern two thirds of the present state of Washington—which was the principal bone of contention. Britain based its claims on British subjects' exploration, discovery, and occupation of the region. American claims also were based on exploration and occupation, including Captain Gray's original discovery of the Columbia River in 1792, the Lewis and Clark expedition of 1804-1806, and the American missionaries and settlers who inhabited the area in the 1830's and 1840's.

During Anglo-American negotiations in 1818 the United States proposed the boundary line of 49° to the Pacific Ocean, but Britain was unwilling to relinquish its claims to the Columbia River, the "St. Lawrence of the West." The two nations, unable to reach a satisfactory agreement, settled upon a treaty of ten-year joint occupation of the disputed area. The treaty was renewed in 1827 for an indefinite period, with the provision that either party could terminate it on a year's notice.

Neither in 1818 nor at any other time until 1845 did the United States or Britain provide for civil government in Oregon. No marshal, no sheriff, no jury, no judge was empowered to carry out legal procedures. No laws could be executed because none had been enacted, there being no enacting authority. Often men took justice, or what they deemed was justice, into their own fallible hands. A missionary, without the shadow of authority, might name a constable or a magistrate. There were times when American traders and trappers tried alleged culprits for murder and other crimes. But maintenance of order, while frequently successful, was unofficial at best. Indians did not become subject to the slightest American

OREGON BOUNDARY DISPUTE

United States Claim — British Claim

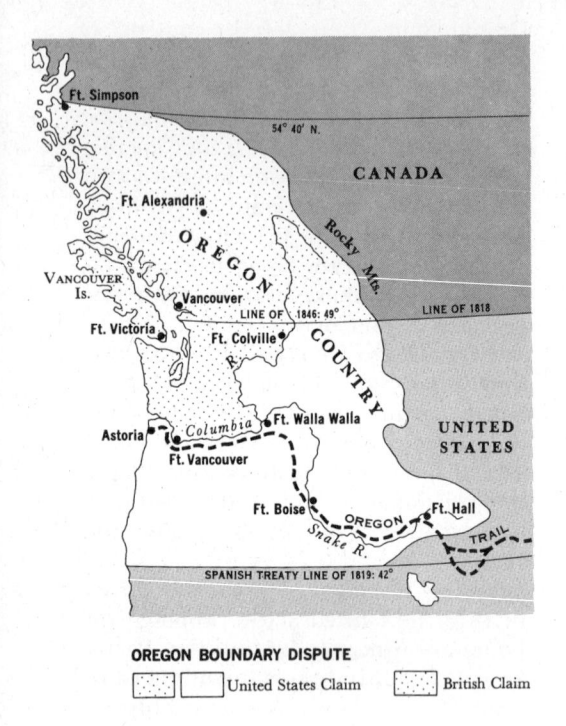

official authority until 1843, when President Tyler appointed Oregon's first Indian agent.

That was the year when the first large body of American immigrants arduously entered the Willamette valley. It was also then that a committee, composed of American pioneers and their French-Canadian neighbors, took a stand at Champoeg favoring the establishment of a provisional government. Once the government came into being, it was effective almost from the start. Men of stamina and initiative determined to do in Oregon what Washington agencies had not done.

Soon the "Oregon fever" had hit the eastern United States, and British settlers in Oregon began to find themselves vastly outnumbered by Americans. This rapid influx of Americans prompted both Britain and the United States to try once again for a peaceful boundary settlement.

Soon after the Democratic victory in the election of 1844 the newly elected President Polk, involved in war with Mexico, once again proposed to Great Britain the boundary line of 49°. When the British minister in Washington peremptorily rejected the American offer, the United States on April 26, 1846, gave the required one year's notice to terminate the joint-occupation treaty of 1818. Later that year the British government, realizing that the United States meant business, decided to settle for the 49° line. Britain submitted a draft treaty to this effect to the United States; Polk submitted the treaty to the Senate, which approved it on June 12 and formally ratified it a week later.

The Anglo-American settlement did not meet with unanimous approval in the United States: Northwestern exponents of Manifest Destiny and antislavery men charged that they had been betrayed by a South which, smugly complacent over the annexation of all of Texas, had been satisfied with less than all of Oregon. But the Oregon Treaty did have the important effect of preventing a possible third war between the United States and Great Britain at a time when the United States was involved in a war with Mexico over the question of Texas.

Settlement of Texas. In the 1820's and 1830's a number of Americans—mostly Southerners—took Mexico's liberal colonization law at face value and migrated to Texas. With the help of Negro slaves and cotton gins they farmed the fertile soil and conducted business under the aegis of Stephen Austin and other *empresarios* who had contracted with the Mexican government to settle a certain number of families in Texas in return for grants of land.

In three centuries the Spanish government had brought only four thousand subjects to Texas. Yet now the Austin communities alone expanded

Democracy and Manifest Destiny

from two thousand in 1828 to more than five and a half thousand three years later. By 1836 more than 25,000 white men, women, and children were scattered between the Sabine River and San Antonio de Bexar. Anglo-Saxon residents far outnumbered those of Spanish ancestry.

Friction between Mexicans and Americans in Texas was probably inevitable. Mexicans, long accustomed to Spanish paternalism, were unprepared for the administrative and legislative responsibilities so readily assumed by Anglo-Saxons. Blunt and self-assertive Americans in Texas were certain that their way of life was freer, healthier, happier, and in all ways superior to that of the Mexicans. Americans looked upon themselves individually and collectively as proper agents to impose reform and progress on what they deemed to be a benighted society, handicapped for generations by superstition and sloth. The average newcomer failed to recognize the spirituality and gentility of the Latin civilization; he criticized the fact that many Mexicans were illiterate and ignorant of his world, but he overlooked the equally pertinent truth that they were sensitive and proud.

Americans in Texas were distressed by gyrations in Mexican policy and the uncertainty of their own status. The Mexican government appeared indifferent to educational needs and law enforcement, and it did nothing to strengthen the Americans' hopes that Texas might be separated from the state of Coahuila, to which it had long been joined. This neglect, as well as divergent attitudes toward religion and slavery, contributed to a drift that endangered the future of Anglo-Saxon and Latin neighbors.

War for Independence. In Mexico City, meanwhile, a growing trend toward dictatorial rule reduced the likelihood of conciliation. The master spirit of despotism was Antonio Lopez de Santa Anna, who became president of Mexico in 1833. Santa Anna, "the Napoleon of the West," was ambitious, adept at intrigue, and an able field commander as long as fate favored him. As president he ruthlessly crushed every semblance of liberalism in Mexico's central government, then turned his attention to Texas, where Americans were vehemently protesting Santa Anna's abandonment of the eleven-year-old "enlightened" Mexican constitution. The Texans' protests ended in a proclamation of independence from Mexico on March 2, 1836.

Four days later Santa Anna and his Mexican troops swept into Texas and massacred every one of the 188 Americans at the Alamo mission in San Antonio. Davy Crockett, Jim Bowie, and William B. Travis were among the American heroes who died defending the Alamo. That same month, at Goliad on the south bank of the San Antonio River, the severely wounded James Walker Fannin surrendered his tiny command to Mexican General José Urrea, with the understanding that Fannin and his soldiers would be accorded the humane treatment normally extended to prisoners of war. Instead, acting under Santa Anna's orders, Urrea mercilessly executed most of the prisoners in cold blood, with Colonel Fannin the last to go. If the shots that killed them were not heard 'round the world in the tradition of Concord bridge, "Remember the Alamo!" and "Remember Goliad!" long served as rallying cries in Texas.

During the war for Texan independence the young republic's forces were in the capable hands of General Sam Houston. This robust native of Virginia had moved in his youth to Tennessee, fought under Andrew Jackson in the War of 1812, studied law, and served as congressman and governor of Tennessee. He settled in Texas after Jackson sent him there to negotiate an Indian treaty in 1832.

Houston demonstrated his leadership at the Battle of San Jacinto on April 21, 1836—not quite two months after the Texans' stunning defeats at the Alamo and Goliad. Houston's troops surprised and defeated Santa Anna's forces and captured the Mexican dictator himself. Houston forced Santa Anna to sign the Treaty of Velasco, by which Mexico agreed to withdraw its forces from Texas and to recognize the Rio Grande as the southwestern boundary of the new Republic of Texas.

The Republic of Texas. Soon after the Texans declared their independence from Mexico they submitted a formal proposal for annexation to the United States, but the proposal was rejected by President Van Buren, who feared precipitating a serious sectional controversy over the extension of slavery into that area. Thus the young republic, under the leadership of Presidents Sam Houston (who served two nonconsecutive terms) and Mirabeau B. Lamar, proceeded to develop its own foreign and domestic policies.

One of the republic's first problems was Mexico's refusal to recognize its independent status. Because Santa Anna had signed the Treaty of Velasco under duress, while a prisoner of war, the Mexicans denied its validity. Thus, while both Europe and the United States officially recognized Texan independence, Mexico withheld recognition.

Though the sizable volunteer army of the San Jacinto campaign was disbanded in 1837, Texas maintained armed troops against the danger of another military campaign by Mexico. The Texas Rangers, loosely organized until then, were developed into a tight-knit corps. Naval troops were maintained in the Gulf of Mexico; as late as 1843, Texan sailors fought against Mexican steam warships.

Maintenance of the navy and defenses against marauding Indians demanded more money than Texas possessed. The republic's civil government also desperately needed financial support. Though bond issues were floated with varying degrees of success, the fiscal structure never was very solid in the period of the republic.

But Texas prospered, despite its shaky financial foundation and its heavy defense expenditures. Texas' population grew rapidly, most of its immigrants continuing to be Americans. Large in territory and rich in untapped resources, Texas was regarded with covetous eyes by those American politicians who viewed it as a promising field for expansion, exploitation, and slavery extension.

Annexation of Texas. Presidents Jackson and Van Buren had been concerned about the North's opposition to the annexation of Texas. Jackson favored annexation and was more outspoken about it after he retired from the presidency. Van Buren marked time, but neither Tyler nor Polk had qualms about working toward annexation. Both were slaveholders, but neither seems to have been thinking primarily about considerations of slavery. (Polk's diary gives abundant evidence to this effect.) Both Tyler and Polk couched their motives in terms of expansion: Would it be to the country's advantage to undergo curtailment of the federal domain? This was substantially the same question Jefferson had asked himself in 1803 with reference to the Louisiana Purchase—and, as Jefferson had, Tyler and Polk answered with a ringing "No!"

But antislavery elements in the North viewed the situation differently. Most Northerners—excluding the tiny minority of abolitionists—agreed with their Southern brothers that the Constitution protected slavery where slavery then existed. Extension of slavery into the West, however, wafted dark clouds of trouble into the skies; the addition of Texas as a slave state was opposed by many citizens north of the Mason-Dixon line.

Early in 1844 President Tyler, anticipating the presidential campaign of that year, sent a treaty for the annexation of Texas to the Senate. When the Senate rejected the treaty by a vote of 35-16, Tyler recommended that Texas be annexed by joint resolution of both houses of Congress, since a joint resolution would require for passage only a simple majority in both houses plus the President's signature, in contrast to the two-thirds Senate majority needed for treaty ratification. Congress adjourned before the measure could be brought to a vote, but when the second session of Congress convened on December 2, 1844, Tyler again urged a joint resolution to annex Texas. This time the resolution passed both House and Senate, and Tyler signed it on March 1, 1845. Under the terms of the resolution, Texas was offered statehood with the understanding that its territory might be subdivided into not more than four states. The Missouri Compromise line of 36°30′ was extended westward to permit slavery in Texas.

Before the annexation resolution was passed, there had been hints and fears of British involvement in the fate of the Texas Republic. It was to England's, as well as to Mexico's, interest to see that Texas stayed out of the United States' orbit; a pending arrangement whereby Texas would ship cotton directly to Liverpool, for example, would mean the tightening of mutually advantageous Anglo-Texan economic ties.

The London government tried to induce Mexico to recognize Texan independence on the condition that the Lone Star Republic would not become part of the United States. Mexico did assent to this proposal in May 1845, and Texans had a choice of annexation to the United States or negotiating such a treaty with Mexico. The offer came too late, however; now that annexation to the United States was its for the taking, Texas found this alternative the more desirable.

War with Mexico. The Mexican government, irate over Texas' independence, became exceedingly resentful when in 1845 its erstwhile possession was formally annexed by the United States. Mexico had threatened to declare war on the United States if Texas were annexed; now, when the congressional resolution for annexation was passed, Mexico withdrew its minister to the United States and severed official relations with the American government.

In June 1845 President Polk ordered General Zachary Taylor and his troops into Texas to defend the territory; Taylor set up camp on the south bank of the Nueces River, about 150 miles from the Rio Grande.

In November of the same year Polk dispatched John Slidell to Mexico on a special mission to discuss the outstanding issues between Mexico and the United States. Slidell was to propose that the United States assume the $2 million in claims of American citizens against the government of Mexico, in return for Mexico's recognition of the Rio Grande as the southwestern boundary of Texas (Mexico claimed the Nueces River as the southwestern line). Polk also authorized Slidell to offer $5 million for New Mexico or $25 million for both New Mexico and California.

But the new Mexican government under President José J. Herrera refused to receive Slidell. Polk, hearing of Slidell's failure, ordered Taylor to proceed to the Rio Grande; when on April 25, 1846, Taylor's troops were attacked without warning by Mexican contingents, Congress declared war on the Republic of Mexico.

The Battles of Palo Alto and Resaca de la Palma followed; the first was an inconclusive artillery duel, the second a smashing American victory that sent the troops of Mariano Arista scuttling back over the river past Matamoros and safely out of the American range. These opening engagements of May 1846 were followed by the major encounters of Monterey the next September and Buena Vista in February 1847. General Taylor, bearing battlefield and theater responsibility in the Monterey-Saltillo area, displayed great gallantry and was popular with his men. However, he did not make much progress in the direction of Mexico City, partly because Polk transferred most of the seasoned soldiers from Taylor's command to that of Major General Winfield Scott.

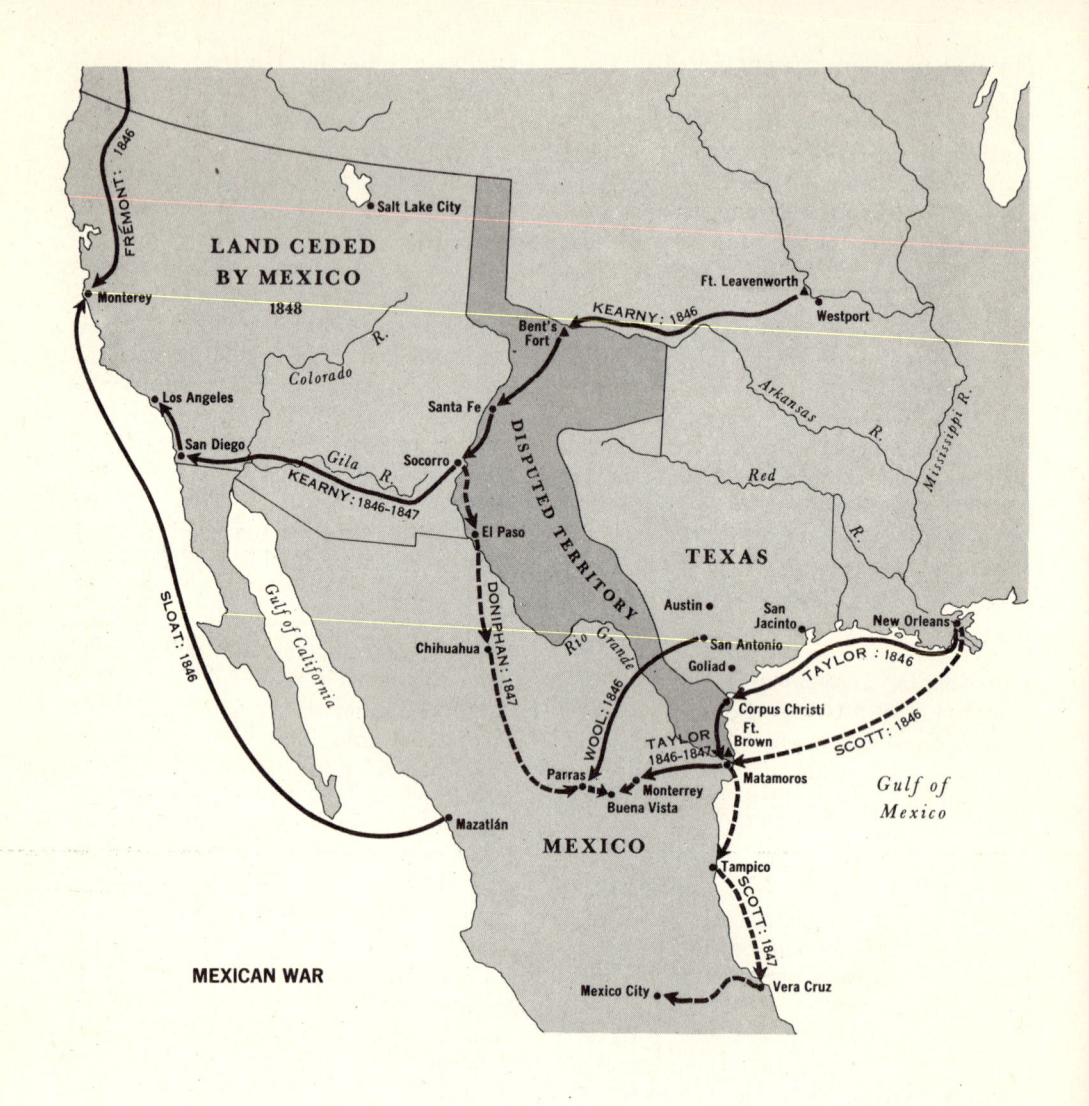

It was Scott, who, landing at Vera Cruz in March of 1847, made that Gulf port his supply base and advanced inland to the mountain pass of Cerro Gordo, where he routed Mexican General Santa Anna. Other battles under Scott were Contreras, Churubusco, Molino del Rey, and Chapultepec. All took place in 1847 and all, like Taylor's four encounters, were American victories. Scott entered Mexico City in September, but it was bloodsoaked Buena Vista more than half a year

152 Democracy and Manifest Destiny

before that would make Taylor the next President.

Although war between the United States and Mexico broke out in May 1846, the news did not reach California for a number of weeks. Meanwhile, a group of California settlers, aided by explorer John C. Frémont and by American naval officers, had revolted against Mexican rule and proclaimed California an independent republic. They raised a flag on which a grizzly bear, a red star, and the legend "Republic of California" were juxtaposed. When news that the United States had declared war against Mexico was received, however, the significance of the Bear Flag Revolt was greatly diminished.

In the summer of 1846 Colonel Stephen W. Kearny and a detachment of about 1700 troops took possession of Santa Fe in the name of the United States. Polk subsequently ordered Kearny to take charge of American operations in California. The American elements, previously led by naval Commodore R. F. Stockton, were brought together under Kearny, and by autumn of 1846 the conquest of California was complete.

Treaty of Guadalupe Hidalgo. In April 1847 President Polk, eager to end the fighting as quickly as possible, delegated Nicholas P. Trist, chief clerk of the State Department, as peace commissioner to Mexico. Trist's instructions were to negotiate a treaty recognizing the Rio Grande as the southwest boundary of Texas and ceding to the United States for $15 million all Mexican territory between the Rio Grande and the Pacific Ocean above the latitude of El Paso. The United States also would assume the claims of United States citizens against Mexico up to $3.25 million.

Once in Mexico, Trist badly bungled the negotiations and was peremptorily recalled by Polk. Trist, however, refused to return to Washington and, with no official authority, signed on February 2, 1848, a treaty which incorporated all the provisions of his annulled instructions. Polk was furious at Trist's disobedience, but he immediately sent the treaty to the Senate for ratification. Though the Treaty of Guadalupe Hidalgo was denounced by two vocal minorities—those who had demanded the cession of all of Mexico and those who wanted none of the southwestern territory—it was ratified by the Senate on March 10, 1848. The United States found itself in possession of the mammoth region which includes the present states of California, Nevada, and Utah, most of Arizona and New Mexico, and parts of Colorado and Wyoming.

Eruption of the Slavery Issue. Northern reactions to the War with Mexico were even more intense than they had been to Texas' annexation. No matter how moderate they had previously been, antiextension Northerners began to heed abolitionists' propaganda that a vicious "slave power" must be checked. According to this version of affairs, the South had dominated the federal government since its establishment. Southerners had occupied the presidency forty-six out of fifty-eight years. Three out of five Chief Justices had been Southerners. Southerners had held and were then holding key cabinet offices and other appointive posts. Although the South was in a minority, slave states had equality in the Senate and a disproportionate share of policy-making positions.

Now the South (so the story went) was afraid that the North's population growth and the prospect that northwestern territories would come into the Union as free states would destroy the South's political advantage. Therefore, it was argued that a nefarious "power" —arrogant, determined, and utterly unscrupulous—sought to strengthen itself by spreading an evil which enlightened men righteously deplored.

The threat would affect the Southwest (as a result of the Mexican War), the West as a whole, and northern states as well. The "slave power," the argument continued, would try to annex every Mexican mile and Central America and the West Indies in the bargain.

At the same time, there were Southerners who saw the North as the fundamentally culpable aggressor section. The pamphlets of abolitionists stirred up Negroes, they asserted; slave insurrections had resulted and would continue to result from senseless agitation. Antislavery virulence had long been limited to a few Northern hotheads, but now the zealotry was epidemic. Northerners petitioned to do away with slavery in the District of Columbia and on federal property in the South. The same intolerance had been manifested in opposition to annexing Texas. And did not northern states abysmally fail to live up to constitutional commitments when they repeatedly refused to enforce the Fugitive Slave Law of 1793? So ran the Southern arguments.

As the world has often seen in situations where emotion interferes with reason, there were exaggerations on both sides rather than complete departures from truth. On the one hand, there simply was no "slave power" in the abolitionist sense of the term. There was no unanimity of Southern opinion as to policies. From Jefferson's day through Jackson's to Polk's, all Southern officeholders in high places had not been of one political mind. Chief Justice Taney, for example, did not invariably hand down Supreme Court opinions resembling those of Chief Justice Marshall. Taney was a Marylander and Marshall a Virginian, yet their legal tenets and those of other Southerners were poles apart. Contrary to what was charged in certain circles, there was no widespread Southern *or* Northern conspiracy. Indeed, mingled with accusations of "slave power" influence and with abolitionist rancor were extremists' attacks on the continuing moderation of many fellow sectionalists.

In the 1840's, the issues of slavery and antislavery, expansion and containment became intermeshed. If the Civil War had never taken place, Americans might not now be inclined to stress North-South antipathies respecting the West. But in the light of the battles and campaigns from Fort Sumter and Bull Run to Cold Harbor and Five Forks, moderns are tempted to point out that the slavery question was potential dynamite even in the 1840's.

Filling Out the West. While settlement of Texas and the Oregon country was proceeding apace, other areas were luring pioneers westward in search of land or mineral wealth. Some who had started out on the Oregon Trail bound for the Northwest changed their destination to California. The path to California followed the Oregon Trail to the Continental Divide where, turning southwestward, it became the California Trail and led through the Sierra Nevada into California.

Before 1840, only fur traders penetrated to California, and whaling ships stopped for supplies occasionally. In the early 1840's some farmers began to move into the Pacific Coast valleys, but, when war with Mexico broke out in 1846, there were only about seven hundred non-Mexican Americans in California. The discovery of gold at Sutter's Mill near Sacramento in 1848 started the "gold rush," which brought the total population of the area to ninety thousand when California became a state in 1850. The gold seekers came by sea around Cape Horn, or partly by sea after crossing the Isthmus of Panama or other parts of Central America and Mexico on foot, or by various routes overland across the North American continent. The latter route was chosen by most immi-

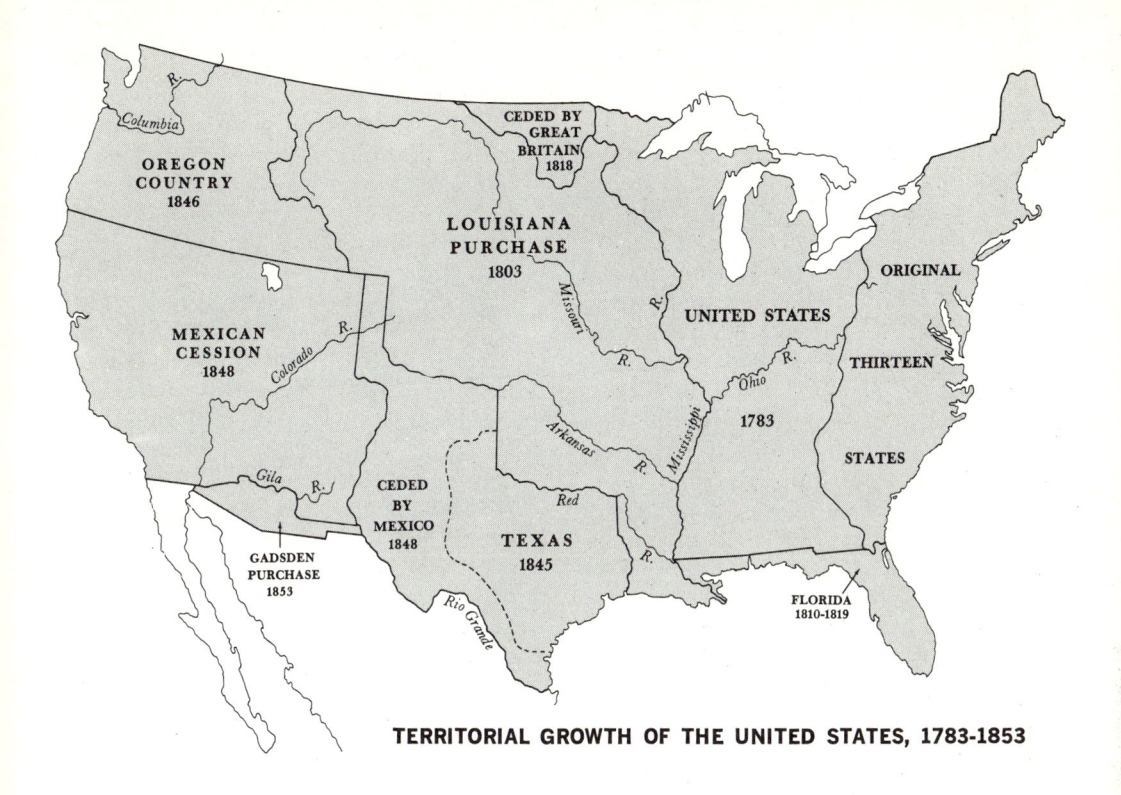

TERRITORIAL GROWTH OF THE UNITED STATES, 1783-1853

grants, an estimated 40,000 using it in 1849 alone.

By the 1850's there were two frontiers in America, one moving westward beyond the Mississippi and the other moving eastward from California and Oregon into the Rocky Mountain area. The first settlement to fill this gap was made by the Mormons, who moved to Utah in 1847. This religious group had been founded by Joseph Smith in New York state in 1827. They had moved to Ohio in 1831 and to Illinois in 1839 to escape persecution, and then, for the same reason and under the leadership of Brigham Young, they decided to move to a desert valley around the Great Salt Lake, where they hoped to find peace. They had some misfortunes and near disasters in the first few years but eventually became prosperous. With the close of the Mexican War the Mormons lost the nominal Mexican jurisdiction under which they had been free to do as they pleased.

The U. S. Congress organized the Mormon lands into Utah Territory in 1850, naming Brigham Young as territorial governor. By 1860 there were forty thousand persons in Utah, but it was not admitted as a state until 1896 because the Mormon church did not renounce the practice of polygamy until 1890. For a few years after 1849 the Mormons profited substantially from the sale of supplies to gold seekers on the way to California.

The treaty ending the war with Mexico filled out the present continental limits of the United States—with one exception. The one exception was a strip of land in what later became southern New Mexico and Arizona, which was purchased from Mexico in 1853 because it was thought to provide the best route for a railroad to California. This transaction is commonly referred to as the Gadsden Purchase. With it the American "empire" was complete from Atlantic to Pacific.

Westward Expansion and Economic Growth, 1824-1848

THE ECONOMICS OF EXPANSION

The West and the Transportation Revolution. From the beginning of human life on earth, man has lived in close association with rivers and streams. Water transportation was the natural way for men to transport both themselves and their goods, for rivers cut through wildernesses men could not penetrate. Therefore, when the settlers moving into the American frontier were forced to return to the most primitive conditions of living, rivers naturally became their first important means of inland transportation.

One of the great drawbacks to river transportation is that the river does not always go where the traffic needs to go. That became true in the United States as soon as the territory west of the Appalachian Mountains was opened for settlement. Rivers descended eastward from the Appalachian watersheds to the Atlantic or westward to meet the Ohio and Mississippi, but no waterway connected East and West. Thus the great enthusiasm for building national roads during the "Turnpike Era" from 1800 to 1830 was occasioned partly by the fact that they were to connect the Ohio River system with the Atlantic coastal rivers. However, transportation over these road and river routes was prohibitively expensive except for light and very valuable merchandise. The best outlet for the bulky Western produce was not eastward but southward on flatboats down the Ohio and Mississippi Rivers to New Orleans. To try to propel flatboats back up the river against the current, however, was still impractical; manufactured products needed by Western settlers—such as guns, ammunition, traps, axes, plows, tools, and even shoes and cloth—still had to come in overland from the East.

Thus, because America's immediate economic problem was the accomplishment of great distances practically and inexpensively, the new steam power developed in England in the eighteenth century was applied in America to water transportation even earlier than to industry. Beginning with John Fitch in 1786, a series of American inventors worked on the problem of driving a boat with steam, culminating with Robert Fulton's commercial success in powering his *Clermont* up the Hudson River in 1807. In the following decade steamboats were successfully tried on the Ohio and Mississippi Rivers. By 1829 there were 200 steamboats in operation on the western rivers, and by 1842 the number had reached 450. A decade later there were considerably over 1000. Partly because of the special needs of the West and partly because early steamboats were too fragile for ocean use (trans-Atlantic steamer service was not frequent until mid-century), more steamboats were in service on the Mississippi River system than anywhere else in the world. Pittsburgh, Cincinnati, and Louisville began as river towns, and New Orleans became one of America's greatest ports.

Meanwhile, in an attempt to avoid the roundabout route through New Orleans, Northerners turned their attention to canal building, which had been so successful in England in the 1760's and 1770's. The first such waterway of great importance was New York's Erie Canal, connecting the Great Lakes and the Hudson River (and thus the port of New York). Upon its completion in 1825, freight charges from Buffalo to New York City were cut from $100 to $10 a ton, the time of the trip from twenty days to six. Migrants began to use the canal to gain access to the West, and Buffalo, Cleveland, Detroit, Chicago, and other cities began to sprout around the Great Lakes, with the area beginning to fill up with settlers just as the Ohio valley had earlier. As a result of the canal trade, New York City grew rapidly in wealth and population, becoming the greatest port on the Atlantic seaboard. The nation was propelled into the "Canal Era" (1825-1840), with other sections from Illinois to Massachusetts trying to imitate the success of New York.

Yet rivers and canals had their shortcomings. During winter, frozen waterways could not be used in the North; rivers followed inconvenient courses, and canals could not be built in rough or hilly country. The coming railroads would overcome all of these limitations.

Steam-powered rail locomotives had already won success in England when the Baltimore and Ohio Railroad instituted the first few miles of American rail service in 1830. Soon other short lines were built elsewhere, and by 1840, 2808 miles of track had been laid. By 1850 the mileage had more than tripled, to 9029 miles, and by 1860 it had tripled again, to 30,626 miles (as compared to industrial Britain's 10,410 miles). The railroads, which connected the Atlantic coast to Chicago and St. Louis by the 1850's, for the first time provided the West with exactly the kind of transportation it needed. Western products, no matter what their bulk, could now be moved regardless of weather or terrain directly to Eastern markets for overseas shipment. Manufactures from the East and abroad could come in freely. Traffic on the rivers and canals declined. With the coming of the rails, the commercial and industrial East and the agricultural West were tied more closely together in common economic bonds.

The Northeast and the Industrial Revolution. Under the impact of continually expanding trade, each section of the country underwent a characteristic economic evolution of its own. New England, for example, the section which achieved the lead in population in the colonial era, was the first to pass from agriculture to commerce and industry. The absence of good soil for agriculture and the abundance of good harbors adjacent to ample supplies of pine and hardwood had turned its people to shipbuilding and overseas commerce in colonial days. It was no accident, too, that the Industrial Revolution should have entered America through New England, for towns well located for commerce were also attractive for manufactures. Mills and factories need to be near shipping points.

Other circumstances contributed to the growth of industrialism in the Northeast. In the early stages of the Industrial Revolution, streams were still a must for turning the water wheels that turned the machinery of mills and factories, and the Northeast was favorably endowed with water power. In Chapter 5 we saw how the Embargo and the War of 1812, in restricting overseas trade, had driven idle commercial capital into investment in domestic industry. The tremendous potentialities of trade with the West, facilitated first by the Erie Canal and then by the railroads, provided further incentive for the manufacture of industrial products. Finally, even after steam had replaced water power in industry, manufacturing continued for a time to be located where capital and labor were already concentrated—in the Northeast.

The rise of industrialism in the northern United States had economic and social consequences of such a revolutionary character that it has been called —as in England—the Industrial Revolution. It revolutionized the nature of business organization, of labor, of population distribution, and of the life and welfare of all Americans.

The Corporate Revolution. The arrival of industrialism meant the beginning of the growth of large factories and large railroad networks. And as the size of businesses increased, the old methods of organizing and financing business enterprises by means of individual ownership or partnership became inadequate. The costs of maintaining fleets of trading ships or small mills did not exceed the personal fortune of individuals, but with the coming of railroads and large-scale manufactures, the enormous costs of buildings, equipment, and stock began to run into millions of dollars, far beyond the financial resources of even the wealthiest person, and the risks were too great to be undertaken singly. As a consequence, entrepreneurs turned increasingly to the corporate form of enterprise.

The chief disadvantage of the partnership was its "unlimited liability" for business debts: that is, if the firm failed, creditors could force the sale of the owners' personal property, as well as their business property, to satisfy their claims. The partnership, therefore, usually comprised a very few individuals who knew and trusted one another, and who were willing to take the risks together. Moreover, the partnership had no permanence; it dissolved and the company collapsed when any single member took it into his mind to withdraw. The corporation, on the other hand, is a separate legal entity or "person," distinct from its owners. An owner may sell his stock in the corporation without the assent of the other owners, and the corporation remains *permanent*. Most important is the feature of "limited liability." If the corporation fails, the owners are liable to lose only what they paid for stock in the corporation; the creditors have no claim on their personal resources. Finally, by the issuance of stock, the corporation can draw on the contributions of literally thousands of investors and accumulate the large amounts of capital needed for big industry.

In spite of its advantages, the corporate form was not without its opponents in the Jacksonian period. Jackson, Jefferson before him, and even the father of free enterprise or laissez faire, the English economist Adam Smith, had attacked corporations as according "exclusive privilege" and limiting "free competition." But what they were attacking was the kind of incorporation that was known before the 1830's. Corporation charters had been obtainable only by special enactment of a legislature and had usually been granted for some specific enterprise that had to be run as a monopoly in order to be profitable. Thus turnpikes, canals, bridges, and banks—enterprises of a semipublic character—were often conducted under charters granting exclusive privileges. Part of Jackson's hostility toward the Bank of the United States can be traced to its monopolistic character. And even less clearly beneficial to all the public was the construction of industrial establishments.

However, the wider markets in the West and the new technical processes made increased capital so necessary to industry that corporation charters were sought more and more in spite of possible public opposition. Moreover, to make incorporation democratic and consonant with Jacksonian equal-rights principles, Whigs and like-minded Democrats urged "general incorporation laws" (as distinct from special legislative grants) which would make corporation charters available to all who could meet certain legal requirements. Beginning in the 1830's and continuing into the 1840's and 1850's corporations began to proliferate under the new system of general laws.

The Whig party, which generally favored business interests (as would later its successor, the Republican party), had advocated free incorporation as a method of inaugurating a kind of "democratic" capitalism; that is, business would no longer be dependent upon rich men but could gather the combined resources of countless small investors. However, this multiplication of ownership eventually resulted in a revolutionary change in the nature of business organization. As the number of stockholders or owners in a corporation rose into the thousands and as they were dispersed about the country, actual management or "control" of the company fell into the hands of individuals who were not dominant owners or perhaps not even stockholders at all. Under the system of individual proprietorship or partnership, ownership and control had been in the hands of the same person; the corporate system began the process of divorcing ownership from control and of creating a vast class of investors dependent, in so far as their profits were concerned, on the actions of others, of corporate managers. The inherent danger was that the managers might not act in the interests of the owners. In former days when the owner managed his own business, an owner who defrauded the company defrauded himself. However, with the separation of ownership and control, the "insiders" or managers could systematically loot a company for their own profit. Said a contemporary observer concerning the stock market scandals of 1854:

The spring trade of '54 opened gloomily. . . . In June it was discovered that the Parker Vein Company had flooded the market with an immense and unauthorized issue of stock. The first of the next month New York was startled by the intelligence that Robert Schuyler, President of the New York and New Haven Railroad, had been selling some 20,000 illegal shares at par,—and was now a defaulter for two millions. Almost simultaneously it was ascertained that Alexander Kyle, Secretary of the Harlem Railroad Company, had made an issue of forged stock to the amount of $300,000. Other developments of breaches of trust came flocking from the inland cities.[1]

Following the Civil War, several more such scandals came to light, most notably the case of Crédit Mobilier involving the building of the Union Pacific Railroad.

The Rise of Industrial Populations. The Industrial Revolution led to an entirely new evaluation of the forces affecting the location of industry. Before the steam engine was developed, the use of water power tended to scatter manufacturing among a large number of small or medium-sized towns, for the capacity of any given dam site was limited. The triumph of steam reinforced the tendency of manufacturing to concentrate in large cities.

Industrial employment brought new problems not imaginable in the previous handicraft period of individual workshops. In America, as in England, little was understood of proper precautions for safety and health in the new factories; people did not know how to cope with such problems because never before had they existed; factory laws even in England were not introduced until the 1840's. Moreover, congested living quarters in the growing industrial cities of New England and the Middle Atlantic states often resulted in a deplorable lack, not only of sanitation, but also of the minimum requirements for decent or comfortable human existence. Hours of work were usually long, wages low, and schools inadequate for the children of workers. Workers whose wages were low could afford little for housing. The idea of public transportation had not been developed, so that workers had to live within walking distance of their source of employment. All of these conditions worked together to produce a type of housing for industrial workers which could become slums of the worst sort.

Perhaps the greatest evil was the increasing employment of children; while the earlier hand industries required skilled male workers, the new steam-driven machines required such minimal skill to operate that even women and children could perform the simple but arduous and monotonous tasks of factory work. On the other hand, conditions were perhaps not so disagreeable as they were in England, and there were bright spots on the American industrial landscape. The novelist Hawthorne in one of his rambles about the New England countryside remarked on the bright, cheerful faces looking out through the factory windows, and the factory girls of Lowell, Massachusetts,

---

[1] James K. Medbury, *Men and Mysteries of Wall Street* (Boston: Fields, Osgood, 1870), p. 309.

were known to dress neatly and to publish a literary weekly. But these pleasant scenes were fast fading into the past.

Urban industrialism resulted not only from new production techniques and new Western markets but also from increased efficiency in agriculture. Improved farm methods and farm machinery permitted more people to be siphoned off into industrial production. As a result, the cities grew between 1820 and 1850 much faster than the population as a whole. In 1820 only one person in fourteen lived in a city of 2500 or more; in 1850 nearly one person in six lived in such a city. This meant an increase of more than fivefold in the population of cities, while the whole population had increased just over twofold during those years.

The rapid growth of industrial cities in the North gave consternation to many Americans who had associated crowded cities and the factory grind with a Europe of decadence and oppression. Overwhelmingly most Americans were still rural, still untouched by conditions developing in the Northeast; but those few Americans who were witnessing cities filling with immigrants and developing slums, vice, and crime were deeply disturbed. The traditional Jeffersonian view of America—the land of democratic simplicity—seemed to be threatened by new problems of industrial complexity.

The Rise of Labor. Among the first to react to these unsatisfactory conditions were the workers themselves. The rise of industry was followed by the rise of unionism. However, it was most often the skilled artisans of the building trades and other industries who made the most effective protest. The unskilled workers, who were the worst off, contributed little to the support of movements from which they would be the greatest beneficiaries.

The oldest labor organizations in America date back to the late eighteenth century, when various skilled craftsmen banded together to obtain higher wages, shorter hours, and other benefits from their merchant-artisan employers. But it was not until the late 1820's and the 1830's that aggressive union activity began with the establishment of strong craft unions in Philadelphia, Boston, New York, Providence, and other cities. An attempt was even made to form a National Trades Union in 1834, but although the group held conventions for several years, the effort failed to achieve an enduring result. The most successful of the early unions were local groups which were primarily political in their objectives, working especially hard for various social reforms like free public schools. Aided by favorable public opinion, labor was able to make substantial gains by legislative action. By the middle of the nineteenth century the idea of free public education, at least through the primary grades, was pretty generally accepted. Beginning in the late 1840's, a number of important states began to establish the ten-hour day as the legal maximum work day. But it was usually possible for a worker to make a special contract with his employer to work longer, and economic necessity frequently drove him to do so, nullifying the effect of the statutory provision. Nevertheless, such laws represented a gain for labor, since they helped to establish the idea of a ten-hour limit.

Finally, in the 1850's, unions less interested in political activity than in "bread-and-butter" issues (wages, hours, and working conditions) gathered momentum. During this period, the first permanent national unions of separate trades were set up, beginning with the National Typographical Union in 1852.

The appearance of solid and enduring national unions was a sign of the end of America's industrial adolescence. Many more decades were to pass before economic conditions were to convince even a substantial minority of American workers or employers that unions were a good and permanent element in industrial relations. The individualistic tradition and conditioning of both workers and employers prevented that result sooner. But national unions were here to stay, and their very existence testified to the arrival of a new period in American economic history.

The South and King Cotton. While the commercial and industrial North and the agricultural West were closing together in common economic bonds, the South remained exclusively agricultural and largely dependent upon Europe and the outside world to absorb its products. Basically, the South was pulling away from its earlier common interests with other parts of the country and was tying itself to an international market economy in which it became the specialized producer of seven eighths of the world's cotton fiber.

However, there were certain financial obstacles which prevented the South from completely freeing itself from dependence on the North. A growing demand for slaves meant continually rising prices for them. To buy land and slaves for the expansion of cultivation required new increments of capital, which the planter class—a leisure-loving and cultured social aristocracy—could not provide for itself. New capital, therefore, had to be acquired in the financial markets of the North and Europe in competition with an expanding and increasingly productive mechanized industry. The shipping and sale of cotton tended to be handled by mercantile agencies in the principal Northeastern seaports, because the highly specialized shipping requirements of the Southern economy could not be met efficiently except in conjunction with the more general trade of the major ports. Southern ports did not offer such possibilities of pooling cargo and warehouse space, and Southerners complained that their own business was taken away from them by Northern merchants who obtained the profits of the cotton trade and kept the Southern planters dependent upon them for mercantile credit.

Nevertheless, the South continued to follow its policy of determined divergence from the economies of the other sections of the nation and to seek a free world market. In the end, Southerners felt that they could escape submission to the North and West on economic policies which they thought would destroy slavery and the plantation system only by seceding from the Union, and that was the path they chose. It was the path to the most destructive event in our national history, the Civil War.

CHAPTER 9

THE AMERICAN RENAISSANCE

AMERICAN TRAITS

The Frontier Individualist. No other trait of the Jacksonian American was more marked than what we might call his "frontier individualism." There was grubbiness on the frontier. There could be narrow-mindedness. And this individualism was not necessarily "nonconformist," that is, marked by willingness to act differently from one's fellow Americans; most Americans, indeed, took the cue for their behavior from the majority. However, in the main, men who invaded the wilderness and established settlements in the West looked upon themselves as economically self-reliant and capable of almost any exertion or achievement. Whether chasing Indians or felling forests or probing the bend and stretch of streams, they developed such qualities as versatility, robustness, and resilience, together with the physical courage which was expected of the frontiersman.

In part, these character tendencies were a heritage from colonial times, when bravery and imagination characterized the Atlantic frontiersman. In part, they resulted from the recent immigrants' impression that the way to get ahead was to make a virtue of necessity and emulate the older Americans. A third reason lay in the nature of the country—particularly in its combination of incessant, often cruel, demands and boundless opportunities.

American Nationalism. Closely linked to this "rugged individualism" of a largely economic sort was the social trait of national pride. In the half century preceding 1830, the United States had made astounding progress from the year of the Battle of King's Mountain through that of Jackson's first inauguration. The victory of Yorktown, the Constitution, the Bill of Rights, the Louisiana Purchase, the Battle of New Orleans, the Missouri Compromise, and the Monroe Doctrine were landmarks passed within the memory of many living citizens. The increase of the population, growth of the national domain, and development of cities and industries were only a few of the reasons for Americans' sense of gratification.

As earnestly as any other interpreter, the nationalistic historian George Bancroft put into words the story of America's glory. In his *History of the United States,* which began appearing in 1834, the scholar lauded the colonial past in terms of divine origin and lofty mission. In politics Bancroft was a partisan Democrat, and his volumes were criticized on the score that every page "voted for Jackson." Bancroft expressed in his history what fellow Democrats like John L. O'Sullivan of New York and Robert Rantoul of Boston wrote in their essays and what other Americans echoed in Fourth of July orations.

Romanticism Revisited. The growth of democratic government during the Jacksonian period reflected a new emphasis on the value of the individual, or the "common" man, apart from his role as an atom in the complex structure of society. This rising ideal of individual worth was a prominent feature of American Romanticism, another leading cultural trend of the pre-Civil War period. Although the Romantic view of society has been discussed in Chapter 6 (see pp. 109-10), a review of its characteristics will help in the understanding of American intellectual and cultural development from 1824 to 1848.

Romantic writers and artists placed new emphasis on imagination, emotion, experimentation, informality, the appreciation of external nature, and the capturing of transient—rather than static—aspects and moods of life. They tended toward the picturesque, the exotic, the sensuous, and the supernatural. In contrast to men of the Enlightenment, who had emphasized reason and intellect, the Romanticists believed that human intuition and poetic sensibility were more likely than reason to lead man to truth. They viewed society as an evolving organism susceptible to refashioning and improvement, and their goal was the "liberation" of man—the full development of his individual potentialities.

The Romanticists' view of society as an evolving organism susceptible to improvement led naturally to the growth of reform movements against customs and institutions which they felt were hindrances to individual development. Since the Continental nations had not yet achieved representative democracy, European efforts at reform were often political; but because Americans found in their own nation the necessary political foundations for rapid progress toward perfection, American Romantics tended to concern themselves less with political reform than with social and humanitarian reforms and the cultivation of the arts. For example, the period saw great emphasis on the temperance movement; the extension of social and political rights to various classes and to women; the first important work with the handicapped and mentally ill; and a vocal attack on the Southern institution of slavery. The various reform movements of the pre-Civil War era are analyzed in Chapter 12.

RELIGION, PHILOSOPHY, AND THE ARTS

The Unitarian Influence. The Romanticist's emphasis on the innate value of the individual and the importance of self-development was closely related to the religious view of man held by the loosely knit group of Unitarians who had challenged the doctrines of the strict, theocratic Puritans of New England (see pp. 49-52, 113-15).

Unitarians accepted some of the traditional Christian revelation, but only so far as that revelation was in accordance with man's reason. They rejected the Calvinistic belief in the doctrine of election, since such a belief implied that God was arbitrary and capricious; instead, Unitarians stressed God's benevolence. They believed that Christ was divine in the sense in which all men are divine or have an element of divinity in their nature. Christ's life represented to the Unitarians an example to be emulated by men who were already innately good and spiritually free.

Indeed, an intellectual and spiritual bridge between the Unitarianism of 1800-1820 and the transcendentalism of the 1830's was provided by William Ellery Channing. Implicit in his ideas was the prominence of the individual—

independent, yet one with God—spiritually obliged to "transcend" his individualistic self by intimate identification with the Deity. Although Channing had been reared in the creed of Calvinism, he came to deny the doctrine of original sin and to believe strongly in freedom of the will.

Channing himself helped in the formation of the American Unitarian Association in 1825. This was ironic, because he personally deplored "the narrow walls of a particular church"— that is, an organized church which the very establishment of an association seemed to imply. Indeed, under the association's aegis, a Unitarian ministry and church membership did develop, and far more attention than Channing approved of was paid to such formalities as creeds, church offices, and church organization.

The revolt against this trend took two forms: one type of "dissent from the dissenters" was that of Ralph Waldo Emerson; a second was that of Theodore Parker. Each of these ministers was convinced that religion should be a vital personal experience, hinging upon inspiration rather than upon forms and doctrines. The manner of the two men, however, differed drastically. Parker's harsh, sarcastic language ignited burning resentment among the conservative majority of the older Unitarian ministers and laymen. While denying such things as miracles and denouncing popular ignorance and corrupt leadership, he demanded that "we worship, as Jesus did, with no mediator, with nothing between us and the Father of all." A learned scholar in both philosophies and sciences, Parker urged that theology embrace scientific methods of inquiry.

Emerson and Transcendentalism. Emerson gave up his Boston ministry in 1832 because he considered the Unitarianism of his day—which by then had become "orthodox" in its turn—too cold, too formal, too ritualistic. He felt, too, that Unitarianism did not go far enough toward the rehabilitation of the individual. The new doctrine of which Emerson became the chief interpreter is known as transcendentalism; Emerson's first book, *Nature* (1836), was the bible of the early transcendentalists.

Transcendentalism has been defined philosophically as "the recognition in man of the capacity of knowing truth intuitively, or of attaining knowledge transcending the reach of the senses." Unitarianism had prepared the way for transcendentalism by insisting that man is essentially good and may trust his own perceptions of religious truth. But the transcendentalists carried this reliance upon the intuitive perceptions of the individual much further than conventional Unitarianism would warrant; in fact, some carried it so far as to set aside even the authority of the Christian Bible. Emerson renounced all authority, all standards and laws externally imposed: "Nothing is at last sacred but the integrity of your own mind."

Emerson viewed the many different aspects of the universe as diverse manifestations of one all-encompassing central spirit, which he called the Over-Soul. The individual man, according to Emerson, could become a channel for the higher truths of the Over-Soul if he would only develop his intuitive powers to the fullest. A logical result of Emerson's doctrine of the Over-Soul was his belief in self-reliance, as expounded in his famous essay of that name. According to this doctrine, every man has something of the divine in his nature and is capable of establishing a direct relationship with the universal spirit. To do so, he must rely upon his own spiritual perceptions; he must be spiritually self-reliant. Said Emerson, "Trust thyself; every heart vibrates to that iron string."

The philosophy which Emerson taught was essentially a variety of idealism—idealism as distinct from materialism. Broadly speaking, idealism and materialism are opposing philosophies —an idealist being one who believes that the basic reality is spiritual and the materialist being one who believes that the basic reality is physical or material. The temper of the times in which Emerson lived—which accorded prime attention to nation building, the exploitation of resources, and scientific thought—aided and abetted a materialistic view. Yet Emerson became one of the outstanding idealists of modern times. However, Emerson was no mere ivory-tower thinker. His idealism was applied. He was concerned ultimately with the conduct of life. He felt in both a practical and an idealistic way that man can draw upon a power greater than his own. He suggested a spiritual energy of the universe and the availability of this energy to man in facing the tasks of life.

Communitarianism. Emerson's transcendentalist disciples, usually more interested in practice than in theory, attempted to apply Emerson's individualistic doctrines in various ways. One result was a movement known as "communitarianism," which was popular in the 1830's and 1840's. Much of the enthusiasm for communal living, however, had come from Britain and the continent of Europe long before *Nature* was published. The idea was for a limited number of people to live together in a little community, wholly or mainly self-sufficient in terms of economics, culture, and religious worship, and more or less separated from the general society surrounding it. These communities could be either religious or secular. Among the Christian communitarians were the Shakers, who established settlements in New England, New York, Kentucky, and elsewhere, and who believed in separation from the world, simplicity of language, and an austere way of life. Religious communities also were founded by the Mormons as well as by several Adventist sects.

Secular communitarianism resembled the Christian kind in that the purpose was to join people together in order to face collectively the challenge of the frontier or to solve collectively the hazards of living in an industrialized New England society. Among the better-known experiments were New Harmony in Indiana, the North American Phalanx in New Jersey, and Brook Farm and Fruitlands in Massachusetts. Secular and religious communitarianism usually shared such features as vegetarianism, prohibition of alcoholic beverages, the dignifying of labor through mutual help, and community ownership and control of property. While most of the secular communities originated from the social contract theories of the eighteenth century, Fruitlands and Brook Farm are worthy of special mention—for these are identified with transcendentalism.

Both of these Massachusetts communities were composed largely of transcendentalists who sought an atmosphere conducive to transcendental thinking, transcendental discussion, and cultivation of reason in a place set apart from a society intent upon materialistic gain. Emerson's influence was distinctly, if indirectly, felt in both communities; but, though Emerson paid them visits, he never became closely identified with either except through his writings and his pupils. Like most such secular experiments, neither community lasted long—perhaps because of the absence of explicitly Christian zeal which, in the case of the Mormons and the Shakers, proved a reliable source of community strength.

Henry David Thoreau. As the leading spirit of the transcendentalist movement and of self-reliant individualism, Emerson significantly influenced communitarianism. As a disciple of nature, he encouraged a back-to-nature movement and counseled men to live in simplicity, according to the prescriptions of nature. Compared with Henry David Thoreau, however, Emerson was merely a theorist; Emerson was "civilized," dignified, and prosperous; he lived in a good house in Concord and wore good clothes. Thoreau, on the other hand, was ascetic, primitive, even "eccentric" in comparison. It was he who most thoroughly put Emerson's mandates of individualism into practice; Thoreau's life was a practical application of Emerson's ideas of plain living. Fourteen years younger than Emerson, Thoreau graduated without distinction from Harvard College in 1837, taught school, helped his father manufacture lead pencils in the early 1840's, did odd jobs in the Emerson household, and in general was a jack-of-all-trades, engaging in fence building, house painting, carpentering, gardening, berry picking, and surveying.

Thoreau's greatest experiment in plain living, or living close to nature, was his two-year residence in a shack on the edge of Walden Pond near Concord, Massachusetts. Here he dwelt among the woods, the birds, and the beasts, read and wrote with few distractions, and shunned the established social order. "I went to the woods because I wished to live deliberately," Thoreau wrote, "to front only the essential facts of life. . . . I had not lived there a week before my feet wore a path from my door to the pondside. . . . How worn and dusty, then, must be the highways of the world, how deep the ruts of tradition and conformity!" From this experience at the pond came Thoreau's famous work, *Walden*, published in 1854.

Independence and self-reliance dominated Thoreau's life. He refused support of any organized church: "Men call me a skeptic, but I'm only too conscientious to go to church." In his detestation of slavery, he actively helped the "underground railway" to convey runaway slaves to the freedom of Canada, and he spent a night in jail rather than pay a small tax in support of a government that prosecuted what he considered an unjust war against Mexico in order to extend slave territory into the Southwest. Out of this latter experience came his essay "Civil Disobedience," perhaps the most famous political essay ever written in America and one which Henry S. Canby has called "Gandhi's textbook in his campaign of passive resistance against British government in India." In it Thoreau inveighed against any government which did not conduct itself in accordance with high moral principle and declared it a citizen's duty to deny support or allegiance to a government that one deeply felt to be wrong. It can be said in Thoreau's favor that such an attitude is essential to the health of a democracy; it is the opposite of apathy—so destructive of an effective public opinion—that cannot exert itself to take a stand and allows contests of great moment to go by default. Thoreau was not antisocial; he merely took his duties as a citizen more seriously than many Americans.

The Boston Brahmins. The period from the triumph of Jacksonian democracy to the Civil War was one of the greatest eras in American literary development, and the cultural influence of New England loomed so large in this period that it has been referred to as "The Renaissance of New England," "The Golden Day," or "The Flowering of New England." Boston, as the cultural center of New England, was the home of a social and intellectual aristocracy so highly respected in their own day that they did much to make literature "respectable" in an era preoccupied with politics, technology, and economic advancement. Oliver Wendell Holmes, the most articulate spokesman of this group, applied the label "Brahmin caste of New England" to the small, cultivated, and exclusive class into which he had been born and which he typified. Holmes and other well-known members of the Brahmin caste—including Henry Wadsworth Longfellow and James Russell Lowell—contributed a great deal to New England ideals of culture and scholarship.

The Brahmin conception of literature was that it should be lofty, pure, and noble; they recoiled from the sort of literary unpleasantness which characterized the writings of Hawthorne and Melville. And as with literature, so with life: the Brahmins—Holmes and Longfellow, in particular—strove consistently to erect barriers against unpleasant or perplexing social and philosophic questions. They neither wanted nor expected such romantic utopias as were visualized by Emerson, Thoreau, and the founders of communitarian experiments like Brook Farm. Rather, they were benevolent toward their fellow men, yet satisfied to savor the pleasant intellectual life of Cambridge and Boston. Holmes considered Boston "the thinking center of the continent, and therefore of the planet."

Nathaniel Hawthorne. The New England writer who most brilliantly opposed transcendentalist tendencies was Nathaniel Hawthorne of Salem, Massachusetts. He was the chief inheritor, in literature, of the old Puritan tradition; and his writings—particularly his novel *The Scarlet Letter* (1850)—embodied Puritan ideals and the Puritan way of life. His seventeenth-century ancestors had been Puritan magistrates charged with persecuting Quakers and condemning the "witches" at Salem court, and he felt deeply his connection with these forebears. Despite his disapproval of their bigotry and cruelty, he recognized the ancestral tie: "Strong traits of their nature," he said, "have intertwined themselves with mine." Thus in opposing the Emersonian view, Hawthorne was essentially criticizing both the optimism inherent in transcendentalism and the reform movements abetted by transcendentalism on the grounds that man is innately sinful, that evil is an ever present reality, not an illusion to be brushed aside, and that self-reliant individualism alone does not save man from destruction. Hawthorne is a striking example of the persistence of the Puritan point of view in an age of liberalism and progressivism.

Unlike Emerson, who denied that evil existed in an ultimate form, Hawthorne not only acknowledged evil but made it central in his stories, sketches, and novels. *The Scarlet Letter* deals with secret guilt, the effects of a disgraceful crime on man and woman, and the need for expiation through confession or love. In *The House of the Seven Gables* (1851) evil appears as a hereditary taint visiting the sins of the fathers on the children in a study of degeneration and decay. *The Blithedale Romance* (1852) was, in part, a satire on Brook Farm—the villain showing how the zealotry of a reformer can become enmeshed with unconscionable ambition and thus serve evil rather than good.

Herman Melville. Another writer close to Hawthorne in his concern with the "deep mystery of sin" and his revulsion against the contemporary currents of optimism was Herman Melville, a novelist neglected during his own lifetime but "rediscovered" in the 1920's by literary critics whose post-World War I mood of disillusionment and despair vibrated sympathetically with the mood of *Moby Dick* and *Billy Budd*. Born in New York and raised in the Berkshires of Massachusetts, Melville as a youth shipped as a sailor on a merchantman plying the Atlantic and later on a whaler traveling the South Seas, and in these voyages he saw first-hand a world of violence, crime, brutality, and misery.

Unlike Emerson but like Hawthorne, Melville was a philosophical pessimist who found it difficult to accept many of the assumptions of Emersonian Romanticism. However, he had arrived at his pessimism along intellectual avenues that differed from Hawthorne's in at least three key ways: (1) while Hawthorne cherished Calvinist values, although ever critical of them and all others, Melville rebelled against the religious conservatism which he knew in his home as a boy; (2) both in Liverpool and in the South Seas, Melville was shocked by the rough and cruel ways of "civilized" men—brutalities which neither Hawthorne nor Emerson had ever experienced at first hand; (3) whether or not the restless and questing nature of his mind sprang wholly from these causes, he lacked the resignation of Hawthorne just as he lacked the optimism of Emerson. Said Hawthorne in reference to a meeting with Melville in England in 1856:

Melville, as he always does, began to reason of providence and futurity, and of everything that lies beyond human ken, and informed me that he had "pretty much made up his mind to be annihilated"; but still he does not seem to rest in that anticipation; and, I think, will never rest until he gets hold of a definite belief. It is strange how he persists—and has persisted ever since I knew him, and probably long before—in wandering to-and-fro over these deserts, as dismal and monotonous as the sand hills amid which we were sitting. He can neither believe, nor be comfortable in his unbelief; and he is too honest and courageous not to try to do one or the other.

Melville's dilemma was the dilemma of many other serious modern minds in an age of materialism and scientific revolution of thought.

Southern Romanticism and Realism. The South produced many writers during the period of sectional controversy that preceded the Civil War, yet it took little part in the American literary renaissance that had its center in New England. Put increasingly on the defensive, the South tended more and more to withdraw from intellectual contact with the North. As it became apparent to Southerners that the institution of slavery must be maintained and permitted to spread, political and economic leadership in the South passed to men who no longer felt the need to apologize for slavery; instead they attempted to defend it—indeed, to praise it. Southerners tended to idealize the cotton plantation as a happy feudal domain where slaves were humanely ruled by highborn gentlemen. They pointed to the Greek ideal of democracy, in which *inequality*, rather than *equality*, was recognized as the fundamental condition of nature. In such a society the competent and worthy individuals, acting in the interest of all, voluntarily assumed the care and direction of the incompetent. This theory, in effect, denied the eighteenth-century idea that all men had certain natural rights.

Because of this emphasis on the pleasantness of feudal life, the dominant Romantic literary influence in the South from the mid-1830's to the mid-1840's was the fiction of the English novelist Sir Walter Scott. Scott's re-creation of the Middle Ages, his knights in shining armor, his defenders of glamorous ladies in distress, the pageantry of his scenes, and the exemplary character of his heroes accorded with Southern notions as to what Southern chivalry was and always would be—in contrast to Northern commercialism and reformism.

A number of American writers attempted to create romantic and idyllic pictures of life in the "feudal" area of the old South. One of the first and best of such novels was John P. Kennedy's *Swallow Barn* (1832), a depiction of Virginia rural life in the 1820's. Kennedy strung together sketches of plantation aristocracy on an episodic thread so thin that the plot is minimal. Substantially all the characterization and what little action develops are only marginally "true to life." Thus the master of Swallow Barn is genial, generous, and bland; his relatives and friends are virtuous and benevolent; their hospitality is bountiful; and the Negroes are cheerful. *Swallow Barn* enjoyed an enviable vogue during the 1830's, but the South it depicted existed largely in the author's imagination.

Indeed, the South was not all gentility and plantation virtue. The Old Southwest—Arkansas, Louisiana, Tennessee, Mississippi, Alabama, and parts of Georgia—still had its small farmers and reckless frontiersmen; and these became the subject of wildly humorous yarns by a series of frontier writers, including Augustus B. Longstreet, J. J. Hooper, George Washington Harris, and William T. Thompson. Writing with a keen awareness of the bumptious comedy inherent in the backwash of the frontier and aiming to depict authentically the rascally people, speech, customs, and scenery of these regions, they produced tales characterized by a robust realism found nowhere else in Southern—or Northern—literature of the times.

George Washington Harris' fictional character Sut Lovingood is a good example of the breed of men inhabiting the pages of these Southwestern humorists. Sut, a lanky mountaineer and a self-confessed "nat'ral born durn'd fool," loves liquor and women but hates Yankees and circuit-riding preachers, whom he describes as "durn'd, infurnel, hiperkritical, potbellied, scaley-hided, whisky-wastin'." His adventures are full of mischief-making and comic situations.

Edgar Allan Poe. Raised as a foster child in Virginia, Edgar Allan Poe can be treated nevertheless only partially as a Southerner. In his personal life he was—or wanted to be—a conservative Southerner and consequently he opposed the New England group; moreover, he supported the works of Southern writers and even praised the Southern defense of slavery. But his writings rarely reveal a Southern tone or setting. In literature he was more strikingly influenced by the "Gothic tradition" in English fiction—the kind of fiction which employed certain stock properties like old castles, decayed houses, dungeons, secret passages, ancient wrongs, supernatural phenomena, and the like. In addition, Poe was not concerned with portraying contemporary scenes or providing moral reflections on life. He believed that poetry should exist for its own sake, never as an instrument of instruction; it may be that no other American has maintained more consistently that literature exists primarily and perhaps solely to entertain.

The West from Fenimore Cooper to the Tall Tale. The disparity between the dream of a peaceful, democratic society in the virgin wilderness and the reality of frontier life is frequently reflected in American thought and literature of the Romantic Age. The real western frontier posed many problems of adjustment for its settlers. Life was harsh and there was little time for social amenities; land speculation, political corruption, and immorality were common in the poorly organized towns of the West. In short, the real frontier bore little resemblance to the literary legend or to the popular tall tale.

The first major writer of fiction to exploit the literary potential of the frontier was James Fenimore Cooper, whose series of "Leatherstocking Tales" both romanticized the wilderness and conveyed the loss many Americans felt when they became aware of the crude fashion in which the frontier was being settled. For instance, Cooper convincingly expressed the tragedy of the American Indian who was pushed out of his ancestral lands by the advancing white man.

At his best, Cooper was a captivating storyteller with a talent for both description and perceptive social criticism. Although modern critics often lampoon his didacticism, stock characters, heavy-handed style, and strained and starchy dialogue, Cooper made a singular contribution toward recording and extolling the frontier experience. The Leatherstocking Tales represent a romantic view of the West, just as Sir Walter Scott's novels romanticized with charm and skill the people and places of a lost Europe. Cooper's West, however, was mainly confined to the old upper New York State, and he himself never saw the prairie, never neared the Rocky Mountains, never crossed the Mississippi River.

If Cooper's West was greatly romanticized, the works of a series of other writers went beyond the romantic and became almost epic or legendary. This glorification of the westward movement is suggested in the words of the historian Frederick Jackson Turner about a half century later in 1893:

> To the frontier the American intellect owes its striking characteristics. That coarseness and strength combined with acuteness and inquisitiveness; that practical, inventive turn of mind, quick to find expedients; that masterful grasp of material things, lacking in the artistic but powerful to effect great ends; that restless, nervous energy, that dominant individualism, working for good and for evil, and withal that buoyancy and exuberance which comes with freedom—these are the traits of the frontier, or traits called out elsewhere because of the existence of the frontier.

If Turner's interpretation of the influence of the frontier on American life is now considered by historians to be rather overstated, the paragraph above nevertheless suggests how the vastness of the American wilderness seemed to affect the thinking of Americans. The great plains, the towering mountains, and the endless forests emphasized bigness—a bigness wholly unknown to the Americans' forebears across the Atlantic in Europe. Felling the forests and turning the soil in the course of creating civilization were in themselves immense tasks.

As if things in America were not big enough, some writers came forward to exaggerate the bigness and generate a new genre of literature called the "tall tale." Such fiction introduced men who could wrestle alligators and whip their weight in wildcats. In Thomas B. Thorpe's *The Big Bear of Arkansas* (1845) we are introduced to a frontier where "varmints ar large, . . . trees ar large, . . . rivers ar large," and where the biggest bear in creation "loomed up like a *black mist,* he seemed so large." Sometimes these tales grew up about such real-life frontiersmen as Davy Crockett. Sometimes legendary figures were introduced, like Paul Bunyan, the mythological giant who became the hero of northwestern logging camps. Chauvinism, boastfulness, and exaggeration here all reflected the influence of the vast wilderness on American thinking and on reading tastes. Recently historians have become more and more convinced that the "starting point of a truly American literature" can be located on the western frontier more logically than in the East.

Other Art Forms. If literature was the form in which Americans did their finest artistic work in the Jacksonian period, an exception existed in the case of the drama; of American playwrights before the Civil War, the less said the better. Similarly, American music was insignificant when measured against the European achievements of composers like Beethoven, Schubert, Chopin, Verdi, or Liszt.

American sculptors, however, had a remarkable vogue both in Europe and at home. Among the most famous sculptors were Hiram Powers, an Ohioan whose "Greek Slave" was greeted with admiration in London, and Thomas Crawford of New York, whose "Armed Freedom" surmounts the Capitol in Washington, D.C. The heroic classic poses—the equestrian statues and idealistically delineated marble busts—were highly regarded in that nationalistic age.

As in the earlier national period, portrait painters were in great demand;

and the most popular were Thomas Sully, Matthew H. Jouett, and Chester Harding. However, "storytelling" or anecdotal painting—in which common human situations were depicted nostalgically or humorously—was growing in popular favor. Scenes down on the farm or among raftsmen poling their flatboats upstream or among the prairie schooners and Indians of the West were present in the canvasses of painters like George Caleb Bingham, William Sidney Mount, and Alfred Jacob Miller. Finally, Romanticism and American pride in the land combined to produce a group of painters known as the Hudson River School, the chief of whom were Thomas Doughty, Asher Brown Durand, Thomas Cole, and George Inness. Landscapists all, they romantically portrayed the wilderness of forests, mountains, and streams.

If American architecture was largely derivative, many stately and indeed beautiful structures were erected during the age of Jackson. The columns of Greek Revival and Roman Revival dwellings and business buildings continued to demonstrate the influence of Jefferson and Benjamin Latrobe. In the 1840's, however, the Romanticist approach made itself felt as rather widespread acceptance of the Gothic style prevailed, in which the engineering achievements of skeletal construction, rib vaulting, and pointed arches current in the Middle Ages were revived.

AMERICA: SLAVERY AND DEMOCRACY

Antislavery Agitation. When Eastern writers such as Thoreau and Melville turned their attention to the South, they were concerned not with the writings of Longstreet, Kennedy, or Hooper, but with the institution of chattel slavery. Yet with rare exceptions, cultured and creative Easterners entered the antislavery cause on a wave of popular sentiment; few of them pioneered actively in the movement for abolition of the South's "peculiar institution."

In the 1820's, relatively humble men like the Philadelphia Quaker Benjamin Lundy were in the vanguard of the abolition fight. But in Boston in 1831 a Massachusetts journeyman printer named William Lloyd Garrison founded *The Liberator,* a violently abolitionist paper. Garrison could see no good in the legal sanctions which protected slavery in half the country. Fanatical in his single-track idealism, he attacked the Constitution of the United States as "a convenant with death and an agreement with hell." It was hardly surprising that neither Emerson nor Hawthorne nor Holmes would underwrite such extremism in a day when John Quincy Adams, himself antislavery but no Garrisonian, described the Abolition party as both small and shallow.

From 1833 on, the self-educated New England Quaker, John Greenleaf Whittier, contributed poems as well as prose and organizing ability to the abolitionists' campaign. Longfellow in 1842 published a few antislavery poems but never became a Garrison adherent. Lowell wrote for the *National Anti-Slavery Standard.* Other younger authors—Thoreau, Melville, and Walt Whitman—were repelled by slavery and said so. Then, while the conservative Holmes and Hawthorne continued to abstain from the agitation, Emerson swung around in the 1850's to laud the almost certainly insane John Brown (see p. 190) and to compare his gallows to the cross of Jesus. It is not astonishing to find Parker, Channing, and other Unitarians of their individualistic bent among the most outspoken antislavery recruits. Nor does it seem strange that Harriet Beecher Stowe, author of *Uncle Tom's Cabin* (1852), was the daughter, wife, and sister of Calvinist ministers—and a woman abundantly aware of her own powerful New England conscience. Mrs. Stowe contended that *Uncle*

Tom's Cabin, which depicted the separation of families, maternal loss, and other evils inherent in slavery, was inspired by God. Inspired or not, it turned out to be the greatest propaganda book ever written by an American. Southern fiction, produced by way of reply, had no comparable punch.

The ablest Southern arguments were in the sphere of nonfiction and came mostly from politicians and educators. Many slaveholders agreed with John C. Calhoun and William Harper of South Carolina and Thomas R. Dew of Virginia that—instead of being harmful—slavery was a positive good. Other Southerners merely saw—or thought they saw—a practical necessity of retaining the slave labor system. When *The Impending Crisis of the South,* a book attacking slavery on economic grounds, was published in 1857, its author, Hinton R. Helper of North Carolina, was violently assailed by Southern spokesmen for spreading slanders against their section. On the other hand, the writings of a Virginian, George Fitzhugh, were warmly praised by some of the men who denounced Helper. In *Sociology for the South,* Fitzhugh said slavery was a social, political, and economic blessing—and avowed that men trying to eliminate it were blind to Southern realities.

De Tocqueville's America. The antislavery crusade was only one aspect of the reform spirit manifest throughout the North (see pp. 223-25). As slavery and abolition interests held no monopoly on Americans' conversations and activities, foreign visitors did not limit their observations to the subject. Indeed, many travelers evinced more abiding interest in other features.

Alexis de Tocqueville, a young French magistrate and member of a noble family, spent nine months in the United States in 1831 and 1832. Although his official purpose was to study the penal system, De Tocqueville's noteworthy contribution to political science and historical analysis was his *Democracy in America* (1835). The Frenchman concluded that American democracy was functioning successfully; that its success depended chiefly on separation of church and state, and on the absence of centralization; that American political morality was important; and that American democracy was not for export to Europe until such time as Europeans elevated their standards of governmental morality.

De Tocqueville was particularly struck by what he saw as an American tendency toward the practical, an avoidance of traditions, and an optimistic hope that in the new American social system men would be able to progress rapidly toward perfection. One of his principal theses was that the American system of government derived from a dominant principle—popular sovereignty—which had unfolded over the course of the nation's history and finally, in Jackson's time, was presenting its consequences, good and ill, for reflection.

De Tocqueville was not without his doubts concerning the American experiment. He saw a potential danger to freedom of the individual in the possibility that majorities would crush minorities or nibble away at minority rights. He also thought he discerned a trend toward mediocrity in popular leaders and in American culture. While De Tocqueville made some wrong guesses—for instance, he failed to grasp the importance of the Industrial Revolution—he was remarkably correct in the aggregate.

BIBLIOGRAPHY

Volumes 4 and 5 of Edward Channing's *A History of the United States*, 6 vols. (New York: Macmillan, 1905-1925) chronicle the growth of democratic government from 1824 to 1848. For a briefer assessment of the period by an expert in political theory, see Charles M. Wiltse, *The New Nation: 1800-1845* (New York: Hill and Wang, 1961). Chilton Williamson, *American Suffrage from Property to Democracy, 1760-1860* (Princeton: Princeton University Press, 1960) contains specific data on voting which had never before been compiled.

The most famous discussion of democracy in the Jacksonian period is contained in the French observer Alexis de Tocqueville's *Democracy in America*, 2 vols., published in several editions since 1835-1840. Arthur M. Schlesinger, Jr., won a Pulitzer Prize for *The Age of Jackson* (New York: New American Library, 1945). Claude Bowers vividly describes *The Party Battles of the Jackson Period* (Boston: Houghton Mifflin, 1922). For other interpretations of the age of Jackson, see: Glyndon G. Van Deusen, *The Jacksonian Era, 1828-1848* (New York: Harper, 1959); Leonard D. White, *The Jacksonians* (New York: Macmillan, 1954); Marvin Meyers, *The Jacksonian Persuasion* (New York: Vintage Books, 1957); and Francis J. Grund, *Aristocracy in America* (New York: Harper, 1959). John W. Ward, *Andrew Jackson: Symbol for an Age* (New York: Galaxy Books, 1955) places emphasis on nonpolitical aspects of the Jackson period; and Marquis James, *Andrew Jackson: Portrait of a President* (New York: Grosset and Dunlap, 1956) is a sympathetic account of "Old Hickory" and his political career. Still one of the best biographies of Jackson, containing selections from many contemporary letters and documents, is James Parton, *Life of Andrew Jackson*, 3 vols. (New York: Appleton, 1860). Fascinating insight into Jackson's personality and beliefs will be found in *The Correspondence of Andrew Jackson*, 7 vols. (Washington, D.C.: Carnegie Institution, 1926-1935).

Charles S. Sydnor, *The Development of Southern Sectionalism, 1819-1848* (Baton Rouge: Louisiana State University Press, 1948) is a scholarly treatment of this important Southern trend. A detailed discussion of the important nullification controversy will be found in Chauncey S. Boucher, *The Nullification Controversy in South Carolina* (Chicago: University of Chicago Press, 1916). Jackson's anti-Bank policies are thoroughly discussed in Ralph C. H. Catterall, *The Second Bank of the United States* (Chicago: University of Chicago Press, 1903). Robert G. Gunderson has written a delightful account of events surrounding the election of 1840 in *The Log-Cabin Campaign* (Lexington: University of Kentucky Press, 1957). Robert J. Morgan deals with Tyler's presidency from the viewpoint of a political scientist in *A Whig Embattled* (Lincoln: University of Nebraska Press, 1954). Bray Hammond, *Banks and Politics in America from the Revolution to the Civil War* (Princeton: Princeton University Press, 1957) is valuable for politico-entrepreneurial interpretations of the period.

Bernard De Voto, *Year of Decision: 1846* (Boston: Houghton Mifflin, 1961) is a dramatic treatment of Western developments. Commercial interests and westward expansion are discussed in Norman A. Graebner, *Empire on the Pacific* (New York: Ronald Press, 1955). Frederick J. Turner, *Frontier and Section* (Englewood Cliffs, N.J.: Prentice-Hall, 1961) is an important collection of essays by an influential scholar. *The Oregon Trail* (New York: New American Library, 1950) by Francis Parkman is standard historical fare by a brilliant stylist. For a provocative reëvaluation of the West in history and literature, see Henry N. Smith, *Virgin Land* (New York: Vintage Books, 1957). Walter P. Webb, *The Great Plains* (New York: Universal Library, 1957) is a regional study by a master of the subject. A classic of the frontier, Josiah Gregg's *Commerce of the Prairies* (Philadelphia: J. B. Lippincott, 1962), presents the retouched account of a Santa Fe trader. Other scholarly and readable surveys of the period of Western expansion are Grant Foreman, *Indian Removal* (Norman: University of Oklahoma Press, 1932) and Paul W. Gates, *The Farmer's Age: Agriculture, 1815-1860* (New York: Holt, Rinehart, and Winston, 1960).

Volumes 5, 6, and 7 of a pioneer work in the field of social history, John B. McMaster's *A History of the People of the United States*, 8 vols. (New York: D. Appleton, 1883-1913), deal with social currents in the first half of the nineteenth century. Social and economic aspects of the Jacksonian era are discussed in Carl Russell Fish, *The Rise of the Common Man, 1830-1850* (New York: Macmillan, 1927). Van Wyck Brooks, *The Flowering of New England* (New York: E. P. Dutton, 1936) treats New England literary developments in detail. For an Englishwoman's view of Jacksonian America, see Frances Trollope, *Domestic Manners of the Americans* (New York: Vintage Books, 1949). A valuable assessment of transportation, manufacturing, and the wage earner is contained in George R. Taylor, *The Transportation Revolution, 1815-1860* (New York: Rinehart, 1951). *Fluctuations in American Business, 1790-1860* (Cambridge: Harvard University Press, 1935) by Walter B. Smith and Arthur H. Cole is an invaluable reference work.

PART 4: INTRODUCTION

A HOUSE DIVIDED

■ By 1850 the United States had attained the size and physical resources of a powerful nation, but it was not yet a nation in the full sense. In fact, there was some doubt as to whether it was a nation at all, or whether it could become one.

It is surprising that any country which was not a strong nation could have grown as rapidly as the United States had already grown. Within a space of forty-seven years this country had moved its western border from the Mississippi River to the Pacific Ocean and had almost trebled its area. What had begun as a string of states along the Atlantic coast had now become a transcontinental two-ocean republic, looking out toward Hawaii, Alaska, and the Far East, as well as toward Europe. The vast resources of the trans-Mississippi in copper, timber, petroleum, fertile soil, water power, and uranium were as yet scarcely recognized; but they had been added to the country's inventory of assets and only awaited the time when they would furnish the sinews of national strength.

This rapidly expanding republic had made great progress in solving some of the problems that had to be solved if the United States was to be both a democracy of free citizens and a nation with strength among nations. In previous history the governments of large countries had been made strong at the expense of individual freedom and local self-government. Political strength for an empire had meant tyranny for its people, and freedom had meant weakness. But America had escaped the choice between internal tyranny and external weakness through the device of a federal system, which left many domestic questions for local action while throwing the collective weight of all the states behind the action of the Union in matters which concerned them as a group. Under this arrangement, freedom did not involve weakness, and strength was not gained at the sacrifice of democratic self-rule. Freedom and local responsibility on the one hand and strength and collective power on the other were effectively reconciled.

America had also enjoyed remarkable success in maintaining a cohesion which at first seemed threatened by the sheer dimensions of continental expansion. Before the nineteenth century, when distances were great enough to make communication and the exchange of goods too difficult, too slow, or too expensive, governments which

Abraham Lincoln, portrait by G. P. A. Healy (1868).
"As I would not be a *slave,* so I would not be a *master.* This expresses my idea of democracy. Whatever differs from this, to the extent of the difference, is no democracy."—Lincoln (1858).

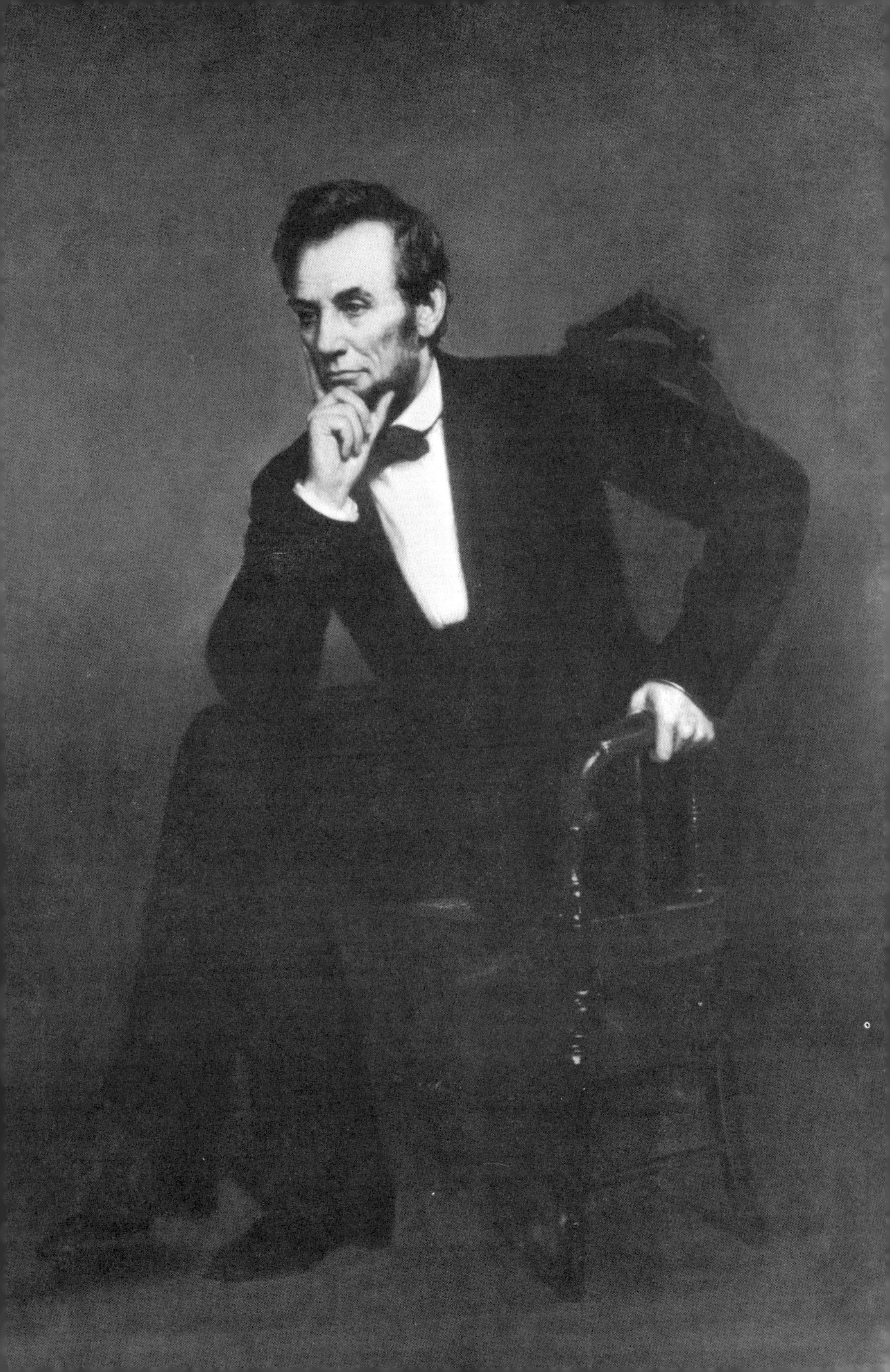

The Metropolitan Museum of Art, Gift of Mrs. Frank B. Porter, 1922.

tried to span these distances had tended to break to pieces unless they concentrated all power in absolute rulers. But in America the development first of turnpikes and canals and then of steamboats and railroads—not to mention the telegraph—was making travel and communication swift and the movement of goods cheap and easy. Consequently, the country was acquiring greater cohesion even as it was growing larger.

Thus, nationalizing forces had already made great strides, but at mid-century it was still uncertain whether they would complete the forging of a nation, or whether the very pressure of these forces would cause a disruption of the rather loose-jointed Union, which for some seven decades had seemed in part a nation and in part a mere association of states. Indeed, the fact that stronger ties were developing brought the question to a crisis more sharply, for the growth of federal power led many Americans to believe that their country ought to maintain uniform values throughout the Union and enforce basic American ideals in all the states. When this concept led to an attack upon Negro slavery, which was a basic institution of labor in the southern states, these states were prompted, in turn, to defend a theory that ultimate power lay in the states and not in the Union, that the Union was a voluntary association of separate and autonomous states rather than a consolidated nation consisting of states welded into a single unit, and that the states could go out of the Union by their separate act in the same way in which they had come into it.

The effort of the southern states to put this idea into operation led to a four-year Civil War (1861-1865), which constituted the greatest internal crisis in American history. The waging of the war settled the question of the nature of the American system. The Union became a single nation, consisting of member states which possessed a restricted (and diminishing) power to deal with essentially local affairs. After the war, the Civil War amendments imposed limitations upon the states and thus wrote into the Constitution the ultimate ascendancy of the federal authority in the Republic.

(Left) *Prisoners from the Front,* painting by Winslow Homer (1866). The Civil War was foremost a war of civilian armies. (Above) *Border Ruffians Invading Kansas,* wash drawing by F. O. C. Darley. In "Bleeding Kansas" civil war had its fanatic rehearsal, as Northerners and Southerners fought for control. (Right) *American Slave Market,* painting by "Taylor" (1852). "A slave market!... husbands, wives, brothers, sisters, fathers, mothers, and young children, to be 'sold separately or in lots to suit the convenience of the purchaser.' "—*Uncle Tom's Cabin.*

Thus, a basic problem was confronted and solved. The fact that the United States was a nation and not a loose association of weak states was to be of vital importance in the twentieth century when conflicting values (or "ideologies") were defended by rival "powers" and the survival of democracy seemed to depend in large part upon the strength of the "power" that defended it. In a broader sense, the United States had proved that self-government is not inconsistent with power, that democracy does not necessarily mean weakness, and that in the words of Abraham Lincoln, "popular government is not an absurdity." The victory of the Union had vested in the central government immense potential strength which would remain largely untapped until the twentieth century. The emancipation of the slaves had broadened the application of democracy and had reaffirmed—at least in principle—the worth of each human being and his right to freedom. But unfortunately this affirmation was only in principle; and at the end of the "Reconstruction" which followed the Civil War, the whole nation acquiesced in Negro segregation and disfranchisement. Thus, a vital problem of democracy in the realm of race relations was left unsolved, to arise again in acute form in the twentieth century.

Like all men everywhere, the men of the Civil War generation could hope only to solve the problems of their own time. By fighting the war, they did solve a major problem in a way that was crucial for the future of America. But they shared the irony which overtakes each generation of people: namely, that even the solutions which they achieve involve unforeseen challenges for the values they defend. The preservation of the Union meant also the triumph of industrial America, which presented new problems. This triumph meant that Americans were moving into a different world— a world where the cherished values of democracy, of freedom, of individualism, and of the general welfare would have to be reinterpreted and reaffirmed in a new kind of republic which was not only stronger and greater but also infinitely more complicated than the one which the Founding Fathers had established or which Abraham Lincoln had fought a war to save.

A House Divided

CHAPTER 10

THE SECTIONAL CRISIS, 1848-1861

THE ORIGINS OF SECTIONALISM

The Transcontinental Republic. Between 1846 and 1848, with the settlement of the Oregon question and the Treaty of Guadalupe Hidalgo, the United States became in the full sense a two-ocean transcontinental republic. Except for Alaska, Hawaii, and a small segment of Arizona which would be acquired by the Gadsden Treaty in 1853, the country had reached its present territorial limits. Growth had been remarkable; within forty-five years the western boundary had moved from the Mississippi River to the Pacific Ocean.

In one sense, the acquisition of the Southwest marked a fulfillment of American nationalism. No other nation on earth had grown so rapidly, and no people were prouder of their nation than the Americans, who boasted incessantly of the superiority of republican institutions. Yet, ironically, the climax of national growth also brought with it a crisis of national unity, for it precipitated a bitter rivalry between two dissimilar sections of the country—areas divided by the Mason-Dixon line and the Ohio River.

The problem of geographical rivalries was not a new one in the United States. In a country larger than all of western Europe with immense diversity of soil, terrain, and climate, conflicts had arisen more than once between economic interests of one area and those of another. In fact, American history has been full of such conflicts, and they have often been marked by a division between East and West. This was true, for instance, in the contest over the Bank of the United States in the time of Jackson, and again in the battle between the advocates of the coinage of silver and the defenders of the gold standard in 1896. The theme of sectional rivalry has been so persistent that historians sometimes dispute whether the deepest antagonisms in American history have been between conflicting social classes or between conflicting sections.

Thus, the sectional crisis between North and South, which approached its climax between 1848 and 1860, was in no sense unique, but it did reach a unique pitch of intensity. Usually, competing sectional forces have sought only to gain advantage over one another within a Union which both accept, but on this occasion the South became so alienated that it made a titanic effort to withdraw from the Union.

The Southern Way of Life. Historians have never been able to agree on any one factor as the primary cause of this division, but they do agree in recognizing a cluster of contributing factors. As far back as the seventeenth century, North and South had developed along dissimilar lines. Virginia,

Maryland, and the colonies to the South had based their economy on crops which were limited to latitudes of warm climate and a long growing season. Tobacco, the first of these to be introduced in the colonies, was followed by rice and indigo in Carolina, sugar in Louisiana, and, most important, by cotton throughout the lower South. For the cultivation of these crops the plantation had evolved as the economic unit of production, and within the plantation system the labor supply had grown to consist of Negroes imported from Africa as slaves. Slave labor did not become dominant until the eighteenth century, but even before the American Revolution, slaves had come to outnumber free persons throughout the plantation districts. In 1850, 32 per cent of the total population of the South was held in slavery, and in South Carolina, Georgia, and Mississippi a majority of the population consisted of slaves. The Southern system, its rural life, and its slave labor, had led to the development of a somewhat conservative temper, a marked stratification of social classes, and a paternalistic type of society. The power of every landowner to rule his own workers on his own plantation had prevented the growth of a strong public authority. As a result, violence was frequent and qualities of personal courage and physical prowess were especially valued in the society. For instance, the practice of dueling, which had died out in the North, still prevailed in the South.

The Northern Way of Life. It would be a mistake to think of the North as presenting a total contrast, for the majority of people in the free states also engaged in agriculture and lived a rural life. But the Northern economy and Northern life were more diversified. In the absence of a valuable export crop such as tobacco or cotton, New England Yankees had turned early to commerce as a means of securing money to buy the imports they needed.

During the Napoleonic wars, when their commerce was disrupted and the supply of imported manufactures was cut off, they had begun a manufacturing industry. As manufacturing grew, cities grew with it. Prosperity and rapid economic growth fostered a belief in progress and innovation quite different from the more traditional (or static) attitudes of the South. Although the factory system brought with it a certain amount of exploitation of labor through low wages, the fact that all men were free made for greater mobility, greater equality, more democracy, and less sharply defined social stratification than in the South. The North grew to value the commercial virtues of thrift, enterprise, and hard work, in contrast to the more military virtues which held a priority in the South.

Such differences as these can easily be exaggerated, for a great deal of frontier Americanism prevailed in both the North and the South. Evangelical Protestantism was the dominant religion of both sections. The materialistic pursuit of wealth motivated cotton planters as well as Yankee industrialists. To a European, all Americans seemed bumptiously democratic, and in Southern politics the Whig party, favored by most planter aristocrats, could not have competed against the Democratic party at all unless it had adopted the democratic symbols of the log cabin, the coonskin hat, and the cider barrel.

THE BASES OF SECTIONAL ANTAGONISM

Regional dissimilarity, however, need not lead to conflict. In the United States today, states of the farm belt differ greatly from those of the Atlantic seaboard, but we tend to think of these differences as making the areas complementary, rather than antagonistic to each other. The antagonism which drove North and South to war in the mid-nineteenth century, therefore, needs to be explained.

Economic Causes. In one sense the antagonism was economic, for the dissimilar economic interests of the North and the South caused them to favor opposite economic policies and therefore to clash politically. Essentially, the South, with its cotton economy, produced raw materials for a textile industry centered in Britain. Accordingly, the South sold on the world market, and in return it needed to buy its manufactured goods where they were cheapest, which was also in the world market, and to keep down taxes and governmental costs as much as possible.

For the North, the need was different. Eastern manufacturers, who could not produce as cheaply as the British, needed a tariff to protect them against ruinous competition (or to increase their margins of profits), and Western grain farmers who had no good way of sending their crops to market needed turnpikes and canals ("internal improvements"). Henry Clay, when he devised his American System, had perceived the possibilities in an alliance by which the Northwest would support the protective tariff needed by the Northeast, and the Northeast would support the internal improvements needed by the Northwest. Not only could each gain its objective, but also each would serve as both a market and a source of supply for the other. Eastern cities would consume Western grain and provide manufactures for the West, while the grain belt would buy manufactured goods from the cities and provide foodstuffs for them.

But the South failed to fit into this scheme. For the South, internal improvements meant only that the South would be paying part of the governmental costs of a program from which it did not benefit, and, indeed, which diverted trade away from the South's own Mississippi River system, which drew trade southward toward New Orleans. The tariff meant only that the South would be prevented from buying its manufactures from those who bought its raw materials and would be forced by law to pay a higher, tariff-supported price for its manufactures. As the Virginian, John Randolph of Roanoke, had angrily declared, "we shall only pay more for worse goods."

Because of these economic factors, North and South tended to vote against each other on questions of tariff, internal improvements, and the extension of the power of the central government in general. Their rivalry had reached a crisis at the time of the Nullification Controversy in 1833, when South Carolina was ready to defy federal law (see page 132). The crisis had been averted only when other southern states had not supported South Carolina. The South as a whole resented federal economic policies but never opposed them to the point of breaking up the Union, to which most Southerners felt strong patriotic loyalty.

The Growth of the Slavery Issue. A deeper cause of division, however, was the institution of slavery. In the eighteenth century, slavery had scarcely been regarded as a moral question at all—except by the Quakers—and pious Yankee shipowners of stern Puritan faith had engaged in the slave trade to Africa just as readily as Southern tobacco and rice planters had bought slaves for labor. As late as 1780 there was no division of slave states and free states; slaves were held in every state of the Union, and they were less numerous in the North only because they were less profitable there. But in the late eighteenth century (during the Age of Reason, or the Enlightenment), slavery came under attack from believers in natural law, human equality, and the rights of man. At the same time, emphasis in the churches shifted from a limited concern with the personal salvation of the individual to a fuller application of Christian teaching in relation to human society. Thus, the savage penal code of earlier times was modified, various social reforms were adopted, and slavery came under attack.

The states from Pennsylvania northward shared in this movement against slavery. By 1804 all of them had adopted laws for the gradual or immediate emancipation of their slaves, and in 1808 Congress had prohibited the importation of any more slaves from Africa. For a time it appeared that the South might also participate in this movement. Southern enlightenment leaders like Jefferson condemned slavery; antislavery societies were active in the South; and the restriction of slavery to the rice and tobacco economy, which was static and no longer very profitable, meant that the Southern economy as a whole did not depend on slave labor.

But the introduction of cotton gave a new vitality to the slave system in the South. In one generation, the cultivation of short staple cotton spread across the lower South from middle Georgia to the banks of the Brazos in Texas. Every decade from 1800 to 1860 the value and the volume of the crop doubled. In this dynamic and expanding economy, the price of slaves rose and fell with the price of cotton. Slavery went with cotton into the new areas, and by 1820 it was completely interwoven into the whole Southern system.

While this was happening, the humanitarian crusade against slavery in Great Britain (which abolished slavery in the West Indies in 1833), in France (which abolished it in 1848), and in the northern states (where the abolitionists became increasingly militant in their denunciations) led the South to a defensive reaction. By 1830 Southern leaders were no longer saying, as they had said earlier, that slavery was an evil but was too deeply rooted to be abolished at once. Instead, they were beginning to assert that slavery was a positive good. They defended it with claims that it had been sanctioned in the Bible; that the Negro was biologically inferior to the white; that the exploitation of Negro workers by the slavery system was not so harsh as the exploitation of white workers by a wage system in which the worker received only a bare subsistence when he was working and no subsistence at all when he was not; and that, since social divisions were inevitable, assigning leadership to one class and subordination to another was better than having an endless struggle between classes.

Soon the South became so defensive about criticism that it would not tolerate the expression of antislavery opinion. An intellectual blockade, as it has been called, was imposed upon antislavery ideas. Meanwhile, in the North, the growth of reform activity and humanitarian feeling created a more and more widespread conviction that slavery was morally wrong.

In spite of this disagreement on the ethics of slavery, several factors prevented a clash over the question. To begin with, slavery was widely regarded as a matter for the states locally rather than for the federal government nationally. At that time, people regarded the federal system more as a loose association of states and less as a consolidated nation, and they were willing to leave many important questions to state action. Further, it was generally understood that the Constitution, in its "three-fifths" and fugitive slave clauses (see p. 76), protected the South's right to practice slavery. It was on the basis of such provisions that the southern states had agreed to join the Union.

Apart from the question of legal or constitutional obligation, many Americans took the position that the harmony of the Union was simply more important than the ethics of slavery—that the slave question must not be permitted to weaken the Union and that the abolitionists were wrong to keep up constant agitation on an issue which caused sectional antagonism. The abolitionists, who were in the minority, felt that the Union was not worth saving unless it was based upon freedom.

The Question of Extending Slavery. All this meant that as long as the institution of slavery was confined to the existing slave states, few Northerners were willing to act against it, and it was not an explosive question politically. But when the question of extending slavery to new areas arose, the opposition was far more determined. As early as the Ordinance of 1787, the old Congress under the Articles of Confederation had agreed to exclude slavery from the region north of the Ohio. Not only were sincere antislavery men determined to "contain" slavery, as we might now express it, but also many people who cared nothing about the evils of slavery wanted to reserve unsettled areas for white men only, and many others wanted to bring these new areas to the support of the North in the economic struggle between North and South. The South, conversely, was equally convinced that the growth of the country should not be all on the side of the North, thus reducing the South to a defenseless minority. This feeling made the South unwilling to concede even the areas where there was little prospect of extending slavery.

Because of these attitudes, the acquisition of any new area, the organization of any new territory, or the admission of any new state had always involved a possible flare-up over the slavery question. There had been such a crisis in 1820, when Missouri applied for admission to statehood as the first state (except Louisiana) to be formed out of the Louisiana Purchase. In the same way, the prospect of acquisition of territory from Mexico as a result of the Mexican War brought on another more protracted and more serious crisis beginning in 1846.

A few months after the beginning of the Mexican War in 1846, President Polk asked Congress to appropriate $2 million to be used in negotiating for land to be acquired from Mexico at the termination of the war. Many Northern Democrats were at this time angry with Polk, partly because he had supported a low tariff and partly because they felt he had violated the promise on which he was elected. His platform, calling for the "reoccupation" of Oregon and the "re-annexation" of Texas, and for "all of Oregon or none," had put the question of expansion on a bisectional basis by promising Oregon, sure to be free territory, for the North, and Texas, which already had slavery, for the South. But after becoming President, he had compromised on Oregon, accepting the boundary at the 49th parallel instead of at 54° 40′, while pushing expansion toward the southwest to the fullest extent by waging war with Mexico.

The Wilmot Proviso and the Calhoun Resolutions. This was the state of affairs when David Wilmot, a Democrat from Pennsylvania, introduced a resolution in the House of Representatives that slavery should be prohibited in any territory acquired with the $2 million which Polk requested. This free-soil resolution passed the House, where the North was stronger, but failed to pass in the Senate, where the South was stronger. The disagreement of Senate and House marked a deadlock in Congress which lasted for four years, blocked the organization of governments for the new areas, and caused a steady increase in sectional tension.

In 1848, at the end of the Mexican War, the victorious United States acquired the present states of Nevada, California, and Utah, most of Arizona and New Mexico, and parts of Colorado and Wyoming by means of the Treaty of Guadalupe Hidalgo; in this treaty also, Mexico relinquished all claims to Texas above the Rio Grande.

In the same year gold was discovered in California, and by 1849 the Gold Rush was in full swing. The need for organizing the new land was urgent, and the territorial question became the foremost issue in public life. At one extreme on this question stood Wilmot and the "free-soilers," both Whig and Democrat, who demanded the exclusion of slavery from the new areas by act of Congress. At the other extreme, most Southern Whigs and Democrats adopted the position of John C. Calhoun. Calhoun argued that the territories were owned in common by all the states (rather than by the federal government, which was only a joint agent for the states), and that all citizens had an equal right to take their property (including slaves) to the common territory. Therefore, Congress had no power under the Constitution to exclude slavery from any territory.

The Doctrine of Popular Sovereignty. Political leaders who wanted some kind of adjustment or middle ground were not satisfied with either Wilmot's or Calhoun's alternative, one of which conceded nothing to the South, the other nothing to the North. They sought a more "moderate" position, and some of them advocated an extension of the Missouri Compromise line at 36° 30′ to the Pacific. But most of them were more attracted by a proposal sponsored by Lewis Cass, senator from Michigan, for what was called "popular sovereignty" or "squatter sovereignty." Cass contended that the fairest and most democratic solution would be to let the people in the territories decide for themselves whether they would have slavery, just as the people in the states had already decided. Cass' proposal offered an attractive means for keeping the slavery question out of federal politics, but it contained one ambiguity which he adroitly refused to clarify: it did not specify *when* the people in the territories should make this decision. If they could make the decision as soon as the territory was organized, free soil could be attained by popular vote as easily as by congressional vote. According to Calhoun, popular exclusion would be just as wrong as congressional exclusion, for it would mean that Congress was giving to the territory a power which Congress did not have and therefore could not give. But if the voters in a territory could decide on slavery only when they applied for statehood, this would mean that popular sovereignty left the territories open to slavery quite as much as Calhoun's position did.

Far from reducing the amount of support for popular sovereignty, however, this ambiguity actually added to the attractiveness of the doctrine: antislavery men argued that popular sovereignty would result in free territories, while proslavery advocates contended that it guaranteed slavery a fair chance to establish itself during the period before statehood.

THE COMPROMISE OF 1850

While these various positions on the territorial extension of slavery were being developed, the impasse in Congress continued. For three entire sessions covering most of the Polk administration, nothing could be voted for California or the Southwest, and it was only after long delay that an act to organize Oregon Territory without slavery was adopted.

In 1848, when the two national parties faced this question in a presidential election, both of them evaded it: the Democrats by nominating Cass, on a platform which still did not say whether the people of a territory could prohibit slavery during the territorial period; the Whigs by nominating a military hero, Zachary Taylor, who had never been in politics, without any platform whatever. In the election campaign, which was a kind of contest between frank evasion and concealed evasion, Taylor was triumphant, and he became President in 1849.

Early Secessionist Sentiment. Meanwhile, the House of Representatives had repeatedly voted in favor of Wilmot's principle of free soil by congressional action. The seeming imminence of a free-soil victory had, in turn, aroused bitter resentment in the South, and for the first time many Southerners began to think of withdrawing from the Union if Congress voted to prevent them from taking their slaves into areas which they had helped to win and to pay for. By 1848, Southerners in Congress were beginning to speak rather freely of disunion. After Taylor was elected, Southerners realized that, although he was a Louisiana slaveholder, he was not going to block free-soil legislation, and they began to organize Southern resistance. In October 1849, a state convention in Mississippi called for a convention of Southern state delegates to meet at Nashville, Tennessee, the following June to work out a united Southern position. Five southern states officially elected delegates to such a convention, and representatives were unofficially chosen by political party conventions or by other means from four others.

Thus, when Taylor's first Congress met in December 1849, the need for organizing the area acquired from Mexico was urgent, and the relations between North and South were at a crisis. This crisis became more acute when Taylor announced his support for admitting California directly to statehood, without going through a territorial stage, and his intention to support the same plan for New Mexico in due course. Technically, this plan bypassed the question of congressional exclusion, but in substance it would represent a free-soil victory, for the proposed states seemed fairly certain to be free states. At this prospect Southern protests were intensified, and though historians today disagree as to whether the country was close to disunion, there were certainly many prominent leaders at the time who feared that it was.

The Clay Compromise Proposals. Among these leaders fearing disunion was Senator Henry Clay of Kentucky. As a spokesman of the border states, which were always anxious to promote sectional harmony, and as one who had played a leading part in arranging the compromises of 1820 and 1833, Clay was a natural leader of compromise. Although a Whig, he was at odds with President Taylor. Accordingly, Clay came forward, early in the congressional session of 1850, with an elaborate compromise designed to cover the slavery question on all its national aspects. Clay's plan called for: (1) admitting California as a free state; (2) organizing the rest of the Mexican cession into two territories, Utah and New Mexico, which were to decide for themselves whether slavery should be permitted or abolished; (3) awarding New Mexico part of the area on the upper Rio Grande claimed by Texas, but compensating Texas through federal payment of the Texas debt contracted before annexation; (4) abolishing the sale of slaves in the District of Columbia but guaranteeing slavery itself in the District; (5) enacting an effective law to compel the return of fugitive slaves who had escaped into the free states.

Clay's proposal brought on a long, brilliant, and famous series of debates in Congress. Clay himself made an immensely eloquent appeal for his plan as a means of saving the Union. Calhoun, who did not support the compromise directly, helped it indirectly by coming into the Senate almost in a dying condition to warn solemnly of the danger to the Union and the determination of the South to maintain its rights. The most important speech of

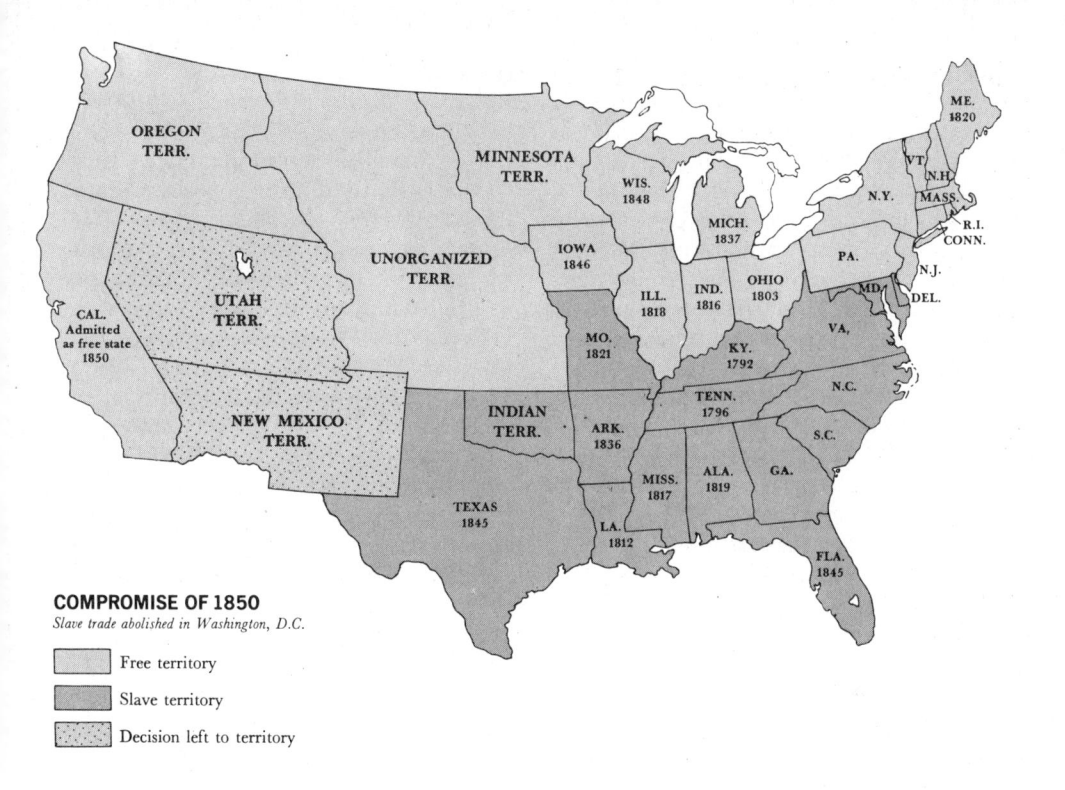

COMPROMISE OF 1850
Slave trade abolished in Washington, D.C.

- Free territory
- Slave territory
- Decision left to territory

the session was made by Daniel Webster, who was Clay's only peer as an orator and who was generally regarded as an antislavery man. On the seventh of March, Webster announced his support of the compromise and made a powerful argument that slavery was naturally excluded from the West by climatic, physical, and agricultural conditions and that there was no need to bring on a crisis by adopting an antislavery law, such as the Wilmot Proviso, to accomplish what had already been settled by physical environment. "I would not re-enact a law of God," said Webster, impressively, "I would not reaffirm an ordinance of nature."

Despite great oratorical support, Clay's "omnibus bill," incorporating all his proposals in one measure, faced heavy opposition. President Taylor was waiting to veto it, and in July it was cut to pieces on the floor by a process of amendment in which Northern and Southern extremists voted together to prevent its passage. Clay—old, worn out, and badly discouraged—went off to Newport for a rest.

The Douglas Strategy. Even before this vote was taken, however, the tide had turned. Early in July, President Taylor had been taken suddenly ill and five days later had died. His successor, Millard Fillmore, favored the compromise and immediately began to exert presidential influence to support it.

Meanwhile, Stephen A. Douglas, a young and vigorous senator from Illinois, took over the management of the compromise forces in Congress. Douglas was not a great orator, but he was a supremely effective rough-and-tumble debater, a man of immense energy ("a steam engine in breeches" was the phrase), and a most sagacious political tactician. He perceived that there was not a clear majority in favor of the compromise and that it could not be passed in the form in which Clay had presented it, but that if Clay's proposals were taken up one by one, each could be passed by a combination of those who favored the compromise and those who favored the particular measure. (For instance, California would be admitted by a majority composed of compromise men and antislavery men, while the Fugitive Slave Act would be adopted by a combination of compromise men and proslavery men.) Douglas applied this strategy so effectively that within a few weeks Clay's entire program was enacted into law.

The adoption of the "Compromise of 1850" ended the crisis. It also broke the long deadlock and gave badly needed political organization to California and the Southwest. Because it brought a great sense of relief to those who had feared for the safety of the Union, it was hailed as a great and final settlement which removed the slavery issue once and for all as a source of discord in the Union.

The Fugitive Slave Act. In fact, the Great Compromise of 1850 settled far less than it appeared to settle. For Utah and New Mexico it still left open the explosive question which Lewis Cass had so carefully avoided: could the citizens of the territory outlaw slavery in the territory? More important, while laying to rest the explosive issue of the Wilmot Proviso, it brought to life the even more explosive issue of the fugitive slave. For the question of the slave in the territories was a legal and abstract question—a question of what was later called "an imaginary Negro in an impossible place"—but the question of the runaway slave was dramatic and real, involving a human creature in quest of freedom who was being hunted down by his fellow man. Finally, the compromise had never commanded a real majority and had been enacted only by finesse. The southern states accepted it somewhat reluctantly, but Georgia spoke for the rest of them when her legislature voted resolutions that if the compromise were not fully enforced, Georgia would withdraw from the union. In fact, while the Southern disunionists were agreeing not to demand secession at this time, the Southern unionists were almost forced to agree to the *principle* of secession in order to get the secessionists to agree not to exercise it. Meanwhile, in the North the antislavery forces were pouring their denunciations upon the Fugitive Slave Act and upon Daniel Webster for supporting it. Political invective had perhaps never before in American politics been so bitter.

For a time, the fugitive slave question raised a terrific furor. To appreciate the uproar, one must understand that the law contained a number of very extreme features. It denied trial by jury in the case of alleged fugitives and provided for their cases to be decided by a special federal commissioner. Further, it paid the commissioner a fee that was higher in cases where he returned the alleged fugitive to slavery than in cases where he set him free; though this arrangement was defended on the ground that there was much more paper work in one case than the other, it led to severe criticism. Still further, the law stipulated that any citizen could be called upon to participate in the enforcement process, which meant that antislavery men must not only permit the capture of fugitives but might possibly be made to help in their capture.

Apart from these features of the law itself, the act aroused criticism because in operation it applied not only to slaves who were then running away but also to any slaves who had ever run away. There were many fugitives who had lived quietly in northern cities for many years and who had been quite safe from arrest under the relatively ineffectual Fugitive Slave Law of 1793, but now, under the act of 1850, they found themselves in real danger. In 1851 a Negro who had lived in Indiana for nineteen years was torn from his family and sent into slavery. Throughout the North, Negroes were terrorized by the law, for Negroes who were not fugitives had reason to fear being kidnapped quite as much as actual runaways had reason to fear being arrested. Consequently, a wave of migration to Canada set in, and several thousand Negroes moved to Ontario.

Resistance Against the Fugitive Slave Law. A series of fugitive slave episodes followed which kept the country at a high pitch of excitement. In Boston, leading citizens openly asserted their intention to violate the law, and in October a "vigilance committee" headed by one of the foremost citizens of Boston, the Reverend Theodore Parker, smuggled two undoubted slaves out of the country. Four months later a crowd, mostly Negroes, seized a prisoner, Shadrach, from the courtroom and spirited him away to Canada. Finally, in April 1851 the government succeeded in returning a slave from Boston, from which city it was boasted that no slave had ever been returned, but this was accomplished only after mobs had surrounded the courthouse for several days. Only once again was a slave, Anthony Burns, returned from Boston; in his case a mob stormed the courthouse in an effort to rescue him, and a large military force was required in order to prevent his rescue.

In other cities, also, rescues and attempted rescues kept the pot boiling, and the fugitive slave question became for a time the foremost issue of the day. Yet the excitement and emotion which the issue generated have made it hard to get at the facts about whether the escape of slaves from the South was numerically significant. On the one hand, Northern antislavery men boasted of their resistance to the law and claimed that they were operating a vast "underground railroad" which had helped 80,000 slaves to escape their pursuers. On the other, spokesmen of the South, indignant at the open violation of the law, complained bitterly that 100,000 slaves had been abducted over a forty-year period. But the censuses reported 1011 fugitives in 1850 and 803 in 1860 —which represented less than one slave out of every 3000—and it showed a relatively slow rate of increase among free Negroes in the Northern population. It seems likely that the underground railroad was primarily a weapon of psychological warfare rather than an escape route for slaves, and it also appears that in many parts of the North the act received public support and effective enforcement.

There is no doubt, however, that the fugitive question dramatized the issue of slavery to a spectacular degree. The human being in quest of freedom, pursued by man-hunters, was an immensely moving figure, and by changing the focus of the slavery question from the legal status of an imaginary chattel in a remote territory to the human plight of an individual human being in a nearby street, the Compromise of 1850 had, perhaps, created more tension than it relieved.

It is by no means an accident that *Uncle Tom's Cabin* (1851-1852), the classic literary protest against slavery, was published less than a year after the enactment of the fugitive law; that the book's most dramatic scene was that of the fugitive slave girl, Eliza, crossing the icebound Ohio River as she was being pursued by bloodhounds; or that the book, one of America's all-time best sellers, wrung sympathy and tears from countless people who had never previously been moved by the abolitionists.

Support of the Compromise: The Election of 1852. If the fugitive slave law dramatized the issue of slavery, the crisis preceding the Compromise had dramatized the issue of Union. Many Northerners who thoroughly disapproved of slavery felt that the question of Union was more important and must have priority. Consequently, despite fugitive slave episodes, the Compromise received strong support throughout the country, and though there had not been a clear majority in favor of adopting it, there was certainly a clear majority in favor of maintaining it.

The firmness of public support for the Compromise showed up clearly in the election of 1852. As the election approached, Millard Fillmore, who had signed the compromise acts while serving out the term of Zachary Taylor, aspired to a term of his own. But in the party convention, Northern Whigs blocked the effort of Southern Whigs to nominate Fillmore and forced the nomination instead of General Winfield Scott, who had captured Mexico City in the Mexican War. Scott was the Whigs' third military hero, and they hoped that, like Harrison and Taylor, he would get to the White House on his military record. The adoption of a platform revealed a deep division among the Whigs; though the majority secured the adoption of a plank accepting the Compromise of 1850, including the Fugitive Slave Act, as a final settlement, the opposition was very strong and consisted mostly of delegates who supported Scott. Scott, who was pompous and politically clumsy, tried to get out of this dilemma by saying merely, "I accept the nomination with the resolutions attached," but it was clear that he was not a thoroughgoing supporter of the Compromise.

The Democrats settled their differences between rival candidates by agreeing upon a dark horse, Franklin Pierce of New Hampshire, who had served with gallantry in the Mexican War. Pierce later proved a weak man, but he was an attractive candidate—handsome and pleasing in his manner—and the Democrats gave him united support on a platform which proclaimed the finality of the Compromise.

The position of the two parties gave the voters a fairly clear choice on the question of compromise—Pierce and his party were united on it, the Whigs were not—and the voters exercised their option in a decisive way. They gave Pierce the largest plurality any President had received up to that time, and he carried all but four states—two in the North, two in the South. This was the last time until 1912 that any candidate for the presidency carried a majority of both northern and southern states (except in 1868, when most southern states were under carpetbag control). The defeat smashed the Whig party, which was already badly divided between the "Cotton Whigs" of the South and the "Conscience Whigs" of the North, and though many important figures—including Abraham Lincoln—remained in the Whig organization somewhat longer, it was never a national party after 1852. This meant

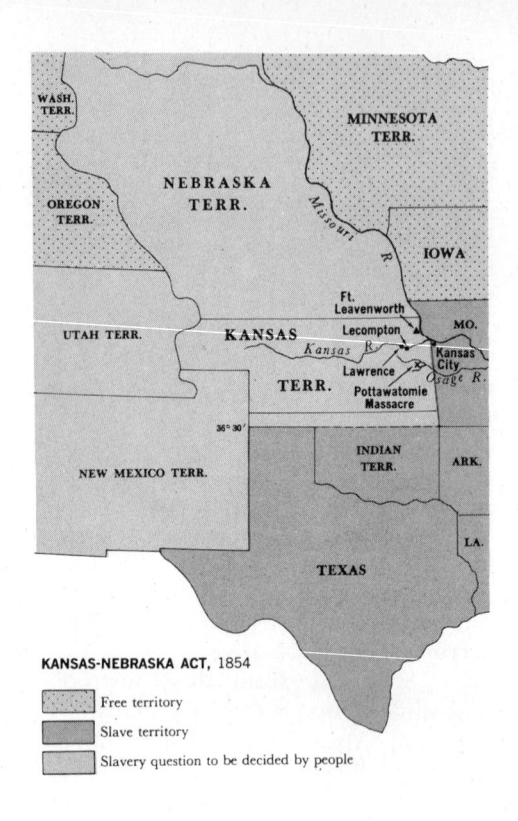

KANSAS-NEBRASKA ACT, 1854

Free territory
Slave territory
Slavery question to be decided by people

188   A House Divided

that only one national party—the Democratic—was left, which in turn meant that there was now only one remaining political organization in which Northern and Southern leaders were still seeking to smooth out sectional disagreements for the sake of party victory.

KANSAS AND NEBRASKA

The Douglas Bill. Pierce's campaign had promised harmony for the Union and finality for the Compromise, but his administration brought just the opposite. His first Congress had barely met in December 1853, when the territorial question arose again in a new form. Stephen A. Douglas wanted to organize territorial government for the region west of Iowa and Missouri. This area lay within the Louisiana Purchase, and since it was north of 36° 30′, it had been closed to slavery by the Missouri Compromise of 1820. Douglas, therefore, at first introduced a bill to organize free territories.

But Southern senators voted against his legislation and thus blocked it. They did this in part because they knew that Douglas wanted to promote a transcontinental railroad west from Chicago or some other Northern terminus to the Pacific. They were equally eager to run such a road west from New Orleans; there was simply no reason for them to give their votes to organize another free-soil territory for the purpose of facilitating a Northern railroad. Douglas felt that he had to have their votes, and thus in January 1854 he was led to take the fatal step of agreeing to change his bill so that it would leave the status of slavery in the Kansas-Nebraska region to be settled by popular sovereignty. Douglas made the plausible argument that what he advocated was nothing new, and that the legislation of 1850 had already replaced the principle of geographical division with the principle of popular sovereignty.

"Appeal of the Independent Democrats." In a widely disseminated tract entitled "Appeal of the Independent Democrats," antislavery men rejected Douglas' argument with furious indignation. They insisted that the act of 1850 applied only to the Mexican cession and was thus merely supplementary to the Missouri Compromise. The South, they asserted, was violating a sacred pledge; in 1820 it had promised to recognize freedom north of 36° 30′ in return for the admission of Missouri, and now it was defaulting on the agreement. This argument was not entirely accurate, for, to mention but one point, a majority of Southern congressmen had voted against the act of 1820 to begin with. But the act had stood for thirty-four years and Douglas was at least reckless, if not wrong, to tamper with it.

The furious blast of indignation which greeted his amended Kansas-Nebraska bill must have told him that he had made a major blunder. But Douglas was bold, aggressive, and tenacious. After committing President Pierce to his bill, he staged an all-out parliamentary battle for enactment. His own resourcefulness in debate enabled him repeatedly to throw his attackers on the defensive, and he conducted a brilliant campaign by which he succeeded in forcing the bill through both houses of Congress.

The Election of 1854. Douglas' success came at a terrible price. He himself had correctly foreseen that the repeal of the Missouri Compromise would "raise the Hell of a storm," but he had not foreseen, as he later said, that he would be able to travel to Chicago by the light of his own burning effigies. Six months after the act was adopted, the congressional elections of 1854 were held. The Whigs were too weak to capitalize on the public reaction; the Republican party had not yet emerged; but the Democrats suffered a stunning setback in the North.

Bloody Kansas. The worst thing about the new Kansas-Nebraska Act was that, even at the price of causing the bitterest kind of sectional hostility, it did not create a real basis for stability in the new territory. It merely changed the terms of the contest, for Douglas and many Northern Democrats believed that popular sovereignty could make Kansas and Nebraska free territories just as well as congressional action could, while proslavery leaders took the repeal of the Missouri Compromise to mean that slavery should prevail in at least one of the two new territories.

Both antislavery and proslavery groups prepared to rush supporters into Kansas to defend their respective positions there. From Missouri, proslavery men, known as Border Ruffians, had a way of riding over into Kansas on election day to vote and to intimidate the free-soilers and then riding back to Missouri. In New England, antislavery men organized an Emigrant Aid Society to send free-soil settlers to Kansas, and though the society never officially purchased weapons for these settlers, the leaders of the society bought rifles with separate funds to arm the emigrants against the proslavery men.

It would have taken a strong President to keep order in Kansas, and Pierce was not strong. He appointed a succession of able governors for the territory, but he would not vigorously support them when they needed his backing. Affairs, therefore, went from bad to worse. After the proslavery men had stolen an election and Pierce had given recognition to the government thus elected, the free-soil men formed another government of their own. Kansas then had two governments—a proslavery one at Lecompton, legal but not honest; an antislavery one at Lawrence, honest but not legal.

It is a great mistake to think of frontier Kansas as inhabited entirely by men who went there as missionaries for slavery or for freedom. Many settlers were simple, land-hungry frontiersmen like those who swarmed into all new territories. Such men were always quick to violence, and all the shooting that took place in Kansas was not because of slavery. But the slavery issue did accentuate the violence and give a pattern to the lawlessness of the frontier.

Thus, with President Pierce denouncing the free-soil government for its illegality, the proslavery forces secured an indictment of the free-soilers by a grand jury which was, of course, of the proslavery men's own choosing. With this indictment an armed mob, or "posse," as it called itself, marched on the free-soil headquarters at Lawrence, where they destroyed the printing press and burned or looted a good deal of property. It was a shocking episode, but only one life was lost. Four days later events took a far grimmer turn when John Brown, a free-soiler who carried his views to fanatical lengths, led to Pottawatomie Creek a body of men who took five unarmed proslavery settlers from their homes at the dead of night and shot or hacked them to death. After that, terror and violence gripped both sides. Kansas became "Bleeding Kansas," and probably two hundred men met violent deaths before a new territorial government used federal troops to restore order four months later.

"The Crime Against Kansas." Meanwhile, the intensity of sectional ill will was both illustrated and heightened by an occurrence in Washington. Charles Sumner, an antislavery senator from Massachusetts, delivered an oration entitled "The Crime Against Kansas" in which, in addition to castigating the slave power as bitterly as he could, he spoke in extremely personal terms about the elderly Senator Andrew P. Butler of South Carolina. He alluded, for instance, to "the loose expectoration" of Butler's speech. A nephew of Butler's in the House of Representatives, Preston Brooks, went to the Senate chamber when the Senate was not in session, found Sumner seated at his desk, and beat him severely with a cane. For several years thereafter Sumner was incapacitated, either by the blows which he received or, according to the best modern medical opinion, by his psychological reaction to the assault. The public significance of this affair, however, lay less in the attack itself than in the fact that a large part of the Northern press made a martyr of Sumner and pictured all Southerners as barbarians, while the South made a hero of Brooks and typed all Yankees as rabid fanatics.

The Character of Franklin Pierce. By this time the Pierce administration was ending as a disaster, because of the weakness of the President and the extent to which he let himself be dominated by Southern influence. After failing to prevent repeal of the Missouri Compromise, Pierce might still have saved the peace of the country if he had stood firm for real popular sovereignty in Kansas. But he had instead backed a proslavery regime which was palpably fraudulent, had allowed violence to go unrestrained, and had finally given his support to the idea of statehood with a proslavery government. At this point Stephen A. Douglas had broken with the administration and was fighting hard in Congress to defeat this proslavery government. Thus the political division at this point was less between free-soil and proslavery forces than between the honest application of popular sovereignty and the perversion of it.

Indeed, Pierce had backed the South at almost every point. He had negotiated the Gadsden Purchase (1854) for the acquisition from Mexico of what is now the southernmost part of Arizona because the land in question was strategic for the construction of a transcontinental railroad by the southern route from New Orleans. He had permitted three of his diplomatic emissaries in Europe to meet at Ostend, Belgium, in October 1854 and to propose American annexation of Cuba by purchase or, if that failed, by "wresting it from Spain." Cuba had almost 200,000 slaves and would strengthen the power of slavery. (This "Ostend Manifesto," however, aroused such world-wide indignation that the administration was forced to repudiate it.) Moreover, the administration did nothing effective to prevent expeditions by adventurers, called filibusters, who invaded the Latin countries from American shores. One such expedition from New Orleans against Cuba failed, and another, led by William Walker against Nicaragua, was temporarily successful.

ON THE EVE OF WAR

The Election of 1856. At the end of Pierce's term even the Southern Democrats knew that he could not be reelected. Indeed, the Democrats nominated James Buchanan of Pennsylvania, who, as minister to England, had been out of the country at the time of the Kansas-Nebraska Act (although as one of three authors of the Ostend Manifesto, he was particularly acceptable to the South). Buchanan was Secretary of State under Polk and a veteran of American politics—an old Public Functionary, as he called himself. To run against Buchanan, a remnant of the Whigs nominated Millard Fillmore, but the principal opposition came from a new party—the Republicans—formed by "Conscience" Whigs and anti-Nebraska Democrats and springing up very rapidly after 1854. This new party passed over its regular leaders to nominate the dashing but politically inexperienced young explorer of the Rocky Mountains and the Far West, John C. Frémont. In the election that followed, Buchanan carried all the slave states (except Maryland, which voted for

Fillmore) and four free states, thus winning the election. But the majority of the North was now backing a party which denounced slavery, along with polygamy (a jab at the Mormons in Utah), as a "relic of barbarism" and which had no organization whatever throughout half of the Union.

It is questionable whether, by this time, anyone could have brought the disruptive forces of sectional antagonism under control, but certainly Buchanan could not do it. His cabinet, like Pierce's, was dominated by Southern Democrats, and in February 1858 he forfeited his claims to impartial leadership by recommending the admission of Kansas to statehood under the proslavery and fraudulent Lecompton Constitution. Douglas and other Northern Democrats resisted; thus Douglas lost the Southern support which he had won in 1854, and the Democratic party became deeply divided.

The Dred Scott Decision. Meanwhile, the Supreme Court handed down a decision which may have been intended to restore sectional peace but which had exactly the opposite effect. This ruling concerned a Missouri slave, Dred Scott, who had been carried by his master first into the free state of Illinois and then into Wisconsin Territory, which was within the Louisiana Purchase north of 36° 30' and was therefore, under the Missouri Compromise, free territory. After he had been carried back to Missouri, Scott sued for his freedom, and the case was eventually carried up on appeal to the Supreme Court. The justices divided in various ways on several questions that were involved, but essentially the five justices from slave states held that Scott was still a slave, while the four from the free states divided two and two. The principal opinion was rendered by Chief Justice Roger B. Taney, who stated that, during colonial times, Negroes had "been regarded as beings so far inferior that they had no rights which the white man was bound to respect." As a description of the conditions which had existed, this statement was substantially correct, but it was widely quoted as expressing Taney's own attitude and was used against him mercilessly. The majority of the court held that a man born a slave was not a citizen and therefore could not bring suit in federal courts. In strict logic, therefore, the court need not have ruled on the other questions which Scott raised, but it went on to state that even if he could have sued, he still would not have been free, for the Missouri Compromise was unconstitutional; Congress had no power to exclude slavery from the territories.

In a literal sense the Dred Scott decision added nothing new, for it merely declared void a law which had already been repealed by the Kansas-Nebraska Act three years earlier. But in another sense, it had a shattering effect: it strengthened a conviction in the North that an evil "slave power," bent on spreading slavery throughout the land, was in control of the government and must be checked. It justified Southerners, on the other hand, in believing that the free-soilers were trying to rob them of their legal rights. It struck a deadly blow at the one moderate position—that of popular sovereignty—which lay between the extremes of free-soil and proslavery contentions. If, as the Court ruled, Congress had no power to exclude slavery from a territory by its own act, certainly it could not give a power which it did not possess to the territorial legislature, and without such power there could be no effective popular sovereignty. Finally, it made compromise by act of Congress almost impossible.

The Lincoln-Douglas Debates. The effect of the Dred Scott decision in popularizing sectional extremism showed up clearly in 1858, when Stephen A. Douglas ran for reëlection to the Senate from Illinois and was challenged to a series of debates by his Republican opponent, Abraham Lincoln. Lincoln, a former Whig, was deeply opposed to slavery. He regarded it as morally wrong—"if slavery is not wrong then nothing is wrong"—and he insisted that the Dred Scott decision be reversed. Slavery must be kept out of the territories and placed "in the course of ultimate extinction." But he was by no means an abolitionist. He did not advocate Negro equality, and he recognized both the complexity of the slavery question and the fact that slavery was protected by constitutional guarantees which he proposed to respect—even to the enforcement of the Fugitive Slave law. Lincoln defined the dilemma which the Dred Scott decision had created for Douglas and for all moderates. If slavery could not be legally excluded from the territories, how could the people of the territory, under popular sovereignty, exclude it?

Douglas replied at Freeport, Illinois (the "Freeport doctrine"), that unless a territory adopted positive laws to protect slavery by local police regulations, slavery could not establish itself; and thus by merely refraining from legislation, lawmakers could keep a territory free. This answer was enough to gain reëlection for Douglas, but it cost him what was left of his reputation as a national leader with strong bisectional support. At one time, Southerners had applauded him for repealing the slavery exclusion of the Missouri Compromise, but now they saw him as a man who was supporting the free-soilers in Kansas and who was advocating a theory which would deprive the South of rights guaranteed by a decision of the Supreme Court.

John Brown's Raid. If the Dred Scott decision brought to a climax the Northern feeling that freedom was being dangerously threatened by a sinister conspiracy of the "slave power," John Brown's raid on Harper's Ferry created an even more intense feeling below the Mason-Dixon line that abolitionist fanaticism posed an immediate danger to social order and even to human life in the South. After the "Pottawatomie massacre" in Kansas, Brown had dropped out of sight, but during the night of October 16, 1859, he suddenly descended, with a band of eighteen men, on the town of Harper's Ferry, Virginia, seized the federal arsenal there, and called upon the slaves to rise and claim their freedom. Within thirty-six hours Brown was captured, and he was later tried and hanged. But his act had touched the South at its most sensitive nerve—its fear of the kind of slave insurrection that had caused immense slaughter in Santo Domingo at the beginning of the century. Southern alarm and resentment would perhaps have been less great if the North had denounced Brown's act—as many Northerners, including Lincoln, did—but the fact soon came out that Brown had received financial backing from some of the most respected figures in Boston, and the day of his execution became one of public mourning in New England. John Brown was called Saint John the Just, and Ralph W. Emerson declared that Brown would "make the gallows glorious like the cross."

The Election of 1860. By this time, developments were rapidly moving toward a crisis. For more than a decade, sectional dissension had been destroying the institutions which held the American people together in national unity. In 1844 it had split the Methodist church; the Baptist church had divided into separate Northern and Southern bodies in 1845. Between 1852 and 1856, sectionalism had split the Whig party, and as matters now stood, the Democratic party was the only major national institution, outside of the government itself, which still remained. In 1860, with another presidential election at hand, the Democratic organization, which had already been strained by the tension between the Buchanan and the Douglas Whigs, also broke apart.

The Democrats. Meeting at Charleston, the Democratic convention divided on the question of the platform. Douglas Democrats wanted a plank which promised in general terms to abide by the decisions of the Supreme Court but which avoided explicit expression of support for slavery in the territories. Southern Democrats, led by William L. Yancey, a famous orator from Alabama, wanted a categorical affirmation that slavery would be protected in the territories. When the Douglas forces secured the adoption of their plank, Yancey and most of the delegates from the cotton states walked out of the convention. The accusation was later made that they did this as part of a deliberate plan or conspiracy to break up the Union by splitting the Democratic party, letting the Republicans win, and thus creating a situation which would cause the South to secede. But, in fact, many of those who bolted were hoping to force Northern Democrats to come to terms or to throw the election into Congress, where there was a chance that the South might have won. For weeks, desperate efforts were made to reunite the Democrats, but in the end the Northern wing of the party nominated Douglas and the Southern wing nominated John C. Breckinridge of Kentucky, Vice-President under Buchanan.

Some of the conservative successors of the Whigs, now calling themselves Constitutional Unionists, nominated John Bell of Tennessee for President and Edward Everett for Vice-President on a platform that said nothing about the territorial question, and called only for "the Constitution, the Union, and the enforcement of the laws."

The Republican Victory. The principal opposition to Douglas, it was understood, would come from the Republicans, whose convention was meeting at a new building called the Wigwam in Chicago. The leading candidate before the convention was William H. Seward, U.S. senator from New York, who had been the leading Republican for some years. But his talent for coining memorable phrases—"a higher law than the Constitution" and "the irrepressible conflict between freedom and slavery"—had won him a reputation for extremism, and the Republicans, who smelled impending victory after the Democratic split, decided to move in a conservative direction in order not to jeopardize their prospects. Accordingly, they nominated Abraham Lincoln, a former Whig from Illinois, who had made his reputation in the debates with Douglas but who had never been militant on the slavery question. To balance this nomination they made Hannibal Hamlin, a former Democrat from Maine, their vice-presidential candidate.

To attain victory, the Republicans needed only to hold what they had won in 1856 and to capture Pennsylvania and either Illinois or Indiana, which Buchanan had carried. As the election turned out, they won every free state except New Jersey (part of which went to Douglas), while Breckinridge won all the slave states except Virginia, Kentucky, and Tennessee (which went to Bell) and Missouri (which went to Douglas). Douglas ran a strong second in popular votes but a poor fourth in electoral votes, while Lincoln was in the curious position of winning with only 39 per cent of the popular vote. His victory resulted not from the division of his opponents, however, but from the fact that his strength was strategically distributed. His victories in many of the free states were narrow, and he received no votes at all in ten southern states. Thus his popular votes had maximum effectiveness in winning electoral votes.

Secession. Lincoln's victory at last precipitated the sectional crisis which had been brewing for so long. As we can now see in the light of later events, Lincoln was moderate-minded and would have respected the legal rights of the South even though he deplored slavery. But to the South, fearful of Northern aggression, his victory was a signal of imminent danger. Here was a man who had said that a house divided against itself could not stand and that the Union could not continue permanently half slave and half free. To the South he denied rights in the territories which the Supreme Court had said the South possessed. He was supported by swarms of militant antislavery men. And his victory clearly represented the imposition of a President by one section upon the other, for 99 per cent of his vote was concentrated in the free states.

In view of these facts, proponents of Southern rights felt that the South must act before it slipped into the position of a hopeless minority, at the mercy of men who had approved of John Brown. Therefore, states' rights leaders invoked the doctrine that each state had retained its sovereignty when it joined the federal Union and that, in the exercise of this sovereignty, each state, acting through a special convention like the conventions which had ratified the Constitution, might secede from the Union. Putting this doctrine into action, South Carolina called a convention which adopted an Ordinance of Secession on December 20, 1860. By February 1, 1861, Mississippi, Florida, Alabama, Georgia, Louisiana, and Texas had followed. The secession of the lower South was complete.

The Failure of Compromise. The actual arrival of disunion, which had been dreaded for so long, evoked strenuous efforts at compromise—especially by leaders in the border slave states, where loyalty to the Union was combined with sympathy for the South. From Kentucky, Senator John J. Crittenden, heir to the compromise tradition of Henry Clay, introduced

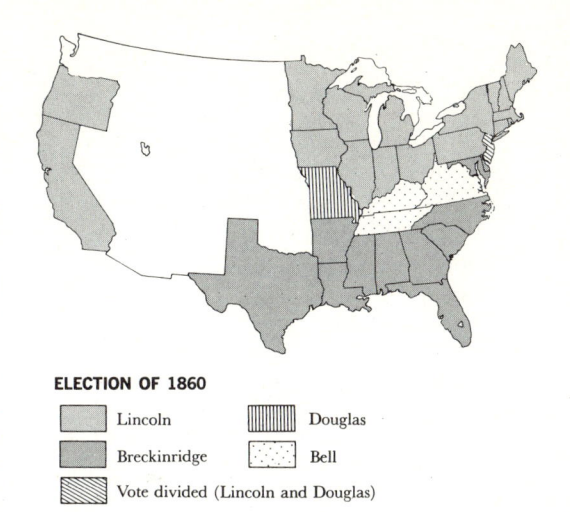

ELECTION OF 1860
Lincoln Douglas
Breckinridge Bell
Vote divided (Lincoln and Douglas)

proposals in Congress to revise and extend the Missouri Compromise line by constitutional amendment. Virginia took the lead in convening a Peace Convention, with delegates from twenty-one states, which met in Washington in February. Congress actually adopted a proposed amendment which would have guaranteed slavery in the states which wanted to keep it, and this amendment was submitted to the states for ratification before the war came and made it obsolete. But concessions on the territories were the only terms that might possibly have conciliated the South, and this was an issue upon which Lincoln was not willing to yield at all. As a result, compromise failed and the rift widened. By the end of February the seven Gulf Coast states had formed a new government, the Confederate States of America, with a capital at Montgomery, Alabama, and with Jefferson Davis of Mississippi as President.

Fort Sumter. Thus, when Lincoln was inaugurated on March 4, 1861, he was faced by a new Southern republic where seven states of the Union had been. This new Confederacy had seized federal post offices, customs houses, arsenals, and even federal forts, with the exception of Fort Sumter in Charleston harbor and Fort Pickens in Pensacola

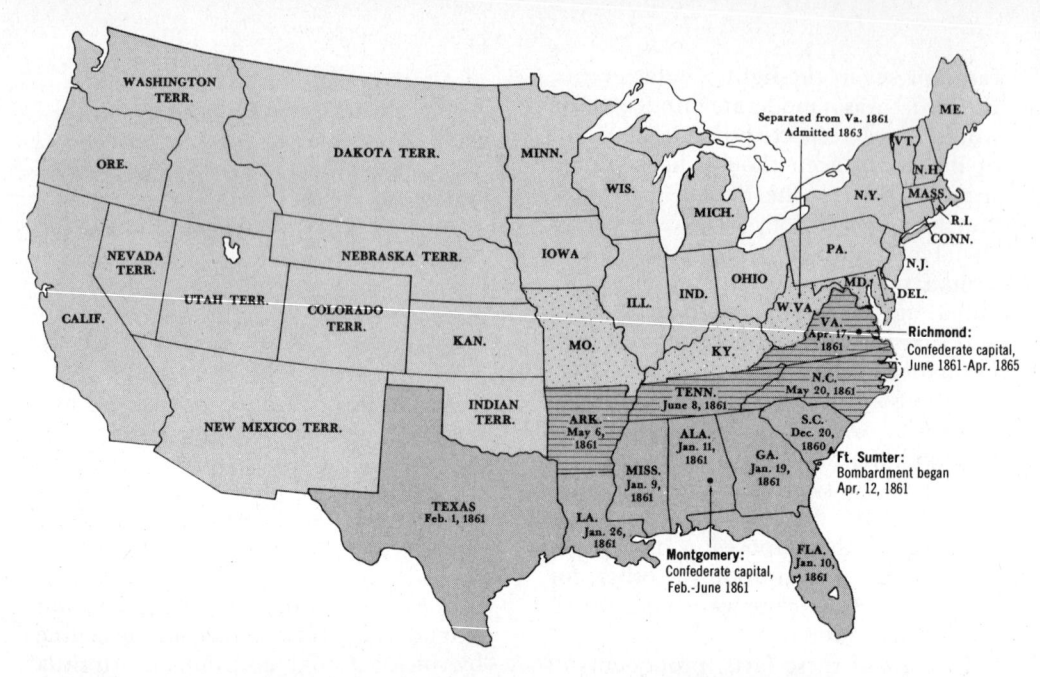

THE UNITED STATES ON THE EVE OF CIVIL WAR *(Dates of secession are given under state names)*

- Free states
- Border slave states that did not secede
- Slave states seceding before firing on Ft. Sumter, Apr. 12, 1861
- Slave states seceding after firing on Ft. Sumter, Apr. 12, 1861

(Slavery abolished in territories: 1862)

harbor. From North Carolina to the Rio Grande, these were the only two places where the Stars and Stripes still flew. There was great speculation at the time as to what position Lincoln would take, and there has been great dispute among historians since then as to what position he actually *did* take. Certainly, he made it absolutely clear that he denied the right of any state to secede and that he intended to preserve the Union. But whether he intended to wage war in order to preserve it is not so clear. There were eight slave states (Virginia, North Carolina, Kentucky, Tennessee, Missouri, Arkansas, Maryland, and Delaware) still in the Union. Lincoln was extremely eager to keep them loyal, and so long as they remained in the Union, they might help to bring the other slave states back. This split among the slave states represented a failure on the part of the secessionists to create a united South. Thus, Lincoln had every reason to refrain from hasty action.

If he had been able to maintain the federal position at Fort Pickens and Fort Sumter, or even at one of them, he apparently would have been prepared to play a waiting game. But less than twenty-four hours after becoming President he learned that Major Robert Anderson, commander at Fort Sumter, was running out of supplies and would soon have to surrender unless food were sent to him. Lincoln apparently gave serious consideration to the possibility of surrendering Sumter, and if he had been able to reinforce Fort Pickens and to make it the symbol of an unbroken Union, he might have done so. But attempts to reinforce Pickens were delayed, and on April 6

Lincoln sent a message to the governor of South Carolina that supplies would be sent to Sumter. If they were allowed in, no reinforcement would be attempted.

Historians have disputed whether this was a promise not to start shooting if supplies were allowed or a threat to start shooting if they were not allowed. But the Confederate government decided that the supplies could not be allowed, and before dawn on April 12, 1861, Confederate batteries opened a bombardment which forced Fort Sumter to surrender after twenty-six hours of furious shelling. This bombardment marked the beginning of a war which lasted four years and which was, with the exception of the Napoleonic wars, the greatest military conflict the world had seen up to that time.

"CAUSES" OF THE CIVIL WAR

Ever since 1861, writers have disputed what caused the Civil War and whether it was an "irrepressible conflict" in the sense of being inevitable. Southerners have argued that the war was fought not over slavery but over the question of states' rights; several of the Confederate states, they point out, seceded only when the others had been attacked. Economic determinists have contended that the Northern public never would support the abolitionists on any direct question (which is certainly true), that Lincoln did not even venture to issue the Emancipation Proclamation until the war had been in progress for a year and five months (which is also true), and that the conflict was really between an industrial interest which wanted one kind of future for America and an agrarian interest which wanted another. Other historians, going a step beyond this, have pictured the North and the South as two "diverse civilizations," so dissimilar in their culture and their values that union between them was artificial and unnatural. In recent years another group of writers, known as revisionists, have emphasized the idea that Northerners and Southerners had formed distorted and false concepts of each other and that they went to war against these images rather than against the people they were really fighting. The war, they would argue, grew out of emotions, not out of realities.

Every one of these points of view has something to be said for it, and the causes of the Civil War were certainly not simple. But though each of these explanations points to something other than slavery, it is significant that the factor of slavery was involved in all of them. It is true that the South believed in the right of the states to secede whereas the North did not, but this belief would have remained an abstraction and never been acted upon if the Republican crusade against slavery had not impelled the South to use the secession weapon. It is also true that the economies of the North and of the South were very different, but the United States has always had certain great regional diversities in economy—for instance between the urban, industrial Northeast and the rural, grain-producing Middle West—and these diversities have not led to war.

It is hard to believe that without slavery the general dissimilarities of North and South—their economic divergence, their specific disagreements on issues like the tariff, or even their social and cultural separateness—would have been brought into such sharp focus as to precipitate a war. That North and South could live together in harmony despite great dissimilarities was proved by experience before 1846 and again after 1877. Furthermore, when one speaks of a "distinctive Southern civilization," one is speaking to a very great extent of slavery, for slavery lay at the foundation of the plantation system, which was the very heart and center of Southern society. Finally, it is true that in the 1850's extremist leaders came to the fore and each section formed an emotional stereotype rather than a realistic picture of the other. But this is a process which always occurs as antagonism deepens.

The point is that slavery furnished the emotional voltage that led to deep distrust and dislike in each section for the people of the other. In his second inaugural, Abraham Lincoln said, "all know that slavery was somehow the cause of the war." The operative word in his statement was "somehow," for the war was not in any simple sense a fight between crusaders for freedom all on one side and believers in slavery all on the other. Robert E. Lee, to name but one Southerner, did not believe in slavery at all, and many a Northern soldier who was willing to die, if need be, for the Union was deeply opposed to making slavery an issue of the war. But both antislavery Southerners and proslavery Northerners were caught in a web which could never have been woven without the issue of slavery.

Could this issue have been settled without war? Was the crisis artificial? Was the territorial question a contest over "an imaginary Negro in an impossible place"? Was war really necessary in a situation where it seems doubtful that a majority of Southerners wanted to secede (only seven out of fifteen slave states seceded before the firing on Fort Sumter) or that a majority of Northerners wanted to make an issue of slavery? (Lincoln had only 39 per cent of the popular vote, and he promised security for slavery where it was already established.) Were the American people, both North and South, so much alike in their religion (overwhelmingly evangelical Protestant), their speech (an American variant of English), their ethnic descent (mostly from British, Irish, and German stock), their democratic beliefs, their pioneer ways, their emphasis upon the values of self-reliance and hard work, their veneration for the Constitution, and even their bumptious Americanism—were they so much alike that a war between them could and should have been avoided? This question raises the more general question whether disagreements are any less bitter when the parties disagreeing share much in common.

What was happening in America was that the center of gravity was gradually shifting from a loosely organized agricultural society to a modern industrial society with much greater concentration of power. As this happened, the government was being transformed from a loose association of separately powerful states to a consolidated nation in which the states would be little more than political subdivisions. In America's startling growth the North had outstripped the South and the equilibrium which previously existed between them had been destroyed. The proposal of the victorious Republicans to confine slavery—and in this sense to exclude the South from further participation in the nation's growth—dramatized this shift in equilibrium. It seems most unlikely that the South would ever have accepted the political consequences of this basic change without a crisis. Whether this crisis had to take the form of armed conflict and whether this phase of armed force had to occur precisely when it did, or might have come a month, or a year, or a decade sooner or later, would seem to be a matter for endless speculation.

CHAPTER 11

CIVIL WAR AND RECONSTRUCTION, 1861-1877

THE BLUE AND THE GRAY

The "American" War. The American Civil War lasted four years, from April 1861 to April 1865. It was fought over more than half of the United States, for battles took place in every slave state except Delaware, and Confederate forces made incursions into Pennsylvania, Ohio, West Virginia, Kansas, and (raiding from Canada) Vermont.

Out of a total of 14,000,000 free males of all ages, 2,800,000 were in uniform—2,000,000 for the Union and 800,000 for the Confederacy. This is a higher proportion than has been attained in any other American war. A total of 618,000 men died in service, either as battle casualties or as the victims of camp maladies (360,000 Union troops and 258,000 Confederates). This means that more than one soldier in five lost his life—a far heavier ratio of losses than in any other war in our history.

Partly because the cost was proportionately so heavy, and partly because of the fact that the Civil War was distinctly an American war, this conflict has occupied a place in the American memory and the American imagination which other wars—more recent, greater, and more crucial in terms of survival—have never held. On both sides, men were fighting for what they deeply believed to be American values. Southerners were convinced that their right to form a Confederacy was based on a principle of the Declaration of Independence—that governments derive their just powers from the consent of the governed. Northerners were equally zealous to prove that a democracy is not too weak to hold together, and that, as Lincoln said, the principle of self-government is not an absurdity.

The Resources of North and South. In later years, after the Confederacy had gone down to defeat, men said that the Lost Cause, as Southerners called it, had been lost from the beginning and that the South had been fighting against the census returns. In many respects this seems true, for the South was completely outnumbered in almost all the factors of manpower and economic strength which make up the sinews of modern war. The eleven Confederate states (not counting Kentucky and Missouri, which were divided) had a white population of 5,450,000, while the nineteen free states had 18,950,000. These figures leave out both the population of the four border slave states of Missouri, Kentucky, Maryland, and Delaware and the slave population of the Confederate states. Slaves strengthened the Confederate war effort indirectly, since by serving as workers they could release some of the whites to serve as soldiers.

The Union was far ahead of the Confederacy in financial and economic strength, too. It had a bank capital two and a half times as great as that of the South. It led the South in the number of manufacturing enterprises by three and a half to one; in the number of industrial workers by six to one; and in the value of its manufactures by five and a half to one. In railroad mileage, it led by approximately two to one.

But against these ratios of strength must be placed the fact that the Union was undertaking a vastly more difficult military objective. It was seeking to occupy and subdue an area larger than all of western Europe. This meant that armies had to be sent hundreds of miles into hostile territory and be maintained in these distant operations. This necessity involved the gigantic task of transporting the immense volume of supplies which are required by an army in the field and defending long lines of communication, which would be worthless if they were cut even at a single point. In wars prior to the Civil War, armies had depended upon the use of great wagon trains and immense numbers of horses to bring supplies. As the supply lines lengthened, the animals ate up in fodder a steadily increasing proportion of the amount which they could haul, until there was scarcely any margin left between what the supply lines carried and what they consumed in carrying it. Thus, the problem of supplies has always been a severely limiting factor to advancing armies. During the Civil War, for the first time in the history of warfare, railroads played a major part in the supply services. If these more efficient carriers of goods had not changed the whole nature of war, it is questionable whether invading armies could ever have marched from the Ohio to the Gulf of Mexico. Ten years earlier the United States had not possessed the railroad network which supplied the Union armies between 1861 and 1865. At an earlier time the defensive position of the South would have been far stronger.

But even with railroads, superior munitions, and superior industrial facilities, the military tasks of the Union were most formidable. America was a profoundly civilian country. The peacetime army numbered only 13,000, and few people on either side had any conception of the vast problems involved in recruiting, mobilizing, equipping, training, and maintaining large armies. It was an amateur's war on both sides, and many of its features seem inconceivable today. Most of the troops were recruited as volunteers rather than by conscription. There were no conscription laws in operation until the war was more than half over, and when these laws were adopted their real purpose was not to put recruitment on a conscription basis but rather to stimulate volunteering. Even when conscripted under the Union's law, a man could still gain exemption by paying a fee of $300 or by hiring a substitute. Conscription was applied only in localities which failed to meet their quotas by volunteering, and thus communities were impelled to pay "bounties" to encourage men to volunteer. This resulted in the practice of "bounty-jumping"—under which a man would enlist, collect his bounty, desert, enlist again in some other locality, collect another bounty, and desert again.

Volunteers often enlisted for limited periods, and when their terms of enlistment expired there was nothing to prevent them from quitting the service and going home, even if the army in which they were enrolled was on the eve of battle. Volunteer units in most cases elected their own officers, up to the rank of colonel, and they frequently preferred officers who were not strict in matters of discipline.

Preparation for military service was negligible. Physical examinations for recruits were a farce. Men were placed in positions of command without prior training as officers, and recruits were often thrown into combat without any

NORTHERN ADVANCES IN THE CIVIL WAR, 1861-1865

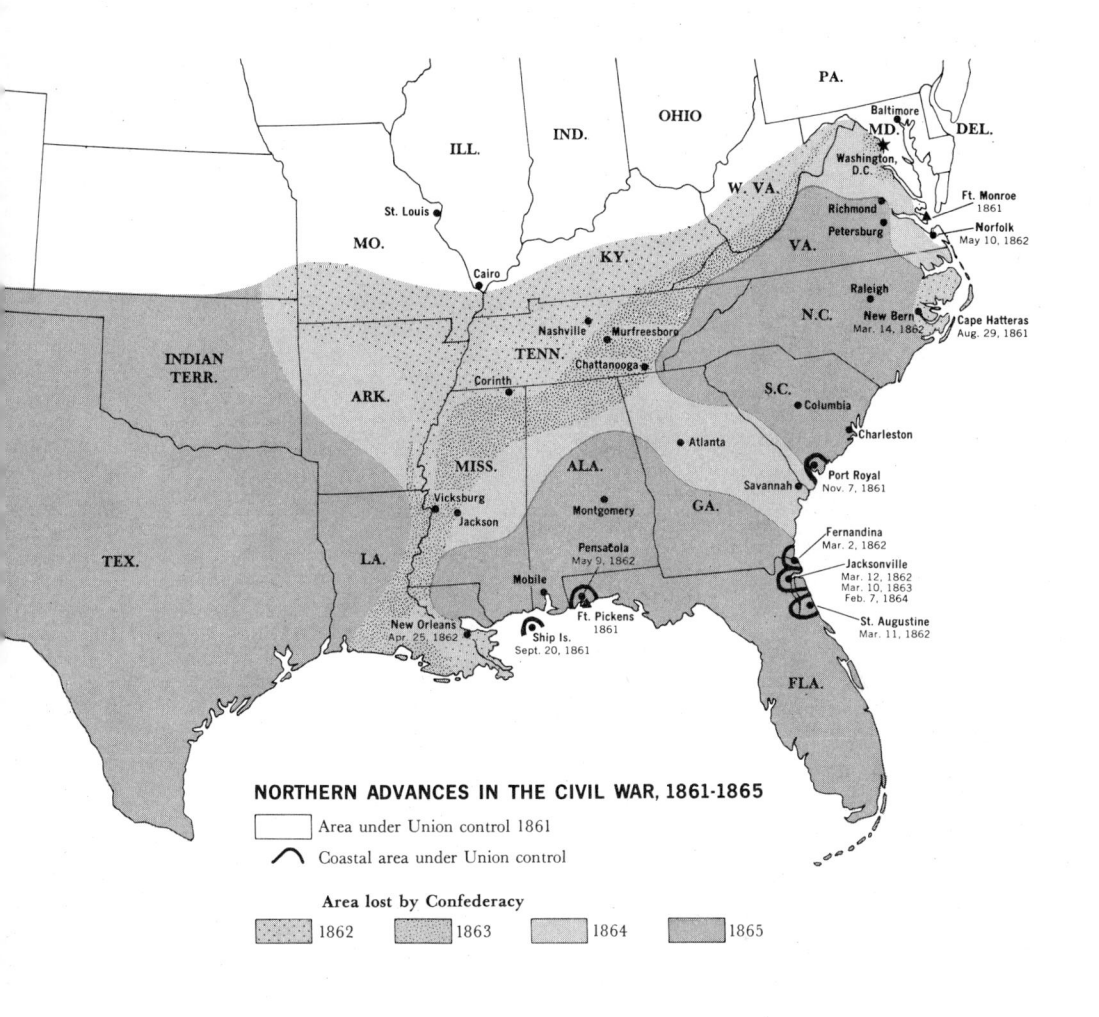

- Area under Union control 1861
- Coastal area under Union control

Area lost by Confederacy: 1862, 1863, 1864, 1865

basic training as soldiers. This was, to a great extent, a do-it-yourself war.

THE WAR IN THE FIELD

The Virginia Front. From the very outset of the war, attention was focused on the Virginia front. After fighting had begun at Fort Sumter and the states of the upper South had joined the Confederacy, the Confederate government moved its capital to Richmond, Virginia, about one hundred miles south of Washington. With the two seats of government so close together, the war in the East became a struggle on the part of the Union to capture Richmond and on the part of the South to defend it.

Between Washington and Richmond a number of broad rivers—the Potomac, the Rappahannock, the York, the Chickahominy, and their tributaries—flow more or less parallel with one another from the Allegheny Mountains in the west to Chesapeake Bay in the east. This grid of rivers afforded a natural system of defense to the South and presented an obstacle course to the North. Southern armies on the defense could lie in wait for their attackers on the south banks of these streams, as they did at Fredericksburg or at Chancellorsville. If the Southern army was driven back after going on the offensive, it could recross to safety, reorganize, and recoup, as it did after Antietam (Sharpsburg) and Gettysburg.

The principal army of the North, the Army of the Potomac, struggled against the principal army of the South, the Army of Northern Virginia, for four years over this terrain. Here each side placed its foremost commander; Robert E. Lee headed the Army of Northern Virginia after Joseph E. Johnston was wounded in 1862, while Ulysses S. Grant was brought east to command in 1864 after his great successes in the West. Public attention centered primarily upon these campaigns, and they have continued to receive more than their share of attention in history.

During the first half of the war, the Union met with a long succession of disappointments and defeats on the Virginia front. In July 1861, when both armies were still raw and unseasoned, the Union sent General Irvin McDowell south with the slogan "Onward to Richmond," and with expectations of an easy victory. But when he encountered the Confederate armies of Generals Pierre Beauregard and Joseph E. Johnston at Manassas Junction (the first battle of Bull Run), he was defeated, and his army, which was too green to absorb a defeat, lost all organization and retreated in panic to Washington. McDowell was replaced by George Brinton McClellan, who had campaigned successfully in West Virginia—a little man of supremely self-confident manner who was inevitably compared with Napoleon. McClellan possessed real ability as an organizer, and he had the good sense to realize that he must make his troops into an army before he took them campaigning. Consequently, there was no more major fighting on the Virginia front for almost a year. When McClellan did at last move in April 1862, he persuaded President Lincoln to let him transport his troops by ship to a point (Fort Monroe) on the Virginia coast within striking distance of Richmond. From this point he proposed to move up the peninsula between the York and the James Rivers (hence called the Peninsula Campaign) and to capture the Confederate capital.

McClellan's plan was a brilliant solution to the difficult problem of supply, for he could now bring provisions to his army by ship without fear of Confederate raiders getting to his rear and cutting his lines. But the plan had one important drawback: it left, or appeared to leave, Washington exposed to the Confederates. President Lincoln therefore insisted on withholding, for the defense of the capital, part of the troops that McClellan wanted, and McClellan, who was never willing to fight unless he had a sure thing, refused to push the offensive without these troops.

While these developments were in progress, the Confederate commander, Joseph E. Johnston, was badly wounded and was replaced by Robert E. Lee. Lee, a Virginia aristocrat, mild of speech and gentle of manner but gifted with a daring which was terrible to his adversaries, quickly perceived that he could play upon the Union's fear that Washington was too exposed. Accordingly, he sent his brilliant subordinate, Thomas J. ("Stonewall") Jackson, on a raid up the Shenandoah Valley, appearing to threaten Washington and causing the administration to hold there defensive troops which had previously been promised to McClellan. When Jackson returned from his raid with phenomenal speed, Lee's reunited forces took the offensive against McClellan's original forces in a series of engagements known as the Seven Days' Battles (June 26-July 1, 1862). McClellan fought hard and was not decisively defeated, but he lost his nerve, moved back to a base on the James River, and sent Washington a series of

THE CIVIL WAR IN VIRGINIA

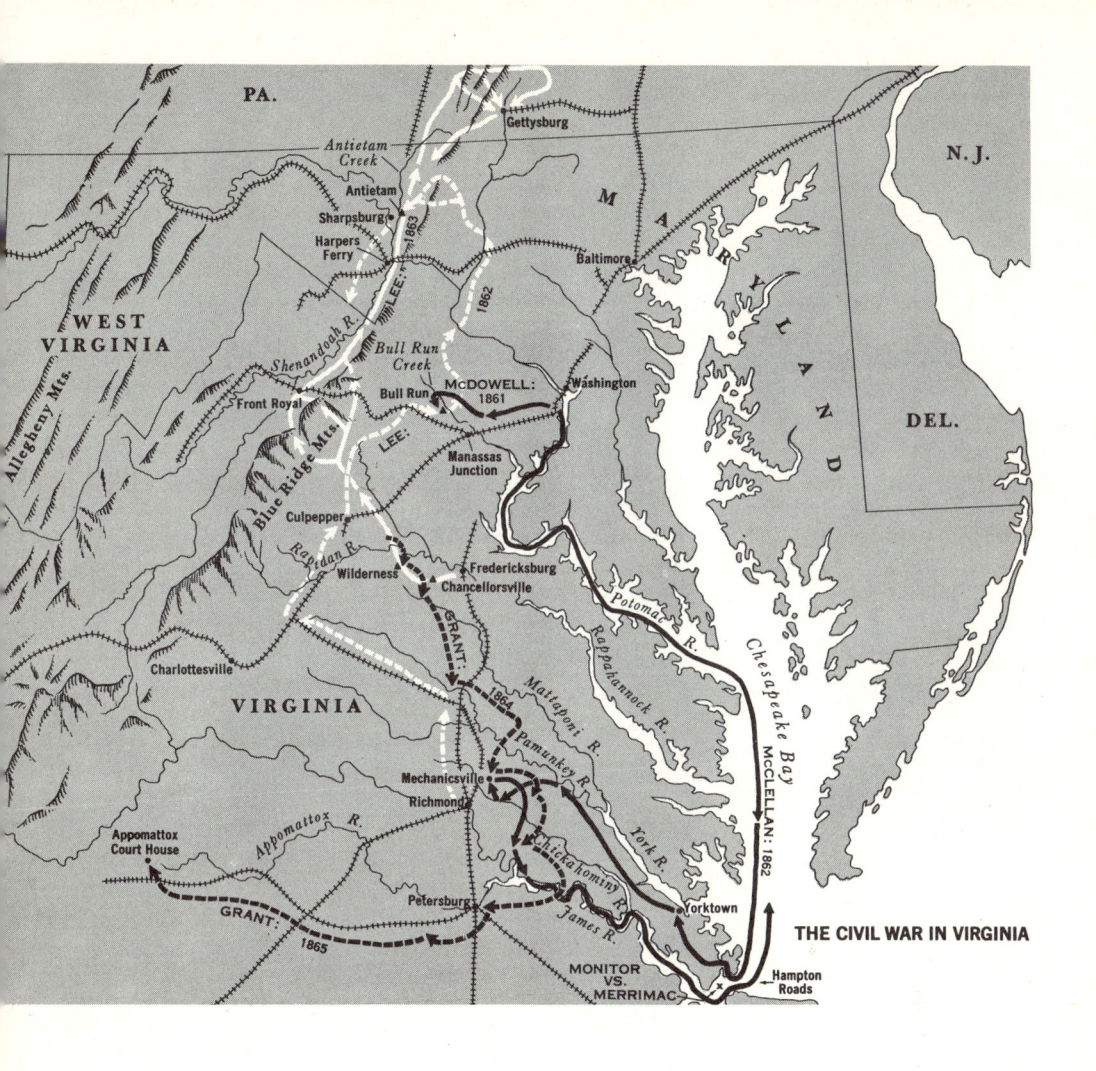

hysterical messages that the government had deserted him. Lincoln, who had never fully accepted the basic idea of operating by sea, removed him from command and placed most of the troops under John Pope, who had gained a reputation in the West.

Pope promptly ran afoul of the Lee-Jackson combination at the Second Battle of Manassas (the second battle of Bull Run) in August 1862, and McClellan was restored to command and given a second chance. When Lee marched north, crossed the Potomac, and advanced into Maryland, McClellan shadowed him. Again Lee divided his forces, sending part of his army to capture Harper's Ferry. But even when a copy of Lee's secret orders fell into McClellan's hands and he knew exactly what to expect, he still did not move quickly or decisively. After a supremely hard-fought engagement at Antietam (Sharpsburg), Lee withdrew, undefeated and unpursued, to the south bank of the Potomac. Lincoln again replaced McClellan, this time with Ambrose E. Burnside.

In December 1862 Burnside made an unimaginative frontal attack across the

Civil War and Reconstruction, 1861–1877   203

THE CIVIL WAR IN THE WEST

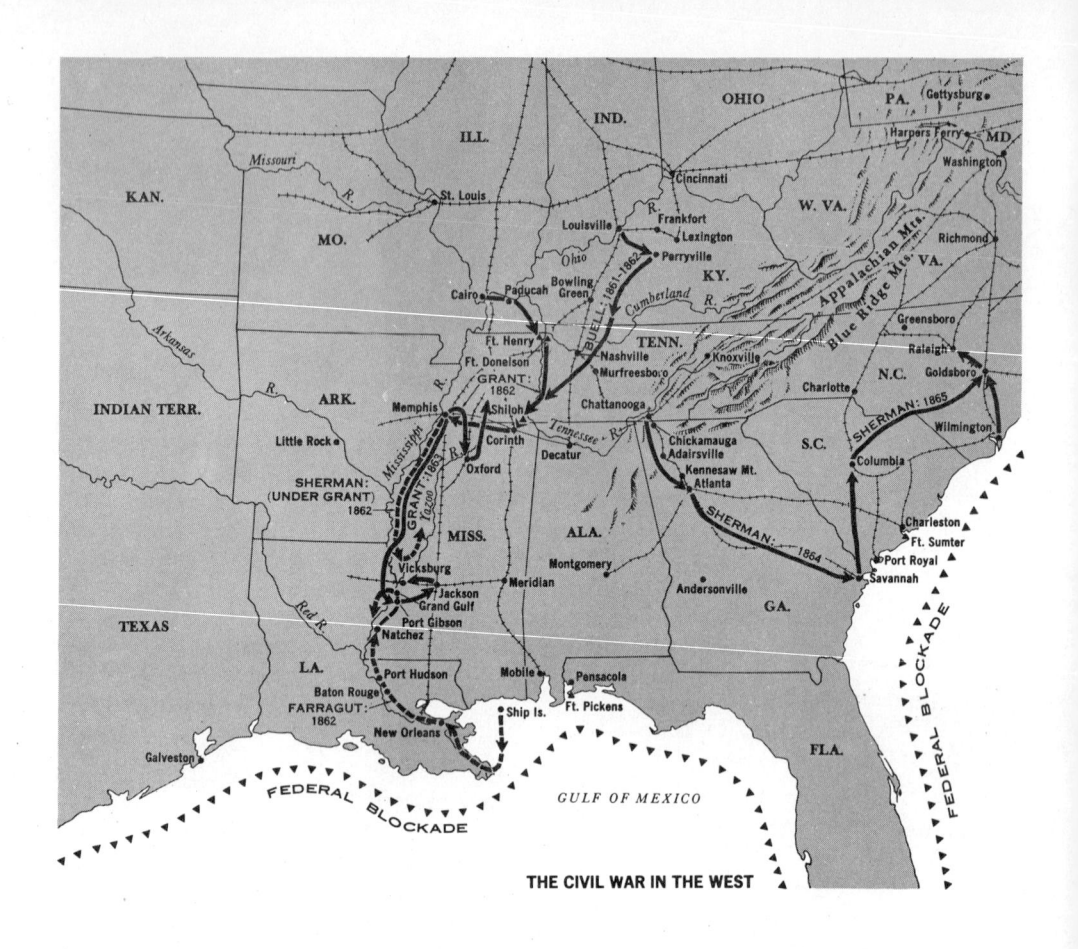

Rappahannock at Fredericksburg, Virginia, against prepared Confederate defenses. Fighting the Confederates on ground of their own choosing, he sustained terrible losses and was replaced by Joseph Hooker. Hooker seemed a man of boldness and decision, but in May 1863, when he was trying to cross the Rappahannock at Chancellorsville, Lee and Jackson caught him with his army straddled across the river. The Confederates won another victory, but Hooker saved his army and the South paid a fearful price: Jackson was accidentally shot by a Confederate and died of his wound a few days later.

Hooker remained in command until Lee launched a second offensive against the North, this time into Pennsylvania. When Lee escaped from Hooker on the northward march, Lincoln again changed commanders, turning this time to George Gordon Meade. Meade's army and Lee's army met at Gettysburg, though neither side had planned it that way, and on July 2 and 3, 1863, the South made its supreme effort at a little town in Pennsylvania, which became the scene of the greatest battle ever fought in North America. Lee, facing Meade across a valley, threw his troops against the Union positions in a series of bold and gallant attacks, the most famous of which was Pickett's Charge. But Meade was too strong to be dislodged. Lee's forces, which had been fearfully punished, waited for more than a day to receive a counterattack which never came and then marched south. Meade did not pursue until too late, and ten days after the battle Lee recrossed the Potomac unmolested. The Army of Northern Virginia had still never been driven from a battlefield, but its great offensive power was forever broken.

The War in the West. On July 4, 1863, the day on which Lee began his uncontested withdrawal, another Confederate general, John C. Pemberton, at Vicksburg, Mississippi, surrendered an army of about thirty thousand men —the largest that has ever been captured in North America. The man to whom he surrendered was Ulysses S. Grant, and the event marked the culmination of a series of campaigns in the West which had been much more decisive in their results than the eastern campaigns.

The whole region beyond the Alleghenies was far vaster and more broken up geographically than the Virginia theater, and the campaigns in the West never had a single focus as they did in Virginia. Operations along the Mississippi were scarcely coordinated with operations in the central and eastern parts of Tennessee and Kentucky, and neither of these was synchronized with activities "west of the River" in Missouri, Arkansas, most of Louisiana, and Texas. Essentially, however, it was the objective of the Union to gain control of the Mississippi and thus to cut off the western wing of the Confederacy. In this way Confederate armies would be deprived of reinforcements and supplies—especially of Texas cattle—which they vitally needed. A further division of the Confederacy would be undertaken by driving southeast through Kentucky and Tennessee, cutting vital Confederate rail connections at Chattanooga in eastern Tennessee, and continuing thence into the heart of the Confederacy, across Georgia to the sea. Such an operation would cut off the Gulf Coast region from the Atlantic seaboard and leave only Virginia, the Carolinas, and part of Georgia to support a hopeless cause.

It took three years and eight months for the Union to carry out these plans, but they began sooner than the great campaigns in Virginia. In February 1862, Ulysses S. Grant, a man who had left the army in 1854 as a failure because of excessive drinking, successfully captured two forts, Henry and Donelson, in western Kentucky, which controlled the Tennessee and the Cumberland Rivers. Unlike the streams of Virginia, which cut across the paths of advancing armies, each of these rivers flowed in a "U" shaped course from the southern Appalachians southward into northern Alabama (in the case of the Tennessee) or central Tennessee (in the case of the Cumberland) and then, reversing their course, almost due north to the Ohio River. Control of these river highways gave Grant easy entry deep into the South. On the Cumberland, Nashville, the capital of Tennessee, fell to the Union as soon as Fort Donelson was captured, and by April Grant had advanced up the Tennessee almost to the border of Mississippi. In that same month, when all was still very "quiet along the Potomac," the Union army and navy, by skillful combined operations, captured New Orleans, which was the largest city of the Confederacy.

After these early successes, the Union forces found themselves blocked for some time. A Confederate army under Albert Sidney Johnston struck Grant unexpectedly at Shiloh, Tennessee, on April 6, 1862, drove Grant's army to the edge of the Tennessee River, and might have destroyed it if Johnston had not been killed in action. When Grant was later able to resume the initiative, he turned his attention to the Confederate stronghold at Vicksburg, where towering bluffs command the

Mississippi. Deep in enemy country, Vicksburg was rendered almost impregnable by vast swamps, a succession of steep hills, and by the river itself. Grant made a series of unsuccessful moves against this natural fortress, but at last he hit on the bold and unorthodox plan of moving down the west side of the river, crossing below Vicksburg, abandoning his lines of communication, and living off the country during his final drive against the Confederate defenses. It was by this plan that he finally captured Pemberton's entire army at Vicksburg on July 4, 1863, and gained complete control of the Mississippi artery.

Grant Takes Command. After Vicksburg, in March 1864, Lincoln brought Grant east to serve as general-in-chief and to take personal charge of the Army of the Potomac (Meade was not removed but was under Grant's command).

By this time the Confederacy, outnumbered from the beginning, was fearfully handicapped by losses of men who could not be replaced as Union losses could. Grant, recognizing this handicap, settled upon a plan of operations that was far less brilliant than his operations in the West, but no less decisive. By steadily extending his flanks he forced the Confederacy to extend also and to make its lines very thin; by continuing pressure, he gave his adversaries no rest. Lee resisted with immense skill, and Grant sacrificed men so freely in the Campaign of the Wilderness (May 5-6, 1864) that his losses exceeded the total number of men in Lee's army. In June 1864, after being terribly punished at the Battle of Cold Harbor, Grant decided to move his base to the James River (as McClellan had done two years earlier), to attack from the south. He succeeded in this maneuver and thus pinned Lee's forces at Petersburg, which is actually south of Richmond. With Petersburg under siege and Lee no longer mobile, it was only a question of time, but Lee held on for nine long months while Richmond remained the Confederate capital.

Sherman's March. While Grant and Lee faced each other across the trenches at Petersburg, the Confederacy was being cut to pieces from the rear. Grant had first cut it at Vicksburg on the Mississippi, and the next cut was to take place from central Kentucky and Tennessee. By the end of 1863, the Union armies had won control of eastern Tennessee through a series of battles which took place principally at Chickamauga and at Missionary Ridge outside Chattanooga. When Grant left for Virginia, William T. Sherman, a trusted subordinate of Grant's, was left to face the Confederate forces under Joseph E. Johnston in the mountains of north Georgia.

Johnston was a "retreating general" but a resourceful obstructionist, and he blocked and delayed Sherman at every step, all the way to Atlanta. There he was removed because of his unwillingness to take the offensive, and John B. Hood was put in his place. Hood made the mistake of challenging Sherman in a general engagement and was so badly defeated that Sherman, after taking Atlanta on September 2, 1864, was able to march unopposed across Georgia to the sea. Sherman reached the port of Savannah on Christmas 1864, while Grant was still outside Petersburg.

Appomattox. From this time, the South was completely fragmented and the Confederacy's cause was hopeless. But Johnston, having returned to his command in the Southeast, held together a force which retreated across the Carolinas, with Sherman pursuing and burning Columbia, South Carolina, as he pursued. Lee, meanwhile, held against steadily increasing odds at Petersburg. By April 1865, however, the inevitable defeat could be put off no longer. Petersburg fell and Richmond was evacuated. Lee met Grant on April 9 at a farmhouse near Appomattox Court House, and in a moving scene surrendered the Army of Northern Virginia to Grant, who accorded generous terms and told his troops not to cheer because, he said, "the rebels are our countrymen again." Johnston also surrendered at Greensboro, North Carolina, before the end of the month, and the Confederate government, which had fled south after the fall of Petersburg, simply evaporated.

THE WAR BEHIND THE LINES

The Problems of the Confederacy. Writers on the Civil War have piled up a vast literature—one of the largest bodies of literature on any historical subject—detailing the military aspects of the war: the battles and leaders, the campaigns and maneuvers, the strategy and tactics. This military record, however, does not fully explain the outcome of the war. For, in terms of strategy and tactics, the Confederate performance equaled that of the Union and, on the Virginia front, surpassed it until the last year of the war. The final result was registered on the battlefield, but the basic factors which caused Confederate defeat lay behind the lines. Essentially, the Confederacy failed to solve the problems of organizing its society and its economy for war. It faced these problems in a particularly difficult form, and when it proved unable to solve them, it went down to defeat.

One basic handicap of the Confederacy lay in the fact that while the North had an economy of industrialism, which was invigorated by war, the South had an economy of cotton production, which was dislocated and almost paralyzed by the war. In the North, war stimulated employment, caused wage increases, and in general kept up civilian morale. In the South, economic conditions deteriorated so badly that what may be called economic morale declined even while fighting morale remained good.

Essentially, the Confederacy, with its rural and agricultural society, needed two things. First, it needed access to the products of European—especially British—industry. Second, it needed to stimulate economic production of food, of horses, and of strategic supplies within the South. Ultimately, it was unable to meet any of these needs.

In order to be able to draw on British industry the Confederacy needed to have buying power in the European market and to be able to ship goods freely to and fro across the Atlantic. Once war broke out, the South knew that President Lincoln would try to stop the foreign trade of the Confederacy. Lincoln proclaimed a blockade, which meant that federal naval vessels would try to seize the merchant vessels of any neutral country bringing goods to Confederate ports. But Southerners thought that the blockade would not work, partly because there were not enough Union ships to enforce it, and even more because they believed in what has been called the "King Cotton delusion." They were firmly convinced that cotton was an absolute economic necessity to Britain, because textiles were the heart of British industry, and without cotton this industry would be prostrated; Britain's factories would stand idle; its workers would be unemployed and would literally starve. When this started happening, the British government would decide to intervene to get cotton, and the British navy, which still dominated the seas, would break the blockade. Southerners were so confident of this idea that they were quite willing to see the British supply of cotton cut off for awhile. In the first months of the blockade, while it was still largely ineffective, they deliberately kept their cotton at home instead of sending a part of it abroad to be held in British warehouses so that it could later be sold to give them funds for the purchase of supplies. Thus, their only important economic asset, a store of cotton which was worth ten times as much as the gold supply of the Confederacy, was never put to constructive use.

The Importance of Sea Power. This faith in cotton ultimately proved to be a fallacy for several reasons. Britain succeeded in getting a certain amount of cotton elsewhere; British antislavery sentiment generated a strong resistance to taking steps that would help the Confederacy; and Britain was pleased to see America adopting a doctrine of international law concerning the right of blockade which she had always advocated and which was bound to be favorable to a nation with large naval power. But most of all, British industry was not paralyzed because Northern wartime purchases stimulated it. Britain, as a neutral, enjoyed an economic boom from supplying war materials to the Union—a boom very similar to the booms which the United States later enjoyed in 1914-1917 and 1939-1941 as a neutral supplying war materials to Britain.

Consequently, Britain and France, which was following Britain's lead, stood aloof, and the Confederates waited for an intervention that never came. In November 1861 their hopes were high when an overzealous Union naval officer, Charles Wilkes, stopped a British ship on the high seas and took off two Confederate envoys to Britain, James Mason and John Slidell. Britain, at this point, actually prepared to fight, but President Lincoln wisely admitted the error and set the commissioners free. Meanwhile, the blockade steadily grew tighter. One Confederate port after another was sealed off. Small Confederate vessels, built for speed and based in the Bahama Islands, continued to delight the South by running the blockade freely and bringing in cargoes of goods with high value in proportion to their bulk. But their volume was small, and they did not in any sense provide the flow of goods which the Confederacy so vitally needed.

In addition to depending on British naval might, the Confederacy made two important efforts to establish sea power of its own. To begin with, it fitted out the first large ironclad vessel which ever put to sea. A powerful steam frigate, the U.S.S. *Merrimac*, which the federals had scuttled in the Norfolk Navy Yard, was raised, renamed the *Virginia*, covered with armor plate, and sent out in March 1862—an iron giant against the wooden vessels of the Union navy. In its first day at sea it destroyed two large Union vessels with ease. The entire Union navy appeared to be in acute danger, and there was panic in northern coastal cities. But the Union had been preparing a metal-clad vessel of its own—a small craft which lay low in the water, with a powerful revolving gun turret. This *Monitor*, as it was called, challenged the *Virginia* on March 9, 1862. The battle ended in a draw, but with Monitor-type vessels the Union navy was again safe.

The Confederacy's second major endeavor at sea was to buy in England vessels and equipment which, under the technicalities of British law, could be fitted out on the high seas as naval vessels without violating neutrality. These vessels could then raid merchant vessels flying the Union flag. There were five such commerce raiders, most famous of which was the *Alabama*. This great marauder, commanded by Admiral Raphael Semmes, roamed the seas for two years, from Newfoundland to Singapore, captured sixty-two merchant ships (most of which were burned, after careful attention to the safety of their crews and passengers), and sank the U.S.S. *Hatteras* in a major naval battle. She was at last cornered and sunk off Cherbourg, France, by the

U.S.S. *Kearsarge,* but her career had made the American flag so unsafe on the high seas that prohibitive insurance costs caused more than seven hundred American vessels to transfer to British registry. The American merchant marine never again attained the place in the world's carrying trade which it had held before the *Alabama* put to sea.

The Confederacy sought to have additional raiders built in British shipyards, and two immensely formidable vessels—the Laird rams—were actually constructed. But strenuous American diplomatic protests, coupled with British awareness that in spite of technicalities this was really a violation of neutrality, led the British government to stop their delivery in October 1863. After this the Confederate cause was lost by sea as well as by land, and the federal blockade tightened like a noose to strangle the Confederacy economically.

Economic Failures of the South. Meanwhile, on the home front, the Confederacy failed economically because it was caught between the need to stimulate production and the need to keep down prices and to control inflation. The Southern government began with almost no financial assets other than land and slaves, neither of which could be readily transformed into negotiable currency. It faced the dilemma of being able to encourage production only by buying goods in the open market at an uncontrolled price, in which case inflation would mushroom; and it could control inflation only by a system of requisitioning goods for its armies at arbitrarily fixed prices, in which case production would be discouraged rather than stimulated. Only a program of heavy taxation, by which the government would take back the inflationary dollars which had been spent, could have helped at all in reducing this problem, but the Confederacy was afraid to use its taxing power. It raised less than one per cent of its revenue from taxes—a smaller proportion than any nation in a modern war—and it procured funds by borrowing, which is the most inflationary method of all. Ultimately it failed either to stimulate production or to control inflation. Goods grew scarcer while money grew more plentiful, and it was grimly said that at the beginning of the war people took their money to market in a purse and brought their goods home in a basket, but that by the end they took the money in a basket and brought their purchases home in a purse.

In short, the Confederacy died of economic starvation—an insufficiency of goods. Its government was too weak to cope with the nearly insoluble economic problems which the war had caused. President Jefferson Davis was a bureaucrat who thought in legalistic rather than in dynamic terms; he was not an innovator but a conservative miscast as a revolutionist. The state governments competed against the Confederate government for the control of manpower and supplies, and they insisted upon their sovereign status so strenuously that it has been said that the Confederacy was born of states' rights and died of states' rights. The only chance the Confederacy ever had, and it was perhaps a fairly good one, was to win a short war before the results of economic malnutrition set in. Once that failed, the cause was hopeless. A few Confederates, like Josiah Gorgas in the Ordnance Department, improvised brilliantly, and others did so desperately; but in a country where a vitally necessary rail line could be laid only by tearing up the rails somewhere else and re-laying them, a long war against a dynamic adversary could have but one ending.

Northern Industrialism and Republican Ascendancy. The problems and limitations of the Confederacy—problems of localism and decentralization, of an agricultural economy and of small-scale economic activities—were characteristic features of the kind of folk society which the Confederacy was defending. But while the South was making a last stand against the forces of the modern mechanized world, the war was rushing the North along the path toward industrial domination. Before the southern states withdrew from the Union, they had blocked some of the governmental measures most conducive to the new industrial economy. Southern secession, however, left the new Republican party in control; and, though this party seemed what we call liberal in its opposition to slavery, it was from the outset Whiggish, or conservative, in its economic policies. It believed in using federal power to promote economic growth through the encouragement of various forms of private enterprise; and, while this was believed to work to the advantage of everyone, it meant in direct terms the encouragement and sponsorship of measures favorable to industry and to private capital. Thus, in February 1861, while the empty seats of the departing Southern congressmen were still warm, and even before President Lincoln took office, Congress adopted the Morrill Tariff, which, though not very high, was higher than the existing tariff of 1857. This was the first of many tariff increases; there was not another perceptible reduction until 1913, and meanwhile Congress repeatedly strengthened the measures by which it gave American industrial producers more exclusive control in the American market, even if this forced American consumers to pay higher prices than they would have had to pay on the world market.

The Transcontinental Railroad. In 1862 Congress broke the long deadlock which the sectional conflict had created over the building of a railroad to the Pacific. For a decade, advocates of a southern route and supporters of a northern route had blocked each other; but now, with the Southerners absent, Congress created the Union Pacific Railroad Company, incorporated with a federal charter, to build westward from Omaha and to meet another road, the Central Pacific, a California corporation, building eastward from Sacramento. To encourage this enterprise, Congress placed very large resources at the disposal of the railroads. It gave to the roads ten square miles of land, running back in alternate blocks from the tracks, for each mile of track built, and it granted loans (not gifts) of between $16,000 and $48,000 a mile—according to the difficulty of the terrain where construction took place. The value of the lands at that time was not great, and the munificence of this largesse has often been exaggerated. But the point is that the government was paying most of the costs of construction, and it might well have controlled or even owned the railroad. Instead, it placed these resources in the hands of private operators, who, if they succeeded, would become owners of the world's greatest railroad and, if they lost, would be losing the government's money rather than their own. It was "venture capitalism," as it is now called, but the government was doing most of the venturing, while the private interests which constructed the road were getting most of the capital.

In 1869, four years after the war ended, the Union Pacific and the Central Pacific met at Promontory Point in Utah, and a golden spike was driven to mark the event. Travelers to California no longer were obliged to sail around Cape Horn, and the United States was a long step closer to being a transcontinental, two-ocean republic in an operative sense as well as in a purely geographical one.

The National Banking System. One other major economic measure resulting from Republican ascendancy was the creation of a new and far more centralized system of banking and money for the republic. Ever since Andrew Jackson's overthrow of the Bank of the United States in 1832, the country had had a decentralized, loose-jointed financial system—one which today it is difficult even to imagine. The United States, of course, issued coins and also bills which were the equivalent of gold or silver, since a corresponding value of precious metal was held in the Treasury for each bill in circulation and could be claimed by the holder of the bill. The government handled all its own transactions in such currency and was thus on a "hard money" basis. Actually, this kind of money was not nearly sufficient to meet the economic needs of the country for a circulating medium. The principal circulating medium, therefore, had been provided by notes issued by banks operating under charters from the various states. State laws governing the incorporation of banks naturally varied, which meant that the financial soundness of the various banks also varied; this in turn meant that some of the notes circulated at face value, and others circulated at various degrees of discount from face. The government was on a hard money basis, but the economy of the country was not, and the federal government exercised no control whatever over the principal component in the monetary system of the country.

The National Bank Act of 1863, which changed all this, grew out of the government's need to raise the immense sums that are needed for fighting a war. At times the government's need of funds was so acute that it resorted to the issue of "greenbacks"—bills which could not be redeemed in bullion. But primarily the Treasury relied upon borrowing—that is, upon selling bonds—and to borrow it had to make the bonds attractive as holdings for the banks. Accordingly, the National Banking Act provided that a bank which purchased government bonds to the amount of one third of its paid-in capital (not less than $30,000) might receive federally guaranteed notes, known as national bank notes, in an amount equal to 90 per cent of its bond holdings. The bank would, of course, lend out the notes at interest, and thus would receive interest both on the bonds and on the notes which it received for holding the bonds. At the same time, a tax was laid on the notes issued under state authority by state-chartered banks; the tax had the effect of making these notes unprofitable and thus driving them out of circulation. As a result of government borrowing policy, therefore, the United States acquired a new, uniform, federally sanctioned circulating medium of national bank notes. These notes became the principal form of money for the next fifty years, but they had the great defect that they made the amount of money dependent upon the volume of federal debt rather than upon the economic needs of the country. They were inflexible, and in 1913 they were largely replaced by the establishment of the Federal Reserve System. But the principles that the United States should have a uniform currency in use throughout the nation, and that the federal government should be responsible for this currency, had come to stay.

EMANCIPATION AND RECONSTRUCTION

The Road to Reunion. Wars always bring results which are not intended by the men who fight them. The Civil War hastened the growth of industrialization and economic centralization in the North; it also caused an increase in federal power at the expense of the states, for no government could spend the funds, organize the forces, and wield the strength which the federal government did, without increasing its power. But the main purpose of the war was to reunite a broken union of states, and there was a question whether the abolition of slavery was necessary to the objective of reunion. Some Republicans wanted to make emancipation one of the objects of the war, simply because they deplored slavery and did not believe that a Union which had slavery in it was worth saving. Others, who were relatively indifferent to the welfare of the Negroes, believed that the slaveholding class, which they called the "slave power," was guilty of causing disunion; that to make the Union safe this power must be destroyed; and that the way to destroy it was to abolish slavery. Still others, including many of the War Democrats and the Unionists in the border states, regarded the war as one against secession, having nothing to do with slavery.

Emancipation. For his part, Abraham Lincoln had stated his belief, long before he became President, that the Union could not endure permanently half-slave and half-free. He knew, however, that he could not free any slaves unless he won the war and that he could not win the war if he antagonized all the Unionists in the slave states of Delaware, Maryland, Kentucky (his own birthplace), and Missouri. As a result, he moved very slowly on the slavery question, and when two of his generals tried to move more quickly by emancipating slaves in the areas which they had occupied, he countermanded their orders very decisively. Few people realize it today, but the war had raged for seventeen months and was more than a third over before Lincoln moved to free the slaves in the Confederacy. In July 1862 he made up his mind to proclaim the freedom of slaves in the insurrectionary states, but he decided to wait for a victory before doing so. The Battle of Antietam (Sharpsburg) in September was not a great victory, but it sufficed; in that month Lincoln issued a proclamation that after January 1, 1863, all slaves in areas which were at that time in rebellion should be "forever free." This still did nothing about slaves in places like New Orleans, which was occupied by federal forces, nor in the border slave states, and it gave all the states of the Confederacy more than ninety days during which they could save slavery by coming back into the union before January 1863. Strongly believing in persuasion rather than force, Lincoln in December 1862 proposed a constitutional amendment for the gradual emancipation of slaves in the border states by the year 1900, with compensation to the owners. But this was defeated in Congress by a combination of proslavery men who thought it went too far, and antislavery men who thought it did not go far enough.

As late as 1864, the House of Representatives defeated a constitutional amendment for the abolition of slavery. The Thirteenth Amendment was not finally voted by Congress for submission to the states until January 3, 1865. Maryland and Missouri abolished slavery by state action at about this same time, but slavery was still legal in Kentucky and Delaware when the Civil War ended, and the amendment for the abolition of slavery was not ratified until eight months after Lincoln's death.

The Question of the Former Slave. If the Union was slow to face the question of slavery, it was even slower to face the question of racism in America. For the perspective of the twentieth century we can now see the great misfortune of the Civil War; while it solved the problem of slavery, it did nothing whatever to solve the problem of racism, which was so closely linked with slavery. People recognized that slavery must end, but this was a negative decision, for it did not clarify what should be put in slavery's place. Was the former slave to occupy a subordinate status in American society, or was he to be put on the path toward equality? The answer was by no means clear, for although there were twenty-one free states, only a part of these permitted Negroes to vote, and though Abraham Lincoln opposed slavery ("If slavery is not wrong, then nothing is wrong"), he did not accept the idea of racial equality ("I am not, nor ever have been, in favor of bringing about in any way the social and political equality of the white and black races"). In fact, to the end of his life he wanted to colonize the former slaves in Haiti or Central America because he believed that whites and Negroes could not live harmoniously together. (This belief, it should be noted, did not necessarily mean that he was discriminatory in his personal attitude; it might mean simply that he was pessimistic about biracial adjustments.)

Lincoln's Policy of Reconstruction. Along with this lack of conviction concerning Negro equality, Lincoln and the Northern moderates were deeply impressed by a feeling that victory in war could not really restore the Union; it could only prevent secession. After that, if the Union were really restored, it would be because the Southern people again accepted the Union and gave their loyalty to it. To bring them back, Lincoln wanted a moderate and conciliatory policy. When in 1864 Congress adopted a measure known as the Wade-Davis Bill, imposing drastic terms for the restoration of the former Confederates, Lincoln vetoed it, and when people raised technical questions about the legal status of the Confederate states (Were they still states, or conquered territories? Had they committed "state suicide"?), he was impatient about such "pernicious abstractions." All that mattered was whether the states could be brought back into their proper relationship with the Union.

In Louisiana and Arkansas the Union had regained enough control by 1864 to start a process of restoring these states to the Union, and Lincoln laid down generous terms on which this could be done. Lincoln would grant amnesty to former Confederates who took an oath of allegiance, and when as many as one tenth of the number who had been citizens in 1860 did so, he would permit them to form a new state government. When this government accepted the abolition of slavery and repudiated the principle of secession, Lincoln would receive it back into the Union. It did not have to recognize Negro rights nor give the vote to a single Negro. Louisiana was the first state reorganized on this basis, and despite its denial of Negro suffrage Lincoln accepted it, though he did ask the governor "whether some of the colored people may not be let in, as for instance the very intelligent, and especially those who have fought gallantly in our ranks." In Virginia, Tennessee, and Arkansas, also, Lincoln recognized state governments which did not enfranchise the Negro. But it was clear that Republicans in Congress were suspicious of these states—more because of their leniency toward the former Confederates than because of their treatment of the Negro—and that Congress might deny them recognition by refusing to seat their newly elected senators and representatives.

In 1864, when the time came for a new presidential election, the Democrats nominated General McClellan to run against Lincoln. Some of the so-called "Radical" Republicans, who were dissatisfied with Lincoln's leniency, tried to block his renomination and put up the Secretary of the Treasury, Salmon P. Chase, in his stead. But this effort failed, and Lincoln was, of course, renominated. In an effort to put the ticket on a broad, bipartisan basis, the party dropped the name Republican, called itself the Union party and nominated for the vice-presidency a Southern Democrat and former slaveholder who had stood firmly for the Union, Andrew Johnson of Tennessee.

In November 1864 Lincoln and Johnson were elected, carrying all but three states (New Jersey, Delaware, and Kentucky). In the following March, the new term began and Lincoln delivered his second Inaugural Address, calling for "malice toward none and charity for all," in order "to bind up the nation's wounds." The occasion was marred by the fact that Johnson, who was recovering from an illness and had taken brandy to fortify himself for the occasion, was visibly intoxicated and delivered an embarrassing harangue. On April 9, Lee surrendered the Army of Northern Virginia; it was clear that the work of Reconstruction must now begin in earnest. On April 14, Lincoln attended a performance at Ford's Theater, where he was shot by an assassin, John Wilkes Booth. He died the next morning, without ever recovering consciousness, and Andrew Johnson became President of the United States.

Johnson's Policy of Reconstruction. Although a Southerner, Johnson was expected to be more severe in his Reconstruction policy than Lincoln. Johnson, a former tailor who had been illiterate until his wife taught him to write, and a man of strong emotions, hated both aristocrats and secessionists. But when his policy developed, Johnson proved even more lenient toward the southern states than Lincoln had been.

On May 29, 1865, he issued a broad amnesty to all who would take an oath of allegiance, though men with property valued at more than $20,000 (in other words, planters) were required to ask special pardon, which was freely given. In the six weeks after May 29 he appointed provisional governors in each of the remaining southern states to reorganize governments for these states. Only men who had been voters in 1860 and who had taken the oath of allegiance could participate in these reorganizations. This meant, of course, that Negroes were excluded. When the new governments disavowed secession, accepted the abolition of slavery, and repudiated the Confederate debt, Johnson would accept them. As to what they were going to do about the Negro, no questions would be asked.

The southern states moved swiftly under this easy formula. Before the end of the year, every state except Texas, which followed soon after, had set up a new government which met the President's terms. But two conspicuous features of these governments were deeply disturbing to many Republicans. First, these southern states had adopted a series of laws known as "Black Codes," which denied to Negroes many of the rights of citizenship—including the right to vote and to serve on juries— and which also excluded them from certain types of property ownership and certain occupations. Unemployed Negroes might be arrested as vagrants and bound out to labor in a new form of involuntary servitude. Second, the former Confederates were in complete control: the newly organized states, between them, elected to Congress the vice-president of the Confederacy, four Confederate generals, five Confederate colonels, six Confederate cabinet officers, and fifty-eight Confederate congressmen.

Congressional Radicals. When Congress met at the end of 1865, it was confronted by the fact that Reconstruction (on the President's terms) had been virtually completed without Congress having any voice in the matter. At this point, the Republicans were far from ready for the kind of all-out fight against Johnson which later developed, but they were not willing to accept the reorganized states, especially since they felt that these states would now claim a larger representation in Congress because of the free Negro population (only three fifths of the Negroes had been counted when they were slaves), without actually allowing the Negroes any voice in the government. It would be ironical indeed if the overthrow of slavery should increase the representation of the South in Congress and if the Rebels should come back into the Union stronger than when they went out.

For some months, the Republicans in Congress moved slowly, unwilling to face a break with a President of their own party, and far from ready to make a vigorous stand for Negro rights. But they would not seat the Southern congressmen-elect, and they set up a Joint Committee of the Senate and the House, under the chairmanship of Thaddeus Stevens, to assert their claim to a voice in the formulation of Reconstruction policy. Also, they passed a bill to extend the life and increase the activities of the Freedmen's Bureau—an agency created to aid the Negroes in their transition from slavery to freedom. When Johnson vetoed this measure and also vetoed a Civil Rights bill, tensions tightened, and in June 1866, Congress voted a proposed Fourteenth Amendment. This amendment clearly asserted the citizenship of the Negroes; it also asserted that they were entitled to the "privileges and immunities of citizens," to the "equal protection of the laws," and to protection against being deprived of "life, liberty, and property without due process of law." The determination of exactly what these terms meant has kept lawyers busy for almost a century now, but one thing was clear: the amendment did not include a right of Negro suffrage. It did, however, provide that states which disfranchised a part of their adult male population would have their representation proportionately reduced. It almost seemed that Congress was offering the Southerners a choice: they might disfranchise the Negroes if they were willing to pay the price of reduced representation, or they might have increased representation if they were willing to pay the price of Negro suffrage. This might not help the Negroes, but it was certain to help the Republicans: it would either reduce the strength of Southern white Democrats or give the Republicans Negro political allies in the South.

The Fourteenth Amendment also excluded from federal office any person who had held any important public office before the Civil War and had then gone over to the Confederacy. This sweeping move to disqualify almost the entire leadership of the South led the southern states to make the serious mistake of following President Johnson's advice to reject the amendment. During the latter half of 1866 and the first months of 1867, ten southern states voted not to ratify.

Radical Reconstruction. Southern rejection of the Fourteenth Amendment precipitated the bitter fight which had been brewing for almost two years. Congress now moved to destroy the Johnson governments and to set up new governments of its own. Between March and July 1867, it adopted a series of Reconstruction Acts which divided ten southern states into five military districts under five military governors. These governors were to hold elections for conventions to frame new state constitutions. In these elections adult males, including Negroes, were to vote, but many whites, disqualified by their support of the Confederacy, were not to vote. The constitutions which these conventions adopted must establish Negro suffrage, and the governments which they established must ratify the Fourteenth Amendment. Then and only then might they be readmitted to the Union. Thus, two years after the war was over, when the South supposed that the postwar adjustment had been completed, the process of Reconstruction actually began.

The period that followed has been the subject of more bitter feeling and more controversy than, perhaps, any other period in American history, and the intensity of the bitterness has made it hard to get at the realities. During 1867 the military governors conducted elections; in late 1867 and early 1868 the new constitutional conventions met in the southern states. They complied with the terms which Congress had laid down, including enfranchisement of the Negro, and within a year after the third Reconstruction Act (of July 1867), seven states had adopted new constitutions, organized new governments, ratified the Fourteenth Amendment, and been readmitted to the Union. In Virginia, Mississippi, and Texas the process was for one reason or another not completed until 1870.

All of these new governments, except the one in Virginia, began under Republican control, with more or less Negro representation in the legislatures. In one state after another, however, the Democrats, supporting a policy of white supremacy, gained the ascendancy. Military and "Radical" rule lasted for three years in North Carolina; four years in Tennessee (never under military government) and Georgia; six years in Texas; seven years in Alabama and Arkansas; eight years in Mississippi; and ten years in Florida, Louisiana, and South Carolina.

These various time spans were the period of so-called "carpetbag government," "military despotism," and "Negro rule." Southern whites remembered the experience bitterly as "a long and cheerless night of misrule," and they pictured this period in terms of certain extreme images which were later adopted by a pro-Southern school of Reconstruction historians. According to this version, the South was at the outset the victim of military occupation in which a brutal soldiery maintained bayonet rule. Then came the "carpetbaggers"—unscrupulous Northern adventurers whose only purpose was to enrich themselves by plundering the prostrate South. To maintain their ascendancy, the carpetbaggers incited the Negroes, who were essentially well-disposed, to assert themselves in swaggering insolence. Thereupon, majorities made up of illiterate Negroes swarmed into the legislatures, where they were manipulated by the carpetbaggers. A carnival of riotous corruption and looting followed, until at last the outraged whites, excluded from all voice in public affairs, could endure these conditions no longer and arose to drive the vandals away and to redeem their dishonored states.

This picture of Reconstruction has a very real importance, for it has undoubtedly influenced Southern attitudes in the twentieth century, but it is an extreme distortion of the realities. As for bayonet rule, the number of troops in the "Army of Occupation" was absurdly small. In November 1869 there were 1000 federal soldiers scattered over the state of Virginia and 716 over Mississippi, with hardly more than a corporal's guard in any one place. As for the carpetbaggers, there were indeed looters among the newcomers who moved into the South, but there were also idealists: many Northern women came to teach; many men came to develop needed industry; many others worked with integrity and self-sacrifice to find a constructive solution for the problems of a society devastated by war and left with a huge population of former slaves to absorb and provide for. Many native Southerners, who joined with the "carpetbaggers" in their programs and who were therefore denounced as "scalawags," were equally public-spirited and high-minded.

As for Negro rule, the fact is that the Negroes were never but once in a majority in the government of any southern state, and that was in the convention and the first legislature of South Carolina. Elsewhere they were a minority, even in Georgia, Mississippi, and Louisiana, where they constituted a majority of the population. In view of their illiteracy and their political inexperience, the Negroes handled their new responsibilities well. They tended to choose educated Negroes for public office, and many of the Negro legislators, congressmen, and state officials were well qualified. They were, on the whole, moderate and self-restrained in their demands; they did not challenge the principle of segregation in the schools (only Louisiana and South Carolina definitely provided for desegregated schools), nor the laws against racial intermarriage, nor the practices of biracialism in social life; and they gave major support to certain policies of long-range value, including notably the establishment of public school systems which the South had not had in any broad sense before the Civil War.

As for the "carnival of corruption," it is true that the post-Civil War era was marked by corruption throughout the country and that corruption presented especial hardships for the southern states, already stripped of their resources by the war. Carpetbag governments in several states issued state bonds, pledging the state to pay one hundred cents on the dollar, and then sold these bonds at immense discounts for whatever they would bring, pocketing the money as it came in. In South Carolina, corruptionists even stole a fund which was created to buy homesteads for Negroes. But corruption was not confined to the South, and within the South it was not confined to the Republicans. Democrats also were among the guilty.

Finally, it should be noted that the Southern whites were never reduced to abject helplessness, as is sometimes imagined. From the outset they were present in all of the Reconstruction conventions and legislatures—always vocal, frequently aggressive, and sometimes dominating the proceedings.

The Fall of Radical Reconstruction. For an average of six years the regimes of Radical Republican Reconstruction continued; then they gave way to the Democratic Redeemers—delaying further action on the question of the Negroes' rights until the twentieth century. When one considers the fact that the South had just been badly defeated in war, that Radical Reconstruction was the policy of the dominant party in Washington, and that Negroes constituted an actual majority of the potential electorate in several southern states (with a certain proportion of the former Confederates disfranchised), it is difficult to understand why the Radical regimes were so promptly—almost easily—overthrown. Several contributing factors must be recognized. First of all, of course, the former slaves were poorly fitted to assume political responsibility. Largely illiterate and conditioned for many decades to defer to the white man, they grasped their opportunity with uncertain hands. Very often they seemed to wish, quite realistically, for security of land tenure and for education more than for political rights. Second, and more important, one must recognize the importance of the grim resistance offered by the Southern whites. With their deep belief in the superiority of their own race, these Southerners were convinced that civilization itself was at stake, and they fought with proportionate desperation, not hesitating to resort to violence and terror. In 1867 a half-whimsical secret society formed in Tennessee and known as the Ku Klux Klan began to take on a more purposeful character and to spread across the South. Soon every southern state had its organization of masked and robed riders, either as part of the Klan or under some other name, who, by use of threat, horsewhip, and even rope and gun, spread fear not only among the Negroes but perhaps even more among the Republican leaders. The states and even Congress passed laws to break up this activity, but the laws proved almost impossible to enforce, and the Klan ceased to operate only when its purposes had been accomplished.

The dramatic quality of the Klan has given it a prominent place in the public's mental picture of Reconstruction. But though the Klan played a prominent role, the white South had other, less spectacular weapons which were no less powerful. Southern whites owned virtually all of the land; they controlled virtually all employment; they dominated the small supply of money and credit which was to be found in the South; and they could, in unspectacular ways, make life very hard for individuals who did not comply with the system. This, perhaps more than the acts of night riders and violent men, made the pressure against Radical rule almost irresistible.

But still more important, perhaps, than either the limitations of the Southern Negroes or the fierce determination of the Southern whites was the fact that, when all was said and done, neither the Republican party nor the Northern public was really committed to Negro equality. Patterns of discrimination against the Negro, which still prevail today, had become well established in the northern states long before the Civil War. Even antislavery men like the Free Soilers had taken the position they did because they wanted to keep Negroes—whether slave or free —out of their bailiwicks. More than one free state had laws to prevent Negroes from entering the state. Significantly, after emancipation all efforts to provide the former slaves with land ("forty acres and a mule") or to set up a federal program of education for the Negroes failed even in Congresses with large Radical majorities.

There were just not enough people who really cared about the freedmen. The decision to give the vote to the Negro was reached very reluctantly, as has been shown above, and it was really adopted not because of any belief that it was right in principle but because Negro participation in politics appeared to be the only alternative to Confederate rule—an unwelcome choice, but the only one. Later, Republicans found that the Northern voters did not support them in this choice; that the white South would not consent to a real reunion on this basis; and that the former Confederates had political objectives quite similar to the Republicans' objectives. As a result, the Republicans let the existing forces in the South find their own resolution— which was one of white supremacy.

Johnson versus the Radicals. The Radicals did not abandon their program all at once. Indeed, it faded out very gradually. While Johnson remained President, the Radicals remained militant, and in 1868 they tried to remove him by impeachment. Though Johnson had denounced the Radicals in intemperate terms, he had done nothing to justify impeachment proceedings except to remove the Secretary of War, Edwin M. Stanton, from his post in the cabinet. In March 1867 Congress had passed a law, the Tenure of Office Act, which forbade such removals without senatorial consent and which has since been held by the courts to be unconstitutional. But when Johnson removed Stanton, who was reporting to the Radicals what went on in administration councils, there had been no judicial ruling, and the House of Representatives voted to impeach Johnson, which meant that he must be tried by the Senate on the articles of impeachment. The trial was conducted in a tense atmosphere and not in a very judicial way. Immense pressure was put on all Republican senators to vote for conviction. When a vote was finally taken on May 16, 1868, conviction failed by one vote of the two thirds required. Seven Republicans had stood out against the party; Johnson was permitted to serve out his term; and the balance between executive and legislative power in the American political system, which had almost been destroyed, was preserved.

The determination of the Republican leaders in Congress to beat down the opposition regardless of cost showed up in a parallel attack on the judiciary. When a Mississippi editor named McCardle appealed to the Supreme Court to rule on the constitutionality of one of the Reconstruction Acts, under which he had been arrested by the military, Congress in March 1868 passed an act changing the appellate jurisdiction of the Court so that it could not pass judgment on McCardle's case.

The Grant Administration. In 1868 the country faced another election, and the Republicans turned to General Grant as their nominee. He was elected over the Democratic candidate Governor Horatio Seymour of New York, by a popular majority of only 300,000—a surprisingly close vote. Grant was not supported by a majority of the white voters: some 700,000 Negro votes helped to elect him. (The importance of the Negro vote in this election inspired Congress to propose the Fifteenth Amendment, forbidding any state from denying any citizen his right to vote "on account of race, color, or previous condition of servitude.")

President Grant supported the measures of the Radicals and in some ways gave his backing to their policies. Like the good military man that he was, he believed that where violence broke out, it should be put down uncompromisingly. Accordingly, he favored the adoption of Force Acts for the use of federal troops to break up the activities of the Ku Klux Klan. When these laws were adopted, he did not hesitate to invoke them, and troops were sent in on a number of occasions.

Fundamentally, however, Grant did not care much about politics or the rights of the Negro. He wanted to see tranquillity restored, and this meant reuniting North and South on any basis which both would be willing to accept. Accordingly, he urged a broader extension of amnesty to all former Confederates, and he grew to resent the frequent appeals of Republican governments in the South for troops to uphold their authority. Though he realized that the tactics of the Redeemers were very bad—"bloodthirsty butchery," "scarcely a credit to savages"—he became convinced that constant federal military intervention was worse in the long run.

During the eight years of Grant's presidency, while the Radicals controlled the Congress and presumably the presidency, Radical governments were overthrown in eight of the southern states. As Grant's second term neared its end, only three states—Louisiana, Florida, and South Carolina—remained under Radical rule.

The program of Radical Reconstruction still remained official policy in the Republican party, but it had lost its steam. The country was concerned about other things. In the realm of foreign affairs, Secretary of State Hamilton Fish was busy putting through an important settlement by which Great Britain and the United States adopted the principle of international arbitration as a means of settling American claims that had grown out of the raiding activities of the *Alabama,* which British shipyards had built for the Confederacy.

In financial circles there was a bitter contest over what to do about the greenback dollars issued during the war. Since greenbacks were not backed by gold, people had saved the more valuable gold dollars and spent the less valuable greenback dollars, thus driving gold out of circulation. The government was willing to give gold for greenbacks even though such a policy would tend to increase the value of the dollar. Debtor interests (such as farmers), who wanted a cheap dollar, fought hard against the policy of redemption, but the policy was adopted in 1875 in spite of such opposition.

In politics, public confidence in the government was very much shaken by a series of disclosures concerning government corruption. In 1872 it was revealed that several congressmen had accepted gifts of stock in a construction company, the Crédit Mobilier, which was found to be diverting the funds of the Union Pacific Railroad—including the funds which the government had granted to it—with the knowledge of the officers of the road. In 1875, Grant's private secretary was implicated in the operations of the "Whiskey Ring," which, by evading taxes, had systematically defrauded the government of millions of dollars. The following year, the Secretary of War was caught selling appointments to Indian posts. Meanwhile, in the New York City government, the Tweed Ring, headed by Tammany boss William Marcy Tweed, was exposed as guilty of graft and thefts which have seldom been equaled in size and never been surpassed in effrontery.

The political condition of the Republican party was so bad that in 1872 many members of the party, in a "Liberal Republican" movement, went over to the Democrats and secured the Democratic nomination of Horace Greeley, long an ardently Republican editor of the New York *Tribune*. Grant was easily reëlected, however, over Greeley's opposition.

In the economic orbit, the country was trying to weather the financial depression which began with the panic of 1873. All in all, the questions of the South and the Negro seemed more and more distant, less and less important, to the people of the North.

The Hayes-Tilden Election of 1876. The election of 1876 brought to an end the program of Reconstruction which probably would have ended soon in any case. In this election the Republicans, who were badly divided, turned to a Civil War veteran and Governor of Ohio, Rutherford B. Hayes, as their nominee. Hayes was a conspicuously honest man, and so was his Democratic opponent, Samuel J. Tilden of New York, who owed his reputation to his part in breaking up the Tweed Ring.

When the votes were counted, Tilden clearly had a popular majority and was within one vote of an electoral majority. But there were three states—Florida, Louisiana, and South Carolina—in which the result was contested, and two sets of returns were filed by rival officials. Congress had to count the votes, and the House of Representatives, with a Democratic majority, was in a position to prevent an election by refusing to go into joint session with the Senate, which the Constitution requires for the count. Congress agreed to appoint an Electoral Commission to provide an impartial judgment, but the commission divided along party lines, voting eight to seven for Hayes. As late as two days before the inauguration it was doubtful whether the Democrats in the House would allow the electoral count to proceed.

Many Northern Democrats were prepared to fight to a finish against what they regarded with considerable justice as a stolen election, but the Southern Democrats had found that one civil war was enough. Moreover, various negotiations had been in progress behind the scenes. Important groups of Southern Democrats who had been left out when the government largesse of the Union Pacific-Central Pacific was distributed now hoped for a Texas and Pacific Railroad which would provide bountiful federal grants for Southern interests. They received assurances from friends of Governor Hayes that he would look with favor upon such programs of internal improvement. Moreover, they were assured that he would withdraw the last remaining federal troops from Louisiana and South Carolina, which meant that their Republican governments would collapse and the score of states would be: redeemed, eleven; reconstructed, none.

With these understandings in mind, Southern congressmen voted to let the count proceed so that Hayes would be elected. Later, when they were explaining their conduct to their constituents, they thought it best to say quite a great deal about how they had ransomed South Carolina and Louisiana and very little about their hopes for the Texas and Pacific and other such enterprises. Thus a legend grew up afterwards that there had been a "compromise" by which Reconstruction was ended. What had really happened, however, was that Southern Democrats and Northern Republicans had discovered that there were many features of economic policy on which they were in close harmony. The slaves were emancipated; the Union was restored; bygones were bygones; and the harmony of their views made reconciliation natural and Reconstruction unnecessary. There was still the Negro question; but hardly anyone had ever supported Negro suffrage or Negro equality for its own sake. It had been an expedient, and now that the expedient was no longer needed, it could be laid aside. Such was the spirit of reconciliation.

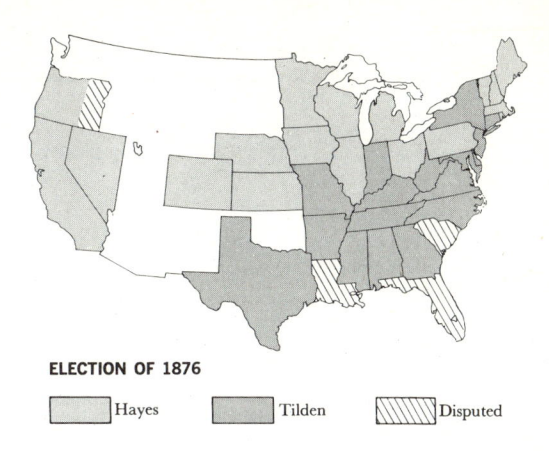

Thus, the country ended a period of intense friction and entered upon a long era of sectional harmony and rapid economic growth. This was done at the expense, however, of leaving the question of racial relations still unattended to, although slavery itself had, at immense cost, been removed.

ELECTION OF 1876

Hayes   Tilden   Disputed

CHAPTER 12

THE CHANGING NATION

THE ERA OF REFORM

Progress and Perfectibility. In the world of today, which has experienced almost two centuries of industrialization, we have had time to see that the great changes of the industrial age brought with them many problems. We tend to think about industrialization very much in terms of these problems: the concentration of economic power; the deterioration of our cities; the congestion of our highway traffic; the waste of natural resources; the poisoning of our environment by smoke, water pollution, and the reckless use of chemicals; the population explosion; the serious gap between rich countries and poor ones; the destructive potentialities of atomic power; and, in general, the failure of social progress to keep pace with technical progress. We have been disillusioned by the fact that victory in two world wars has brought neither peace nor democracy to the world; and the highest living standards in history have not eliminated many social ills such as alcoholism, drug addiction, delinquency, and crime, as might have been hoped.

It is difficult today, therefore, to understand what a deep vein of optimism and faith in progress permeated nineteenth-century thought. The experience of Americans confirmed their optimism, for they saw republics replacing monarchies; they saw equality spreading with the broadening of the suffrage and with frontier land selling at a price that would enable everyone to own a farm; they saw the wilderness brought under cultivation, the productivity of labor increased, the living standard rising, and opportunity broadened to reach an ever larger proportion of people.

The religion of nineteenth-century Americans contributed to their belief that man could become perfect and that society was making progress toward perfection. Most Americans believed in a Protestant version of Christianity which taught that man could achieve salvation—but that he must strive against the forces of evil in order to do so. This religious idea of personal salvation was easily extended to the secular field of social thought, with the belief that society must practice right and must rid itself of evil, and that when all the evils were eliminated one by one, it would become a perfect society. The old Puritan theology, with its intense concentration upon a future existence in heaven or hell, was breaking down, but even when it did so, the spiritual drive which had been so strong a part of Puritanism was not lost. Instead, it was channeled into the field of social thought, where it gave impetus to a crusade, on a broad front, for many kinds of reforms.

Emerson and the Reform Movement. The spiritual drives and ideals underlying the reform movement of the pre-Civil War period are well illustrated in the career of Ralph Waldo Emerson, whose belief in self-reliance has already been mentioned. Emerson was the descendant of a long line of Congregational ministers, and he began his career as a Unitarian minister. He had all the old Puritan concern with spiritual values, but instead of believing, as the Puritans did, in the depravity ("original sin") and unworthiness of man, he believed that man is inherently good and that, as he himself said, "God is in every man." Because of his belief in the direct relation of God and man, he rejected orthodox theology and soon gave up his ministry.

If man is inherently good, Emerson thought, it must follow that man has the potentiality of perfecting his own nature and perfecting his society. The steps that man made toward perfection would constitute progress, and in proportion as perfection was fulfilled, man would become truly free. Thus, in Emerson's thought, progress did not mean material gain ("success") as it has meant to many Americans. Rather it meant the fulfillment of man's spiritual potentialities and the progressively broader recognition of the worth of every man. Emerson took the eighteenth-century Enlightenment idea that men are equal and added to it the idea that every man has infinite capacity for goodness and greatness. His beliefs had an immense appeal, for they gave a spiritual dimension to the whole democratic principle which America was adopting at this time. But to fulfill their potentialities, men, according to Emerson, must give up everything by which they degraded or exploited others. In personal terms, this meant that a man must be independent and must not follow the crowd—"Whoso would be a man," Emerson said, "must be a non-conformist." In social terms, it meant that there must be a constant drive to elevate the condition of man by means of various reforms.

The Reform Movement. The reform movement, of course, was immensely broader than Emerson, and he alone did not create the philosophy behind it, but his importance lies in the fact that he expressed its basic attitude, better perhaps than anyone else. Sometimes he even spoke satirically of the excesses of some of the reformers ("What a fertility of projects for the salvation of the world!"). But he himself went to live for a time at Brook Farm, where a group of transcendentalists were trying to create a perfect community. The reform impulse led to the launching of many such communitarian experiments, including the Mormon society.

The major way in which reform expressed itself, however, was not through a withdrawal from society but through efforts to improve society. Such efforts were a dominant feature of American activity from the age of Jackson to the Civil War, and indeed, down to the present. Reform expressed itself in a great variety of ways: in the abolition of imprisonment for debt; in prison reform and the abolition of flogging; in humane care for the mentally ill (previously treated like animals); in campaigns to limit labor to ten hours a day; in programs for the training of blind people. On a broader front, the temperance movement became an immense crusade. It began by appealing for voluntary abstinence and by campaigning against the bad influence of barrooms, where workingmen often squandered wages which were needed for the support of their families. By the 1850's, it had changed its character and had become a drive for the adoption of prohibitory laws. Maine led the way with a prohibition law in 1851, and within ten years all of the New England states, New York, and most of the Middle West except Illinois had followed. The laws were poorly enforced, especially in New York, and most of them were soon repealed, but for a while nearly half of the country was legally "dry."

Women's Rights. Another great crusade, but one which did not gain success so quickly, was the movement for women's rights. This was no mere matter of the ballot, for women in mid-nineteenth-century America were denied full rights to own property, to be educated, or to enter many occupations. The first colleges were opened to women in the 1830's, but very few institutions followed their lead for many years. In 1839, Mississippi took the first steps toward correcting the common law rules which made even a wife's personal clothing the property of her husband, and between 1844 and 1850 about fifteen states changed their laws to abolish the more extreme legal disabilities of women. In 1848, at a convention at Seneca Falls, New York, the feminists demanded general social and political equality. But the majority, even of women, did not actively support this demand, and it was to be another forty years before women gained the ballot in even a single state.[1] In the decade of the fifties, however, women began to hold most of the teaching positions in schools, and by their right to independent earnings they were undercutting the economic dependency which had been the basis of their traditional subordination.

Education. Another major development of the mid-nineteenth century was the development of public education. Although not usually counted in the list of reforms, the campaign for state-supported schools drew upon the same motives which sparked the reform movement and was led by reformers, the most notable of whom was Horace Mann. When Mann accepted the post of secretary of the Massachusetts state board of education in 1837, he wrote, "so long as I hold this office I devote myself to the supremest welfare of mankind upon earth. . . . I have faith in the improvability of the race —in their accelerating improvability." (Here, again, was the theme of the perfectibility of man.)

At that time, education in the United States was not generally regarded as a matter of public responsibility. At the primary level, the New England towns did follow the old Puritan practice of maintaining primary schools so that no child need be unable to read the Bible. In other states, people paid for their children to learn reading and writing, just as one might pay for lessons in music or art today. Some states did provide schools for the poor, but the very fact that these were for paupers caused people to shun them to avoid the embarrassing admission of poverty. Beyond the primary level, the work which is now done by high schools was then done by private "academies," of which there were more than 6000 (but with only 12,000 teachers) in the United States by 1850.

At the college level, there were a number of state universities, but most of these received paltry support from their states and were kept going mostly by tuition fees. The characteristic institution of "higher" learning was the small, church-supported denominational college, with a faculty of five or ten and a student body of anywhere from 100 to 300. College was still the privilege of a limited few. More than 500 such colleges were founded in the United States before the Civil War, and all of these were strictly teaching institutions, with little or no idea of actually increasing the body of knowledge.

Mid-century saw many developments in the educational field. At the level of primary education, the pauper schools were largely eliminated during

---

1. Wyoming Territory adopted woman suffrage in 1869, and the territory became a state in 1890. Colorado followed in 1893, Utah and Idaho in 1896, but there were no others until the twentieth century.

the 1830's, and taxation for at least partial support of the schools became widespread except in the South. But many states still required parents to pay part of the costs of schooling, and in some states these rates were not abolished until the 1860's. As late as 1827, more than half the children in Pennsylvania were not attending school at all (250,000 out of 400,000), and education was not compulsory anywhere until 1852, when Massachusetts passed the first compulsory attendance law. As late as 1870 the average American had received less than twenty-two months of schooling in his entire life, and until the 1860's girls fared far worse than boys in the amount of schooling they received.

High schools were still in their infancy. In 1860, half the high schools in America were in the three states of Massachusetts, New York, and Ohio, and the total number of public high schools (321) was less than the total number of colleges.

Colleges continued to increase in number, and 165 new institutions were founded between 1850 and 1870, but the total number of colleges was less significant than the development of truly advanced studies. Some of the old church-dominated colleges, where students had recited their classroom lessons almost like grammar school pupils, were turning into secular universities dedicated to free inquiry. In 1869 Harvard, for instance, inaugurated a chemist, Charles W. Eliot, to succeed a long line of clergymen in the presidency. In 1868 Andrew D. White launched another real university at Cornell, and in 1876 Daniel Coit Gilman started America's first true research university at Johns Hopkins. These institutions had broad curricula and a commitment to advance knowledge as well as to teach.

To many Americans who hailed the new schools with enthusiasm, public education meant vocational training—that is, better preparation for better-paying jobs. But to the leaders who fought the battle for free schools, universal education, education beyond the three R's, and teaching which emphasized understanding rather than mere memorization—to such leaders the new education, like other reforms, was important because it would help to make the ideal of equality a reality by giving all men a comparable opportunity to develop their talents. If man was perfectible, education would take him along the path toward perfection.

During the 1850's one other reform movement—the campaign against Negro slavery—attracted much public attention and excited so much controversy that for a time it eclipsed all the other reform movemets. The antislavery movement has been discussed in Chapter 10, and some of its consequences appear in Chapter 11.

The Underlying Ideals of Freedom and Individualism. Looking at all the varied activities of the mid-nineteenth-century reformers, one must ask, what was the basic drive that motivated them all? The question is perhaps too complex to answer in full, but clearly one important ideal which most of them shared was the ideal of the individual freed from all handicaps which interfered with the fulfillment of his potentialities as a human being. The public education movement was sparked by the belief that ignorance and illiteracy must not be allowed to retard the development of the abilities of poor persons. The movement for women's rights was based on a belief that the opportunities open to individuals ought not to be restricted because of their sex. The antislavery movement aimed fundamentally at removing a harsh set of restrictions imposed upon individuals who happened to be Negroes. Even the temperance and prohibition movements were designed to protect all individuals from a certain form of temptation.

This ideal of individual freedom was based upon the concept of a society in which power would be so widely diffused or atomized that no one individual or group could control other individuals or groups or do much injury to them. The ideal of freedom, then, would be fulfilled by the double condition of (1) removing inequalities and handicaps and (2) maintaining a dispersal of power such that no one could really control anyone else.

When nineteenth-century Americans thought of power, they pictured it in terms of privileged economic groups, and they believed that concentration of power could be avoided simply by devising a system to limit the action of government and by maintaining impartial rules for all elements in the economy. Accordingly, in politics they cherished the idea that the power of government should be restricted by a written constitution and that, where power was conferred, it should be divided between three branches of officials—legislative, executive, and judicial—who would restrain one another by a system of checks and balances.

In economics, they believed that a system of unrestricted buying and selling in a free market by unregulated producers and consumers (laissez faire) would prevent buyers from exercising power over sellers, or vice versa, and would leave all parties free to follow whatever occupation they preferred, to sell their products to anyone who would buy, and to buy what they needed from anyone who would sell. The rivalry (competition) among buyers would protect the seller from the power of any one buyer, and the rivalry among sellers would protect the buyer from the power of any one seller. The classic statement of this economic philosophy was made by the British political economist Adam Smith in *The Wealth of Nations* in 1776. Americans tended to adopt Smith's views as basic doctrine, although they accepted deviations in practice, such as the protective tariff and the activities of state governments in building railroads, chartering banks, and regulating businesses.

Because of their confidence in what could be accomplished merely by freedom from controls in a system of diffused power, the idealists of the mid-nineteenth century sometimes fell unrealistically short of their purposes. In the case of slavery, for instance, they failed deplorably to advance any constructive program for creating a new role for the former slaves, simply because they had thought of a vast social problem in the purely negative terms of doing away with the ownership of one man by another and not at all in terms of the fact that emancipation would disrupt an old way of life without creating a new one. In the case of temperance, they assumed that alcoholism could be ended by destroying the power of the distillers and the saloons, and they ignored the fact that alcoholism is usually a response by the individual to problems which are or which seem insoluble to him—so that laws against distillers cannot prevent some kind of pathological response as long as the problem remains.

Many critics today believe that the reformers also idealized the free individual too much. They wanted to free him so that he could fulfill his best potentialities of mind and spirit. But very often he used his freedom in order that he might more readily take advantage of his fellow man in the race for wealth. This disparity in purpose was particularly evident in the field of educational reform, for the leaders of education advocated education for the purpose of giving men a better understanding and appreciation of life and the universe, but the public supported it for vocational reasons, as a quicker means to better-paying jobs.

The believers in individualism especially emphasized the virtues of the frontiersman as the epitome of the independent, self-reliant man. But critics today argue that democratic reform came from the city more than from the frontier. They assert that the pioneer experience did more to brutalize the frontiersman than to ennoble him. He may have been truly self-reliant, they contend, but he was hardly individualistic in the sense of holding values different from those of his fellows. Instead, the rigors of frontier life forced him to adapt in a very specific way, leaving him little opportunity for individual self-development and self-expression. According to this negative verdict, he ended by killing the Indians, by exterminating the buffalo, by exploiting the natural resources, and by despoiling the beauty of primitive nature which he pretended to love. At the end, he was impoverished rather than enriched in spirit—so isolated by his experience as an individual that he had become to some degree antisocial, distrustful of everything beyond his own limited horizon, and indifferent to the interests of the community and the possibilities of community life.

THE INDUSTRIAL SOCIETY EMERGENT

Competition versus Concentrated Power. What the believers in a system of diffused power failed to foresee was that the new sources of energy, such as steam, the new technology of heavy machinery and assembly lines, and the new scale of economic organization would all combine to make it difficult to maintain a diffusion of power. The laissez-faire theorist purposes to keep competitors ever vying with one another, but the actual competitor in the system seeks to eliminate his competitors and have the field to himself. In the old economy of local markets, small shops, and hand production, this eradication of competition had been impossible, but in the new economy of national markets, vast corporate organizations, and mechanized production it was an attainable goal; and before the end of the Grant administration some industrialists and railroad enterprises were noticeably succeeding in eliminating their competitors and getting their fields to themselves.

The reformers, in short, had worked earnestly to solve the problems of a society that was primarily agricultural, with a system of diffused power. But even while they improved their model of society, the model itself was undergoing a great industrial transformation which tended to make some of the improvements obsolete even as they were being devised.

Urbanism. As Americans developed a more advanced economic system for the country they steadily shifted the normal basis of life from an economy of subsistence, where the average family produced most of its own needs ("making a living"), to an economy of exchange, where the average family produced one crop or did one job and sold its product or its labor for money with which to buy its needs from other specialized workers ("making an income"). As this shift took place, opportunities for nonagricultural work increased and the number of people who were drawn into the tasks of distribution (trade and commerce) or into the processing of goods (industry) multiplied far more rapidly than the total population.

This shift in economic occupations meant also a shift from country to city. Thus, even in the classic age of the American frontier, when the westward movement was still advancing across the plains and over the Rocky Mountains and when the migration west seemed the great American migration, it was already true that a reverse migration was setting in. This migration drew people from the farm to rapidly growing American cities—cities larger than colonial America had ever dreamed of. It also drew migrants from Europe in greater numbers than ever before. American urban growth was changing the population patterns of two continents.

In 1870 New York was the only city in the United States with a million population. But there were twenty-five cities which were larger than any city had been in 1790, at which time Philadelphia had 42,000 and New York 33,000. Between 1830 and 1870, America's rural population increased about two and a half times from 11 million to 28 million, but urban population increased no less than nine times from 1.1 million to 9.9 million. The number of farms was increasing so much less rapidly than the population of cities that it would appear that the number of farm boys who moved to the city must have been several times more than the number of city boys who went to the frontier to occupy farms.

Another major source of recruits for the cities lay across the Atlantic in western Europe. In the first fifty years of the republic, European immigrants did not come in large numbers, but in 1842, for the first time, their annual total surpassed 100,000. By 1855 it exceeded 200,000 and, after declining during the Civil War, reached 318,000 in 1866 and 459,000 in 1873. Immigration was still far below the peaks of 1,000,000 or more which it was to attain six times between 1905 and 1914, but by 1850 the proportion of foreign-born in New England and the Middle Atlantic states was already 15 per cent, rising to 20 per cent by 1870. By the latter year, the proportion of population which was either foreign-born or of foreign-born parentage was to rise to 33 per cent in New England and to 42 per cent in the Middle Atlantic states (54 per cent and 50 per cent respectively by 1900).

The Technological Effects of Urbanism. The growth of such metropolitan clusters of population and the heavy concentrations of immigrants in the cities required complex changes in American life. At the purely technical level, the sheer size of these urban concentrations presented many problems unfaced by the small town. Since distances within the new cities were too great for walking, public transportation became a necessity—first horse-drawn cars and later steam-driven elevated railways and trolley cars. To control the dangers of fire—an immense hazard in nineteenth-century wooden cities—cities required more than the volunteer bucket brigade of rural districts, and fire engines were developed, though they continued to be operated by volunteer companies rather than by regular fire departments. Despite these facilities, the city of Chicago was virtually destroyed by fire in 1871, in what still remains America's worst conflagration.

Similarly, the old-fashioned county constable was inadequate to cope with crime in the cities, and full-scale police departments evolved. (The first policemen were put in uniform in New York in 1853.) But no police could make cities safe after dark as long as the only illumination came from dim and flickering oil lamps. Boston and New York met the need for better illumination by installing gas street lights in 1822 and 1823. The improved gas arc light replaced these in the 1870's, and electric lighting came to American cities in the 1880's.

Another serious problem was the protection of public health and the control of epidemics, for scourges of disease, the worst of which was yellow fever, killed one person in every twenty in Philadelphia in 1798, one in twelve in New Orleans in 1850, and one in eight in Memphis in 1878. The installation of public water supplies and sewage systems and the establishment of municipal health departments all were forms of response to this danger.

Community Relations. Essentially, these were technical problems—often very difficult ones—but problems on which everyone could agree and to which the technical solution could be sought. But at another level, the cities presented a problem which could not be solved without deep social adjustments—namely, the problem of new kinds of relationships among new groupings of people. The city was too large and complex to form a natural community of people most of whom were personally acquainted with one another, as was the case in a village or small town. The city tended to separate its groups of people. The poor were situated in one district, the well-to-do in another. The community, therefore, could more easily forget about the condition of the poor, and landlords who thought only of maximum profits could build windowless, unheated tenement houses without adequate plumbing—tenements which soon became slums. Thus, as immigrant groups came in, they tended to be crowded into districts apart from the rest of the population.

The New Immigration. Students of American immigration have traditionally made a major distinction between what they call the "old immigration" and the "new immigration." The old —mostly before the Civil War—consisted largely of stock from northern and western Europe and especially from Germany, Ireland, and, to a lesser extent, Scandinavia. Predominantly, these immigrants were Protestant (except for the Irish); many of them had some education and some small savings. Culturally, it is said, they were similar to native Americans.

The new immigration, mostly since the Civil War, came heavily from eastern and southern Europe, especially from Italy, Poland, the Balkans, and Russia. To a great extent these were peasant folk, illiterate and poor; in religion they were Catholic or Jewish, and culturally they contrasted sharply with the Yankees. A measure of validity endures in this contrast, for these differences were all real, but possibly this formula leaves out the most crucial factor: earlier immigrants, as farmers or agricultural laborers, came and adjusted to a country that was still basically rural and possessed rural values; beginning with the Irish, later immigrants, mostly unskilled industrial workers, arrived in an America that was rapidly becoming urban, and their adjustment was to the urban society. In concrete terms, they were forced to adjust to residential segregation, labor exploitation, and slums. As a result, they were not readily drawn into the mainstream of American life but remained overwhelmingly in a lower economic class and became the objects of prejudice.

It was in this variegated urban society, with its diversity of ethnic groups, cultural components, and religious faiths, that the traditional qualities of pioneer Americanism failed to fit adequately. Early Americanism had stressed individualism and self-reliance so much that it was not easily recognized that the problems of slums were in many respects social problems requiring action by society and not personal problems requiring action by the individual. Early American society had demanded the virtues which were needed on the frontier, and it was not cosmopolitan in recognizing the virtues of other cultures. American Protestantism, with its ancient memory of persecution at the hands of the Catholic Church and with its Old Testament scorn for faiths unlike its own, was not a tolerant religion, and separation of church and state had been adopted more because of a fear of other religions than because of a respect for them.

The Know-Nothings. Thus it happened that, in spite of the tradition of the "melting pot" and in spite of the new opportunity which America gave to a great many immigrants, there grew up a kind of barrier between the native stock and the immigrant stock, with serious tensions between them. These tensions showed up very clearly for the first time in the 1850's with the development of what was called the Know-Nothing movement. The Know-Nothings—a secret fraternal order, the Supreme Order of the Star-Spangled Banner, organized in 1850—were opposed to foreigners and to Catholics and, when questioned about their secrets, would reply, "I know nothing." Between 1854 and 1856 the Know-Nothings moved into politics, and their strength was so great that they won a number of smashing election victories in Massachusetts, Pennsylvania, New York, and Maryland. By 1858 the Know-Nothing movement had subsided as suddenly as it had flared up, but the social divisions of which it was symptomatic had not disappeared at all and were to appear again in the American Protective Association of the 1880's, in the Ku Klux Klan of the 1920's, and in continuing patterns of prejudice and discrimination against foreigners, Catholics, and Jews.

"Americanization." For the immigrant, acceptance was possible, upon certain terms. These terms were that he must become "Americanized." Americanization meant not only that he must substitute the American version of English for his native speech but even more that he must accept a whole range of American attitudes, values, and customs. He must accept the American goal of economic success and must reach this goal. He must dress, talk, and act like a native American; and he must sandpaper out of his personality any distinctive quality which made him "different." When Alexis de Toqueville came from France to visit America during the era of Andrew Jackson, he observed that in a country which repudiates aristocracy, as America did, the standards of the aristocrats cannot dominate, as they did in European society; instead, the standards of the majority will become the standards of the society. The majority will insist that everyone conform to its standards, and the power of the majority will be so great that even in a land of liberty the principle of conformity will often be stronger than the principle of freedom. This is, in a sense, what happened to the immigrants, and it meant that even when the melting pot succeeded and the immigrant became Americanized, the success was gained at the expense of forcing him to renounce important parts of his cultural heritage, including portions that might have enriched American life had our society been tolerant and cosmopolitan enough to accept them.

The Negro. For the immigrant, Americanization was possible at a price. But there remained one group, forming one tenth of the population and consisting of native Americans of old colonial stock, for whom Americanization was not permitted on any terms, no matter how fully they adapted themselves to American standards. This was the Negro population, held mostly in slavery until 1865. As we have seen in the two preceding chapters, America gave far more attention to the plight of the Negro than it ever gave to the plight of the immigrant, and it paid a greater price, in the Civil War, for the solution of the problem of slavery than it has paid for the solution of any other social problem. Beginning about 1830, when William Lloyd Garrison started publishing the *Liberator*, the abolitionists kept America in an uproar off and on for thirty years because of the slavery issue. After the Civil War, the Negro question embittered an entire decade.

Yet after the Civil War, the Negro remained in a separate status. Having been a landless agricultural worker, he became a landless sharecropper. Having been an unenfranchised slave, he found himself excluded from voting or otherwise participating in political life and became a disfranchised freedman. Once subordinated by slavery, he was now subordinated by segregation.

By the 1890's, his subordination was so firmly fixed that the U.S. Supreme Court accepted the principle of segregation in the case of *Plessy* v. *Ferguson* (1896), in which it declared that a requirement that Negroes and whites use separate facilities (in this case, railroad cars) was not discriminatory so long as equally good facilities were provided for each group. Even the foremost leader of American Negroes, Booker T. Washington, despaired of trying to gain recognition of Negro equality and urged Negroes to work for economic advancement as individuals rather than for their civil rights as a group. It was not until the twentieth century that a leader of a different kind, W. E. Burghardt Du Bois, reasserted the Negro's claim to civil rights; and a new organization, the National Association for the Advancement of Colored People, founded in 1909, began a long, hard fight to secure these rights.

The men of the nineteenth century had seen the Negro question too narrowly as a legal and moral question of the right of one man to own another. They had not seen it in its broader sense as a social question of the relation of one ethnic group to another. Hence, while solving the legal question, they had made only a fumbling attempt to solve the social question; and they had failed to handle it because, while they disagreed over the moral question and fought over it, they did not really disagree over the social question but in all parts of the country treated the Negro as an inferior.

By the beginning of the nineteenth century, America had developed a system of democracy appropriate for a rural, frontier society of homogeneous culture. The men of the mid-nineteenth century accomplished much to fulfill the objectives of this system—saving the Union, freeing the slaves, and realizing the democratic ideal on a number of important fronts. They had accomplished, perhaps, as much as can be asked of one generation. But they could not foresee what the future held; they could not even recognize some of the vast social changes going on around them. By the end of the century, America was far along the way toward an urban, industrial society of many elements with great diversity of culture; but much unfinished business remained in adapting the democratic system to the conditions of this new society.

BIBLIOGRAPHY

On the entire period 1850-1877, J. G. Randall and David Donald, *The Civil War and Reconstruction*, 2nd ed. (Boston: D. C. Heath, 1961) provides a masterful condensation of a vast amount of scholarly literature. For the prewar and war periods, the most comprehensive, detailed, and authoritative treatment is Allan Nevins, *Ordeal of the Union*, 2 vols.; *The Emergence of Lincoln*, 2 vols.; and *The War For the Union*, 2 vols. still in progress (New York: Charles Scribner's Sons, 1947-   ).

On the background of the Civil War, the view that unrealistic emotionalism and blundering leadership played a large part is expressed in Avery O. Craven, *The Coming of the Civil War* (New York: Charles Scribner's Sons, 1942) and in various writings of J. G. Randall, including *Lincoln the President*, 4 vols. (New York: Dodd Mead, 1945-1955). Important essays by Arthur Schlesinger, Jr., and Pieter Geyl, controverting this view, are in Edwin C. Rozwenc (ed.), *The Causes of the American Civil War* (Boston: D. C. Heath, 1961). A major account of the last four years preceding the war is Roy F. Nichols, *The Disruption of the American Democracy* (New York: Macmillan, 1948).

On slavery, the two best modern treatments are Kenneth Stampp, *The Peculiar Institution: Slavery in the Ante-Bellum South* (New York: Alfred A. Knopf, 1956), and Stanley M. Elkins,

Slavery (Chicago: University of Chicago Press, 1960); but on economic aspects the studies of Ulrich B. Phillips on *American Negro Slavery* (New York: Macmillan, 1918) and on *Life and Labor in the Old South* (Boston: Little, Brown, 1929) are still essential. The most balanced general account of the antislavery movement is Louis Filler, *The Crusade Against Slavery 1830-1860* (New York: Harper, 1960).

Much of the best and most indispensable history is in the form of biographies. Thus, on the Compromise of 1850, see Holman Hamilton, *Zachary Taylor*, 2 vols. (Indianapolis: Bobbs-Merrill, 1941, 1951); Charles M. Wiltse, *John C. Calhoun*, 3 vols. (Indianapolis: Bobbs-Merrill, 1944-1951); and Claude M. Fuess, *Daniel Webster*, 2 vols. (Boston: Little, Brown, 1930). On the disintegration of the Union between 1850 and 1860 see David Donald, *Charles Sumner and the Coming of the Civil War* (New York: Alfred A. Knopf, 1960); Philip S. Klein, *President James Buchanan* (University Park: Pennsylvania State University Press, 1962); and Gerald M. Capers, *Stephen A. Douglas, Defender of the Union* (Boston: Little, Brown, 1959). For the career of Lincoln up to 1858, see Albert J. Beveridge, *Abraham Lincoln, 1809-1858*, 2 vols. (Boston: Houghton Mifflin, 1928).

On the period of the war itself, see Nevins, Randall, and Randall and Donald, as cited above. Also, from the Northern perspective, Carl Sandburg, *Lincoln, the War Years*, 4 vols. (New York: Harcourt, Brace, 1936) and Margaret Leech, *Reveille in Washington* (New York: Harper, 1941). For the Confederacy, the most complete single volume is E. Merton Coulter, *The Confederate States of America, 1861-1865* (Baton Rouge: Louisiana State University Press, 1950); but Clement Eaton, *A History of the Southern Confederacy* (New York: Macmillan, 1954) is an admirable concise account.

In the realm of military history, among scores of good writers three are especially outstanding: Douglas S. Freeman treated the Confederate armies in his classic *R. E. Lee*, 4 vols. (New York: Charles Scribner's Sons, 1934-1935), and *Lee's Lieutenants*, 3 vols. (New York: Charles Scribner's Sons, 1942-1944); Kenneth P. Williams died before completing his account of the Union armies, entitled *Lincoln Finds a General*, 5 vols. (New York: Macmillan, 1949-1959); and Bruce Catton has written both a trilogy on the Army of the Potomac—*Mr. Lincoln's Army, Glory Road,* and *A Stillness at Appomattox* (Garden City, N. Y.: Doubleday, 1951-1954)—and the first volume of a Centennial History of the War, entitled *The Coming Fury* (Garden City, N. Y.: Doubleday, 1961).

On Reconstruction, the traditional histories are pro-Southern. One of the best of these is William A. Dunning, *Reconstruction: Political and Economic, 1865-1877* (New York: Harper, 1907). An excellent summary of recent scholarship and interpretation is John Hope Franklin, *Reconstruction After the Civil War* (Chicago: University of Chicago Press, 1961). One of the most important books in developing the "revisionist" view is Eric L. McKittrick, *Andrew Johnson and Reconstruction* (Chicago: University of Chicago Press, 1960).

For cultural and intellectual developments, see Ralph H. Gabriel, *The Course of American Democratic Thought to 1860*, 2nd ed. (New York: Ronald Press, 1956); Merle Curti, *The Growth of American Thought*, 2nd ed. (New York: Harper, 1951); Carl Bode, *The Anatomy of American Popular Culture, 1840-1861* (Berkeley: University of California Press, 1959); and Allan Nevins, *The Emergence of Modern America, 1865-1878* (New York: Macmillan, 1927). For a broader view of industrial developments, see Thomas C. Cochran and William Miller, *The Age of Enterprise* (New York: Macmillan, 1942). On education see Edgar W. Knight, *Education in the United States*, 3rd ed. (Boston: Ginn, 1951), and Freeman R. Butts and Lawrence A. Cremin, *A History of Education in American Culture* (New York: Holt, 1953). On immigration consult Marcus Lee Hansen, *The Atlantic Migration, 1607-1860* and *The Immigrant in American History* (both Cambridge, Mass.: Harvard University Press, 1940), and Oscar Handlin, *The Uprooted* (Boston: Little, Brown, 1951). On nativist reactions against the immigrant see Ray A. Billington, *The Protestant Crusade, 1800-1860* (New York: Rinehart, 1952). On the American Negro see John Hope Franklin, *From Slavery to Freedom*, 2nd ed. (New York: Alfred A. Knopf, 1956).

PART 5: INTRODUCTION

THE AGE OF INDUSTRIALISM

■ Americans in the post-Civil War decades lived in a nation quite different from that of their fathers—a nation where traditional ideas of democracy were modified by the values of a new industrial and urban society. The most important change was the burgeoning of industrial and financial corporations controlling nation-wide industries and supplanting the small, locally owned factories and businesses, around which the national economy had been constructed. In addition, American life was fundamentally altered by other far-reaching events: the passing of the frontier and much of the old West; the eclipsing of countryside and farm by city and factory; the dramatic improvement of communication through telegraph and transcontinental railroads; the new blood added to American stock by the flood of immigrants; the formation of large-scale labor unions; and the emergence of the United States as a world power.

The triumph of industrialism in the post-Civil War generation launched the United States on the road to becoming the richest and most powerful nation in the world. But at the same time it transformed the country from one of economic democracy and opportunity for all to one of economic plutocracy and opportunity for only a few. Industrial growth led to extreme economic inequities and sharpened class differences. At the end of the nineteenth century few Americans could regard themselves as economically secure and independent; most of them were dependent for their livelihood on the workings of a vast, complex economic system.

Although the old agrarian ideals of freedom, personal dignity, and worth steadily gave ground under the impact of industrial expansion, they still remained the core of the American view of life in the industrial age. Abraham Lincoln restated these ideals in a message to Congress in 1861; the hired laborer, Lincoln said, was not "fixed to that condition for life. . . . Men, with their families—wives, sons and daughters—work for themselves, on their farms, in their houses, and in their shops, taking the whole product to themselves, and asking no favor of capital on the one hand, nor of hired laborers or slaves on the other. . . . The prudent, penniless beginner in the world labors for wages for awhile, saves a surplus with which to buy tools or land for himself, then labors on his own account another awhile, and at length hires another new beginner to help him. This is the just and generous and prosperous system which

John D. Rockefeller, Sr., portrait by Eastman Johnson (1894). In an age characterized by few American statesmen and by Presidents and lawmakers now half-forgotten, history was made by the economic giants— men like Rockefeller who dominated vast industrial combines like Standard Oil.

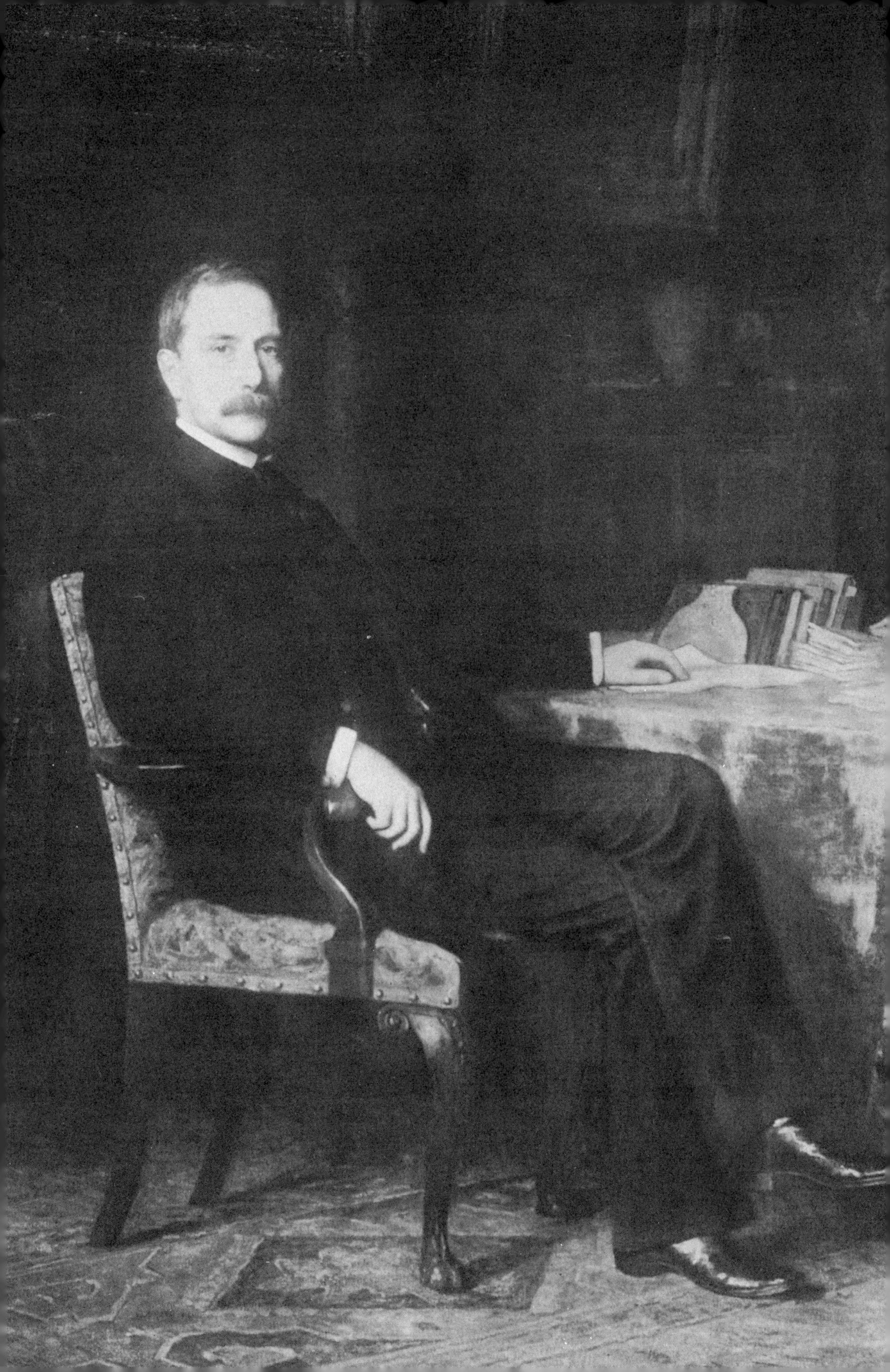

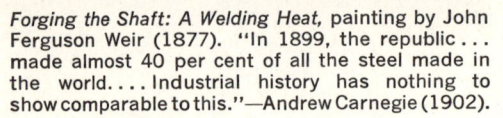

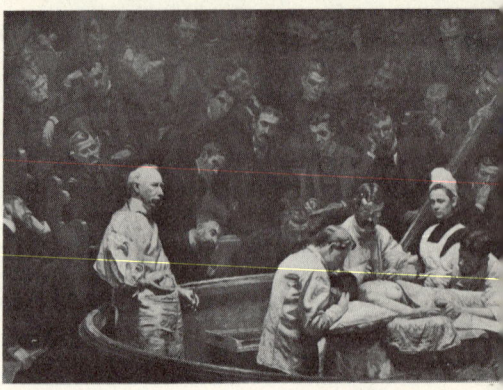

Forging the Shaft: A Welding Heat, painting by John Ferguson Weir (1877). "In 1899, the republic... made almost 40 per cent of all the steel made in the world.... Industrial history has nothing to show comparable to this."—Andrew Carnegie (1902).

The Agnew Clinic, painting by Thomas Eakins (1889). American scientists and physicians flocked to German universities and brought "modern" research techniques and educational methods back to American schools.

opens the way to all—gives hope to all, and consequent energy and progress and improvement of condition to all."

Most Americans desired this kind of society throughout the industrial age of the post-Civil War years, and many of them continued to insist—in spite of evidence to the contrary—that equality and freedom were being realized in their country. They still believed or hoped that the existence of big business was compatible with the old agrarian ideals. But they were either misled or confused about what was going on, because industrial growth could not help but produce inequities. Industrial expansion needed a large supply of both capital and labor. A small capitalist class, whose economic stakes were protected by the government, organized American industry and employed in its factories a large class of workers who enjoyed practically no economic rights. In the process a fundamental change occurred in American life. The ordinary American was transformed from an independent property owner to a hired employee of a large corporation; as a consequence the wage earner lost nearly all his freedom and much of his sense of responsibility and initiative. Economic equality had given way to economic progress.

American workers at first accepted this economic inequality with considerable docility, because they believed it necessary to economic progress and because they did not understand what they were sacrificing. The mass of immigrants from southern and eastern Europe who provided the bulk of the labor for the new industrialism were accustomed to exploitation and inequality. To them America was still the land of opportunity and a place for riches and independence. But as banking and industrial corporations gained a tighter grip on the economic system, and as depressions occurred more frequently in the last quarter of the nineteenth century, a growing number of Americans began to realize that the power of big business was often used in ways inimical to the public interest. More Americans came to believe that industrial monopolies constituted a threat to democracy and that their powers must be checked. They were receptive to the ideas of such radical reformers as Henry George, who

Steelworkers' Noontime, painting by Thomas P. Anshutz (c. 1890). Unskilled workers remained largely unorganized—the victims of long hours and low pay.

assailed the economic inequities of industrialism: ". . . The enormous increase in productive power which has marked the present century . . . , has no tendency to extirpate poverty or to lighten the burdens of those compelled to toil. . . . In factories where labor-saving machinery has reached its most wonderful development, little children are at work; . . . amid the greatest accumulations of wealth, men die of starvation, and puny infants suckle dry breasts. . . . This association of poverty with progress is the great enigma of our times." Near the end of the nineteenth century Americans demanded and secured national regulation of business combinations. They also organized national labor unions, and the country witnessed a series of widespread and often violent strikes as labor fought business for the right to organize and for higher pay, shorter working hours, and better working conditions.

The most important and persistent political problem of the post-Civil War decades was the adjustment of our national political life to industrial America. American workers and farmers—especially the latter—found their economic position steadily worsening under the impact of an expanding and exploitative industrialism. Both organized to strike back and to improve their lot, the farmer in a more active and politically significant way than the workers. The farmer, who expected to play an important role in the new industrial order and who hoped to be one of its chief beneficiaries, instead found himself its victim. A steady decline in farm prices for almost thirty years, combined with stationary or increased costs of taxes, consumer goods, and transportation, prompted the farmers to seek relief. But American politics during most of the Gilded Age suffered a certain remoteness from public opinion; the public for a long time was not sufficiently aroused to express its resentment or to demand action against the abuses of big business. The agrarian revolt did not become a potent force in American politics until the very end of the nineteenth century, and even then it met defeat. In a sense its defeat underscored the fact that now in American politics the old Jeffersonian alliance of the agricultural South and West no longer could command a majority. A new American nation of cities and industries had taken over.

CHAPTER 13

INDUSTRIALIZATION AND URBANIZATION, 1865-1900

THE AMERICAN INDUSTRIAL REVOLUTION

The Growth of Industrial Capitalism. In the years that followed the Civil War there occurred in the United States a series of notable economic changes that resulted in what is popularly known as the American Industrial Revolution. The most important feature of this phenomenon was a rapid and vast economic expansion. Between 1860 and 1900 the total railroad mileage increased from 30 thousand to 193 thousand, while the capital invested in manufacturing jumped from $1 billion to almost $10 billion, the number of workers from 1.3 million to 5.3 million, and the value of the annual product from under $2 million to over $13 million. Industry had come of age, and the United States had become the greatest industrial nation in the world.

This enormous economic growth not only made the United States potentially the most powerful country in the world but transformed it from a rural and agrarian nation into an urban and industrial one. By 1890 the value of this country's manufactured goods exceeded that of its agricultural products; and ten years later manufactured products were worth twice as much as agricultural products.

Big business came to dominate economic life. Ante-bellum factories and plants—where the relationship between the owner and his help was close, where the workshop was small and the market was local, where the ownership comprised an individual or a partnership—gave way to large, impersonal corporations. The hitherto scattered banking institutions now became concentrated in four or five financial centers. And east of the Mississippi River large, sprawling cities sprang up around industrial centers. Into these centers swarmed millions of immigrants from Europe, who were to alter the racial composition of the nation.

Although the Civil War is generally regarded as marking the beginning of the triumph of industrial capitalism, it did not produce the Industrial Revolution. The forces responsible for the rapid postwar expansion of American industry had been developing for more than half a century. In the 1850's railroads revolutionized transportation, and, at about the same time, certain inventions transformed both industry and agriculture. The sewing machine paved the way for the ready-made clothing industry, and a similar machine, adapted to leather, provided the possibility of factory-made boots and shoes. The Hoe rotary printing press brought large-scale mechanization to the newspaper business.

In agriculture, the introduction of such machinery as the reaper brought

238 The Age of Industrialism

new methods of farming to this country. The new machines enabled the North to meet the food needs of its military forces and yet have a surplus of wheat for shipment to Europe. At the time of the Civil War, Colt revolvers were considered the best in the world; vulcanized rubber was commonplace; American iron manufacturers had experimented with the Bessemer process; and Boston was the leading boot and shoe center in the world.

The Effect of the Civil War. It has been customary to credit the Civil War with a major role in bringing about the Industrial Revolution through the great impetus that it supposedly gave to the growth of manufacturing in the North. In fact, however, the Civil War probably retarded American industrial development, for growth rates slowed during the conflict. Between 1839 and 1899 total output of commodities, including agricultural products, increased elevenfold, or at an average rate per decade of slightly less than 50 per cent. But growth rates varied widely from decade to decade. The 1840's and 1880's were periods of considerably more rapid advance than the 1850's, 1860's and 1870's, and the lowest level of industrial growth occurred during the decade of the Civil War.

Nevertheless, the government gave strong encouragement to entrepreneurs during the Civil War. The Republican party, seeking the votes of businessmen in the 1860 campaign, promised them favorable legislation. In power, the Republicans carried out their pledges and through tariff, railway, banking, and immigration legislation created conditions suitable for industrial capitalism.

The Post-Civil War Boom. A number of factors were responsible for the post-Civil War industrial boom. The United States possessed bountiful raw materials, and the government was willing to turn them over to industry for little or no money. Coupled with the abundance of natural resources was a home market steadily expanding through immigration and a high birth rate. Both capital and labor were in abundance. The increase in trade and manufacturing in the Northeast in the years before the war produced an accumulation of savings, while additional millions of dollars came from European investors. Unbroken waves of European immigration provided American industry with workers as well as with customers. From 1860 to 1900 about 14 million immigrants came to the United States, most of whom settled in cities and became industrial workers.

The Role of Government in Business. An essential factor in the growth of industrialism was the continuation of the government's friendly attitude toward business. The protective tariff —beginning with the Morrill Tariff of 1861 and expanded by the McKinley bill of 1890, the Wilson-Gorman law of 1894, and the Dingley Tariff of 1897— allowed American manufacturers to charge high prices without fear of foreign competition. The national banking system and the financial policies pursued by the Treasury Department resulted in a currency deflation that benefited creditors at the expense of debtors. Additional favors to businessmen came in the form of grants of land and of natural resources.

Equally helpful to the development of business was government inertia. There were no sweeping investigations of business practices, no legislation to protect labor and consumers, and no effective regulatory commissions or laws. Businessmen knew they could with impunity do very nearly what they wished. This fitted in well with the prevalent idea in post-Civil War America that the government, beyond protecting property rights and maintaining law and order, should not meddle with the economic and social life of the country. American businessmen professed to believe in the laissez-faire economic theory set forth by the English economist

Adam Smith in his *Wealth of Nations* (1776). But the protective tariff violated the laissez-faire economic doctrine, for it was a form of government intervention in the economy on behalf of American manufacturers.

The Role of the Courts. Just as beneficial to business as protective tariffs and a hands-off attitude was the protection given by the Supreme Court in its interpretation of the Fourteenth Amendment. This amendment, added to the Constitution in 1868, was presumably designed to safeguard the newly emancipated Negro. But the original intent of the amendment disappeared, and it became instead a refuge for private enterprise.

The Fourteenth Amendment declares in its first section that "No state shall make or enforce any law which shall abridge the privileges or immunities of citizens of the United States; nor shall any state deprive any person of life, liberty, or property, without due process of law." It is true that in the first postwar cases involving the question of governmental regulation of business, the Court interpreted this "due process" clause in favor of the state governments. In the Slaughterhouse Cases of 1873, involving a Louisiana law that granted a monopoly of the slaughterhouse business in New Orleans to one corporation, the Court declared the law to be a legitimate exercise of the police powers of a state to protect its citizens. In *Munn* v. *Illinois* (1877) the Court approved an Illinois law that fixed maximum storage rates for grain elevators on the grounds that a state could regulate "a business that is public in nature though privately owned and managed."

These decisions so alarmed American businessmen, however, that some predicted the end of private property. Others believed that the only remedy lay in a constitutional amendment to protect business against state regulation. Then a change occurred in the make-up of the Court with the appointment of more conservative justices. The end of the depression years of the mid-eighties quieted radical demands, and a series of decisions beginning in the Santa Clara case of 1886 and culminating in *Smyth* v. *Ames* in 1898 made the Fourteenth Amendment into something quite new. In these cases the Court greatly broadened the scope of the Fourteenth Amendment by holding that the word *person* in its first section included corporations as well as individuals. It widened the application of the "due process" clause (which had originally been intended only to prohibit confiscation of property or other arbitrary violations of individual rights) to invalidate any regulation that would prohibit a corporation from making a "reasonable" profit on its investment. And finally, the Court held that the courts and not the states should decide how much profit was reasonable. With these last cases the Fourteenth Amendment had practically been rewritten. Businessmen who denounced the rule laid down in *Munn* v. *Illinois* found protection in these later decisions. Lower courts handed down injunctions that tied the hands of regulatory commissions, and the Supreme Court became the stronghold of laissez faire.

THE RAILROAD AGE

The new industrialism could never have been possible without the tremendous expansion of the railroad systems in America. In fact, they played such a dominant role that the period could well be called the railroad age. Between 1831 and 1861, 30,000 miles of railroad created a network connecting the Atlantic seaboard and the Mississippi Valley. The war slowed down construction, but between 1867 and 1873 about 30,000 miles of railroad were added, and during the 1880's a record breaking 73,000 miles were constructed. In 1900 the American railroad system, extending into every section of the country, measured 193,000 miles. This represented 40 per cent of the world's railroad mileage and was more than the mileage of all European countries combined. Railroad building increased more rapidly than the population. In 1865 there was one mile of track in operation for every 1150 Americans; twenty years later there was one mile for every 450. Capital invested in railroads jumped in this period from $2 billion to nearly $10 billion.

After the war most of the short lines were consolidated into a few large systems. Cornelius Vanderbilt, who had already made a fortune in steamboats, led the way. Before his death in 1877 he had extended the New York Central System to give through service between New York and Chicago, offering improved service at reduced rates.

The New York Central's chief competitor for the traffic between the East and the Middle West was the Pennsylvania Railroad, which, under J. Edgar Thompson, T. A. Scott, and G. B. Roberts, became the most important railroad and one of the foremost business enterprises in the country. At the end of the nineteenth century the Pennsylvania had lines tapping the most important Middle Atlantic and North Central industrial centers.

The Erie Railroad was a competitor for much of this traffic, but in the 1860's and 1870's it suffered from being in the hands of three of the most disreputable railroad manipulators of the era: Daniel Drew, Jay Gould, and Jim Fisk. Through bribery, chicanery, and fraud they made the Erie synonymous with all the vices of the Industrial Revolution. Consolidation enabled the Baltimore and Ohio to push into the Middle West, and the New York, New Haven, and Hartford to fan out into New England. By 1900 railroad consolidation had reached such vast proportions that more than two thirds of the railroad mileage of the country was controlled by groups led by Cornelius Vanderbilt, James J. Hill, E. H. Harriman, Jay Gould, John D. Rockefeller, and John Pierpont Morgan.

The Transcontinentals. More spectacular and more important than railroad building in the older sections of the country was the construction of the transcontinentals. In 1862 Congress chartered the Union Pacific and the Central Pacific railroads (see p. 210). Upon their completion in 1869, together the two railroads had received 54 million acres of government land and government loans amounting to about $60 million. In addition the Union Pacific issued one million shares of stock at $100 a share.

A great deal of profiteering accompanied the building of both roads, and a large measure of this profiteering could be ascribed to the fact that ownership and control were becoming divorced in modern corporate enterprise (see pp. 158-159). Managers systematically bled their companies for their own profit. The country was first made aware of this on a large scale in 1872, when it was discovered that the officers of the Union Pacific Railroad had had the road built by a construction company (the Crédit Mobilier) which they owned, and had turned over most of the assets of the road, including loans from the government and investments by shareholders, to themselves as constructors, paying, by the most conservative estimate, $73 million for a $50 million job. The fact that they bribed congressmen in connection with this deal is incidental. The diagnostic evil was simply the fact that the executives were placed in a position which gave them constant opportunity to enrich themselves at the expense of the investors and of the enterprise itself.

The Crocker Company, which built the Central Pacific, amassed a profit of about $63 million on an investment of $121 million. Most of this went to the four leading officials of the Central Pacific—Leland Stanford, Collis P. Huntington, Charles Crocker, and Mark Hopkins—each of whom left a fortune of $40 million or more at his death.

Government Aid to Railroads. While individual initiative and enterprise played a large part in the building of America's great railroad empire, it is doubtful that American railroads would have become so highly developed had it not been for the generosity of the federal, state, and local governments. Between 1850 and 1871 the railroads received from the federal government alone more than 130 million acres of land—an area as large as the New England states, Pennsylvania, and New York combined—and from the states about 49 million acres of land. It is nearly impossible to assess the value of this land, but a conservative estimate (based on $2.00 an acre) would place the value at $360 million. Some estimates have been as high as $2.5 billion.

Because they failed to meet all the conditions under which this land was granted, the railroads were able to retain only about 116 million acres. Even so, at the end of the land-grant era it was discovered that railroads had been granted one fourth of the entire area of Minnesota and Washington; one fifth of Wisconsin, Iowa, Kansas, North Dakota, and Montana; one seventh of Nebraska; one eighth of California; and one ninth of Louisiana. And at one point (1882) Texas discovered that her donations of land to railroads exceeded by 8 million acres the amount remaining in the public domain.

To such grants of land were added loans and subsidies. Towns, cities, and counties gave the railroads about $300 million and the states, at a conservative estimate, furnished an additional $228 million. The federal government made loans of approximately $65 million, most of which went to the Union and Central Pacific. A town was at the mercy of a railroad which could by-pass it and thereby cause the town to dry up. By this threat the railroads were able to secure cash grants, loans, exemption from taxation, and subscription to their stocks. Yet many loans were made voluntarily and enthusiastically in order to get local railroad advantages. For, as the governor of Maine asked in 1867, "Why should private individuals be called upon to make a useless sacrifice of their means when railroads can be constructed by the unity of public with private interests, and made profitable to all?" By 1870, according to one estimate, public subsidies plus land grants contributed 60 per cent of the costs of all railroad construction.

THE INDUSTRIALISTS

"Robber Barons" or "Captains of Industry"? It is important to recognize that the foregoing factors were not wholly responsible for the American Industrial Revolution. It required the superb talent found among those Americans who mobilized the nation's productive energies to build the railroads and factories. The new industrialists were ambitious, resourceful, and extremely able. At times they were ruthless and dishonest but probably no more so than many other Americans of their day. They displayed the vigor, cleverness, and strength of will that have characterized the great entrepreneurs of all epochs of capitalistic expansion. They lived at a time when the highest goal was to acquire wealth and when one's position in society was determined by the amount amassed. In their day they were known as Captains of Industry and praised for the economic growth of modern America; but in time they came to be described in many quarters as Robber Barons who exploited the working class and exacted tribute from the public.

Few of the industrialists were guided by the same morality and ethics that had prevailed in business long before the Civil War. To eliminate competitors and get around legal and political obstacles, they did not hesitate to use trickery, bribery, and corruption. Their attitude toward complaints about their methods was summed up in William Vanderbilt's famous "The public be damned," uttered in reply to a reporter's question about the motives for his management of the railroads. H. O. Havemeyer boasted that he did not know enough about ethics to apply them to business; Cornelius Vanderbilt exclaimed, "Law, what do I care about law? Haint I got the power?"; and J. P. Morgan told a reporter that he "owe[d] the public nothing."

The industrialists came mostly from lower- or middle-class families. The majority of them were native white and of Anglo-Saxon and New England descent. They had little or no formal education. Usually they were Protestants, strict denominationalists and pious men; scarcely any were high livers like Jim Fisk, who had a flair for publicity, splendid gestures, and the gilded life. Many of them had bookkeeping training and experience. Nearly all of them expressed a strong craving for riches, a fact that should not set them apart from other Americans.

A number of the new industrialists were of military age during the Civil War, but most of these took advantage of a law that allowed them to hire a substitute or to pay a certain amount of money in lieu of military service. Writing from Pittsburgh in 1863, Thomas Mellon, the founder of an aluminum fortune, declared that "such opportunities for making money had never existed before in all my former experience." When his son James asked permission to enlist, the elder Mellon wrote, "Don't do it. It is only greenhorns who enlist. Those who are able to pay for substitutes do so, and no discredit attaches." Then he added, "It is not so much the danger as disease and idleness and vicious habits. . . . I had hoped my boy was going to make a smart, intelligent businessman and was not such a goose as to be seduced from his duty by the declamations of buncombed speeches."

Simon Cameron, as Secretary of War, handed out war contracts left and right and asked only for production in return. Gigantic frauds and great fortunes resulted from shoddy contracts and shady deals. Vanderbilt supplied the government leaky ships. J. P. Morgan, who was twenty-four years old in 1861, purchased 5000 discarded carbines and sold them back to the army for $112,000. Both Morgan's and Vanderbilt's deals were exposed, but neither man was punished. Jim Fisk went south to smuggle out cotton and sell it in the North for large profits. Jay Gould's inside information enabled him to cash in on railroad deals and speculation in gold. And so it went during the war years.

Social Darwinism. Invaluable to the new industrial order was social Darwinism. Herbert Spencer, a leading English disciple of Charles Darwin, applied Darwin's law of biological evolution to social and economic life. Spencer held that evolution was leading inevitably to a society in which men would enjoy "the greatest perfection and the most complete happiness" and that competitive struggle was the means by which this would come to pass. In this unremitting strife the weak fell by the wayside, and the strong pushed forward. Any governmental attempt to alter this situation impeded progress.

The Darwinian theory seemed to prove that those who survived were the fittest. Translated into economic and social terms, this assumption brought science to the support of predatory capitalism. Spencer enjoyed a great vogue in the United States from 1870 to 1890, and his theories considerably helped the new industrialism. In fact, they provided American businessmen with a rationale for their conduct. John D. Rockefeller told his Sunday school class, "The growth of a large business is merely the survival of the fittest. . . . The American Beauty rose can be produced in the splendor and fragrance which bring cheer to its beholder only by sacrificing the early buds which grow up around it. This is not an evil tendency in business. It is merely the working-out of a law of nature and a law of God." Andrew Carnegie exclaimed when he first read Spencer, "I remember that light came as in a flood and all was clear. Not only had I got rid of theology and the supernatural, but I had found the truth of evolution."

According to Spencerianism the American economy was governed by a natural aristocracy that had risen to the top through the struggle for profits that rewarded the strong and eliminated the weak. The country could be served best by the economic independence of this natural aristocracy. The new doctrine crippled reform movements by justifying poverty and slums. These conditions were natural for the unfit who, by lack of thrift and industrious habits, had not survived the economic struggle, and any governmental effort to relieve poverty was a perversion of the natural law, for as Spencer declared, "there shall not be a forcible burdening of the superior for the support of the inferior."

Somewhat paradoxically, philanthropy also was expected to play a part in the behavior of a businessman. On the one hand, he was expected to be humanitarian and to relieve distress in whatever form it appeared; on the other, he was forbidden by the dictates of social Darwinism to offer any aid that might undermine self-reliance, initiative, and ambition. The solution to this dilemma was offered by Andrew Carnegie in *The Gospel of Wealth* (1889). While asserting that wealth must necessarily be concentrated in the hands of the few, Carnegie also set forth the maxim that the man who dies rich dies disgraced. The duty of the man of wealth, he maintained, was to administer his surplus funds as a trust to yield the greatest value to the *community*. Funds should be given, for example, to help found public libraries, improve education, and promote world peace. To support a needy *individual,* on the other hand, was wrong. Carnegie argued that every man maintained by charity was a source of moral infection to his neighborhood and asserted that of every thousand dollars spent for poor relief nine hundred fifty would better be thrown into the sea.

The Trust. Before the Civil War, American business was highly competitive and consisted of small units, mostly individual enterprises or partnerships. After the war, however, businessmen sought ways to check increasing competition, which they had come to regard as inefficient, wasteful, and threatening to their profits. They thus established trade agreements, associations, and pools to limit competition; but because these devices depended upon voluntary cooperation and were not enforceable in the courts, none proved sufficiently reliable. The answer seemed to lie in the formation of industrial trusts, which provided businessmen with more efficient control over the policies of all members within a single industry.

Under the trust system the stock of several competing companies was placed under the control of a group of trustees in exchange for trustee certificates. Ownership remained with the original companies, but management was consolidated in a single board of directors. John D. Rockefeller was by far the most important figure in the trust movement, and the formation of his Standard Oil Company in 1879 established the trust pattern in the United States.

Rockefeller and the Standard Oil Trusts. Rockefeller was a young merchant in Cleveland, Ohio, when he decided to enter the oil industry during the Civil War. Here he found violence, lawlessness, and waste, and, being no exponent of such free enterprise, he took steps to end this competitive spirit. Rockefeller adopted the most efficient methods of production, saved regularly a part of his profits, and surrounded himself with some of the ablest men in the industry. By 1867 he was the largest refiner of oil in Cleveland, and in 1870 he organized the Standard Oil Company of Ohio with a capitalization of one million dollars and eliminated his Ohio competitors. He now proceeded to take on the refiners in New York, Pittsburgh, and Philadelphia. Those who accepted Rockefeller's terms shared in the large profits, but those who continued to resist him were attacked with every weapon in cutthroat competitive warfare. He usually crushed his competitors with ruthless price cutting, but he also had an immense competitive advantage in the rebates and drawbacks (see footnotes, p. 248) which he received from the railroads. By 1879 Rockefeller controlled about 90 per cent of America's refining industry.

Within a comparatively short time after entering the highly competitive oil industry, the Standard Oil Company was able to dominate it. In accomplishing this domination, Rockefeller created the original trust, a word that came to be applied to any large combination with monopolistic powers. Of all the trusts that appeared in the eighties and nineties, none aroused more alarms or pointed up more moral issues than the Standard Oil Trust.

And how Rockefeller was able to gain a monopoly in the oil industry produced conflicting opinions. "I ascribe the success of the Standard Oil Company to its consistent policy of making the volume of its business large through the merit and cheapness of its products," declared Rockefeller. But Senator James K. Jones of Arkansas offered another explanation on the floor of the United States Senate in 1889: "The iniquities of the Standard Oil Company have been enumerated and recounted until some of them are familiar to everyone," said Jones, "and the colossal fortunes which have grown from it, which in all their vastness do not represent one dollar of honest toil or one trace of benefit to mankind, nor any addition to the product of human labor, are known everywhere." And the controversy has continued. Some writers see in the rise of Standard Oil a dark record of unfair trade practices, railroad favors, bribery and blackmail, and an alliance between the corporation and politics by which legislators, officials, and judges closed their eyes to practices that violated the law. Others have argued that Standard Oil straightened out a disorderly industry and, by introducing efficiency and competency, lowered prices and created a great industry. Both sides, however, agree that Standard's methods frequently were ruthless and that they would not be tolerated today.

Rockefeller had a way of being ahead of the law most of the time, and William Vanderbilt, testifying about the leaders of Standard Oil before a congressional committee in 1879, expressed an opinion prevalent in his time. "Yes, they are very shrewd men. I don't believe that by any legislative enactment or anything else, through any of the States or all of the States, you can keep such men down. You can't do it! They will be on top all the time. You see if they are not." Be that as it may, in 1892 the Supreme Court of Ohio ordered the dissolution of the Standard Trust on the grounds that it was designed to "establish a virtual monopoly" and was "contrary to the policy of our state." But this decision did not produce the desired results, for the Standard trustees, although they returned the stock to the stockholders, continued to manage the member concerns as "liquidating trustees" until 1897, when the court forced them to abandon this stratagem.

Prior to this, in 1889, New Jersey had changed its corporation laws in such a way as to make legal the formation of a holding company—a company which owned a majority of the stock in a number of subsidiary corporations and was established to unify their control. In 1899 the various subsidiaries of Standard were legally combined through the creation of a giant holding company, the Standard Oil Company of New Jersey, capitalized at $110 million (as compared to the first Standard Oil Company of Ohio, capitalization of $1 million). Standard's control over the refining business continued as complete as ever. In 1911 the United States Supreme Court held that Standard had violated the Sherman Antitrust Act, but this decision, like earlier ones in the state courts, had little effect upon the management of Standard's affairs.

Carnegie and Steel. Just as Rockefeller captured the refining market from his competitors, so Andrew Carnegie captured much of the steel market from his rivals, although he never achieved a monopoly. He had made money in various ways in the fifties and sixties and was already a millionaire when he turned to steel production in the early seventies. Like Rockefeller, Carnegie secured rebates from the railroads. He also was materially aided by the depression of the seventies, for as he said about it afterward, "so many of my friends needed money, that they begged me to repay them [for their investments in early Carnegie enterprises]. I did so and bought out five or six of them. That was what gave me my leading interest in this steel business."

From this time on, Carnegie led the field in the steel industry. He bought out and took into his business Henry Clay Frick, who in the seventies had gained control of most of the coke ovens around Pittsburgh. Together they created a great vertical combine of coal fields, coke ovens, limestone deposits, iron mines, ore ships, and railroads. In 1892 the Carnegie Steel Company was formed at a capitalization of $25 million; it controlled all its sources of supply and was soon making one fourth of all unfinished steel in the United States. At the turn of the century it became a New Jersey corporation with a capitalization of $160 million.

Carnegie was essentially an industrial capitalist in that his money came from industry and not from bankers. He put a large part of his profits back into his business, and he did not allow his corporation's stock to be sold to persons outside his organization. He was successful because of his efficient business methods and driving energy and because he skillfully chose partners of almost equal ability, such as Frick and Charles Schwab. Like most of the corporation leaders of this era, his labor policy was one of long hours, low wages, and hostility to trade unions. He was a daring man in business, ready to discard equipment whenever better came along. He made improvements in times of depression, and when prosperity returned he was ready to produce. Carnegie was a skeptic and also something of an intellectual. He had many friends in the political and literary worlds and contributed pieces to serious magazines.

The Growth of Trusts. Soon after Standard Oil Company had set the trust pattern, other business enterprises of this type appeared. The McCormick

Harvester Company of Chicago secured almost a monopoly of mechanical farm equipment. James B. Duke's American Tobacco Company, established in 1890, and Henry O. Havemeyer's American Sugar Refining Company, founded in 1891, gained almost complete monopolies, while Philip D. Armour and Gustavus Swift won domination of the meat packing business. Other consumer goods controlled by trusts were salt, whisky, matches, crackers, wire, and nails.

Eventually, prosecution by states or state legislation declaring trusts illegal ended these organizations. Although the original form of trust disappeared, the term "trust" continued in use and was applied to any type of monopoly. Many of the former trusts reorganized themselves into holding companies under the friendly corporate laws of New Jersey. Others became corporate combines created by mergers of separate firms. Fewer combinations occurred during the depression of 1893-1897, but after this they increased at an extraordinary rate.

Opposition to the Trusts. As the American people watched the proliferation of trusts and millionaires, they became convinced that something must be done to restore competition. There arose a popular outcry against monopolies, and by the eighties public speakers and writers began to condemn them. In 1881 Henry D. Lloyd attacked the Standard Oil Trust in "The Story of a Great Monopoly" in the *Atlantic Monthly*; similar articles against other examples of big business followed. Edward Bellamy in his *Looking Backward* (1887) assailed economic conditions of the time and pictured a future socialist Utopian state where life's necessities and luxuries would be produced by a cooperative society for the benefit of all. Henry George in his *Progress and Poverty* (1879) maintained that the problems of the times were largely the result of a monopoly of land. "All who do not possess land," he argued, "are toiling for those who do, and this is the reason why progress and poverty go hand in hand." Land took on value not because of anything that the owner did, but because people came to live on it. George proposed, therefore, that the unearned increments in land values be confiscated by the government in the form of a single tax on land. This would benefit the whole of society and adjust those economic disparities from which American society in the industrial age suffered.

During the eighties a number of states passed laws prohibiting trusts, but these failed to check the increasing concentration of industry. Some trusts appeared more powerful than the states that attempted to regulate them, and when one device for creating monopoly ran afoul of the law, another was substituted. State legislation also proved ineffective so long as such states as New Jersey, Delaware, and West Virginia placed few restrictions on the chartering corporations and permitted the creation of holding companies.

The Interstate Commerce Act. These frustrations aroused the opponents of monopoly to demand federal action. Between 1873 and 1885 more than thirty measures were introduced in the House of Representatives providing for the regulation of interstate railroads. Some of them were passed, only to fail in the Senate. But under the pressure of Easterners as well as Westerners the Senate yielded at last and appointed the Cullom Committee to investigate. In 1886 the committee made its report, concluding: "It is the deliberate judgment of the Committee that upon no public question are the people so nearly unanimous as upon the proposition that Congress should undertake in some way the regulation of interstate commerce." This recommendation together with the Wabash decision in 1886, forbidding the states to continue their regulation of *inter-*

state railroad traffic, led to the Interstate Commerce Act of 1887.

This law provided that all railway rates "shall be reasonable and just." It prohibited such discriminatory practices as rebates[1] and drawbacks[2] and made illegal some of the long and short haul abuses[3]. It forbade pooling agreements[4] and required that all rates and fares be printed and publicly posted. The act established a five-man Interstate Commerce Commission, with power to investigate the railroads and to require reports from them. The Commission could hear complaints of violations of the law, but it had to depend upon the courts to enforce its rulings; thus the Commission did not receive the powers necessary to regulate the transportation system. Also, the commissioners were virtually required by the act to be inexperienced in railroad practices, so they had difficulties fully understanding and acting on the complaints of the shippers. The chief weakness of the law, however, was its vagueness: what were "reasonable and just" rates? Such grave defects in the act were recognized even by such a staunch opponent of federal regulation as Senator Nelson Aldrich of Rhode Island, who described the new law as a "delusion and a sham, an empty menace to great interests, made to answer the clamor of the ignorant and unreasoning."

The Commission soon discovered that it could not compel witnesses to testify and that appeals to the courts produced endless delays. Even in those cases that reached the Supreme Court the decisions generally favored the railroads over the Commission. Between 1887 and 1905 the Court heard sixteen cases appealed by the I.C.C., and in fifteen it upheld the railroads.

The Sherman Antitrust Act. When the states proved unable to curb the industrial trusts it was clear that the federal government would have to step in, and Senator John Sherman of Ohio outlined the issue when he said in 1890:

Congress alone can deal with the trusts, and and if we are unwilling or unable there will soon be a trust for every production and a master to fix the price for every necessity of life.

In 1890 Congress passed the Sherman Antitrust Act by an almost unanimous vote. Although Sherman introduced it, it was written mainly by Senators George F. Edmunds of Vermont and George F. Hoar of Massachusetts. The act declared that "every contract, combination in the form of trust or otherwise, or conspiracy in restraint of trade or commerce" was illegal. But Congress left it to the courts to determine the meaning of the terms and phrases in the law, and the law could not be enforced without the cooperation of the Attorney General. Senator Orville Platt of Connecticut in commenting on the act stated that "The conduct of the Senate . . . has not been in the line of honest preparation of a bill to prohibit and punish trusts. It has been in the

---

1. Powerful industrial shippers, in a strong bargaining position with railroads, often demanded—and received—secret "rebates," or discounts from publicly posted shipping rates. Rebates sometimes were given in return for a specified volume of business or in return for the shipper's distributing his traffic in accordance with a pooling agreement made among competing lines.

2. In exchange for the privilege of transporting the freight of a large shipper (*e.g.*, Standard Oil), railroads agreed to pay the shipper "drawbacks," or subsidies drawn from a percentage of all receipts of its competitors.

3. The "long and short haul" abuse pointed up the fact that railroads charged rates based not on operating costs but on what the public could be forced to pay. Over "long hauls"—*e.g.*, from Chicago to New York—competition between railroads was keen and freight charges were low (sometimes lower than operating costs); but over "short hauls"—*i.e.*, between local points serviced by only one line—a railroad, in a noncompetitive situation, could charge rates as high as the public could bear, thereby recouping whatever losses the railroad may have suffered on long hauls.

4. By means of "pooling agreements" competing railroads sometimes agreed to maintain uniformly high rates in a particular locality by apportioning traffic among themselves or dividing accumulated earnings. Pooling was intended to avoid competitive rate wars.

line of getting some bill with that title that we might go to the country with." Senator Shelby Cullom of Illinois thought that if the act "were strictly and literally enforced the business of the country would come to a standstill."

But it was not enforced. From 1890 to 1901 the Justice Department instituted only eighteen antitrust suits. And the Supreme Court—in *U.S.* v. *E.C. Knight Co.* (1895)—vitiated the law by holding that manufacturing, being wholly intrastate in character even though ultimately affecting interstate commerce, was not subject to federal regulation. This limited definition of the "commerce clause" in the Constitution put trusts beyond federal control.

The Growth of Finance Capitalism. During the 1890's industrial capitalism began to give way to finance capitalism as investment bankers became more influential in the development of American industry. The industrial capitalists like Rockefeller and Carnegie were producers who had grown up with their own industries. Finance capitalists like J. P. Morgan and August Belmont came to power not because they were skilled industrial organizers but because they had enormous sums of money with which they could purchase control of an industry. The influence of the bankers derived from their control of funds available for investment. A corporation in need of capital could ask a banking house to sell the corporation's securities. In return the investment banker demanded a share in the management of concerns in which his customers had invested. Hard-pressed industrialists could not refuse, and gradually the bankers assumed supervision of corporate policies. By the turn of the century a number of corporations had passed from the control of industrialists to that of bankers.

The leading American finance capitalist was J. P. Morgan, who was also a dominant figure in the entire national economy, but the New York banking houses of August Belmont and Co. and Kuhn, Loeb and Co. and the Boston banking houses of Lee, Higginson and Co. and Kidder Peabody and Co. were also important. Morgan worked to bring about order and stability in one industry after another, for he wanted to make sure that dividends would be paid regularly to stockholders. He disliked competition because he felt it would lead to cutthroat price cutting, which would be bad for business. Instead, he wanted corporations to make prices and markets. Morgan's policies gave more protection to stockholders but higher prices to consumers.

Probably the biggest of Morgan's ventures was his launching of the United States Steel Corporation in 1901. He bought out the Carnegie Steel Corporation and combined it with ten other steel companies into one vast corporation capitalized at the unprecedented figure of slightly over $1 billion plus a bonded debt of over $303 million. The Bureau of Corporations later estimated that the total value of the combined assets of all the merged companies was $676 million. Thus, only two thirds of the $1 billion capitalization represented real assets; the remaining one third was in the form of "watered" stock, representing fictitious values. The bonded indebtedness and the $75 million which Morgan personally drew from the corporation to pay for his services made the corporation worth even less than $676 million.

With Carnegie's sale to Morgan the era of industrial capitalism came to a close. Finance capitalism brought even greater economic consolidation. In 1893 there were twelve great companies with an aggregate capital of less than $1 billion. In 1904 there were 318 industrial combinations with an aggregate capital in excess of $7.25 billion. Aside from Morgan's United States Steel, ten were capitalized at above $100 million and thirty were capitalized for more than $30 million.

Labor. Labor had a difficult time in the industrial age. While businessmen solicited government assistance in the form of tariff protection and did not regard this as government intervention, they bitterly opposed any attempt to improve the conditions of labor by legislation on the ground that this would be unwarranted interference with the economic system. Most businessmen regarded as absurd the notion that employees had the same right to government protection and aid as had already been afforded business. Businessmen believed that they alone had the right to determine terms and conditions of employment, and they dismissed the idea of collective bargaining.

But as business formed combinations, so did labor. The National Labor Union, organized in 1866, was mainly a reform organization that summed up the grievances that labor had had since the 1840's. It demanded an eight-hour day, the abolition of slums, and the establishment of cooperatives. It favored arbitration over strikes in labor disputes, and it frowned, at first, upon independent political action. Its most important leader was William Sylvis, who died in 1869 after heading the organization for only a year. Had he lived longer the union might have played a greater role in the history of labor. But after his death the union turned more and more to political activity, and its trade-union aspect disappeared in 1873 when it became the National Labor Reform party. Although the National Labor Union was short-lived, it prepared the way for more effective labor organizations.

One of these was the Knights of Labor, organized in Philadelphia in 1869 under the leadership of Uriah Stephens. The main objective of the Knights was to secure the solidarity of labor by means of secrecy, by the organization of cooperatives, and by education and propaganda. Secrecy was of prime importance to the members, for their jobs were at stake. Industries locked out workers belonging to unions. Even the name of the organization was not made public until 1881. Their secrecy caused the Knights trouble with the churches: only the intercession of Cardinal Gibbons of Baltimore kept the Pope from excommunicating the Catholics in the federation.

The Knights were of national importance from 1879 to 1893, while Terence V. Powderly was their Grand Master Workman. Although Powderly himself was opposed to use of the strike as a weapon, and was willing to come to terms with capital at almost any price, the Knights did engage in strikes and were so successful at winning them that their membership shot up to 700,000 in 1886, their peak year. The hard times of the mid-eighties had led to boycotts and strikes, notably on the Union Pacific in 1884 and Jay Gould's Wabash in 1885. Spontaneous strikes by shopmen and trainmen had caught the companies off guard and compelled Powderly's support of his followers. These were labor's first major victories, and they forced Gould to negotiate with the Knights. An illusion of easy success arose, and suddenly the Knights were flooded with members.

But fast on the heels of success came the Great Southwestern Strike of 1886 and failure. Powderly had agreed in the Wabash settlement to have no more strikes without notifying the railroads in advance. It was an agreement he could not enforce; the strikes that had occurred were not of his making, but were strikes of local origin that had drawn him in only after they had begun. In the Southwestern strike Gould refused to negotiate, because the Knights had given no advance notice to the railroad.

Of all the labor upheavals of the period, none was more frightening to men of property and order or did more damage to the prestige of labor than the bombing at Haymarket Square in

Chicago in 1886. On May 1, a number of independent trade unions struck for recognition of the eight-hour day, and two days later the police shot and clubbed some of the strikers who were beating up strikebreakers. The violence of the police prompted growls of resentment and threats of retaliation in the labor press. The next day, May 4, a group of anarchists called a protest meeting in Haymarket Square. As the speeches were coming to a close almost two hundred policemen arrived on the scene and ordered the crowd to go home. Before anyone could move, however, a bomb exploded, killing one policeman outright and fatally wounding several others. Almost immediately the police opened fire on the workers and soon a riot was in full swing. A number of civilians were killed, dozens of them wounded, and in the confusion and excitement several of the policemen shot each other. The reaction in Chicago and throughout the nation was one of horror. In the resulting hysteria, eight men were arrested, tried, and convicted on what later has come to be seen as flimsy, inconclusive evidence. Four were executed and the others imprisoned.

Although the Knights of Labor had nothing to do with the Haymarket Riot, they were identified in the public mind with the anarchists, and skilled workers began to desert the Knights in large numbers. From this time on, the Knights declined in influence, and by 1890 the membership had fallen to 100,000. Other reasons, such as the failure of their cooperatives and their identification with some of the other labor violence of the eighties, also contributed to the downfall of the Knights.

With the onset of depression in the summer of 1893, however, unrest and dissatisfaction among the working class deepened. Among the most violent of the labor upheavals, which aroused national apprehension, was the Pullman strike called by the American Railway Union in sympathy for the distress of Pullman workers. By the end of June 1894 some twenty thousand railroad men were on strike in and around Chicago, tying up every Midwestern railroad. In retaliation the railroad companies appealed to a federal court for an injunction against the strikers on the basis of the Sherman Antitrust Act, arguing that the strike was a restraint on trade such as the act forbade. The court issued the injunction.

At the same time, violence broke out in Chicago, and President Cleveland (over the protest of Governor Altgeld of Illinois) sent in two thousand federal soldiers to "protect the mails." Before order was restored, some twenty people were reported killed and two thousand railway cars destroyed. Eugene V. Debs, president of the American Railway Union, and other labor leaders were arrested, convicted of contempt of court —for violating the injunction—and sentenced to six months to a year in jail.

The conviction of the A.R.U. leaders was upheld later by the Supreme Court of the United States, which declared the injunction issued against the union to be a legitimate device for the protection of interstate commerce and the mails. For thirty years after the Debs case, a federal court injunction was a potent weapon in the hands of employers threatened with a strike. It was not until 1932 that organized labor was able to induce Congress to pass the Norris-LaGuardia Act, which limited the courts' authority to interfere in labor disputes.

Outside of the railroad brotherhoods, the only national union of sizable membership which weathered the anti-labor pressures of these years was the American Federation of Labor, founded in 1886. However, the A.F.L. at this time was a somewhat reactionary movement. Under the presidency of Samuel Gompers, it devoted itself solely to trade unionism, organizing skilled workers but doing little for the unskilled. By

1904 the A.F.L. claimed 1,676,200 of the nation's 2,072,700 unionists.

CITY AND COUNTRY

Urban Growth. The Industrial Revolution brought far-reaching social and cultural changes to American cities. Cities grew at a phenomenal rate and were subject to the many dislocations caused by economic expansion. To them came many new ethnic groups, who, uprooted from long familiar surroundings, confronted one another with deep mistrust while they strove to put down their new roots among strangers. A new society emerged. The individualism and self-reliance which had prevailed in the earlier America gave way to interdependence and the need for greater social regulation in a newer America.

Statistics show dramatically the extraordinary growth of urbanism in the industrial age. In 1790 only 5.1 per cent of the population lived in centers of more than 2500 inhabitants. By 1860 the percentage had gone up to 19.8, and by 1900 to 39.7. By the turn of the century one of every three Americans lived in urban areas and one of every two made his living in urban pursuits.

Most cities grew in a haphazard manner. They usually followed the gridiron design with straight streets running at right angles to one another. The chief aim was to crowd as many people as possible into the smallest possible space. Jacob Riis, the reformer, estimated in 1890 that in New York, for example, about 330,000 persons were living in a single square mile of the Lower East Side. In contrast were the surroundings of the newly made rich. Many lived in overstuffed mansions of pretentious architectural designs, whether in the cities or on the outskirts, or on country estates.

The mushrooming of cities brought many new problems. Unwholesome living conditions, inadequate sanitation, and lack of public health services led to frequent outbreaks of epidemic diseases. Fires became so numerous and destructive that they were estimated in the 1880's as costing the country $100 million a year. With the spread of slums came a rapid increase in crime and general lawlessness, and in the large cities gangsterism and prostitution flourished in certain areas.

The West. While industrial expansion was transforming post-Civil War America there took place another movement of momentous consequence, the settlement of the western half of the country. It was a migration probably unparalleled in the history of the world. In one generation Americans established more than a million farms in this last West and occupied more new land than earlier Americans had settled in two and a half centuries. From 1607 to 1870 Americans had occupied 407 million acres and had placed 189 million of them under cultivation. In the last three decades of the nineteenth century they took up 430 million acres and brought 225 million of them under cultivation.

The Mining Frontier. Miners were the first to reveal to the nation the resources and potentialities of the territory between the Missouri River and the Pacific. The discovery of gold in 1849 had lured many miners to California, and later, throughout the 1860's, miners hurried to "strikes" in Colorado, Arizona, Idaho, Montana, and Wyoming. In each case gold attracted the first settlers, the miners. When the pay dirt was exhausted, ranchers and farmers, aided by the government and railroads, laid the foundations of the territory.

The discovery of gold in the foothills of the Rocky Mountains close to Pike's Peak, near Lake Tahoe on the eastern slopes of the Sierra Nevada, on the reservation of the Nez Percé Indians in the eastern part of the Washington territory, in Last Chance Gulch in Montana, and in the Black Hills region of South Dakota on the reservation of the Sioux Indians, brought thousands upon thousands of persons to these areas. Into them crowded all the elements of a rough and active civilization. A large number of the miners, such as those in Idaho, "were like quicksilver," said H. H. Bancroft, the historian. "A mass of them dropped in any locality, broke up into individual globules, and ran off after any atom of gold in their vicinity. They stayed nowhere longer than the gold attracted them." Others, as in Colorado, once the mining boom had spent itself, stayed on to farm and to help their area become a territory.

The story of the mining towns is a familiar one in fiction and motion pictures. Their lawlessness has attracted much attention. To be sure, it existed. But it would be a mistake to represent the mining communities as mere nests of lawlessness, or to argue, as most Easterners did, that mining camps had abandoned the institutions of civilized society. Mining camps did have few churches, schools, newspapers, theaters, and so forth, but they quickly established them. For example, the town of Deadwood, South Dakota, consisting mainly of two long rows of saloons, had the reputation of being the most lawless place in the country, although a stage company played Gilbert and Sullivan's *Mikado* there for a record run of 130 nights. Miners did not conform to the standards of society or of law that existed elsewhere. They made their own. Each mining camp was a separate administrative and judicial district which had its own governing officials and passed and enforced its own laws. The legal codes and practices of these mining camps were eventually recognized in American courts, and a number of them were incorporated into constitutions and laws of the western states.

The miners' frontier came to an end in the 1880's. No more important discoveries were made, and the individual prospector was gradually replaced by big corporations usually run by Eastern financiers. Between 1860 and 1890, $1,242,000,000 in gold and $901,000,000 in silver were taken out of the mines in the West. These amounts enabled the federal government to resume specie payment and helped to precipitate the money question, which became a major political issue during the last quarter of the nineteenth century.

The Settlers. The opportunities for obtaining cheap or free land induced many a settler to go West. He could buy a farm outright from the national government under the terms of the Preemption Act of 1841, which allowed him to obtain a quarter section or 160 acres at the nominal price of $1.25 an acre. Or he could purchase his quarter section from one of the land-grant railroads or from any one of the states whose holdings of public domain were enormously increased by the passage of the Morrill Act of 1862. (The Morrill Act had given every state establishing a public agricultural college 30,000 acres for each senator and representative then in Congress.) Finally, the Western settler could secure his quarter section free of charge under the Homestead Act of 1862. This law made it possible for any American citizen, or any alien who had declared his intention of becoming a citizen, to acquire 160 acres of unoccupied government land by living on it or by cultivating it for five years. If the homesteader wished to gain ownership sooner, he could, after six months of residence, buy his quarter section at the prevailing minimum price, usually $1.25 an acre, though the residence requirement went up to fourteen months in 1891.

The Homestead Act has been called "the greatest democratic measure of all history," but it had a number of faults. It was not adaptable to the area to which it applied. The best farming lands east of the 100th meridian (the line approximately bisecting the Dakotas and Nebraska east and west) were largely preëmpted by 1862, and the law applied chiefly to the region from the Great Plains to the Pacific, where small homesteads were inadequate. Moreover, the Homestead Act did not end land speculation. In fact, larger purchases than ever were made by individuals. For example, William S. Chapman bought 1,000,000 acres in California and Nevada, and Francis Palms and Frederick E. Driggs procured 486,-000 acres of timberland in Michigan and Wisconsin. There was also fraudulent administration of the law. False claims were made; claims were turned over to speculators and to land, mining, and timber companies, and perjury and bribery of land officials were common. In practice the act was a perversion of the land reformer's ideas.

A generous Congress passed other measures during this period to dispose of the public domain. The Timber Culture Act of 1873 provided free grants of 160 acres in certain regions on condition that the settler plant 40 acres (later reduced to 10 acres) in trees and keep them growing for ten years. Under the terms of the Desert Act of 1877 the government offered semiarid lands in 640-acre tracts to those who would irrigate them. But since irrigation projects usually required more capital than most settlers had, the law primarily benefited large-scale grazing companies. The Timber and Stone Act of 1878 permitted the sale of quarter sections of land not suited for agriculture but valuable for timber, and large corporations and speculators managed to get possession of more than thirteen million acres of such government lands.

The Indian. An essential step in the conquest of the last West was the solution of the Indian problem. The Indians of the Great Plains and the Rocky Mountains, about 250,000 in number, presented a formidable obstacle to white settlement. The strongest and most warlike were the Sioux, Blackfoot, Crow, Cheyenne, Comanche, and Apache tribes. They clung tenaciously to their land and put up a good fight. Mounted on swift horses and armed with bows and arrows, they had fire superiority over the white man until he perfected the repeater rifle. The Plains Indians were doomed to defeat in the end, but they taxed the resources of the white man to the limit.

During the Civil War, savage fighting occurred with the Apache and Navahos in the Southwest and with the Arapaho and Cheyenne tribes on the Great Plains, and for the next twenty-five years Indian warfare recurred constantly. In the mountain areas most of the tribes were persuaded to give up their lands and move to reservations, but the tribes on the Great Plains proved to be more militant. Between 1869 and 1875, for example, more than two hundred battles took place between the army and the Indians. One of the most famous of the Indian conflicts occurred in 1876 at the Battle of the Little Big Horn River in Montana. There the Sioux under Chief Sitting Bull annihilated the 264-man command of General George A. Custer. But the Indians gained little by their victory. Shortages of ammunition and food forced the Sioux to scatter, and by October of the same year their largest group had been captured. Sitting Bull escaped to Canada but, facing starvation, returned in 1881. The Nez Percés in Oregon continued to resist until they succumbed to disease and starvation. In the 1880's the Apaches went on the warpath until their chief, Geronimo, was captured in 1885, and another Sioux uprising was easily suppressed in 1890. Indian resistance to the white man's conquest of the last West had come to an end.

The Indian wars after 1865 cost the federal government millions of dollars and hundreds of lives, and yet a solution to the problem seemed to be nowhere in sight. Much of the failure rested with the national government, which held to the theory that each tribe was a sovereign but dependent nation. Indians frequently misunderstood the terms of the tribal treaties and many individual Indians did not feel bound by them. Moreover, authority over Indian affairs was divided between the Department of the Interior and the War Department, and each pursued different policies and objectives. Then, too, frontiersmen in general believed that the only good Indian was a dead one, and most soldiers agreed. Easterners, far removed from the scene of strife, had a different attitude. Here churchmen and reformers united to urge a policy of humanitarianism toward the Indians.

As the War Department followed its policy of fighting the Indians, new ideas about the problem began to have some influence at Washington. A new Board of Indian Commissioners, composed of civilians, was created in 1869. It attempted to convert the Plains Indians, who were nomadic and wild, to agriculture on the reservations, onto which they had been forced, and to persuade the government to break down tribal autonomy. In 1871 Congress abolished the policy of dealing with tribes as though they were independent nations. In the seventies, too, the government began to establish Indian boarding schools removed from the reservations. And year after year the Indian Commissioners recommended that Indians be given individual holdings and that the system of reservations gradually be eliminated. Books began to be written on behalf of the Indian, among which Helen Hunt Jackson's *Century of Dishonor* (1881) had the greatest influence in stirring up public opinion behind efforts to improve the lot of the Indians.

Finally, in 1887, the Dawes Act initiated a government policy of dealing with the Indians which, with a number of modifications, lasted until 1934. It provided for the dissolution of tribal autonomy and the division of the tribal lands among individual members. To protect the Indian in his property the right of disposal was withheld for twenty-five years. At the end of this probationary period, the Indian received full rights of ownership and full United States citizenship. In 1906 the Burke Act gave the Secretary of the Interior discretionary authority to reduce the probationary period, and in 1924 the United States granted full citizenship to all Indians.

The new policy did not work well. The Indians were too easily persuaded to sell their land and many became degenerate alcoholics after selling. Some of the tribes, especially in Arizona and New Mexico, continued to hold their land in tribal fashion and to retain their tribal organizations. Most disheartening was the lack of incentive on the part of the Indians to cultivate the land they kept. Large numbers of them became paupers, and the feeling increased that it had been a mistake to have the Indians abandon their traditional way of life. In 1934 the Indian Reorganization Act reversed the government's Indian policy and allowed the tribes to hold their land as communal property.

CHAPTER 14

THE POLITICS OF CONSERVATISM AND DISSENT, 1877-1900

POLITICAL DOLDRUMS

Critics of the Gilded Age. American political activity in the post-Reconstruction years seemed to lack the vitality and productivity of earlier periods. The Presidents had executive ability and high principles, but they, like most of the important men in Congress, proved to be mediocre and uninspiring leaders. "No period so thoroughly ordinary has been known in American politics since Christopher Columbus first disturbed the balance of power in American society," wrote Henry Adams, that mordant commentator of the Gilded Age. "One might search the whole list of Congress, Judiciary, and Executive during the twenty-five years 1870 to 1895 and find little but damaged reputation. The period was poor in purpose and barren in results."

This era in American politics has been kicked and scuffed among historians until little remains of its reputation. Most critics believe that at no other time in American history was the moral and intellectual tone of political life so uniformly low, or were political contests so preoccupied with patronage. "Even among the most powerful men of that generation," said Henry Adams, speaking of the politicians, there was "none who had a good word for it." It has become a historical convention to censure the politicians of these years for degenerating into a group of spoilsmen who served the business community as they were themselves served by business.

The most serious charge leveled against the major parties was that they failed to meet the problems generated by the Industrial Revolution. Far-reaching economic changes necessitated extensive social readjustments, and problems arising from recurrent industrial crises and depressions demanded vigorous governmental action. But both parties chose to ignore these new issues and to revive old ones; problems of the new economic order were seldom aired in the political arena except when the third parties joined battle.

The Parties. The common explanation for this failure is that there were no important differences on major issues between Democrats and Republicans. "Neither party has any principles, any distinctive tenets," wrote James Bryce, a contemporary English observer of the American party system. "The two major parties in this period," concluded Bryce, "were like two bottles. Each bore a label denoting the kind of liquor it contained, but each was empty." Historians have called this period the "age of negation" and "the politics of dead center."

To account for the seeming impotence of political parties during this era it must be remembered that the concen-

256 The Age of Industrialism

sus of opinion in America was that government should "let well enough alone"; consequently, government rarely concerned itself with economic and social problems. However, there were other deterrents to governmental action. Probably most important was the sharp contest between the parties and the failure of either to control the national government for any appreciable length of time. Contrary to popular belief, these were not years of Republican supremacy; rather, they were a period of party stalemate and equilibrium.

In the six presidential elections from 1876 to 1896, the Republicans, while winning four, gained a majority of the popular vote in only one (1896) and a plurality in only one (1880), but even that plurality was less than one tenth of one per cent. In three of these elections the difference between the popular vote for the two major party candidates was less than one per cent, although electoral vote majorities ranged from one in 1876 to 132 in 1892. The Democrats, while electing a President twice (1884, 1892), won a majority of the popular vote in 1876 and a plurality in 1884, 1888, and 1892. The Republicans managed to control both the presidency and Congress at once for only six years (1889-1891 and 1897-1901), and the Democrats were able to do it for only two years (1893-1895).

Victory depended heavily on the "doubtful" states, which had enough shifting voters to swing the results either way. These were Connecticut, New York, and New Jersey in the East and Ohio, Indiana, and Illinois in the Midwest. These states, especially New York and the three Midwestern ones, enjoyed strong bargaining power with which they secured favorable posts for their politicians and obtained most of the funds from the campaign treasuries at election time. The doubtful states were wedded to neither party but courted by both. The parties chose presidential and vice-presidential candidates from these areas and awarded their congressmen important committee assignments.

Congressional Supremacy. National political power was then vested chiefly in Congress and not in the presidency. A group of arrogant Republican politicians had overthrown President Johnson, gained nearly complete control of Grant, and set out to put succeeding Presidents at their mercy. The office of President was at a low ebb in power and prestige. Senator John Sherman, Republican leader of Ohio, himself a perpetual aspirant to the office, wrote that "The executive department of a republic like ours should be subordinate to the legislative department. The President should [merely] obey and enforce the laws." Congressional leaders acted accordingly. "The most eminent Senators," observed George F. Hoar, Republican of Massachusetts, about his colleagues in the Senate, "would have received as a personal affront a private message from the White House expressing a desire that they should adopt any course in the discharge of their legislative duties that they did not approve. If they visited the White House, it was to give, not to receive advice."

Big Business in Politics. The considerable power that business wielded also contravened governmental action. Businessmen were usually able to obtain what they wanted from either party, because rival political machines either could be purchased or were so tractable that they did not need to be bought. It should be remembered that a majority of Americans were sympathetic to business. They believed that laissez faire and free competition reduced prices and assured a higher rate of employment; therefore, they considered government regulation unnecessary, unjust, and immoral. Even the reformers crusaded for only the most urgent reforms, and then only after a careful study had confirmed the need. "Government supervision among Anglo-Saxons is apt to degenerate into jobbery," wrote Charles Francis Adams, Jr. "In America, particularly, the whole instinct of the people leads them to circumscribe rather than to enlarge the province of government. This policy is founded in wisdom."

But despite its favorable position, business did not control American politics. Businessmen had to pay heavily for political favors, and often they were blackmailed by threats of regulation or withdrawal of government assistance. Businessmen complained that politicians treated them simply as customers, compelling them to pay for protection, selling political benefits to the highest bidders, and refusing to do the proper thing without pay. These facts alone furnish proof of the independence of the politician, so complete that it was necessary for the businessman to bribe him. Politicians were eager to deal with businessmen because they were well organized and had money to spend. Farmers and workers also were able to win political favors once they became organized and began to put pressure on politicians.

The Republicans. The Republican party was a loose combination of Northeastern business groups and upper Midwestern farming groups—an alliance that had been formed in 1860 and had fought and won the Civil War. In much of the North and West, Republicans were the party of wealth and respectability.

Two other large groups attached to the party were Negroes and Union army veterans. However, the freedmen, abandoned by the Republicans in 1877, became more openly critical of the party and rapidly began to lose the political influence they had enjoyed in the days of Reconstruction. War veterans, on the other hand, increased their political importance by organizing the Grand Army of the Republic in 1866 and pressuring Congress into voting for generous pension laws.

Sharply divergent views between Northeastern businessmen and Western farmers occasionally threatened party unity, but Republican orators tried to side-step their differences by "waving the bloody shirt"—equating party loyalty with national patriotism and charging the Democrats with having fought under the Confederate flag.

The Democrats. The Democratic party was a more regional coalition than the Republican. Its support came chiefly from the "solid South" and the city machines of the Northeast, but it also had some support from those Northeastern bankers and merchants—"sound money" men—who opposed the protective tariff and government subsidies to special interests and who favored contraction of the currency.

In the South the Democrats were the party of white supremacy. Southern party leaders, often of Whig background, called themselves "Conservatives" and frequently were labeled "Bourbons" by their opponents. They had much in common with Democratic leaders in the Midwest, who shared their conservative economic views and were also known as "Bourbons." In large northern cities the Democratic party had the allegiance of most immigrants, who were attracted by the name of the party and by the fact that some of their own leaders had risen to places of influence in it.

The Party Bosses. The political rulers of the day were not the titular leaders but the party bosses, many of them United States senators, who headed powerful state machines and rewarded their followers with public offices. The most important bosses were Senators James G. Blaine of Maine, Roscoe Conkling of New York, Zachariah Chandler of Michigan, James Donald Cameron of Pennsylvania, Oliver P. Morton of Indiana, and John A. ("Black Jack") Logan of

Illinois, all Republicans; and Arthur P. Gorman of Maryland, a Democrat. Before 1883 these party bosses had at their disposal an enormous amount of spoils in the form of federal, state, and local offices. They controlled a hierarchy of workers down to the ward heelers, to whom they gave offices in return for faithful service. The assessment of office holders and the sale of nominations and offices tightened the bosses' grip on local machines.

When the Civil Service Reform Act of 1883 (see pp. 263-64) began to remove these resources, politicians turned increasingly to businessmen for money and support. A new type of political boss appeared—a business type who resembled and worked closely with the corporation executive, made few speeches, and conducted his activities in anterooms, caucuses, and committees. Matthew S. Quay of Pennsylvania, Leland Stanford of California, Philetus Sawyer of Wisconsin, Thomas Platt of New York, and Nelson W. Aldrich of Rhode Island were bosses of the new type. Some had been prosperous bankers and businessmen and had entered the Senate to protect their interests. In 1889, William Allen White could say that "a United States Senator . . . represented something more than a state, more even than a region. He represented principalities and powers in business." According to White, one senator "represented the Union Pacific Railway System, another the New York Central, still another the insurance interests of New York and New Jersey. . . . Coal and iron owned a coterie from the Middle and Eastern seaport states. Cotton had half a dozen senators. And so it went." Contemporaries labeled this imposing body the "Millionaires' Club." What these men thought of themselves was expressed by one of their own, Senator George Hearst of California: "I do not know much about books; I have not read very much; but I have traveled a good deal and have observed men and things and I have made up my mind after my experiences that the members of the Senate are the survivors of the fittest."

The principal effect of the spoils system was to transfer party control from publicly elected leaders to "inside" rulers or bosses. The most flagrant examples of "invisible government" occurred in the cities, many of which were run by corrupt political machines. Whether Democratic, like Tammany Hall in New York, or Republican, like the Gas Ring in Philadelphia, their methods were the same. Bryce expressed the opinion that municipal government was "the one conspicuous failure of the United States," and Andrew D. White in an article in *Forum* in 1890 stated that "with very few exceptions, the city governments of the United States are the worst in Christendom—the most expensive, the most inefficient, and the most corrupt."

New York City furnished the country its most notorious example of a municipal machine. There Tammany Hall, an organization dating back to the eighteenth century, controlled the Democratic party and the local government. William Marcy Tweed and his followers A. Oakey Hall, the mayor, Peter B. Sweeney, county and city treasurer, and Richard B. Connally, the city controller, ran Tammany Hall and plundered the city. By every type of peculation this repulsive crew robbed the city treasury year after year until at the height of their power they were splitting among themselves 85 per cent of the total expenditures made by the city and county. Their technique was simple. Everyone who had a bill against the city was instructed to pad his bill—at first by 10 per cent, later 66 per cent, finally 85 per cent. Tweed's gang received the padding. For example, the courthouse, originally estimated at $3,000,000, cost the taxpayers $11,000,000. The plastering bill alone amounted to $2,870,000 and the carpeting to $350,000, "enough to cover the whole City Park three times." The loot taken by the Tweed Ring has been variously estimated at from $45,000,000 to $100,000,000.

Although respectable citizens protested, they were powerless for several years to move against Tweed because he controlled every arm of the government. Finally, courageous editorials in the New York *Times* and the cartoons of Thomas Nast in *Harper's Weekly* exposed the corruption of the Tweed Ring and aroused the general public. His own followers, Tweed said, could not read, but they could "look at the damn pictures." Tweed offered George Jones, owner of the *Times,* a million dollars to quiet his paper and Nast a half million to study art in Europe, but they refused. A citizens' committee headed by Samuel J. Tilden and Charles O'Conor launched an investigation that was able by the end of 1872 to drive every member of the Tweed Ring out of office. Tweed himself died in jail.

The Reformers. In this age of cynicism and corruption, voices such as those of the "single-tax" advocate Henry George and the socialist Edward Bellamy called for reform. Probably the most respectable of all the reformers were the "Mugwumps," as they were called by their opponents. (The term was first used politically in 1884 to describe the independent Republicans who refused to support presidential candidate James G. Blaine.) Mugwumps generally were newspapermen, scholars, and intellectuals, earnest men of high ideals and prominent social position, of conservative economic views, and usually of Republican background. Foremost among them were George William Curtis, editor of *Harper's Weekly;* E. L. Godkin, editor of the *Nation;* Carl Schurz; William Cullen Bryant; Whitelaw Reid; and Samuel Bowles. They lashed out against the spoils system and armed to purify politics through civil service reform. Since they believed in laissez faire they restricted their economic program to tariff reform and sound money.

The Mugwumps spoke in moralistic terms rather than in economic ones. They appealed primarily to the educated upper classes, for they seldom identified themselves with the interests of the masses, whom they viewed with an aristocratic disdain. They regarded the reform movements of labor and farmers as radical and dangerous and had little use for other reform movements of the period. But this is a characteristic of all contemporary reform movements. They had little in common and had great difficulty in understanding one another. Thus the reformers were divided and mutually suspicious and exerted little influence.

FROM HAYES TO HARRISON

Hayes and the Presidency. Historians have portrayed Rutherford B. Hayes as a respectable mediocrity with an average capacity and an impeccable public and private life. True, there was no dramatic flair in his personality, and he lacked brilliance, but he was a man of integrity and honest intentions, and his determination and steadfastness of purpose eventually frustrated even his bitterest foes. Hayes' presidency is an excellent illustration of how party stalemate and equilibrium hamper effective executive leadership. Hayes worked under severe handicaps that have not been fully appreciated. His right to the office was disputed (see p. 220), and Republicans and Democrats alike referred to him as "the *de facto* President" and "His Fraudulency." His programs for the South and for civil service reform plus his show of independence caused such a deep split within his own Republican party that he was nearly read out of it. At one time Hayes had but three supporters in the U.S. Senate, one of them a lifelong friend and relative. Moreover, the Democrats controlled the House of Representatives throughout his administration and the Senate the last two years of his term. Under these circumstances it is amazing that he could accomplish anything.

Hayes endeavored to reëstablish presidential power and prestige and to redress the balance between the executive and legislative branches. He first challenged congressional dominance in the make-up of his cabinet when he picked men who were most unwelcome to the bosses, particularly the liberal Republican Carl Schurz for Secretary of the Interior and the Southern Democrat and former Confederate David M. Key for the important patronage-dispensing position of Postmaster General. At first the Senate balked and refused to confirm the entire cabinet list, but under much public pressure it finally gave in to the President.

Hayes gained another victory over congressional encroachment by refusing to yield the right given him by the Force Acts of 1870-1871 to intervene in federal elections in the states. Democratic majorities in Congress sought to nullify these Reconstruction laws by attaching to army appropriation bills riders aimed at removing federal supervision of elections. Hayes fought these attempts because they would have placed him under the "coercive dictation" of a "bare" majority in Congress and because he wanted to make the executive "an equal and independent branch of the government." He vetoed eight such bills, and Congress lacked enough votes to override him.

Hayes struck a daring and spectacular blow for reform against the spoils system and its greatest champion, Senator Conkling. Hayes had already vexed the bosses with his inaugural statement that "he serves his party best who serves his country best," and he angered them with his declaration that "party leaders should have no more influence in appointments than other equally respectable citizens." He appointed a commission headed by John Jay of New York, grandson of the first Chief Justice, to investigate the largest patronage office in the federal service, the New York Customhouse—long an example of the spoils system at its worst. The commission found that most of the employees had been appointed in the interest of the Conkling machine, that twenty per cent of them were superfluous, and that the place was ridden with "ignorance, inefficiency, and corruption." When Conkling's lieutenants, Collector of the Port Chester A. Arthur and Naval Officer Alonzo B. Cornell, refused to clean up the corruption or to resign, Hayes boldly removed them and named two others to the posts. On Conkling's insistence the Senate refused to confirm the nominations, but Hayes persisted and within a year his choices were approved. He had won a battle, but he had not routed the spoilsmen.

The End of Reconstruction. Hayes removed the last of the federal troops from the South and ended military Reconstruction. He acted to restore harmony between North and South and between whites and Negroes. He responded to a general demand for a change in policy in the South. He considered that Reconstruction governments had lost so much support that they had become entirely unable to sustain themselves even by the use of force. And he dreamed of building in the South a strong Republican party that would no longer depend upon the Negro for its main strength and that could command the esteem and support of Southern whites. He became the first Republican President to experiment with the plan of appointing regular Democrats to important posts in the South in the hope of gaining Republican success there. He seldom was credited with any honest motives, for the public in 1877 and long thereafter believed that this was part of the bargain that had made him President. His experiment was a sharp departure from the strategy of the Radicals during Reconstruction; had it worked, the "solid South" as a Democratic stronghold might not have come into being.

Depression and the Silver Question. When Hayes entered the presidency, the country was experiencing the worst years of a depression that had begun in 1873. Almost immediately he was confronted with the first great industrial conflict in our history—a railroad strike that began on the Baltimore and Ohio and spread through fourteen states, affecting two thirds of the railroad mileage in the country outside of New England and the South. At the request of four state governors, Hayes sent federal troops to intervene in the strike and restore order.

Hayes ran further afoul of labor, especially on the West Coast, when he vetoed a bill passed in 1879 to restrict Chinese immigration. He felt the bill violated the Burlingame Treaty of 1868, which had given the Chinese the right of unlimited immigration to the United States. (However, Hayes sent a mission to China to negotiate a new treaty, and the resultant Treaty of 1880 gave the United States the right to regulate or suspend Chinese immigration. The Exclusion Act, passed by Congress in 1882, suspended such immigration for ten years.)

The President also took an unpopular stand on the currency question. Discontented agrarians wanted "cheap money" and the repeal or modification of the Resumption Act of 1875, which obligated the Treasury to redeem greenbacks in specie at full face value on January 1, 1879. Many predicted that such redemption would wreck the monetary system, for everyone would want gold rather than paper notes. But Hayes resisted the pressure and aided Secretary of the Treasury John Sherman in accumulating a gold reserve to redeem the currency. Greenback dollars, which were worth only sixty-seven cents in 1865, rose to one hundred cents before the deadline of resumption, and people realizing this preferred the notes, which were easier to handle; thus no run on the gold reserve developed.

Inflationists now pushed demands for free coinage of silver, and once again Hayes took the unpopular side. The old ratio between gold and silver had been sixteen to one: there was sixteen times as much silver in a silver dollar as there was gold in a gold dollar. But when the Gold Rush of 1849 lowered the price of gold, an ounce of silver became worth more than one sixteenth of an ounce of gold, and Americans sold their silver on the open market rather than have it coined at a loss. Silver dollars nearly disappeared from circulation, and in 1873 Congress abolished their coinage. Then silver mines in Nevada, Arizona, and Colorado produced such large quantities of silver that the price of silver fell, and miners and agrarians called for a return to the coinage of silver at the old ratio.

Congress responded by passing over Hayes' veto in 1878 the Bland-Allison Act, authorizing the Treasury to purchase not less than $2 million and not more than $4 million worth of silver each month and coin it into dollars at the former ratio of 16 to 1. The act, however, did not fully meet the demands of the silverites, who wanted the "free and unlimited coinage of silver"; moreover, the Treasury consistently purchased only the minimum amount of silver required by the act.

The Election of 1880. Hayes did not seek reëlection, and the Republican convention of 1880 was divided in its support: the "Stalwart" faction, led by party boss Roscoe Conkling, sought a third term for Ulysses S. Grant; but James G. Blaine of Maine and John

Sherman of Ohio also had Republican supporters. When it became clear that none of the three could secure a majority, the delegates nominated Congressman James A. Garfield of Ohio on the thirty-sixth ballot. To appease the Stalwarts, second place on the ticket went to one of Conkling's closest associates, Chester A. Arthur, whom Hayes in 1878 had dismissed as head of the New York Customhouse. When Samuel J. Tilden declined to run, the Democrats picked General Winfield Scott Hancock, a Pennsylvanian and a Union hero in the Battle of Gettysburg. His running mate was William H. English of Indiana.

The platforms of the two parties revealed few basic differences on policy and no real understanding of the country's problems. The campaign turned largely on personalities and irrelevant issues which produced a great deal of sound and fury but nothing of importance. Five sixths of the voters turned out, and Garfield won by fewer than 40,000 popular votes, although his electoral vote was 214 as compared to 155 for Hancock. Despite the failure of the major parties to discuss the vital issues of the day, less than 4 per cent of the electorate voted for a protest party candidate (General James B. Weaver of Iowa of the Greenback Labor party, which advocated inflationary policies and stricter federal regulation of interstate commerce).

Garfield and Arthur. Garfield had been an effective speaker and an able party leader in the House, but his friends found him timid and vacillating. Overwhelmed with the demands of office seekers, he exclaimed, "My God! What is there in this place that a man should ever want to get into it?" After accepting the aid of the Stalwarts during the campaign and apparently reaching some understanding with them on patronage matters, Garfield antagonized Conkling by making Conkling's great rival, Blaine, Secretary of State, and by appointing a Conkling opponent in New York Collector of the Port. In the ensuing fight between the President and the Stalwarts, Conkling and his colleague from New York, Thomas "Me Too" Platt, resigned their seats in the Senate and were not reelected by the New York legislature. At the height of the conflict, on July 2, 1881, Charles J. Guiteau, a madman and disappointed office seeker, shot Garfield and shouted, "I am a Stalwart and Arthur is President now." Garfield died of the wound on September 19, and Arthur became President.

To many Americans the succession of Arthur was a calamity, for he had the reputation of a New York machine politician. Reformers shuddered at the thought of a spoilsman in the presidency, and there was a widespread feeling that the Stalwarts would take over. But, in spite of his unsavory past, Arthur was personally honest and did have ability. The responsibilities and dignity of the high office caused him to rise to the occasion and to give the country a good administration. He did not turn over the patronage to Conkling, as many thought he would. He supported civil service reform, prosecuted frauds in the Post Office, cleared the way for the construction of a modern navy, and had the Chinese immigration question settled. He also tried to check federal spending on unnecessary public works by vetoing an $18 million rivers and harbors bill and to bring about a reduction in the tariff, but both efforts were defeated by Congress.

The Civil Service Act. The most important legislation during Arthur's presidency was the Pendleton Civil Service Act of 1883. Since the end of the Civil War, reformers had been denouncing the spoils system and advocating the establishment of a permanent civil service based on merit. Garfield's murder dramatically advanced their cause. The Pendleton Act authorized the President to appoint a Civil Service Commission of three members to provide "open competitive examinations for testing the fitness of applicants for the public service now classified or to be classified." In addition, the act forbade the levying of political campaign assessments on federal office holders and protected them against ouster for failure to make such contributions. At first the act affected only the lowest offices—about fourteen thousand or 12 per cent of the total number of federal employees, leaving the remainder under the spoils system—but the President was given authority to extend the classified list at his discretion. Arthur demonstrated good faith by making excellent appointments to the Commission. Every subsequent President extended the classified list, and at the end of the century it included 40 per cent of all federal positions.

The Election of 1884. In 1884 the Republicans turned their back on Arthur and nominated James G. Blaine of Maine for President. The Democrats named Grover Cleveland of New York. Viewing Blaine as an old guard politician inimical to good government, William Curtis, Carl Schurz, and other reformist Mugwumps bolted the Republican party and supported Cleveland. As in 1880 there were few real issues, and the campaign degenerated into one of personal abuse and vilification. "The public is angry and abusive," observed Henry Adams. "Everyone takes part. We are all doing our best, and swearing like demons. But the amusing thing is that no one talks about real issues." The Democrats publicized the "Mulligan letters" to prove that Blaine, as Speaker of the House, had been guilty of unethical conduct in connection with land-grant railroads, and the Republicans retaliated with the charge that Cleveland was the father of an illegitimate child, a fact which Cleveland himself had acknowledged. Since Blaine seemed to have led an impeccable private life but a delinquent public one, and Cleveland just the reverse, one Mugwump suggested that "we should elect Mr. Cleveland to the public office he is so admirably qualified to fill and remand Mr. Blaine to the private life which he is so eminently fitted to adorn." Overall, the decision in 1884 was even closer than in 1880. Cleveland's plurality in popular votes was only 29,000 and his electoral vote was 219 to Blaine's 182. So narrow was the margin of victory for Cleveland that he carried the pivotal state of New York by a mere 1,149 votes.

Cleveland and the Presidency. Cleveland, a strapping figure of well over two hundred pounds, came to the White House in 1885 with a reputation as a reformer and a man of courage, integrity, and prodigious work habits. Actually he was unimaginative, stolid, obdurate, brutally forthright and candid, and he lacked a sense of timing. He was also a thoroughgoing conservative, a believer in sound money and a defender of property rights. In his inaugural he promised to adhere to "business principles," and his cabinet included conservatives and business-minded Democrats of the East and South. His administration signified no break with his Republican predecessors on fundamental issues.

Cleveland faced the task of pleasing both the Mugwumps and the hungry spoilsmen of his own party who had been cut off from federal patronage for twenty-four years. At first he refused to yield to the bosses on appointments and thereby won the acclaim of reformers. But, faced with a revolt within his own party, Cleveland gave in to the spoilsmen and replaced Republicans with "honest Democrats." Carl Schurz wrote, "Your attempt to please both reformers and spoilsmen has failed," and Cleveland broke with the Mugwumps. At the end of his presidency he had removed about two thirds of the 120,000 federal officeholders. On the credit side he increased the civil service classified list to 27,380, almost double the number when he took office.

Cleveland had more success as a watchdog of the Treasury. He halted the scandalous pension racket by vetoing hundreds of private pension bills that congressmen pushed through for constitutents whose claims had been rejected by the Pension Office. Cleveland signed more of these bills than had all his predecessors since Johnson put together, but he was the first President to veto any. The Grand Army of the Republic screamed at the vetoes, and in January 1887 Congress responded by passing a Dependent Pension Bill, which provided a pension for all honorably discharged disabled veterans who had served as little as three months in the Union army, irrespective of how they had become disabled. Cleveland vetoed it and angered the G.A.R.

Aside from the Interstate Commerce Act (see pp. 247-48), for which Cleveland deserves no credit and which he signed with reluctance and "with reservations," little significant legislation was enacted during his term. He did compel railroad, lumber, and cattle companies to give up 81 million acres of public land that they had fraudulently occupied. In 1886 Congress passed a Presidential Succession Law, which provided that after the Vice-President, the succession should pass to the members of the cabinet, beginning with the Secretary of State, in the order of the creation of their departments. In 1887 the Dawes Act inaugurated a new Indian policy (see p. 255).

The Tariff Issue. For the first time in this era both major parties were forced to take a position on the tariff issue. Cleveland devoted his entire annual message of December 1887 to the tariff question, advocating a drastic reduction in duties. The Democratic-controlled House responded with a low tariff measure, but the Republican-dominated Senate turned it down and passed a highly protective measure that the House would not accept. This led to a deadlock and the injection of the tariff question into the 1888 election.

The Election of 1888. The Democrats renominated Cleveland and chose the elderly ex-Senator Allen G. Thurman of Ohio as his running mate. The Republicans nominated Senator Benjamin Harrison of Indiana for President, and Levi P. Morton, a wealthy New York banker, for Vice-President. Two labor parties, voicing the industrial unrest of the period, entered the campaign. The Union Labor and the United Labor parties condemned the major parties for being under the control of monopolies and for being indifferent to the welfare of workers.

The campaign was waged largely on the tariff issue, with Republicans defending protection and Democrats advocating a reduction of duties. The Republicans appealed to the manufacturing interests, who would profit from a high tariff, and to veterans, who were promised generous pension legislation. Both parties used money freely, and throughout the country voters were bribed in probably the most corrupt presidential election in our history. Although Cleveland had a plurality of more than 90,000 popular votes, Harrison carried the crucial doubtful states of Indiana, New York, and Ohio, and gained 233 electoral votes to Cleveland's 168. Despite all the campaign talk about the tariff, the vote did not indicate a national decision against Cleveland on that issue. Cleveland carried the manufacturing states of New Jersey and Connecticut and increased his strength of 1884 in such pro-tariff states as Ohio, Michigan, and California. The decisive factors were probably the efficiency of the Republican organization with Senator Quay at its head and the purchase of the floating vote in the doubtful states.

Harrison and the Republicans. Harrison possessed intellectual gifts and was an eloquent orator, but he was very cold in his personal relationships. "Harrison sweats ice water," became a popular phrase, and one of his associates remarked that "Harrison can make a speech to ten thousand men and every man of them will go away his friend. Let him meet the same ten thousand in private, and every one will go away his enemy." Although Harrison had ability, he lacked forcefulness, and the leadership passed largely to the Republican leaders in Congress, especially to Senator Nelson W. Aldrich of Rhode Island and Speaker of the House Thomas B. Reed of Maine. Reed pushed through the House a revision of the rules that gave him almost dictatorial powers over proceedings and earned for him the title of "czar."

For the first time since 1875 the Republicans had the presidency and a majority in both houses of Congress, and they began to pay off their political debts. The McKinley Tariff of 1890 raised rates to a higher level and protected more products than any previous tariff in American history. In the same year the Dependent Pension Act, substantially the same measure vetoed by Cleveland, granted pensions to all G.A.R. veterans suffering from any disability, acquired in war service or not, and to their widows and children. In the same year, in order to meet the demands of the silverites, the Sherman Silver Purchase Act increased the amount of silver to be purchased by the Treasury to 4.5 million ounces a month. To appease the popular clamor against monopolies, the Sherman Antitrust Act was also passed in 1890 (see p. 248). However, this Congress acquired the unsavory label of the "Billion Dollar Congress." By distributing subsidies to steamship lines, passing extravagant rivers-and-harbors bills, offering large premiums to government bondholders, and returning federal taxes paid by northern states during the Civil War, this Congress handed out so much money that by 1894 the Treasury surplus was gone, and the United States has never had a surplus since.

Instead of the widespread support that such policies were expected to bring, the public reaction was one of hostility, and in the congressional elections of 1890 the Republicans were severely rebuked. They retained only 88 of the 332 seats in the House and had their majority in the Senate reduced from 14 to 6. The appearance of nine new congressmen representing farm interests and not associated with either of the major parties indicated that a third-party revolt was shaping up and that a new phase in American politics was under way.

THE AGRARIAN REVOLT

The Plight of the Farmer. The third-party revolt took the form of agrarian insurgency in the West and South, which had been coming on since the Civil War and which reached its culmination in the 1890's. There were a number of causes for agrarian discontent. The conversion of American agriculture to a commercial basis made the farmer a specialist whose role was to produce a surplus by which the United States could adjust an unfavorable balance of trade. But unlike the manufacturer, the farmer had no control over his market or prices. He worked alone and competed with other farmers of America and the world. Rather than benefiting from the new order of things, he was its victim.

Moreover, prices for agricultural products had declined. Between 1870 and 1897 wheat prices dropped from $1.06 to 63.3 cents a bushel, corn from 43.1 to 29.7 cents a bushel, and cotton from 15.1 to 5.8 cents a pound. These were market prices, after warehouse and transportation charges were added; the net prices paid to the farmer were even lower. Farmers of the Old Northwest received only 42 cents a bushel for wheat which government economists estimated cost 45.1 cents a bushel to produce. In Kansas, in 1889, corn sold for ten cents a bushel and was commonly used for fuel, and in 1890 a farmer in Nebraska stated that he had shot his hogs since he could neither sell nor give them away.

Farmers increasingly were shackled with debts and loss of proprietorship over their land. In 1900 nearly one third of the country's farms were mortgaged. In the Middle West the percentages were highest—45 per cent in Wisconsin, 48 per cent in Michigan, and 53 per cent in Iowa. Mortgages were few in the South because of the crop-lien system, by which local merchants advanced seed, equipment, and personal necessities to planters in return for a first lien on the planter's future cotton crop. Throughout the country the number of tenant farmers increased from 25.9 per cent of all the farms in 1880 to 29.4 per cent in 1890 and to 35.3 per cent in 1900.

Naturally the farmer blamed others for his plight, in particular the railroads, the middlemen, and the banks. He resented railroad rate differentials and discriminations against him. On through routes and long hauls rates were low, because the railroads competed with one another, but on local or short hauls, where there was little or no competition, rates were high. Sometimes the Western local rate was four times that charged for the same distance and commodity in the East, where rail lines were more numerous. Farmers paid more to ship their grain from Minnesota towns to St. Paul or Minneapolis than a shipper in Minneapolis had to pay for a haul to New York. Farmers also disliked the way railroads favored big shippers and dominated state politics.

The farmer also believed himself to be at the mercy of the middlemen—local merchants, grain dealers, brokers, and speculators. He attacked the national banks because their rules precluded loans on real estate and farm property and because they did not respond to his seasonal needs for money.

The farmer complained that he bore the brunt of the tax burden. The merchant could underestimate the value of his stock, the householder might exclude some of his property, the owner of securities could conceal them, but the farmer could not hide his land. Finally, the protective tariff hurt the farmer because he purchased his manufactured goods in a highly protected market and sold his crops in an unprotected one. He shared none of the benefits of protection; instead, he contributed heavily to the subsidization of business. This injustice was all the more difficult to bear in view of his belief that the tariff was "the mother of trusts."

The Granger Movement. The farmers, feeling they were being left behind and suspecting politicians of indifference and even hostility to their interests, decided to organize and protest against their condition. In 1867 Oliver Hudson Kelley, a government clerk, founded the Patrons of Husbandry, which became better known as the Grange. The farmers saw in the Grange a weapon with which to fight their foes. By 1874, its peak year, it had an estimated membership of 1.5 million. The Grangers established a number of cooperatives in an effort to eliminate the profits of the middleman, but mismanagement and business opposition doomed most of them. The Grange officially declared itself "nonpolitical," but individual members joined various agrarian third parties organized in the Midwest, which in coalition with one of the old parties gained control of several state legislatures and enacted Granger laws to regulate the rates charged by grain elevators and railroads. They were challenged in the courts, but in *Munn* v. *Illinois* in 1877, the most important of these cases, the Supreme Court upheld the "police power" of state regulation. After 1875 Grange membership decreased rapidly; out of the twenty thousand local granges extant in 1874 only four thousand remained in 1880. Many farmers had been attracted by its novelty and vogue, and others believed it would provide a panacea for all their ills; they left when they found there was not immediate and universal success.

The Greenback Movement. Farmers next were attracted to the Greenback movement, which arose from demands to increase the amount of currency in circulation in order to check the downward trend in prices. From 1867 to 1872, in the social-reform or wage-earners' period, Eastern labor dominated the movement; its primary objectives were to lower the interest rate on money and to reduce taxation. After 1873, in the inflationists' or farmers' period, farmers favored an expansion of the currency in the hope it would bring higher prices for their products. When the panic of 1873 intensified the agricultural depression and the Granger movement failed to relieve the situation, farmers took over the Greenback movement. Its high-water mark was the election of fifteen congressmen in 1878. But with the resumption of specie payment in 1879 and with the rise of the price of corn in 1880, the farmers lost interest in Greenbackism and its support rapidly declined. In the presidential election of 1880 the Greenback candidate, James B. Weaver of Iowa, received only 300,000 votes, about 3 per cent of the total, and by 1888 the party was dead.

The Farmers' Alliance. With the decline of the Grange and the disappearance of Greenbackism, a new set of farm groups appeared. Most important were the Farmers' Alliances, two distinct organizations of different origins. The Northwestern Alliance was organized by Milton George in Chicago in 1880. The Southern Alliance was formed in 1875 in a frontier county of Texas for protection against horse thieves and land sharks. It remained small until 1886, when it expanded throughout the South under the vigorous leadership of C. W. Macune and absorbed rival farmers' organizations. For Negroes there was a colored Farmers' National Alliance and Cooperative Union.

The Alliances experimented with cooperatives more than the Grange had, but with no greater success. A merger of the two Alliances was unsuccessfully attempted in a meeting at St. Louis in 1889. The Southern Alliance insisted upon the retention of its secret rituals and the exclusion of Negroes, at least from the national body. The Northwestern Alliance wanted a federation in which each organization would keep its identity. Then the Southern Alliance changed its name to the National Farmers' Alliance and Industrial Union and induced the three strongest state alliances of the Northwestern Alliance, those of Kansas and North and South Dakota, to join it. In the same year it gained the endorsement of the Knights of Labor.

The Emergence of Populism. Though the Alliances proclaimed themselves nonpolitical organizations, each year they issued demands which could be realized only by political means. For example, the Ocala, Florida, platform of 1890 called for the abolition of national banks, establishment of subtreasuries, a graduated income tax, direct election of United States senators, and government control of communication and transportation facilities. By 1890 the Northwestern Alliance concluded that nonpartisan activities were a failure and decided to enter politics. Kansas led the way by organizing a People's (Populist) party in June 1890, and Alliancemen in other western states set up independent parties under other names. The West was in the throes of a mighty upheaval; a later commentator called it "a pentecost of politics in which a tongue of flame sat upon every man and each spoke as the spirit gave him utterance."

"Sockless" Jerry Simpson, Ignatius Donnelly, Mary Ellen Lease, Anna L. Diggs, and General James B. Weaver were among the leaders of Western Populism. The party, though hastily constructed, was successful in Kansas, where it elected five congressmen and one senator in the 1890 elections; in Nebraska, where it gained control of both houses of the legislature and elected two congressmen; and in South Dakota, where it elected a senator.

In the South the Alliance, fearing that the establishment of a third party might bring the Negro into power, first tried to gain control of the Democratic party machinery. It attacked the industrial and urban leadership of the Democratic party and endorsed candidates who pledged themselves to the Ocala platform. The Alliance appeared to have captured the Democratic party in the elections of 1890 when four governors, eight state legislatures, forty-four congressmen and three senators promised to support Alliance demands, but nearly all these elected officials reverted to Democratic orthodoxy once in office. This disillusioning experience, plus the prospects of Cleveland's renomination by the Democratic party, stimulated southern Alliancemen to become Populists. In July 1892 the national People's party was formally organized in Omaha.

The Election of 1892. The Populist platform of 1892 restated earlier Alliance demands, including the free and unlimited coinage of silver at the ratio of sixteen to one; government ownership and operation of railroads and the telephone, telegraph, and postal systems; prohibition of the alien ownership of land; restriction of immigration; and a graduated income tax. The death of L. L. Polk of North Carolina just before the convention met in Omaha on July 4 probably deprived the Populists of their strongest candidate. They nominated General James B. Weaver of Iowa for President and General James G. Field of Virginia for Vice-President. Both Cleveland and Harrison were renominated, and their running mates were Adlai E. Stevenson of Illinois and Whitelaw Reid, editor of the New York *Tribune*. The free silver plank was the only exciting issue in the campaign, and Weaver polled 1,040,000 popular votes and 22 electoral votes. Populists became the first third party since the Civil War to break into the Electoral College. They also elected 10 representatives, 5 senators, 3 governors, and 1500 members of state legislatures. Cleveland defeated Harrison with 277 to 145 electoral votes and 5,555,426 to 5,182,690 popular votes.

Cleveland and the Depression of 1893. Shortly after Cleveland entered the presidency in 1893, the country began to experience its worst economic depression. At the end of the year 158 national banks and several hundred state and private banks had failed, and 15,000 business firms had gone into bankruptcy. Factories and mines were closed, and thousands of workers were unemployed. The failure of the corn crop and the continued decline in the price of agricultural products increased the suffering in the West. But the worst would come during the next four years.

Like his predecessors in office, Cleveland believed it was not the duty of the federal government to alleviate suffering in a depression, and he complacently stated in his second inaugural that "while the people should patriotically and cheerfully support their Government, its functions do not include the support of the people." In his view the Sherman Silver Purchase Act had caused the depression, and his proposed remedy was to repeal the act and maintain the gold standard. The silverites disagreed. They contended that the cure lay in the free and unlimited coinage of silver at a ratio of sixteen to one of gold and that the Sherman Act had provided inadequate relief. Many debtor agrarians agreed.

But Cleveland was convinced that the silver certificates issued under the Sherman Act and redeemed in gold were responsible for the drain on the gold reserve that was being lowered to the established minimum of $100 million. This was an oversimplification, for there were several causes for the drain on gold. Cleveland summoned Congress into special session in 1893 and, through a combination of Gold Democrats and Republicans, had the Sherman Act repealed. Most Western and Southern Democrats voted against the Democratic administration and widened the split within the party on the currency issue.

Repeal failed to restore prosperity. The Treasury's gold reserve continued to fall, and in order to remain on the gold standard Cleveland had the Treasury sell government bonds for gold. A group of bankers headed by J. P. Morgan absorbed three bond issues in 1894 and 1895, but it was not until 1897, when the depression had finally run its course, that the Treasury crisis ended. The gold purchases enabled the Treasury to meet its obligations, but the bond sales intensified the silverites' hatred of the President. Many Americans became alarmed over the government's dependence upon a syndicate of New York bankers.

Cleveland failed to bring about any substantial reduction of the tariff. The Democrats, fulfilling their campaign promises, had passed a tariff bill in the House drawn up by William L. Wilson of West Virginia, which provided for a modest reduction in rates. In the Senate, though, a group of protectionists from both parties, led by Senator Arthur Gorman, influential Democrat from Maryland, attacked the bill with more than 600 amendments restoring some old rates and raising others. The Wilson-Gorman Tariff of 1894, which Cleveland denounced as "party perfidy and party dishonor" and which became law without his signature, was a far cry from reform. It did provide for a small income tax of 2 per cent on incomes over $4000, but the Supreme Court, as unpopular as Cleveland, held the income tax unconstitutional, even though an income tax had been collected during the Civil War.

For the remainder of his presidency, Cleveland confined his role to that of protector of the status quo. He vetoed the Seigniorage bill, which would have increased the supply of the currency. Through subordinates he rudely rejected the petitions of "armies" of unemployed workers who, under the nominal leadership of men like Populist Jacob S. Coxey, marched on Washington in 1894 to plead for public works relief programs. In the same year, Cleveland sent federal troops to crush the Pullman strike.

The Election of 1896. The agrarians looked upon Cleveland as an enemy; he personified the Northeastern conservatism against which they were in revolt. Within the Democratic party insurgency was rampant. In the elections of 1894 the Democrats had barely retained control of the Senate and lost the House. The Democratic convention of 1896 was not a sudden coup. The movement had been well-planned and organized. Insurgent Democrats prepared to outdo the silverites in denouncing Cleveland and advocating free silver. They hoped to win back the Populists and to take over the Democratic party. Their work was so effective that by the summer of 1896 they had gained control of every state Democratic organization south of the Potomac and west of the Alleghenies except South Dakota, Minnesota, and Wisconsin.

The Republicans met in St. Louis in June and nominated William McKinley of Ohio for President and Garret A. Hobart, a corporation lawyer of New Jersey, for Vice-President. Marcus Alonzo Hanna, a wealthy Ohio industrialist, had been largely responsible for McKinley's nomination. On the monetary question McKinley's record was not consistent. He had voted for both the Bland-Allison Act and the Sherman Silver Purchase Act. Yet in 1891, in running for governor, he condemned the free coinage of silver and advocated international bimetallism. Hanna had already decided upon a gold standard plank, but at the convention he gave the impression that he had to be "persuaded" by Eastern delegates that "the existing gold standard must be maintained." Upon the adoption of the gold plank a small group of silver advocates led by Senator Henry M. Teller of Colorado dramatically left the hall and organized the Silver Republican party.

The Democrats were torn by bitter strife when they met in Chicago in July. The silverites dominated the convention, and Cleveland was denounced in resolutions and speeches. The platform repudiated the Cleveland program and attacked the protective tariff, national banks, trusts, and the Supreme Court; it called for an income tax and the free coinage of silver at the ratio of sixteen to one. The leading contender for the nomination was Congressman Richard P. "Silver-Dick" Bland of Missouri, who had fought for free silver since the seventies. But the convention passed him over and on the fifth ballot nominated William Jennings Bryan of Nebraska, who had captivated the silver delegates with a speech that rose to a stirring peroration: "You shall not press down upon the brow of labor this crown of thorns, you shall not crucify mankind upon a cross of gold." Bryan's nomination has the appearance of being won by the accident of a spontane-

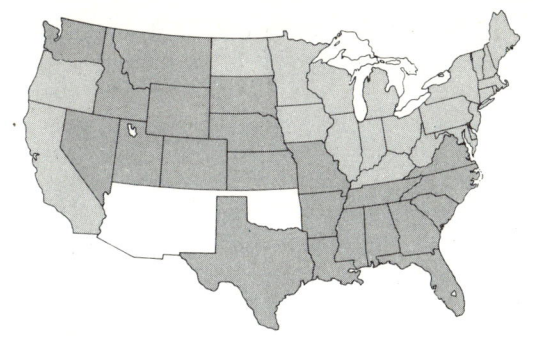

ELECTION OF 1896: ELECTORAL VOTE

McKinley: 271 Bryan: 176

ous speech. But Bryan, only thirty-six at the time, had been rounding up support for several years and had presented his ideas many times to other audiences. His convention speech was simply the last step, and that step became certain when the silverites gained control of the convention. Bryan's running mate was Arthur Sewall of Maine, a wealthy shipbuilder, banker, and protectionist, but an advocate of free silver.

The Populists faced a dilemma when their convention met in St. Louis in July. If they nominated their own candidate, they feared they would split the reform vote and permit McKinley to win. If they endorsed Bryan, they would surrender their identity to the Democrats and sacrifice their broad program of reform for one that placed a disproportionate emphasis on the silver question. Western Populists were eager to nominate Bryan, but Southern Populists, who regarded fusion with the Democrats as anathema, wanted a separate ticket. The Populists finally were induced to nominate Bryan through trickery. Senator William V. Allen of Nebraska, chairman of the convention, told the Southerners that the Democrats had promised to withdraw Sewall and accept Thomas E. Watson, Populist leader of Georgia, as their vice-presidential candidate if the Populists would nominate Bryan. Watson's decision to accept this compromise persuaded Southern opponents of fusion to vote for Bryan's nomination. This would have created a true Democratic-Populist partnership, but the Democrats refused to withdraw Sewall. Henry Demarest Lloyd watched the convention with great disgust and concluded that "The People's party has been betrayed, . . . but after all it is its own fault."

The campaign was a highly emotional and dramatic one. In an unprecedented manner Bryan spoke in 21 states, traveled 18,000 miles, made more than 600 speeches, and talked to some 5,000,000 persons. McKinley remained at his home in Canton and read well-prepared speeches from his front porch to carefully coached delegations that visited him. But Hanna did the real work. The powerful response to Bryan's appeal frightened Eastern conservatives, and Hanna took advantage of their panic to collect campaign funds. From trusts, banks, railroads, and tycoons he raised a sum estimated at between $3.5 million and $15 million as against a bare $300,000 for Bryan.

Hanna used the money lavishly but wisely, and he received great assistance from the press, which heaped all kinds of abuse upon Bryan. The *Louisville Courier Journal* called Bryan "a dishonest dodger . . . a daring adventurer . . . a political faker," and the New York *Tribune* referred to him as a "wretched, rattle-pated boy." The Philadelphia *Press* described the "Jacobins" of the Democratic Convention as "hideous and repulsive vipers," and Theodore Roosevelt was reported as saying that the silver men might well "be stood up against the wall and shot." John Hay, writing to Henry Adams in London, said of Bryan, "The Boy Orator makes only one speech—but he makes it twice a day. There is no fun in it. He simply reiterates the unquestionable truths that every man who has a clean shirt is a thief and should be hanged, and there is no goodness or wisdom except among the illiterates and criminal classes." In addition there were dire warnings that Bryan's victory would bring disaster. Farmers were told that mortgages would not be renewed. Workmen were informed that factories would be closed or wages cut.

Out of almost 14 million popular votes McKinley won with a margin of over a half million and with 271 electoral votes to 176 for Bryan. Bryan failed to carry a single industrial and urban state, and he did not win a single state north of the Potomac and east of the Mississippi. Despite the widespread unrest among labor, Bryan failed to elicit its support, and this failure was one of the principal reasons for his defeat. But also he had nowhere near the material resources that backed McKinley, and he represented the party that had been charged with the depression. The Republicans gained a majority in both houses of Congress.

McKinley and the End of an Era. The McKinley administration was ushered in under highly favorable circumstances. Businessmen knew that their interests would be safeguarded for four years. There was a return to prosperity which was to continue for several years. Farmers largely dropped politics and were busy raising crops. Politicians were happy and looked forward to a long period of abundance. McKinley, well aware of the economic distress that had affected Americans, promised in his first inaugural that this would be his chief concern. To maintain recovery he advocated two principal measures— a higher tariff and a gold standard act. Congress responded with the Dingley Tariff of 1897, which raised duties to an average of 52 per cent, the highest in our history, and the Gold Standard Act of 1900, which declared the gold dollar from that time on would be the sole standard of currency.

With these two laws the McKinley administration made good its campaign promises. Beyond this neither the President nor Congress intended to interfere with the country. They planned to let it alone and to allow business to create prosperity. McKinley's inauguration marked the beginning of the greatest consolidation movement in American industry (1897-1904). This, coupled with the Spanish-American War, produced the golden years of prosperity under McKinley and Hanna.

McKinley's presidency marked the beginning of a new era not only in national politics but in the running of the national government. Professor Wilfred Binkley, a leading authority on the President and Congress, writes that "Not since the presidency of Thomas Jefferson, had there been achieved such an integration of the political branches of the federal government and such consequent coherence and sense of direction in its functioning." The equilibrium and stalemate of the preceding two decades had given way to Republican supremacy.

CHAPTER 15

INDUSTRIALISM AND AMERICAN CULTURE

THE ECONOMICS OF INDUSTRIALISM

The Gilded Age. The term most commonly used by historians to describe the decades that followed the Civil War is "The Gilded Age," taken from the title of a novel by Mark Twain and Charles Dudley Warren published in 1873. It seemed a fitting epithet for the tawdry gilt that characterized many features of American life in this period. It reflected the cynical spirit and crudeness of the new age and the graft, corruption, and praise of material values that accompanied it. The United States, wrote E. L. Godkin in *The Nation* in 1866, is a "gaudy stream of bespangled, belaced, and beruffled barbarians. . . . Who knows how to be rich in America? Plenty of people know how to get money; but . . . to be rich properly is, indeed, a fine art. It requires culture, imagination, and character." Godkin spoke for a number of perceptive Americans who were appalled by what they called the materialism, crassness, and immorality that had accompanied the new industrialism. They were alarmed especially that the men of new wealth — the new plutocracy — lacked the "restraints of culture, experience, the pride, or even the inherited caution of class or rank." The ideals, character, and moral values of a rural and agrarian America seemed outmoded in industrial America.

But even though perceptive social critics of the Gilded Age, as well as some modern historians, assailed the captains of industry as robber barons who undermined our moral fiber and imposed their coarse tastes upon the nation, the typical American saw these industrialists only in their role as respected members of society, pillars of the churches, and philanthropists who occupied positions of prestige and power both here and abroad. As a consequence, millions of Americans admired and emulated the successful businessmen. This favorable view of industrialists was given further support by the prevailing economic and social theories of the period — laissez faire and social Darwinism — both of which extolled the rugged individualism practiced by the captains of industry.

Industrialism and Laissez Faire. The dominant economic philosophy of the times was laissez faire: beyond what was necessary to maintain law and order and to protect life and property, the government was not to interfere in the conduct of business or in personal matters. According to this view, men pursuing their business interests free of government meddling would achieve the best possible use of resources,

274   The Age of Industrialism

would promote steady economic progress, and would be rewarded, each according to his deserts. Acquisition of wealth was considered evidence of merit, for did not wealth come as a result of frugality, industriousness, and sagacity? And poverty carried with it the stigma of worthlessness, for did it not result from idleness and wastefulness? During most of the late nineteenth century these attitudes prevailed in America and were upheld by prominent educators, editors, clergymen, and economists.

Social Darwinism. Free competition and government nonintervention were sanctioned not only by the laissez-faire economic theories of Adam Smith and the English classical school; rugged individualism also found "scientific" support in social Darwinism (see pp. 243-44). Spencer's ideas were especially attractive to American businessmen since they justified free competition and made successful businessmen feel that they themselves were the finest flower of evolution. Most of the industrialists cited Spencer's views to defend their business activities and to oppose government regulation. The new doctrine opposed poor relief, housing regulations, and public education, and justified poverty and slums; Spencer believed that these conditions were the proper lot of the unfit who had been bested in the economic struggle and that any governmental effort to relieve poverty was an interference with the operation of the natural law.

Spencer's ideas had an enormous vogue in the United States in the last quarter of the nineteenth century. By the time of his death in 1903 Americans had bought nearly 400,000 copies of his books, an incredibly high figure for a sociological or philosophical work. Numbered among his many devoted followers in America were Edward Livingston Youmans and John Fiske, who spread the gospel of social Darwinism all over the country through magazine articles, popular books, and lectures. Such leading universities as Harvard, Johns Hopkins, and Yale included the Spencerian philosophy in courses on religion, biology, and social science.

Spencer's most influential American disciple was William Graham Sumner, who taught sociology and political economy at Yale from 1872 until his death in 1910. Sumner vigorously supported economic individualism and hailed the millionaires as products of natural selection. He scornfully derided reformers and their programs to protect the weak; he ridiculed democracy as the "pet superstition of the age"; and he repudiated the idea of equality among mankind. Sumner was interested in the welfare of the "forgotten man," who to him was the middle-class citizen who worked hard, minded his own business, paid his taxes, and never asked the government for help. Sumner remained true to his individualism and incurred the hostility of social Darwinists who were businessmen when he attacked the protective tariff for violating genuine individualism.

Reform Darwinism. The social Darwinists took the position that since society was the outcome of natural processes, man could not hope to control it. Hence they considered the efforts of reformers both mischievous and futile. In the 1880's, however, a number of sociologists and economists revolted against the individualism and fatalism of social Darwinism. These "reform Darwinists" maintained that societies could command their own destinies and that human intelligence could improve the existing system.

A leader among the dissenters was Lester Ward, a largely self-educated sociologist. He came from a poor family in Illinois, endured privations in his early life, worked in factories, fought in the Civil War, and for many years was a government official. When he was 65

Ward became Professor of Sociology at Brown University, where he taught "A Survey of All Knowledge." His ideas were first presented in his *Dynamic Sociology* (1883) but were more readable in *The Psychic Factors of Civilization* (1893). Ward opposed the prevailing theory that "neither physical nor social phenomena are capable of human control," asserting "that all the practical benefits of science are the result of man's control of natural forces." Ward argued that man must use his intelligence to plan and direct his future. He distinguished between "telic" forces—those governed by human purpose—and "genetic" forces—those resulting from blind natural processes—and maintained that there was "no natural harmony between natural law and human advantage." Thus he believed that a laissez-faire economic system did not necessarily advance human progress, and he advocated state management and social planning. "Those who dismiss state interference," Ward said, "are the ones who most frequently and successfully invoke it."

Younger professors of sociology, such as Albion Small of Illinois, Charles Horton Cooley of Michigan, and Edward Allsworth Ross of Wisconsin, seconded Ward's assault on social Darwinism. Contrary to Spencer's notion that society was composed of separate individuals operating independently of one another, they asserted that each individual personality was shaped by social institutions which were themselves amenable to social control. In *Sin and Society* (1907) Ross argued that in the new industrial society morality required the impersonal corporation to accept full responsibility for its antisocial acts. Followers of Spencer and Sumner declined in numbers and influence in the universities. When the American Sociological Society was founded in 1906 Ward became its first president. His ideas on government social planning took root and grew to dominate American social thinking in the twentieth century.

The New Economists. Similarly the viewpoint of economists changed. Leading university economists in the Gilded Age—men like Francis Amasa Walker of the Massachusetts Institute of Technology and J. Lawrence Laughlin of Harvard and Chicago—believed in the orthodox laissez-faire economics of the classical school. They taught that natural economic laws could function properly only in an unregulated society.

In the mid-1880's, however, a new group of scholars, many of whom had been trained in German universities, began to challenge these sentiments. In 1885 they founded the American Economic Association, which boldly declared that the state was "an agency whose positive assistance is one of the indispensable conditions of human progress" and that "the doctrine of laissez-faire is unsafe in politics and unsound in morals." Among the leaders of this revolt were Richard T. Ely of Johns Hopkins and Wisconsin, Simon Nelsen Patten of Pennsylvania, John R. Commons of Wisconsin, and Wesley C. Mitchell of Columbia. Although they differed in their economic and political programs, they all dissented from the classical belief in absolute economic laws valid for all societies. They insisted that society, constantly changing, had to be examined in terms of process and growth. Using the historical approach to study economic realities, they discovered that there were great differences between what actually happened and what, according to classical economics, was supposed to have happened.

Thorstein Veblen. The leading academic rebel was Thorstein Veblen. Born in Wisconsin of Norwegian immigrants and educated at Yale and Johns Hopkins, he taught at Chicago, Stanford, and Missouri. Veblen bitterly assailed what he called the "kept classes" and their "pecuniary" society. He derided the idea that the wealthy leisure class was the most biologically fit and the millionaires were a product of natural selection. Veblen argued that the millionaire was not responsible for the creation of the industrial technology but rather had taken possession of the wealth produced by the skill and labor of other people.

In his most widely read book, *The Theory of the Leisure Class* (1899), and in a number of other volumes Veblen analyzed the role of the upper class in American society. Although Veblen had little popular appeal, he did wield a great deal of influence among intellectuals of the twentieth century, particularly after the Great Depression of 1929.

Reformers. Outside academic circles, increasing numbers of radical reformers began to attack the existing social and economic system and to propose new plans of economic organization. They too rejected Spencer's fatalism and the idea that progress resulted from the struggle for existence and the consequent removal of the unfit.

The most important of these reformers was Henry George. Born in Philadelphia, he moved to San Francisco as a young man, where for twenty years he watched a frontier society become transformed into a wealthy and class-stratified society. What was the cause of this imbalance that deepened the poverty of the masses and increased the wealth of a few? George believed the explanation lay in the inequities of private land ownership that allowed landowners to enrich themselves solely through the rise of real-estate values. Land took on value not because of anything the owner did but because people lived on it. George believed that the unearned increment, instead of going to private individuals, ought to be taken by the government in the form of a "single tax" on land values; this would make other taxes and other forms of government intervention unnecessary, leave individual enterprise otherwise free, and promote "the Golden Age of which poets have sung and high-raised seers have told us in metaphor!"

George set forth his theories in *Progress and Poverty* (1879) and found a wide audience both in the United States and abroad. George spent the rest of his life working for the single tax program and continued to develop his theme in subsequent books. In addition, he edited a newspaper, gave many speeches, and came close to being elected mayor of New York City in 1886.

Far more radical than George's program was that of his contemporary, Edward Bellamy. Also rejecting the fatalism of the social Darwinists, Bellamy concentrated his attack on the competitive system itself. He had long been troubled by the suffering and poverty seen in industrial America, and he turned to socialism as a cure for these ills. In his utopian novel, *Looking Backward* (1888), Bellamy portrayed an ideal socialist community in the year 2000 whose beauty and tranquillity contrasted sharply with the ugly industrial towns of his day. Bellamy believed the Golden Age he depicted would come after the nationalization of great trusts and the "substitution of scientific methods of an organized and unified industrial system for the wasteful struggle of the present competitive plan with its countless warring and mutually destructive undertakings."

Bellamy's book reached a wide public; at least 500,000 copies were sold. He called his system "Nationalism," and "Nationalist" clubs sprang up to spread the new faith. "Nationalist" magazines advocated public ownership of railroads and utilities, civil service reform, and government aid to education. This served to renew interest in socialism and caused the American public to consider socialist ideas and programs. Bellamy, however, avoided the word "socialism" because he found it distasteful and because he realized that in the United States the term was often identified with "anarchism" and "communism," words that frightened most Americans.

PHILOSOPHY IN THE AGE OF INDUSTRIALISM

"Common Sense" and Idealism. Laissez faire and social Darwinism were thus increasingly criticized as the nineteenth century came to a close; similarly, formalism in social thought and orthodoxy in philosophy were being subjected to reëxamination. The traditional philosophy prevalent in the United States was Scottish or "commonsense" realism. Its main purpose was to explain traditional Protestant theology, but it also justified the *status quo* and conservative thought. First introduced in the late eighteenth century, it still dominated academic circles. Its leading exponents were the Reverend James McCash of Princeton and the Reverend Noah Porter of Yale.

From the 1870's on, the most important new influence was German idealism, particularly as expressed by Georg Wilhelm Friedrich Hegel (1770-1831). Hegel viewed the whole course of history as the working out of divine purpose by certain general laws of nature and culminating in the achievement of perfect freedom. But Hegelianism, like the Scottish philosophy, rationalized existing conditions, and what Hegel meant by "freedom" was very different from the traditional American conception. Hegel's philosophy glorified the state and taught that the individual could be free only by subordinating himself to his national government and to his social institutions. These ideas coincided well with the policies of the Republican party during the Civil War and Reconstruction.

Thus, in philosophy as in economics the initial stimulus toward a new outlook came from Germany. Most of the young men who founded new schools of philosophy in America had studied at German universities and had been influenced by Hegel, although they did not accept German idealism uncritically. The earliest centers of new philosophic thought were outside the colleges and universities. Very influential was the Philosophical Society of St. Louis, whose leading figure was William T. Harris, commissioner of schools first for St. Louis and then later in the federal government. Other well-known institutions were the Fellowship of the New Life, founded in 1884 by Thomas Davidson; the Concord Summer School of Philosophy and Literature (1879-1888); and the Society for Ethical Culture, founded in 1876 by Felix Adler.

An idealist movement displaced the common-sense school in academic circles in the 1880's. It was strongest in New England, where its leaders were Josiah Royce of Harvard and C. E. Garman of Amherst, but it was not confined to any one part of the country. The idealist awakening was evident also at such universities as California, Columbia, Cornell, Johns Hopkins, Michigan, and Princeton. The idealists believed in the priority of mind over matter and in the fundamental unity of the universe, but they modified these concepts to support American individualism.

Probably the most influential American idealist was the California-born Josiah Royce, who taught at Harvard from 1882 until his death in 1916. Royce accepted the German belief that individuals were parts of a single absolute mind, but unlike the orthodox Hegelians he asserted that each separate individual was an essential part of this whole and made his own singular contribution to it. Thus he gave to the individual a more significant, active role in the universe.

American Pragmatism. Meanwhile a school of philosophy more distinctively American and opposed to idealism was growing in popularity. Pragmatism, unlike most earlier philosophies, did not offer theories about God and the universe. It presented instead a way of evaluating acts and ideas in terms of their consequences in concrete experience. Pragmatism says that we cannot reject any hypothesis if consequences useful to life flow from it. The pragmatist's decision regarding the truth or falsity of an idea, then, is based on experimental test; "workability" is the correct method for finding truth. This concept was closely associated with two ideas that had gained wide currency in American thought—the idea of progress through evolution, and the idea of truth obtained through scientific investigation. The forerunners of pragmatism were Chauncey Wright and Charles S. Pierce, but two other men, William James and John Dewey, developed it.

William James, philosopher and psychologist at Harvard, rejected Spencerian determinism, which afforded no place for chance or human will. He upheld the independence of the mind and "the right to believe at our own risk any hypothesis that is live enough to tempt our will." At times he was inclined to suggest if someone felt happier or behaved better as a result of believing some idea, that idea should be regarded as true. While James repudiated absolutes, he also spoke out against a skepticism that would inhibit impulsively generous commitment. He distrusted all general laws and abstractions that denied man's capacity for free action. James contended that man's decisions would influence the course of events and that in spite of the existence of God, good or evil would result from human device and intelligence.

In his *Principles of Psychology* (1890), James made the first important American contribution to the scientific study of the mind. In later books he expounded his views on pragmatism. Theories to him were "instruments, not answers to enigmas." Pragmatism "has no dogmas, and no doctrines save its method," which was a method for reaching the truth. "The true is the name of whatever proves to be good in the way of belief," James said, "and good, too, for definite, assignable reasons." Such views were a sharp departure from nearly all the philosophies and religions of the past, and they captivated many Americans. Yet they also laid James open to the charge that pragmatism was simply another name for expedience: anything is good that works.

James' chief disciple was John Dewey, who considered himself an instrumentalist rather than a pragmatist. Born in Vermont in 1859, Dewey taught at Michigan, Chicago, and Columbia and remained an active force in American thought until his death in 1952. Originally an idealist, Dewey was converted to pragmatism in the 1890's after reading James. Though he lacked James' lucidity he developed his ideas in greater detail.

Dewey believed philosophy should become a tool for society to use in meeting its problems. To him no thinking was valid that did not spring from experience, for while ideas led to action it was only through action that men could acquire sound ideas. As he himself put it, his philosophy stemmed from the "growth of democracy—the development of the experimental methods in the sciences, evolutionary ideas in the biological sciences, and the industrial reorganization." Dewey put much faith in intelligence as a tool for social reform; he considered the mind "at least an organ of service for the control of environment." Like other social dissenters of this period, Dewey criticized laissez faire and social Darwinism and argued that life need not be accepted passively, but could be shaped by man. Since his instrumentalism meant using philosophy to advance democracy, he urged philosophers to leave their ivory towers, stop speculating about what he felt were meaningless trifles, and occupy themselves with politics, education, and ethics.

The New Legal Theory. There was also a revolt against formalism in law. The preceding generation regarded the law as fixed and unchanging and as a standard measure which the judge applied to the question at hand. But Oliver Wendell Holmes, son of the poet of the same name and friend of William James, declared in his book, *The Common Law* (1881): "The life of the law . . . has not been logic; it has been experience. . . . The felt necessities of the time, the prevalent moral and political theories, intuitions of public policy, avowed or unconscious, even the prejudices which judges share with their fellowmen, have a good deal more to do than the syllogism in determining the rules by which men should be governed." Law, Holmes felt, should be based upon changing social needs or political policies rather than upon logic or precedent. "It is revolting," he said, "to have no better reason for a rule of law than that it was laid down in the time of Henry IV. It is still more revolting if the grounds upon which it was laid down have vanished long since, and the rule simply persists from blind imitation of the past." A new school of legal theorists arose who not only accepted Holmes' reasoning but went on to contend that the meaning of any general legal principle must always be judged by its practical effects.

RELIGION IN THE AGE OF INDUSTRIALISM

Protestantism and Darwinism. The churches also had to adapt themselves to industrialism and to some of the main currents of thought. This proved to be difficult for the Protestant churches. Most Protestants considered the Bible to be the supreme authority and closely identified their ethics with the economic individualism of the middle class; but the Darwinian theory of evolution undermined confidence in the authority of the Bible, and the rise of large corporations weakened belief in the virtues of economic individualism.

In the eighties and nineties an increasing number of Protestant clergymen accepted the theory of evolution and reconciled it with religious beliefs. Henry Ward Beecher, one of the most celebrated preachers of the time, declared in his *Evolution and Religion* (1885) that evolution was merely "the deciphering of God's thought as revealed in the structure of the world." A few clergymen went beyond this to deny some of the supernatural events in Christianity; this alarmed the "fundamentalists," who reasserted their literal belief in the supreme authority of the Bible as the only solid foundation for religious faith. A struggle ensued between the fundamentalists and their opponents, the liberals.

Conservative Protestantism. Throughout the Gilded Age most Protestant clergymen believed the existing economic order was just. For instance, Beecher condemned the eight-hour day, insisted that poverty was a sign of sin, and advocated the use of force, if necessary, to put down strikes. Commenting in 1877 on the sharp wage cuts suffered by railway workers, Beecher concluded:

> It is said that a dollar a day is not enough for a wife and five or six children. NO, not if the man smokes or drinks beer. . . . But is not a dollar a day enough to buy bread with? Water costs nothing; and a man who cannot live on bread is not fit to live.

Perhaps Beecher and other clergymen like him were conservative because wealthy businessmen in their congregations made heavy contributions to church funds. In any case, the conservative sentiments of many of the clergy and their lack of sympathy for the workingman's demands caused a drop in working-class attendance in the churches.

The Social Gospel. In the 1880's a few of the socially conscious Protestant clergymen took issue with Beecher's teachings on current economic questions and began to preach the Social Gospel. They insisted that the problems created by industrialism could be solved only by a universal application of the teachings of Christ. Among the chief exponents of the Social Gospel were ministers Josiah Strong, Washington Gladden, and Walter Rauschenbusch. In his writings and sermons Gladden upheld the right of labor to organize and recommended that industrial disputes be eliminated by an "industrial partnership" that would allow workers to receive "a fixed share" of industry's profits. Gladden espoused the idea of government ownership of public utilities, although he rejected socialism as a system. Rauschenbusch severely censured industrial capitalism as a "mammonistic organization with which Christianity can never be content."

The Catholic View. The Roman Catholic Church's attitude toward social reform was more negative than positive, more tolerating than approving. Only in part was the hierarchy moved by considerations of justice and charity. James Cardinal Gibbons, Archbishop of Baltimore, insisted that Catholics cultivate a patriotic citizenship in keeping with the nation's civil institutions and customs. Gibbons asserted, "The accusation of being un-American—that is to say, alien to our national spirit—is the most powerful weapon which the enemies of the Church can employ against her." Only in this sense—as an aspect of Americanization—did the Catholic Church display any marked interest in social reform before the second decade of the twentieth century.

Archbishop John Ireland of St. Paul minimized the economic problems of the time and advocated only temperance and conservative trade unionism. In 1903 he said publicly, "I have no fear of great fortunes in the hands of individuals, nor of vast aggregations of capital in the hands of corporations." Ireland's friendship with James J. Hill, the railroad builder, and President McKinley brought him under the criticism of reformers. Yet he did often express strong sympathy for organized labor; he said on one occasion, "Until their material condition is improved it is futile to speak to them of spiritual life and duties."

Through this indifference to social reform, the Church jeopardized its hold on the loyalty of its communicants. Catholics in large numbers lost interest in a Church which seemed indifferent, if not hostile, to movements for the promotion of their economic welfare. Many Catholics turned to socialism. As the Church began to lose its members to Protestantism and socialism, it developed a greater interest in social problems. Also helping to change the Church's attitude was Pope Leo XIII's famous encyclical *De Rerum Novarum* (1891), which condemned the exploitation of labor and asserted that it was the duty of the state to bring social justice.

CULTURE IN THE GILDED AGE

Tastes and Manners. The Gilded Age has often been characterized as one of the most sterile periods in the cultural history of the United States. Everywhere in this generation, according to some critics, materialism so abounded that it perverted tastes and debauched the intellectual life of the country. There is ample evidence to suggest this point of view. But the age has too often been measured by its political record, which frequently misfired, and this criterion alone is not sufficient. The age was roundly condemned by such contemporary critics as Walt Whitman, Mark Twain, and Henry George, but their reasons were mostly superficial.

It was an age of crassness and vulgarity, and its unhappy aspects must be recognized. But historian and socio-literary critic Vernon L. Parrington, though sharply critical of the period, was fascinated by it. He interpreted the Gilded Age as one in which the energies dammed up by frontier life and inhibitions of backwoods religion were suddenly released.

One of the better known aspects of the Gilded Age was society's freedom to revise its morals and manners. The new rich of the industrial age were unsure of themselves and employed gaudy display to impress outsiders. The conspicuous waste of money was the measure of social status; it prompted the American craze for antiques and European collections, and launched perhaps the greatest plunder of the Continent since the sack of Rome.

Nothing exhibits better the excesses of the Gilded Age than its architecture and interior decoration, which declined to a new low. Houses were copied from European styles, and it was an age of the jig-saw, the cupola, the mansard roof with its dormer windows, and an orgy of decoration. "A stuffy and fussy riot of fancy," Parrington says of it, "restrained by no feeling for structural lines, supplied the lack of creative imagination, and architecture sank to the level of the jerry-builder. Bad taste could go no further." The same excess can be found in dress with its bustles, paddings, and corsets, in furniture, and even in machinery. In morals low and broad standards commingled with Victorian morality.

Achievements. Yet despite these obvious cultural excesses, intellectual and artistic developments of the Gilded Age were among the most fruitful this country has ever seen. We have already observed how the original and creative thinkers of the eighties and nineties made these two decades perhaps one of the most intellectually fertile periods in the whole of American history. Unfortunately, too many observers of the period have been preoccupied with the second-rate thinkers and artists and have neglected those who made contributions of the first order.

In the field of scholarship, the age saw the birth of two new social sciences: Lewis Henry Morgan founded anthropology and Lester Ward fathered American sociology. The period also witnessed a revolution in higher education. Until this time institutions of higher education concentrated on training ministers and lawyers, but now learning began to shake off its fetters and to range freely in the physical, natural, and social sciences, the arts, and the humanities. The most famous of the daring new university presidents were Charles W. Eliot of Harvard and Daniel Coit Gilman of Johns Hopkins. At Harvard, Eliot greatly expanded the curriculum and sponsored the elective system, which had originated at the University of Virginia at the time of its founding. He also drastically reformed Harvard's medical and law schools and gave them true professional status. At Johns Hopkins, Gilman built the first great graduate school in America. The graduate school and the seminar method were introduced from Germany in the 1870's, and some graduate work was done at Harvard and Yale in the 1870's. But Johns Hopkins, designed primarily as a center for graduate work at its founding in 1876, took the lead in this field and held it for the next quarter of a century. At that time also, professional schools got under way—

the Columbia School of Mines (1864), the Massachusetts Institute of Technology (1865), Stevens Institute (1871), and the Johns Hopkins Medical School (1893).

Arts and Letters. During the two or three decades following the Civil War, the most popular form of American literature was the regional short story. Bret Harte and Hamlin Garland in the West, George Washington Cable and Joel Chandler Harris in the South, and Sarah Orne Jewett in New England gave readers a fresh and exciting view of regional America and contributed to the reunification of the country.

Mark Twain, whose works were written in this period, was in his own day considered a regional author, but his novels, essays, and sketches have made a lasting reputation for him as a humorist, moralist, and social critic. The materials for Twain's best narratives—*The Adventures of Tom Sawyer* (1876), *Life on the Mississippi* (1883), and *The Adventures of Huckleberry Finn* (1884) —were his boyhood home, Hannibal, Missouri, and the great Mississippi River which rolled before it.

Twain, along with many other writers of the period, pointed out the evils of crass materialism and ridiculed the get-rich-quick schemes of his money-mad countrymen. In *The Gilded Age*, for example, Twain and Charles Dudley Warren pointed out that sober industry and contentment with a modest income honestly earned are infinitely preferable to frantic money-making schemes.

Growing social ills of the Gilded Age called forth specific indictments which became increasingly prominent in the literature of the late nineteenth and early twentieth centuries. William Dean Howells, who by 1900 was considered by many young writers to be the dean of American letters, exhibited the grime and squalor of New York City in *A Hazard of New Fortunes* (1890); Stephen Crane's *Maggie: A Girl of the Streets* (1893) exposed the ugly life of New York's Bowery; and Hamlin Garland in *Main-Travelled Roads* (1891) described the hardships and injustices suffered by farmers in Iowa and Wisconsin. While they emphasized the injustices and abuses of the new industrial order, however, treatment by writers of the captains of industry was for a good many years comparatively gentle. In Howells' *The Rise of Silas Lapham* (1884), for example, the author implied that the great majority of American financiers were honest—that robber barons were the exception, not the rule. The novelist and literary critic Henry James (brother of William James), who lived abroad most of his life, considered the ethics of the American financiers who vacationed in Europe to be fundamentally sound. The principal characters of James' *The American* (1877) and *The Golden Bowl* (1904) were businessmen of integrity and charm.

The literature of social criticism contained proposals for specific utopias, the most influential of which was Edward Bellamy's *Looking Backward* (1888). Bellamy, believing that economic inequality was the cause of all social ills, described a socialist utopia in which wealth was distributed equally among its members. Other writers of the period who proposed a socialist solution were Howells in *A Traveller from Altruria* (1893) and Upton Sinclair in *The Jungle* (1906). Most of the literature dealing with social problems, however, proposed reforms rather than a radical alteration of the American system of free enterprise.

Because many poets—Bryant, Longfellow, Holmes, Lowell, Emerson, and Whittier—whose careers had begun in an earlier period, continued to satisfy and to determine tastes after the war, much of American poetry showed remarkably few effects of the changing intellectual climate. By the end of the century, however, American poets and prose writers were feeling the full impact of the scientific movement. For example, much of Stephen Crane's poetry inferred from the biological struggle for survival and the astronomical immensity of the universe that man is unimportant:

> A man said to the universe
> "Sir, I exist!"
> "However," replied the universe,
> "The fact has not created in me
> A sense of obligation."

The Gilded Age knew nothing of Emily Dickinson, because only seven of her poems were published during her lifetime (1830-1886), but she is today considered one of the leading poets of the post-Civil War period and America's chief woman poet. She began to write poetry in the mid-fifties and continued until her death in 1886, but she spent the last half of her life as a recluse in Amherst, Massachusetts. Walt Whitman, whose volume of poetry, *Leaves of Grass*, had been published in three editions before the Civil War, continued to be an important figure in American poetry of the postwar period despite the fact that many critics objected to Whitman's departures from the conventions of versification and style and to his frank treatment of sex. Whitman's Quaker inheritance contributed to the independence, love of peace, and sense of brotherhood celebrated in so many of his works—among them *Drum Taps* (1866), a volume of poems recounting the experiences and suffering shared by both North and South, and the richest account of the Civil War to be found in our poetry.

Increasing wealth and leisure after the Civil War contributed to a new awareness of art among Americans, and such high caliber painting was done by George Inness, Thomas Eakins, Winslow Homer, Albert Pinkham Ryder, and Eastman Johnson that the Gilded Age could be called the most important one in American painting. Inness pioneered a new landscape school. Homer and Eakins were the leading American representatives of the naturalistic movement in painting; Homer grounded his art in direct observation of nature, while Eakins depicted the ordinary middle-class city life of the United States in the late nineteenth century. Johnson's illustrations of contemporary domestic scenes were enormously popular with the public. Ryder, haunted throughout his life by the sea, was the most original Romantic of his time. Two American expatriates, James McNeill Whistler and John Singer Sargent, both of whom lived for most of their lives in London, enjoyed international reputations—Whistler for his portrayals of contemporary life, Sargent as the most sought-after portraitist of the Anglo-Saxon world.

Although in architecture, as has been noted, the Gilded Age marked the nadir of taste, fine and outstanding architects did exist. Henry Hobsen Richardson and Louis H. Sullivan were the first major architects to meet the demands of industrialism upon their art; to these men, buildings had a sociological function as well as an artistic one. In his *Autobiography of an Idea*, Sullivan wrote, "that masonry construction was a thing of the past . . . that the old ideas of superimposition must give way before a sense of vertical continuity."

Most of these first-rate writers and artists worked in obscurity and did not receive the recognition they deserved from their contemporaries. Americans of the post-Civil War generation regarded others we now consider second-rate to be the leading figures in their respective fields, and because of this the Gilded Age has often been characterized as one of the most sterile periods of American culture. But viewed from the perspective of history it proves to have been one of America's richest and most fruitful eras.

BIBLIOGRAPHY

A good survey of industrial growth can be found in Edward C. Kirkland, *Industry Comes of Age: Business, Labor, and Public Policy, 1860-1897* (New York: Holt, 1961). Thomas C. Cochran and William Miller, *The Age of Enterprise: A Social History of Industrial America* (New York: Macmillan, 1942) covers industrial and business expansion since 1800. Roger Burlingame, *Engines of Democracy* (New York: Scribner, 1940) emphasizes inventions and technology. Stewart H. Holbrook, *The Age of the Moguls* (New York: Doubleday, 1953) contains entertaining anecdotes and dramatic incidents of the lives of business leaders. William Miller (ed.), *Men in Business: Essays in the History of Entrepreneurship* (Cambridge: Harvard University Press, 1952) has scholarly studies of the business community. The now somewhat discredited view that the nineteenth-century industrial leaders were "predatory capitalists" is to be found in Matthew Josephson, *The Robber Barons: The Great American Capitalists* (New York: Harcourt, Brace, 1934). Joseph Dorfman, *The Economic Mind in American Civilization, 1865-1918*, vol. 3 (New York: Viking, 1949) and Edward C. Kirkland, *Dream and Thought in the Business Community, 1860-1900* (Ithaca: Cornell University Press, 1956) analyze the dominant ideas in the business world. The trust problem is analyzed in H. R. Seager and C. A. Gulick, *Trust and Corporation Problems* (New York: Harper, 1929).

Rendigs Fels, *American Business Cycles, 1865-1897* (Chapel Hill: University of North Carolina, 1959) is an excellent study of the cyclical course of American economic development in post-Civil War America. Samuel P. Hays, *The Response to Industrialism, 1885-1914* (Chicago: University of Chicago Press, 1957) studies the impact of industrialism upon American life.

Thomas C. Cochran, *Railroad Leaders, 1845-1890: The Business Mind in Action* (Cambridge: Harvard University Press, 1953) studies the attitudes of leading railroad executives toward such matters as expansion, innovation, competition, and labor. R. E. Riegel, *The Story of Western Railroads* (New York: Macmillan, 1926) is the most useful general account of the transcontinentals. R. A. Billington and J. B. Hedges, *Westward Expansion*, 2nd ed. (New York: Macmillan, 1960) is an excellent survey of the westward movement. T. A. Richard, *A History of American Mining* (New York: McGraw-Hill, 1932) is the standard account of the miners' frontier. Roy M. Robbins, *Our Landed Heritage: The Public Domain, 1776-1936* (Princeton: Princeton University Press, 1942) is excellent on the disposition of the public lands.

Matthew Josephson, *The Politicos, 1865-1898* (New York: Harcourt, 1938) is the liveliest and the most comprehensive, but not the most detached, account of the political history of this period. H. U. Faulkner, *Politics, Reform, and Expansion, 1890-1900* (New York: Harper, 1959) is a recent synthesis of the nineties. Two excellent sectional studies of politics are C. Vann Woodward, *Origins of the New South, 1877-1913* (Baton Rouge: Louisiana State University Press, 1951) and H. S. Merrill, *Bourbon Democracy of the Middle West, 1865-1898* (Baton Rouge: Louisiana State University Press, 1953). A brilliant but mordant commentary on the period may be found in the appropriate chapters in Henry Adams, *The Education of Henry Adams* (New York: Houghton, 1907). James Bryce, *The American Commonwealth*, 2 vols. (New York: Macmillan, 1888) is a classic contemporary account of American government and American politics by a brilliant Englishman. Leonard D. White, *The Republican Era, 1869-1901: A Study in Administrative History* (New York: Macmillan, 1958) traces the federal administrative history of these years.

E. F. Goldman, *Rendezvous with Destiny: A History of Modern American Reform* (New York: Knopf, 1952) and Richard Hofstadter, *The Age of Reform: From Bryan to F. D. R.* (New York: Knopf, 1955) deal with the mentality of reform. Ari Hoogenboom, *Outlawing the Spoils: A History of the Civil Service Reform Movement, 1865-1883* (Urbana: University of Illinois Press, 1961) surveys the course of the civil service reform movement in this period.

F. A. Shannon, *The Farmer's Last Frontier: Agriculture, 1860-1897* (New York: Farrar & Rinehart, 1945) examines agricultural conditions and movements. The political repercussions of the depression of the nineties are handled in excellent fashion by G. H. Knoles, *The Presidential Campaign and Election of 1892* (Stanford: Stanford University Press, 1942). John D. Hicks, *The Populist Revolt* (Minneapolis: University of Minnesota Press, 1931) is the standard work on Populism, although a good brief survey can be found in S. J. Buck, *The Agrarian Crusade* (New Haven: Yale University Press, 1920). Two works giving a more specialized treatment of ideas in this generation are Richard Hofstadter, *Social Darwinism in American Thought*, rev. ed. (New York: Braziller, 1959) and M. G. White, *Social Thought in America* (New York: Viking, 1949). Perry Miller, (ed.), *American Thought: Civil War to World War I* (New York: Rinehart, 1954) is a first-class anthology of the leading thinkers of the period.

PART 6: INTRODUCTION

THE EMERGENCE OF A MODERN NATION

■ By the late 1890's the transformation of the United States from an agricultural to an industrial nation had created a number of urgent problems. Their resolution would often have profound effects, sometimes decisively determining the future both of the United States and of the world.

On the surface, the domestic issues were obvious. Could the alliance of businessmen and politicians be broken and the needs of labor, agriculture, and the consumer be met? Could a rational plan for the development and use of America's matchless natural resources be devised? Could the spread of slums be halted and the millions of new immigrants assimilated? Could American Negroes be given greater opportunities to uplift themselves? And above all, could monopoly be controlled and business malpractices be stamped out?

On various fronts throughout the nation there were signs that some of these things could be done. Reform movements were building up in many cities and states. Skilled labor had regrouped its forces under the American Federation of Labor and was poised for an assault on limited objectives. Legislation to regulate the railroads and to curb the trusts—the Interstate Commerce Act of 1887 and the Sherman Antitrust Act of 1890—was already on the statute books, and the demand to enforce the regulatory laws was growing stronger. Equally important, the intellectual foundations of laissez faire had been undermined by the reform Darwinists, a small, but articulate, band of intellectuals and clergymen who were strongly prepared to fight for social and economic reform. Meanwhile the reconstruction of philosophy begun by Josiah Royce and William James was being completed by John Dewey, who would become the most noted American philosopher of the twentieth century.

Nevertheless, the advocates of progress—or, to put it another way, of adjustment —faced formidable obstacles. Politically they were scattered through both major parties and comprised an insignificant minority of the power elements of each. Intellectually they constituted an extraordinarily small percentage of the citizenry at

Theodore Roosevelt, portrait by John Singer Sargent (1905)·
"We demand that big business give the people a square deal; in return we must insist that when any one engaged in big business honestly endeavors to do right he shall himself be given a square deal."—T. Roosevelt (1913).

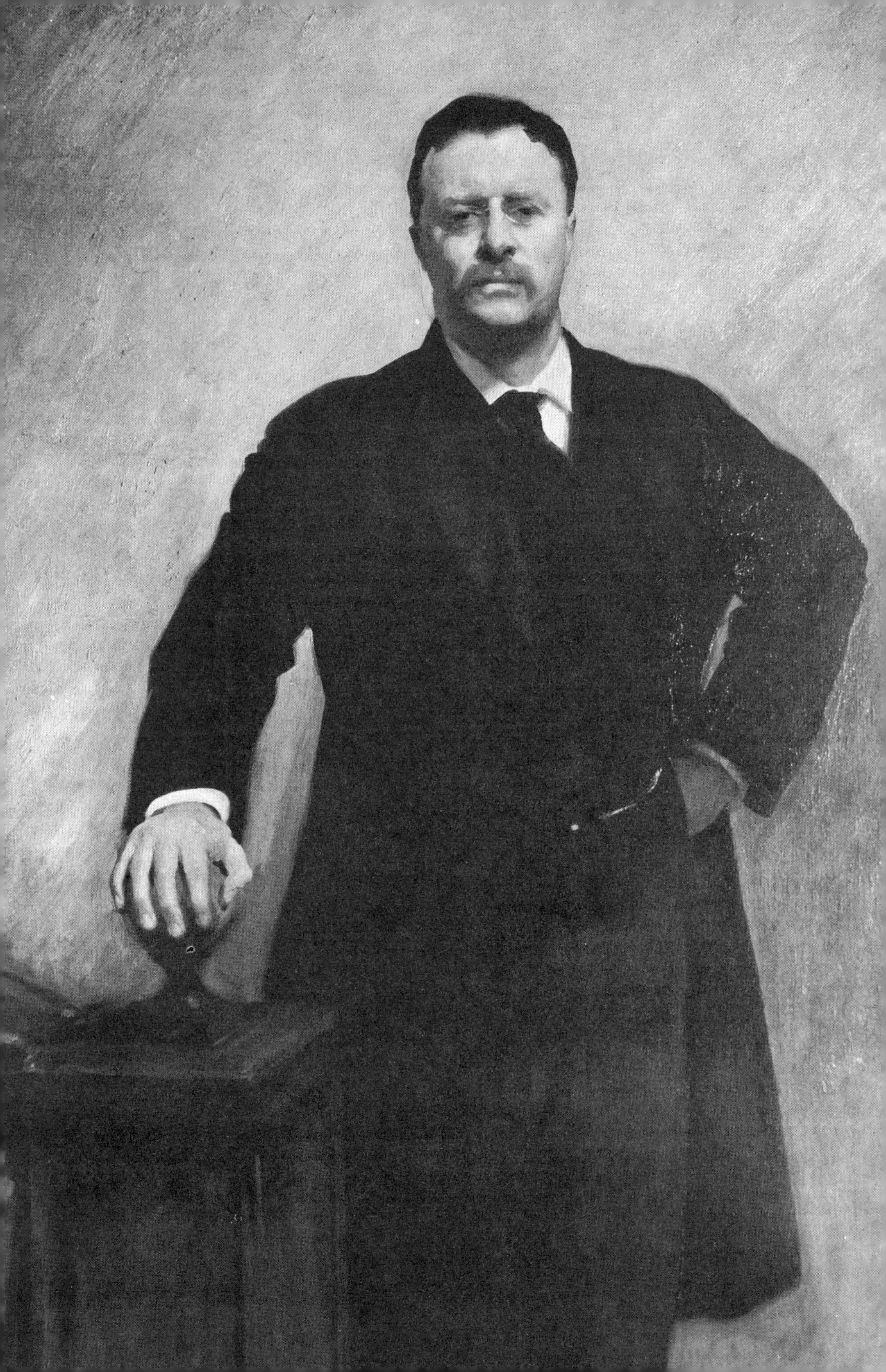

Armistice Night, 1918, painting by George Luks (1918). It was "over over there," as the song went, and America then retreated from twenty years of progressivism at home and "great crusades" abroad.

large. Yet to achieve their ends they would have to induce changes in American institutions as far-reaching in some respects as those wrought by the Civil War. For in spite of the growth of cities and the infusion of new ethnic and religious strains, the dominant values of American society remained rural, individualistic, and Protestant.

At the least, the powers of government would have to be increased. Executive agencies would have to be created and staffed by experts—by scientists, social workers, and economists who understood the forces which were molding the new industrial America. Even more basic changes would have to be made by the judiciary; if business were to be regulated effectively, federal and state courts would have to restrain their impulses to strike down acts of Congress and the state legislatures. The judicial abuse of the injunctive power would have to cease if labor's drives for living wages and human conditions of employment were to be fulfilled. And liability for industrial accidents would have to be shifted from employees to employers if thousands of accident victims were not to be reduced to poverty.

It was the achievement of the progressives, as the reformers came to be called, that they forced partial gains in all these areas and substantial gains in some of them. By the time the United States entered World War I the American political system had become reasonably responsive to the changing needs of the industrial and urban order. The machinery to regulate big business had been strengthened, and a modest program to uplift agriculture had been instituted. Labor's standard of living had risen, and the conditions of work had begun to improve in many industries. The courts had started to reinterpret the law. And the nation's educational system had been partially reconstituted.

Significant as these developments were, they paled in comparison to those in foreign affairs. Here, too, the currents of change had begun to flow long before they became a torrent in the Spanish-American War of 1898; and here, too, the wellsprings

Dewey at Manila, painting by Rufus F. Zogbaum (1899). The summer-long Spanish-American War—"a splendid little war" John Hay had termed it—thrust America's sea power on an imperialist course in the farther Pacific and in the Caribbean.

Cliff Dwellers, painting by G. Bellows (1913). "The shame of our cities," the misery of "how the other half lives," the "bitter cry of the children," and "the jungle" all gave titles to books decrying urban-industrial conditions in America.

were fed by the Industrial Revolution. Yet—and this is the crux of the great debate over isolationism that lasted from 1899 to 1941—the issues were so confused and their solutions so costly and radical that a large portion of the American people and their leaders failed either to understand them or to sustain long-term efforts to resolve them. Geographical and intellectual isolation made it hard for farmers and small town residents to realize that there was no escaping a power position which the Spanish-American and First World Wars had dramatized but which the nation's industrial might had forged. The ethnic backgrounds of most recent immigrants predisposed them against cooperation with the United States' great natural ally, the British. A belief in economic determinism convinced many progressives and most labor leaders that war was a uniquely capitalistic phenomenon. Selfishness and ultranationalism caused many conservatives to reject the moral responsibilities of the world power they themselves had fostered.

Except for one or two critical issues, however, these attitudes contributed more to the disillusionment of the 1920's than to decision-making in the years between the defeat of William Jennings Bryan in 1896 and the election of Warren Gamaliel Harding in 1920. The American people went exuberantly to war against Spain in 1898 and almost incidentally acquired a colonial empire in the process. During the next two decades their government built the Panama Canal and emerged as both policeman and protector of the Caribbean. Meanwhile it projected itself decisively into the affairs of Europe and the Far East by mediating the Moroccan Crisis of 1905 and the peace that ended the Russo-Japanese War in the same year. It then turned the tide for the Allies in World War I. Finally, in an action that graphically demonstrated the American people's failure to make their temporary agreements a permanent consensus, the United States turned its back on the League of Nations, which their President Woodrow Wilson had largely created.

CHAPTER 16

THE FORGING OF MODERN GOVERNMENT, 1900-1917

PROLOGUE TO CHANGE

Enter Theodore Roosevelt. On a September afternoon in 1901, at the Pan-American Exposition in Buffalo, New York, a young anarchist professing belief in the assassination of rulers approached President William McKinley and shot him with a revolver at close range. Eight days later the President died; and with his death an old era gave way to the youngest man (age forty-two) ever to hold the highest public office in the nation: Vice-President, now President, Theodore Roosevelt.

On December 3, 1901, two and one half months after a madman's bullet had put him in the White House, Roosevelt sounded the note of American politics in the twentieth century. The old political system, he declared in his first annual message to Congress, would have to be changed to meet new social and economic problems. "When the Constitution was adopted, at the end of the eighteenth century," wrote Roosevelt, "no human wisdom could foretell the sweeping changes . . . which were to take place by the beginning of the twentieth century. At that time it was accepted as a matter of course that the several States were the proper authorities to regulate, so far as was then necessary, the comparatively insignificant and strictly localized corporate bodies of the day. The conditions are now wholly different and wholly different action is called for."

Northern Securities Co. and the Anthracite Coal Strike. Action soon followed words. On February 14, 1902, Roosevelt invoked the Sherman Antitrust Act against the Northern Securities Company, a mammoth railroad holding corporation controlled by the bankers J. P. Morgan and Company and Kuhn, Loeb and Company and the railroad operators James J. Hill and Edward H. Harriman.

Morgan was stunned. He exclaimed that Roosevelt had not acted as a "gentleman" and later tried to treat the President like a rival operator. Hill was even more embittered. "It really seems hard," he complained, "that we should be compelled to fight for our lives against the political adventurers who have never done anything but pose and draw a salary." But the proceedings went forward. Two years later the Supreme Court, by a five to four decision, ordered the Northern Securities Company to dissolve.

Roosevelt had added further dimension to presidential leadership by the time the Northern Securities case was settled. John M. Mitchell, leader of the United Mine Workers, had called anthracite miners of northeastern Pennsylvania out on strike in May 1902. The strikers demanded an eight-hour day, wage increases, and recognition of their union. The eight railroad companies which dominated the industry would neither recognize the United Mine Workers nor mitigate the workers' near subhuman conditions of life. "[The miners] don't suffer," the operators' chief spokesman exclaimed at one point; "why, they can't even speak English." And so the strike continued through the summer and into the fall.

Roosevelt feared a coal shortage and was infuriated by the operators' arrogance; he considered filing an antitrust suit against the coal combine. But the Attorney General advised that it would fail for lack of evidence, and Roosevelt decided to invite the contesting parties to the White House. The operators deeply resented this implied recognition of the U.M.W. and vehemently refused to make any concessions at the ensuing conference in October. Roosevelt was determined to end the strike; he thereupon issued secret orders to the army to prepare to seize the mines and sent a warning to Wall Street. These measures sufficed. The operators agreed to accept the recommendations of an independent arbitration committee appointed by the President. Their plan to crush the U.M.W. had failed. "This is the great distinguishing fact," the Springfield *Republican* proclaimed at the time, "for while the operators still nominally refuse to recognize the mine workers' union, that union nevertheless is a party to the President's plan of arbitration and is so recognized by him."

The political importance of both the Northern Securities suit and the President's intervention in the coal strike far transcended their immediate economic significance. Roosevelt, by striking out boldly on his own, had asserted his independence of big business, revitalized the executive office, and helped prepare the way for the "progressive movement" to reach the national level.

THE REVOLT OF THE MIDDLE CLASSES

The New Consensus. The program that Theodore Roosevelt and Woodrow Wilson were to press on Congress and the nation from 1905 to 1916 was neither revolutionary nor original. Many reforms of the progressive era had been spelled out in the Populist party platform of 1892; almost every major measure that Roosevelt and his successors would sign into law had been suggested earlier by William Jennings Bryan. Even the attack on the Northern Securities Company had been based on the Sherman Antitrust Act, a law enacted twelve years before. Why, then, did progressivism succeed where Populism and Bryanism had failed?

The critical reason was the character of progressivism's constituency and leadership. Populism, despite its attempt to win labor support, had been essentially a movement of rural protest. Bryanism had been more broadly based. But Bryan had failed in 1896 to win essential middle-class support, even among more substantial farmers and workers. They were frightened mainly by Bryan's alleged financial heresies. "How intellectually snobbish I was about 'sound economics,'" the Kansas editor William Allen White remembered. "I was blinded by my birthright.... It seemed to me that rude hands were trying to tear down the tabernacle of our national life."

Progressivism triumphed because White and tens of thousands of other civic-minded Americans who shared both his prejudices and his virtues were drawn into it. They took with them a white-collar middle class almost six million strong. Predominantly old stock, Protestant, and urban, this group had numbered less than a million when the Mugwumps had vainly defied the old Republican bosses in the 1870's and 1880's. By 1900, however, these progressives constituted the new balance of power. Even as they were reëlecting William McKinley to the presidency, they were supporting candidates for municipal and state offices on platforms embodying much that post-Civil War reformers had always demanded. "Populism shaved its whiskers, washed its shirt, put on a derby and moved up into the middle of the class—the upper middle class," White also remembered. The result was an urban and rural consensus that cut across the old party lines, changed the character of both major parties, and profoundly altered the course of American history.

Wellsprings of Reform. For the vast majority of its silent, white-collar supporters, progressivism was an economic movement fired by moral indignation. Progressives fed on resentment toward poor schools, street car and water monopolies, rising prices, and soaring tax rates induced partly by collusion between politicians and businessmen. They wanted only to "turn the rascals out" and reëstablish honest government. They were as yet not much concerned with labor's problems. They were more interested in policing the slums than in eradicating them. They suspected that the influx of southern and eastern European immigrants was the cause of urban blight.

For all their limitations, progressives had both the ability and the desire to gain political control. They were generally well educated and accustomed to active participation in local affairs. They were not shackled by the tribal loyalties that made political machines irresponsible agencies of municipal government. They shared with farmers a puritanical heritage that made them fundamentally intolerant of corruption. Most important, they were capable of concerns that transcended their immediate economic interests. They responded enthusiastically when their leaders and spokesmen—editors and clergymen, college presidents and school principals, and, above all, civic-minded businessmen and lawyers—went on to conceive an ever growing reform program.

Their leaders were also partly moved by self-interest. They resented the waste of tax dollars, blamed high prices on the "trusts," and deplored the discriminatory practices of the railroads. They also feared aggrandizement of power by organized labor, the growth of a non-Protestant population, and the morally corrosive effect of slums. Moreover, many of them thought that they were being squeezed by the upper and nether elements of society. Some may even have been moved by a desire to regain a status supposedly stolen by the new financial and business leaders, those *nouveaux riches* whom one critic described as being "without restraints of culture, experience, the pride, or even the inherited caution of class or rank." Actually, however, their program was based more on hope than on fear, more on moral indigation than on personal resentment, more on a disinterested view of the commonweal than on ordinary self-interest.

The Social Problem. Everywhere that progressives looked they saw poverty, injustice, and political corruption in the midst of growing abundance and seemingly limitless opportunity. One per cent of the nation's families owned seven eighths of its wealth and ten million Americans lived in abject circumstances. The average worker toiled sixty hours a week. Almost two million children worked in fields or factories, frequently on night shifts. Thousands of workers were killed annually on the railroads alone—by one estimate over seven thousand. As late as 1913 industrial accidents annually caused twenty-five thousand deaths. Nor did there seem to be much hope that employers would or could cope with these problems. Wages were fixed by supply and demand. In the absence of a strong labor movement or minimum wage laws, even those manufacturers who wished to be humane had to pay subsistence wages in order to survive competition.

Labor's attempts to organize and strike for higher wages and shorter hours had been systematically weakened by judicial injunctions and, more important, by management's use of immigrants as strikebreakers. There was no pension system, no automatic compensation for injuries or death sustained on the job. The widow who received $250 from her husband's employer could consider herself blessed, and so could the one who had resources to go to court under the inadequate liability laws. Relief, when it was available, came largely from private sources.

The Business Problem. The consolidation of several firms into large industrial combines, a movement described in Chapter 13, threatened to make conditions worse rather than better. By 1904 combinations of one form or another controlled two fifths of all manufacturing in the United States. Six great financial groups dominated about 95 per cent of the railroads. Some 1320 utilities companies were organized under a handful of giant holding companies. And as early as 1902 the United States Industrial Commission had reported, "In most cases the combination has exerted an appreciable power over prices, and in practically all cases it has increased the margin between raw materials and finished products." The Commission added that the cost of production had probably decreased, and that profits had doubtless increased. A subsequent report revealed that the cost of living actually increased 35 per cent between 1897 and 1913.

As we have seen, efficiency was the economic justification for these developments. But the consolidation movement, like the protective-tariff movement, was based primarily on fear of competition and its attendant instability. No one, not even J. Pierpont Morgan, whose very gaze "forced the complex of inferiority . . . upon all around him," was immune. Fear of competition had driven him and his associates to buy out Andrew Carnegie and organize the United States Steel Corporation in 1901. The desire for stability and assured profits had also prompted him and James J. Hill to organize the Northern Securities Company in 1901.

The consolidation movement tended to destroy competition; more important, it made it difficult for the nation to solve its festering social and political problems. Great corporations had the power to prevent organization of basic industries and used this power ruthlessly. They also transformed economic power into political influence in various ways. If railroad, sugar, oil, and steel interests could not "buy" state legislatures as openly as they could twenty-five years earlier and if they could no longer send hand-picked men to Congress, they nevertheless exerted great influence over both elections and legislative decisions. They made huge contributions to the Republican party, controlled countless newspaper editors and publishers, and maintained powerful lobbies in Washington and in state capitals.

Actually, the chief and most active opponents of social and economic change were the small industrialists, organized in the National Association of Manufacturers, which was founded in 1895. These and other small businessmen and real estate promoters were chiefly responsible for the already widespread desecration of America's cities and countryside. Small industry fought minimum wage, child labor, and factory safety bills. Small businessmen lobbied most vigorously for low local and state taxes and thus for inadequate schools and social services.

However, the role of small business should not obscure the major issue that Roosevelt and progressives faced on the national level. The inescapable fact was that big business in 1901 constituted the most potent threat to American democracy. The post-Civil War transfer of power from Washington to Wall Street had been accelerated under President McKinley. The presidency by the time of Roosevelt's ascension had become a kind of branch brokerage office, with the President himself little more than the Washington director of a nation-wide financial operation. There was nothing particularly sinister or even secret about the system. Republican politicians like McKinley and his friend Mark Hanna believed that national welfare depended upon cooperation between business and government. National policies should promote the prosperity of big business. But there could be no national progressive movement until the reign of big business was effectively challenged. This was why Roosevelt's action against the Northern Securities Company had such great symbolic importance.

Social Idealism. The men who would march to battle when Theodore Roosevelt disrupted the Republican party in 1912 were ten years younger than the stalwarts who manned the bastions for conservatism and the G.O.P. Progressives were college students or impressionable young men of affairs when the intellectual revolution described in Chapter 15 challenged the economic and social values of their fathers in the 1880's and 1890's. They may not have heard of Lester Ward and his *Dynamic Sociology* (1883), but they were thoroughly familiar with Henry George's indictment of poverty and Edward Bellamy's utopian vision of the potentialities of the new technology. In the main, they accepted the postulates of reform Darwinism as distinguished from Spencerian social Darwinism. In brief, they believed that man could and should shape his environment creatively and socially.

To be sure, they continued to hold vestiges of older theories—theories of race, for instance, which argued Anglo-Saxon superiority, still hindered their full acceptance of the importance of environment as a social conditioner. Even John R. Commons, economist, historian, Christian layman, and zealous friend of labor, favored immigration restriction on genetic grounds. But progressives, unlike old-line conservatives, worked hard to create a better environment for the millions of southern and eastern European immigrants who had already come. And the restriction movement, while partly influenced by genetic theories, was based also on a purely practical economic belief that immigration caused low wages. One of the noblest chapters in the history of the United States was written by Jane Addams at Chicago's Hull House, a settlement house devoted to the improvement of community life in the Chicago slums. She worked to restore the immigrants' sense of personal dignity and encouraged them to preserve the best of their own cultures. Roosevelt's appointments of Negroes and members of other minority groups were based on more than political expediency. "I grow extremely indignant at the attitude of coarse hostility to the immigrant," he wrote the Protestant clergyman and editor Lyman Abbott in 1906:

I have one Catholic in my Cabinet . . . and I now have a Jew . . . and part of my object in each appointment was to implant in the minds of our fellow Americans of Catholic or of Jewish faith, or of foreign ancestry or birth, the knowledge that they have in this country just the same rights and opportunities as every one else.

Scientism. Another thing which exerted great influence on the progressives' outlook was the impact of the new technology. By 1910, when the progressive movement began to reach full flower, there were a half million automobiles on American roads. By 1917, after adoption of the assembly line had enabled Ford to cut the price of his Model T from $950 to $290, there were close to five million. By 1915 over six million telephones were in use, and more than fifty corporations were supporting industrial research. When the United States entered World War I in 1917 the country was well on the way to being thoroughly serviced by electricity; by the end of the war more than half of American industry was run by electric power. Meanwhile, scientific management techniques devised by Frederick Winslow Taylor were increasingly applied. Production increased 76 per cent between 1899 and 1909, although the labor force had increased by only 40 per cent. Progress in medicine and development of public health programs reduced the death rate from 17 to 12.2 per thousand and increased life expectancy from 49 to 56 years between 1897 and 1917.

Not all progressives reacted the same way to these developments. Some were more impressed by large-scale production and scientific management than were others. But virtually all agreed that production was the key to abundance and that the personal indignities and social effects of poverty could be substantially modified. They further agreed that the art of government had not kept pace with the science of industry. They proposed, accordingly, to apply the new techniques to management of public affairs. And they turned with remarkable unanimity to experts—scientists, economists, social workers, and public health specialists—for counsel, political support, and the staffing of commissions, which were formed to deal with the bewildering complexities of modern society.

Moral Idealism. To their conviction that man could shape his environment creatively by the application of science, progressives added a full measure of Christian idealism. Even the atheists and agnostics among them were demonstrably influenced by a Christian movement called the Social Gospel. It began in the 1870's and 1880's, when a group of zealous and socially conscious Protestant clergymen called for the application of Christian principles of brotherhood and compassion to the problems of labor. The active proponents of the Social Gospel never numbered more than a fraction of the Protestant clergy, and they were concentrated in urban churches.

The movement's most important figure, Walter Rauschenbusch, was a professor of church history whose studies drove him to the conclusion that capitalism was inherently sinful and that the righteous alternative was Christian Socialism. His socialistic proposal was decisively rejected by churchmen, but his graphic analysis of the brutalizing impact of industrial life was widely accepted. In 1908, one year after publication of Rauschenbusch's most important work, *Christianity and the Social Crisis,* the Methodist Episcopal Church came out for abolition of child labor and for a host of other reforms. In that same year the Federal Council of Churches of Christ in America was founded on a platform that placed official Protestantism squarely behind the movement to end exploitative capitalism by means of social welfare legislation.

During the progressive era, however, American Protestantism actually spent far more energy campaigning for prohibition than fighting against man's exploitation of his fellow man. Nor was the influence of Pope Leo XIII's memorable encyclical, *Rerum Novarum* (1891), substantial among Roman Catholics. The Pope's charge that "a small number of very rich men have been able to lay upon the masses of the poor a yoke little better than slavery itself" spurred numerous parish priests to compassionate works. But for twenty-five years the American hierarchy largely ignored the encyclical.

Nevertheless, the Social Gospel movement had a considerable impact. It quickened many lay consciences. It raised profound questions about business ethics and the morality of the laws of the market place. Most important, it broadened and strengthened the moral foundations of the progressive movement.

Muckraking. Of all influences affecting progressives, the most sensational was the literature of exposure. In 1902 a group of journalists, later called "muckrakers," began to publish articles about social, economic, and political problems in such middle-class magazines as *McClure's*, *Collier's*, *Everybody's*, and *Cosmopolitan*. Their subject matter ranged from the traffic in prostitutes to the perversion of democracy in city halls, state houses, and the United States Senate. Their output varied greatly in quality. Some were like Ida M. Tarbell, who carefully documented the impersonal ruthlessness of John D. Rockefeller and his associates in the *History of the Standard Oil Company* (1904). These scholarly muckrakers established standards of research and reporting which few journalists have ever surpassed. Others resembled David Graham Phillips, author of *The Treason of the Senate* (1906), who unfortunately obscured, by means of innuendo and misrepresentation, much of the real truth that underlay his work.

One muckraker, Lincoln Steffens, brought to his work extraordinary insight into contemporary practices of American politicians, businessmen, and ordinary citizens. His two chief contributions were *The Shame of the Cities* (1904) and *The Struggle for Self-Government* (1906). Steffens was neither unaware of the defects of character that made public officials accept bribes nor indifferent to the moral lassitude that made average citizens indulgent of bad government. However, he was much more interested in the bribegivers than in the bribetakers. Refusing to play to the anti-immigrant biases of his middle-class readers, he showed that the old-stock Republican machine in Philadelphia was worse than Irish-dominated Tammany Hall. He revealed that in Rhode Island it was rural Yankee legislators, not urban Italians, who had sold out to the traction and other interests. And he described how the Pennsylvania Railroad in New Jersey and the Public Service Corporation had engineered the New Jersey legislature into perpetuating low taxes and other special privileges for railroads and public service corporations.

The muckrakers' impact was enormous. Their analysis of political corruption confirmed the progressive leaders' belief that the American republic must be reformed or become a businessman's oligarchy. And the widespread circulation of their articles aroused voters and helped to create the political support necessary for successful action. But it is important to remember that muckraking was not a prime generator of reform. It reached its height in 1906, long after reform Darwinism, scientism, moral idealism, and the Social Gospel had made their impact.

THUNDER IN THE CITIES AND STATES

Early reform. The foundations of progressivism were laid during the six years between Bryan's defeat in 1896 and Roosevelt's intervention in the coal strike of 1902. During the next decade the movement spread through the entire country, including the South, in one of the most creative political upheavals that the nation has ever experienced.

Starting most often as reformers intent upon restoring honesty to city government, progressive leaders soon found that the trail of privilege and corruption led from the cities to the states and thence to powerful business interests. They also found, as their Mugwump predecessors rarely did, that honesty was not enough. Government, they came gradually to conclude, had to be transformed from a negative to a positive force. Only then could utilities corporations be brought under control, exploitation of men, women, and children be stopped, and most other urban evils be eradicated.

The movement began with the eruption of municipal reform movements in New York City and Chicago between 1894 and 1897. A year later Theodore Roosevelt, who had stamped himself as a brilliant but traditional civic reformer, was elected governor of New York on an "honest government" platform. Once in office he pushed through a corporation tax, strengthened the factory and tenement inspection laws, and flouted business interests on so many other counts that the G.O.P. machine eased him into the vice presidency in 1900. Meanwhile, Robert M. La Follette abandoned Republican orthodoxy and won the governorship of Wisconsin in 1900 on the most advanced platform of the period. Tom Johnson, a wealthy and humane industrialist, was elected mayor of Cleveland on a municipal-ownership platform in 1901.

The Reform Program. Concluding that they must break the business-political nexus before economic reforms could be enacted, progressives sought both to transfer power to the people and to apply scientific procedures to government. In city after city they campaigned successfully for the commission or city-manager plans, for home rule, and for honest elections. And in state after state they won the direct primary, the short ballot, the initiative and the referendum, and the recall of elected officials.

In addition, progressives strengthened child labor laws, created commissions staffed by experts to regulate utilities and railroad rates, and began to impose inheritance, corporation, and graduated income taxes. They also made increasingly large appropriations for schools, state universities, mental and penal institutions, and welfare programs in general. Maryland enacted the first workmen's compensation law in 1902. Oregon limited women workers to a ten-hour day in the next year. Illinois established a public assistance program for mothers with dependent children in 1911. And Massachusetts in 1912 created a commission to fix wages for women and children. By the end of the progressive era the number of students in high schools had almost doubled, most of the great industrial states had workmen's compensation laws, and the number of industrial accidents had been dramatically reduced by both forced and voluntary adoption of safety procedures.

True, the mechanical reforms were not as effective as hoped. The initiative, referendum, and recall were little used; the commission plan could be subverted by corruption. Bosses eventually returned in some cities. But not even they could hold back the progressive tide, and the movement for social justice advanced steadily down through the 1920's. The epilogue that Senator La Follette wrote in his *Autobiography* in 1913 was in reality a prologue:

> It has been a fight supremely worth making, and I want it to be judged . . . by results actually attained. If it can be shown that Wisconsin is a happier and better state to live in, that its institutions are more democratic, that the opportunities of all its people are more equal, that social justice more nearly prevails, that human life is safer and sweeter—then I shall rest content in the feeling that the Progressive movement has been successful.

PROGRESSIVISM MOVES TO WASHINGTON

In 1904 President Roosevelt was girding for a mighty struggle with conservatives in his own party. Roosevelt's revitalization of the Sherman Antitrust Act in 1902 had fired the public's imagination and restored a measure of authority to his office. But the legislative record of his first administration had been modest. A Democratic-sponsored reclamation measure, the Newlands Act, had been passed in 1902 with the President's support. The Elkins Act to prohibit railroad rebates had gone through in 1903 because the railroads favored it. And a Department of Commerce and Labor, including a Bureau of Corporations with investigatory powers, had been created the same year. But a handful of conservatives, called Old Guardsmen—Nelson W. Aldrich of Rhode Island, William B. Allison of Iowa, Marcus A. Hanna of Ohio, Orville H. Platt of Connecticut, and John C. Spooner of New York—had otherwise kept the legislative hatches closed.

Wealthy, able, and intelligent, these senators were also arrogant and dogmatic on social questions. Except for Mark Hanna—who had sought rapprochement with labor in 1900 by joining with Samuel Gompers in forming the National Civic Federation, an agency devoted to promoting mediation of labor disputes—these senators were insensitive to social and economic injustice. But they supported governmental subsidies and other favors to business even while they invoked the survival-of-the-fittest concept against the mildest reforms. They did not want Roosevelt to run for a full term in 1904. But he captured the party machinery, and they and the financial and business interests in general helped him win a rousing victory over the conservative Democrat, Judge Alton B. Parker. As the New York *Sun* put it, it was better to have "the impulsive candidate of the party of conservatism than the conservative candidate of the party which the business interests regard as permanently and dangerously impulsive."

Roosevelt would find little support by turning to the Democrats. Bryanism was stronger outside Congress than in it. And although Democrats were willing to abandon states' rights on some issues, the ancient predilection persisted in softened form, especially among Southerners. They had scant sympathy for Roosevelt's desire for a more centralized government. Even if they had approved this desire, their strength in the Senate was too slight for Roosevelt to have forged a viable coalition with them and the small minority of progressive Republicans. Roosevelt had no choice, therefore, but to work through the men who held the party—the conservative Republican leaders.

Still, there were offsetting factors. The President controlled the patronage. He could enforce acts of Congress vigorously or indifferently. He could appoint fact-finding commissions. And he could use the vast moral force of his office to influence public opinion and thus, indirectly, the Congress. Reinforced by his understanding of these powers and emboldened by his popular mandate and the angry excitement whipped up by the muckrakers, Roosevelt prepared in December 1904 to present Congress with a full program of reform.

Railroad Regulation. His first major achievement was the Hepburn Act for railroad regulation. Roosevelt had asked for, and failed to get, a regulation measure in 1905. Meanwhile, Ray Stannard Baker, one of the scholarly muckrakers, published a devastating account of railroad malpractices in *McClure's*. A concerted demand for action arose in the Middle West and the South. The demand came not only from farmers but also from merchants, manufacturers, and civic leaders. Their national organizations—among the most active were the National Board of Trade, the National Business League, and the United States Chamber of Commerce—protested less against high rates than against the long-and-short-haul evil[1], the curtailment of services induced by the consolidation of lines, and similar abuses.

---

1. See footnote, p. 248.

These were formidable pressures, and a number of conservative Republican senators swung partly to the President's side. Then, following a series of brilliant manuevers by Roosevelt, a coalition of Republicans and Democrats passed a compromise measure in 1906 which the President accepted. La Follette cried "betrayal" because the bill failed to authorize the Interstate Commerce Commission to evaluate a railroad's worth in determining rates. But, in fact, the Hepburn Act was a momentous step forward.

The Hepburn Act empowered the I.C.C. to investigate and fix rates on complaint, and it required railroads to adopt a uniform system of cost accounting. It expanded the I.C.C.'s jurisdiction to express, sleeping-car, and pipeline companies, strengthened the law against rebating, and forbade free passes. Finally, it required railroads to divest themselves of outside properties.

Public Health Controls. The President, shortly after adoption of the Hepburn Act, signed two other significant measures—the Pure Food and Drug Act and the Meat Inspection Amendment to the Agricultural Appropriations Act. Each was necessitated by the callous disregard of the public's health by the industries concerned. Each reflected a sharpened awareness by responsible men that federal regulation was the only means of safeguarding the people's health against irresponsible businessmen.

The Pure Food and Drug Act was a testament both to the new scientism and to the single-minded dedication of the Department of Agriculture's chief chemist, Dr. Harvey W. Wiley, "a very mountain among men, a lion among fighters." Wiley had long been pressing for a law to prevent the manufacture and sale of adulterated, misbranded, or poisonous foods and drugs. With powerful help from President Roosevelt, the American Medical Association, and the muckraker Samuel Hopkins Adams, his bill finally came to the floor of the Senate in the spring of 1906. Sneering openly at chemists in the Department of Agriculture, Senator Nelson W. Aldrich of Rhode Island said that "the liberty of all the people" was at stake. But Senator Porter J. McCumber of North Dakota rejoined that the real issue was the public's right to receive what it asked for and "not some poisonous substance in lieu thereof." The Old Guard's defenses eventually collapsed. An imperfect, but pioneering, pure-food-and-drug measure became law on June 30, 1906.

The fight for the Meat Inspection Amendment was even more exciting. Upton Sinclair's muckraking novel, *The Jungle* (1906), graphically exposed conditions in the meat-packing industry:

There was never the least attention paid to what was cut up for sausage; there would come all the way back from Europe old sausage that had been rejected, and that was mouldy and white—it would be doused with borax and glycerine, and dumped into the hoppers, and made over again for home consumption. There would be meat that had tumbled out on the floor, in the dirt and sawdust, where the workers had tramped and spit uncounted millions of germs.... [A] man could run his hand over these piles of meat and sweep off handfuls of the dried dung of rats.

Roosevelt read *The Jungle* in page proof. Finley Peter Dunne's humorous character Mr. Dooley had Roosevelt rising from his breakfast table, crying, "I'm pizened," and throwing sausages out of the window. He ordered an immediate investigation. Meanwhile, lobbyists for the meat-packing industry charged that an inspection measure drawn by Senator Albert J. Beveridge of Indiana was "unconstitutional" and "socialistic." However, when European sales dropped precipitously following partial publication of the presidential commission's findings, the meat-packers abruptly reversed themselves. What they and their powerful employers now wanted, wrote the muckraker Mark Sullivan, was "an inspection law . . '. strong enough to still public clamor, while not so drastic as to inconvenience them too greatly." The result was conflict and, in the Rooseveltian pattern, compromise. The measure as finally approved forbade the manufacture, sale, or transportation of adulterated or fraudulently labeled food and drugs sold in interstate commerce.

For Generations Yet Unborn. By now the President was also deep in a bitter struggle for rational control and development of the nation's natural resources. On his side were a great host of governmental scientists and experts headed by Gifford Pinchot, uncounted public-spirited citizens from all over the nation (but especially from the East), numerous homesteaders, and the great lumber corporations. Arrayed against him were small lumber companies, grazing, mining, and power interests of all types, most western state governments, and, in the end, a decisive majority in Congress.

The issues were simple in some instances and complex in others. Should homesteaders be sacrificed to big cattle and sheep men for reasons of efficiency? Should giant lumber corporations, which had the means to pursue scientific forestry, be favored over small companies, which did not? In any event, the moralistic and scientific assumptions of Roosevelt and his supporters were clear enough: namely, that the country's natural resources belong to the people as a whole; that "the fundamental idea of forestry is the perpetuation of forests by use"; that the federal government should reclaim arid lands; that "every stream is a unit from its source to its mouth, and all its uses are interdependent"; and that the electric monopoly is "the most threatening which has ever appeared."

Early in his administration Roosevelt saved what became the heart of the Tennessee Valley Authority in the 1930's by vetoing a bill that would have opened Muscle Shoals on the Tennessee River to haphazard development by private interests. He then set aside governmental reserves in Nebraska for a tree-planting experiment that served as a model for a more comprehensive program under the New Deal. In 1905 he rehabilitated the Bureau of Forestry, renamed it the Forest Service, and appointed Gifford Pinchot as its chief.

A small revolution followed. The new agency was staffed with trained and dedicated foresters. The development of water-power sites by utilities corporations was subjected to enlightened controls. Numerous bills for development under conditions injurious to the public interest met Rooseveltian vetoes. More than 2500 potential dam sites were temporarily withdrawn from entry in order to assure orderly and constructive development. In addition, 125 million acres were added to the national forests; half as many acres with coal and mineral deposits were transferred to the public domain; and most large lumber corporations (though not the small ones) were persuaded to adopt the selective-cutting techniques that alone assured both the perpetuation and the proper use of timber resources.

Western congressmen beholden to private interests responded with near-hysterical charges of "executive usurpation" and destruction of states' rights. But Roosevelt was undaunted. He skirmished for the preservation of the country's natural monuments even as Congress passed laws depriving him of authority to create new national forests. Before he left office in March 1909 the number of national parks had been doubled, sixteen National Monuments like California's Muir Woods and Washington's Mount Olympus had been created, and fifty-one wildlife refuges had been established. "Is there any law that will prevent me from declaring Pelican Island a Federal Bird

Reservation?" Roosevelt had asked. Informed that there was not, he had replied, "Very well, then I so declare it."

Meanwhile the President appointed a commission to investigate and make recommendations for multipurpose river valley developments such as the Tennessee Valley Authority later became. Then in May 1908 he urged the first conference of governors to implement the conservation movement in their states. No governor espoused the movement with Roosevelt's zeal and understanding, but spadework for moderate state programs had nevertheless begun. "When the historian . . . shall speak of Theodore Roosevelt," the President's bitter enemy Senator La Follette later wrote, "he is likely to say . . . that his greatest work was inspiring and actually beginning a world movement for . . . saving for the human race the things on which alone a peaceful, progressive, and happy life can be founded."

Variations in Antitrust Policy. Neither La Follette nor most other progressives were altogether enthusiastic about Roosevelt's later attitude toward big business. The President had followed up action against the Northern Securities Company with a spate of suits, and twenty-five indictments had been obtained and eighteen proceedings in equity had been instituted by the end of his second term. His successor, William Howard Taft, intensified the pace, bringing forty-three indictments in four years. Meanwhile, the Supreme Court had expedited proceedings with a unanimous verdict against the meat-packing trust in 1905. Finally, in 1911 the Supreme Court implicitly reversed the Knight decision of 1895 in two verdicts decreeing dissolution of the Standard Oil Company and the American Tobacco Company. These decisions made it clear that manufacturing combinations were not exempt from the Sherman Antitrust Act, even though the Court qualified this somewhat with the "rule of reason," which said that bigness *per se* was no crime.

These proceedings and decrees certainly had some impact. They halted consolidation at the top and prevented countless malpractices. "The example of these basic decisions served as a powerful negative factor in business affairs," concludes one recent scholar. "Certain lines of development were denied to ambitious men." Yet they wrought few basic changes in the American economy. Price leadership continued, as the producers in a single industry followed the price lead of a few dominant corporations like United States Steel. Moreover, control over credit remained highly concentrated in Wall Street.

As his administration progressed, Roosevelt himself experienced a metamorphosis in his attitude toward the "trusts." Because he appreciated the advantages of large-scale production and distribution, he sought to distinguish between "good" and "bad" trusts. He put his faith primarily in regulation rather than in antitrust proceedings; and he repeatedly called on Congress to strengthen and expand the regulatory Bureau of Corporations. After he left office he came out openly for government price fixing in basic industries.

Meanwhile Roosevelt maintained cordial relations with the Morgan-U.S. Steel axis. In order to prevent the spread of a severe financial panic that struck New York in 1907, he acquiesced in U.S. Steel's absorption of a southern competitor, the Tennessee Coal and Iron Company. In the next year he accepted without protest the inadequate Aldrich-Vreeland banking bill, which progressives and agrarians bitterly opposed. He did not make a serious effort to revise the tariff at any time during his presidency.

Trouble on the Labor Front. Labor continued to make modest advances during the Roosevelt and Taft administrations, mainly because of the progressives' work in the states. The American Federation of Labor grew by fits and starts, and the standard of living of its highly skilled members rose appreciably. Real wages throughout the manufacturing industries seem to have increased all through the progressive period—for a total of 37 per cent from 1897 to 1914—while the average work week declined from sixty to fifty hours.

The A.F.L. failed, however, to organize basic industry, mainly because of the massive counteroffensive by employers, spearheaded by the National Association of Manufacturers. The N.A.M. resorted to weapons ranging from propaganda to violence in order to prevent labor from organizing. Their most effective tactic was maintenance of the open shop (a shop in which union membership is not a precondition of employment); their most important ally was the middle class, including many of the men who had strongly supported the progressive movement. The employers understood that in practice an open shop meant a nonunion shop, but middle-class progressives often did not. Even when they saw the point, a lingering devotion to natural law and rights made it difficult for them to accept the idea of the closed shop (a shop in which an employer may hire only union members). Roosevelt was unsure on the issue. And men like Woodrow Wilson, president of Princeton, and Charles W. Eliot, president of Harvard, were adamant; Eliot actually acclaimed the strikebreaker as "a very good type of modern hero." In consequence, labor received virtually no support during the progressive era for the one measure that would have assured it success—active governmental support of the organizing process. In fairness to progressives it should be added that labor's spokesmen at this time would not have welcomed such support.

To compound labor's difficulties, the basic right to strike was often grossly impaired by management's resort to violence, the actions of corporation-dominated state governments, and the use of injunctions by judges who cared more for property than for human rights. In speech after speech from 1905 to 1912 Roosevelt inveighed mightily against the abuse of the injunction. But the N.A.M. was so influential in Republican councils that he failed to get an anti-injunction plank in the G.O.P. platform in 1908.

Campaigns to organize the steel industry meanwhile suffered a series of setbacks and collapsed altogether during the period 1909-1910. The United Mine Workers were successful in the East, but they failed in two bloody efforts in Colorado. The first, in 1903-1904, ended in a rout climaxed by the deportation of strikers to the desert. The second, in 1913-1914, ended in tragedy when National Guardsmen burned a striker's tent colony at Ludlow on April 20, 1914, accidentally killing eleven women and two children. Although the resultant investigation spurred John D. Rockefeller, Jr., to institute reforms in the management of his Colorado mines, he insisted on management's right to fight organization.

Against this background of bitter conflict the formation in 1905 of the freewheeling and often violent International Workers of the World (I.W.W. or "Wobblies") was almost inevitable. It was concentrated in the West and fought the battles of frontier miners, lumbermen, and migratory workers. Also inevitable was the tremendous growth of the influence of the Socialist party, especially after the A.F.L. decided to concentrate on winning procedural reforms through the Republican and Democratic parties.

Forecasts of the Welfare State. By 1907 the Republican majority in Congress had had their fill of Theodore Roosevelt. They approved no major domestic legislation during his last two years in office and repudiated him openly on several occasions. Nevertheless, the executive power continued to expand. The President appointed a number of new investigatory commissions. He made further advances in conservation. And he repeatedly lectured Congress and the people on the need to mitigate the harsh inequities of capitalism by welfare measures. He was outraged by the Supreme Court's ruling in *Lochner* v. *New York* (1905), which held that a maximum-hours law for bakers was unconstitutional on the grounds that it was an unreasonable interference with the right of free contract and an unreasonable use of the state's police power. And after a New York tenement law was invalidated and a workmen's compensation law declared unconstitutional, he wrote Justice William R. Day that, unless the judiciary's spirit changed, "we should not only have a revolution, but it would be absolutely necessary to have a revolution, because the condition of the worker would become intolerable."

Finally, on January 31, 1908, Roosevelt sent Congress the most radical message ever penned up to that time by a President. He charged that businessmen had revived the doctrine of states' rights in order to avoid all meaningful regulation. He observed that there was "no moral difference between gambling at cards . . . and gambling in the stock market." He called for stringent regulation of securities, imprisonment of businessmen who flouted the law, and a comprehensive program of business regulation. He upbraided "decent citizens" for permitting "those rich men whose lives are evil and corrupt" to control the nation's destiny. He lashed the judiciary for "abusing" the writ of injunction in labor disputes. He contemptuously dismissed editors, lawyers, and politicians who had been "purchased by the corporations" as "puppets who move as the strings are pulled." Moreover, he came out for workmen's compensation, compulsory arbitration of labor disputes, and acceptance of big unionism as a countervailing power to big business.

THE DISRUPTION OF THE G.O.P.

Taft's Background. Roosevelt's chosen successor, William Howard Taft, lacked the energy, conviction, and political skill to carry on Roosevelt's policies. He had been an enlightened and compassionate civil governor in the Philippines, and he seemed to be sympathetic to Roosevelt's progressive views. But he had marked limitations. He believed implicitly in natural law. He was a good but painfully conventional lawyer, and he had no zest for the give-and-take of politics. Although he possessed a strain of courage, he completely lacked boldness or energy.

The Republican convention of 1908 readily endorsed Roosevelt's selection of Taft even while it was rejecting the President's proposed labor plank. Big and small business heartily concurred, and in the autumn Taft handily defeated the Democratic candidate, William Jennings Bryan, by 321 to 162 electoral votes. However, Taft's plurality in the popular vote was one half of Roosevelt's in 1904, and the Democrats elected a number of progressive governors and defeated several reactionary Republican congressmen.

No sooner were the returns in than Taft's troubles began. The troubles stemmed in large part from his own limited view of his role as President and leader. He conceived his mission to be to consolidate the Roosevelt reforms (giving them the "sanction of law," so he privately phrased it), not to embark on new ventures. Taft was too steeped in legal traditionalism to accept the dynamic conception of the Constitution that Roosevelt had outlined in his first annual message. He failed, consequently, to seize the executive reins. He believed, moreover, that the counsel of lawyers was superior to that of scientists and other experts, and he deplored Roosevelt's reliance on investigatory commissions.

The Tariff Fiasco. Popular opposition to the high rates of the Dingley Tariff of 1897 had grown by leaps and bounds. Many persons blamed the tariff for the rise in the cost of living that had accompanied the McKinley prosperity. By 1908 agitation was so strong in the Republican Middle West that Roosevelt and Taft agreed that the tariff reform could no longer be ignored. In the Republican platform of 1908 they won incorporation of a plank promising tariff revision. Taft called a special session of Congress in the spring of 1909 to honor this promise. The House responded by reducing the schedules only to have Nelson W. Aldrich and the Old Guard in the Senate revise them upward after a furious battle for lower rates by certain Midwestern Republican senators. The President accepted a compromise (the Payne-Aldrich Tariff of 1909), then defended the measure in the Middle West as "the best bill that the Republican party ever passed." Midwestern Republicans were stunned.

Two years after the Payne-Aldrich Tariff disaster Taft negotiated a reciprocity agreement with Canada which La Follette and other Midwesterners charged was partial to Eastern interests. This time the President fought his bill through the Senate successfully, only to have Canada reject it because of loose talk that it presaged annexation by the United States. Thereupon a coalition of Republican insurgents and Democrats passed three new tariff reduction bills. Taft vetoed them on the grounds that they were not "scientific."

The Rise of Insurgency. Meanwhile, Taft was besieged with troubles on other fronts. In 1909 a group of progressive Republicans in the House of Representatives, led by George W. Norris of Nebraska, moved to unseat Speaker Joseph G. Cannon and break his arbitrary and partisan control over legislation and committee appointments. Taft refrained from supporting them on the urgent advice of Roosevelt and Senator Elihu Root. The insurgents then blamed Taft for their failure. Norris renewed his fight in 1910 and stripped Cannon of his dictatorial power. Taft was secretly pleased, but both insurgents and the public continued to link the President with the uncouth and reactionary Speaker.

Taft's rather curious stand on conservation led to additional, even worse, difficulties. He believed in conservation, but he also abhorred the freewheeling methods that Roosevelt had used to achieve his objective. He was determined to pursue a more cautious policy. Accordingly, he replaced Secretary of the Interior James R. Garfield with Richard A. Ballinger, an anticonservationist who had earlier resigned from the Land Office because he disagreed with Roosevelt's view that the public's interest in natural resources was paramount to that of entrepreneurs. Construing the law rigidly when government interests were at stake and loosely when private interests were at issue, Ballinger soon provoked Gifford Pinchot, chief of the U.S. Forest Service, to charge that Ballinger was promoting a "giveaway" of Alaskan mineral lands to the Guggenheims, the great mining industrialists. Incensed, Taft ordered Pinchot's removal from office.

A joint congressional committee, established in 1910 to inquire into the administration of the Interior Department, eventually exonerated Ballinger, but Taft was fatally stamped as an anticonservationist. The mark was not wholly inaccurate. Although Taft actually withdrew more lands from entry than Roosevelt and put millions of acres of forest lands into new reserves, he never did grasp the Roosevelt-Pinchot conception of controlled development or of multi-purpose river valley projects.

The Triumph of Insurgency. Returning from a big-game hunt in Africa in June 1910, Roosevelt expressed high indignation over Taft's ineptness and Pinchot's dismissal. The former President soon drove deeper the wedge that was splitting him and the insurgents from Taft. At Osawatomie, Kansas, on September 1, Roosevelt restated and amplified the social welfare program announced in his memorable message of January 31, 1908. He now called his program the "New Nationalism." It put the national need "before sectional or personal advantage," he said. He quoted Lincoln's assertion that "Labor is prior to, and independent of, capital." He asserted that the judiciary's primary obligation was to protect "human welfare rather than ... property." And he called for graduated income and inheritance taxes, workmen's compensation legislation, a federal child labor law, tariff revision, and more stringent regulation of corporations.

The Taft administration—marked by the fight over high tariffs, the revolt against Speaker Cannon, and the Ballinger-Pinchot controversy—was not without constructive achievement. However, the President and his supporters could claim small credit, for it was through the alliance of insurgent Republicans and progressive Democrats that a great body of reform measures were pushed through Congress. Some reforms were supported warmly by the President, others half-heartedly, and some not at all. But all owed their success to the widening progressive movement. The Sixteenth, or income-tax, Amendment was passed by Congress in July 1909 (and ratified by the states in February 1913). The Mann-Elkins Act of 1910 strengthened the Interstate Commerce Commission and extended its authority to telephone, telegraph, cable, and wireless companies. On Taft's recommendation a postal savings bank system was also created in 1910. And with the President's approval safety measures were adopted for mines, an Employers Liability Act covering work done on government contracts was passed, and a Children's Bureau was created.

Armageddon. Nothing Taft could do by this time would win the support of Republican progressives. By now they were demanding the nomination in 1912 of either Roosevelt or La Follette. La Follette made an early and earnest bid and then refused to bow out gracefully after his most devoted followers admitted that he could not win. Pressure on Roosevelt to make an open fight against Taft was strong, especially in the Middle West. When he threw his hat into the ring in February 1912, one of the bitterest preconvention campaigns in Republican history ensued. Roosevelt outpolled Taft two to one in the thirteen states that held presidential primaries, but the President still controlled the party machinery. His friends took over the national convention in Chicago in June and awarded most of the crucial contested delegates to Taft. Thereupon more than 300 Roosevelt delegates stormed out of the hall. Six weeks later they returned to Chicago to form the Progressive or "Bull Moose" party, nominate their hero, and hear him deliver his "Confession of Faith." It was one of the classic political testaments of American history. It synthesized the progressives' aspirations for democracy, elimination of injustice, and equality of economic opportunity.

Roosevelt did not lack a large and loyal following, including Social Gospel devotees, college professors and presidents, businessmen and editors, Gifford Pinchot and his fellow conservationists, and social workers by the score. They were all excited by the opportunity to write their social and economic theories into law. But when the Democrats nominated a moderate progressive and extraordinarily able man, Governor Woodrow Wilson of New Jersey, Theodore Roosevelt was foredoomed to defeat.

In the election of 1912 Wilson carried forty states with 6,296,547 popular votes, 42 per cent of the total. Roosevelt ran more than two million popular votes behind Wilson; Taft ran a poor third. Nearly a million voters registered desire for more fundamental economic reforms than either Wilson or Roosevelt proposed by casting their ballots for the Socialist candidate, Eugene V. Debs.

THE TRIUMPH OF PROGRESSIVISM

Wilson's Background. Woodrow Wilson was born in a Presbyterian manse in Virginia in 1856 and reared in a South convulsed by Civil War and Reconstruction. As a Ph.D. candidate at Johns Hopkins University, he had argued in a brilliant dissertation, *Congressional Government* (1885), that the basic weakness in the American political system was its separation of executive from legislative leadership. He had taught at several institutions and made a distinguished record as president of Princeton University from 1902 to 1910. Elected governor of New Jersey in 1910, he changed quickly from a rather academic conservative into a practical progressive. He also revealed superb political intelligence. He boldly seized control of the Democratic state machine and pushed a comprehensive reform program through a divided legislature. He then gave eloquent voice to high ideals and moderately progressive aspirations on a nation-wide tour that eventuated in his nomination for President.

The New Freedom. Wilson called his program in 1912 the New Freedom. It differed sharply from the New Nationalism—chiefly in that Wilson advocated regulated competition, while Roosevelt advocated regulated monopoly. The New Freedom's core was the destruction of monopoly by downward tariff revision, relentless enforcement of strengthened antitrust laws, and the freeing of banks from dependence on Wall Street. These were important objectives, and their fulfillment would have been a momentous achievement. But they fell short of the New Nationalism's social goals. Wilson during the campaign of 1912 approved these goals but said that they should be accomplished only by the states and localities. The New Freedom in essence was a call for the federal government to restore conditions that would permit free competition to flourish on all fronts.

Tariff and Banking Reform. In 1913 Wilson began his tenure auspiciously by calling a special session of Congress on the day of his inauguration. Later he broke tradition by addressing a joint session in person. His first objective was drastic tariff reduction to destroy the Republican system of special privilege to industry and producers of important raw materials. Threatened immediately with revolt by Democrats from sugar and wool states, he used patronage to win their support for his measure, the Underwood Tariff. Meanwhile he charged publicly that Washington had seldom seen "so numerous, so industrious or so insidious a lobby" as the interests which opposed his program. The result of this masterful exertion of leadership was the first substantial reduction of tariff schedules since before the Civil War.

By the time that he signed the Underwood bill in October 1913, Wilson was embroiled in conflict over banking legislation. There was widespread agreement about the urgent need for a new banking and currency system but little consensus about the right solution. Old Guard Republicans wanted a single great central bank controlled by private bankers. Conservative Democrats insisted on a decentralized reserve system under private control. Bryan Democrats and progressive Republicans called for a reserve system and currency supply owned and controlled by the government.

Uncertain of his ground, the President authorized Representative Carter Glass to prepare a preliminary bill. The unimaginative Virginian responded with a measure that failed to provide for central direction (which was the gravest failing of the existing National Banking System, enacted in 1863), and Wilson himself insisted that Glass redraw the bill to remedy this defect. Meanwhile, roused by the Pujo Committee's sensational revelations of Wall Street's influence over the nation's financial structure, Bryan Democrats and progressive Republicans fought bitterly for public controls. Wilson, after consulting with Louis D. Brandeis, his most influential adviser on domestic matters, worked out a series of constructive compromises that were adopted as the Federal Reserve Act in December 1913.

The measure created twelve Federal Reserve Banks owned and controlled by private bankers but responsible to a seven-member central Federal Reserve Board appointed by the President. The reserve banks were authorized to issue currency from a sound, yet reasonably flexible, base and to perform numerous other central banking functions. Provision was also made to meet the seasonal needs of agriculture. The Federal Reserve System was not intended to be revolutionary and, for example, destroy private ownership and initiative in banking. But it was a powerful factor in creating new centers of financial power to offset Wall Street's overweening control.

A Touch of Reaction. Wilson's next great objective was revision and strengthening of the Sherman Antitrust Act. This along with downward revision of the tariff and creation of a new

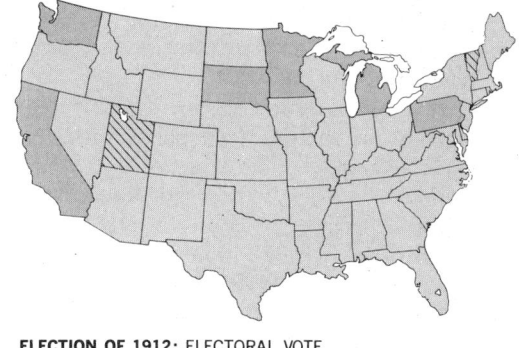

ELECTION OF 1912: ELECTORAL VOTE

Wilson: 435   Roosevelt: 88   Taft: 8

banking and currency system would complete the New Freedom program. There would be no legislation to give special benefits to labor, no rural-credits measure, no such conservation program as Roosevelt had envisaged. Child labor, women's suffrage, workmen's compensation, and all the rest would have to come, if they came at all, by action of the separate states. In at least one area, moreover, there was a positive repudiation of social justice in 1913. With the President's acquiescence, the Secretary of the Treasury and the Postmaster General segregated some Negro employees.

A second blow to the social justice movement came soon afterwards. Over the protests of states' rights Southerners fearful of the extension of federal power, a child labor bill sponsored by the National Child Labor Committee passed the House in 1914. When it reached the Senate, however, Wilson refused to fight for it on the grounds that it was probably unconstitutional. It got nowhere in the upper house.

Moving Toward the New Nationalism. By 1914 the progressive movement had gathered too much momentum to be long halted by presidential indifference. While the child labor forces were regrouping for a second assault, new pressures were bearing so heavily on the White House that Wilson had either to accommodate them or risk loss of his office in 1916. They were first felt when the administration introduced its antitrust program in 1914.

Wilson's original measures included legislation to outlaw specific unfair trade practices and to create a federal trade commission with only fact-finding powers. Progressives in both parties did not think much of the first and refused to support the latter proposal because it did not grant the commission the power to act on its findings. Wilson learned a great deal during these discussions. Conversations with Brandeis and others convinced him that it was impossible to outlaw every conceivable unfair trade practice. They also persuaded him that something like the Rooseveltian solution was the only possible alternative. He lost interest in his first measure, known as the Clayton Antitrust Bill. As finally adopted in 1914, it was full of ambiguities and qualifications. Meanwhile, Wilson espoused and pushed through Brandeis' measure, the Federal Trade Commission Act. This act called for the creation of a Federal Trade Commission empowered, in effect, to define unfair trade practices on its own terms and to suppress them on its own findings, subject to broad court review. The Federal Reserve Act had given first proof that Wilson might be willing to consider expanding federal power over economic affairs. The Federal Trade Commission Act was a sure sign that he had moved toward dynamic use of the federal authority.

In the meantime, the President found himself involved in a bitter quarrel with organized labor over the Clayton Antitrust Bill. Samuel Gompers and the A.F.L. hierarchy demanded provisions to exempt labor unions from prosecution for the secondary boycott, blacklist, and other weapons which the Supreme Court had declared were in violation of the Sherman Act. In effect, labor wanted special privileges to offset management's power. At this point Wilson adhered rigidly to the New Freedom line. But he did accept an affirmation of rights that labor already possessed in law, if not always in fact, and a few other moderate provisions.

Adhering to New Freedom doctrine on this one important point did not signify that Wilson was not ordinarily sympathetic to the needs of labor. His Secretary of Labor was a former secretary-treasurer of the United Mine Workers. The A.F.L. lobby spoke more decisively in Washington during his administration than the N.A.M. Moreover, Wilson signed, although he did not originate, the La Follette Seamen's Act of 1915, which released sailors from bondage to labor contracts.

"We Are Also Progressives." It was perhaps inevitable that Wilson should have moved decisively toward an advanced progressive position in 1916. For one thing, experience alone had proved that the New Freedom ideology was too confining to permit achievement of Wilson's own expanding social and economic goals. He also had to win a large minority of the disintegrating Progressive party if he were to have a chance for reëlection in 1916.

Wilson seems to have embarked quite deliberately upon new policies aimed at bringing the progressive movement to fruition and, incidentally, at assuring a Democratic victory in the impending election. He began by nominating Brandeis to the Supreme Court in January 1916. Old Guard Republicans protested bitterly. Brandeis had upset legal tradition in 1908 by presenting a mass of sociological data to the Supreme Court in his successful defense of an Oregon law establishing maximum working hours for women. But Wilson forced Brandeis' confirmation. Next, he came out for a languishing rural-credits bill that he had condemned as class legislation two years before. He urged, successfully, creation of a tariff commission because he feared that Europe would dump its surplus goods in America at the end of the war. Wilson threw strong support behind the child labor bill and won its adoption. Enacted in the summer of 1916, it was declared unconstitutional two years later in *Hammer* v. *Dagenhart*. He also won approval of a model federal workmen's compensation bill.

The flow of nationalistic, social justice legislation continued until the very eve of the election. A measure was adopted to extend federal assistance to the states for the construction of highways. The Revenue Act adopted in the late summer of 1916 increased income taxes sharply and imposed a new estate tax. The President in September personally pushed through Congress the Adamson bill to establish the eight-hour day for railroad workers.

Altogether, Wilson's administration pushed through the most imposing and important program of reform legislation in American history up to that time. Wilson could claim truthfully, as he did during the presidential campaign that followed, that he and his party had in fact put the Progressive platform of 1912 on the federal statute books.

CHAPTER 17

THE RISE OF AMERICA AS A WORLD POWER, 1898-1919

THE NEW FRONTIER

Years before 1893, when historian Frederick Jackson Turner announced the closing of the western frontier in American life, an influential minority of Americans were straining to extend the nation's power and influence to the remote reaches of the globe. These expansionists included romantic nationalists like the Reverend Josiah Strong, whose best-selling *Our Country* (1885) equated Christianity with those "peculiarly aggressive traits" that would impose Anglo-Saxon civilization "upon Mexico, down upon Central and South America, out upon the islands of the seas, over upon Africa and beyond." Young and bellicose politicians like Theodore Roosevelt, Henry Cabot Lodge, and Albert J. Beveridge were captivated by visions of a grandeur at once real and illusory. (Captain Alfred Thayer Mahan, in *The Influence of Sea Power upon History* (1890), argued that only a large navy could protect the trade that would be the lifeblood of the new American empire.)

Americans for two centuries had believed that it was the "manifest destiny" of a superior people to occupy the North American continent; to many, penetration of the Far East and Latin America seemed but a logical corollary. They were ready to accept, and for a while to sustain, an imperialistic thrust in the simple conviction that growth was the natural order of things.

Beneath the rhetoric and beyond the mystique, however, were the harsh realities described in Chapters 13 and 14. Workers and farmers were restive. The American industrial and agricultural plants seemed to be producing more than the people could consume, while capital seemed to be accumulating more rapidly than domestic outlets. "Commerce follows the flag," Henry Cabot Lodge warned in 1895. "The great nations are rapidly absorbing for their future expansion and their present defense all the waste places of the earth. . . . The United States must not fall out of the line of march."

Samoa. Hard on the completion of the first transcontinental railroad in 1869, American business and naval groups, in expectation of a quickening of the Asian trade, arranged a treaty for a naval station and commercial coaling rights in Samoa. A decade of jockeying for power by Germany, Great Britain, and the United States followed. Open conflict was narrowly avoided in 1889, and the German government proposed that the islands be divided. But at the United States' insistence it was agreed instead to establish a tripartite protectorate. Rivalry continued, and in 1899, after the Spanish-American War had committed the United States openly to imperialism, the fiction of Samoan in-

310   The Emergence of a Modern Nation

dependence was abolished. Germany and the United States divided the islands, and Great Britain was compensated with the Gilbert and Solomon Islands.

Hawaii. Meanwhile, another group of naval officers and Hawaiian-American businessmen was conspiring to formalize American control of Hawaii, the crossroads of the central Pacific. Provoked by native misgovernment, the white men who dominated the Hawaiian economy virtually disenfranchised the natives in 1887. Native resentment was soon compounded by the depressing impact of the McKinley Tariff (1890) on the sugar industry, and Queen Liliuokalani in 1892 abrogated the whites' special political privileges. Supported by the American minister and American marines, the whites overthrew the Queen in 1893 and sent a mission to Washington to negotiate a treaty of annexation in the hope that they could avoid the sugar tariff and assure orderly government in their interests.

President Cleveland's refusal to approve the treaty set off a four-year debate. American imperialists argued that possession of Hawaii would give naval protection to the Pacific Coast, prevent Japanese annexation, and enable the United States to penetrate the Far East commercially and even militarily. They also viewed annexation as part of a "Large Policy" embracing construction of a Nicaraguan canal and acquisition of Canada.

Many influential newspapers and periodicals also supported Hawaiian annexation; the Republican platform of 1896 endorsed it; and William Jennings Bryan came out tentatively for it the next year. To be sure, President McKinley upon taking office announced that he opposed all acquisition of territory, but he soon changed his mind. Three months after his inauguration he submitted a new annexation treaty to the Senate, and the islands were annexed by joint resolution of Congress in July 1898, after naval operations in the Pacific had dramatized Hawaii's usefulness as a base. "As I look back upon the first steps in this miserable business and as I contemplate the outrage," ex-President Cleveland wrote to his former Secretary of State Richard Olney, "I am ashamed of the whole affair."

Venezuela and the Monroe Doctrine. Yet Cleveland himself had contributed during his second administration to the jingoism that made the imperialists' triumph possible. Angered by Great Britain's refusal in 1895 to accept American arbitration of a boundary dispute between British Guiana and Venezuela, Secretary of State Olney had bluntly informed the British Foreign Secretary that "The United States is practically sovereign on this continent, and its fiat is law." The British testily replied that the Monroe Doctrine was not recognized in international law and did not apply to boundary disputes in any event. Cleveland then sent a message to Congress requesting money for an independent investigation. He also warned that British failure to accept the American findings would constitute "a willful aggression." The British thereupon began slowly to back down, and the boundary was fixed by an international commission in 1899 (although largely in accord with Britain's original claims).

Cleveland's rude threat of force made the Monroe Doctrine a viable instrument of national policy. In addition, it prompted Great Britain to reappraise its American policy in the context of imperial Germany's rise to world power. Britain's decision that the United States should be courted rather than alienated had a profound impact upon subsequent events.

THE SPANISH-AMERICAN WAR

Trouble in Cuba. Meanwhile, Cleveland was handling a festering crisis in

Cuba with consummate restraint. Cubans had always resented Spain's misrule of their island. When their sugar economy collapsed under the weight of European competition, the United States' depression of 1893, and the restrictive duties of the Wilson-Gorman Tariff of 1894, their smoldering hostilities flamed into a full-scale revolt in the summer of 1895. Determined to suppress it, Spain sent over its ablest general, Valeriano "Butcher" Weyler, who soon drove much of the civilian population into concentration camps at an estimated cost of 200,000 lives.

The American people's instinctive sympathies for the Cuban people were intensified by an outpouring of propaganda from a revolutionary junta in New York and by the yellow journalism of the New York *World* and New York *Journal.* "You furnish the pictures," *Journal* publisher William Randolph Hearst wired one of his artists who had reported during a lull in hostilities that there was no war in Cuba to portray, "and I'll furnish the war." But it was the press as a whole, feeding voraciously on the junta's releases and reprinting indiscriminately the *World*'s and the *Journal*'s atrocity stories, that incited the nation-wide hysteria.

Genuine sympathy for the Cubans combined with less altruistic factors to create a growing demand for a war to liberate the Cubans. Conservative Republicans and Democrats hoped that a war would divert attention from the silver issue. Senator Lodge pointed out, "Free Cuba would mean a great market to the United States" and "an opportunity for American capital." Protestant clergymen said that American intervention would alleviate suffering and, incidentally, open Cuba to Protestantism. Ultranationalists saw war as a means of testing the nation's military might, uniting the North and South, and even resolving the unemployment problem. "The South dearly loves a fighter," an Atlantan wrote the President; "if you will show yourself strong and courageous in defense of Cuba, you will have a solid South at your call.... Strengthen the Army and Navy of this country and in this way give employment to the thousands of idle men who need it."

But Grover Cleveland had a different conception of his duty. Convinced that the Cuban insurrectionists were as barbarous as the Spaniards, he went out of office in March 1897 without having yielded to the emotion-wrought calls for a positive policy.

Submission. Cleveland's successor, William McKinley, lacked his stubborn courage and iron principle. Neither McKinley nor the industrialists and bankers upon whom he leaned wanted war. The President set out, accordingly, to overcome the raging fever by forcing Spain to make a settlement satisfactory to the insurrectionists. Under American pressure Spain recalled General Weyler in the summer of 1897 and promised abolition of the concentration camps and autonomy for Cuba similar to Canada's. Although McKinley responded graciously to these moves, he also intimated that the United States would act if hostilities continued.

The war fever again rose in February 1898, when Hearst published a stolen letter written by the Spanish Minister Dupuy de Lôme, which said that McKinley was a "peanut politician," a "bidder for the admiration of the crowd." Western Republicans introduced three separate resolutions for recognition of Cuban belligerence. And the President was bombarded with demands for action. "We will have this war for the freedom of Cuba in spite of the commercial interests," Assistant Secretary of the Navy Theodore Roosevelt boasted.

Soon after the De Lôme letter was published, the battleship *Maine* was destroyed in Havana Harbor (February 15). The Hearst press, the New York *Tribune,* and a few other newspapers blamed the disaster on Spain and called for war. Lodge, Beveridge, and other militant politicians joined them. The *Maine* "was sunk by an act of dirty treachery on the part of the Spaniards," Roosevelt charged. But McKinley and most of Wall Street still hoped for peace. So the President appointed a commission of inquiry and resumed negotiations with Spain.

As passions mounted, administration circles began to fear that McKinley could not be reëlected if he refused to submit. Important men in the business and financial community—men who had little active interest in the "Large Policy" and none whatsoever in liberating the Cubans or avenging the destruction of the *Maine*—now reluctantly joined the war hawks. Thus Elihu Root warned: "Fruitless attempts to hold back or retard the enormous momentum of the people bent upon war would result in the destruction of the President's power and influence, in depriving the country of its natural leader, in the elevation of the Silver Democracy to power." Under the weight of such counsels McKinley lost the will to resist. "I think . . . possibly the President could have worked out the business without war," one of his intimates later wrote, "but the current was too strong, the demagogues too numerous, the fall elections too near."

On March 27, 1898, the United States sent an ultimatum to Spain demanding an immediate armistice, closing of the concentration camps, and Cuban independence if the United States decided it was advisable. Even before Spain responded, however, the President began to compose his war message. Then on April 11, two days after Spain had capitulated to his first two demands, he sent the unrevised message to Congress, adding only that Spain had agreed to an armistice. Within two weeks Congress enthusiastically passed, and the President signed, a joint resolution authorizing use of force to compel the Spaniards to evacuate. The Teller Amendment to the resolution pledged the United States to withdraw from Cuba as soon as its independence had been established.

Military Operations. Only the American navy was prepared for hostilities. Modernization and expansion of the fleet had roughly paralleled the rise of interest in the Far East, and by 1898 the United States navy was the fifth largest in the world. The Asiatic squadron was especially strong. Ten days before the destruction of the *Maine*, moreover, Assistant Secretary of the Navy Theodore Roosevelt had used his superior's temporary absence to order Commodore George Dewey to attack the Philippines in the event of war with Spain.

Dewey confronted an antiquated Spanish fleet in Manila Bay less than two weeks after the war resolution was signed. Five hours later it had been destroyed and the course of history changed. Troops were hastily dispatched from the United States, and the Spanish garrison in Manila surrendered on August 13.

Meanwhile, land operations in Cuba proceeded less smoothly. The regular army of 28,000 men were dispersed throughout the United States and lacked any training in large-scale maneuvering. The War Department was inefficient and unimaginative. It proved incapable of properly equipping the new regular and volunteer forces that Congress soon authorized. The army that landed in Cuba was short of every basic supply from arms to medicine.

The original strategy of commanding General Nelson A. Miles was to occupy Puerto Rico in the autumn and then to proceed to Havana, where Cuban insurrectionists would augment his forces. When the Spanish Atlantic fleet slipped into Santiago harbor in Cuba, however, he decided to send his army to Cuba immediately.

A force of 17,000, including Theodore Roosevelt's volunteer Rough Riders, landed amidst incredible confusion outside Santiago in June. They drove toward the city, winning a fierce engagement at El Caney and a major battle at San Juan Hill. The campaigns produced the usual complement of heroes, but none so dramatic as Roosevelt. "The instant I received the order I sprang on my horse," he later wrote of his exploits, "and then my 'crowded hour' began."

The end of the war swiftly followed. On July 3 the Spanish fleet sailed to its destruction by the American squadron that lay in wait outside Santiago harbor. On July 17 the Spanish army commander in Santiago surrendered on generous terms. Meanwhile, United States troops occupied Puerto Rico almost without opposition. Then, an armistice was signed on August 12. The United States had suffered 450 dead in battle or of wounds and had lost 5200 on account of disease. Wrote John Hay to Theodore Roosevelt: "It has been a splendid little war."

The Triumph of Imperialism. The Teller Amendment had been a weak straw in the wind. Imperialistic sentiment had grown to gale-like proportions during the war. The Hawaiian annexation resolution rolled through Congress three months after hostilities began. Soon afterward the President decided that Puerto Rico and Guam should be ceded to the United States. Meanwhile, he made plans to retain Manila and finally decided to annex the entire Philippine archipelago.

McKinley later explained his decision to a delegation of Methodist clergymen:

I went down on my knees and prayed God Almighty for light and guidance more than one night. And one night late it came to me this way—I don't know how it was, but it came: (1) That we could not give them back to Spain—that would be cowardly and dishonorable; (2) that we could not turn them over to France or Germany—our commercial rivals in the Orient—that would be bad business and discreditable; (3) that we could not leave them to themselves—they were unfit for self-government—and they would soon have anarchy and misrule over there worse than Spain's was; and (4) that there was nothing left for us to do but to take them all, and to educate the Filipinos, and uplift and civilize and Christianize them, and by God's grace do the very best we could by them, as our fellow men for whom Christ also died. And then I went to bed and went to sleep and slept soundly.

The President's explanation was a good one as far as it went. The evidence at hand indicated that Spanish rule had actually been worse in the Philippines than in Cuba, that the Filipinos were unprepared for self-government, and that they could not long remain independent on their own. An even more fundamental consideration, however, was McKinley's desire to satisfy the people's will.

The victory at Manila had broadened horizons dramatically. All through the summer and autumn of 1898, newspapers, religious publications, and civic leaders called for retention of the Philippines for substantially the same reasons that the President gave the Methodist clergymen. Furthermore, the prospect of an expanding trade with China had drawn a large and influential phalanx of businessmen and their journals into the imperialist camp. "If it is commercialism to want the possession of a strategic point giving the American people an opportunity to maintain a foothold in the markets of . . . China," Mark Hanna declared, "for God's sake let us have commercialism."

McKinley, however, first wanted to test public opinion. He toured the Middle West in October with a stenographer at his side to time the applause accorded his various soundings. Only after he had convinced himself of the preponderant sentiment for annexation did he cable his peace commissioners in Paris to demand cession of the entire Philippine archipelago.

The Treaty of Paris. By the terms of the treaty signed on December 10, 1898, Spain ceded the Philippines to the United States for $20 million.

THE CONTINENTAL UNITED STATES AND PRINCIPAL OVERSEAS STATES AND TERRITORIES
Dates of acquisition appear below place names

Spain also acknowledged Cuban independence and ceded Puerto Rico and Guam outright to the United States. The Senate ratified the treaty two months later. The treaty would probably have been defeated if Bryan had not influenced a handful of Democrats to vote for ratification on the erroneous assumption that the election of 1900 could be waged squarely on the issue of imperialism.

The Aftermath. By 1900 the United States was tasting the first bitter fruits of imperialism. Filipino partisans had begun to fight for independence from Spain before the Americans arrived. They turned against their new American masters in 1899 and inflicted losses on the American occupation troops as heavy as those suffered in the war with Spain. Not until the Americans resorted to methods as ruthless as those used by the Spanish in Cuba were the Filipinos finally suppressed in 1902.

Partial restitution followed. McKinley, and especially Theodore Roosevelt, took literally the poet's charge "to take up the White man's burden / Send forth the best ye breed." McKinley instituted and Roosevelt greatly strengthened a political system designed to prepare the Filipinos for self-government. Schools were built; a yeomanry was installed on lands purchased from the Catholic Church; and numerous other reforms were instituted.

Meanwhile, the United States observed the form of the Teller Amendment by granting nominal independence to Cuba. There, too, the natives benefited enormously from the American occupation, especially in public health. After assuring itself of control of Cuba's foreign relations through the Platt Amendment to the Cuban Constitution of 1901, the United States withdrew.

In the long view, American imperialism was the most enlightened of any in the world. Such minor economic advantages as accrued to the United States were offset by the expenditure of vast sums for civic and social improvement. In every possession, stable and eventually democratic government was instituted. Unfortunately, however, economic development did not always keep pace. Hawaii prospered, but it remained the virtual fief of a half dozen giant corporations. Puerto Rico suffered from overpopulation, inadequate natural resources, and absentee ownership. And the Philippines concentrated too much on the production of raw materials for the American market, though the standard of living on the archipelago rose dramatically.

THE FAR EAST

The Open Door. The drive for commercial expansion soon thrust the United States into the vortex of Far Eastern affairs. During the Spanish-American War the great powers had continued to carve out spheres of influence in China, and the British in 1899 began to evade payment of the tariff, the Chinese government's main source of revenue. Such action, if taken generally, could only cause the collapse of the Peking government. China would then be dismembered, and American trade, which was privileged by a most-favored-nation agreement, would be foreclosed.

McKinley's new Secretary of State, John Hay, accordingly proposed in September 1899 that the powers agree to respect the rights of all nationals within all spheres of influence. Specifically, Chinese officials were to continue to collect the tariffs, and the powers were to refrain from discriminating in levying port duties and railroad charges within their spheres. Reluctant to offend the United States, the powers responded equivocally to Hay's proposal. When the Secretary boldly announced their "final and definitive" acceptance in March 1900, Japan alone protested.

The policy thus inaugurated was the ultimate triumph of the proponents of the "Large Policy." Based on the assumption that trade with the Orient was essential to American prosperity, the policy "commanded a measure of interest and support over the years second only to that accorded the Monroe Doctrine." It led to deep and continuing commitment by the United States in the affairs of the Far East.

The first complications came in the spring of 1900 when a group of fanatical Chinese nationalists, the Boxers, killed foreigners, occupied Peking, and besieged the foreign legations. The United States joined in suppressing the revolt and imposing a huge indemnity on the impotent and impoverished Chinese government. Meanwhile Hay issued a second round of Open Door notes. The new notes extended the demand for equal trade rights to the entire Chinese empire and underlined American concern for the preservation of Chinese territorial and administrative integrity.

The Roosevelt Far Eastern Policies. In 1901 Theodore Roosevelt came into office determined to realize the fruits of America's venture into the Far East. "Before I came to the Pacific slope I was an expansionist," he told an export-conscious audience in San Francisco in May 1903, "and after having been here I fail to understand how any man . . . can be anything but an expansionist." Even as Roosevelt spoke those words, however, he realized that the United States could maintain its foothold in the Far East only by accommodating itself to the aspirations of the Japanese. Alone among twentieth-century American Presidents, Roosevelt perceived that Japan's need for raw materials and markets impelled it to look outward. He believed, moreover, that Japan's abandonment of designs on Hawaii and the Philippines, coupled with its alliance with Great Britain in 1902, made it the natural counterpoise to Russia, whose failure to withdraw from China in 1902 he considered an act of "well-nigh incredible mendacity." Roosevelt's first major move was the secret recognition in 1905 of Japanese suzerainty in Korea in return for an explicit disavowal of Japanese designs on the Philippines.

By this time Roosevelt was already mediating the Russo-Japanese War of 1904-1905 at the request of the victorious but nearly insolvent Japanese. His basic objectives were to preserve the balance of power and to protect the Open Door. But he also believed that it was his moral duty to end the carnage as soon as possible. He further hoped to cement Japanese-American relations. His mediation fulfilled the first three of these goals and failed in the fourth, the Japanese blaming him for Russia's refusal to pay a war indemnity or to cede to them all of Sakhalin Island.

A decision by the San Francisco board of education to segregate the ninety-three Japanese students in the city's public schools dealt Japanese-American relations a more serious blow in October 1906. Roosevelt labeled the segregation order "a crime against a friendly nation" and threatened to use "all the forces, civil and military," at his command to rectify it. He then called the board members to the White House. They agreed to reverse the order if Japan would curb the emigration of peasants and laborers. A "Gentlemen's Agreement" to that effect was arranged in 1907.

Having thus deferred to Japanese sensibilities, Roosevelt characteristically decided to flaunt American strength by sending the battle fleet on a world cruise in 1907. Even before the fleet returned, however, the President had made another realistic concession to Japan. By the Root-Takahira Agreement of November 1908 the United States implicitly recognized Japan's economic ascendancy in Manchuria in return for a reaffirmation of the *status quo* in the Pacific and the Open Door in China.

New Far Eastern Policies. Neither Taft nor Wilson shared Roosevelt's view that the United States should accept Japanese preëminence in East Asia. Roosevelt warned Taft as early as 1910 that China was "weak and unreliable" and that the United States should abandon its commercial aspirations in Manchuria. But Taft believed too strongly in the fiction of Chinese independence to pursue so realistic a course. He followed instead a policy of "active intervention to secure for our merchandise and our capitalists opportunity for profitable investment." He permitted his Secretary of State Philander C. Knox to demand American participation in an international bankers' consortium to build a network of railways in China. Taft also allowed Knox, who was alarmed by the consolidation of Japanese and Russian influence in Manchuria, to propose the internationalization of that province's railways.

President Wilson proved equally assertive. "Our industries have expanded to such a point that they will burst their jackets if they cannot find a free outlet to the markets of the world," he declared in 1912. "Our domestic markets no longer suffice. We need foreign markets." Thus Wilson opposed the bankers' consortium because it failed to give the United States the controlling voice and threatened to lead to European domination, not because he deemed it advisable to withdraw from the Far East. The United States intends "to participate, and participate very generously, in the opening to the Chinese and to the use of the world the almost untouched and perhaps unlimited resources of China," he declared at the time. He then urged American bankers to act independently.

Furthermore, Wilson perceived that the outbreak of World War I in 1914 had created a power vacuum in China. When Japan tried to make China into a satellite by imposing twenty-one far-reaching demands on China in 1915, Wilson vigorously defended Chinese integrity and independence. When Japan then resorted to economic penetration, the President and Secretary of State Robert Lansing proposed formation of a new four-power consortium to supply China with private capital. With Wilson's approval, Lansing also rejected Tokyo's demand that the United States recognize Japan's paramount interest in China just as Japan had recognized America's in Mexico. Finally, however, they arranged a *modus vivendi*—the Lansing-Ishii Agreement of November 1917. By this document the United States recognized Japan's special interests in China while Japan reaffirmed its support of the Open Door and agreed not to use the war situation to seek new privileges in China.

THE CARIBBEAN

Panama. The main thrust of President Roosevelt's diplomacy was destined to establish U.S. supremacy in the Caribbean. Soon after taking office he arranged negotiation of the second Hay-Pauncefote Treaty (1901), by which Great Britain granted the United States the right to build and defend an Isthmian canal. Early American planning envisioned a Nicaraguan canal. But when an opportunity to buy out a French company's rights to the more desirable Panama route presented itself in 1902, Roosevelt responded enthusiastically. He agreed to pay $40 million for the French company's rights. He also had Secretary of State Hay draw up a treaty to grant Colombia, which owned Panama, $10 million and $250,000 annual rental for the right of way.

When the Colombian senate indignantly rejected this arrangement, Roosevelt lost both his patience and his self-control. Privately castigating the Colombians as "Dagos" and "inefficient bandits," he tacitly encouraged agents of the French company to stimulate a Panamanian revolution against Colombia. When the revolution broke out on November 3, 1903, he sent an American warship to the scene under conditions that assured the revolution's success. He thereupon recognized the new Republic of Panama on November 6 and approved a treaty, negotiated by Panama's new minister, Philippe Bunau-Varilla (an agent of the French company), authorizing the United States to build the canal.

Roosevelt later claimed that "our course was straightforward and in absolute accord with the highest standards of international morality." But in 1911 he blurted, "I took the canal zone and let Congress debate, and while the debate goes on the canal also does." Ten years after that confession, the United States agreed to pay Colombia $25 million. By then Roosevelt was dead.

Meanwhile, the first great government corporation in American history overcame extraordinary health and engineering problems to complete construction of the Panama Canal. It was opened to the commerce of the world on August 15, 1914, on equal terms to all nations—but only because President Wilson had persuaded Congress to repeal an act of 1912 that the British said violated the Hay-Pauncefote Treaty by exempting American coastwise traffic from payment of tolls.

The Roosevelt Corollary to the Monroe Doctrine and "Dollar Diplomacy." The need to defend the Panama Canal soon drew the United States deeply into the affairs of the Caribbean. Neither Roosevelt nor his successors wanted this development. Referring to the Dominican Republic, Roosevelt later averred that he had "about the same desire to annex it as a gorged boa constrictor might have to swallow a porcupine wrong-end-to." But the poverty, instability, and corruption of the Caribbean republics lent themselves so readily to penetration by European countries that even such an apostle of peace as William Jennings Bryan saw no recourse but to make the Caribbean Sea an American lake.

The first serious incident involving European powers occurred in December 1902, when the Germans, cooperating with the British in a blockade of Venezuela, bombarded a port town and threatened to take control of Venezuelan customs. The American people and Roosevelt reacted militantly. Kaiser Wilhelm II, reluctant to offend the United States because of Germany's growing isolation in Europe, accepted Roosevelt's suggestion for mediation of the dispute. The matter was settled by the Hague Tribunal in 1904.

Meanwhile, the Dominican Republic had been forced by the German, Italian, and Spanish governments to sign protocols for the payment of debts to their nationals. The Dominicans thereupon requested Roosevelt "to establish some kind of protectorate over the islands," as the President phrased it. The United States took control of the Dominican customs in 1905. It was just such dangers of European intervention which prompted Roosevelt, in his annual message of December 6, 1904, to announce what became known as the "Roosevelt Corollary to the Monroe Doctrine":

Chronic wrongdoing, or an impotence which results in a general loosening of the ties of civilized society, may in America, as elsewhere, ultimately require intervention by some civilized nation, and in the Western Hemisphere the adherence of the United States to the Monroe Doctrine may force the United States, however reluctantly, in flagrant cases of such wrongdoing or impotence, to the exercise of an international police power.

President Taft, like Roosevelt, was concerned primarily with protection of the Panamanian life line, and he was even more ingenious than Roosevelt in devising new approaches. One was the outright use of troops in Nicaragua in 1912 to install and maintain a conservative pro-United States party in power. Another was what contemporaries called "dollar diplomacy"—use of American private capital to displace European bondholders and concessionaires.

The Wilson-Bryan Policies. President Wilson was not averse to using "dollar diplomacy" when circumstances seemed to demand it. However, he and Secretary of State Bryan were eager to play active personal roles. They believed so strongly that Latin Americans could be taught democracy that they tried to impose it on the revolution-ridden and corrupt Caribbean republics. "We can have no sympathy with those who seek to seize the power of government to advance their own personal interests or ambition," Wilson warned in a public statement on March 11, 1913. "As friends, therefore, we shall prefer those who act in the interest of peace and honor, who protect private rights and respect the restraints of constitutional provision." The consequence of Wilson's and Bryan's activism was unparalleled diplomatic and military intervention in the Caribbean, to say nothing of Mexico. The Wilson administration regularized the occupation of Nicaragua (which re-

LATIN AMERICA, 1914

••••••• New York to San Francisco via
Panama Canal: 6,059 miles

– – – New York to San Francisco via
Cape Horn: 13,932 miles

mained occupied by U.S. marines until 1933). It dispatched marines to Haiti and imposed a puppet regime in 1915. It sent marines to the Dominican Republic in 1916 and governed it directly through military officers. At the same time, however, it fostered road-building, school-building, and many other constructive projects.

Triumph and Tragedy in Mexico. Upon becoming President in 1913, Wilson had embarked on a bold new policy toward Mexico, where the classic Latin American alliance of dictator, Church, and foreign investors had provoked a convulsive political upheaval.

By 1911 more than half of Mexico's oil, two thirds of its railroads, and three fourths of its mines and smelters had come under the ownership of Americans. Much of the remaining oil was owned by the British. The Catholic Church was the largest landowner, though William Randolph Hearst and other Americans also had huge holdings. The average Mexican, whether peon or industrial worker, lived in abject poverty. Against this background, a revolution erupted in 1910, and the dictator Porfirio Díaz was finally driven out in May 1911 by a group of middle-class intellectuals headed by a constitutionalist named Francisco Madero. However, less than a year later, Madero himself was overthrown and murdered by counterrevolutionary forces under the army's chief general, Victoriano Huerta, who became president of Mexico amid revolutionary upheaval.

Wilson's first break with tradition came when he withheld recognition from the dictator Huerta on the grounds that the United States should henceforth cooperate only with governments based on the unquestioned consent of the governed. Next he persuaded the British to withdraw their support from Huerta. Then he brought his new policy to fruition by offering to aid Huerta's chief antagonist, the constitutional reformer, Venustiano Carranza. Carranza wanted only arms; and on February 3, 1914, Wilson lifted an arms embargo instituted by Taft.

Huerta's strength nevertheless continued to increase, and Wilson's sense of frustration became more acute. Seizing finally on a trivial incident at Tampico, he asked Congress for authority to move against the Mexican dictator. Congress had not responded when he ordered the fleet on April 21, 1914, to occupy Vera Cruz to prevent a German ship from unloading ammunition. In the resultant action, 126 Mexicans were killed.

The President's militant action horrified peace-loving Americans and provoked even Carranza to threaten full-scale resistance should American troops march on Mexico City. Thus abandoned by the liberals of both Mexico and the United States, Wilson resolved his dilemma by agreeing to mediation by the "ABC powers"—Argentina, Brazil, and Chile—with the eventual result that Huerta resigned in favor of Carranza, who became *de facto* president of Mexico. Wilson continued, however, to press Carranza to accept his guidance. He warned him against mass executions and made it clear that he would oppose expropriation of the vast holdings of Americans and other foreigners.

Wilson was by no means oblivious to the relationship between economic well-being and political democracy. Wrongly concluding that Pancho Villa, an unlettered, unscrupulous military adventurer, was an honest social reformer, he soon shifted his support to him. Carranza thereupon broadened his own reform program while his leading general crushed Villa's armies in the field.

In Washington, meanwhile, the President was subjected to tremendous pressures from American conservatives to mount a full-scale invasion of Mexico. The American Catholic hierarchy, the Hearst press, oil and other corporate interests, and ultranationalists like

Theodore Roosevelt all urged him to act. But Wilson held firm and extended *de facto* recognition to the Carranza regime in October 1915.

Reduced to banditry, Villa now strove to regain his power by inciting the United States to war. Early in 1916 he murdered fifteen American engineers in northern Mexico, and Wilson once again braved a nearly overpowering call for war. Then Villa made a bold sortie into Columbus, New Mexico, killing seventeen Americans. The President had no alternative but to order Brigadier General John J. Pershing to pursue the outlaw into Mexican territory. The inevitable "incidents" followed, intensifying anti-American feeling in Mexico, and for the third time conservatives and ultranationalists in the United States called angrily for an all-out invasion. Wilson responded by mobilizing the National Guard along the Mexican border, but he refused to divert the punitive expedition from its limited objective.

The impending war with Germany finally impelled the President to withdraw Pershing's force in late January 1917. Six weeks later the grant of *de jure* recognition to Carranza's government ended one of the most ironic episodes in American history. Had Wilson at any time supported Huerta or mounted the invasion that American conservatives and ultranationalists demanded, the Mexican revolution would have collapsed. But his interference in Mexican affairs had been so maladroit that he ended by alienating the very group whom he had helped to rise to power.

WORLD WAR I

Initial Reactions. On June 28, 1914, an obscure Serbian nationalist shot the heir to the Austro-Hungarian throne, Archduke Francis Ferdinand, and plunged all Europe into war. Serene in the belief that geography would save the United States from the holocaust, President Wilson at once issued a proclamation of neutrality; he then adjured the American people to be "impartial in thought as well as in action."

However great their resolve to stay out of the "action" of war, the American people were not disposed to be neutral in thought. The dominant bias in favor of the Allies headed by Britain and France was compounded of ethnic, business, and cultural ties. It was intensified by a rational, though vaguely formed, conviction that a German victory would adversely affect American interests because it would put an aggressive military regime in the European saddle.

In these circumstances, Germany's violation of Belgium's neutrality and subsequent resort to indiscriminate submarine warfare were the real catalysts acting on American opinion. British propaganda served merely to sharpen perceptions and inflame passions already present. "The principle of Anglo-Saxon liberty seems to have met the irreconcilable conception of the German State," wrote Elihu Root at the time, "and the two ideas are battling for control of the world."

To be sure, these sentiments were far from unanimous. The great majority of the country's 8,000,000 Germans or German-Americans were strongly attached to the fatherland. The spokesmen of the nation's 4,500,000 Irish-Americans were almost universally anti-British, and several million Poles and Jews were almost fanatically anti-Russian. From the outset these groups fed on German propaganda in their foreign-language newspapers and religious journals; neither the pro-Allied cast of the regular press nor German actions changed their alignment. Because these groups were overwhelmingly lower or lower-middle class, however, they never exercised an influence proportionate to their numbers.

The American people's divisions were accentuated by the impossibility of genuine neutrality. German might was based on dominance of the land mass of central Europe; Great Britain's on control of the seas. To impose an embargo, as the pro-Germans and many pacifists demanded, would be to deal Britain a paralyzing blow; to supply the Allies, as the United States soon did, was to strengthen them in relation to Germany. Hence the impossibility of complete neutrality.

Accordingly, President Wilson made the only possible decision consistent with the best adherence to traditional rules of neutrality. He decided during the first six months of the war to accept Britain's control of the seas. True, he did so under protest, for the British were moving toward nothing less than completely halting trade with Germany. They expanded the contraband list (goods which they could intercept under international law) to include even food. But at no time did Wilson consider military action to uphold the United States' shifting, and in some cases historically untenable, constructions of its neutral rights.

Indeed, as the war progressed, the President permitted positive action to assure the flow of supplies to the Allies. Anticipating a strain on American gold reserves in the summer of 1914, he had permitted Secretary of State Bryan to declare that the administration disapproved of loans to the Allies because they violated the spirit of neutrality. He modified this policy in March 1915 by permitting the house of J. P. Morgan to extend a $50 million credit to the French government. He rejected a German-American proposal to prohibit the export of all war materials. Then, in the summer of 1915 he completely lifted Bryan's ban on loans.

The President was undoubtedly influenced by the realization that American prosperity had become dependent upon war production. By 1916 exports to the Allies exceeded $3 billion in value, four times their 1914 level. "To maintain our prosperity, we must finance it," Secretary of the Treasury McAdoo warned Wilson in August 1915. "Otherwise it may stop and that would be disastrous." But it does not follow that the United States entered the war to maintain this prosperity or to assure repayment of these loans.

The German Response. The German Admiralty on February 4, 1915, marked out a broad war zone around the British Isles in which all enemy vessels and probably many neutral ones would be sunk without warning by German submarines. Six days later Wilson replied that Germany would be held to "strict accountability" for illegal destruction of American ships and American lives.

The issue was first joined in March when an American was lost on a British liner torpedoed without warning. Arguing passionately that the United States should not indulge the technical right of its citizens to sail through war zones on belligerent ships, Bryan proposed that the government warn them against it. But before a decision was reached, an event of tragic proportions virtually destroyed all hopes of such a solution. On May 7 off the coast of Ireland the British liner *Lusitania* was sunk without warning, with a loss of 1198 lives, 124 of them American.

The nation was appalled by the immensity of the disaster, but few voices were raised for war. From all over the country, in fact, came fervent appeals for peace, and from Democratic leaders in Congress came a warning that Wilson probably could not obtain passage of a war resolution. As a Kansas progressive leader informed Roosevelt, the Midwest's sense of outrage "died down as suddenly as it had risen." When the President soon afterward declared that "There is such a thing as a man being too proud to fight," Roosevelt was almost alone in denouncing him.

Determined to find a peaceful solution, Wilson called on the imperial German government to renew its allegiance to "the rights of humanity" by conforming to the traditional rules of war. The second of his three notes was stern enough to prompt Bryan to resign in protest. But the President neither contemplated nor threatened war; he was prepared at the most to sever relations. The Germans proved unwilling to gamble on his intent, however, and on June 6 the Admiralty ordered U-boats to spare large liners. When on August 19, 1915, a submarine provoked a severer crisis by sinking the British liner *Arabic,* the German government was able to avoid a break with America only by giving a definite pledge of safety for unarmed passenger liners.

Preparedness. Meanwhile Wilson had begun to prepare the nation for the hazards of an uncertain future. He was reluctant to do so; but under the hammering of Roosevelt and a substantial element of the Republican party, he finally faced the implications of his "strict accountability" policy. He took the first tentative steps in the summer of 1915, came out for major increases in the navy and army in December, and then toured the Middle West in January and February 1916.

No other issue of the period proved to be so revealing of the configuration of isolationist sentiment. Progressives of all three parties, including the secondary leadership of the disintegrating Bull Moose organization, opposed preparedness as a movement of munitions makers in particular and capitalists in general. Farmers in upstate New York, in California, in the Carolina Piedmont, and in the valley of Virginia, no less than in Kansas and Nebraska, charged that preparedness would lead to war. Organized labor all over the country—in New York and San Francisco as well as in Chicago, Milwaukee, and St. Louis—agreed.

Conversely, conservatives from every section of the nation supported preparedness enthusiastically. The Chamber of Commerce in almost every state endorsed it overwhelmingly. Bankers' and manufacturers' associations in the Midwest and South came out militantly for it.

The main opposition in Congress came from Bryan Democrats and a few Republican progressives. Attributing the movement to conservative Republicans, they resolved to make them bear its cost. "I am persuaded to think that when the income tax will have to pay for the increase in the army and navy," wrote Claude Kitchin of North Carolina to Bryan, "they will not be one-half so frightened over the future invasion by Germany." Not until Wilson agreed to accept their inheritance, munitions-profits, and progressive income tax program did they relax their opposition; and then it was to approve a severely compromised program. The defense legislation of 1916 provided for only moderate increases in the army.

The Election of 1916. Prewar progressivism had reached full flower by the spring and summer of 1916 (pp. 307-09). In convention at St. Louis in mid-June, the progressive-agrarian Democrats ignored the President's orders to make "Americanism" their keynote and indulged instead in one long and tremendous demand for peace. "He kept us out of war" became their campaign theme, and Wilson had little recourse but to accept it. By comparison to the extreme measures advocated by the Roosevelt and Old Guard wings of the reunited Republican party, Wilson's was in fact the policy of moderation. This was widely recognized at the time. It, along with the Democrats' remarkable legislative record, had a powerful pull on independents and ex-Bull Moosers.

Divisions within the Republican party also rebounded to Wilson's advantage. Although the G.O.P. platform criticized the Democratic preparedness program as inadequate and virtually called for war against Mexico, it deferred to the sensibilities of the more than one hundred German-American delegates at the Republican convention by equivocating on neutral rights. The Republican campaign consequently lacked consistency. The Republican presidential candidate, former Justice Charles Evans Hughes, was forced, on the one hand, to call for a hard policy toward Germany and to contend, on the other hand, that such a policy would assure peace. The St. Louis *Post-Dispatch* graphically described his dilemma:

> To satisfy the pro-Germans he must quarrel with the pro-British, who demand war with Germany. To satisfy Wall Street, he must quarrel with the western radicals. To satisfy the jingoes and the Munitions Trust, he must quarrel with most of the country. To satisfy privilege and plutocracy, he must quarrel with the people. Even as a candidate Mr. Hughes dare not have a policy, because to have a policy is to antagonize one element or another of his followers.

Wilson's reëlection by a half million plurality was not surprising. The resentment of Irish-, German-, Jewish-, and Polish-American voters probably cost him much of the East and such Midwestern states as Illinois and Wisconsin. But he swept most states where isolationism reflected agrarianism rather than ethnocentrism and where the progressive impulse was strong.

The Failure of Mediation. Hardly were the returns in than the President sought to end the war. For almost two years he had been striving to persuade the belligerents to accept a negotiated peace. His efforts had failed because both the Allies and the Central Powers still aspired to victory in the field. Taking new hope in a German peace overture of December 12, 1916, Wilson, six days later, called on the belligerents to define their war aims. The British replied privately that they would negotiate on liberal terms (even though the Allies had returned a belligerent public answer), but the Germans answered evasively.

The President thereupon appealed to world opinion in a speech before the Senate on January 22, 1917. He asserted the right of the United States to share in laying the foundations for a lasting peace, set forth his plan for a League of Nations, and added the noblest of all his perorations: "It must be a peace without victory. Victory would mean peace forced upon the loser, a victor's terms imposed upon the vanquished. . . . Only a peace between equals can last."

Men of good will the world over were intoxicated by Wilson's great vision. But realists knew that it was hopeless to expect the German military party to will its own destruction. On January 31 the German government submitted terms that would have assured its hegemony in Europe. It also announced resumption of unrestricted submarine warfare. At that point President Wilson severed diplomatic relations with Germany.

Although Wilson still hoped to avert war, the onrush of events soon overtook him. From British intelligence on February 25 he received a transcript of the "Zimmermann note," a diplomatic message sent by German Foreign Secretary Zimmermann proposing to Mexico that in the event of war between the United States and Germany, Mexico should join Germany against the United States. As reward Mexico should recover "the lost territory in Texas, New Mexico, and Arizona." On the next day the President asked Congress for authority to arm American ships for defense and to employ other measures to protect American commerce on the high seas. Bolstered by the public's militant reaction to the Zimmermann note, Wilson castigated progressive senators who prevented adoption of the armed-ship bill as "a little group of willful men representing no opinion but their own." He then ordered ships armed under the authority of earlier statutes.

A succession of events followed. Three American ships were sunk with heavy losses on March 19. Also in March a liberal revolution in Russia overthrew the tsar, thereby giving the Allied cause more the aspect of a popular crusade. Great throngs of Americans called for war in mass meetings in New York and other cities. Reports that the Allies were in such desperate straits that only American intervention could save them came to the White House from London.

Weighed down by these enormous pressures, the President sorrowfully decided for war. He briefly considered a limited naval war; but he quickly dismissed the idea, perhaps because he thought that the end of the war was near and wanted a large role at the peace conference. But he knew that the risks of participation would be great. As President Wilson told a friend on April 2, 1917:

Once lead this people into war, and they'll forget there ever was such a thing as tolerance. To fight you must be brutal and ruthless, and the spirit of ruthless brutality will enter into the very fibre of our national life, infecting Congress, the courts, the policemen on the beat, the man in the street.

At eight-thirty in the evening of the same day Wilson asked a joint session of Congress to recognize that Germany was at war against the United States and mankind. "The world must be made safe for democracy," he said, " . . . for the right of those who submit to authority to have a voice in their own Governments, for the rights and liberties of small nations, for a universal domination of right by such a concert of free peoples as shall bring peace and safety to all nations and make the world itself at last free."

Four days later, on April 6, 1917—the Senate having voted 82 to 6 for a war resolution, the House 373 to 50—the United States entered World War I as an associate of the Allied powers.

A PEOPLE AT WAR

The President and his advisers soon learned that disaster loomed on almost every side. On the western front a French offensive had been stopped, and ten French divisions had already mutinied. In the Balkans the Allies were being pushed back. In Italy the Austrians, reinforced by the Germans, were soon to win a great victory at Caporetto. In the east the Russian armies were demoralized. On all fronts the Allies were running out of reserves. More ominous still, the Germans were destroying three times as much shipping each month as the Allies were building. Britain faced starvation unless something could be done.

The Washington administration responded boldly. The U.S. navy at once began to patrol the Western Hemisphere and to give assistance to the antisubmarine campaign around the British Isles. By July thirty-five American destroyers were based at Queenstown, Ireland; by the end of the war almost four hundred American ships were overseas. Meanwhile, the American navy virtually coerced the British into adopting the convoy system. The results of this critical decision were spectacular. Shipping losses fell from 881,027 tons in April to half that figure in December. By May 1918 they had dropped to 200,000 tons per month, thus destroying the calculations on which the Germans had based their decision to risk hostilities with the United States.

The War on Land. Six weeks after adoption of the war resolution a selective service law that applied to rich and poor alike was enacted, and a great army was in process of formation by the summer of 1917. During the winter of 1917-1918 the small American expeditionary force held a quiet sector of the front and served generally to bolster sagging Allied morale.

Meanwhile the American commander, General John J. Pershing, systematically prepared a major offensive. Appalled by the defense-mindedness of Allied generals, Pershing was determined "to draw the best German divisions to our front and consume them." Before he could do so, however, he had to throw two divisions into Château-Thierry to support the French in May 1918. Two months later 85,000 Americans helped the Allies turn back the last great German drive to break through the Marne pocket and take Paris. Finally, in mid-September Pershing's army, now greatly reinforced, took the offensive at St. Mihiel in its first independent action. It attained its objective after a two-day battle that cost six thousand in dead and wounded. Now more than half a million strong, the Americans turned west and won a fiercely fought battle in the Meuse-Argonne area. This victory, coupled with British and French successes in the central and northern sectors, brought Germany to its knees. An armistice was signed on November 11, 1918. Although the American contribution was critical, it was slight by comparison to that of the Allies.

Mobilization for Victory. Three months after American intervention the War Industries Board was created to coordinate purchases, allocate raw materials, control production, and supervise labor relations. The WIB made rapid progress in some areas but failed to control military purchases. "The Military Establishment . . . has fallen down," a Democratic senator exclaimed in January 1918. "It has almost stopped functioning . . . because of inefficiency in every bureau and in every department of the Government." Rejecting a Republican demand for a coalition cabinet, Wilson boldly conferred such sweeping authority on the WIB's new head, Bernard Baruch, that the industrial machine was soon hammered into shape. Congress later confirmed the President's action in the Overman Act of May 1918.

Meanwhile Herbert Hoover, director of the Food Administration, stimulated dramatic agricultural increases by pegging prices. Food exports to the Allies doubled in 1917-1918 and tripled in 1918-1919. The Fuel Administration was not so spectacularly successful, but it too performed effectively. Conversely, the ship-building program proved a failure, less than a half million new tons being afloat by the end of the war. Only by commandeering three million tons already under construction in private yards and by seizing a million tons of German and Dutch shipping did the United States acquire the fleet that saved the Allies. The railroad situation was even worse for a while. The eastern freight system nearly collapsed in December 1917. But conditions rapidly improved after the President put all railroad transportation under the control of William G. McAdoo, and the demands of the great military effort of 1918 were fully met.

Progressivism in War Time. The administration's tax and labor policies continued the powerful progressive surge of 1916. Over the bitter protests of conservatives, almost one third of the $38.5 billion total war bill was raised by war profits, income, and luxury taxes. The income tax eventually reached seventy-seven per cent in the highest brackets. Although progressives demanded even higher rates, the wealthy classes actually suffered a sizable economic loss during the war.

Moreover, the government threw its power decisively to labor's side. The National War Labor Board, under the joint chairmanship of former President Taft and Frank P. Walsh, promoted harmony between labor and management. The A.F.L. increased its membership from 2,072,702 to 3,260,168.

Hours of labor declined from 53.5 per week in 1914 to 50.4 in 1920. And real wages rose sharply—14 per cent above the prewar level in 1917 and 20 per cent above it the following year.

Propaganda and Civil Liberties. The administration's record on civil liberties proved far less exemplary, partly because of the need to create a solid front. Millions of Americans believed on April 6 that the United States should not have entered the war. In 1917 mayoralty candidates of the antiwar Socialist party polled close to half the vote in Dayton, Ohio, more than a third in Chicago, and nearly a quarter in New York and Buffalo—impressive evidence of both the magnitude and geographic spread of antiwar sentiments.

The administration struck back with a vast propaganda program and legislation to bridle criticism of the war. The Committee on Public Information under George Creel induced the press to accept voluntary censorship and organized some 15,000 writers, scholars, and businessmen into a public-speaking and pamphlet-writing bureau. The result was the creation of a necessary national will to fight. The American people accepted the draft, subscribed liberally to numerous bond drives, and adjusted reasonably well to the dislocations and inconveniences wrought by mobilization. They came also to believe the President's reiterated assertions, echoed again and again by Creel and his speakers and writers, that Americans were fighting to make the world safe for democracy. At the same time, however, they indulged in an orgy of intolerance and bigotry. State committees of public safety repressed and persecuted almost capriciously. One German-American was lynched. Conservatives read "Bolshevist" and "German socialist" into almost any sign of labor strife.

From the outset, moreover, the administration was determined to suppress opposition that might cripple the war effort. The Espionage Act of June 1917 forbade interference with the draft or any action calculated to help the enemy. The administration broadened its restrictive program as the war progressed, partly because the activities of the "Wobblies" (the Industrial Workers of the World) caused production of copper to decline precipitously. The Trading-with-the-Enemy Act of October 1917 and the Sedition Act of 1918 imposed virtual closure on free speech in the United States. By war's end some 1500 people had been convicted for violating their provisions and the Espionage Act.

The Lost Peace. As early as the spring of 1916 President Wilson had been committed both to a liberal peace and to American participation in a postwar league of nations. He had amplified this program in his "Peace without Victory" speech of January 22, 1917, and had spelled out its details in the memorable "Fourteen Points" address a year later.[1] Determined to impose this

---

1. Wilson's "Fourteen Points," pronounced on January 8, 1918, may be paraphrased as follows:
(1) "Open covenants openly arrived at."
(2) Freedom of the seas in peace and in war alike.
(3) The removal of all economic barriers and the establishment of an equality of trade conditions among all nations.
(4) Reduction of national armaments.
(5) A readjustment of all colonial claims, giving the interests of the population concerned equal weight with the claims of the government whose title was to be determined.
(6) The evacuation of Russian territory and the independent determination by Russia of its own political development and national policy.
(7) The evacuation and restoration of Belgium.
(8) The evacuation and restoration of France and the return of Alsace-Lorraine.
(9) A readjustment of the frontiers of Italy along national lines.
(10) Self-determination for the peoples of Austria-Hungary.
(11) Evacuation of Rumania, Serbia, and Montenegro and access to the sea for Serbia.
(12) Self-determination for the peoples under Turkish rule and freedom of the Dardanelles under international guarantee.
(13) The independence of Poland, with free access to the sea guaranteed by international covenant.
(14) The formation of a general association of nations (*i.e.*, the League of Nations) under specific covenants for the purpose of affording mutual guarantees of political independence and territorial integrity to great and small states alike.

program on the Allies in spite of their secret treaties for the division of the German, Austro-Hungarian, and Turkish empires, he set out for the peace conference in Paris in the first week of December 1918.

The President faced imposing obstacles. A narrow Republican victory in the congressional elections in November 1918 had weakened his moral authority. Many Republicans had already expressed opposition to his program, and Roosevelt and Lodge would soon write Prime Minister David Lloyd George of Great Britain and Premier Georges Clemenceau of France that Wilson did not speak for the American people. Nor did Wilson help matters by failing to select a single prominent Republican as a member of his five-man peace commission.

The President reached France convinced nevertheless that he might conceivably deliver all Europe from the tyranny of history. Triumphal tours of Paris, London, and Rome confirmed his sense of mission. "Wilson heard from his carriage, something different, inhuman or super human," wrote a correspondent who had seen the great men of the age on parade. Hardly conscious of the fear, lust, and vindictiveness that would shatter his hopes, he sat down with Lloyd George, Clemenceau, and Vittorio Orlando of Italy to forge a lasting peace.

The President first rejected a proposal by the French, who were obsessed with the need for security against Germany, to convert the west bank of the Rhine into buffer states under French control. But he did agree that the west bank should be permanently demilitarized and occupied by the Allies for fifteen years. He also acquiesced in the return of Alsace-Lorraine to France, the reduction of the German army and navy to cadre strength, and the mandating of Germany's colonies to victor nations under the League of Nations. Finally, he won Clemenceau's acceptance of the league idea by agreeing to join Britain and France in a treaty of mutual defense against Germany.

More victories and more concessions followed. A new Poland was created without violating unduly the principle of self-determination. Italy was granted control of the Brenner Pass for security reasons, but her plea for a long strip of the Dalmatian coast to include Fiume was rebuffed. And the Covenant of the League of Nations was firmly embedded in the peace treaty. On the other hand, Germany was subjected to a potentially astronomical reparations bill and was impelled to admit war guilt. More important still, nothing was done to remove economic barriers within Europe or throughout the world. Thus Wilson had won considerably more than his critics later conceded and a great deal less than he had hoped.

Returning to the United States on July 8, 1919, the President threw down the gauntlet two days later. "Our isolation was ended twenty years ago," he warned the U.S. Senate. "There can be no question of our ceasing to be a world power. The only question is whether we can refuse the moral leadership that is offered, whether we shall accept or reject the confidence of the world."

Wilson's words fell on a divided country. The German-Americans and their powerful journalistic ally, the Hearst press, opposed the treaty's harshness toward Germany. Italian-Americans sulked over Wilson's refusal to allow Italy to take Fiume. Irish-Americans mounted a virulent opposition because of President Wilson's failure to support the movement for Irish independence. Furthermore, a small group of sincere and irreconcilable isolationists in the Senate pledged themselves to complete defeat of the treaty because of the provision for the League of Nations. Many intellectuals and idealists were revolted by the treaty. "The European politicians who with American complicity have hatched this inhuman monster," said the *New Republic,* "have acted either cynically, hypocritically or vindictively."

Nevertheless, Wilson might still have won the fight for ratification had he not been so uncompromising, and Senator Henry Cabot Lodge and a small group of Republicans so partisan. More than two thirds of the Senate approved the League Covenant in broad principle. When the President was greeted by a tremendous response on a trip through the West in September 1919, it looked as though he must win. "My clients are the children; my clients are the next generation," he exclaimed with tears in his eyes to a cheering throng in Pueblo, Colorado. "I intend to redeem my pledges to the children; they shall not be sent [to France]." Seven days after this memorable peroration the President suffered a stroke that paralyzed his left side.

The battle now ground slowly to its tragic end. Lodge as chairman of the foreign relations committee presented the treaty to the Senate on November 6 for approval subject to a number of reservations. The most important had been suggested earlier by Elihu Root. It asserted that the United States assumed no obligations under Article X of the League Covenant to preserve the territorial integrity or political independence of any country, to interfere in controversies between nations, or to use its armed forces to uphold any article of the Treaty for any purpose, *unless Congress by joint resolution so provided.*

The ailing President refused to accept the Lodge reservations on the grounds that they crippled the Covenant, and Democrats on November 19 dutifully followed his command and voted against the treaty with reservations. Their vote was sufficient to prevent approval.

So strong was pro-League sentiment throughout the country, however, that the Treaty was brought to a second vote on March 19, 1920. By this time Wilson had recovered sufficiently to take an active part in the controversy. "Either we should enter the League fearlessly," he wrote in a public letter, "accepting the responsibility and not fearing the role of leadership which we now enjoy . . . or we should retire as gracefully as possible from the great concert of powers by which the world was saved." If the Senate failed to ratify without crippling reservations, he concluded, the election of 1920 should then be a "great and solemn referendum" on the issue. In spite of, perhaps because of, Wilson's last stand, the Senate again refused to approve ratification of the Versailles Treaty. But the final vote was close. A change of seven Democratic votes would have been enough for Senate approval.

CHAPTER 18

CULTURE AND THOUGHT IN THE PROGRESSIVE ERA

THE PROGRESSIVE MIND AND RACISM

Old and New. The momentous political and social reforms of the Roosevelt, Taft, and Wilson administrations testified eloquently to the richness of the progressive mind. Although most of the ideas which nurtured it had come earlier, the progressive mind was extraordinarily constructive; it was unafraid to apply the imperfect new insights of psychology, philosophy, and science to individuals and society. Almost every aspect of American life felt its impact: theology became infused with social theory; education was transformed; new art forms emerged; the study of history deepened and narrowed; and the law became more creative.

The "New" Immigration and Racism. The most significant exception to these trends was in race relations, which deteriorated during the progressive era, partly because the immigration of eastern and southern Europeans—people supposedly unlike the "Nordic" stock who had ancestored most old-line Americans—continued on an immense scale until the outbreak of the First World War. Between 1901 and 1914 the proportion of "new" immigrants grew to 72 per cent, as some 3 million Italians, 1.5 million Jews, and 4 million Slavs poured into the United States.

The influx of such a vast number of people would cause social tensions in any case, but the growth of racist theory compounded the problem. Superficially the racist views of the period seemed convincing. The neo-Darwinian belief that individual characteristics were passed on through the germ plasm regardless of environment was widely accepted by eugenicists. And if historically Anglo-American political institutions had proved more stable than those of other nations, might not the reason for the stability be that Anglo-Americans represented a superior race of men? For a while the findings of psychologists also buttressed this plausible body of racist theory. They disclosed, for example, that Americans of northern European derivation scored markedly higher than southeastern Europeans on intelligence tests.

During World War I, however, new research suggested that such cultural or environmental factors as rural-urban origin or educational advantages were more important than biological differences. Thus Southern whites scored lower than Northern whites in army intelligence tests, and Negroes from some northern states scored higher than whites from some southern states.

Furthermore, long before the startling findings of the army intelligence tests, the environmentalist emphasis of

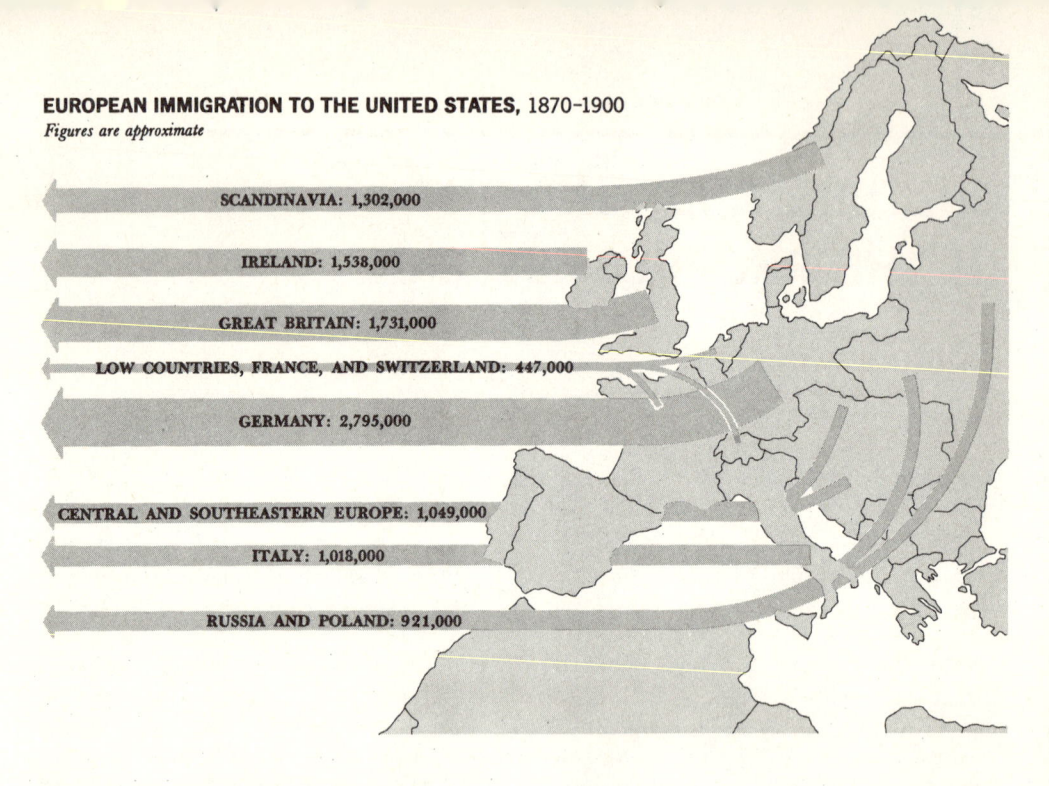

EUROPEAN IMMIGRATION TO THE UNITED STATES, 1870–1900
Figures are approximate

SCANDINAVIA: 1,302,000
IRELAND: 1,538,000
GREAT BRITAIN: 1,731,000
LOW COUNTRIES, FRANCE, AND SWITZERLAND: 447,000
GERMANY: 2,795,000
CENTRAL AND SOUTHEASTERN EUROPE: 1,049,000
ITALY: 1,018,000
RUSSIA AND POLAND: 921,000

The "old" immigration, from 1776 down to the 1890's, consisted chiefly of immigrants from northern and western Europe—so-called "Nordics," in the racist language of an earlier day. About 85 per cent of the immigrants arriving before 1883 came from these areas; and they continued to predominate, though in a steadily lessening degree, in the final decades of the nineteenth century.

reform Darwinism had modified the racism of the progressives, if not of the conservatives. Nevertheless, while most progressives neither accepted completely nor rejected totally the neo-Darwinian belief in heredity, they did equate race with cultural nationalism. They did believe in "superior" cultures, into which immigrants had to be assimilated. America's political institutions were Teutonic or Anglo-Saxon in nature; and they concluded that the "new" immigrants should eventually be "Americanized." But almost all believed that the "new" immigrants were coming in too rapidly to be absorbed at the time; hence they resorted to the literacy test as a device to curtail drastically, though not to cut off entirely, the "new" immigration.

Negroes and Racism. Whatever the moderation of their racial views, progressives were almost as slow as conservatives to resist the wave of intolerance toward Negroes that swept the country during the progressive era. From 1895 to 1907 all the southern states except Maryland, Tennessee, and Kentucky disfranchised Negro voters. Violence or the threat of violence continued to be an important means of race control. And though the total number of lynchings decreased as the result of a sharp decline in lynching in the North, the number actually increased in the South. In 1906 a race riot in Atlanta degenerated into a mass slaughter. Two years later an anti-Negro riot occurred a half mile from Lincoln's home in Springfield, Illinois. Meanwhile, Southern orators like South Carolina's "Pitchfork Ben" Tillman carried the message of white supremacy to receptive Northern audiences. And

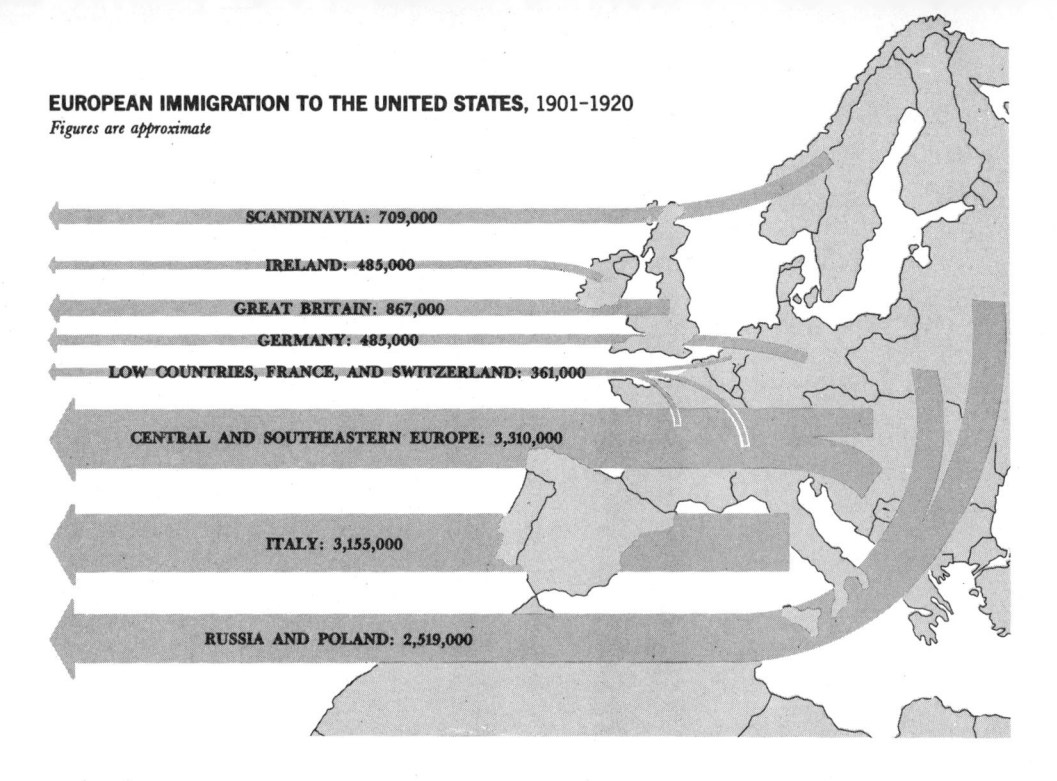

EUROPEAN IMMIGRATION TO THE UNITED STATES, 1901-1920
Figures are approximate

SCANDINAVIA: 709,000
IRELAND: 485,000
GREAT BRITAIN: 867,000
GERMANY: 485,000
LOW COUNTRIES, FRANCE, AND SWITZERLAND: 361,000
CENTRAL AND SOUTHEASTERN EUROPE: 3,310,000
ITALY: 3,155,000
RUSSIA AND POLAND: 2,519,000

From the turn of the century to 1920, the "new" immigration from southern and eastern Europe took the lead; in the year 1907, for example, immigrants of "Latin," Jewish, and Slavic origin comprised 85 per cent of the total. The restrictive immigration acts of the 1920's (see pp. 355-56) were designed to cut back severely on this "new" immigration, in favor of older racial stocks.

in 1915 the production of Thomas Dixon's violently racist book, *The Clansman*, as a motion picture titled *The Birth of a Nation* stimulated more incidents.

The bright spots were few. Negroes decreased their illiteracy rate from 44.5 per cent to 30.1 per cent in the first decade of the century. They also benefited slightly from the general upswing in prosperity. A handful of Northern philanthropists expanded their support of Negro colleges. A minority of Southern whites welcomed Negroes into the Progressive party in 1912. And the prestige of the Negro leader Booker T. Washington continued to grow. But as late as 1910 only 8251 Negro youths attended high school. Nor did any southern state make a very serious effort to provide adequate or equal educational opportunities for Negroes.

The first real ray of hope came when the National Association for the Advancement of Colored People was founded on Lincoln's birthday, 1909, by a group of Negro intellectuals and a number of white educators, clergymen, editors, and social workers. They dedicated the NAACP to the abolition of all forced segregation and to the promotion of equal justice and enlarged educational opportunities for Negroes. For tactical reasons, most NAACP leaders were whites, and only one Negro served as an official during the NAACP's first years; he was W. E. Burghardt Du Bois, a Harvard-trained historian and political activist who had repudiated Booker T. Washington's program of vocational education and political quiescence and reasserted the Negro's claim to civil rights. Du Bois was NAACP director of publicity and research for 24 years.

SCHOOL AND CHURCH IN THE PROGRESSIVE ERA

Public Education. Far more important in the long run than the exploitation of immigrants or the rise of racism was the revolution in education. The public school system was in deplorable condition at the start of the progressive era. Politics, corruption, and incompetence were rife; rote instruction, oversized classes, and an out-of-date curriculum were the rule. Teachers were poorly prepared and even more poorly paid. They averaged $42.14 per month in 1900, less than a day laborer. The proportion of male teachers had dropped from 43 per cent in 1880 to 30 per cent in 1900; by 1920 it would fall to 15 per cent. Children averaged three years of schooling in the South, seven years in the North. Southern states spent an average of $9.72 per pupil each year; northern states, $20.85.

The most dramatic changes occurred in the South, which was swept by an educational revival comparable to the one that had transformed Northern and Midwestern schools before the Civil War. By 1910 school budgets had doubled, the enrollment of white children had risen almost a third, and the average school term had been lengthened from five to six months. Meanwhile the illiteracy rate of whites declined from 11.8 to 7.7 per cent.

At the same time, a revolution in educational theory and practice was changing the character of the nation's school system. It was spurred by imaginative teachers and experimental psychologists and was already under way when the instrumentalist philosopher John Dewey (see p. 279) assumed leadership around the turn of the century. Dewey's desire to reconstruct society gradually by applying intelligence to social problems made it almost inevitable that he should turn first to educational reform. "The pragmatic theory of intelligence," he said, "means that the function of the mind is to project new and more complex ends—to free experience from routine and caprice."

Dewey called for an educational curriculum that prepared children to live in an urban, democratic society. Subject matter, he felt, should be adapted to the needs and capabilities of children; the learning process should be centered on the child's own experiences; and "learning by doing" should supplant the memorization of data. "To do this," he wrote in *School and Society* (1899), "means to make each one of our schools an embryonic community life, active with types of occupations that reflect the life of the larger society, and permeated throughout with the spirit of art, history, and science."

Against the sustained and often irrational opposition of traditionalists, Dewey and his followers accomplished one of the major cultural revolutions of the century. By the outbreak of World War I, Teachers College of Columbia University was well on the way to inculcating a whole generation of teachers with a creative approach to teaching. Dewey's most influential work, *Democracy and Education,* appeared in 1916, and three years later the Progressive Education Association was organized to advance further the dynamic new program.

As in most creative acts, however, the costs proved high. Traditionalists within the universities failed at first to grasp the intellectual foundation of the reconstruction of education. Moreover, in one of the most critical decisions in American educational history, they irresponsibly refused either to encourage or to cooperate with the proponents of teacher-training. Forced thus to organize outside the liberal arts faculties, departments and colleges of education within universities tended to become autonomous. As a result, they lost contact with the psychologists, philosophers, and historians who might have had a leavening influence upon their curricula. The situation in state teachers colleges was even more paradoxical: they were a distinct improvement over the two-year normal schools from which they had sprung, yet they failed tragically to fulfill their promise. Directed by men and women trained as vocationalists, they offered such a proliferation of overlapping education courses as to make a mockery of the word "education." (As late as 1960 it was common for prospective elementary school teachers to take more than half their course work in education, or education-related, courses.) On no level—B.S., M.S., or Ph.D.—did the quality of an education degree compare favorably to a degree in one of the traditional disciplines.

Meanwhile, professional educationists began to gain control of the certification of new teachers. Mixed results followed. The quality of teachers and teaching in rural areas and small towns improved dramatically, and many well-educated older teachers in the cities and suburbs began to use the new methods imaginatively and constructively. But at the same time, the new certification requirements discouraged countless men and women of superior intellect and liberal education from entering public school systems. More ironical still, thousands of poorly prepared English, history, and science teachers began to spend summers taking graduate education courses, rather than content courses, in order to qualify for salary increases or administrative positions. And most ominous of all, an increasing number of physical education teachers with minimal background in the liberal arts began to qualify for principalships and superintendencies by taking courses in education during the summer.

Higher Education. Colleges and universities were favorably influenced by the deepening of knowledge, the specialization induced by the new technology, and their own growing commitment to excellence. The quality of graduate and professional study rose notably. States greatly expanded their aid to higher education. Municipal colleges and universities multiplied. Major strides were made in adult education. And from 1900, when the Association of American Universities was founded, until 1914 the total enrollment in colleges and universities increased from 109,929 to 216,493. Concurrently, the status and salaries of college professors rose; the percentage of Ph.D.'s increased; the concept of tenure broadened; and in spite of numerous violations by college presidents or boards of trustees, the principle of academic freedom received wider and wider acceptance. In part these developments reflected the influence of the American Association of University Professors, organized in 1915; but in the main they marked the coming to age of American higher education.

Increased specialization, expanded research opportunities, and freedom to create led to epochal contributions to almost all areas of knowledge. By the end of the progressive era American scholarship had surpassed European scholarship in some fields and equaled it in many others. But once again the cost proved high: the social sciences developed their own vocabularies, often unnecessarily; historians wrote more and more for each other even as the quality of their research improved remarkably; and scientists, physicians, and engineers lost contact with the humanities and social sciences because of their need to specialize early in their undergraduate careers.

Legal education was beset by the same paradoxes. Pre-law training was steadily upgraded; by World War I the best law schools required an A.B. degree for admission. But except for a handful of law schools attached to the great universities, the nature and theory of law were largely neglected. Even though a law degree became a virtual prerequisite for election to public office, most law schools turned out competently trained technicians and little more.

Meanwhile, undergraduate education became increasingly watered with nonacademic subject matter. The burgeoning land-grant colleges sustained an extraordinary amount of theoretical research, especially in the physical and natural sciences. Hardly less than the teachers colleges, however, they fell far short of fulfilling their promise. Partly because of the influence of Dewey and largely because of the demands of the taxpayers, they too opened their doors to vocationalism.

Agriculture students gained impressive knowledge of agricultural principles, but they often returned from college with little more appreciation of culture or understanding of society than they had had when they entered. Nor were they unique. Many coeds spent their energies on home economics courses at the very time that the great Eastern women's colleges were decisively proving the ability of women to excel in academic disciplines. And colleges or departments of business administration committed to the narrow or technical aspects of business education began to be formed in almost all but the finest private colleges and universities. Meanwhile, much of the worst teaching in America was done by college professors who remained impervious to, or contemptuous of, the revolution in teaching wrought by Dewey and his disciples.

Theology. Another striking phenomenon of the prewar period was the survival of Protestantism after the violent intellectual storms of the last quarter of the nineteenth century. To be sure, the progressive era was marked by radical, and often paradoxical, change. Organizations like the Young Men's Christian Association, the International Sunday School Association, and the American Bible Society blurred denominational lines. Modernism, fundamentalism, and the Social Gospel movement cut across them. And the formation of the Federal Council of Churches of Christ in America by thirty-three evangelical bodies with a membership of 17 million created a loose unity after 1908.

At the same time, however, a large number of disgruntled Methodist and Baptist fundamentalists formed new Protestant sects, and the northern Presbyterian church preserved the purity of its doctrines only by expelling several of its most distinguished ministers and losing control of its leading seminary, the Union Theological Seminary in New York. Modernist clergymen largely captured the northern Methodists, the northern Baptists, and the urban Congregationalists. And perhaps a majority of intellectuals left the church in spirit.

Even the Social Gospel ministers failed to agree on a common body of assumptions. Thus one leader of the movement, the Congregationalist Washington Gladden, blamed the world's ills on Protestantism's theological rock bed—the belief that salvation is a private matter between man and God. The result, he charged, was a failure to apply the law of love to the resolution of social problems. Christians must realize that although God did not reveal Himself fully in nature, His partial immanence could be seen in the ever increasing force of sympathy, love, and self-sacrifice. They should further understand, Gladden held, "that human nature is modifiable, and is constantly being modified, under the influence of the divine Spirit, so that social standards and ruling ideas are gradually changing from generation to generation."

But another eminent Congregationalist, George Herron, argued with great fervor that Christ would be revealed fully with the Second Coming. He would come, however, only after such a self-sacrificing imitation by Christians as would transform the world. The dualism of contemporary life was intolerable:

A corporation, greedy, godless, vicious in many of its operations, consists of men famous for their piety and benevolence. A nation governed by men of eminent Christian character goes mad with the spoils of unrighteousness. . . . A church containing many sincere, teachable, self-sacrificing Christians is as powerless a moral institution in the community as the town pump.

The two most prominent modernists of the times, Edward Scribner Ames, a Disciple of Christ, and Shailer Mathews, a Baptist, broke still more sharply with traditional theology. Rejecting the supernatural, Ames emphasized both the scientific method and democratic idealism. Man was to revere life, love his fellow man, and have faith in his ability to improve the world. For Ames, as for most of the intellectuals who left the church, social justice rather than individual salvation became the ultimate ideal.

Mathews was more representative of those who stayed in the church. Like Ames, he was enamored of both science and democracy; but unlike Ames, he continued to have faith in the supernatural. Mathews believed that man must be regenerated, and he and a majority of modernists fastened on incarnation as the means to that end. "God's spirit," writes historian Stow Persons, "was believed to be incarnate in the world, working through the social historical process, expressing itself in the highest values of the community, such as love, brotherhood, justice, and good will."

Yet it would be wrong to assume that these views characterized Protestantism as a whole. For every Christian Socialist or near-socialist clergyman, there were probably hundreds of theological and social conservatives. And for every layman whose social conscience was aroused by a Washington Gladden or his like, probably a thousand were moved to acceptance of the existing theological and social order by the Rev. Russell Conwell's exhortation to get rich—"to make money honestly is to preach the gospel"—or by the Rev. Billy Sunday's thundering fundamentalism.

ARCHITECTURE, PAINTING, AND LITERATURE

Architecture. The paradoxes of progressivism were even more graphically set off by the popular taste in architecture. Two striking originators, Louis Sullivan and Frank Lloyd Wright, conceived organic styles and profoundly influenced European architecture; and a number of talented designer-engineers built functional and often esthetically inspiring bridges and factories of steel and reinforced concrete. But most architects and their businessmen-clients emphasized form rather than function. The overwhelming majority of the progressive era's buildings were more banal than creative, more pretentious than graceful. The same held for private houses. Sullivan, Wright, and a few others did imaginative work, but the preponderance of new construction was eclectic. When historical styles such as Cape Cod, Georgian, or Greek Revival were used, the end product almost invariably violated the lines and proportions that had given the originals their distinction.

Sullivan attributed this failure of taste to the appeal of the Roman façades, false monumentalism, and harmonious lagoons of the Great White City fashioned for Chicago's Columbian Exposition of 1893. "The damage . . . has penetrated deep into the . . . American mind," he wrote, "effecting there lesions of dementia." More likely, however, the Exposition's imperial style touched the same impulses for grandeur that would ordain the acquisition of an empire after the war with Spain in 1898.

Sullivan's pupil, Frank Lloyd Wright, also failed to exercise much immediate influence on the American skyline. "Early in life," Wright once wrote, "I had to choose between honest arrogance and hypocritical humility. I chose honest arrogance." Wright's great distinction was his development of Sullivan's concept of "organic" architecture. Professing a regional style (he was in fact influenced by the Japanese), he designed from the inside out, emphasizing always the unique texture of his materials. His use of native woods, horizontal planes, and deep overhangs often succeeded brilliantly in harmonizing man and nature. As early as 1900 the *Architectural Review* recognized Wright's genius, and by 1905 his work had deeply affected the modern movement in Germany, Holland, and France. But only as Wright's ideas were brought back to the United States by Europeans like Walter Gropius did Wright make a vigorous imprint on American architecture. Meanwhile, the skilled traditionalists Stanford White, Ralph Adams Cram, and their disciples continued both to form and to reflect the widespread preference for Roman and Gothic.

On the other hand, the maligned Columbian Exposition did serve at least one creditable purpose: its classic spaciousness sparked a nation-wide movement to beautify American cities. Uncounted open spaces in cities were converted into parks, and sums commensurate with the nation's wealth were poured into public buildings. Unfortunately, little attention was given to the flow of traffic, and even less was given the needs, interests, and habits of pedestrians. And the buildings erected were almost always more derivative than original in design.

Painting. "There is a state of unrest all over the world in art as in all other things," the director of the Metropolitan Museum complained in 1908. "It is the same in literature, as in music, in painting and in sculpture." This was the year that eight young painters spearheaded by the realists Robert Henri, George B. Luks, and John Sloan protested against the National Academy's near blackout of their work and staged a private show in New York. The realists rebelled not against the old painting techniques—they never mastered the new ones—but against the class bias that failed to see reality in all human activity, including the seamy. Theirs was a work of social protest closer to the political ferment of the era than to the revolution in art forms that had already swept Europe. Inevitably, Victorian-minded critics dismissed them as "apostles of ugliness," "the revolutionary gang," "the black gang," and, most often, "the ash-can school."

Meanwhile, more creative European currents were beginning to affect American artists. By 1912 the work of the post-impressionists was familiar to sophisticated habitués of the New York gallery of the revolutionary camera artist Alfred Stieglitz. The next year sixteen hundred paintings, drawings, prints, and pieces of sculpture representing almost every mode in modern art were exhibited in a spectacular show at the New York Armory. Picasso, Matisse, Brancusi, Duchamp, Kandinsky, Cezanne, Van Gogh, Gauguin, and virtually all other prominent artists had their work displayed to the extreme discomfort of conservative critics. The *New York Times* labeled the show "*pathological.*" *Art and Progress* compared many of its artists to "anarchists, bomb-throwers, lunatics, depravers." And an official of the Chicago Law and Order League demanded that the exhibition be banned from his city because the "idea that people can gaze at this sort of thing without it hurting them is all bosh."

The vehemence of the conservatives' criticism and the desperation of the counterattack they soon mounted served only to underscore their artistic bankruptcy. As the art historian Sam Hunter writes, "They were soon unable to pose with real conviction or enthusiasm a possible alternative, since even the art they defended was becoming a retarded and diluted academic derivative of some form of modernism." Nevertheless, the public proved as slow to accept the highly individualized abstractionism of the new painters, the foremost Americans of whom were Max Weber and John Marin, as it did the architecture of Sullivan and Wright.

The Novel. The trend toward realism in literature reached its highest form in the works of Nebraska-born Willa Cather, author of *O Pioneers!* (1913) and *My Ántonia* (1918). More popular were Booth Tarkington, Winston Churchill, and several literary journalists like William Allen White, who blended realism with optimism much as the progressive political leaders were doing.

Meanwhile, Jack London and Frank Norris were writing a raw version of the survival-of-the-fittest doctrine into a host of brutal novels ranging in subject from man's struggle against the elements to his battle with the trusts. But it was in the writings of Theodore Dreiser, the era's only literary giant, that naturalism, as literary determinism was called, proved the most profound. The son of German Catholic immigrants who settled in Indiana, Dreiser early disavowed belief in religion and conventional morality. "Man was a mechanism," he wrote, "undevised and uncreated, and a badly and carelessly driven one at that." Yet Dreiser, no less than his predecessors, was a moralist at heart. All his work was charged by a tension between determinism and its antithesis; in the very act of denying free will and the importance of man, he affirmed them. "To have accepted America as he has accepted it, to immerse oneself in something one can neither escape nor relinquish, to yield to what has been true and to yearn over what has seemed inexorable," this, concludes Alfred Kazin, "has been Dreiser's fate and the secret of his victory."

Dreiser's first novel, *Sister Carrie* (1900), was withdrawn by his publisher because of its harsh reception; critics, many of whom objected to the novel's sympathetic treatment of a "fallen woman," failed to see that its account of the purposelessness of life was counterbalanced by its emphasis on life's sheer vitality. His second book, *Jennie Gerhardt* (1911), like *Sister Carrie* the story of a "kept woman" who was otherwise virtuous, struck at the failure of the conventional moral code to correspond to reality. Similar themes pervaded *The Financier* (1912) and *The Titan* (1914), though they were widely regarded as progressive-type indictments of the "robber barons."

Poetry. The years before World War I also witnessed a remarkable renaissance in poetry. Perhaps the most powerful voice was Edwin Arlington Robinson, a traditionalist who dealt with the abiding theme of the individual's search for God and truth amidst darkness and suffering. Robinson failed in his quest; life and human destiny remained mysterious. Yet in the "black and awful chaos of the night" he felt "the coming glory of the Light." Rescued from obscurity by Theodore Roosevelt, who gave him a government sinecure after reading his *Children of the Night* (1897), Robinson failed nevertheless to receive full recognition until after the war.

By 1912, the year Harriet Monroe established the magazine *Poetry* in Chicago, the renaissance was at hand. Vachel Lindsay, now remembered more for his jazz-like odes than his sensitive lyrics, published his "General William Booth Enters into Heaven" in the first issue of *Poetry*, then went on to exalt the common people in numerous other works. Edgar Lee Masters, Clarence Darrow's law partner, startled traditionalists with his masterpiece, *Spoon River Anthology*, in 1915. There he laid bare the sham and moral shabbiness of small-town America in a brilliant compound of irony, sadness, and humor that closed, paradoxically, on an affirmative note. A year later Carl Sandburg's first volume appeared. A Whitmanesque romantic who employed free verse, Sandburg glorified Chicago as the roaring, brawling butcher and steel-maker to the world. During these same years Robert Frost was writing deceptively simple free verse against a rural New England backdrop that masked his passionate, almost terrifying, life-force:

> Now no joy but lacks salt
> That is not dashed with pain
> And weariness and fault;
> I crave the stain
>
> Of tears, the aftermark
> Of almost too much love,
> The sweet of bitter bark
> And burning clove.[1]

At the same time another revolt against the genteel tradition was brewing among a group of American and English poets in London, the so-called imagists. Led by Ezra Pound and Amy Lowell, they asserted that the poet should re-create impressions caught in the fleeting image. They held that meter and rhyme made the creation of a pure image difficult, if not impossible, and they accordingly rejected them. They also rejected Romanticism as being the literary expression of a decadent humanistic culture. They were soon joined by T. S. Eliot, whose now classic "The Love Song of J. Alfred Prufrock" met a hostile reception when first published in *Poetry* in 1915. In "Preludes," dealing with the images of dreary urban life, Eliot points up the frustrations of the individual:

> His soul stretched tight across the skies
> That fade behind a city block,
> Or trampled by insistent feet

> At four and five and six o'clock;
> And short square fingers stuffing pipes,
> And evening newspapers, and eyes
> Assured of certain certainties,
> The conscience of a blackened street
> Impatient to assume the world.
>
> I am moved by fancies that are curled
> Around these images, and cling:
> The notion of some infinitely gentle
> Infinitely suffering thing.
>
> Wipe your hand across your mouth, and laugh;
> The worlds revolve like ancient women
> Gathering fuel in vacant lots.[2]

THE SOCIAL SCIENCES

Psychology and Economics. Man's understanding of himself was further deepened by rapid advances in psychology. Freed from its old metaphysical and theological commitment by the Darwinian revolution, psychology began now to explore the whole range of human activity. By World War I two definite schools—the instinct and the behaviorist—had emerged. Both were European in origin; both found a receptive audience in the United States and exerted considerable impact on American thought.

The founder of the instinct school, William McDougall, felt strongly that psychology should concern itself with social behavior. He contended that man was ruled by deep-seated instincts rather than by rational or moral considerations. And his charge that classical economic theory was "a tissue of false conclusions drawn from false psychological assumptions" reinforced the insights Thorstein Veblen had already

---

[1] From "To Earthward" from *Complete Poems of Robert Frost*. Copyright 1923 by Holt, Rinehart and Winston, Inc.; renewed 1951 by Robert Frost. Reprinted by permission of Holt, Rinehart and Winston, Inc., and Laurence Pollinger, Ltd.

[2] From "Preludes," *Collected Poems 1909-1935* by T. S. Eliot. Copyright 1936 by Harcourt, Brace & World, Inc., and reprinted with their permission, and with the permission of Faber and Faber, Ltd., London.

written into his *Theory of the Leisure Class*. In *The Instinct of Workmanship and the State of the Industrial Arts* (1914) Veblen echoed McDougall's strictures against the inadequate psychological base of classical economics. He especially charged that modern industrial institutions had failed to play upon man's constructive instincts. F. W. Taussig argued in *Inventors and Money-Makers* (1915) that the instinct of contrivance, or workmanship, did not depend necessarily on prospective gain, as the defenders of the profit-making system contended. However, although instinct psychology undermined classical economic thought, it produced no systematic theory of its own.

The behaviorist psychology of the Russian Ivan Pavlov and the Americans E. L. Thorndike and John B. Watson proved more receptive to the dominant environmentalism of the times. Passing over everything that could not be verified by direct observation, the behaviorists sought to measure all human behavior in terms of stimuli and response. "It is the business of behavioristic psychology," wrote Watson, who later became an executive in an advertising agency, "to be able to predict and control human activity." Since consciousness was not observable, it should not be studied; thought was to be treated as latent speech.

Behaviorism offered too restricted and shocking a view of human nature to be universally acceptable; humanists rejected it decisively. Nevertheless, it sired a powerful school of psychology and markedly influenced all subsequent social science. At its best, behaviorism contributed enormously to social engineering of a constructive sort; at its worst, it lent itself to social manipulation. Its dramatic rise was paralleled by the equally spectacular rise of capitalism's one unique institution, advertising. On the one hand, that institution served powerfully to spur economic growth. On the other, it inculcated attitudes far removed from the socially desirable values of the school and the church and stimulated, even urged, materialistic social values.

The New History. The writing of history proved no more immune to the new intellectual currents than did other disciplines; nor did it escape their paradoxes. The influence of German methodology, first felt at Johns Hopkins, continued as historians now severed almost completely their ties with literature. Seeking scientific truth by the use of rigorously exact techniques, they destroyed hallowed beliefs, stripped history of its individual drama and romance, and lost some of their popular audience. Yet they added immeasurably to the general body of knowledge, contributed important new insights about the forces that molded America, and provoked much constructive controversy inside and outside the profession.

The foremost characteristic of much of the new history was present-mindedness. As James Harvey Robinson and Charles A. Beard confessed in their pathfinding *The Development of Modern Europe* (1907), they had "consistently subordinated the past to the present" in the "ever-conscious aim to enable the reader to catch up with his own times." Implicit in this approach was a belief in laws of behavior as formulated by social scientists; the insights of philosophers, poets, and observers no longer sufficed. Implicit, also, was a desire to use history to create a better future. This last was not new. From Thucydides' time historians had concerned themselves with the usable past; some had been great moralists, finding in the past examples of virtue to be imitated in the present. When Robinson and Beard wrote, however, probably a majority of America's professional historians conceived their task as being merely descriptive. It was against them and their failure to search for causal explanations that might indirectly bear on the present—to be, in the new view, truly scientific—that Robinson and Beard revolted.

The seeds of revolt had earlier been sown by Frederick Jackson Turner. Notwithstanding his effort to cut off Americans from their European past, Turner's environmentalism had opened new vistas to many historians. As Eric Goldman puts it, "The vogue of Turner's idea pulled men away from thinking in terms of political abstractions and shifted their minds to a concept that was close to economic." One of Turner's students, Algie M. Simons, wrote the first semischolarly Marxist history of the United States. Numerous others proved sensitive in some degree to the influence of economic forces on history.

Meanwhile a storm was brewing over the Constitution. In 1907 J. Allen Smith published *The Spirit of American Government,* in which he argued that the Constitution was written by property-holders who aimed to prevent the masses from controlling the government. "The powerful corporate interests . . . ," said Smith in a passage that summed up the progressives' criticism of the judiciary, "are securely intrenched behind a series of constitutional and legal checks on the majority which makes it extremely difficult for public opinion to exercise any effective control over them."

Six years later Charles A. Beard buttressed Smith's hypothesis with mountains of seemingly conclusive evidence. "The Constitution," he wrote in *An Economic Interpretation of the Constitution* (1913), "was essentially an economic document based upon the concept that the fundamental private rights of property are anterior to government and morally beyond the reach of popular majorities." He then set forth data to prove that through their interest in public securities, money, manufacturing, trade, and shipping, the framers of the Constitution had stood to gain directly from the establishment of the new government.

Beard always protested that his work was American-inspired. James Madison, he repeatedly pointed out, had offered "one of the earliest, and certainly one of the clearest" statements of economic determinism. As Morton G. White has observed, however, *An Economic Interpretation of the Constitution* actually reflected the worst, or at least the simplest, aspects of both Marx's and Madison's thought. Thus Marx neither denied man's capacity for high-minded action nor accepted the idea that every political action derived directly from an economic interest. Conversely, Madison believed with Aristotle that factions and interests were rooted in human nature —not, as Marx contended, in economic systems. But in Beard's analysis the framers had been moved by a narrow Marxian view of the deterministic force of economic systems and a similarly narrow Madisonian view of a direct relationship between self-interest and action. Recent scholarship has demolished, or at least seriously challenged, the evidence on which Beard based his economic thesis.

Beard also denied that he had written a tract for the times. "I simply sought to bring back into the mental picture of the Constitution," he said, "those realistic features of economic conflict, stress and strain, which my masters had, for some reason, left out of it, or thrust far into the background as incidental rather than fundamental." Whatever his intentions, the work drove deeper the wedge between progressives and conservatives. In the span of a decade many men's attitudes toward the Constitution and the judiciary that upheld it had moved from reverence to begrudged respect to unbridled contempt.

The impact of *An Economic Interpretation of the Constitution* on the historical profession proved even greater than its impact on progressive politicians. Two generations of historians were nourished on it; and though many were skeptical from the beginning, few failed thereafter to give due attention to economic factors in their teaching and writing. Perhaps the fairest judgment of Smith and Beard's work is the one that Roosevelt passed on the Armory Exhibition of Modern Art: "The necessary penalty of creativity is a liability to extravagance."

LEGAL AND POLITICAL MAIN CURRENTS

Sociological Jurisprudence. The vast changes in American thought and institutions wrought by progressivism were mirrored in the law. Admittedly, the old absolutes died hard. Not until the new industrial problems became acute did the liberating force of Oliver Wendell Holmes' *The Common Law* begin to be felt; not until judges came abreast of the new psychological and sociological currents did a progressive synthesis begin to be formed. In crudest form the new accommodation reflected the judiciary's realization that since it lacked the power of the purse or sword it could not indefinitely hold back a nation bent on reform. As Mr. Dooley phrased it, "Th' Supreme Court follows th' ilection returns." But in its broadest and highest form it reflected the same impulses that had inspired the progressive movement in general—the quest for social justice, the belief in progress, the urge to create, and the faith in scientism. Thus Harvard's Dean Roscoe Pound, who synthesized the historical insights of Holmes, the methodology of the social scientists, and the pragmatism of James and Dewey, conceived the law as an agency for social reconstruction:

> The sociological movement in jurisprudence is a movement for pragmatism as a philosophy of law; for the adjustment of principles and doctrines to the human conditions they are to govern rather than to assume first principles; for putting the human factor in the central place and relegating logic to its true position as an instrument.

In spite of lingering opposition, the force of these and similar ideas was immediate and widespread. Judges began to probe beyond the crime into its social or psychological origins. Juvenile delinquency came to be viewed as environmental rather than hereditary in origin. And children's courts modeled on the one that Judge Ben Lindsey established in Denver spread throughout the nation and even to Japan.

The law also began to adjust creatively to labor problems. The common law concepts of "fellow-servant rule" and "contributory negligence," which had exempted employers from liability for most industrial accidents, withered away as the courts upheld liability and workmen's compensation laws grounded on sociological realities. No one put the case more graphically than Roosevelt in his epochal message of January 31, 1908:

> It is hypocritical baseness to speak of a girl who works in a factory where the dangerous machinery is unprotected as having the "right" freely to contract to expose herself to dangers to life and limb. She has no alternative but to suffer want or else to expose herself to such dangers. . . . It is a moral wrong that the whole burden of the risk incidental to the business would be placed with crushing weight upon her weak shoulders.

The most celebrated manifestation of sociological jurisprudence was Louis D. Brandeis' successful defense in 1908 of an Oregon statute regulating the working hours of women. Disposing of the legal precedents in the first two pages of his brief, he spent 102 pages on sociological data designed to prove that excessive hours of labor were injurious to the health of women and to the general well-being of the community. Actually, lawyers had long invoked extralegal evidence to support their arguments; from John Marshall's time, moreover, Supreme Court justices had read their own social and economic biases into their opinions. The "Brandeis Brief," however, served to make more scientific and dramatic an established practice. He would have the justices form their extralegal views on the best available evidence rather than on personal prejudice.

Hardly less important than the inroads made by sociological jurisprudence was a renewed emphasis on judicial restraint. This was the belief, best exemplified by Holmes, that the legislature should be reasonably free to pass experimental legislation:

I think that the word liberty in the Fourteenth Amendment is perverted when it is held to prevent the natural outcome of a dominant opinion unless it can be said that a rational and fair man necessarily would admit that the statute proposed would infringe principles as they have been understood by the traditions of our people and law.

The majority of the Court did not adhere consistently to this doctrine. It struck down the Child Labor Act of 1916, and it ruled numerous state statutes unconstitutional. Yet, as a recent student of the Supreme Court concludes, the vision of judicial tyranny was an exaggeration. The Court did uphold most of the basic progressive legislation of the period even though much of this legislation struck at the core of the free enterprise system—for example, an employer's right to fix prices and wages.

Political Thought. While Dewey, Pound, and Beard were reconstructing education, law, and history, three young humanists—Herbert Croly, Walter Lippmann, and Walter Weyl—were calling for a reconstitution of politics. They charged that the existing system was geared to minority interests, and they deplored especially the failure of spiritual and esthetic progress to keep pace with material progress. The remedy, they concluded, was to infuse the political order with the new social and psychological concepts.

In 1909 Croly published the first of the new blueprints, *The Promise of American Life*. Croly accepted Veblen's and the instinct psychologists' charges that industrialism had repressed man's finer instincts. He directed his fire, accordingly, at laissez-faire capitalism's basic precept—the belief that freedom to pursue individual gain led inevitably to social progress. In words that came close to paraphrasing Theodore Roosevelt's presidential messages of 1907 and 1908, Croly called for the replacement of anarchic individualism by social cohesion. By the rigorous exercise of self-discipline, man must create a community loyal to an elevating ideal—a nation-state that would fulfill man's great promise.

Believing in big business' potential for good and despairing of the Democrats' devotion to states' rights, Croly at first fastened on the Republican party as the vehicle to achieve his purposes. He considered Roosevelt almost the ideal statesman: "The whole tendency of his programme is to give a democratic meaning and purpose to Hamiltonian tradition and method. He proposes to use the power and resources of the Federal government for the purpose of making his countrymen a more complete democracy in organization and practice." Like Roosevelt, however, Croly finally concluded that Republican nationalism served special interests almost exclusively. In 1912 *The Promise of American Life* became the Bull Moose party's bible and Croly its prophet.

The following year Walter Lippmann wrote a Freudian analysis into his synthesization of the current social wisdom, *Preface to Politics* (1913). Lippmann professed little faith in direct democracy, and he seemed to call for a superman to lead the nation to an unspecified destiny. "He who has the courage of existence," he proclaimed, "will put it triumphantly, crying 'yes' as Nietsche did." Yet Lippmann had too sharp an appreciation of the representative character of American institutions to believe in dictatorship. He really sought leadership that would give voice to the "dynamic currents" and "actual needs" of the people and destroy the corruption, political indifference, and cultural apathy that prevailed almost everywhere. Constitutional fetishism, the conscious belief in the sanctity of private property, vested rights, and competition—all this, said Lippmann, should be reëxamined. "The same energies," he wrote, "produce crime and civilization, art, vice, insanity, love, lust, religion. . . . Only by supplying our passions with civilized interests can we escape their destructive force."

Walter Weyl, a young economist well trained in statistics, added solid knowledge in his *The New Democracy,* published in 1912. A democracy, he said, had to soften the harsh condition of its poor classes in order to survive. Croly, Lippmann, and Weyl all found a public forum in *The New Republic,* a weekly magazine of comment that began publication in 1914 and remained until the 1920's the chief clearing house of progressive political opinion and thought.

Historians have tended in recent years to pass off the progressive intellectuals as superficial and to term their times an age of innocence. These generalizations are not without truth if we measure the progressives by their failures rather than by their triumphs. They are even more persuasive if we tear the progressives from their historical context and fail to compare their program with that of the conservatives or traditionalists. For it was the conservatives, not the progressives, who failed to see that workers had to be treated as more than subhumans in an age of growing abundance; that crime and vice were largely environmental in origin; and that the study of personality by psychologists, and of man and society by sociologists and anthropologists, opened rich possibilities for further human development. More important still, it was the conservatives, not the progressives, who failed to see that big government was all that prevented the American republic from becoming the feudal domain of the new industrial barons; that the advance of technology and the rise of pure science and the social sciences stripped traditional educational curricula of a large part of their reason for being; and that the law was neither created in a social vacuum nor could long remain static. And most important of all, it was the conservatives, far more than the progressives, who clung to the fiction that nation-states could indefinitely survive under the law of the jungle.

To be sure, the progressive mind had its faults. It expected and demanded more than most men could give. It was slow to understand that to solve one problem is to create another; and when it did grasp that truth after World War I it became disillusioned. It flirted dangerously with political authoritarianism because of its uncritical acceptance of the new scientism. It distorted history even as it made history meaningful to its own generation. It placed its faith in an environmental interpretation of society that emphasized physical conditions too heavily and thus proved too simple. And it submitted to a philosophical relativism of epochal proportions. It was also enamored of means—with the initiative, the referendum, and the recall as well as with government by commission—at the cost of a clear definition of its ends. And it failed, consequently, to realize that the need to change the power structure of American society was more critical than the need to change the forms of democracy. Finally, it fell far short of achieving the synthesis its theoreticians—Croly, Lippmann, and Weyl—envisioned.

But to point up the progressive mind's flaws is not to deny its worth. No cynical appraisal of its motives, no reasoned critique of its paradoxes, no sophisticated rejection of the idea of progress—the virtual hallmark of progressivism—can deprive it of its rightful dignity and historical eminence. If it built imperfectly, it for the most part built humanely. And if it cast down the ancient absolutes, its act of negation was one of affirmation. For above all else, the progressive mind sought to create a society in which individual dignity could withstand the fearful onslaught of raw industrialism.

BIBLIOGRAPHY

George E. Mowry, *The Era of Theodore Roosevelt: 1900-1912* (New York: Harper, 1958) is an admirable synthesis of progressivism's early phases. The same author's *Theodore Roosevelt and the Progressive Movement* (Madison: University of Wisconsin Press, 1946) is illuminating, but somewhat dated. Arthur S. Link, *Woodrow Wilson and the Progressive Era: 1910-1917* (New York: Harper, 1954) is the best account of Democratic progressivism. A good regional survey is Russel Nye, *Midwestern Progressive Politics: 1870-1958*, rev. ed. (East Lansing: Michigan State University Press, 1959). Richard Hofstadter, *The Age of Reform: From Bryan to F. D. R.* (New York: Alfred A. Knopf, 1955) is suggestive although its central theses have been subjected to sharp attack. For insight into the extreme left see Ira Kipnis, *The American Socialist Movement: 1897-1912* (New York: Columbia University Press, 1952).

A number of works cover selected aspects of the era. Lincoln Steffens' highly readable contemporary articles are reprinted as *The Struggle for Self-Government* (New York: McClure, Phillips, 1906) and *The Shame of the Cities* (New York: Peter Smith, 1959). The relations between business and politics are explored in Robert A. Wiebe, *Businessmen and Reform: A Study of the Progressive Movement* (Cambridge, Mass.: Harvard University Press, 1962). Louis Filler, *Crusaders for American Liberalism*, rev. ed. (Yellow Springs, Ohio: Antioch Press, 1950) describes the muckrakers. Samuel P. Hays, *Conservation and the Gospel of Efficiency* (Cambridge, Mass.: Harvard University Press, 1959) analyzes the conservation movement's scientific base. The same author's *Response to Industrialism: 1885-1914* (Chicago: University of Chicago Press, 1957) should also be consulted, as should the autobiographies of Theodore Roosevelt, Robert M. La Follette, Lincoln Steffens, George W. Norris, and William Allen White.

Contrasting interpretations of President Roosevelt are offered in Henry F. Pringle, *Theodore Roosevelt*, rev. ed. (New York: Harcourt, Brace, 1956); John M. Blum, *The Republican Roosevelt* (Cambridge, Mass.: Harvard University Press, 1954); and William H. Harbaugh, *Power and Responsibility: The Life and Times of Theodore Roosevelt* (New York: Farrar, Straus and Cudahy, 1961). Paul W. Glad, *The Trumpet Soundeth: William Jennings Bryan and His Democracy, 1896-1912* (Lincoln: University of Nebraska Press, 1960) surveys Bryan's career from 1896 to 1912 with sympathy and understanding. Henry F. Pringle, *The Life and Times of William Howard Taft* (New York: Farrar and Rinehart, 1939) is a standard biography. Belle Case and Fola La Follette, *Robert M: La Follette: 1855-1925*, 2 vols. (New York: Macmillan, 1953) is a loving but substantial account of the life of Roosevelt's great rival. The first three volumes of Arthur S. Link's *Wilson* (Princeton, N.J.: Princeton University Press, 1947-1960) carry its subject's career to late 1915.

The most informed and judicious survey of foreign affairs for this period is in Richard W. Leopold, *The Growth of American Foreign Policy* (New York: Alfred A. Knopf, 1962). Margaret Leech, *In the Days of McKinley* (New York: Harper, 1959) redeems McKinley and adds a little luster he never had. Ernest R. May, *Imperial Democracy* (New York: Harcourt, Brace and World, 1961) gives a dispassionate account of the decision to go to war against Spain. Howard K. Beale, *Theodore Roosevelt and the Rise of America to World Power* (Baltimore: Johns Hopkins Press, 1956) is a seminal, and surprisingly favorable, account of TR's diplomacy as President. TR's post-presidential career, Taft's handling of foreign policy, and Wilson's record up to the outbreak of war are treated in the previously cited works by Harbaugh, Pringle, and Link. They should be supplemented by Tyler Dennett, *John Hay: From Poetry to Politics* (New York: Dodd, Mead, 1933); Richard W. Leopold, *Elihu Root and the Conservative Tradition* (Boston: Little, Brown, 1954); and Daniel M. Smith, *Robert Lansing and American Neutrality, 1914-1917* (Berkeley: University of California Press, 1958).

Frederic L. Paxson, *American Democracy and the World War*, 3 vols. (Boston: Houghton Mifflin, 1936-1948) is still a useful survey of the nation at war. H. C. Peterson and Gilbert C. Fite, *Opponents of War, 1917-1918* (Madison: University of Wisconsin Press, 1957) offers a bitter account of the suppression of civil liberties. A highly sympathetic account of Wilson and the peacemaking is Arthur Walworth, *Woodrow Wilson: World Prophet* (New York: David McKay, 1958). It should be read against John A. Garraty, *Henry Cabot Lodge* (New York: Alfred A. Knopf, 1953). Thomas A. Bailey, *Wilson and the Peacemakers* (New York: Macmillan, 1947) retains much of its original value.

Among the important intellectual histories are Henry F. May, *The End of American Innocence* (New York: Alfred A. Knopf, 1959) and especially Stowe Persons' difficult but extremely perceptive *American Minds: A History of Ideas* (New York: Holt, 1958). John Higham, *Strangers in the Lane* (New Brunswick, N.J.: Rutgers University Press, 1955) is severely critical of old-stock Americans' response to immigration. John Hope Franklin, *From Slavery to Freedom: A History of American Negroes*, rev. ed. (New York: Alfred A. Knopf, 1956) is the best broad survey of Negro history. Lawrence A. Cremin, *The Transformation of the School* (New York: Alfred A. Knopf, 1961) is a work of considerable insight but insufficient criticism. For architecture, see John E. Burchard and Albert Bush-Brown, *The Architecture of America* (Boston: Little, Brown, 1961). On literature, Alfred Kazin's classic *On Native Grounds* (New York: Harcourt, Brace, 1942) should be supplemented by Charles C. Walcutt, *American Literary Naturalism, A Divided Stream* (Minneapolis: University of Minnesota Press, 1956).

PART 7: INTRODUCTION

BETWEEN TWO WARS

■ World War I had not in itself brought marked changes in American life or forced civilians to make many sacrifices. Yet the climate of 1920 was strikingly different from that of 1914. The course of events in Europe during the five years from 1915 through 1919 had robbed the progressive movement and progressive thinking of their energy. While attention was directed abroad, interest in domestic reform survived in only a few areas. By the time the full force of American emotional energy was again directed toward domestic affairs, the progressive years seemed nearly as far away as the conservative years of the turn of the century. Nevertheless, Americans of 1920 who seemed to want to return to an earlier period found it quite impossible to recapture the past.

In historical perspective, changes during the period between the two wars may be seen as forcing the abandonment of traditional attitudes and beliefs and demanding adjustment to a new society with a different physical environment and changed cultural values. Technological progress was changing conditions of working and living. Automobiles had been multiplying for two decades, but the true motorization of the United States came in the 1920's. Electric power and gasoline transportation, which were rapidly making existing patterns of population and industry obsolete, presented metropolitan areas with a staggering collection of new problems. For the first time, the nation came face to face with mass production of durable goods and what this would imply for the future.

In many other ways the period was one of profound change. The motion picture achieved maturity with both sound and color, and it displaced "live" entertainment from all but a few score theaters in the larger cities. Radio, unknown to the general public at the beginning of 1920, had reached a high level of social importance by the time Franklin Delano Roosevelt's opening words "My friends..." began to be heard in 1932. Automobile buses brought consolidated schools and lessened the inadequacy of rural education. Women gained the vote and assumed a new leadership in changing Victorian ideas of manners and morals. Externally the United States had become the most powerful nation, responsible for the peace and prosperity of the world to a degree that few Americans could recognize and accept.

Franklin D. Roosevelt, portrait by Frank O. Salisbury (1935).
"The Federal Government has always had and still has a continuing responsibility for the broader public welfare.... I pledge you, I pledge myself, to a new deal for the American people."—F. D. Roosevelt (1932).

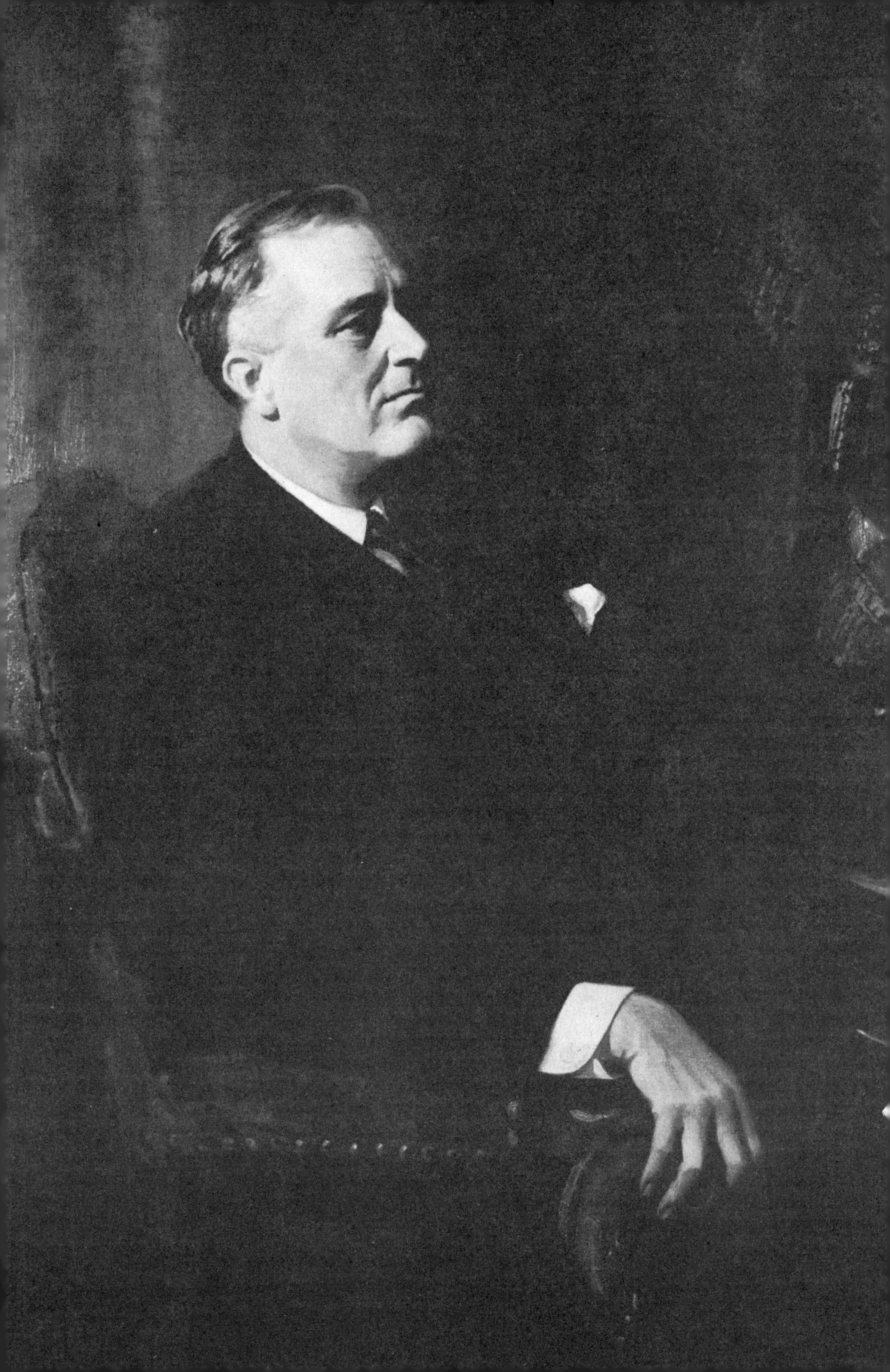

American Tragedy, painting by Philip Evergood (1937). The "Little Steel" companies' stand against unionization brought such violence as the bloody riot at Republic Steel's South Chicago plant on Memorial Day, 1937. Depicted here are police using guns and clubs to break up the union demonstrators. Ten strikers were killed

Lulled, perhaps, by middle-class prosperity, Americans of the twenties seemed as reluctant to face their changed domestic situation as they were to see the implications of their international power. The old faith in the self-regulating economy persisted among businessmen and business-minded intellectuals. A beneficent evolution seemed to be advancing society, and deliberate efforts at planning were viewed as threats to initiative and innovation. But the forces of change could not be pushed aside. Even in the prosperous years the physical situation forced government action in many fields. Expenditures by state and local authorities for roads, sewers, schools, and buildings soared during the twenties, and some local governments went deeply into debt.

The Great Depression of the thirties thrust the idea of the self-regulating economy into the category of attractive but impractical theory. Businessmen joined farmers and workers in demanding government action, and Republicans joined Democrats in formally ushering in the welfare state. From the beginning of 1932 on, regardless of the personal wishes of many political leaders, the federal government was forced to assume responsibility for the nation's economic welfare.

Important as these social and economic changes were, it may be that inner changes in ideas and values were still more important. For more than a generation the traditional patterns of child rearing, schooling, and adult behavior based on Protestant Christian morality had been under attack from a battery of ideas stemming initially from the methods of science. In the twenties the victory of the attitudes of science in large sections of the urban middle and upper classes was fairly complete. Child rearing became experimental and scientifically guided, and schooling became increasingly progressive. Inspired by John Dewey, education for social adjustment rather

(Left) *The Passion of Sacco and Vanzetti,* painting by Ben Shahn (1931-32). This example of "social protest" art portrays the coffined corpses of Sacco and Vanzetti being paid "pious" homage by the Lowell commission, while in the background hangs the portrait of a "self-satisfied" Judge Webster Thayer. (Above) *Tattoo and Haircut,* painting by Reginald Marsh (1932).

than moral training reached its peak and produced a younger generation with less firmly held beliefs.

Two of the most upsetting impacts of science reached most educated adults in the twenties: Freudian psychology and the implications of modern physics. From 1920 on, Freud's ideas of the unconscious and its force in motivating conduct gained wide acceptance. Implicitly Freud ridiculed the hopes for progress through human reason and perfectibility that had so inspired the reformers of the prewar days. Late in the twenties the popularization of mathematical physics forced intellectuals, at least, to recognize still greater inadequacies in human perception and in the simple verbal logic by which men had always reasoned.

The force of this total scientific attack, from child rearing to symbolic logic, on central values of the culture—this "inner revolution"—was accentuated by the economic breakdown of the thirties. To the older generation it seemed nearly impossible to maintain the traditional values of Christian belief; to the younger generation brought up in the atmosphere of science all fixed values seemed questionable. This confusion, far deeper than the economic maladjustment, helps to explain the avidity of intellectuals in the United States and abroad for the "scientific" certainties of Marxism.

In spite of confusion about the nature of man and the universe, many of the traditional values governing American social activity persisted, and some thrived under adversity. The basic beliefs in individualism and freedom of choice were surprisingly resistant to mass unemployment. Radical departures from the traditions of American government never gained any lasting support. In many walks of life the New Deal strengthened the old ideals of equality and democracy. Americans seemed to be striving to retain as much of their heritage as new circumstances would permit.

CHAPTER 19

PROSPERITY IN ISOLATION, 1919-1929

THE SWING TOWARD CONSERVATISM

Postwar Reaction. Nineteen-nineteen was a year of disillusionment. During the war progressives, once satisfied with welfare legislation and national regulation of trusts, had raised their hopes for such fundamental changes as federal control of railroads, shipping, prices, and employment. John Dewey, America's most famous philosopher, had predicted in 1918 that "no matter how many among the special agencies for public control decay with the disappearance of war stress, the movement will never go backward." But during 1919 the movement toward a public-regulated economy not only receded but was lost altogether in a wave of reaction.

Like all sweeping changes in opinion, the swing to conservatism between early 1919 and 1920 had many causes. The unsatisfactory peace in Europe, publicized in the worst light by opponents of the League of Nations, cooled the popular enthusiasm that President Wilson had temporarily aroused. The result appears to have been an apathy about America's role in world affairs that carried over into domestic issues as well.

Along with this indifference to further reform there was undoubtedly a real fear on the part of middle-class Americans that revolution on the Russian model might spread. Socialism had ceased to be a utopian goal, safe to discuss at women's club meetings, and had become a gray world of commissars and secret police supported by the intrigues of a foreign power. As a result, the unprecedented series of strikes in 1919 by which labor kept wages abreast of soaring prices were widely regarded as dangerous indications of revolutionary sentiment. In some cases management publicly condemned the strikers as Reds.

Political demagogues were, of course, ready to ride to power by playing upon such fears. On January 1, 1920, agents of Attorney General A. Mitchell Palmer arrested nearly three thousand allegedly alien radicals and held them without hearings under the Sedition Act of 1918. Friends who subsequently inquired about those arrested were also jailed. The ailing President protested mildly against Palmer's activities, but the anti-radical campaign gained momentum. Of the thousands of aliens rounded up by the Attorney General, 556 were deported, after trial, for radical activity.

Seventeen states passed "criminal syndicalist" laws providing for the arrest of agitators. The New York state legislature carried out a lengthy investigation of revolutionary radicalism and refused to seat Socialist representatives from New York City. Meanwhile, Congress refused to admit Victor Berger from Wisconsin until this very moderate Socialist had again been elected by his Milwaukee constituents.

At the height of this "Red scare," the arrest and conviction of two alien anarchists, Nicola Sacco and Bartolomeo Vanzetti, for the murder of a factory paymaster and guard during a robbery in South Braintree, Massachusetts, turned out to be the *cause célèbre* of the 1920's. Because at the trial Judge Webster Thayer allegedly displayed bias against Sacco and Vanzetti and because the prosecuting attorney, limited by thin evidence, exploited their evasion of the wartime draft and their unpopular opinions in order to prejudice them in the eyes of the jury, many liberals protested that the men had been convicted for their radicalism rather than for the stated crime. In the six years following their conviction in 1921, Judge Thayer denied appeals for a rehearing, the Massachusetts supreme court refused to intervene, and both the governor and a special commission headed by Harvard president A. Lawrence Lowell, after inquiries, found the trial fair and the defendants guilty. In those same years, protest meetings took place all over the world, and prominent men like Albert Einstein and Anatole France gave their support to petitions urging clemency or a retrial. In Massachusetts, however, public opinion remained hostile, and on August 23, 1927, Sacco and Vanzetti were electrocuted in an atmosphere of martyrdom.

The most alarming aspect of the wave of anti-Red hysteria in the 1920's was not the injustices visited upon a few hundred leftists and aliens but the general suppression of free thought that accompanied the unrelenting efforts of the Attorney General and certain "patriotic" societies. Teachers became afraid to impart normal, necessary criticisms of American leaders or society. Business employees were afraid to be associated with men or organizations branded by the superpatriots as subversive. Liberal journals were called revolutionary, and people were afraid to be seen reading them. Compared to the Red scare of the 1950's, that of the early twenties was less serious in its impact on government but probably more repressive in its effect on the ordinary citizen.

In the back country, especially in the South, the hysteria gave a sinister impetus and direction to the Ku Klux Klan, which was revised in 1915 "to unite white male persons, native-born Gentile citizens, who owe no allegiance of any nature to any foreign government, nation, institution, sect, ruler, person or people." The Klan had shown little tendency to grow until the postwar anti-Red campaign got under way, but in 1920 Edward Y. Clarke, a professional organizer and fund raiser, became the Imperial Kleagle and rapidly made the Klan into a powerful force both socially and politically. The Klan, with its unity against Negroes, Catholics (who were held to owe allegiance to a foreign ruler), Jews, and foreigners, grew rapidly, reaching a total of several million members by 1924. Since the initiation fee was $10, large resources were at the disposal of Klan leaders, who used them to influence—in some cases to control—state politics.

At the level of the local den, however, the Klan was largely an organization for leisure time enjoyment, community economic pressure, and irresponsible use of force. A congressional investigation revealed that Negroes and foreigners were intimidated into selling property to Klan members at low figures, and into heeding warnings to avoid business competition. Citizens defending Negroes, foreigners, or Catholics might also incur the vengeance of the Klan. The hooded parades, secret meetings, fiery crosses, beatings, and lynchings given their victims enlivened the otherwise drab existence of many Klansmen.

Against the ominous rise of lower middle-class reaction, the stuff of which fascism was to be made in Germany, must be placed the continuation of liberal or even radical farmer movements in the Northwest. Led by the old Non-Partisan League, a Farmer-Labor party was formed which ran second to the victorious Republicans in the election of 1920 in Minnesota, South Dakota, and Washington. Thus, the decentralized character of American politics sustained minority movements while making it difficult for them to win national power.

Triumph of the Conservatives. In the middle of the confusing year 1920 the two national conventions met to nominate candidates for the presidency. The leading Republican contenders—Governor Frank O. Lowden of Illinois and General Leonard Wood—fought each other to a deadlock. The compromise candidate supported by a group of business representatives and conservative congressional leaders was Senator Warren G. Harding of Ohio, a man virtually unknown to the American public but one who had the gracious, commanding look of a President. For Vice-President the convention nominated Calvin Coolidge, the Massachusetts governor famous for his stand against organized labor in the Boston police strike of 1919.

The Democrats had even greater difficulty in choosing a candidate. During thirty-seven indecisive ballots, Attorney General Palmer, the anti-Red champion, fought William G. McAdoo, the liberal ex-Secretary of the Treasury and son-in-law of Woodrow Wilson. Then the convention compromised on a progressive who had been twice reëlected governor of Ohio, James M. Cox. While Cox was as little known to the general public as Harding, the Democratic ticket was strengthened by the vice-presidential nomination of Assistant Secretary of the Navy Franklin D. Roosevelt.

Partly in deference to President Wilson, Cox and Roosevelt made entry into the League of Nations a major issue of the campaign. The Republicans avoided commitment on the League question and instead advocated higher tariffs and tax reduction. The Republicans, reading the popular temper correctly, were extremely confident. During the campaign Harding stayed on his front porch in Marion, Ohio; his speeches, according to McAdoo, were "an army of pompous phrases moving across the landscape in search of an idea." In spite of—or perhaps because of—the assurance of victory, the Republicans were aided by an $8 million campaign fund.

The Republican landslide was the greatest since the second election of James Monroe. Harding carried every state outside the "solid South," and there he carried Tennessee. He received 61 per cent of the popular vote, as much as Franklin D. Roosevelt was to poll in his greatest victory. In Congress the Republicans could not score quite so great a sweep as the Democrats in 1936, because of the Democratic representatives of the South, but the Republican majority was 167 in the House and 22 in the Senate.

Harding Administration Scandals. Although Harding was probably not far below the average intelligence of the less prominent Presidents of the United States, he was lacking in ideas, vigor, and moral conviction. Easygoing and affable, he delegated all responsibility. Harding appointed old friends to important posts, but he offset these weak appointments by naming Charles E. Hughes Secretary of State; Andrew Mellon, Secretary of the Treasury; Henry A. Wallace, Secretary of Agriculture; and Herbert Hoover, Secretary of Commerce.

Harding's friends, with whom he often played poker late into the night, soon began taking bribes and misusing funds on a scale that could not be concealed. Late in 1922 Harding learned that Charles R. Forbes had stolen millions from the Veterans' Bureau. By the summer of 1923 there was a rumor that the House, now controlled by Democrats and Progressives, might try to impeach Harding. But on August 2, in the midst of the increasing revelations of corruption, Harding died of an apoplectic stroke.

Ultimately investigations and trials revealed that Attorney General Harry M. Daugherty had profited from the enforcement of prohibition and the handling of alien property; Secretary of the Interior Albert B. Fall had received many thousands of dollars from oil men Harry F. Sinclair and E. L. Doheny for leasing them valuable government oil reserves in Teapot Dome, Wyoming, and in Elk Hills, California; Forbes had cost the taxpayers some $250 million more than necessary for hospitals and other veterans' benefits; and many lesser men had profited from the President's lack of judgment and rigor.

With Vice-President Calvin Coolidge now succeeding to the presidency, the Republican party had a man superbly qualified to make amends for the laxity of the Harding administration. Coolidge, a slight, dry-looking, diffident Vermonter who after graduation from Amherst had won success in Massachusetts law and politics, seemed to personify the traditional virtues of thrift and frugality. He would not be betrayed by his intimate friends, because he had none. At a time when business and most of the middle class seemed satisfied with the status quo, Coolidge could be relied upon not to rock the boat.

Republican National Policy. Led for eight years either by Harding, who had been installed by the right wing of the Republican party, or by Coolidge, whom Hoover called a "real conservative," the administration tried to lessen or remove controls over business activity. In this policy the President was often at odds with Democratic-Progressive coalitions in the House and the Senate, but the presidential powers of appointment and veto proved effective weapons in cutting down federal activities.

With the exception of the Shipping Board, the Democrats had liquidated most of the new agencies set up for war purposes and had returned the railroads to their stockholders. Ocean shipping, however, presented special problems. At the end of the war the government owned some two million deadweight tons of hastily constructed freighters which were slow and inefficient in comparison with new turbine or diesel electric vessels coming from English and Continental yards. In addition, United States wages and manning requirements made it impossible to compete on an equal basis with foreign operators. To keep some of the ships at sea the Shipping Board for a decade pursued a policy of selling the freighters for $5 to $10 a ton and granting mail subsidies for operation on strategically important routes.

One of the first conflicts between the conservative President and the less conservative Congress was over the soldiers' bonus bill. This provided a twenty-year endowment policy totaling $1 for each day a veteran had served in the United States and $1.25 for each day overseas. President Harding in 1921 and President Coolidge in 1924 vetoed the bill; the Harding veto was sustained, but a more generous Congress overrode Coolidge's veto.

Immigration Quotas. A major change in American political policy in the 1920's was the regulation of immigration on a quota basis. While the Chinese and Japanese had been excluded by diplomatic agreements and other Asian and African people had not migrated voluntarily in any large numbers, the United States had held the door open for most Europeans. Organized labor and "old stock" Americans had long tried to restrict this vast flood, which in peaceful and prosperous years brought over a million newcomers annually. The deluge of Russian and other eastern European peoples which resumed in 1919, mounting unemployment in late 1920, and the Red scare led Congress to restrict annual immigration to 3 per cent of the people born in a particular foreign area and resident in the United States in 1910. Opposed vigorously in Congress only by Catholics, the bill met a veto by Wilson. Passed again in the special session of 1921, it was signed by Harding. During the first year of operation the restrictions reduced immigration from around the million level to 300,000.

To organized labor and nativists, however, the number of "undesirable" or "unassimilable" immigrants from eastern Europe still seemed too large. The National Origins Act of 1924 set up a temporary quota of 2 per cent of the foreign born of 1890 and established a commission to work out quotas by a formula based on numbers of foreign-born over the whole range of United States census data. The bill excluded Orientals; Japan, which had been voluntarily restricting emigration to the United States, regarded this as an affront to national dignity, but the Japanese protest was brushed aside by Congress. The final report of the Commission on National Origins, which reduced southern and eastern European quotas to negligible size and held the total to about 150,000 annually, was enacted into law in 1929.

Tariffs, Taxes, and Federal Regulation. High tariff continued to be a major Republican policy. Ironically, the protectionist group in Congress in the early 1920's was led by Midwestern farmers who feared Canadian, Irish, and Argentine competition. Their first bill for increased agricultural duties was vetoed by Wilson on the basis that American farmers also needed foreign markets. The Harding administration favored higher duties, but the increases in the Fordney-McCumber Tariff of 1922 were generally moderate. Although agricultural products gained protection, the principle of a tariff that would equalize prices of domestic and foreign products was generally maintained. The farm bloc managed to get some manufactures like shoes and wagons on the free list. On the other hand, some industries received very high protection. The Tariff Commission still had the right to recommend changes and the President had power to alter the rates by 50 per cent. Neither Harding nor Coolidge made important use of this power.

The Republican Presidents appointed conservative, business-minded members to federal regulatory commissions. This led to such a relaxation in vigilance that, in the words of a famous authority, the Federal Trade Commission "tried to commit *hari-kari*"—to cease functioning as a regulatory agency. Moreover, the antitrust division of the Justice Department seldom prosecuted mergers. The Federal Power Commission, established in 1920 to regulate interstate electric power, did little to justify its existence. The efforts of the Interstate Commerce Commission to bring about railroad consolidation and recapture excess earnings were without significant effect.

Freed from fear of federal regulation, businessmen also were gradually relieved of the higher taxes of the war period. Andrew Mellon, formerly head of the Aluminum Company of America and one of the richest men in the world, believed sincerely that high income taxes retarded economic growth. As Secretary of the Treasury he immediately sponsored a tax bill that repealed the excess profits tax and sharply reduced the surtaxes on personal income. After amendments by the Republican farm bloc and by Democrats in the Senate, the Revenue Act of 1921 repealed the excess profits tax but reduced the maximum surtax on personal income only from 65 to 50 per cent. Nevertheless, since revenues steadily exceeded expenses, there was increasing pressure for tax reduction. By 1929 four subsequent revenue acts had reduced the maximum surtax to 20 per cent and the effective initial rate to ⅜ of 1 per cent. The tax on corporate income was slightly reduced, to 11 per cent.

These tax reductions, which retarded repayment of the national debt and left it at $16 billion at the beginning of the Great Depression, have been vigorously criticized. Yet the administration faced a real economic dilemma. To have repaid the debt more rapidly would have released as much, or more, cash to the money markets than came from the untaxed savings of high incomes. Only if the government could have found a way to use the money so as to increase lower incomes or to pay it to some of the two million unemployed could the surplus have been kept from feeding the inflation in stocks and mortgage bonds. Such a fiscal policy would have been directly contrary to the firmly held beliefs of the conservative majority and, as an explicit policy, probably beyond the imagination of most of their opponents.

One proposed use for federal funds which would not have involved the government in new types of business or competed with private industry was the support of farm incomes. Farmers had been led by the demands of World War I to expand wheat acreage, which in view of long-run trends was already excessive in 1914. After the collapse of the reconstruction boom in 1920, farm prices fell behind the cost of things the farmer had to buy, and both foreign and domestic markets for staples such as wheat and cotton declined. Farmers were not participating in the general prosperity.

A plan put forward by farm machinery manufacturers Hugh S. Johnson and George N. Peek in 1922 did not involve federal subsidy but merely required a federal marketing agency that could maintain a domestic price in excess of the world price. Written into the McNary-Haugen Bill and endorsed by practically all farmer organizations, the proposal was resisted by conservative Republicans as a dangerous extention of federal power. The bill was passed in 1926 and again in 1927 but killed both times by a Coolidge veto.

Although by the late 1930's the Farm Bureau Federation, the chief agricultural pressure group, was to seem conservative, in the 1920's it formed a rallying point for liberals. In spite of the conservative presidential leadership, progressives of both parties maintained their strength in Congress. The greatest obstacle to liberal or progressive victories during the decade was probably not the relatively small group of conservatives with substantial incomes but the general political apathy bred by prosperity from 1923 to 1929. Presidential elections drew only a little more than half the voters to the polls: Coolidge was sustained in the 1924 presidential election by a mere 28 per cent of the possible electorate.

EXPANSION OF GOVERNMENT ACTIVITIES

Domestic Regulation Increases. Even within the administration there were men like Charles E. Hughes and Herbert Hoover who did not share the Coolidge standpat type of conservatism. Hughes' innovations in foreign policy will be discussed shortly. Herbert Hoover, as Secretary of Commerce, tried to bring more efficiency into business operations. To avoid destructive competition he urged small companies to have trade associations administer their mutual concerns, and he invited them to post their prices with the Commerce Department and to refrain from secret rebates. To lower production costs he put his influence behind the movement for standard sizes. The number of shapes of bottles and the various sizes of bricks, for example, were both cut 90 per cent. After unsuccessfully preaching self-regulation to the young air-transport and radio industries, his department established regulatory agencies in 1926 and 1927 respectively. In these directions Hoover was a planner, but, as he saw it, he was using the power of government primarily to suggest better voluntary planning to private industry.

State and local authorities, still the most important forms of government, were led into a great expansion of their operations. Increasing high school education, in particular, demanded new buildings and bigger school budgets. Skyscrapers concentrated so many workers in the centers of the largest cities that new public transportation was required. On the other hand, automobiles moved so many families to the open areas of the cities or suburbs that new streets and sewers were continually needed. Some states, such as New York, increased the scope and size of their expenditures for welfare. New laws or municipal ordinances regulating business practices, sanitation, and housing required new bureaus and squads of inspectors. From all of these needs of a growing industrial society the expenses of government soared. Between 1922 and 1927 the annual cost of state and local government rose nearly 40 per cent, and the rise had undoubtedly passed 50 per cent by 1929. The debts of these governments increased even faster, up nearly 50 per cent from 1922 to 1927 and perhaps by two thirds, had figures been collected, by 1929. It is also worth remembering that in 1929 these governments cost about two and a half times as much to run as the federal government and had about twice as many civilian employees, exclusive of school teachers. Thus what appears on the federal level to have been a period of low government expenditure and reduction of debt was *in toto* one of rapid increase in expenditure and dangerous accumulation of local indebtedness.

Security in the Pacific. While there was a vigorous movement for the League of Nations and world peace, most of the minority of Americans who thought about foreign relations probably wanted to avoid being involved in either European or Far Eastern affairs. The war against Germany was ended by a resolution of Congress on July 2, 1921, and separate treaties were negotiated with the new governments of Germany, Austria, and Hungary, but Far Eastern problems were not settled.

Meanwhile the Navy Department had plans for building the world's largest battle fleet. In spite of congressional refusal to pass the big-navy bills, England and Japan were deeply worried over the possibility of having to compete with the United States in naval construction. Therefore, they readily accepted Secretary of State Hughes' invitation to meet in Washington in 1921 to discuss naval disarmament. Since a naval agreement would have to be linked with treaties establishing and guaranteeing Far Eastern arrangements, France, Italy, Belgium, the Netherlands, and Portugal, nations with Asiatic territories, were invited together with China to the conference.

Early in 1922 Secretary Hughes led the way to a naval agreement whereby England, Japan, and the United States scrapped hundreds of thousands of tons of battleships, afloat or in construction, and agreed to limit capital ships to 525,000 tons each for England and the United States and 315,000 tons for Japan. To secure Japan's interests in the western Pacific each party agreed not to fortify new bases or enlarge old ones. World War II was to demonstrate that this arrangement could, as planned, give Japan an initial supremacy in its nearby waters. After some argument, France and Italy joined in the treaty, each limiting its capital ships to 175,000 tons. A new Four-Power Pact (United States, British Empire, France, Japan) ended the Anglo-Japanese Alliance and pledged the powers to respect each other's possessions and rights in the Pacific. A Nine-Power Pact, also concluded during the Washington Conference, affirmed the sovereignty, independence, and administrative and territorial integrity of China. The American policy of an "open door" for Chinese trade was reaffirmed.

War Debts and International Cooperation. The Washington treaties established a system of security for Asia such as the Treaty of Versailles was presumed to have done for Europe, but the latter had a major weakness: an unrealistic structure of reparations and war debts. In 1921 Germany was forced to accept a reparations commission bill for $33 billion, but no such sum could be transferred in a few decades from one European country to the others without severely disrupting the economies involved. Similarly the United States tried to collect war debts of $4.6 billion from England, $4 billion from France, and $2 billion from Italy. The European states advised a general cancellation of all international payments that would endanger normal economic growth, but the American Presidents from Wilson to Roosevelt insisted on the principle of collection.

Since such sums could be paid only in goods and since United States tariffs limited imports, payments were regularly more than balanced by new American lending and investment abroad. Throughout the decade bankers sold annually about $1 billion worth of foreign government, municipal, and corporate bonds to American investors. This was a profitable system for the bankers, and it allowed United States manufacturers to maintain large exports, but it meant that world financial stability depended on continued prosperity and an easy money market in the United States.

From the start, Germany was unable to pay the reparations assessed by the commission. In 1924 the so-called Dawes Plan, devised by Owen D. Young and Charles G. Dawes from the United States, cut reparations to what seemed like a manageable level. In 1929 the Young Plan further reduced payments. By now, the $33 billion bill had shrunk to about $2 billion. During the 1920's the Allies paid the United States about $2.6 billion in war debts, and the United States loaned Germany some $2.5 billion, 80 per cent of which went to the Allies. Therefore, in fact, there was nearly a mutual balancing. The Allies paid the United States, which loaned to Germany, which paid reparations to Allies, and the cycle continued. But the American investors and banks that had advanced the money were left with bonds that soon defaulted on their interest payments.

Meanwhile, the United States pursued a rather uncertain course of international cooperation. Secretary of State Hughes started the practice of sending "unofficial observers" to League of Nations sessions and to meetings of the principal League committees, but isolationists in the Senate prevented the United States from joining the World Court. This, however, did not prevent Americans, as individuals, serving as justices. In 1928 Frank B. Kellogg, who in 1925 had succeeded Hughes as Secretary of State, took the lead in negotiating a general agreement to outlaw war as an instrument of national policy. The Pact of Paris, or Kellogg-Briand Pact, was signed ultimately by all the great powers, but Kellogg regarded the pledge as more valuable for appeasing peace sentiment at home than for influencing foreign nations. Providing no means of applying collective sanctions against an aggressor, the pact was an idealistic but empty gesture.

Paradoxically, the idealistic foreign policy of Woodrow Wilson had left the United States deeply involved in occupations and controversies in the Caribbean area. United States troops were in Haiti, Nicaragua, and the Dominican Republic, and diplomatic relations with Mexico had been suspended. On the South American mainland, hostility toward United States occupations interfered with both trade and investment.

Republican Leadership Reaffirmed. In the depression year of 1922 discontented agrarian and labor elements met in a Conference for Progressive Political Action. Continuing its meetings into 1924, the conference agreed to support the presidential nomination of Senator Robert M. La Follette in the Republican convention and, if defeated there, to organize a third party with La Follette as their candidate.

Obviously the progressive minority had no chance of winning the Republican nomination, but they might have been captured by the Democrats if that party had supported an advanced liberal ticket. The Democratic party, however, was disastrously split over such issues as prohibition, the Ku Klux Klan, Catholicism, and immigration restriction. William G. McAdoo, Wilson's son-in-law, was in reality a liberal who might have received wide support, but he had been the lawyer for E. L. Doheny in the scandalous leasing of government oil lands. The liberals, therefore, gave their support to Governor Alfred E. Smith of New York, who because of his urban, Catholic, and immigrant connections was unacceptable to the Southern delegates. Neither McAdoo nor Smith could garner the two-thirds majority necessary for nomination, and on the one-hundred-and-third ballot John W. Davis, formerly of West Virginia, was chosen. Davis, by then a prominent New York corporation lawyer, suited neither major group, and his defeat in the prosperous year of 1924 was a foregone conclusion.

When the Republican convention met and nominated Coolidge on the first ballot, the Progressives held their own convention and put forward La Follette. Supported by the American Federation of Labor, many Western farm organizations, and the Socialist party, La Follette ran on a platform advocating the type of action that Europeans called social-democratic. Nationalization was to apply only to railroads and hydroelectric power; injunctions in labor disputes were to be effectively forbidden; and Congress was to be given power to overrule the Supreme Court.

Coolidge swept the election with 15,718,000 popular votes to 8,385,000 for Davis and 4,831,000 for La Follette. The latter carried only Wisconsin and Davis won only the solid South. The Progressive party had failed to develop the strength necessary for survival.

Few American Presidents have enjoyed four such prosperous, peaceful, and generally pleasant years as those from 1924 to 1928. Coolidge could easily have been renominated and reelected had he chosen to run for a second elected term in 1928. But after keeping the bosses in doubt long enough to preserve his influence in the convention, Coolidge gave his support to Herbert Hoover. Quickly nominated, Hoover ran on a platform of continuing the Harding-Coolidge policies. With these, he said, "we shall soon, with the help of God, be in sight of the day when poverty shall be banished from this nation."

The Democratic managers probably had little hope of defeating a strong Republican, but they hoped that an unusual candidate might bring new voters to the polls. Such reasoning may explain the swing to Governor Smith, who had so many obvious disadvantages as a national candidate. The Democratic platform scarcely differed from the Republican, and on economic questions Smith differed little from Hoover.

Smith made John J. Raskob, a fellow Catholic and chairman of General Motors, the head of the Democratic committee. Raskob gave the utmost assurance to business that there would be no upsetting changes.

Aside from the immense support given the Republicans by the boom prosperity, the issues came to be Catholicism and prohibition. Smith could do nothing about the former except give assurances of his independence from Rome and his religious tolerance, which apparently had little effect in the strongly Protestant back country. In the belief that labor and many businessmen were now in favor of repeal of the Eighteenth Amendment, Smith departed from the plank in the party platform that had been inserted to win the support of the dry South and campaigned strongly against prohibition.

While probably no candidate could have defeated Hoover in the year 1928, Smith lost or miscalculated on all fronts save one. His "me-tooism" in support of business probably changed few votes. His Catholicism and antiprohibition sentiments lost seven southern states and, at the most, gained only two northern ones. But he did have an appeal to the urban masses. This urban swing, scarcely noticeable in the Hoover landslide, was a portent of the basic change in party strength that was to come from the increase in urban Democrats in the decades ahead.

High Hopes for a Prosperous Nation. In his inaugural address Hoover said, "I have no fears for the future of our country, it is bright with hope." His *Memoirs* also show the high hopes with which he started his administration: "Mr. Coolidge was reluctant to undertake much that was either new or cost money, and by 1929 many things were already fourteen years overdue." He had a number of plans for bringing more efficiency into government activity, but his first major act, in calling a special congressional session to redeem

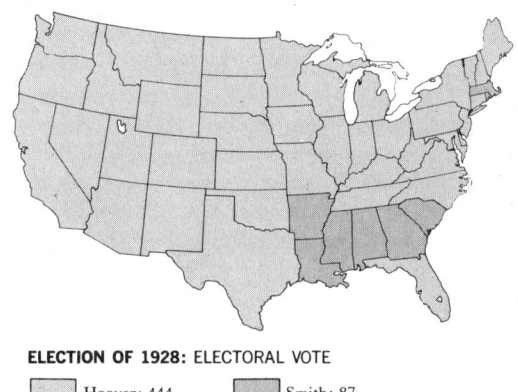

ELECTION OF 1928: ELECTORAL VOTE

Hoover: 444   Smith: 87

Republican promises to farmers, unfortunately misfired. The President sponsored the Smoot-Hawley Tariff bill to raise the rates on agricultural products, but when the bill finally passed the Senate in June 1930 it carried higher rates on numerous manufactured products and raised the general level of rates on dutiable articles about 25 per cent. This was not what the President had intended, but to give assurance to business he signed the bill. Meanwhile, other nations had been raising their tariffs, some in retaliation for the United States' action, and the outlook for world trade and repayment of international obligations steadily grew darker.

In place of the McNary-Haugen scheme, the administration planned to aid the farmer by the Agricultural Marketing Act of 1929. This originally provided for loans to aid cooperative selling, but the progressives added a provision for the use of federal money to stabilize the market price of grain. For these purposes a Federal Farm Board was given a revolving fund of $500 million, the largest single appropriation up to that time for nonmilitary purposes. The plan for buying grain to raise domestic prices and reselling when the market could absorb the surplus might have worked for a time had there been rapid world-wide recovery in 1930. But since the trend toward oversupply in wheat already seemed clear, this cure through manipulating the market was at best a makeshift expedient.

In the effort to bring back prosperity after the panics of 1929, most of President Hoover's plans for efficiency and mild reform were abandoned. "Instead of being able to devote my four years wholly to these purposes," he lamented, "I was overtaken by the economic hurricane. . . . Then the first need was economic recovery and employment." Fearing that reform would upset business and deepen the depression, the President became as conservative as his predecessors.

SOCIAL CHANGE

Motorization and Urbanization. While the advent of radio and the progress in electronics promised great future changes, more obvious and immediate changes in American society centered around the automobile. Up until World War I automobiles had been chiefly used for the recreation of the upper middle class. In 1917 fewer than one farm family in six had an automobile, and in the nation as a whole there were fewer than five million cars. With only four hundred thousand trucks and too few buses to make a census category, these forms of transport were negligible economically and socially.

By 1930 two thirds of the farms, probably all of the prosperous commercial farms, had automobiles. The nation had about 23 million passenger cars. Since there were only about 26 million households, and many prosperous families in big cities did not use private automobiles, the United States had nearly achieved the goal of a car in the garage of every family that wanted one. Even more spectacular than the fivefold increase in passenger cars was the ninefold rise in the number of trucks. Nearly four million commercial vehicles, of which forty thousand were buses, signaled the beginning of the change to a society built around motor transport.

In this new geography main highway intersections would replace villages as shopping centers, cities would be within easy reach of farms, factories would move from the congested areas of cities to the country, and consolidated grammar and high schools would collect children by bus from miles around. Few places would remain remote from the pressures and advantages of an urbanized culture.

The "Automotive Social Ladder." One of the cultural pressures directly connected with the automobile was its rise as a sign of social status. The American automobile, to be sure, depreciated rather rapidly, and for reliable service replacement was desirable in about five to seven years. But social considerations worked for even briefer ownership. To have a new car was a symbol of success and prosperity, and the bigger and more expensive the car the higher the presumed status of the owner. For urban and suburban apartment dwellers the automobile took the place of an elaborate house as a mark of social standing. Only farmers and the very rich seem to have been relatively immune to such pressures.

Quickly observing this "automotive social ladder," producers began to differentiate each year's model and to carry on the most intensive advertising of any makers of durable goods. There were real physical satisfactions in better performance and an increased feeling of adequacy by encasing oneself in a heavy, powerful automobile, but the lure of social approval was perhaps the strongest force behind the continuous demand for new and bigger cars. Since buyers seldom had saved the money to pay cash, the automobile became the most important item in a rapid spread of installment buying.

While the spread of slums had shown the inadequacy of American municipal planning for nearly a century, the automobile more than the slum lay back of the rapid rise of planning commissions and authorities. Although zoning was initiated in New York in 1916 without particular regard to motor transport, the latter, by opening all areas to all types of use, led to the rapid spread of zoning to other cities. The steady migration to major metropolitan areas during the twenties also forced planning on reluctant municipal authorities. By the end of the decade 37 per cent of the city population of the United States lived in zoned communities.

Automobiles and trucks required new bridges, tunnels, and thoroughfares into central city business districts. The Port of New York Authority, established by a "treaty" between New York and New Jersey in 1921, initiated interstate agencies to plan transportation. In spite of such limited recognition of a growing automobile traffic problem, however, urban efforts to alleviate either traffic or slum congestion in the prosperous twenties could be characterized as too little and too late.

Women Become First-Class Citizens. The Nineteenth Amendment, ratified by the states in 1920, established women's right to vote but was symbolic of much broader changes in feminine activity. The nineteenth-century image of the ideal woman had been of one waited on by servants, protected from the world, and limited in ideas and ability. Suffragettes before World War I were attacked as vigorously by other women who clung to the nineteenth-century ideal as by politicians who shied away from the challenge of a new electorate.

Early in the century upper middle-class women had started to lead a more vigorous and less decorous life. They had learned to drive automobiles, smoke cigarettes, and embrace men in the modern dance. On a more serious level they went to college in increasing numbers, became doctors, dentists, and lawyers, promoted organizations for the general welfare, and took an active part in social reform. The cut in the supply of domestic servants at low wages brought about by the war and by immigration restriction further challenged the middle-class ideal of female gentility. Meanwhile, the trend to apartments and smaller houses with electrical aids such as the vacuum cleaner restored some of the leisure lost from lack of servants.

Both the rise of managerial and office employment in relation to that in the plant and the increase in service in relation to manufacturing opened new job opportunities for women. There was, therefore, a gradual but steady rise in the percentage of working women, together with a shift in their activity from domestic service to store and office work. By the 1920's married women working at white-collar jobs were no longer regarded as having lost some of their middle-class respectability; on the contrary, there was a tendency to admire them for their independence.

Independence was the watchword of the "new woman." Upper middle-class women reaching maturity in the early 1920's were determined to live their lives without regard to the older traditions of manners or morals. Freudian psychology gave them a weapon for attacking the old double standard of sex relations and for proclaiming their equal right to infidelity and divorce. They also insisted on their right to go anywhere unchaperoned, to drink, smoke, and swear in public, and generally to behave as men did.

The decorous manners of the Victorian era seemed to disintegrate before the careless onslaught of the emancipated younger generation, but other forces of society speeded the process.

The heightened tempo of manufacturing, transportation, and communication was reflected in social life. The amenities of older societies seemed cumbersome and slightly ridiculous. Migration to cities and from one neighborhood to another led to easy acquaintance and friendship based largely on proximity or convenience.

Prohibition. Superimposed on a society that was undergoing fundamental and confusing changes was America's greatest experiment in increased government control of personal habits. Few nations had a history of more consistent attachment to the consumption of alcohol than the United States. In the decades prior to 1918, however, there had been a trend toward more drinking of beer and wine and less recorded consumption of hard liquor. It seems possible that banning or making the purchase of hard liquor difficult might have produced a more temperate nation without much public resistance, but this experiment was never tried. Instead, the combination of war hysteria over shortage of grain, anti-German sentiment against the brewers, and leadership of the temperance organizations by bone-dry fanatics led to an unsuccessful effort to ban all alcoholic drinks.

The Eighteenth Amendment left interpretation of what was an "intoxicating" beverage to Congress. The Volstead Act of 1919, vetoed by Wilson and repassed by the necessary two-thirds majority, set the limit of alcoholic content at $\frac{1}{2}$ of 1 per cent. While farmers could continue to make wine and other drinks at home, as they always had, city dwellers were now denied the possibility of legally buying even the weakest form of beer. As a result, the big urban areas that had opposed the prohibition movement now refused to abide by the law. And as is usual under such circumstances, there was no difficulty in finding entrepreneurs ready to supply the illicit demand.

It is an interesting paradox of the triumph of the prohibitionists in Congress that, having passed the amendment and the Volstead Act, they settled back and made no great effort to enforce the law. The number of federal agents began at about 1500 and rose to only a little over 2800 at the peak. With a top salary of around $3000 it was not surprising that these men were often corruptible, but even had they been entirely diligent they were too few even to check the imports of liquor. Furthermore, the local authorities in "wet" areas gave them little or no help. In 1923 New York state repealed its law for local enforcement, and politicians in other big metropolitan areas connived, almost openly, with the men supplying the liquor.

As a result, an illegal traffic in alcohol, liquor, and beer, worth hundreds of millions of dollars annually, fell into the hands of underworld leaders. The terms "racket" and "racketeer" came into use, and these newly rich gangsters soon found that they could extort fees for protection from other businesses besides liquor selling. Laundries, dry cleaners, and garages—trades that handled valuable goods belonging to customers—were particularly easy victims of intimidation. Thousands of small proprietors paid weekly fees to keep their stores from being burned.

"Where were the police?" one would logically ask. The answer often was: in the pay of racketeers. Al Capone, head of the liquor racket in Chicago, was as powerful politically as anyone in the municipal government of that metropolis, and he was the undisputed ruler of the suburban city of Cicero. In the suburbs of other great cities such as New York the liquor interests often controlled county or municipal politics. The sheriffs or police chiefs received a portion of the weekly collections from speakeasies and worked against the occasional federal agent who sought to get evidence of violation of the law.

In addition to corrupting politics and breeding contempt for the law, the Volstead Act altered the habits of the upper class in an unwholesome way. Business executives in their clubs and homes ostentatiously flouted the law. Men who had scarcely drunk at all before prohibition now felt it obligatory from the standpoint of social prestige to have a well-stocked cellar and to serve liquor on social occasions. Taking the cue from their elders and spurred by the normal rebelliousness of youth, teen-agers, college students, and young married groups sought to outdo one another in consumption of alcohol.

The national picture was confusing. In dry areas prohibition appeared to work at least as well as it had before the amendment. In wet urban areas, less well represented in Congress, prohibition appeared to be undermining both the young elite and honest government. Some manufacturers thought there was less drinking among their employees, while others were sure there was more. The Republican administration continued vaguely to sponsor "the noble experiment" while the Wickersham Commission, appointed by Hoover, gave an unfavorable report in January 1931 but illogically concluded that prohibition should be continued. In the end it was not moral or temperance issues but the depression and need for government revenue in the desperate year of 1932 that apparently tipped the balance in favor of legalizing the liquor business. There was no serious effort to substitute a new law permitting beer and wine for the unworkable Volstead Act. The Eighteenth Amendment itself was quickly repealed by the Twenty-first in 1933, and the temperance problem was returned to the states.

ECONOMIC CHANGE

A Slower Rate of Growth. In the long run, economic growth depends upon the making of more and more capital goods such as buildings, factories, roads, and machines. For the decade 1919 to 1928 "net capital formation" (that is, the creation of new capital goods) in relation to national income was 14 per cent less than in the previous decade and nearly 18 per cent less than two decades earlier. During the years 1924 to 1929 the annual investment in new capital goods was actually falling. On the other hand, the income of the wealthiest classes was increasing and their savings were rising; these savings or funds for investment were by 1924 beginning to run ahead of the rate at which industry and business were willing or able to use them. In other words, there were more savings each year than there were productive new securities to be bought. As a result, investors were competing for the few available securities, and the price of existing securities went up. A large part of the nation's savings were being used for speculation.

But why should the rate of creation of capital goods slow down when there was plenty of saved money to pay for them? Two explanations can be offered. One is that since there was little change in real wages or salaries from 1924 to 1929, consumer demand did not rise rapidly enough to encourage industrial expansion. The other explanation is more speculative. Changes in technology occur in incalculable ways. Some that promise substantial profits require large new investments, as in the case of railroads, while others do not, as in the case of the phonograph. A series of technological innovations requiring large investment absorb savings and labor and produce an expanding economy; but few major capital-absorbing innovations in technology occurred in the 1920's. To be sure, some of the older developments such as electrification, roads for automobiles, and improvements in steel production were still going forward, but their ranks were not added to substantially, and after 1927 there was a slowing down of the combined rate of growth.

Technological Advance. While the new technological developments of the 1920's did not increase the rate of capital investment, they considerably raised productivity. By 1929 about a thousand large firms were supporting some type of research. Better control of industrial products through careful cost accounting, spot testing, and control laboratories (collectively referred to as "quality control") led to higher efficiency.

Radio broadcasting and air travel first reached the general public in this decade, and automobiles and electricity came into general use. Until 1919 the federal government forbade private use of radio. Broadcasts by Westinghouse's station KDKA of the presidential election of 1920 demonstrated the great public possibilities of the new medium of communication, and within the next few years the industry assumed the general pattern that was to remain for decades: competing national networks would subsist on substantial revenue from large advertisers, and high priced performers would offer variety programs. By 1930 twelve million American families, about 40 per cent of the total, could tune in Rudy Vallee, Eddie Cantor, or sports announcer Graham McNamee on their radio sets.

The airplane, invented before World War I, had never attracted much interest in America. During the war the government made an effort to catch up with European development but produced few planes before the Armistice led to cancellation of contracts. The Post Office started an experimental airmail route between New York and Washington in 1918 and after six years extended service to Chicago and San Francisco. Meanwhile, commercial plane production was negligible, and flying was limited to selling rides at airfields and local fairs. In 1925 the government first made an effort to build commercial transport by allowing the Post Office to grant air-mail contracts to private firms. The following year Congress gave general regulatory authority to the Commerce Department.

The regular use of air service in Europe and a series of spectacular overseas flights culminating in Charles A. Lindbergh's solo crossing of the Atlantic in 1927 gave some Americans confidence enough to travel by plane. Between 1928 and 1930 passengers increased from 1400 to 32,000, and revenue miles flown multiplied about thirty times to a total of 4.3 million. In spite of the depression the young industry continued to grow, but in 1940 the 100 million passenger miles flown were almost negligible compared to the 24 billion passenger miles by rail and the incalculable travel by private car.

In the automotive industry, even in the prosperous years of the 1920's, the smaller assemblers of cars had been dropping out. The early years of the depression reduced the number of competitors to less than a dozen producing similar cars within four or five price ranges. Ford finally had to give up his famous Model T in 1927 and bring out the Model A, a car similar to those of his chief competitors. This episode temporarily convinced American manufacturers that in new cars the public wanted size and luxury rather than cheapness.

Both homes with electricity and total consumption of electrical energy doubled from 1920 to 1930. In urban and suburban areas five sixths of all residences came to have electricity, but farm electrification was only beginning. In 1920 1.4 per cent of farms had electricity and by 1930 only 10 per cent.

The lack of substantial farm improvement during the 1920's illustrates the lag that often occurs between new technological possibilities and their commercial use. Declining markets for the great staple crops—corn, cotton, and wheat—and an excessive number of farm operators left the average farmer without capital or incentive for experimentation with new technology. Yet during the decade advances were made in soil biology and chemistry which made diversification of crops much safer than formerly; hybrid seeds were developed which could increase both corn and wheat yield and resistance to unfavorable weather; and all-purpose tractors were reduced in size and cost. It took World War II with its excessive demand for farm products to bring this new knowledge and technology into general use.

The Decline of Craft Unionism. World War I and the postwar boom brought union membership to a peak of five million workers in 1920, about 12 per cent of the total labor force. While this was a record for the United States, by comparison with western Europe the level of organization was low. A major reason was that American organizations were largely limited to the skilled crafts and older types of industrial activity. The new mass production industries of the twentieth century, such as automobiles, chemicals, and electrical equipment, had successfully resisted efforts at organization.

The union situation of 1920 was essentially unstable. Many union members in war industries and postwar construction soon had to seek other jobs. Employer organizations, held back since 1917 by government policy and competition for workers, were now ready to marshal business-minded people against organized labor. During the Red scare it was easy to convince the middle class that unions had radical intentions.

The American Plan, which was sponsored by the National Association of Manufacturers, representing small and medium-sized business, and which was vigorously pursued by various trade and employer organizations, called for the open shop. Some of the organizations associated with the movement insisted that their members should not enter into any union contracts. Advertisements were placed in newspapers denouncing the closed shop (one restricted to union members) as un-American. Labor spies were hired in larger numbers than before to detect union organizers.

During the war, big companies had established personnel departments to control hiring and firing and to study the causes of labor turnover. While no real theoretical progress was made until the end of the decade, when Professor Elton Mayo developed theories regarding worker morale, the new thought given to labor problems in some big companies brought improvements in plant conditions, plans for incentive pay, group insurance, pensions, and a spread of employee magazines and recreational facilities.

One important "welfare" device for preventing the organization of workers by national unions was the employee representation plan or company union. The government demand that contractors in World War I enter into collective bargaining with their employees led 125 of the largest companies to organize their own unions with some 400,000 members. Since these unions and their officers were controlled and supported financially by the companies, they were not generally regarded as true representatives of labor. Yet in the twenties they constituted the one growing area of labor organization. By 1928 it was estimated that company union membership had grown to 1.5 million, half that of the A.F.L.

In spite of the American Plan, welfare devices, and competing company unions, it may still be argued that the independent unions declined because of the depression of 1920 to 1922 and because business was growing away from the old skilled crafts. The immediate drop in union membership during the two years of depression was 1.4 million.

Two hundred thousand more members were lost during the prosperous years from 1923 to 1929. By 1930 less than 7 per cent of the labor force was organized in independent unions.

Only in coal and textiles were labor leaders engaged in vigorous campaigns during the mid-twenties. Both industries had the same basic problems: the southern areas were not unionized, and Communists were unwilling to support the existing union leadership. While John L. Lewis was able to preserve the United Mine Workers' bargaining position in the older areas, he had to agree to wage cuts during the years of high national prosperity.

Neither the United Textile Workers nor its communist-led rival, the National Textile Workers' Union, was able successfully to invade the South and unionize the new mills. With lower wages in that region the industry continued to drift away from New England and the Middle Atlantic states.

As militancy declined in the ranks of labor, two trends were evident—one toward cooperation with employers, the other toward surrender of union leadership to racketeers. Where employers were small and often poorly informed, as in the clothing business, unions could help to improve shop practices and overall efficiency. Even some of the large railroads found that union-management cooperation increased productivity in their shops. But looking at the labor scene as a whole, the areas of advancing cooperation were small. In unions where the complacency of the mid-twenties made the members careless about attending meetings, dishonest local officials, supported by so-called guerrillas, built up machines that the rank and file dared not oppose. Often these labor racketeers dealt secretly with employers, taking payments from them to prevent the union members from demanding wage increases. The twenties were not a decade of pleasant prosperity for organized labor.

THE NEW ERA IN BUSINESS

Managerial Enterprise. As usual in times of business prosperity, the number of firms and enterprises grew faster than the population as a whole. In 1920 there were probably fewer than 2.5 million firms, in 1929 over 3 million. About two thirds of all firms were in trade and service, and very few of these had more than two or three employees. The overall growth figures, however, conceal a great deal of routine change. Every year of the twenties thirty to fifty thousand new firms started, and every year a slightly smaller number left the business scene. While adequately capitalized small companies that were started by men who knew the business they were entering had good chances of success, a large percentage of potential entrepreneurs lacked both qualifications. At the top, a few medium-sized or large firms disappeared each year through mergers, but these equaled only 1 or 2 per cent of the new firms starting up.

The American business structures appeared to have reached a plateau of stability. Big companies continued to dominate highly capitalized industries in manufacturing, railroads, and utilities. But the rise of true monopoly had been checked by antitrust laws. While in industries dominated by a few companies competition in price was avoided, competition in quality and marketing was generally vigorous.

By the 1920's the stock of most very large companies was widely held and neither the officers nor the directors of the company owned any considerable percentage of the shares. The chief officers were chosen from among men who had made successful careers in management and were professional executives rather than either relatives of an owner or large personal investors. The connection of such men with profit was indirect. Profit for the company was a mark of success, a guarantee of security, and a fund from which larger salaries could be drawn, but it did not directly enrich the non-owning manager. These men were interested in building strong organizations capable of weathering bad times, rather than in reaping quick profits in the market. They favored spending earnings for research, expert advice, and improvement of company morale, rather than for extra dividends to the stockholders. As a result, the common stock dividends of the biggest companies tended to move toward moderate, stable rates rather than to fluctuate with profits.

While scarcely a thousand companies were big enough to have professional, bureaucratic management remote from control by owners, the thousands of top executives of these big companies were leaders of business opinion. Executives commanded specialized knowledge and expert staff work; they hired the best lawyers, lobbyists, accountants, and engineers; and their assistants wrote for them speeches and articles analyzing business problems. Hence America seemed much more a land of big business than was the case statistically.

Shaping Public Opinion. George Creel's Committee on Public Information and similar European agencies during World War I provided new ideas on how to create favorable opinion. About 1920 Edward Bernays and Ivy Lee began to call themselves public relations counselors. Soon the major advertising agencies also had public relations departments. The usual techniques were to publicize events that showed the client in a good light and to "plant" favorable stories in magazines. Much of the content of newspapers in the peaceful years of the twenties originated in public relations offices.

The value of the stockholder as a public relations resource was also exploited. By lowering the price of shares through splitting them two or more ways, and by aggressive selling to small investors, often through agents of the company, it was possible for a big corporation to acquire tens of thousands of new stockholders. American Telephone and Telegraph, which took a leading part in this movement, increased the number of its owners from 50,000 in 1920 to 210,000 in 1930. Stockholders were sent attractive annual reports and letters from the president designed to make them feel that they were an important part of the organization. In return many stockholders undoubtedly used their votes and influence for government policies favorable to the company.

Whether as a result of the new public relations, or prosperity, or for other less obvious causes, the American public seemed to have given up much of its traditional hostility to big corporations. Articles in praise of business signed by corporate leaders made popular reading in mass-circulation magazines, and business periodicals boasted of the dominance of the businessman and his values. In this friendly atmosphere business was bold in the use of direct influence in legislatures, in community pressures through business clubs, and in the use of advertising contracts to influence editors. A basic danger, as illustrated in the thirties, was that business developed no new progressive policy to go with its added responsibility.

Stock Market Boom and Bust. Besides lacking a suitable social philosophy, businessmen and their economic advisers lacked understanding of relationships in the economy. Consequently, the stock market boom from 1927 to 1929, though not reflected in any corresponding upswing in real capital formation, was not regarded as dangerous. A sense of confidence that the severe business cycle was a thing of the past pervaded American finance.

With low taxes and with 5 per cent of the wealthiest classes receiving about a third of disposable personal income, savings were large. Low corporate taxes allowed big companies to accumulate unprecedented cash surpluses. Both personal savings and corporate surpluses were used for speculation. Moreover, brokers, by means of loans, made it easy for investors of even modest income to purchase securities beyond their means. Investors could buy "on margin," that is, deposit only a small percentage of the total price of a block of securities, with the broker advancing the rest of the money. The hope was, of course, that the price of the securities would rise and the investor could sell, making possible not only payment of the loan but a profit as well. Often brokerage houses and banks would lend three quarters of the cost of new securities, the customer depositing only a 25 per cent margin. In practice, margins often were allowed to go down to 10 per cent or less. Not only were the banks happy to lend on this type of demand or call loan, but big business companies also employed unused reserves for stock market loans.

Since the public would readily buy the shares of railroad and public utility holding companies, ambitious entrepreneurs like the Van Sweringen brothers in Cleveland, Samuel Insull in Chicago, and S. Z. Mitchell in New York set up pyramids of one holding company on top of another. Selling stock of these companies to the public, these empire builders secured money to buy dozens of operating companies while keeping personal control of the organization through the top holding company. In theory, economies were being achieved through removal of wasteful competition, but in fact the savings were often consumed by greater managerial costs.

High-pressure selling by the agents of bankers and brokers led investors into buying many other questionable securities. The mortgages on new urban hotels, apartments, and office buildings which were rising all over the nation were divided into small bonds for the investors. Ultimately these buildings would be needed, but in 1929 they were already outrunning the demand for such space. United States investment firms literally coaxed foreign governments into issuing loans that could be marketed to the American public. And in spite of all this manufacture of new securities, the demand exceeded the supply and boosted the price of existing stocks higher and higher.

By the summer of 1929 many insiders, convinced that stock prices were too high in relation to earnings, started to sell. But thousands of speculators on margins could only cling to the limb they were on and hope for some miraculous support. Late in October the limbs broke in a series of panic days on the New York Stock Exchange. Stocks sank so fast that holders on margin were generally wiped out. Efforts by J. P. Morgan and Company to stabilize the market failed. On October 29, the last day of extreme panic, 16 million shares were traded, and at times stocks could not be sold for want of buyers at any reasonable price. By November stocks had lost 40 per cent of their September value.

Stunned by these disastrous panics in what appeared to be stabilized prosperity, business and political leaders insisted that the economy was sound and the market break would not affect industry. Only about half a million people had margin accounts, and only a million and a half had brokerage accounts of any kind. But unfortunately, since this small group included most of the chief accumulators and users of capital, their importance was not to be measured in numbers. Furthermore, the whole economy had become more geared to the stock market than ever before. In the collapse of values, corporations lost their surpluses; brokerage houses were unable to sell fast enough to cover their loans; banks in turn were left with demand loans that could only be liquidated at a fraction of their value; and foreign governments were no longer able to borrow on Wall Street.

CHAPTER 20

THE GREAT DEPRESSION AND THE NEW DEAL, 1930-1941

THE DOWNSWING

Increasing Force of the Depression. In contrast to the severity of the stock market panics, the Great Depression began gradually. At the end of 1929 and the beginning of 1930 employment declined only slightly more than was seasonally normal. A Wall Street economist thought the collapse of inflated security values "a favorable development from the point of view of general business." Secretary of the Treasury Andrew Mellon saw nothing "in the present situation that is either menacing or warrants pessimism."

Influenced by the prevailing expressions of optimism, President Herbert Hoover sought to end the mild recession by encouraging appropriate business actions and by implementing favorable government policies. In conferences with business leaders he urged them to maintain wages, prices, and plans for expansion. In return he promised to continue a normal program of public works; to raise tariffs; and to lower the Federal Reserve System's rediscount rate (the rate of interest at which banks could exchange customers' notes for currency at Federal Reserve Banks) in order to stimulate business activity by making credit more readily available. In addition, the Federal Farm Board, which had been created in 1929, was expected to support agricultural prices by lending funds to marketing cooperatives or to stabilization corporations; the loan funds would be used to purchase basic farm crops and livestock at marketing time so that markets would not be glutted.

The President, however, refused to face realistically the condition of the unemployed and continued to manipulate figures to encourage a false optimism; in the spring of 1930, just before business unemployment climbed sharply, he assured the nation: "The worst effects of the crash upon unemployment will have passed during the next sixty days."

The chief barrier to effective action in dealing with the advancing depression was that President Hoover, most economists, and practically all businessmen adhered to the traditional laissez-faire view that government should not interfere with business; thus they considered private investment the only road to national economic recovery. They did not regard public works projects or other government programs as means of recreating prosperity through increasing demand for goods and services. Furthermore, allied to the conservatives' failure to appreciate the possibilities of artificially increased demand was the traditional attitude that helping individuals by federal food or relief payments would undermine the initiative of the American people.

A slight upturn in early 1931 supported President Hoover's "wait-and-see" policy. But the business indexes soon started down again, and the international financial structure began to disintegrate. In June 1931 banks on the European continent failed; reparations and debt payments soon stopped, and by September England went off the gold standard (that is, refused to pay its foreign obligations in gold). In July President Hoover, with the agreement of England, France, and Germany, declared a one-year moratorium on European debt and reparation payments. He hoped that such a temporary lifting of the burden of intergovernmental debts would promote world trade and stimulate economic recovery. However, the European crisis resulted in continued gold withdrawals from banks in the United States, European sale of American securities, and the freezing of most foreign credits held by banks in this country. These events led to a contraction of bank loans in the United States and an end to the possibility of a quick return to prosperity. While the collapse of 1929 was initiated in the United States, descent into the deep trough from 1931 to 1933 was, as President Hoover claimed, precipitated by European events.

Initiation of the Welfare State. Men of "the business world," wrote President Hoover, "threw up their hands and asked for government action." As voluntary action proved inadequate to counteract the deepening depression, Hoover moved step by step toward federal legislation. In December 1931 and January 1932 the President cooperated with leaders of the politically divided Senate and the Democratic House in creating the Reconstruction Finance Corporation (RFC). This conservatively managed agency, with resources of $2 billion, was to make loans to financial institutions and railroads to prevent bankruptcy and forced liquidation. Aid was given to some 5000 medium-sized to large businesses in order to meet their pressing obligations, such as bond and mortgage interest or short-term debts. The philosophy of aid was to preserve those institutions whose operation was essential to the public and to other businesses; consequently, banks and railroads received the most aid while small business, in general, was not initially helped.

Until this time the "general welfare" clause of the Constitution had never been interpreted to mean maintenance of the economic system by congressional action. While later Democratic acts continuing the RFC and extending aid to agriculture and individuals were to push the doctrine much further, nevertheless the nonpartisan RFC Act can be considered the beginning of the federal "welfare state" or "social capitalism." It demonstrated in the sphere of big business that an advanced industrial economy was so complexly interrelated that government could not stand by and see any essential parts break down.

Other recovery measures enacted in the spring of 1932 included the Glass-Steagall Act, which made government bonds and additional types of commercial paper acceptable as collateral for Federal Reserve notes—thus liberalizing the lending powers of banks—and made available to business about $750 million of the government gold supply. In July the Federal Home Loan Bank Act created twelve regional Federal Home Loan Banks to extend federal financial assistance to building and loan associations, savings banks, and insurance companies that were in trouble because of falling prices. But Democratic efforts at direct aid to individuals were defeated; Hoover continued to view relief as a function of state and local governments, and consequently relief limped along on the basis of small RFC loans to the states.

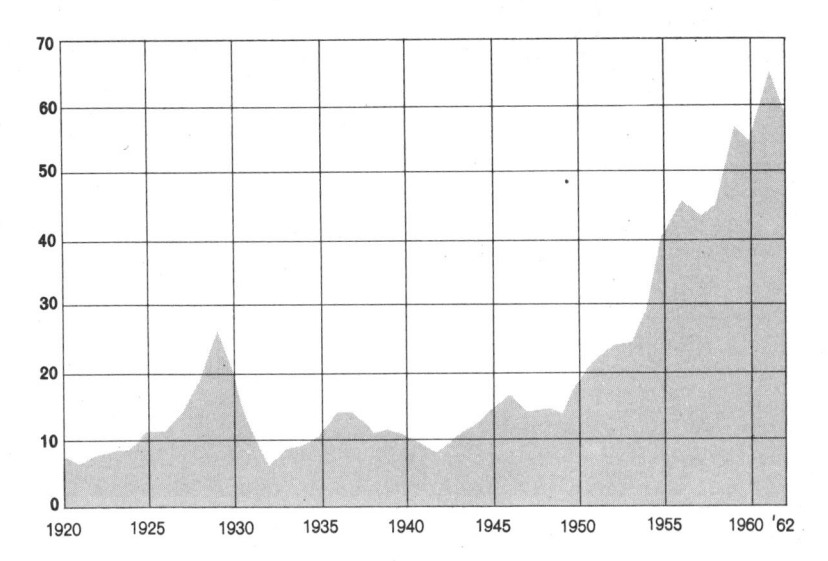

INDEX OF COMMON STOCK PRICES, 1920-1962
Years 1941-1943 Equal 10

By the middle of 1932 about 12 million workers—a quarter of the labor force—were unemployed. Furthermore, since many of those listed as employed were working only part time, man-hours worked were less than 40 per cent of those of 1929. State and local governments had in general exhausted their borrowing power, taxes were partly uncollectable, and federal loans were too little and too late. Many hard-hit industrial areas were trying to feed the unemployed on a few cents a day. While apartments and tenements stood partly empty, evicted families crowded in with more fortunate relatives or built shacks in vacant lots which were soon called "Hoovervilles." All across America there were hunger and misery.

The Election of 1932. By the summer of 1932 the patience of various groups throughout the nation was being exhausted. Organized farmers in Iowa were violently enforcing a "farm holiday" on produce deliveries; an "expeditionary force" of several thousand veterans was encamped in Washington demanding cash payment of the World War I bonus; numbers of unemployed were killed by police in riots around Detroit; and some conservative editors were calling for a dictatorship to preserve the state.

Yet a majority of the leaders of both major parties conservatively opposed any substantial change in policy. Of the Democratic leaders only Governor Franklin D. Roosevelt of New York seemed to lean toward a more progressive approach, favoring the use of governmental power to whatever extent necessary and in whatever ways necessary to reverse the trend of economic events.

Franklin Delano Roosevelt, a fifth cousin of Theodore, had been brought up on a country estate above Poughkeepsie, New York, and educated at Harvard and at Columbia Law School. In 1910 he entered politics and was elected to the New York state assembly, where he stood for progressivism and reform and was an ardent supporter of Woodrow Wilson. President Wilson, aware of the personal charm of the

The Great Depression and the New Deal, 1930–1941

big, strong-jawed, smiling young man, appointed Roosevelt Assistant Secretary of the Navy; the 1920 Democratic convention, aware of the magic of the name Roosevelt, nominated him for the vice-presidency.

Shortly after his defeat as Cox's running mate Roosevelt contracted infantile paralysis, but by 1924 he had recovered sufficiently to appear, supported by crutches, at the Democratic convention and make the nominating speech for Alfred E. Smith. In 1928, at Smith's insistence, Roosevelt ran for governor of New York. Carrying the state by 25,000 votes while Smith lost it for the presidency marked Roosevelt as one of the coming men in the Democratic party. In 1930, after one term as a rather easygoing, liberal governor, he carried the state by a record-breaking 725,000 votes.

These repeated victories made him the party's logical candidate for the presidency in 1932, but Roosevelt, fearful of a strong undercurrent of conservative opposition, left nothing to chance. His able secretary, Louis M. Howe, planned and advised, and New York state Democratic chairman James A. Farley toured the country and talked to politicians. Roosevelt was violently opposed by Al Smith, now firmly on the conservative side, and the William G. McAdoo-William Randolph Hearst forces in California preferred Speaker of the House John Nance Garner of Texas. But at the Democratic convention Farley skillfully negotiated with Hearst and McAdoo for California's support on the fourth ballot in return for Garner's nomination for Vice-President. This shift swung Texas and other states to the Roosevelt bandwagon, but Al Smith held on to his delegates and left Chicago without congratulating the nominee.

The Republicans had no recourse but to renominate Hoover, and, in truth, the prosperous people who financed and ran the national machinery in both parties probably thought that Hoover had done all that could be expected. Yet everyone knew he would not be a strong candidate with the public.

The campaign mirrored the complete confusion in both parties regarding acceptable economic policy. The two platforms were nearly the same, and both candidates talked of public works and relieving misery while reducing spending and balancing the budget. But Garner probably was right when he told Roosevelt that to win "all you have to do is to stay alive until election day." Hoover probably gained no votes by his weary and often bitter campaign, and on election day he polled 15,759,000 votes to Roosevelt's 22,800,000. While many middle-class voters supported Socialist party candidate Norman Thomas as the only candidate with a constructive program, Thomas failed utterly to attract the masses. His 881,951 Socialist votes were fewer than in 1920 and relatively less than half of those of 1912. Artists and intellectuals desiring a thoroughgoing protest supported William Z. Foster, the Communist, but his meager 102,785 votes indicated that the workers did not support him.

Bottom of the Depression. The depression reached its lowest ebb in the four months between the election and Roosevelt's inauguration. During this critical period there was little constructive leadership. Hoover thought that everything justifiable had been done in the domestic field and was interested in stimulating foreign trade. Roosevelt could not accept Hoover's analysis of the domestic situation and was not prepared to work for return to an international gold standard, the keynote of Hoover's plans. As the nation drifted without leadership, silver shirts, white shirts, khaki shirts, and other fascist organizations strove unsuccessfully for mass support. "Technocracy," a vaguely defined plan for placing control of the nation's means of production in the hands of technicians in order to realize the full efficiency of industrial equipment, created a midwinter furor, but it died quickly from lack of immediate, practical proposals. In general, the people waited patiently, putting their hopes in the new administration.

The final breakdown of commercial banking was responsible for bringing the economy to its lowest ebb. Of the 16,000 state banks of 1929 that were not members of the Federal Reserve System, nearly half had closed their doors by 1933. These banks had no system to save them, and many of their officers knew little about banking. Of the 7500 members of the Federal Reserve, however, about 1400 disappeared during the depression, demonstrating that even these banks were too small and poorly connected to stand the strain. Banks that failed drew away deposits kept in the banks of the larger cities. The first metropolitan area to buckle under the pressure was New Orleans. Early in February 1933 the Governor of Louisiana declared a temporary "bank holiday," freezing loans and deposits.

Meanwhile, a Senate committee investigating banking practices had uncovered dishonesty and evasion of responsibility in the highest circles. Major banks had lent money to their officers on no proper security, and bad securities had been sold to banks to save investment subsidiaries or affiliates from disaster. These and other questionable practices had been overlooked by federal examiners. Faced with such uncertainties, depositors began to withdraw their surplus cash from the banks and stuff it into safe deposit boxes.

Closing of the banks in Michigan in mid-February started a chain reaction that ended on March 4, 1933—the day of Roosevelt's inauguration—when Governor Lehman of New York and other governors joined in declaring a "bank holiday" to stop destructive runs as depositors rushed to withdraw savings. The banking crisis had, in turn, hurt business, and unemployment stood at somewhere between 14 and 17 million, perhaps as much as a third of the labor force. The economy was producing at about half the rate of 1929, and the trend was downward.

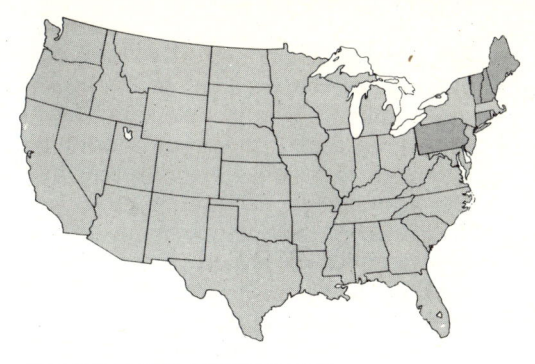

ELECTION OF 1932: ELECTORAL VOTE

Roosevelt: 472   Hoover: 59

FDR: THE FIRST TERM

The Honeymoon. Roosevelt's inaugural address on March 4, 1933, struck a note of hope. The nation was strong, he said, and would recover from this crippling depression. "The only thing we have to fear is fear itself—nameless, unreasoning, unjustified terror which paralyzes needed efforts to convert retreat into advance." He closed by affirming, "The people of the United States . . . have asked for discipline and direction under leadership. They have made me the present instrument of their wishes. In the spirit of the gift I take it."

The nation and Congress, which Roosevelt immediately called into emergency session, responded to his appeal, and quickly the pattern of the "New Deal" began to reveal itself. First, people must be put back on their feet economically as soon as possible by stimulating employment through every means—"our greatest primary task," Roosevelt declared in his inaugural address, "is to put people to work." Preferably the employment should be by private firms, but if necessary the federal government should use its resources to provide employment on the most useful work projects that could be quickly devised. Second, the abuses that aggravated the depression must be corrected. Anyone guilty of criminal acts of financial or corporate manipulation must be punished. Banking laws should be made stricter in some respects, controls over the stock exchanges and the commodity markets should be tightened, and abuse of the holding-company device should be corrected by closer control of its use, especially in the field of public utilities. Finally, after these emergency corrective measures had been taken, Roosevelt proposed a series of long-term, permanent steps to bring about the fuller development of the country and to make the lives of most Americans more secure and prosperous. Roosevelt referred to these three objectives of the New Deal as "Relief, Recovery, and Reform."

On March 6, even before Congress met in special session, the President proclaimed a four-day national bank holiday and a four-day embargo on the export of gold, silver, and currency. When Congress convened on March 9 its first business was to provide for the reopening of banks to relieve the financial emergency. The Emergency Banking Relief Act—introduced, passed, and approved on March 9—confirmed the President's earlier actions and provided steps for the reopening of sound banks.

The special session of Congress subsequently was fed a stream of recovery measures drawn up by groups in the administration, often with differing philosophies; but with the force of the President behind them the bills were enacted by sweeping bipartisan majorities. By the time this famous "Hundred Days" or political "honeymoon" ended in June 1933 the basic emergency legislation was complete. The Federal Emergency Relief Administration (FERA) was created with $500 million in funds to be granted to states for direct relief. A Civilian Conservation Corps (CCC) was set up to put unemployed young men into camps to carry out reforestation and erosion-control projects. Beer and light wine with an alcoholic content of 3.2 per cent or less by weight were legalized and repeal of the Eighteenth Amendment initiated (passage of the Twenty-first Amendment late in 1933 officially repealed prohibition).

Farm and Home Relief. From the standpoint of loss in money income, farmers were the hardest hit of any occupational group. From 1925 on they had been in a vicious circle of increasing overproduction of staple crops and declining prices; prices were so low, too, that farmers could not afford the investment needed to shift to other produce for which there was a better market. Hybrid seeds, soil biology, and mechanization made notable progress in the 1920's, but farms were too small and farmers too poor to experiment with new crops or take advantage of new technology. In 1929, for example, fewer than one farmer in seven had a tractor. Depression turned hardship into disaster: total cash income for farmers fell from an average of nearly $11 billion per year in the late twenties to $4.7 billion in 1932. But even this low total conceals the desperate straits of marginal cotton, corn, and wheat cultivators.

The Agricultural Adjustment Act of June 1933 contained the basic principle of subsequent farm legislation: that the government should subsidize staple crop farmers in order to restrict their acreage under cultivation, thus reducing output and raising the prices of farm products. Money to subsidize the farmers was to come from a tax on millers and other processors of staple products; in this way the law was self-supporting. To get the program going quickly, the Secretary of Agriculture arranged for the plowing up of millions of acres of cotton and the slaughter of six million pigs at less than usual market weights, the pigs to be put to uses other than providing human food. Although millions of Americans considered the destruction of food and cotton positively sinful as long as other millions were hungry and ill-clothed, agricultural prices and income did improve in 1934 and 1935.

Mortgage Refinancing. The government had to try not only to revive farm income but also to take care of hundreds of thousands of defaulted mortgages, both farm and nonfarm. In two initial acts creating the Federal Farm Mortgage Corporation and the Home Owners Loan Corporation, the government offered to refinance mortgages on long terms at low interest.

In addition, the Federal Housing Administration Act of 1934 introduced the plan of the guaranteed packaged mortgage—one that could be paid, principal and interest, by uniform monthly payments. This government guarantee of a high percentage of the total cost of homes in the low-price range constituted the most important change in the history of American home ownership. Now the man with a steady job could afford to build or buy, where he had had to rent before, and repayment of his obligations would occur automatically every month. This also marked an important step in the development of mass production of homes and long-term installment buying.

Regional Development. One of the most revolutionary of the acts passed by the Hundred Days Congress initiated the redevelopment of an entire geographic region—the economically ailing seven-state Tennessee valley area.

The Muscle Shoals-Tennessee Valley Development Act of May 1933 created an independent public corporation, the Tennessee Valley Authority, which was given control of the government property at Muscle Shoals, Alabama, and the power to build and operate other dams and power plants on the Tennessee River and its branches wherever the authority thought advisable. In addition to generation and distribution of electric power, TVA was charged with controlling the flood waters of the Tennessee River and improving its navigation facilities; promoting the conservation of soil in the valley and aiding reforestation; and producing nitrates and other fertilizers for the improvement of the valley's agriculture.

Although the power dams, plants, and distribution systems of TVA were criticized by private power companies as unfair competition (the public facilities were not required to pay the same taxes as private companies, and they received other government subsidy), the constitutionality of the TVA was upheld by the Supreme Court in 1936. The following year President Roosevelt requested Congress to set up six additional regional river valley authorities, but Congress declined the suggestion. The areas in which they were to be located were not quite such distinct units as the Tennessee valley, nor were the people of these other areas in such a distressed condition as those of the Tennessee valley had been in 1933. The general business outlook was brighter in 1937, and the business community supported the widespread contention that private capital could develop these valleys as well as the federal government could.

Industrial Recovery. While banking, currency, mortgages, and agriculture had occupied the President's attention during the first weeks of his administration in 1933, he learned in April that unless he acted quickly Congress would pass a uniform thirty-hour-a-week law governing all industry. Because he regarded such a law as impractical, the President had his advisers prepare a substitute. The resulting National Industrial Recovery Act (NIRA), though hastily improvised, actually was the outgrowth of much business, labor, and governmental thought about how to reconcile "free" private enterprise with effective control of wages and competition.

Excess industrial capacity, unemployed labor, and nearly bankrupt firms had reduced the market to chaos in many industries. With women receiving as little as $5 for a full week's work, companies that tried to maintain fair labor standards found themselves undersold. The solution proposed in the act was to have each industry, through its trade association, agree to a code of "fair competition" defining wages, hours, and minimum prices. Labor would be represented in the making of such industry agreements by representatives of its own choosing without any pressure from the employer. The public would also be represented so that the interests of consumers of the industry's products were not lost sight of. When all three parties were represented in the determination of policies for an industry, the government could overlook the fact that a price agreement would appear to be a clear "conspiracy to restrain trade" under the terms of the Sherman Antitrust Act. The National Recovery Administration (NRA) was set up to administer this section of the law.

The second section of NIRA set up the Public Works Administration (PWA) and authorized the expenditure of $3.3 billion for public works projects designed both to provide work for relief and to stimulate recovery.

When the bill became law in June 1933 the President appointed retired General Hugh S. Johnson head of the NRA. A spreading blue eagle was adopted as the symbol of cooperating firms; those who signed fair competition codes were to be allowed to display the blue eagle symbol on their stores, plants, or merchandise, and the public was strongly urged not to patronize nonsigners. However, the negotiation of codes proved difficult and time-consuming; in July 1933 President Roosevelt, to speed matters, announced a blanket National Reëmployment Agreement, and under this plan millions of Americans were working under the soaring blue eagles within a few months. The original idea of cooperative agreements between the employer, organized labor, and consumer representatives was all but lost in the haste. Furthermore, consumers were unorganized and unable to protect their interests as management and government drew up a flood of codes. As time passed, thousands of cases of noncompliance with codes were reported. Labor was extremely restive because industry often opposed union organization as authorized by NIRA, and the country was plagued by strikes. Employers began to fear that they had made a mistake in agreeing to negotiate with labor in drawing up the codes. The public also began to feel that it was being fleeced by prices that were rising faster than income.

Although the NRA contributed to the raising of wages from the low levels of 1932, did away with child labor, and in some industries helped small business to stay alive, the NIRA experiment illustrated the difficulty of comprehensively regulating the economy and maintaining free enterprise at the same time. The United States Chamber of Commerce and labor leaders as diverse as William Green, John L. Lewis, and Sidney Hillman continued to support the NRA until the Supreme Court ruled the act unconstitutional, but the rising group in the Roosevelt administration had lost interest.

Devaluing the Dollar. Controllable inflation, the President hoped, would raise farm prices and in general lighten the burden of debts in relation to income. The administration felt that such inflation could be stimulated either by heavy government spending or by altering the value of the dollar. Of the two possibilities, devaluing the dollar had the immediate advantages of not adding to government costs and of stimulating exports.

While the President was supporting the inflationist group in Congress, European nations were meeting in June-July 1933 to attack the worldwide depression by attempting to agree on stabilizing national currencies and restoring the international gold standard. However, contrary to this spirit, an amendment to the Agricultural Adjustment Act of May 1933 gave the President the right to inflate U.S. currency by issuing $3 billion in paper currency, freely coining silver, and devaluing the gold content of the dollar up to 50 per cent. For the time being he did none of these things, waiting to see whether the AAA and the NRA would do the inflationary job, but neither would he enter into any international agreement fixing the value of the dollar. As a result, the London Economic Conference was a failure.

Although there was a sharp increase in manufacturing production, employment, and prices between March and July 1933—in part, the result of an effort to produce before the restrictive NRA codes went into effect—by autumn manufacturing and employment were declining, and wholesale prices had again leveled off. At this point the President decided to use his power to devalue the dollar in the expectation that the resulting inflation would lead to higher prices. He reduced the value of the gold content of the dollar to 59.06 cents, a degree of devaluation calculated to restore the price level of 1926. Prices rose slightly, but not nearly so much as the administration had expected; the President's monetary program had no significant effect.

Rise of Conservative Opposition. Early criticism of the New Deal had come primarily from advanced liberals and labor leaders. Some members of Congress, for instance, would have nationalized banking and railroads; these men and even more moderate liberals regarded the restoration of the banking system in relatively unchanged form as the loss of a great opportunity for progress toward a more stable economy. Organized labor was particularly dissatisfied with its treatment by the NRA, which in labor circles came to be called the "national run-around."

On the other hand, monetary manipulation during the last half of 1933 lost the President the support of many leading Democrats who conservatively opposed any tinkering with the monetary system. Efforts at permanent reform of financial operations, as distinct from mere recovery, widened the rift between liberals and conservatives.

The reform program really began with the Federal Securities Act of 1933, by which the Federal Trade Commission was given power to see that issuers of securities fully disclosed to investors all essential details pertaining to new securities issues. A further reform was effected by the Banking Act of June 1933, which divorced investment banking from commercial banking on the premise that the promoting and selling of new security issues by commercial banks gave them an improper amount of power over other businesses and was inconsistent with the policy of caution and prudence which banks should follow. The Banking Act also created the Federal Deposit Insurance Corporation (FDIC) to insure bank deposits up to established limits and prevent losses to depositors. Leading bankers vigorously opposed deposit insurance, and stricter regulation of the securities markets aroused more general business opposition.

The battle between liberals and conservatives was intensified when the Securities Exchange bill was before Congress in the spring of 1934. This bill called for the establishment of a three-member Securities and Exchange Commission to regulate the practices of stock exchanges, including the size of margins; to require full disclosure of details about all securities; and to enforce other parts of the Federal Securities Act of 1933. Stockbrokers and investment bankers complained bitterly about the restrictions this legislation would place on them. But despite bitter debate in Congress the bill was passed in June 1934 and the die-hard opponents of all governmental regulation of the financial community were decisively defeated.

Another development in the spring of 1934 that alarmed some businessmen was adoption of the Reciprocal Trade Agreements Act, which gave the President power to make separate agreements with foreign nations to alter U.S. tariff rates by 50 per cent in either direction. Even moderate Republicans denounced this as a fascist-type surrender of power to the President. But Democrats with strong Southern support held firm and enacted this basic change in American tariff policy.

In the course of debates over security regulation and the tariff, business arguments against the New Deal took their permanent shape. The government was condemned for creating a vast and irresponsible bureaucracy, for depriving individuals of their freedom and initiative, and for increasing the national debt. Direct relief, in particular, was condemned because it ran contrary to the deeply ingrained tradition that self-help was the basis of American greatness.

In August 1934 a group of wealthy Republicans and conservative Democrats formed the Liberty League to defend the rights and liberty of the individual against the New Deal. Backed by DuPont and General Motors executives, the League won the support of previous Democratic presidential candidates John W. Davis and Alfred E. Smith and many other conservative political leaders in both parties. The big city daily newspapers were moving in the same direction. Within a year, at least two thirds of the metropolitan dailies were strongly in opposition to the New Deal, and their influential columnists were attacking the "third-rate college professors" and other "impractical intellectuals" who were held to be guiding the policies of the administration.

Reliance Upon the Masses. The business attack on the New Deal, though backed by adequate finances and the support of newspapers, had the fatal weakness of lacking a positive philosophy. Business leaders could only ask the public again to put its faith in the self-regulating economy. That, in fact, the public would not trust self-regulation was shown in the election of 1934. Normally the administration party loses strength in Congress in the nonpresidential elections; the Democrats, however, gained nine seats in the House and nine in the Senate, with nearly 57 per cent of the popular vote—an off-year administration victory unmatched since before the Civil War.

What had built the Democratic majority? The answer of a number of presidential advisers was that it was the public's desire for security—for assurance that when unemployed or old they would be cared for. At this point, therefore, the New Deal became more equalitarian and humanitarian than any of the previous progressive movements.

In the spring of 1935 a new system of relief through useful work was instituted. Jobs ranging over all levels of skill from mixing concrete to painting murals were to be created from an appropriation of nearly $5 billion. Pay would be at rates above relief but lower than approved wages for private employment. The Works Progress Administration lasted until World War

II and spent some $11 billion. Although it could employ only from two to three million workers, it kept those with the more valuable skills from deteriorating through idleness. Other minor forms of aid were instituted to help students stay in school and to provide potential farmers with subsistence homesteads.

In the President's mind, the most important legislation of this administration was the Social Security Act of 1935. This act created a Social Security Board to administer unemployment compensation, old-age security, and various social services. Payroll taxes were levied on both employers and employees to finance old-age pensions of from $10 to $85 per month for retired workers. Pensions under the new system would not begin until 1942, but meanwhile the federal government would assist the states in paying small pensions. In the beginning many groups, including farm and educational workers, were not eligible for pensions, but in succeeding years coverage was broadened and rates raised to compensate for inflation. The Social Security Act also extended federal-state unemployment insurance to 28 million workers and authorized money grants to states to assist them in relief of the blind, cripples, delinquent children, and other dependents. Now the power of Congress to legislate for the general welfare had a new meaning.

The Supreme Court: Challenge and Response. Early in 1935, with the Social Security bill on its way through Congress, the President regarded his program as virtually complete. Had the Supreme Court upheld the legislation of 1933 and 1934, the Roosevelt administration, like that of Woodrow Wilson, might have turned its attention to matters other than domestic reform. But the Supreme Court had four justices unalterably opposed to the New Deal—Pierce Butler, James C. McReynolds, George Sutherland, and Willis Van Devanter. Two others, Owen J. Roberts and Chief Justice Charles E. Hughes, had grave doubts regarding the constitutionality of the delegation of congressional power to administrative agencies and the use of the commerce power to regulate conditions of production and trade within the states.

The crucial tests came in the summer of 1935, when the Court declared the NIRA and a number of other basic acts of the New Deal unconstitutional. There was little hope that those still to be tested, such as the Agricultural Adjustment Act, would fare any better. (The Supreme Court invalidated the first AAA in January 1936.)

The Court's failure to interpret the Constitution flexibly and to support the type of laws initially planned in cooperation with business leaders pushed the President toward the more extreme believers in regulation. The influence of the administration was now put behind the Wagner Act (National Labor Relations Act) to replace the labor provisions of the outlawed NIRA. The Wagner Act created a new National Labor Relations Board (NLRB) for administrative purposes and upheld the right of employees to join labor organizations and to bargain collectively through representatives of their own choosing.

This support of labor was not the only New Deal measure to antagonize conservatives. A new tax bill introduced in June 1935 had the announced purpose of redistributing the tax burden from the poor to the rich. The Revenue Act of 1935 (Wealth Tax Act) actually made few changes in taxes on income under $50,000 a year, and the graduated corporation income tax stopped at 15 per cent. But high surtaxes on very big incomes and on inheritance of estates further alarmed the wealthy over the "communistic" trend of the New Deal.

Attack by the rich probably strengthened the mass support of the President. More potentially dangerous was the fascist type of attack. In weekly radio broadcasts Father Charles Edward Coughlin, a demagogic Catholic priest from Detroit, denounced Jews and international bankers. In Congress Senator Huey P. Long of Louisiana advocated an ill-defined sharing of the wealth under the slogan "every man a king." After Long was assassinated in the Louisiana state house in the fall of 1935, Coughlin and other unorthodox reformers continued to keep the administration under fire, but without Long they lacked a strong political leader.

The Election of 1936. Many Republicans felt that with Alfred M. Landon, ex-governor of Kansas, they would defeat Roosevelt in 1936. The *Literary Digest's* poll of subscribers, which indicated a Landon presidential victory, helped to sustain this view. Landon promised to do everything that the New Deal was doing for the common man but to do it in ways more satisfactory to business. The President responded with a more advanced liberalism than in earlier campaigns. In his acceptance speech he denounced the "economic royalists" and said that Americans in their achievement of economic and social democracy had a "rendezvous with destiny."

The result was the greatest landslide since 1920. Landon, with 16.7 million votes to the President's 27.8 million, carried only Maine and Vermont. The Coughlin group, supporting a radical farm leader, polled less than a million votes, and the Socialists' and Communists' votes were negligible. No President since Monroe had received such strong second-term support from the people.

THE LAST PHASE OF THE NEW DEAL

Battle Over the Court. In a surprise move soon after the election of 1936 Roosevelt boldly attempted to use his great political strength and national popularity to alter the composition of the ultraconservative Supreme Court—and thus to liberalize the Court's attitude toward New Deal legislation.

In February 1937 the President presented Congress with a bill to reorganize the federal judiciary by adding up to fifty judges to the federal court system as a whole. The bill further proposed to increase the membership of the Supreme Court from nine to a maximum of fifteen by permitting the President to appoint one new justice for each justice over seventy who refused to retire. Roosevelt's ostensible argument for the bill was that federal judges were overworked and decisions too long delayed because the judiciary was "handicapped by insufficient personnel." Furthermore, the President contended that the aging judges were antiquated in outlook—"little by little, new facts become blurred through old glasses fitted, as it were, for the needs of another generation." For the lower courts Roosevelt's argument was valid, but the highest tribunal was not far behind in its case work, and the justices over seventy included some of the most vigorous and liberal members of the Court.

The magnitude of the change from nine to fifteen justices when no previous Congress had ever altered the size of the Court so drastically, and the doubtful sincerity of Roosevelt's argument for the major provision of the bill reacted with unexpected strength against the administration. Liberal Democrats and progressive Republicans joined conservatives in opposing the measure. The press was violent in its denunciation of the type of activity that could lead to fascist dictatorship, and public opinion polls showed popular distaste for so arbitrary an action by the President.

While Congress debated the President's "Court-packing" bill, the Court itself removed much of Roosevelt's reason for the bill by voluntarily liberalizing its stand on New Deal legislation. Justice Roberts and Chief Justice Hughes abandoned the conservative camp and joined Justices Brandeis, Cardozo, and Stone in reversing the legal doctrines of 1935 and 1936: In March 1937 the Court, by a five-to-four decision, upheld a Washington state minimum wage law for women although the previous year it had declared unconstitutional a similar law of the state of New York. In April the Court declared the National Labor Relations Act constitutional, and the next month it upheld the Social Security Act. Furthermore, Justice Van Devanter's resignation from the Court in May 1937 gave Roosevelt a chance to appoint a justice who would convert the liberal minority of the Court to a majority in future decisions. To succeed Van Devanter Roosevelt appointed Senator Hugo L. Black of Alabama, an enthusiastic supporter of the New Deal.

In June 1937 the Senate Judiciary Committee reported the court reform bill unfavorably, and the Senate, after bitter debate, subsequently rejected the proposal by voting 70 to 20 to return it to the Judiciary Committee. Congress did, however, pass a Supreme Court Retirement Act permitting Supreme Court justices to retire, with full pay, at age seventy; it also passed a Judicial Procedure Reform Act which established reforms in the lower courts.

New Dealers found consolation for the defeat of the administration bill in the fact that the few years after defeat of the "Court-packing" plan saw a radical change in the complexion of the Supreme Court. A succession of deaths and resignations enabled Roosevelt to make eight new appointments to the Court and gave him the liberal tribunal which Congress had denied him.

A Government-Protected Labor Movement. Early in 1933 total independent union membership in the United States had fallen to less than 2.7 million, including about 2 million in the A.F.L. Unemployment had reduced company union membership to less than a million. The morale of union leaders was at a low ebb; in general their proposals for recovery were no more imaginative than Hoover's.

Section 7(a) of NIRA (granting to organized labor the right of collective bargaining through representatives of their own choosing) and the subsequent upswing in employment gave organized labor a chance to expand. Organizing drives and some help from the National Labor Board of the NRA raised total union membership to 3.6 million in 1935. Meanwhile, faced with the threat of being forced by code authorities to bargain collectively, the larger employers were setting up company unions. By 1935 this type of membership had passed 2.5 million.

In 1935, also, a group within the A.F.L., led by John L. Lewis of the United Mine Workers, was urging the organization of all workers in a given industry—skilled or unskilled—into a single union, in contrast to the craft union method of organizing specific trades or skills. The A.F.L. as a whole, however, was dominated by craft unions and officially opposed all moves toward industrial unionization.

The Wagner Act of 1935 gave industrial organizers new and effective weapons. The powerful National Labor Relations Board created by the act could, at the request of a union but not of an employer, hold a plant election; if the union received the vote of a majority of workers, it became the bargaining agent for all. Furthermore, the Board could determine the units—plants, companies, or industries—for election purposes, and it could prevent employers from interfering in any way with organizers or trying to influence the election. If the winning union was able to negotiate a closed-shop agreement, the employer was required to deduct union dues from the pay of all workers.

Annual average of
EMPLOYMENT, UNEMPLOYMENT AND UNION MEMBERSHIP, 1920-1960

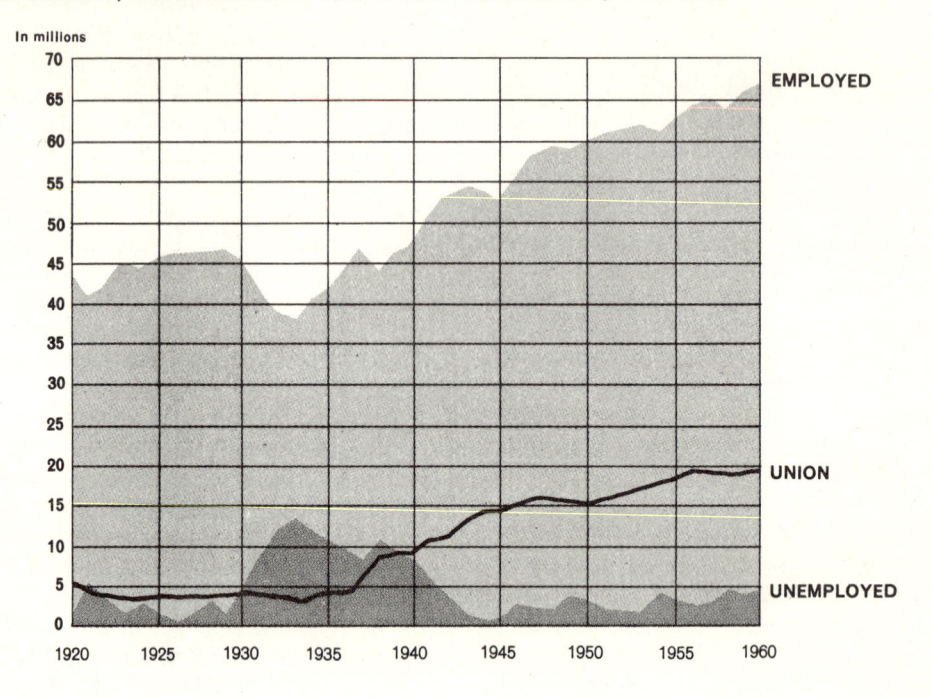

Encouraged by the opportunities of the new law, the leaders of eight A.F.L. unions defied the parent body and formed a Committee for Industrial Organization. Led by John L. Lewis, the C.I.O. refused to compromise with the crafts, and the unions involved were expelled by the A.F.L. in 1937. The following year the committee became the Congress of Industrial Organizations with Lewis as president and a membership roughly equal to that of the A.F.L.

The new drive for industrial organization started in steel in 1936. Myron C. Taylor, chairman of the United States Steel Corporation, decided there was more to be gained in prosperous times by good labor relations than by a prolonged strike; in March 1937 U.S. Steel voluntarily granted the C.I.O. full bargaining authority for its employees. The smaller steel companies, however, hoping the Wagner Act would be declared unconstitutional, continued to defy the National Labor Relations Board. Even after the Wagner Act was upheld by the Supreme Court in its dramatic shift in attitude, the NLRB had to compel the organization of "Little Steel."

Like steel, the automobile industry had resisted organization during the life of the NRA. Ford, in particular, was violently anti-union. To win their initial success, the United Automobile Workers, led by an ex-Baptist minister, Homer Martin, used a new strategy: the sit-down strike. Starting with General Motors, the workers stayed in the plant while food and other necessities were brought to them by their families. This meant that guards could oust the idle workers only by a fight within the factory which might damage highly valuable machinery or by stopping their

384 Between Two Wars

food supply, which would involve attacking women and children.

Refusing to interfere by force, in February 1937 Michigan Governor Frank Murphy, with the backing of President Roosevelt, brought labor and management together in a settlement favorable to the union. Chrysler agreed to a contract in the spring, but Ford resisted until the U.A.W.-C.I.O. won an election at the River Rouge plant late in 1940. (The sit-down strike itself, however, was declared unconstitutional by the Supreme Court in 1939.)

In spite of the sharp downswing of business and employment from mid-1937 to 1939, union strength continued to increase. Enthusiastic young organizers, government protection of the processes of organization and election, and compulsory bargaining were building a labor movement of unprecedented strength. For self-defense the A.F.L. was forced to adopt the principle of industrial organization and compete vigorously with the C.I.O. In 1940 there were nearly 9 million organized workers: over 4 million in the A.F.L., 3.5 million in the C.I.O., and a million in independent unions. Although the total union organization of 22 per cent of all non-agricultural employees was a peak for the United States, it was still substantially less than the 28 per cent organized in Great Britain, the 30 per cent in France, and the 50 per cent in Australia and Denmark.

Return to Depression. Late 1936 and the first half of 1937 appeared to be the early stages of a boom period. Volume of industrial production rose above 1929, and stocks moved rapidly upward. The administration, confident that recovery was sufficiently underway to carry on by itself, ordered a cutback in spending by New Deal agencies. Between January and August 1937 relief roles were drastically cut and the federal budget was reduced by $3 billion. Contrary to the administration's expectations, however—and in part, at least, as a result of its sharp reduction in expenditures—a new nationwide recession soon set in, becoming noticeable by July 1937 and reaching bottom about mid-1938. Not until the beginning of 1940, when the European war and American rearmament had become important economic factors, was there a return to the business volume of 1937. The severity of the depression was about equal to that of late 1931. Unemployment rose above ten million, or a fifth of the labor force, and even with the return toward prosperity in 1940 over eight million people were still looking for jobs.

The depression forced the government to institute new policies to promote recovery. Agricultural production had been sharply cut by a severe drought in 1934 and a more moderate one in 1936. In the latter year Congress passed a soil conservation act to check planting of soil-depleting crops and encourage planting of soil-restoring crops. As a result of these developments agricultural income, including government payments, stood up better in this depression than did the income of other sectors. In addition, the well-organized farmers won substantial new support in the Agricultural Adjustment Act of 1938. Soil conservation was to be encouraged by payments to staple crop producers agreeing to acreage allotments. Marketing quotas could also be imposed by the vote of two thirds of the growers of a staple crop. If Congress appropriated the money, farmers conforming to these regulations would be given "parity payments" whenever actual prices fell below "parity prices"—government-determined prices intended to keep the farmer's purchasing power at the 1909-1914 level. Crop loans were also available to all farmers of crops with marketing quotas, but those who did not accept the quota could borrow only 60 per cent as much as could the cooperators. In spite of many loopholes and much subsequent criticism, this law remained the basic plan of agricultural support.

Wage and hour guarantees attempted in the NIRA were now incorporated in a Fair Labor Standards Act. The labor of children under sixteen was prohibited, the minimum wage was set at twenty-five cents an hour, and beyond forty-four hours a week overtime was to be paid. The Housing Act of 1937, now in operation, stimulated the construction industry. Other parts of the federal budget, including public works and defense, were allowed to grow so that federal expenditures in 1939, more than 25 per cent above 1938, were the highest of any peacetime year in previous American history.

While the New Deal had greatly improved stability and security in the national economy, it had not brought satisfactory recovery. For the first time the gross national product per capita had failed to achieve a level higher than in the previous decade. What had been wrong? Several different answers were possible, depending upon different economic emphases.

It was possible, first of all, to emphasize the fact that from beginning to end President Roosevelt, either from conviction or from political expediency, held down spending and tried to balance the budget. Prior to the depression of 1938, only 1934 and 1936 showed substantial increases in government spending in relation to receipts, and in both cases the level of spending dropped the following year. Put another way, the administration failed to break cleanly with the idea of the self-regulating economy and to develop a philosophy of where and how to spend. Yet, while failing to spend government funds at the level necessary to promote expansion, the government's policies did not encourage expansion through investment by business.

Another line of reasoning pointed to the failure of NIRA and other legislation substantially to redistribute income so as to create sharply increased consumer demand. Still another approach was that by chance too few technological innovations occurred that offered profits in return for large capital investment.

Whatever approach one took, the disturbing question remained: How could expansion and growth be assured in time of peace?

THE APPROACH OF WORLD WAR II

Breakdown of the Security System. Despite prevailing isolationist sentiments, the United States in the 1920's was part of a system of international security which rested on the Washington Treaties of 1922 governing Far Eastern relations (see p. 358); on the structure of international debt and reparations payments as worked out in the Dawes and Young Plans (see p. 359); and on the ability of the League of Nations—or its leading members, England and France—to police the settlement of Versailles. Between 1931 and 1935 this entire security structure was demolished, leaving the world perennially on the verge of war.

Partly because Russia had not been invited to take part in the Washington Conference, the treaties of 1922 did not bring peace to China. During the next decade Russia and China first combined to reunify China and then fought an undeclared war. When peace was restored with Russia, the Chinese Nationalist leader Chiang Kai-shek brought pressure against the Japanese in Manchuria. This gave the strongly imperialist Japanese army the excuse to overthrow the liberal ministry in Tokyo and to wage a war for complete control of Manchuria. The League of Nations, as well as individual nations like Britain and the United States, condemned the Japanese aggression, but Japan ignored the protests, completed its conquest of Manchuria, and in 1933 withdrew from the League. A demonstration that a great power could embark on aggression without effective opposition from League members marked the beginning of the collapse of the League.

International debt and reparation payments depended upon continuing loans from the United States. With the collapse of the Wall Street security market it was only a question of time before payments would end. President Hoover's moratorium in 1931 temporarily eased the debt burden on European nations, but neither the Hoover nor the Roosevelt administration was ready to profit from the inevitable by canceling the war debts. After 1934 only Finland continued to pay, and another part of the World War I settlement had come to an end.

Meanwhile, Italy followed Japan's lead in aggressive expansion. In October 1935, the Italian fascist dictator Mussolini launched a wholesale invasion of the African kingdom of Ethiopia. President Roosevelt declared an arms embargo, and the League of Nations, under British pressure, condemned Italy as an aggressor and imposed economic sanctions. But because of British and French fears of driving Germany and Italy into an alliance, the embargo did not include coal and oil. Furthermore, the League had little machinery for enforcing economic sanctions, and nonmembers like Germany and the United States largely ignored the prohibitions. As a result, the conquest of Ethiopia was quickly completed, and the authority of the League completely undermined.

The conflict over Ethiopia gave the new dictator of Germany, Adolf Hitler, his first big opportunity to use the military force he had been building up in defiance of the Versailles Treaty. In March 1936 Nazi troops marched into the Rhineland, which had been demilitarized by the Versailles Treaty. France mobilized 150,000 troops, but Britain refused to support the use of force to compel German withdrawal. Another World War I agreement had been smashed.

Why had the major military and naval powers of the world failed to enforce the peace? In the first place, Russia, the nation most feared in the long run by Great Britain, was not a party to the Western agreements. The fact that Hitler was a professed enemy of Russia made it difficult for British governments, particularly the Conservative ones, to decide where the ultimate national interest lay. Yet even if the British ministry decided to let Hitler gain strength, they did not want him too strong, and this weakened them in dealing with Italy. Another factor faced by both Britain and the United States was the strength of pacifist and neutralist movements in their own countries. A government embarking on vigorous policies that risked war might find itself lacking in the necessary legislative support. In France many conservatives in the army and government feared Communism much more than they feared Hitler's fascism.

Isolation and Neutrality. The breakdown of the world order led the United States both to strict isolationist legislation and to an effort to weld the Western Hemisphere into a self-sufficient defense system. The latter presented many difficulties. Aside from Canada, the nations of the Western Hemisphere were further removed from the United States by tradition and national culture than were the nations of northern Europe, and the capitals of the three largest South American powers, Argentina, Brazil, and Chile, were also farther removed geographically. Economically as well, the United States had more ties with Europe, and so did each of the major South American nations.

President Roosevelt's inaugural address in 1933 dedicated the United States to "the policy of the good neighbor"—nonaggression, nonintervention, and friendly cooperation to solve mutual problems in the Western Hemisphere. At the seventh Pan-American Conference meeting at Montevideo later the same year, the United States subscribed to a nonintervention pact adopted unanimously by the conference. The American government soon proved that its change of policy was sincere. It refrained from intervention to quell disorders that arose in Cuba and in 1934 abrogated the Platt Amendment authorizing intervention there; in the same year it withdrew its marines, sent during some disorders in 1929, from Haiti; and in 1936 it ratified a treaty restoring to Panama its sovereign powers. Reciprocal trade agreements negotiated with six Latin American nations strengthened economic ties. While the bonds between "good neighbors" 5000 miles apart remained somewhat tenuous, the Roosevelt administration policy marked a great improvement over inter-American relations of the previous thirty years.

Though Americans in the midthirties were fully cognizant of the onrush of fascism in Europe, most of them were confident that the United States could remain a neutral bystander in the impending conflict. As Europe's crises deepened, determination mounted in the United States to "sit this one out." The hastily improvised Neutrality Act of 1935, although reluctantly signed by Roosevelt, prohibited the export of arms or ammunition to belligerents and required the President to forbid American citizens to travel on belligerent ships except at their own risk. A "permanent" Neutrality Act in 1937 retained the earlier restrictions on loans and munitions in time of war and declared travel on belligerent vessels unlawful for American citizens. In addition it provided that for a period of two years belligerent nations could purchase goods, other than munitions, in the U.S. only on a "cash-and-carry" basis.

Rise of the Axis. In 1936 the presumed safeguards of the World War I diplomatic structure were finally swept away. In October and November Germany, Italy, and Japan entered into an anticommunist pact. These powers, having built new mechanized armies, were now too powerful for England and France to attack. Helped by German military engineers and scientists, Hitler had worked a diplomatic revolution that made defeated and penalized Germany the strongest nation in Europe.

Why had this happened? Causes may be traced far back, but three were abundantly clear in 1936: (1) Mutual distrust between England and France on one side and Russia on the other prevented the old World War I alliance against the central powers; (2) the United States could not be relied upon for active support; and (3) England and France had not kept up with military development. To make their plight worse, England and France had guaranteed the independence of smaller nations such as Czechoslovakia and Poland, which they could not possibly defend against Germany. Faced with the choice of arming for possible war or muddling along in the hope that some change would occur in the German situation, the conservative leaders of the Western powers chose the latter course.

Large-scale Japanese inroads in northern China led President Roosevelt in a speech of October 1937 to test American sentiment by advocating a "quarantine" of aggressor nations. He quickly found that Congress was two to one against cooperation with the League of Nations in bringing effective sanctions against Japan. Underlying much of this isolationist attitude was an implicit confidence that England and France were still capable of controlling the situation. From 1938 on, however, as Germany continued to build up its mechanized army, the European situation was quite out of the preventive control of England and France. Hitler was ready to embark on a daring program of expansion, and his territorial demands were to prove limitless.

Hitler's first victim was his neighbor Austria, which Germany invaded and annexed in March 1938. After the Austrian coup, Hitler moved on to his next objective—the annexation of the Sudetenland, a German-speaking portion of Czechoslovakia. Hitler bluntly informed English Prime Minister Neville Chamberlain that he was determined to secure self-determination for the Sudeten Germans. Chamberlain in turn persuaded Edouard Daladier, the French premier, that a sacrifice on the part of Czechoslovakia would save the peace. In September 1938 Hitler, Mussolini, Daladier, and Chamberlain met in Munich and worked out the details of the surrender of the Sudetenland in return for Hitler's promise that he had no further territorial ambitions.

While the Munich Pact gave Britain precious time to build up its air force, British and French hopes that the agreement would appease Hitler's expansionistic cravings were shattered when in March 1939 the German army invaded and seized the remainder of the Czech nation. Mussolini seized Albania the following month, and the two dictators celebrated by signing a military alliance, the "Pact of Steel."

The shock of Hitler's callous violation of a solemn pledge made at Munich ended the appeasement policy of France and Great Britain. Britain launched a tremendous arms program, and in Paris Daladier obtained special emergency powers to push forward national defense.

It was Germany's aggression against Poland, however, that finally precipitated the Second World War. During the summer of 1939 Hitler made increasingly insistent territorial demands upon Poland while Chamberlain, with the French government concurring, warned the Nazi government that "in the event of any action which clearly threatened Polish independence" the British would "at once lend the Polish government all support in their power."

As German threats against Poland increased, Britain and France desperately sought an alliance with Russia. The Nazi and Soviet foreign secretaries, however, were secretly working out an agreement of their own; on August 23, 1939, Russia and Germany signed a nonaggression pact giving Hitler a free hand in Poland—thus precipitating war between Germany and Britain and France. Russia reasoned that such a conflict would give the Soviet Union time to build up its armaments and would weaken the antagonists. The Soviet Union also secured German recognition of Soviet claims in eastern Poland and the Baltic states.

Now Hitler could attack Poland without fear of intervention by his great rival to the east. Without a declaration of war, Nazi troops crossed the Polish frontier on the morning of September 1, 1939, and the *Luftwaffe* began to bomb Polish cities. Hitler hoped that the appeasing governments of France and Great Britain would wring their hands and do nothing, but he miscalculated: the two western democracies, knowing that their own time would come sooner or later, declared war on Germany on September 3. The Second World War had begun.

The Inactive War. War in Europe split American political opinion along new lines. Many liberals opposed defense spending because it would cut down on welfare appropriations. Conservatives who had vigorously opposed domestic spending were, in many cases, willing to support larger military appropriations. Public sentiment, disgusted by Europe's inability to keep the peace, was strongly against anything that would involve the United States in war.

From the start the President favored rearmament and aid to France and England. His political problem was to swing public and congressional opinion behind him. Plans for defense mobilization were drawn up but not acted upon. After the Munich Pact there was a White House Planning Conference which led to a bill in 1939 appropriating a half billion dollars for defense. When polls early in 1940 showed public opinion 60 per cent in favor of aid to England and France, the President secured a revised Neutrality Act which lifted the arms embargo on a cash basis but still prohibited American ships from trading with belligerents and American citizens from traveling on belligerent vessels.

After the rapid conquest of Poland, Germany remained virtually inactive during the winter of 1939-1940. This "Phony War" ended abruptly on April 9, 1940, when Germany simultaneously invaded Denmark and Norway. A month later Nazi armies invaded Belgium, France, and Holland, and in six weeks all had surrendered. After the fall of France the British rescued over 300,000 of their troops from the beach at Dunkirk, but they had to abandon practically all of their equipment. The army returned to an island without land defense against armored columns. On June 10, when the defeat of France was certain, Italy came into the war on the side of Germany.

A Year of Decision. What should American policy be now that Hitler with his ally in Italy controlled western Europe, and military men regarded the conquest of England as likely? The joint planners of the War and Navy Departments thought that the United States should husband its resources at home to prepare for attack. Isolationists, including many leading citizens and scholars, held that while the United States should be prepared, it was in no immediate danger of attack. The President was for as much aid to Britain as he could arrange without being overridden by the antiwar majority in Congress.

The President's decision to take a chance on British survival through all-out U. S. aid was probably the most fateful one of the entire period. He could have pursued a more isolationist policy without alienating his political support. The policy he elected to pursue led almost inevitably to war. The overriding fact in the decisions of both Roosevelt and Wilson appears to have been an unwillingness to permit a Europe in which a militaristic Germany was the dominant power.

In a contest over policy involving military action the President has a great advantage over Congress. He can act and seek support later, whereas Congress, as a nonadministrative body, is always behind a rapid march of events. This is in effect what happened from June 1940 on. The President went ahead administratively to give England as much aid as possible. In so doing, he educated the public toward his point of view, and Congress was usually presented with actions already taken that would be hard to reverse.

In June, for example, Congress thought to restrict the President by passing a law forbidding him to give away military equipment unless the Army Chief of Staff and the Chief of Naval Operations certified it as not essential to the national defense. But on September 2 an executive agreement was signed with England transferring fifty over-age American destroyers in return for British bases in Newfoundland, Bermuda, and the Caribbean. Since the bases increased American security, this action was obviously not a violation of the law, yet it tied the United States to the defense of the British Empire and marked the end of any pretext of neutrality. Germany did not declare war at this time because it did not want the United States in the war. Later in September 1940 Germany, Italy, and Japan formed a military alliance obviously aimed at the United States.

These critical strokes of foreign policy took place during the presidential campaign of 1940. Four days before the Republican convention met in June, the President appointed Republican leaders Henry L. Stimson and Frank Knox to his cabinet as Secretaries of War and of the Navy. Two days before the convention France surrendered. The general confusion favored the internationalists. As none of the leading Republican contenders developed decisive strength, Wendell L. Willkie, a businessman who sympathized with Roosevelt's foreign policy, was skillfully maneuvered to victory. As in 1936, the Republicans had gone far away from the principles of their center and right wing to attract marginal Democratic votes.

The national emergency led the President to seek a third term. Through the manipulations of Harry Hopkins, representing the President, the Democratic bosses were reluctantly forced to accept Henry A. Wallace for the vice-presidency.

During the campaign both those favoring all-out aid and those opposed to risks that might lead to war were nationally organized. The journalist William Allen White of Kansas headed a Committee to Defend America by Aiding the Allies, and business leader Robert E. Wood of Illinois was chairman of the isolationist America First Committee. At first the effect of the controversy on the campaign was not clear, since both candidates were internationalists. But by October, as Great Britain withstood Germany's aerial blitzkrieg and was not invaded, the argument that aid to Britain was more important than keeping out of war lost its immediate urgency. When public opinion pollsters found that the number of those favoring foreign aid had declined to less than half the voters, Willkie shifted his ground. Having failed to gain support on the issues of the third term and mismanaged defense, Willkie now attacked Roosevelt as a warmonger. Alarmed by the apparent success of the Willkie strategy, the President was pushed further and further away from his true beliefs. Just before election he told his listeners: "I have said this before, but I shall say it again and again and again: Your boys are not going to be sent into any foreign wars." In his mind, an attack on the United States would not be a "foreign" war.

The Democratic vote was slightly below that of 1936 and the Republican 5.5 million larger, but Willkie won only 82 electoral votes to Roosevelt's 449. The total minor party vote fell below 200,000. It was hard to call the result a referendum on any policy, since there had been no substantial disagreement; but it could be read as a vote of confidence in Roosevelt personally, or, as Republicans saw it, as proof of the strength of habitual patterns of voting and the Democratic political machine. To the President, it was support for more vigorous foreign aid and military preparation.

Characteristically, the President had put political and foreign problems ahead of domestic ones. By August Congress had appropriated some $16 billion for defense—enough, if it could be used, to move toward a war footing. The following month Congress agreed on a bipartisan basis to a selective service (draft) act. But meanwhile the essential economic organization for defense faltered. Production, the President felt, could be called into existence later when needed.

This was, of course, far from true. Coordination of production was in the hands of a nearly powerless National Defense Advisory Commission. In the words of Donald Nelson, its coordinator for procurement, the commission "began to stagger in the late summer and early autumn of 1940. In November it was punch drunk. It did not fall flat on its face until five days before Christmas." Its successor, the Office of Production Management, had little more success.

The basic difficulty was that private industry did not want to be regimented in time of peace, and, for fear of strengthening the isolationists, the President was reluctant to ask Congress for the necessary power. Fortunately, however, the United States had great capacity for manufacturing the automotive and other steel equipment needed for this war. Incentives such as quick tax write-offs and long-term contracts stimulated big business to undertake much of the new construction that had to precede mass production of military equipment.

By December 1940 the opinion polls indicated around 60 per cent of the American people were in favor of helping Great Britain even at the risk of war. Thus, when Churchill told Roosevelt that British credits for the purchase of war supplies was nearing exhaustion, Roosevelt believed he had popular support for extending more liberal, outright aid. A bill was quickly drawn up and introduced in Congress calling for "munitions of war and supplies of many kinds to be turned over to those nations which are now in actual war with aggressor nations," to be paid back in goods and services at the end of the war. Opposed by Republican leaders, the bill had the compulsion of the situation behind it. On March 11 "Lend-Lease" became law, and the next day the President asked Congress for an initial $7 billion to implement the policy. (Total Lend-Lease aid to all the Allies through the course of the war amounted to over $50 billion.)

The United States had already broken the laws of neutrality beyond repair by aiding only one side and keeping the vessels of the other out of the western Atlantic. Yet Lend-Lease marked the point of no return on the road to war. The bill committed American industrial power, nearly equal to that of all the rest of the world, to the defeat of Germany.

CHAPTER 21

THE AGE OF ANALYSIS

THE INNER REVOLUTION

New World of Uncertainty. In the late nineteenth century, middle- and upper-class Americans subcribed to well-defined values of Christian morality and the doctrine of self-improvement through the use of reason and will. They viewed the physical universe as a coherent, understandable system regulated by simple laws which were rapidly being learned. As a result of the firm beliefs of American society, parents and teachers tended to be authoritative, and political and economic leaders tended to be dogmatic.

During the first two decades of the twentieth century, however, this system of beliefs was attacked from every side. New scholarship cast doubt upon the literal truth of the Bible. Psychology first questioned the older theories of learning and mental discipline, and then, through Freud, attacked reason itself. Furthermore, understanding of the nature of the physical world was lost to all but scientists by the discovery that only mathematics provided a reliable guide to the behavior of matter. None of these new ideas were satisfactory substitutes for the old "truths," however; the new world of science was based on uncertainty and on a continual search for answers that would, at best, be only partial.

In the first two decades of the twentieth century only scientists, ministers, professors, and other intellectuals were much troubled by the changing bases for belief. Only in the 1920's was the impact of the new ideas felt in middle-class child rearing, education, and popular attitudes. But when this stage was reached, the total effect on the educated individual amounted to a revolution in ideas and attitudes.

Changes in Education. The mid-nineteenth-century American view was that education should be directed toward primarily moral or religious rather than intellectual ends. The philosophy of Horace Mann, the most famous American educator of the period, was a "blend of natural law, faith in progress, capitalistic morality, and liberal Protestantism."[1] The teacher's role was to see that the pupils memorized passages that inculcated abstract truths.

But in the late nineteenth century American scholars returned from German universities with new conceptions of psychology and elementary education. By 1900 alert parents were applying the new psychology to child rearing: children were to be trained by reason and interest rather than by display of parental authority. Confined to a few advanced families before World War I, these principles of letting the child experiment and learn for himself were widely held among the urban middle class of the 1920's.

---
1. Lawrence Cremin, *Transformation of the School* (New York: Alfred Knopf, 1961), p. 10.

A radically progressive approach to education based on the new psychology was advanced by John Dewey (see p. 334). Before World War I the impact of Dewey's progressive education was limited to some private schools and the public systems in a few cities, but in the 1920's his principles became dominant in the major teachers colleges and spread throughout the public school system as theory, if not as practice. Dewey's *Democracy and Education,* written in 1916, was the most influential guide; the Progressive Education Association, formed in 1919, was the major pressure group; and Teacher's College of Columbia University was the chief training center for progressive educators.

Often allied with progressivism were new movements for efficiency and utility in education. School superintendents applied business methods of "job-analysis" to their schools. The intellectual worth of teachers was often neglected, while they were rated by their efficiency in performing the "housekeeping" necessities of the school. The ideas of preparing the student for daily life, rather than requiring him to master a body of knowledge, led a writer in 1922 to divide school activities into four major categories: health, fundamental processes, civic and social relations, and recreation. Of these, only the second embraced conventional learning.

From the emphasis on utility came a great growth of vocational education on the secondary level. The Smith-Hughes Act of 1917, granting federal aid to vocational education, started a rapid spread of special high schools and manual or trade departments in older schools. More and more a distinction was made between the minority in high school who expected to go to college, and the majority who should substitute the development of practical skills for "book learning."

In the 1930's the extreme child-centered philosophy was superseded by a community-centered approach. No doubt the depression put emphasis on social and community duties, but, in addition, child-centrism had been pushed to such chaotic extremes that even Dewey had become critical of the results. The newer view stressed good group relations among students and teachers, and schools responsive to the needs and problems of the community. Although it partially restored discipline, this approach did not necessarily place more emphasis on academic learning.

Statistics can only partly suggest the low but improving quality of teaching in the interwar period. In 1920 the average teacher's salary was $871 a year, and the usual school was a small rural building with one or two teachers. The average teacher was not college-educated and was not paid enough to support a family. As a result, most teachers were young single women teaching school until they married or found a more promising job. By 1930 the situation had improved somewhat. The average salary had risen to $1400—still inadequate for a middle-class family—and automobile buses were introducing the consolidated school. By 1940 consolidated schools, with their greater degree of specialization among teachers, were becoming the rule in the more populous areas; a majority of the children were in urban schools; and teachers' salaries had risen about 25 per cent in purchasing power.

College education followed many of these same trends. For the first time utilitarian programs spread rapidly: schools of education in which physical education could be a major subject multiplied; women were offered courses in home economics; and most major universities started schools of commerce or business. For students who wanted a mixture of liberal arts and "useful" subjects, junior colleges offered two-year certificates. In 1920 there were only 52 such colleges; by 1930 there were ten times that number.

Many regarded these developments as a lowering of the standards of college education; nevertheless, colleges and universities showed substantial development as centers of learning and research. The 1920's was the first full decade in which general research was supported by massive endowments such as those of the Carnegie and Rockefeller Foundations. Increasing private donations and state grants enabled American universities to rival those of Europe as centers of research. And at the same time, more and more Americans were going to college. In 1920, 8 per cent of young people aged 18 to 21 were in college; in 1930, over 12 per cent; and in 1940 nearly 16 per cent. College degrees were becoming increasingly important in securing jobs and gaining social prestige.

The Attack on Rationality. While the pragmatic philosophy that underlay progressive education had emphasized the use of reason to alter tradition, psychological theories which emerged in the 1920's questioned man's ability to reason objectively. The ideas of Sigmund Freud, a Viennese physician and psychiatrist, had a profound social impact. In his brilliant writings Freud popularized the idea that people were impelled to think and act by unconscious pressures inaccessible to normal reason. Freud further held that these irrational, unconscious urges were of a "sexual" nature, although he used the term "sex" broadly to include many cravings for pleasure not normally thought of as sexual. Thus, to Freud, what appeared to be rational behavior was often merely the disguise for a mixture of erotic urges and childhood attitudes which, though they were unrecognized by the individual, influenced his behavior in many ways.

One of the great appeals of Freudianism was that it offered help to people who were emotionally disturbed. By free association of ideas in the presence of a psychiatrist, together with the scientific interpretation of dreams, it might be possible to bring the disturbing elements to conscious recognition and thus to lessen or end the feeling of conflict or anxiety.

Early Freudian doctrines lent themselves to a completely sexual view of man's conduct; their emphasis on the *libido,* man's instinctive sexual drive, plus Freud's denial of the validity of religious feelings had a profound effect upon the thinking of well-educated people all over the western world. It turned older theological doctrine upside down: in the place of salvation by abstinence and by the use of reason and will power Freudianism placed no emphasis on abstinence and little on reason and offered salvation through indulgent secular "confession." People who sought Freudian therapy did not necessarily discard their religious faith, and a few clergymen managed to reach a compromise with the new doctrine, but again the scientific approach had weakened or contradicted the values of the nineteenth century.

Freudianism provided an excellent weapon for attack on Victorian formalities, rural Protestant virtues, older educational ideas, and limitations on women's activities. Consequently, Freudianism appeared to have great influence on urban middle-class conduct. Leading intellectuals such as Walter Lippmann, Harold Lasswell, and Jerome Frank applied Freudianism to politics, public opinion, and the law with the general effect of further weakening rationality and traditional standards. Magazines and books were full of the new psychiatric language, and many well-educated people enjoyed being amateur Freudian psychiatrists. Well-informed parents now worried about the danger of suppressing their children's urges, and the child-centered home joined the child-centered school in relaxing discipline.

Physical and Social Theory. A further attack on the nineteenth-century belief that man was on the verge of understanding the nature of things came from physical science. Over the half-century before 1920 a brilliant group of European physicists and mathematicians demonstrated that man could not perceive the nature of physical reality or picture its workings by the ordinary three-dimensional images of the mind; only mathematics had a logic that could handle the four or more dimensions of physical problems. Furthermore, they discovered that matter was not solid substance but a system of electrical energy, and that the only guides to this reality were mathematical equations and readings of complicated electrical recording devices. Discoveries in the infinitesimal world of the atom and the infinite world of outer space made reflective men uncertain whether reality is precise and orderly or, at least, whether man's imagination is capable of grasping its order, if there is one. In 1930 the English physicist, Sir James Jeans, suggested that reality as men were accustomed to thinking of it might be only an illusion.

Some writers predicted that the scientific uncertainty that was brought to the reading public in the late 1920's should lead to a new age of faith. But the immediate effect seemed to be in the opposite direction. Like the earlier evolutionary theory, the new science undermined theology without offering anything positive to replace it. Furthermore, the highly abstract characterizations of God that seemed to suit the physical theories were without much appeal to practical, realistic Americans.

The effect of mathematical logic and the changing scientific knowledge was also upsetting to the social sciences and philosophy. Society no longer seemed so simple as it had at the beginning of the century. If general social laws could be discovered it would only be by highly complex and sophisticated methods. As a result, American social scientists turned to improving their methods and trying them out on limited, carefully defined problems, rather than elaborating general systems. Philosophers, also discouraged by the mysterious character of reality, turned to studies of method. "How can any kind of truth be established?" became their major question. The testing of various systems of logic and representation consumed their time, and the main body of philosophers lost interest in general systems of thought.

While the social sciences as a whole continued their pursuit of more sophisticated methods, the depression brought the pressure of immediate, practical problems to bear on economic thinking. A few academic social scientists embraced Marxism and gave up hope for the capitalist system, but the number was surprisingly small. The majority turned to solutions of the type that were given a rounded theoretical formulation by the British economist John Maynard Keynes.

Keynes' ideas brought the first major revision of economic theory in the twentieth century. Furthermore, they offered a more realistic view of the operation of the entire economy than had existed before. His major work, *The General Theory of Employment, Interest and Money*, published in 1936, shifted the main theoretical emphasis from supply and demand to income and investment, or from the mechanics of the market to the distribution of income. Keynes' most important conclusions were: (1) that increasing the income of the poor stimulated demand, while increasing the income of the rich promoted saving; (2) that increased demand, not increased saving, led to new business investment; (3) that total income could only increase from such investment; (4) that if the functioning of the undisturbed free market did not provide adequate business investment to maintain a sufficient flow of income, the federal government was the only agency with sufficient power to see that this result was achieved.

Obviously these doctrines implying higher wages and government investment were resisted by conservatives. But the theory was already being applied in fact by the New Deal, although President Roosevelt did not subscribe to Keynesianism or any other economic theory. By the end of World War II the prosperity induced by government spending and massive redistribution of income downward was so obvious that politicians of both major parties implicitly acted on the Keynesian assumptions, and academic economists gradually made Keynes' ideas the starting point for their new theoretical models. These things would have happened without Keynes, but he supplied the rationale for the capitalist revolution that emerged from the disaster of the Great Depression.

The Increasingly Social Gospel. While the pressures of clergymen for sweeping social reform lessened in the prosperous 1920's, religious groups became increasingly concerned with secular matters. Urban churches, in particular, acquired game rooms, gymnasiums, and lecture halls and seemed to be shifting their emphasis from worship to social service and recreation. By the end of the decade the Federal Council of Churches of Christ, the liberal ecumenical organization, had commissions for such diverse matters as international justice, social service, race relations, and Christian education. The National Catholic Welfare Conference, formed to help carry out social obligations of the Catholic Church, became a powerful force with a large staff of experts on legislative matters. Missionary activities also were increasingly secularized. By 1920 effectively organized Protestant and Catholic missions in non-Christian areas were emphasizing "civilizing" education, medical care, and various other services.

The increasingly social orientation of the leading Protestant churches was resisted by fundamentalists—Protestants who believed in the literal interpretation of the Bible as a historical record and prophecy, as well as a guide to faith and morality. The conflict between fundamentalism and current scientific views, either religious or secular, was dramatized by the Scopes trial in 1925. John Scopes, a science teacher in a Tennessee high school, was charged with violating a state law forbidding the teaching in public schools of any theories denying the Biblical account of the creation of man—Darwin's theory of evolution in particular. With his prosecution led by William Jennings Bryan, who championed the literal interpretation of the Bible, and his defense conducted by the famous liberal lawyer Clarence Darrow, Scopes was convicted of violating the Tennessee law and fined $100, but the penalty later was set aside. The Scopes trial attracted more national and world-wide attention to American fundamentalism than did any other event of the period between the wars.

Historically the Protestant church in America had been supported by the urban middle class. Neither farmers in remote areas nor the urban lower class generally made the effort necessary to participate actively in the work of a Protestant church, but for status-seeking members of the middle class the church had a definite social value. It was a place to meet leading citizens and develop friendships through cooperation in religious endeavors. Consequently, the great growth of the urban and suburban middle class and the spread of the automobile to outlying areas led to a steady increase in church membership up to 1929. By 1926, 46 per cent of the population were church members.

These reasons for growth go far to explain why the Great Depression reversed the trend in membership. People with only shabby clothes and no money for the collection plate did not want to appear before their more prosperous neighbors. The depression may actually have increased religious feeling, but between 1930 and 1934 the income of Protestant churches declined 50 per cent. For the decade as a whole church membership fell about 6 per cent. That the decline was caused by financial hardships is further indicated by the rapid growth in membership in the prosperous years which followed World War II.

The Great Depression brought liberal Catholic, Jewish, and Protestant organizations closer together. In 1931 the National Catholic Welfare Conference, the General Conference of Rabbis, and the Federal Council of Churches of Christ joined in a conference on Permanent Preventatives of Unemployment. Such efforts were continued by an inter-faith Committee on Religious Welfare Activity. Despite vocal opposition from conservatives within the various denominations who wanted their churches to refrain from raising political and social questions, liberal religious journals became increasingly secular in content and more concerned with economic problems. A large portion of these leading religious spokesmen, perhaps a third, urged some cooperative or socialistic solution for the depression.

MASS COMMUNICATION

Newspapers. The newspaper continued to be the principal reading matter of adult Americans. Where personal interests were involved, such as in attitudes toward the New Deal, readers were obviously prepared to disagree with their newspapers. But by subtle selection and handling of news and comment the papers and press associations undoubtedly influenced readers to accept the ideas of editors and managers.

The major trends in the period between the wars were toward less directly competitive and more elaborate papers. While newspaper chains stopped growing in the 1930's, another ultimately more important limitation on competition came from the merger of competing papers within the same city. In 1930 nine tenths of the cities with a population of more than 100,000 had two or more directly competing papers, but of the smaller cities only a fifth had such morning or evening competition.

In the larger cities competition of a sort was often maintained by an all-day tabloid competing against single full-sized morning and evening papers. The first American tabloid newspaper was the *New York Daily News*, started by Joseph M. Patterson in 1919. Easy to read on subways and buses, by 1924 the *News* had the largest circulation in the city. Other publishers quickly followed Patterson's innovation, and by 1940 there were nearly fifty tabloids.

Another form of potential competition whose effects on the full-sized daily were hard to measure was radio news. To protect themselves, many papers—250 by 1940—bought control of radio stations. In spite of the obvious fact that radio can deliver news more quickly, intimately, and dramatically, the effect of news broadcasts on newspaper circulation was not severe. As the public received increasing amounts of news it appeared to gain more interest in local, national, and international events and to spend more time learning about them.

Improvements in technology and press services produced better quality newspaper illustrations, more detailed last-minute news, and an increase in special departments and columns. The humorous columnist like Mr. Dooley, or Will Rogers, his counterpart in the 1920's, was an old feature, but the column of serious general comment was an innovation in the twenties. People bought papers just to read some favorite columnist like Heywood Broun or

Walter Lippmann. The more popular writers were distributed by press syndicates to newspapers all over the United States.

Magazines. The increasing public appetite for current events was fed by the rise of weekly news magazines. In 1920 only the *Literary Digest*, which took its material on current events largely from the newspapers, was important in this weekly field. In 1923 *Time*, smartly written under the direction of editors Briton Hadden and Henry Luce, made an immediate hit and inspired two other news weeklies. Following English patterns, the weekly picture magazine *Life* was started by the Luce organization in 1936. It also attracted imitators.

Throughout the 1920's the aged *Saturday Evening Post* was supreme among general weekly magazines. Closely mirroring the interests of the satisfied middle class, it mixed good popular fiction with inspirational articles about business leaders and the virtues of the American way of doing things. During the 1930's the *Post*, by turning more liberal, managed to hold much of its circulation, but competitors in its own field as well as other types of magazines were weakening its position.

Surrounded by hundreds of magazines and other sources of news and comment, the educated man of the 1920's frequently felt unable to keep up with what was being written. To help him, Mr. and Mrs. De Witt Wallace started *The Reader's Digest*, a reprint of what they considered the most important magazine articles of the preceding month. As the popularity of their digest grew they also commissioned articles and condensed books for quick reading. By 1940 *The Reader's Digest*'s circulation of three million already surpassed other monthlies, and ultimately it became the most widely read magazine in the world.

Radio. In August 1920, Station WWJ of the Detroit *News* began commercial broadcasting. The mass development of radio was retarded by many problems, including the control of necessary patents by American Telephone and Telegraph, General Electric, and Westinghouse, and the unwillingness of Associated Press, the largest news service, to have its releases broadcast. But in 1926 A. T. & T. agreed to permit network broadcasting by renting its wires, and the same year A.P., pressed by competitors, particularly Hearst's International News Service, amended its rules to allow broadcast of important news. Between 1926 and 1929 three national radio networks were created. Advertising agencies now brought their big clients to the networks, and radio quickly achieved the form that was to characterize it during the next generation.

By 1940 four fifths of American households had radios. These families heard Hoover, Roosevelt, and other political leaders put forth their views; Franklin Roosevelt, in particular, capitalized on his charming radio personality and the pseudo-intimacy of home reception in his "fireside chats."

Since advertisers dictated what was to be performed, there was little sponsorship for serious drama or literature during the popular hours. The leading stars of screen and stage appeared on radio, but usually as special attractions in the middle of variety shows. The only obvious effect of radio on its listeners was to make American culture more uniform in language, humor, and material goals.

THE ARTS

During the prosperous twenties, patronage of the arts was more widespread than ever before, but the Great Depression brought five grim years when most painters, sculptors, and serious composers could sell practically nothing. Rescue came in 1935 from the Federal

Arts Project, a branch of WPA. Forty thousand destitute actors, musicians, writers, and painters were employed at from $60 to $100 a month, and they quickly produced an unprecedented amount of music, drama, and other art for audiences that ran into the millions. This support, meager as it was, won many artists back from rebellion to a more balanced judgment of American society.

Music. The development of the phonograph and the radio gave composers and players of serious music a vastly expanded audience. By the 1920's phonographs and phonograph records had achieved an accuracy of reproduction that made them acceptable to fine musicians. Undoubtedly many more people than ever before became acquainted with operas, symphonies, and other classical works.

Although composers, like other artists, had reacted before the war to the new scientific attitude of experimentalism, trying dissonant, multitonal, nontemporal compositions, this *avant-garde* had few representatives in the United States. The upsurge in American composition was based on native folk melodies, both Negro and white, which produced jazz, more sophisticated popular compositions, and serious concertos and symphonies. Jazz was already mature in 1920. During the following decade the musical comedies of American composers Irving Berlin, George Gershwin, Jerome Kern, and Cole Porter captivated the western world. Carrying the same motifs to a higher plane of serious composition, George Gershwin wrote *Rhapsody in Blue* (1924), *An American in Paris* (1928), and *Porgy and Bess* (1935), all of which won world-wide acclaim. Aaron Copland, Roy Harris, and other Americans also gave classic form to American rhythms and melodies.

Motion Pictures. David W. Griffith's silent movie, *Broken Blossoms*, starring Lillian Gish, was widely acclaimed in 1919 by critics as marking the emergence of a new art form. The *Literary Digest* called it as important as music or poetry. Unfortunately, technological success and the work of this one middle-aged pioneer were not followed by a great burst of high-quality motion picture composition, directing, and acting.

The motion picture as an art medium was subordinated to business interests in marketing the film. The major production studios owned chains of theaters and controlled the circulation of pictures. With an investment of $2 billion to protect by 1930, the managers of the industry were unwilling to risk films that might not appeal to their major public, American adolescents; consequently, motion pictures of the twenties were massive spectacles of courts and armies directed by Cecil B. DeMille, sentimental melodramas starring Mary Pickford, breathtaking exploits by Douglas Fairbanks, Sr., or romantic seductions by Rudolph Valentino. Charlie Chaplin, producing and directing his own pictures, continued in his comedies of the underdog to protest against the current trends of both American society and Hollywood film production.

In the last three years of the 1920's sound and then color made the motion picture potentially the equal of the stage. As a result, local and traveling stock companies and vaudeville practically disappeared, and the professional stage became restricted to a few of the largest cities. From the 1920's to the 1950's the motion picture was the standard form of dramatic entertainment in the United States.

Although the artistic quality of the best pictures of the 1930's was unquestionably superior to that of the previous decade, the industry still feared realism. Accepted doctrine was that the audience wanted to escape into a dream world of wealth and high adventure. Consequently, the motion picture was a conservative force substituting imaginary satisfactions for worries about the daily problems of life. Produced by businessmen, pictures inevitably glorified material values and preserved the legendary American success story during the grim years of unemployment.

Architecture. To many Europeans the most important American artistic achievement of the 1920's was the skyscraper. Many European cities regulated the height of buildings, and none had the urge for lofty display that seized American business. As land values rose in U.S. cities it became economical to increase the height of buildings in the most valuable locations, but the heights achieved in the 1920's far exceeded the economic need. The advertising value that accrued to the company that built a towering building and the extra amount that tenants were willing to pay for the prestige and convenience of such lofty offices led to a race for height that culminated in the 1200-foot Empire State Building, begun in 1929.

The architectural design that was dominant in skyscraper architecture by the late 1920's resulted partly from the New York Zoning Act of 1916, which forced setbacks in buildings rising above certain heights. The plans of the Finnish architect Eliel Saarinen, who designed a series of blocks diminishing in size as the building rose, with windows set in vertical panels between continuous strips of stone or concrete, became a general model for skyscraper design.

Whereas the Saarinen motifs emphasized height, the principles of modern European architecture—often called the international style—often emphasized horizontal lines. A slight influence of Frank Lloyd Wright could be detected in new factories and school buildings, but the major inspiration of American architects such as Joseph Urban seems to have derived from European models.

During both prosperity and depression, older styles of architecture dominated the design of most public buildings and homes. The Capitol in Washington, D.C., was rebuilt by the Hoover and Roosevelt administrations in the classical Greco-Roman style, the style also chosen for most post offices and state buildings. During the 1920's hundreds of thousands of new homes were built by the well-to-do, but they or their architects and builders generally preferred to adopt some past style rather than to experiment with the unfamiliar problems of "modern."

Painting. The mood of experimentation that prevailed in education and the social sciences, and the urge to break with tradition, were reflected in sculpture and painting. In these media the break with the past took two roads: some artists simplified or distorted the objects they represented, while others abandoned reality completely in favor of abstract design. In sculpture these two trends, obviously close together, were harder to distinguish than in painting, and, in any case, American sculptural achievement was minor.

Such European movements as cubism, surrealism, and other forms of abstract painting found proponents in the United States. A predominantly abstract approach to form was adopted by Joseph Stella, John Marin, Marsden Hartley, Stuart Davis, and Max Weber, but during the reaction of the 1920's against prewar enthusiasms such purely abstract painting failed to attract young artists, and it diminished in popularity during the depression. Another group, including Charles Sheeler, Charles Demuth, and Georgia O'Keeffe, emphasized the abstract aesthetic form in machinery, architecture, and nature. Their craftsmanship was exacting, their themes recognizable, and their forms sharply bounded and precise.

The main body of important American painting during the interwar period, however, illustrated a more conventional type of painting which had close enough contact with reality to permit social observations. Thomas Hart Benton, Grant Wood, and John Steuart Curry extolled the rural sights and characters of the Midwest, as opposed to the urban East or Europe. In contrast to the Midwesterners there existed a group of painters who similarly concentrated on the American scene but explored the problem of urban life rather than the virtues of rural life. Ben Shahn, William Gropper, and Philip Evergood were among those stimulated by a strong sense of social justice, engendered primarily by the depression; in their paintings they protested against political corruption, slum life, and strikebreaking. Whereas the ash-can school of the early twentieth century (see p. 338) had seen poverty as picturesque or inescapable, these angry painters of the 1930's saw poverty as an inexcusable result of capitalism.

Never before in American history had so many young men sought careers in art. The prosperity of the middle twenties produced one great wave, which ended for the majority in poverty and nonproductivity during the first half of the 1930's. The second major upswing came in 1935 with the Federal Arts Project. Partly because the subsidized painters had to do so many community murals and other public pictures, and partly because there was a general return to an appreciation for things American, this art tended to embrace the national past. It cannot be said with assurance that during these twenty years any great masterpieces were executed by American painters, but the total product of the abler artists was larger and more impressive than in previous generations.

Literature and Drama. Writers of the 1920's experienced a growing dissatisfaction with and alienation from American society and twentieth-century values. In particular, they were disillusioned by the ease with which Woodrow Wilson and others throughout the world had converted moral idealism into a zeal for war; they were alienated by the triumph of materialism and business values in the postwar period; and they were exasperated by the smug self-satisfaction of the American upper classes. "The younger generation," wrote Harold Stearns, "*is* in revolt; it *does* dislike almost to the point of hatred and certainly to the point of contempt the type of people dominant in our present civilization."[2]

In *This Side of Paradise* F. Scott Fitzgerald complained that the young writers "had grown up to find all Gods dead, all wars fought, all faiths in men shaken." They deplored American materialism, prosperity, Puritanism, and conformity—in short, much of the national heritage. But unlike the confident prewar novelists they did not preach reform, for they saw no immediate way of correcting the situation. This prevailing nonsocial attitude was sweepingly expressed by the leading drama critic, George Jean Nathan: "What concerns me alone is myself and a few close friends. For all I care the rest of the world can go to hell at today's sunset."

To escape from America writers moved to the relative isolation of Greenwich Village in New York City or to the more complete separation of Paris. That critic H. L. Mencken's pungent but superficial and nihilistic attacks on all values were widely read in both his *American Mercury* magazine and in book form revealed the desire of many intellectuals to divorce themselves from American attitudes.

Yet from this alienated generation of writers came as much good drama, poetry, and fiction as the United States had ever seen. Novelists denounced the world in vigorous new prose, used new literary techniques, and wrote with frankness and sincerity. Ernest Hemingway, who gave currency to the phrase "the lost generation," started in *The*

---
2. Harold Stearns, *America and the Young Intellectual* (New York: George H. Doran, 1921) pp. 11-12.

Sun Also Rises (1925) with a rather general repudiation of the postwar world and of the importance of the intellect. In *A Farewell to Arms* (1929) he showed the stupidity of World War I. But by 1940 in *For Whom the Bell Tolls* Hemingway had moved gradually to a more positive position of affirming the need for the social solidarity of man.

Other writers exposed the contradictions and hypocrisies of American culture. Theodore Dreiser's *American Tragedy* (1925), which portrayed a young American hopelessly confused by the false social and religious values of his environment, marked the summit of Dreiser's career. Sinclair Lewis wrote all of his important attacks on American society during the 1920's. *Main Street* (1920) satirized the small town of the Middle West, where "dullness made God." *Babbitt* (1922) parodied the self-satisfied, conformist, materialistic American businessman so successfully that "Babbitt" and "Babbittry" were added to the dictionary. *Arrowsmith* (1925) depicted an America which placed frustrating impediments in the path of a doctor devoted to medical research. *Dodsworth* (1929) satirized the American woman, picturing Fran Dodsworth as a pampered, selfish, superficial, pretentious snob. Sherwood Anderson in *Winesburg, Ohio* (1919) and in subsequent books showed from a Freudian viewpoint how middle-class morals and customs produced a neurotic society. Perhaps the most brilliant attacks on the lack of proper values among the American upper class were in F. Scott Fitzgerald's *This Side of Paradise* (1920) and *The Great Gatsby* (1925).

The rebellion against the world in general and postwar America in particular also produced great drama. The eleven plays of Eugene O'Neill, from *Beyond the Horizon* (1920) to *Mourning Becomes Electra* (1931), all strongly influenced by Freudian psychology, marked the first major United States contribution to serious theatre. Half a dozen other Americans, such as Sidney Howard, Maxwell Anderson, Elmer Rice, and Robert Sherwood, joined in this remarkable upsurge of American drama.

In contrast to the preoccupation of writers in the twenties with individual emotional adjustment as seen in the light of new psychologies, the Great Depression inevitably brought a return to social problems. Poverty amidst plenty was the writers' lot as well as that of the masses. John Dos Passos, who had begun an attack on American capitalism in *Three Soldiers* (1921), achieved his best work in a trilogy, *U.S.A.*, published between 1930 and 1935. His picture of American society was far from accurate, but the writing was sincere and powerful.

A number of writers joined or supported the Communist party as offering the only logical solution and were influenced to write novels of working-class experience. From this forced-draft effort to understand a strange environment, few important novels or poems emerged. In drama Clifford Odets succeeded somewhat better with plays like *Waiting for Lefty* (1935), but here also the proletarian period left no masterpieces.

Three men who placed less emphasis on American political problems produced notable work between 1929 and 1941. James T. Farrell's three-volume *Studs Lonigan* (1932-1935) showed the failure of the traditional character-building institutions—the home, the school, and the church—to prevent the moral ruin of a young Irish immigrant boy. John Steinbeck's *The Grapes of Wrath* (1939), a chronicle of the misery of a family of Oklahoma tenant farmers who migrate to California in search of work, is a vivid portrayal of the difficulties caused by the Great Depression. Many years later Steinbeck was awarded the Nobel Prize for literature. William Faulkner published a dozen volumes dealing both realistically and symbolically with the failure of Southern society to adjust to the twentieth century. Faulkner experimented with many new devices in order to explore both the conscious and unconscious life of his characters, but he gradually moved toward a more conventional style.

Thomas Wolfe, regarded by many critics as a major novelist, wrote four autobiographical novels between 1929 and his death in 1938. Combining both an obsession with his own emotional responses and a devotion to America, his long, loose-jointed books were unique in the depression decade.

THE HISTORICAL VIEW

By 1940 the scientific and technological basis for a new era in the world's history had been achieved, but emotional and institutional adjustment had not taken place. "The old has lingered on as the new has appeared," wrote Walton Hamilton in 1938, "the industrial landscape is all broken up with fault lines. . . . A lingering culture—fiction, drama, music, poetry—tries vainly to bring itself alongside current industrial fact."

Electrification, automobiles, and high industrial productivity made possible a society in which middle-class standards of living could be universal, but up to the mid-1930's the working of the economy was so poorly understood that wrong policies were almost continuously pursued. By the late 1920's the economy needed more mass purchasing power; by the early 1930's the need became acute. But even in the New Deal, government policies were not adequate to correct the situation. Without steadily rising consumer demand there was little incentive to put the new technology to work, and consequently the economy failed to expand at a satisfactory rate.

Economic failure was accompanied by intellectual and spiritual troubles affecting the entire western world. Among the elite of all leading nations the scientific, pragmatic attitude had displaced the traditional "natural" or religious values of the nineteenth century. What had seemed simple and reasonable to their grandfathers seemed infinitely complex and uncertain to men of the second quarter of the twentieth century. School and church, once the guardians of basic beliefs, were now confused and tended to become followers of the new trends rather than sources of authority.

The spiritual uncertainty of the times deeply affected artists and scholars; yet both these groups reacted so vigorously against the obvious shortcomings of their environment that American productivity in both art and scholarship reached new levels. The 1930's, in particular, was a decade of realistic and sharpened probing into American problems.

The probing by historians produced general agreement on the nature, meaning, and inevitability of the New Deal. A handful of Marxists attacked Roosevelt for his unyielding capitalism, and one or two professional historians subsequently supported Republican criticisms of domestic policy, but the great majority took a liberal Democratic view. More and more historians viewed the period from 1900 to 1940 as one of grudging but inevitable adjustment of outworn political ideas to the needs of mass-production industrialism.

Thus, in spite of the nearly revolutionary character of domestic political change from the 1920's to the 1930's, the sharpest disagreements among historians came in interpreting foreign policy. Charles A. Beard, one of the leading American historians (see p. 341), violently attacked the President for taking the nation into World War II. This essentially isolationist view was immediately countered by other respected members of the profession such as Allan Nevins and William E. Langer, who held that no course other than that pursued by FDR would have been strategically or morally justifiable. As in the case of the minor groups that disagreed about domestic policy, a longer perspective has led to the acceptance of America's role in World War II as probably inevitable, considering the character of American culture and the pressure of world-wide forces.

BIBLIOGRAPHY

William E. Leuchtenburg, *The Perils of Prosperity: 1914-1932* (Chicago: University of Chicago Press, 1958) and Harold U. Faulkner, *From Versailles to the New Deal* (New Haven: Yale University Press, 1951) are good general accounts of the swing toward conservatism in the 1920's. On political and social thought see Eric F. Goldman, *Rendezvous with Destiny* (New York: Alfred A. Knopf, 1952), and Richard Hofstadter, *The Age of Reform: From Bryan to F.D.R.* (New York: Alfred A. Knopf, 1955). Arthur M. Schlesinger, Jr., *The Crisis of the Old Order* (Boston: Houghton Mifflin, 1957) is a provocative discussion from a Democratic viewpoint, as is Karl Schriftgiesser's more journalistic account, *This Was Normalcy* (Boston: Little, Brown, 1948). For continuing progressivism see Kenneth MacKay, *The Progressive Movement of 1924* (New York: Columbia University Press, 1947); B.C. and Fola La Follette, *Robert M. La Follette 1855-1925*, vol. 2 (New York: Macmillan, 1953); and Oscar Handlin, *Al Smith and His America* (Boston: Little, Brown, 1958). The best general economic account of the period just prior to the Great Depression is George Soule, *Prosperity Decade: From War to Depression, 1917-1929* (New York: Rinehart, 1947). *Only Yesterday* (New York: Harper, 1931) by Frederick Lewis Allen is a lively comment on society in the 1920's.

For the period of the 1930's, Harris G. Warren, *Herbert Hoover and the Great Depression* (New York: Oxford University Press, 1959) is a judicious account. Brief and readable is Dexter Perkins, *The New Age of Franklin Roosevelt: 1932-1945* (Chicago: University of Chicago Press, 1957); a longer survey is Basil Rauch, *The History of the New Deal, 1933-1938* (Toronto: McClelland and Stewart, 1944). Two more volumes by Arthur M. Schlesinger, Jr., *The Coming of the New Deal* and *The Politics of Upheaval* (Boston: Houghton Mifflin, 1959, 1960), take the Age of Roosevelt to 1936. Three volumes by Frank Freidel bring his *Franklin D. Roosevelt* (Boston: Little, Brown, 1952-1956) to 1932. A good brief biography is James M. Burns, *Roosevelt: The Lion and the Fox* (New York: Harcourt, Brace, 1956). Many of Roosevelt's associates wrote memoirs; of these, Frances Perkins, *The Roosevelt I Knew* (New York: Viking, 1946) is favorable and Raymond Moley, *After Seven Years* (New York: Harper, 1939) is critical. Robert E. Sherwood, *Roosevelt and Hopkins: An Intimate History*, 2 vols. (New York: Harper, 1948) is strong on foreign affairs; while John M. Blum, *From the Diaries of Henry Morgenthau, Jr.* (Boston: Houghton Mifflin, 1959) is chiefly domestic. A good study of the judiciary is C. H. Pritchett, *The Roosevelt Court* (New York: Macmillan, 1948).

For a foreign policy view friendly to Roosevelt see Allan Nevins, *The New Deal and World Affairs* (New Haven: Yale University Press, 1950); for a critical one see Charles A. Beard, *President Roosevelt and the Coming of the War, 1941* (New Haven, Conn.: Yale University Press, 1948). For a more detailed discussion of the American entrance into World War II see William L. Langer and S. E. Gleason, *The Challenge to Isolation; 1937-1940* (New York: Harper, 1952), and *The Undeclared War; September 1940-December 1941* (New York: Harper, 1953).

John K. Galbraith, *The Great Crash, 1929* (Boston: Houghton Mifflin, 1955) is both lively and authoritative. Broadus Mitchell, *Depression Decade, 1929-1941* (New York: Rinehart, 1947) is a general economic account. John D. Black, *Parity, Parity, Parity* (Cambridge: Harvard Committee on Research in the Social Sciences, 1942) discusses agricultural policies. Labor policy is treated in Walter Galenson, *The CIO Challenge to the AFL* (Cambridge: Harvard University Press, 1960) and Irving Bernstein, *New Deal Collective Bargaining Policy* (Berkeley: University of California Press, 1950). A comprehensive social and economic picture of the 1930's is Dixon Wecter, *Age of the Great Depression, 1929-1941* (New York: Macmillan, 1959).

For a general discussion of cultural and intellectual trends between the wars see Merle E. Curti, *The Growth of American Thought* (New York: Harper, 1951). Morton White, *The Age of Analysis* (New York: New American Library, 1955) is lively on trends in philosophy, which are covered more systematically in Herbert W. Schneider, *A History of American Philosophy* (New York: Columbia University Press, 1946).

PART 8: INTRODUCTION

THE GLOBAL CONFLICT

■ When involvement in the Second World War caused Franklin D. Roosevelt to tell newspaper reporters that "Dr. Win-the-War" was taking over from "Dr. New Deal," no one could know how deeply the experience of the Great Depression and the New Deal had cut into the fabric of American history. But the subsequent twenty years amply demonstrated that the great reforms of the 1930's had become integral parts of American life. Neither Republicans nor Democrats, when in power in the years after 1941, sought to alter or to abandon the far-reaching results of the Roosevelt Revolution. Moreover, the political party of Franklin D. Roosevelt now became the party of the nation. In all but two of the twelve congressional elections from 1940 to 1962, the Democratic party won majorities in both houses of Congress. Even an extremely popular Republican President like Dwight D. Eisenhower could not wean the American people from their depression-born allegiance to the Democratic party.

The Second World War was a turning point in history. Not only did it end the reformist impulse of the New Deal, but at long last it also eliminated the Great Depression. Moreover, the war demonstrated how wrong had been those observers who talked learnedly in the 1930's of the stagnation of the American economy. Under the impetus of war, production soared. In a sense, the American contribution to winning the war was to drown the enemy in a flood of goods. True, fifteen million American men and women were mobilized in the fighting forces, and over 321,000 died. But without depreciating these sacrifices, the fact remains that it was the Germans and the Russians who lost millions at home and on the battlefield; the American job was production. Furthermore, thanks to the lavish surpluses of the American economy, the United States was able to fight the war to complete victory on both fronts. Americans had always fought their wars with total victory as their goal, but the Second World War promised to be the last in which they would dare to. The new weapons which came out of the war were so destructive that total victory in any future war might well mean the end of the victors as well as of the vanquished. But limited war was unfamiliar to Americans; they found fighting such a war in Korea bewildering and frustrating.

Domestically, the war shaped a whole generation of Americans. In liquidating the depression, the war ushered in a new era of prosperity. Americans, unlike the Ger-

---

General of the Army Dwight D. Eisenhower, portrait by Thomas E. Stephens (1958). Eisenhower's eminent career spanned the modern era—as Supreme Allied Commander in Europe, 1943-1945; as U.S. Chief of Staff, 1945-1948; as Supreme Commander of the NATO forces, 1951-1952; and as President of the United States, 1953-1961.

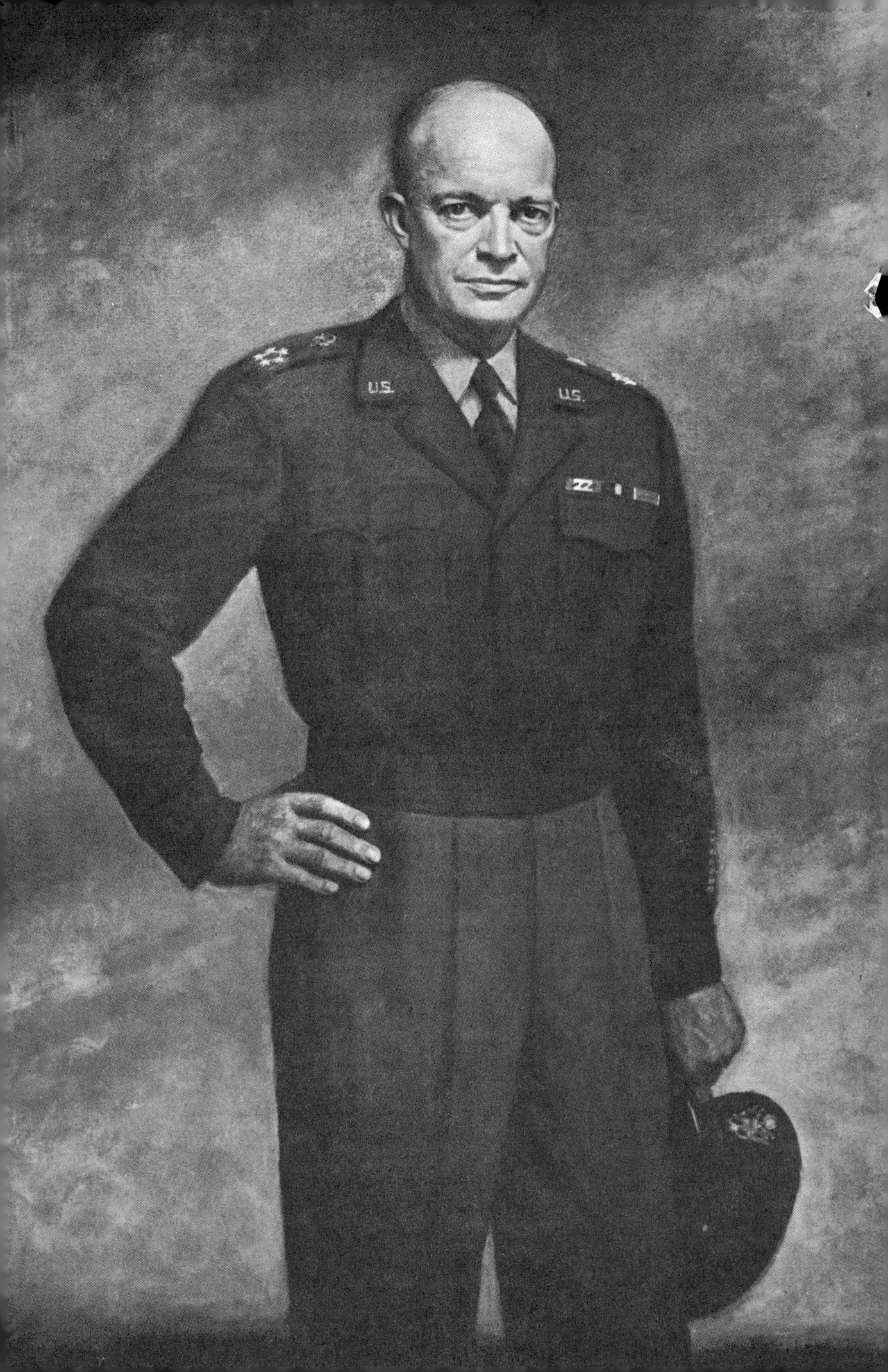
U.S.
U.S.

(Left) *The Rock*, painting by Peter Blume (1948). The nuclear age often bred a strong sense of futility and nihilism in literature and art; yet this surrealist painting connotes optimism, as the smoking ruins suggestive of old, destroyed values give way to the quarrying of materials for new buildings, new values, new hopes. (Above) *Nighthawks*, painting by Edward Hopper (1942).

mans, managed to have guns *and* butter. Never before had so many Americans lived so well. Moreover, the prosperity was enduring and of a kind which lifted whole strata of the poor to higher planes of living. Negroes obtained job opportunities and recognition that three decades of agitation had been unable to achieve. In the years after the war their economic gains were effective in battering down barriers of segregation in the South and in the North. Farmers, whose position under the New Deal had improved over that of the depressed twenties, went on to heights of prosperity during the war and after, rivaling those of the golden days before the First World War. Organized labor emerged from the war so strong that almost immediately thereafter it was subjected to governmental restraints. The war propelled women out of the home into factories in unprecedented numbers, and they continued to swell the industrial labor force after the war.

The prosperity of the war years and after transformed not only American society but also political and social attitudes. Prosperous times after 1945 seemed to breathe life into a new conservatism. For several postwar years a pervading fear of Communist subversion muffled honest dissent and placed limits on critical social thought. Reform ceased to be popular. Though it is true that none of the New Deal measures was abandoned in the postwar years, at the same time it is evident that few, if any, additional advances were made. Democratic Presidents Harry S. Truman and John F. Kennedy, consciously following the steps of FDR, recommended new reforms, but the Congresses, though nominally dominated by the Democratic party, were usually far too conservative to enact reform measures. Nor is it without significance that the conservative Dwight D. Eisenhower proved to be among the most popular Presidents in history. For most Americans these were good years, in which prosperity and private concerns took precedence over public reform.

Of the many unforeseen consequences which flowed from the Second World War, none was more portentous than the emergence of the Soviet Union as a world power. Swiftly moving into the power vacuum left in Europe by the destruction of Nazi Germany, the U.S.S.R. threatened not only to dominate the continent but also to spread its

Collection of the Whitney Museum of American Art, New York.

(Above) *The Senator,* painting by Joseph Hirsch (1941). The congressman popularly pictured with a big paunch, a big cigar, and a small mind is a rarity in real life; actually informed lawyers, teachers, businessmen, and other professionals comprise the overwhelming majority in Congress. (Right) *Woman I,* painting by Willem de Kooning (1950-52).

ideology of Communism and its military control into Asia and Africa. Within two years after the death of Hitler, the United States and Russia, despite their wartime coalition against the Nazis, found themselves engaged in an ominous Cold War.

The Second World War ended for good the historic isolationism of the United States, but it was the menace of Soviet expansion which worked the real revolution in American attitudes toward foreign affairs. The transformation was not only fundamental but amazingly rapid. The military and political Commitments which the American people accepted within a decade after 1945 not only reached around the globe but involved the full power of the United States in resisting Communist expansion. In 1940 such whole-hearted acceptance of the responsibilities of world leadership would have been beyond the wildest imaginings of the most ardent internationalist.

By the middle of the twentieth century the United States was incomparably more powerful than any world leader since Rome bestrode the civilized world, yet its ability to fashion the world to its own taste was more limited than Britain's in the nineteenth century. During Britain's years of world leadership, European technology, wealth, and military power easily overawed and controlled the peoples of Asia and Africa. But the Second World War changed that, undermining the whole structure of European colonialism and sending it crashing to the ground within ten years after 1945. In place of colonialism stood dozens of newly independent nations in Asia and Africa fiercely determined to resist any and all interference with their newly acquired freedom. At the same time they looked to the established nations of the world, especially the United States, to help them realize their nationalist ambitions and to improve the lot of their peoples. Because the Soviet Union also stood ready to aid these new nations, the needs and hopes of the emergent peoples opened opportunities for the further spread of Communism and Soviet power. Nor could such a challenge to American leadership be met by force. In the postwar world, persuasion, not gunboats, was the sanction of leadership. In the contrast between the magnitude of the tasks of world leadership and the narrow uses to which power could be put lay the challenge to the United States in the remaining years of the twentieth century.

CHAPTER 22

THE PRICE OF POWER, 1941-1948

THE CHALLENGE

Roosevelt's Dilemma. The Lend-Lease Act of March 1941 was only the first step that President Roosevelt was prepared to take in order to help Britain resist German aggression. Although each such step would move the nation closer to war, the President knew that he had no alternative. No more forthright position, even if he wanted to take one, was possible. Although Roosevelt probably overestimated the strength of the vocal isolationist minority, he estimated correctly the great reluctance of most Americans to become directly involved in a war. As a result, in his pursuit of what he thought was the defense of American interests, he was not always open and candid. Sometimes he acted secretly, as he did in late April 1941, when he ordered a naval patrol of the North Atlantic to help the British detect German submarines. Other times he acted as boldly as he thought the majority of the people would permit, as in July, when American troops were ordered to Iceland to relieve the British in protecting it from German invasion.

When Hitler, in a surprise move, invaded the Soviet Union on June 22, 1941, Roosevelt followed Churchill in welcoming a new fighting force in the war against Germany, even though few military advisers believed the Russians could hold out more than three months against the German blitz. Acutely aware of the weakness of British and Russian defenses against Hitler, Roosevelt, in early July, asked Congress for an extension of the draft law and repeal of the prohibition on overseas service for draftees. The isolationists, thoroughly aroused, branded the request as yet another of the President's covert efforts to get the United States into war. After acrimonious debate, the draft extension passed by a single vote in the House of Representatives.

Meanwhile, Roosevelt consummated another of his bold strokes. On August 9-12 he and Prime Minister Churchill met secretly on the U.S.S. *Augusta* in Argentia Bay, Newfoundland. The result was the Atlantic Charter, setting forth the aims of the war: no territorial changes would be made in favor of the victors, and all nations would be protected in their right to choose their own governments, without fear of aggressive threats. When announced on August 15, this meeting between a technical neutral and an active belligerent brought loud protests from isolationists in the United States. Nevertheless, upon his return home Roosevelt asked for increased appropriations for Britain and the Soviet Union.

Undeclared War. When in September a German U-boat attacked the American destroyer *Greer*, which, unbeknown to the American public, was

410   The Global Conflict

sending the British navy information on German subs, Roosevelt seized the opportunity to make another move in behalf of the British. He issued a "shoot-on-sight" order to the navy and asked Congress for authority to arm American merchant ships.

With American naval vessels shooting without even waiting to be attacked, it was only a matter of time before a serious incident occurred. On October 17 the American destroyer *Kearny* was torpedoed and damaged off Iceland; eleven Americans were killed. Less than three weeks later the *Reuben James* was sunk by a German U-boat with the loss of 115 lives. Recognizing America's essentially unneutral position, few Americans could really be outraged by the sinking; instead, most seemed to support the President's policy. In early November Congress authorized Roosevelt to arm merchant vessels and permit their entry into the war zone. The fight in Congress had been bitter, but the House victory was 212 to 94, far greater than the single-vote margin of the previous summer.

By the end of November 1941 the United States, though technically at peace, was virtually allied with Britain and Russia. Yet Hitler's armies were deep inside the Soviet Union, seemingly on their way to an early victory. And Japan was obviously readying itself for an offensive against the British and Dutch colonies in Southeast Asia. The dilemma of the President was acute. He could not dispel the nagging fear that Russia and Britain, despite American aid, might yet be overwhelmed by the Germans—an event which would leave the United States alone to face Germany. At the same time he knew that Americans were so divided over the struggle in Europe that he dare not try to lead them immediately into full-scale war against Hitler.

Japanese-American Relations, 1940-1941. Since the early 1930's, Japanese expansionism on the Asian mainland had met gradual but increasing American opposition. Finally in 1939 the United States began to restrict the flow to Japan of some strategic war materials, like oil and scrap iron. But Roosevelt would not embargo all war materials, as some of his advisers urged, because he feared that too strong a stand would push the Japanese into an adventure against the defenseless but oil-rich Dutch East Indies. Yet he believed some measures were necessary during 1939 and 1940 to warn Japan of American opposition to aggression. The Japanese response was to move into northern Indochina in the summer of 1940 and to join the Tripartite Pact with Germany and Italy in September 1940.

By early 1941 the Japanese and American positions in Asia were irreconcilable; Japan's minimal demand was that the United States cease its aid to Chiang Kai-shek, while the United States demanded that Japan terminate its war against China. During 1941, several diplomatic efforts aimed at softening the two positions proved to be futile, though Prince Konoye, the Japanese premier, did his best to constrain Japanese militarists, who believed that war was the only answer to America's interference with Japanese ambitions in Asia. The military's hand was strengthened in April 1941, when the Soviet Union promised to remain neutral in the event of a Japanese-American war. Japan's fear of a two-front war was thus reduced, while Hitler's earlier promise to support Japan in a war against the United States made it clear that, under such circumstances, the United States would be the one forced to fight on two fronts.

Japanese ambitions became clearer and more alarming in July, when Japanese military units invaded southern Indochina in obvious preparation for an attack upon the Dutch East Indies. In retaliation the United States, Britain, and the Netherlands cut off all vital military supplies to Japan.

Meanwhile, Japanese military circles increasingly viewed war with the United States as inevitable. On September 6, 1941, the Supreme War Council voted for war with the United States if American aid to China did not cease within six weeks. Before the six weeks elapsed, General Hideki Tojo, long an advocate of war with the United States, replaced Prince Konoye as premier. Up to the last, Konoye had sought to restrain the military clique and to arrange a personal meeting with Roosevelt, but neither effort had borne fruit. Tojo, though convinced that war with the United States was inevitable, sent a personal representative, Saburo Kurusu, to Washington in early November for further fruitless talks with the Americans. By the end of the month Americans knew, from their breaking of the Japanese codes, that war was coming, but they did not know where in the Pacific it would start.

With diplomacy proving incapable of halting the Japanese, American naval authorities on November 24 sent out warnings of war with Japan to the commanders at Pearl Harbor and Manila. On November 27 these bases were warned again, this time that "An aggressive move by Japan is expected within the next few days." On December 1 the emperor gave his consent to war; already a Japanese task force was steaming across the northern Pacific for a surprise attack on Pearl Harbor. In Washington, the two Japanese envoys, Kurusu and Ambassador Nomura, continued their inconclusive talks with Secretary of State Cordell Hull.

Pearl Harbor. The time was 7:50 on Sunday morning, December 7, 1941. In the sky over Oahu island, Captain Nakaya of the Japanese navy wrote in his log: "Pearl Harbor is still asleep in the morning mist. The orderly groups of barracks, the wriggling white line of the automobile road climbing up to the mountaintop; fine objectives in all directions. . . . Inside the harbor were important ships of the Pacific fleet, strung out and anchored two ships side by side in an orderly manner." Ten minutes later the first wave of Japanese planes struck the great American base. The surprise was complete; some American sailors thought the first bombs were accidentally dropped from American planes. Although the Americans, despite their unreadiness, fought back fiercely, the losses sustained were enormous: all of the eight battleships, the main object of the attack, were put out of action. Two of them never saw action again. Except for the three aircraft carriers, which happened to be at sea, the whole Pacific fleet was damaged or destroyed. Almost all of the aircraft, most of which did not even get off the ground, was knocked out. More than 2400 Americans were killed and 1200 wounded; the Japanese lost 29 airplanes, five midget submarines, and one fleet submarine. Considering the extensive damage, the attack on Pearl Harbor was one of the cheapest victories in the history of warfare.

Despite the devastating success of the raid, the decision to attack Pearl Harbor was a colossal blunder. For some time the administration had feared the Japanese would attack British and Dutch possessions in Asia without involving the United States. In that event the United States would have been helpless to counter Japanese aggression directly; after December 7, however, Americans were united in their opposition.

The strike against Pearl Harbor was only one part of an audacious and grand plan to destroy British, Dutch, and American power in the western Pacific. Soon after the bombing of Pearl Harbor, Japanese planes attacked the Philippines. Again, though this time there had been some warning from Hawaii, the Americans were caught unready. On December 8 the Japanese attacked Hong Kong, Borneo, the Malay Peninsula, and the American island outpost of Guam. The audacity and power of the Japanese advance were brought home on December 10, when Japanese land-based bombers sank the British battleship *Prince of Wales* and the battle cruiser *Repulse* off the coast of Malaya. Never before had air power destroyed a free-moving battleship; the age of the airplane in naval warfare had arrived. Successful amphibious landings in the Philippines and elsewhere also attested to the Japanese' command of the most advanced methods of offensive warfare.

The day after the attack on Pearl Harbor, described by Roosevelt as "a day which shall live in infamy," Congress, at the President's request, voted for war with Japan with only one dissenting vote. Nothing was said about Germany, heretofore the prime concern of the United States. On December 11 Hitler fulfilled his promise to the Japanese by declaring war on the United States; Italy followed soon thereafter. The dilemma was resolved. The United States was now in a position to use to the fullest its great power against aggressor nations in both Asia and Europe.

After the initial shock had passed, many Americans grew suspicious that the astonishing success of the Japanese assault must have resulted from traitorous acts. Actually, exhaustive investigations on the part of both the navy and Congress produced no evidence to support such allegations. Nowhere in government records was there any suggestion that Hawaii might be the object of a Japanese thrust. The fact is that most military experts seriously underestimated Japan's ability to mount the kind of elaborate, multipronged assault of which Pearl Harbor was but a part. There can be no doubt that the commanders at Pearl Harbor were lax in taking precautions after the war warnings of November, but these defects add up to nothing more sinister than inefficiency and carelessness.

WAR IN TWO HEMISPHERES

Creation of the Grand Alliance. Within two weeks after Pearl Harbor Winston Churchill and his chief military advisers arrived in Washington for extended discussions with the President and American military leaders about the long-range strategy of the two-front war in which both countries were now engaged. The basic decision of the conference, as General Marshall later reported, was that "Germany is still the prime enemy and her defeat is the key to victory. Once Germany is defeated the collapse of Italy and the defeat of Japan must follow." Roosevelt, despite pressure to do otherwise, never deviated from this decision, even though Japan appeared to be the greater immediate menace to the United States. The two allies also agreed to pool their resources and military equipment for the duration of the struggle. Finally, the conference created a Combined Chiefs of Staff in Washington to plan and coordinate global strategy. As a public manifestation of the new association, Churchill, Roosevelt, Maxim Litvinov (representing Stalin), and the representatives of 23 other nations at war with one or more Axis powers signed the Declaration of the United Nations on New Year's Day, 1942.

As the arsenal of the alliance, the United States in subsequent months worked out new Lend-Lease agreements with the principal allies. According to these agreements, the costs of the war were to be borne in proportion to ability to pay, thereby avoiding in postwar years the long and acrimonious war-debt wrangles which followed World War I. By the end of the war in 1945, the United States contributed over $50 billion in Lend-Lease, the bulk of which went to Great Britain. In return, the Allies provided $8 billion in goods or services to the United States.

Holding the Line. The first months of 1942 were filled with one Japanese success after another. (As a gesture of defiance the United States dispatched General James Doolittle to lead a small, carrier-borne air strike against Tokyo in April, but its military value was nil.) In a matter of months the Japanese overran all of Southeast Asia. In the Philippines all American resistance to the invaders ceased on May 6. Meanwhile, other Japanese forces pushed down the Malay Peninsula; on February 15, Singapore, the great British naval base, the symbol of Britain's power in Asia, fell to the Japanese. Resisted only by a few available Dutch, British, and American naval units, the Japanese invaded the coveted Dutch East Indies the same month. Early in March, Java, the main island of the archipelago, was in Japanese hands. Another Japanese army, meanwhile, had overrun Siam and Burma and now stood poised on the borders of India. The Japanese by the end of March controlled the western half of the Pacific from the Kuriles to the Solomons, as well as the islands and mainland of Southeast Asia from Indochina to India. Of the once extensive European possessions in the area, only Port Moresby in New Guinea still held out. New Japanese landings in the northern Solomon Islands suggested that Australia itself might soon be outflanked and threatened with invasion.

Strenuous American efforts in the middle of 1942 managed to stop, but not roll back, the Japanese advance. In May the naval-air Battle of the Coral Sea halted the southward naval advance, and the following month the American victory over a large Japanese naval task force off Midway Island ended the westward thrust. Japanese losses at the Battle of Midway were so extensive that thereafter the imperial navy, despite the damage inflicted at Pearl Harbor, was on the defensive. The third effort to contain the Japanese advance comprised a series of combined land and sea operations in the little-known, jungle-covered island of Guadalcanal in the Solomons. The first precarious American landing on Guadalcanal took place on August 7, 1942, but it was not until the fifth major sea and air encounter on November 13-14, 1942, that the southern Solomons rested securely in American hands.

As in the Pacific, the first year of war in Europe brought almost uninterrupted setbacks for the Allies on both land and sea. Although Hitler never captured Moscow, his troops came within cannon shot of the city; in southern Russia the German forces penetrated the Caucasus and reached the shores of the Volga. In the Atlantic, soon after the United States entered the war, German submarines began systematic depredations upon all shipping. German submarines were now much speedier and deadlier, and there were more of them than in the First World War. That spring and summer German submarines sank Allied tankers and merchantmen before the eyes of civilians on the shores of New Jersey and Florida. By the middle of 1942 shipping losses, which had been high in 1941, reached a new peak of 4.5 million tons, or more than in all of 1941; yet in the same six months only twenty-one U-boats were sunk. At the conclusion of eleven months of war and after a furious program of shipbuilding, Allied tonnage was less than it had been on the day Pearl Harbor was bombed. Improved antisubmarine techniques and devices and more destroyers slowly cut down the losses, but the submarine menace hung over Allied preparations until the middle of 1943. Indeed, submarine attacks seriously delayed the assaults upon North Africa and Italy and the great invasion of the European continent.

The Turning Point. In the month of November 1942, Allied forces around the globe assumed the offensive, which they never lost thereafter. November had witnessed the victory on Guadal-

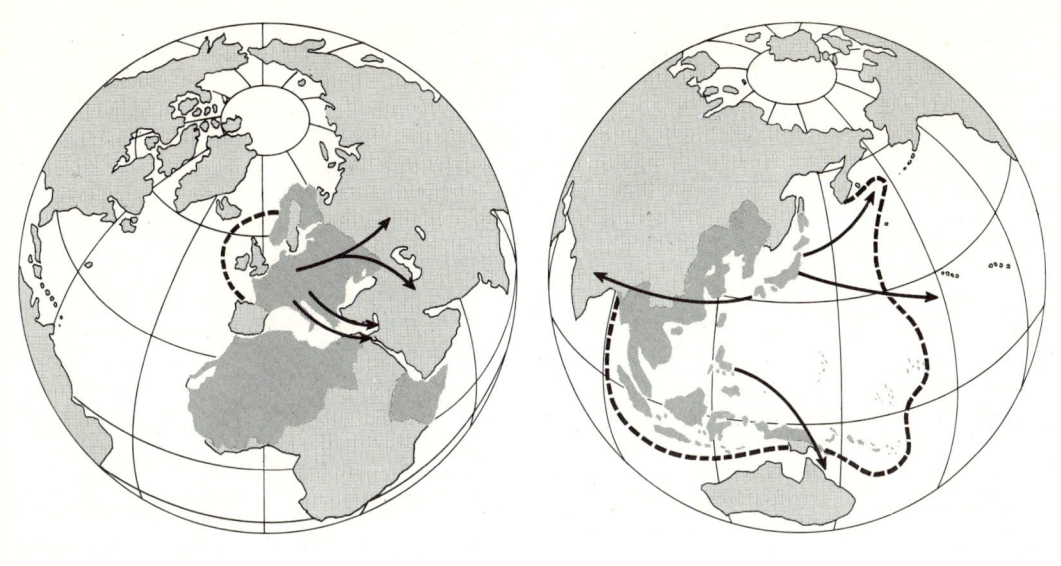

THE MAIN AXIS CAMPAIGNS, 1942

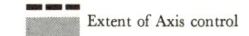

▬▬▬ Extent of Axis control

canal in the southwestern Pacific. At about the same time the Russians, after a heroic defense of Stalingrad on the Volga, seized the offensive against the Germans. On November 8 American forces commanded by General Dwight D. Eisenhower invaded the French North African colonies of Morocco and Algeria. Surprise landings from the giant armada of 500 warships and 350 transports and cargo ships were made successfully at several points along the coast. The Vichy French, many of whom supported the Americans because of previous arrangements with high officers in the French army and navy, offered only scattered resistance. Total Allied casualties amounted to fewer than 2000.

The immediate purpose of the North African landings was to catch the German armies, under General Erwin Rommel, in a giant squeeze; only a week before, General Bernard L. Montgomery's British Eighth Army had begun an offensive at El Alamein in Egypt. As Rommel's forces retreated westward before Montgomery along the North African coast in December and January, they backed up against the now well-established American forces in Algeria and Tunisia. Although it took hard fighting, by the early spring of 1943 Rommel's once invincible Africa Korps was no more. German losses in Africa reached 350,000.

With all of North Africa in Allied hands, the next target was Sicily, which was invaded by air and sea in July 1943. By the time the Sicilian campaign was concluded at the end of August, Italy was out of the war. A new Italian government under Field Marshal Pietro Badoglio had deposed Mussolini and, after surrendering unconditionally on September 3, joined the Allies in the war against Germany. But the Nazi forces quickly disarmed the Italians, thereby rendering the diplomatic coup a military nullity. Despite three amphibious invasions of the Italian peninsula—one from Sicily across the Straits of Messina in September 1943, another at Salerno the same month, and still another at Anzio in January 1944—stubborn German resistance and the Italian mountains kept the Allies fighting in Italy until May 2, 1945.

Setting the Goals of War. In January 1943, soon after the consolidation of the Allied landings in North Africa, Roosevelt and Churchill met in the Moroccan city of Casablanca to discuss war aims. It was at this meeting that Roosevelt, after consulting with Churchill, announced that only unconditional surrender of Germany and Italy would be acceptable to the Allies. Later critics would argue that such uncompromising terms stiffened German resistance and prolonged the war. Certainly the Nazi propaganda machine played upon the argument that victory for the Allies spelled annihilation for the Germans. But at the time Roosevelt was careful to say that unconditional surrender "does not mean the destruction of the population of Germany, Italy, and Japan, but it does mean the destruction of the philosophies of those countries which are based on conquest and the subjugation of other people." Actually, it appears doubtful that the statement influenced German resistance very much; certainly it produced exactly the opposite effect upon the Italians, who surrendered with alacrity nine months later.

Late 1943 saw several meetings of the Big Three powers. At the end of October the foreign ministers of the United States, Great Britain, and the Soviet Union met for the first time in Moscow. There it was agreed that the three nations would consult on "all matters relating to the surrender and disarmament" of their common enemies. They also recognized a need for setting "the earliest possible date" for the planning of an international organization of the "peace-loving states." Victory, in short, was already being anticipated.

En route to a meeting with Stalin in Teheran, Iran, Churchill and Roosevelt stopped at Cairo on November 22-26, 1943, to confer with the Nationalist Chinese leader Chiang Kai-shek. The three allies agreed to prosecute the Pacific war until Japan was forced into unconditional surrender. They also agreed that Manchuria, Formosa, and the Pescadore Islands, earlier seized by Japan, should be returned to China after the war.

The Teheran Conference of November 28-December 1, 1943—the first personal encounter between Stalin, Churchill, and Roosevelt—resulted in no new decisions, although Roosevelt did secure from Stalin, as Hull had from Molotov a month earlier, a promise of Russian help against Japan soon after the end of the war against Germany. Convinced of the need to have Stalin's friendship in the postwar world, Roosevelt did his best to charm the dictator and to dissipate Stalin's obvious suspicion of the two English-speaking allies.

The Battle for Production. In a very real sense the turning of the tide of war from constant defeat to persistent victory was attributable to the astounding production which flooded from American factories and farms. At Teheran even Stalin acknowledged that without American production the Allies would not be winning the war.

Actually the battle for production was almost as laborious, if not so bloody, as the fighting in the field. Conversion of the economy to full wartime production did not really begin until after Pearl Harbor, even though the fall of France in 1940 warned the administration that American production would have to be greatly stepped up if Britain were to survive. During 1940 and 1941 Roosevelt created several agencies, headed by businessmen and labor leaders, to speed up and coordinate production; but, when the Japanese struck, the level of war production was still far from satisfactory. In January 1942 Roosevelt set up the War Production Board with Donald M. Nelson as chief and, though this more centralized control was the best arrangement yet, the organization of production did not achieve optimum efficiency until the creation of the Office of War Mobilization in May 1943 under James F. Byrnes, former Democratic senator from South Carolina.

While building up an armed force of some fifteen million men and women, the United States undertook to expand its productive capacity to feed, clothe, supply, house, and transport this army and the British and Russian armies spread around the globe. To meet this gargantuan assignment required not only the expenditure of billions of dollars but also the execution of a host of plans and arrangements. Priorities for materials had to be established, raw materials gathered, labor recruited to replace the men inducted into the armed services, and civilian industries converted to war work. The automobile industry, for example, was given over entirely to the manufacture of tanks, trucks, and other military vehicles. The aviation industry expanded its working force from 49,000 in 1939 to a peak of 2.1 million in November 1943, when it employed over 12 per cent of the total number of workers in manufacturing. By 1944 airplane production reached 95,000 units annually. To keep supplies moving, the total tonnage of American shipping increased over five times between 1939 and May 1945. Some of the feats of ship construction were incredible. In 1941 the average time required for construction of a Liberty ship was 355 days, but during the war new methods reduced the time to 56 days, and one especially efficient yard completed a Liberty ship in 14 days. Whole new industries sometimes had to be created: the production of synthetic rubber was inaugurated when the Japanese cut off the major source of natural rubber from Southeast Asia. The volume of industrial production increased so rapidly that by October 1943 some cutbacks were made to prevent surpluses.

Agricultural production also expanded. Between 1939 and 1946 agricultural production increased some 30 per cent, even though the labor force on farms *fell* more than 5 per cent. As a result, not only was the United States able to keep the armed forces well supplied with food, but the nation as a whole ate better than ever before, and the Allies were able to draw upon the American larder during the war and after.

The Home Front. Because the needs of the armed forces came first, many kinds of civilian goods ranging from automobiles to toasters were unobtainable, and necessities in short supply like coffee, sugar, meat, and butter were rationed in order to ensure equitable distribution. Housing, especially in areas where new war plants went up, was hard to obtain and housing conditions were crowded and substandard. Bus and train travel was dirty, uncomfortable, and overcrowded, if available for a civilian at all. Many commodities still obtainable on the home front often declined in quality but not in price as manufacturers tried to get around price controls. However, the average citizen did not suffer unduly. As Director of War Mobilization James F. Byrnes said in January 1945, "It is not as if the civilian economy has been starved. Some items are short. But on the whole the volume of consumption has risen. . . . Our level of living is higher than in 1929 or 1940."

Industrial labor was certainly better off. Unemployment dropped from 9 million in July 1940 to 780,000 in September 1943. And although prices rose by about 30 per cent between 1939 and 1945, wages rose faster, increasing about 70 per cent, thanks to raises and overtime pay. The need for additional labor was so great that at one point the government undertook a house-to-house survey to find workers for war industries; by the middle of 1944 war workers accounted for some 45 per cent of the nation's labor force, which included millions of women and teenagers (aged 14-17).

Although more workers went out on strike during the war years than during the depression years, the number was less than 2.5 million in any one year and only a small proportion of the total labor force. Only occasionally did the President have to seize plants in order to keep production going. The most notable labor dispute was with John L. Lewis, who twice in 1943 led his United Mine Workers in strikes against government restraints on wage increases. In retaliation, Congress in June 1943 enacted a general antilabor law, the Smith-Connally Act, which authorized the President to seize any plant where a strike threatened to interfere with the war effort and which imposed criminal penalties on those who called such strikes. Roosevelt vetoed the bill as extreme, but Congress quickly overrode his veto.

The job of fitting a free labor force to the needs of war production was formidable. A War Manpower Commission, created in 1942, undertook this task by freezing workers to their jobs unless more important war work required them elsewhere. To handle disputes between labor and management, now that strikes were voluntarily banned, the President set up the War Labor Board. The board also attempted to hold the line on wages in order to keep prices level, although it did permit a 15 per cent increase to make up for the rise in the cost of living. In the main, the War Labor Board, which amicably settled thousands of labor disputes during the war years, refused to permit the emergency to be used as an excuse for eroding the gains made by organized labor in the previous decade. As a result, union membership increased from nine million in 1940 to almost fifteen million in 1945.

Controlling Inflation. Simply because there was so much money and so few consumer goods, the control of prices was a major problem. Essentially, prices were kept under control by two methods—increased taxes and a price freeze by government order. The Office of Price Administration, which was in charge of controlling inflation, failed to put a tight lid on prices until late in 1942 so that some prices, notably those of foods, rose alarmingly through most of 1942. Thereafter, however, controls were more effective. Prices in general did not rise more than 30 per cent between 1940 and the end of the war.

Because Congress would not follow through on legislation, taxation was not so steep as the administration had hoped. Only the Revenue Act of 1942, which increased the corporate, private-income, and excise taxes, took much of a bite out of civilian purchasing power. In that act, for the first time, the income tax reached into the pockets of the average citizen. About fifty million income-tax payers were recorded in 1943 as compared with thirteen million in 1941. Congress refused to heed Roosevelt's demand for a further increase in taxes in 1943. Yet in spite of government spending at a rate as high as $100 million a year, about 40 per cent of the cost of the war was paid for out of taxes, a proportion which had never been achieved in any previous American war.

Civil Liberties. Fearful of sabotage, the government early in 1942 ordered the rounding up of some 110,000 Japanese living on the West Coast, even though some two thirds of them were American citizens. Although no specific acts of sabotage could be charged against them, these people were held in relocation centers in the interior for most of the war. This action of the government, though later upheld by the Supreme Court, was severely condemned as an indefensible act of racism, since mere Japanese ancestry was the basis for the internment. Ironically, the Japanese in Hawaii, who made up a much larger proportion of the population, were not affected by the order. No comparable interference with civil liberty was taken against Americans of German and Italian ancestry, nor did the population at large indulge in any of the irrational attacks on Germans such as had marred the domestic record during the First World War.

By and large the position of Negroes improved during the war, despite an ugly race riot in Detroit in 1943 and near outbreaks of violence elsewhere. Thousands of Negroes moved into northern cities seeking the new job opportunities. By April 1944 a million more Negroes were employed in civilian jobs than in 1940; during the same period the number of Negroes in skilled jobs and foreman positions doubled. Under pressure from Negro leaders the federal government also undertook to make jobs available for Negroes. The President in June 1941 created a Fair Employment Practices Committee to investigate charges of discrimination against minorities on defense jobs. In 1943 the committee was granted enforcement authority.

The Election of 1944. In the midst of the Second World War, as in the Civil War, the nation conducted a presidential election. The Republicans, who after Pearl Harbor strongly supported the war effort, now entertained high hopes for victory since in the congressional elections of 1942 they had gained forty-seven seats in the House and nine in the Senate. Prominently considered for the Republican nomination was Thomas E. Dewey, who had gained national renown as the first Republican since 1920 to be elected governor of New York state. Dewey spoke for the same internationalist wing of the party that had supported Wendell L. Willkie in 1940, but he did not suffer from Willkie's close identification with the administration. Moreover, Dewey, unlike Willkie, enjoyed the support of the professionals in the party. As a result, the convention nominated Dewey on the first ballot. John A. Bricker of Ohio, who as a Midwesterner and an isolationist brought balance to the ticket, received the vice-presidential nomination. The party platform was internationalist in content, but the convention's enthusiasm for Bricker betrayed the persistence of isolationism in Republican ranks.

Roosevelt waited until just a week before the Democratic convention met in July before he indicated his willingness to seek the nomination, but once he did the matter was settled. The real battle in the convention then raged around the choice of his running mate. Roosevelt's own choice, though not a strong one, was incumbent Vice-President Henry Wallace, but Wallace was unacceptable to conservatives within the party. The President's second choice was James F. Byrnes, the efficient and capable Director of the Office of War Mobilization; however, labor leaders, well organized politically, and liberals in general opposed Byrnes as anti-Negro and perhaps antilabor. As a consequence, before the convention actually voted, party leaders had decided upon Harry S. Truman as a compromise candidate. Truman, nominated on the third ballot, was a senator from Missouri and chairman of a Senate investigating committee which had gained national acclaim for its honest and efficient policing of government war contracts.

His head filled with plans for the postwar settlement, Roosevelt's heart was not in the hustings. Nevertheless, early in the campaign he made one of the most effective political speeches of his career and by the vigor of his few

ALLIED ADVANCES IN EUROPE IN WORLD WAR II

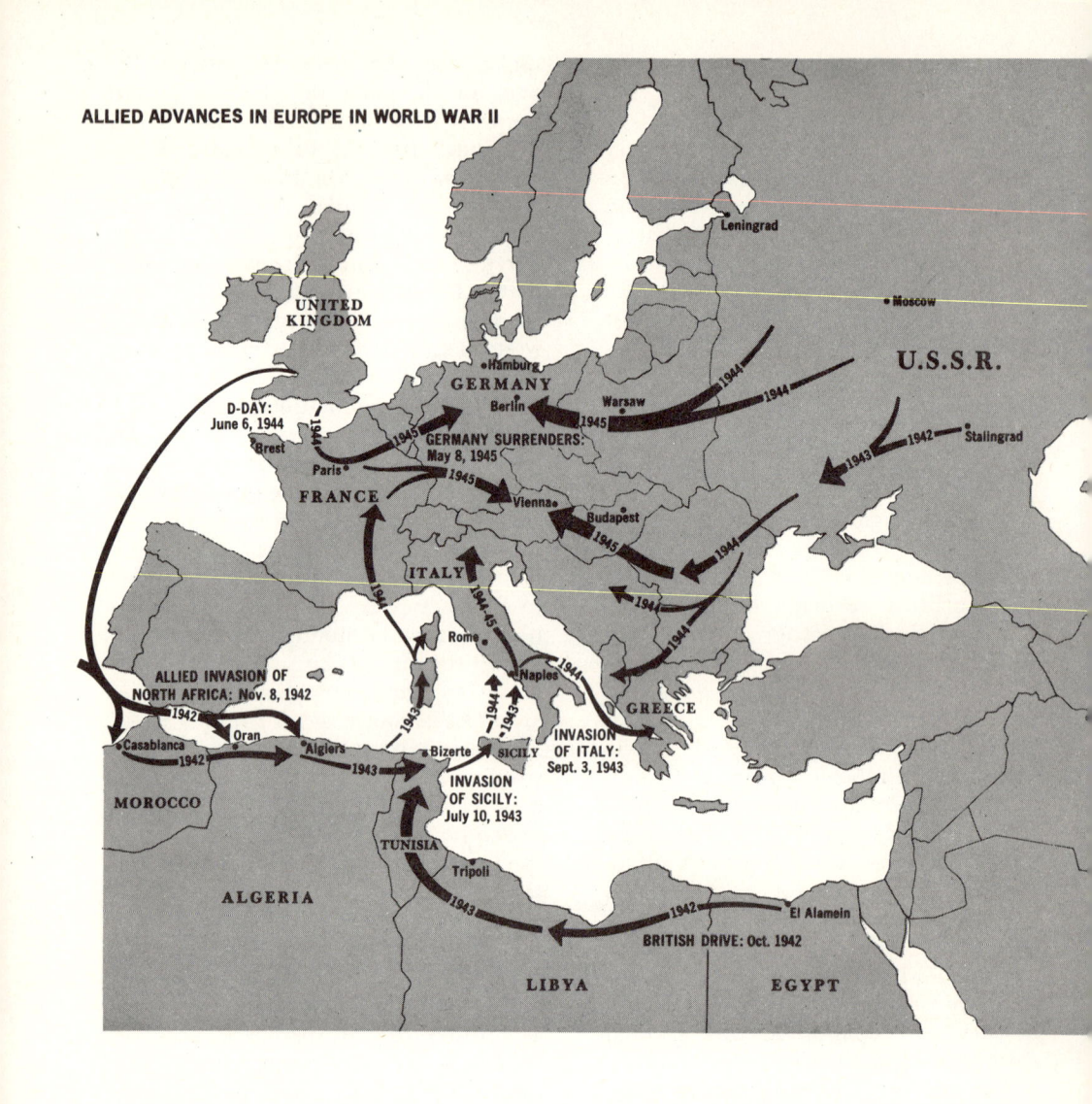

campaign speeches effectively countered Republican charges that he was physically incapable of enduring another term of office. As usual Roosevelt won, though by a smaller margin in the popular vote than ever before, receiving 25.6 million votes to Dewey's 22 million. The Democrats retained control of both houses, gaining twenty new seats in the House of Representatives.

Island Hopping in the Pacific. When the last Japanese resistance ended on Guadalcanal in February 1943, the United States began the long push northward toward Japan. The task was essentially one for the navy and the marines, since the Japanese were dug in on a multitude of small islands scattered throughout the western Pacific. One by one through 1943, Japanese island fortresses fell to air and amphibious attack: the central Solomons in the summer, eastern New Guinea in the fall, and the Gilbert Islands in the late fall. Some of the strong-

420   The Global Conflict

ALLIED ADVANCES IN THE PACIFIC IN WORLD WAR II

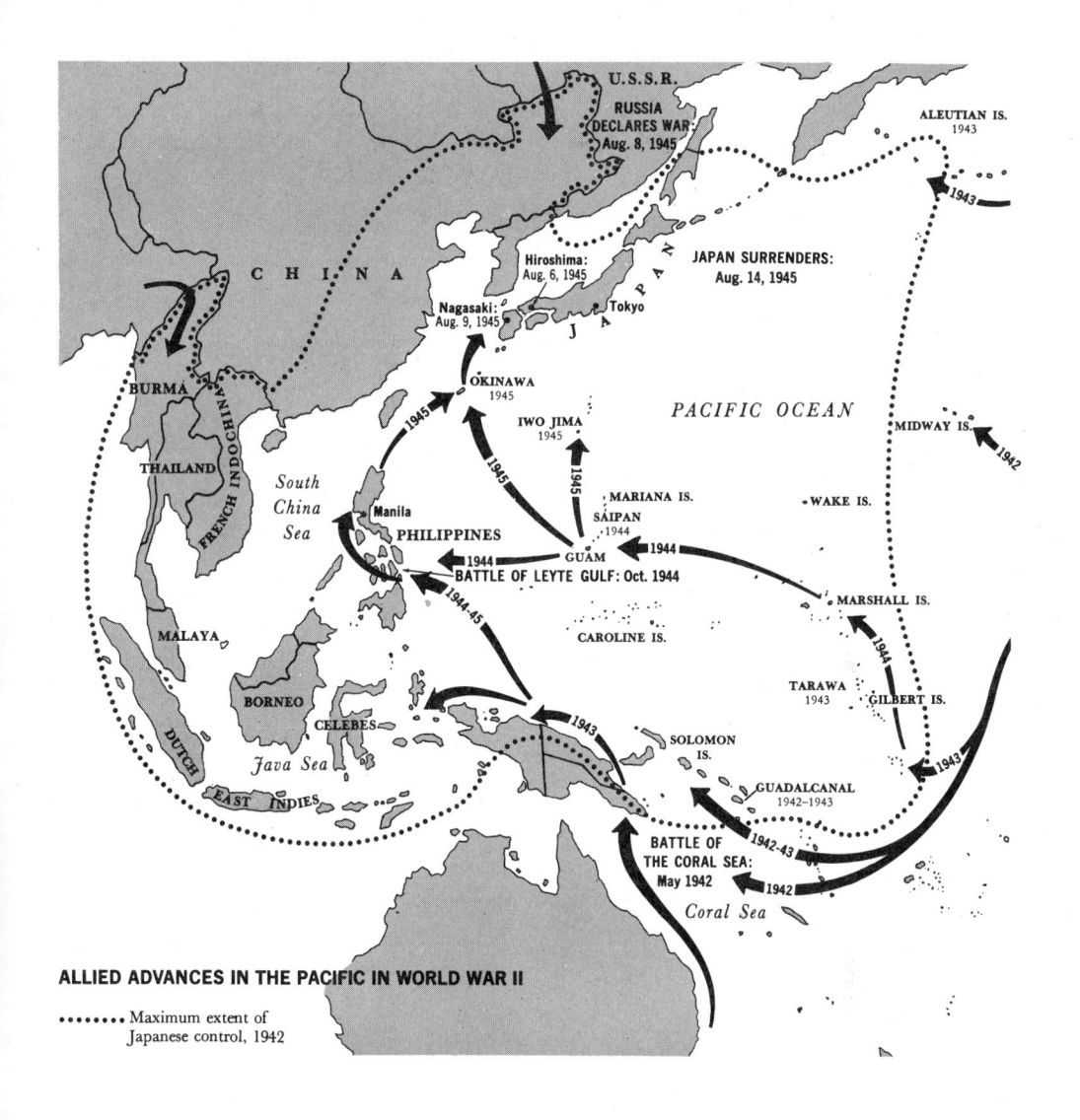

••••••• Maximum extent of Japanese control, 1942

holds, like Tarawa in the Gilberts, were costly encounters, for the Japanese were tough and resourceful fighters and their fortifications deep and well constructed. But as the great naval task forces of the United States moved northward into the Marshall, the Admiralty, and the Mariana Islands, other Japanese outposts were by-passed, their garrisons still intact; cut off from supplies, they would eventually have to surrender without bloodshed. By the end of June 1944 the capture of Saipan in the Marianas placed the air force's giant new B-29 bomber within easy striking distance of Tokyo itself. Systematic bombing of Japan's home islands from Saipan began in November 1944.

The Invasion of Europe. Meanwhile, preparations were well under way for the long-awaited frontal assault upon Hitler's Fortress Europe. Ever since the middle of 1942 Stalin had been urging the Western Allies to open a second front, but aside from the invasion of Italy, which was obviously peripheral, the Allied response had been confined to air bombings of the Third Reich. Nevertheless, by the middle of 1943 these air attacks were formidable. On July 24, 1943, for example, and for six days thereafter, the combined British and American air forces dropped 8000 tons of bombs on the single German city of Hamburg, devastating three quarters of the city. Later, fifty other large German cities each received a similar pounding. During 1943 and 1944 Allied planes dropped ten times the tonnage of bombs which the Germans had dropped on England in 1940. More than 300,000 Germans died in these uninterrupted raids, which by 1944 were deliberately aimed at workers' homes as well as factories in an effort to destroy German morale as well as German industrial capacity. Devastating as they were, the raids cost the Anglo-American air forces some twenty-one thousand bombers and their crews.

On December 6, 1943, in appointing Dwight D. Eisenhower Supreme Allied Commander of the West, the Combined Chiefs of Staff told him: "You will enter the continent of Europe and, in conjunction with other Allied Nations, undertake operations aimed at the heart of Germany and the destruction of her armed forces." For months before the actual invasion began and while supplies, shipping, and men were being accumulated in England, Allied planes bombed and strafed German positions along the Channel coast, knocking out bridges, railroads, and airfields. The Nazis could not help but know in general what was impending, but they guessed wrong, thanks to superb Allied counterintelligence, as to the exact point of the attack on D-day, June 6, 1944. The main concentration of Allied troops on that fateful day was north of the Cotentin peninsula in Normandy, where the massive invasion force quickly established five connected beachheads. Within two weeks after D-day, a million troops landed and moved inland; by the end of July both the British and American armies had broken out of their coastal positions and were striking north and west. On August 15 a new American army invaded southern France, landing at Toulon and proceeding rapidly northward up the Rhone valley. By this time most of northern France was cleared of German troops. Paris fell to French and American troops on August 25.

Concomitantly with the Allied invasion of June 6, the Russians launched a broad offensive on the eastern front, bringing the Russian armies to the Baltic and into Poland and Rumania by the end of the summer. By late autumn of 1944 the armies of the Grand Alliance were poised to strike into Germany from the east and the west.

Despite the overwhelming land and air power being brought against it, Germany made two desperate attempts to forestall the inevitable. The first was a new secret weapon, a fast-flying rocket bomb, the V-2. (The V-1 or "buzz bomb," used somewhat earlier, was a jet-driven aerial bomb and not a rocket.) The first V-2's landed in England in August. Traveling faster than the speed of sound, the V-2 was impossible to intercept, and it hit without warning. Before the launching bases could be destroyed by Allied bombers, the murderous V-2 attacks killed some 8000 Britons.

The other desperate German effort was a great counteroffensive mounted on December 16, 1944, against the American forces in the Ardennes forest of Belgium. The Battle of the Bulge, as it came to be called, caught the Americans by surprise. They retreated before the onslaught. As a result the whole Allied timetable in the west was set back over six weeks. The first Allied troops did not cross the Rhine until March 7, 1945, when the bridge at

Remagen, one of the few remaining Rhine bridges, was unexpectedly taken by soldiers of the American Ninth Armored Division. By that time the Russians stood on the banks of the Oder River, less than forty-five miles from Berlin.

The Big Three at Yalta. As the coils of Allied power tightened around Germany, Roosevelt, Stalin, and Churchill met on February 4-11, 1945, at Yalta, a resort town in the Crimea. Desirous of securing Russian aid against the Japanese and of bringing the Soviet Union into a new world organization, Roosevelt at the Yalta Conference did his best to assure Stalin that the United States recognized Russia's special interests in Europe. It was agreed, therefore, that the new government of Poland would be the one established at Lublin by the Russians and not the one in exile in London. But it was also agreed that final recognition of the Lublin government would await "free and unfettered elections." Also, pending the signing of a German peace, Poland would receive German territory to compensate for portions of eastern Poland taken by Russia in 1939.

Russian insistence upon a large figure for German reparations was also favorably received by the Americans, though no final commitment was made. Stalin asked for and received cession of the Kurile islands from Japan and concessions and bases in China. The territorial and reparations agreements were not made public until after the war. In return, Stalin agreed to participate in the new world organization and to enter the war against Japan within three months after the defeat of Germany.

Despite later criticisms, the so-called concessions by Roosevelt do not seem excessive in the context of February 1945. Poland, after all, was in Russian hands, and Russian military assistance against Japan then seemed eminently desirable and worth the granting of Japanese territory to the Soviet Union. Furthermore, Chiang Kai-shek later consented to the concessions which Roosevelt agreed to support in Stalin's behalf.

The End of the Third Reich. Soon after the Yalta Conference, on April 12, 1945, Franklin D. Roosevelt died at Warm Springs, Georgia. A surprised and shaken Harry S. Truman assumed the presidency the same day. Roosevelt's death plunged the nation and the peoples of the Allied world into sorrow, but the military machine which FDR had helped to forge drove on to total victory over Germany and Italy.

With the Russians already fighting in flaming, bombed-out Berlin, Adolf Hitler on April 30 committed suicide in his underground bunker beneath the Reichschancellery; faithful guards burned his body. Nazi Germany outlasted its founder by no more than a week. On May 2, Admiral Karl Doenitz, whom Hitler had recently named as his successor, tried to surrender to the British while continuing the war against the Russians, but Field Marshal Bernard L. Montgomery contemptuously rejected this last, but not first, attempt to divide the Western and Eastern allies. Germany surrendered unconditionally to all the Allied powers on the morning of May 7, 1945.

The United Nations Organization and Potsdam. FDR's death left President Truman with the completion of the task which Roosevelt considered preëminent: the convocation of the representatives of the Allied nations at San Francisco to draw up a charter for a new world security organization. The completed Charter of the United Nations was signed by all fifty Allied countries on June 26, 1945. Despite the long history of American isolationism and the rejection of the League of Nations after World War I, the U.S. Senate agreed to American membership in the UN after only six days of debate and with only two dissenting votes.

President Truman was also called upon to represent the United States at the last conference of the Big Three powers at Potsdam, Germany. Since no final decisions on Germany had been made at Yalta and since the United States still desired Russia's support against Japan, Truman, Stalin, and Churchill (later replaced by Clement Attlee, representing the newly elected Labour government in Britain) met outside ruined Berlin on July 17, 1945. Differences between East and West were more evident than before; wranglings frequently occurred over details and the meaning of previous agreements. The two Western allies were deeply suspicious of Russian policy in Poland, which Stalin seemed intent upon making a Russian satellite. Stalin also insisted that the new border between Germany and Poland was final, though at Yalta Poland's independence had been agreed upon and the border considered only temporary. Furthermore, the tentative agreements on reparations Stalin now insisted were final. All three powers agreed that Germany should remain united, although, for purposes of temporary military administration, each of the three powers (later France was added) would occupy a separate zone. Berlin itself was to be occupied jointly by the victors. Even though Russia had not yet entered the war in the Pacific, the conference issued a demand for Japan's unconditional surrender.

The End of the War with Japan. As the European war reached its climax in the summer and fall of 1944, the American air force and navy moved ever closer to the Japanese home islands. In October, under the cover of a mighty array of warships and planes, American troops sloshed ashore on the island of Leyte in the Philippines in a move which caught the superior Japanese forces completely by surprise. In the naval encounters in the Battle of Leyte Gulf the American forces utterly defeated the last important remnants of the Japanese fleet. At the end of February 1945, after successful invasions of two other Philippine islands, Luzon and Mindanao, General Douglas MacArthur, the resourceful American commander in the Pacific, announced the capture of Manila. Just three years had elapsed since MacArthur had been ordered by President Roosevelt to leave the Philippines in the face of the Japanese invasion.

That same month of February 1945 the marines landed on Iwo Jima, a small but thoroughly fortified island in the Bonins, only five hundred miles from Japan itself. After fighting which rivaled that at Tarawa for bloodiness, Iwo Jima fell into American hands, its airfield being quickly put to use by fighters flying protection for the B-29's bombing Japan. On March 9, B-29's from Saipan dropped a record load of firebombs on Tokyo, igniting the wooden and paper houses of the city; the resulting holocaust was rivaled only by that at Hiroshima five months later.

Even as fierce fighting continued on the Philippines, the Americans invaded Okinawa, an island of the Ryukyu chain close to the home islands. Once again the Japanese dug in and fought virtually to the last man, while Kamikaze (Japanese suicide pilots) hurled their planes at the Americans, sinking thirty-four ships of the invading fleet. By the end of the campaign in June 1945, some 110,000 Japanese had died on Okinawa; less than 8000 had been taken prisoner. The 49,000 American casualties were the heaviest of any engagement in the Pacific theater and a grisly prefiguring of the costs to be expected from the contemplated assault on the Japanese home islands.

That dreaded encounter, however, never came; at 8:15 A.M. on August 6, 1945, a single B-29 dropped a single atomic bomb on the industrial city of Hiroshima. The tremendous blast waves, fire waves, and radiation leveled 60 per cent of the city and killed over

70,000 people outright; 10,000 more were never found. Because the bewildered Japanese did not surrender immediately, on August 9 a second nuclear bomb was dropped on Nagasaki with equally devastating consequences. A day before, on August 8, the Soviet Union fulfilled its promise by declaring war on Japan and invading Manchuria. Japan's leaders, recognizing that their country faced certain destruction and heeding the Emperor's pleas that no more lives be sacrificed, surrendered unconditionally on August 14. The official surrender took place on September 2 aboard the battleship *Missouri* anchored in Tokyo Bay.

The story of the development of the nuclear bomb began in August 1939, when President Roosevelt received a letter from the noted scientist Albert Einstein informing him that the splitting (fission) of the nucleus of an atom of uranium seemed possible. The consequent release of energy, Einstein wrote, would be enormous. Fearful that Nazi scientists might develop such a bomb, the administration in 1940 began the Manhattan Project to try to beat them to it. In a secret basement under the football stadium at the University of Chicago, a team of scientists in December 1942 successfully constructed the first nuclear pile. Once it had been shown that a nuclear reaction could be controlled in this fashion, the engineers took over, constructing plants at Oak Ridge, Tennessee, and Hanford, Washington, for the manufacture of materials needed for assembling a bomb. After more than $2 billion had been invested in the great gamble, the first test of the bomb took place successfully on July 16, 1945, in the desert outside Alamogordo, New Mexico. The secret of the project had been kept so well that Harry Truman did not learn of it until he became President.

The job of building the bomb was so complicated and time-consuming that the two bombs used against Japan were the total world supply. Later it was learned that the Germans had lagged far behind the United States and Great Britain in the development of nuclear fission and probably would not have been able to construct a bomb for months or perhaps years. But no matter who made the first bomb, once its devastating power had been released, the world could not be the same again. Thus, simultaneously with the coming of peace, the world entered the age of nuclear power—an age which would be at once an era of promise and of fear.

FROM PEACE TO COLD WAR

Reconversion. Soon after the surrender of Japan, the dismantling of the great military establishment began. By January 1946, in response to public clamor at home and unrest among the troops still stationed around the globe, the government was discharging members of the armed forces at the rate of 35,000 a day; by the end of 1946 the armed forces were less than 80 per cent of wartime strength. Simultaneously with the discharging of soldiers, the government began the cancellation of war contracts, of which $35 billion worth were dropped within a month after the surrender of Japan. The end of war work and the glutting of the labor market with discharged veterans seemed to many to presage a severe depression, but the billions of dollars of personal savings and the rapid transition to peacetime production made it turn out otherwise. Instead, inflation became the principal economic problem in ensuing years.

The ending of overtime work at war plants and the upward movement of prices in 1945 and 1946 provoked organized labor into a wave of strikes. In October 1945, for example, the number of man-days lost through strikes doubled over September and continued to rise until February 1946, when the peak was reached. All told about 4.5 million workers went out on strike in 1946. Since the strikes were usually for increased wages, the federal government ran into difficulties trying to hold the line of prices. The popular and congressional demand for tax reductions also meant increased pressure on prices. In November 1945 Congress cut income taxes by some $9 billion and repealed the wartime excess-profits tax as an inducement to increased production.

The big issues of 1946 were prices and labor unrest. The Truman administration tried to hold the line of prices by continuing wartime price controls, but businessmen, most Republicans, and large sectors of the population were anxious to remove all wartime restrictions. The results were inadequate price-control legislation and a steadily rising price curve. With the election of a Republican Congress in November 1946, the Truman administration gave up resisting the drive to normalcy; it abolished virtually all controls over prices. Nevertheless, shortages of all kinds of goods persisted, with the result that prices in 1947 continued to rise to new heights almost every month. Despite the high prices, or perhaps because of them, employment remained high and business activity good. Undoubtedly many workers, especially unorganized labor and white-collar workers, suffered from the steady increase in the cost of living, but the country as a whole enjoyed a boom.

Before it was clear that a boom would be the shape of the postwar era, Congress, fearing a depression, enacted the Employment Act in February 1946, which placed responsibility upon the federal government for the prevention of mass unemployment and economic depression. Although no specific measures were spelled out in the act (because of the need to win conservative support), the act did create a Council of Economic Advisors to the President. In a sense the act was a reflex from the days of the depression and showed the continuing effect of the New Deal revolution.

Truman versus a Republican Congress. The opposition to price controls, the support of labor control bills, and the demand for tax reductions marked a rising conservative tide across the country and in the Congress. This conservatism was clearly reflected in the congressional elections of 1946. Brandishing the slogan "Had Enough?" the Republicans elected majorities in both houses for the first time since 1928. First on the agenda of the new Eightieth Congress was legislation to control labor unions, which since the end of the war had been disrupting the economy through nation-wide strikes. Earlier in 1946 Truman had vetoed a severe anti-labor law, even though he himself, beset by a national railroad strike in May 1946, had threatened to draft rail workers into the army. In June 1947 the new Republican Congress, under the leadership of conservative Senator Robert A. Taft, passed the Labor-Management Relations, or Taft-Hartley, Act. Truman returned the bill with a stinging veto message, but Congress quickly overrode the veto.

The Taft-Hartley Act attempted to meet two public complaints against labor. In an effort to deal with nation-wide strikes which disrupted the economy, the act empowered the President to force a union to accept a 60-day "cooling-off period" before striking. If at the end of the cooling-off period the dispute was not settled, the employer's last offer would have to be presented to the workers in a secret vote. The act was also intended to reverse the alleged favoritism of New Deal legislation toward labor by listing a number of unfair union practices: it banned the closed shop, permitted employers to sue unions for broken contracts or strike damages, required unions to make their financial statements public, forbade union contributions to political campaigns, ended the "check off" system whereby employers collected union dues, and required union leaders to take oaths that they were not Communists. Despite the opposition of labor organizations and of many liberal Democrats, the Taft-Hartley Act has remained unchanged, a measure of the American people's conviction in the postwar era that national labor unions, like business, need some kind of public control.

Although Truman and the Republican Eightieth Congress rarely agreed on domestic policies, on defense and foreign policy they often did (see below, pp. 429-30). An administration bill to unify the army, navy, and air force was not entirely acceptable to Congress, but the services were merged into the Department of Defense under the National Security Act of July 1947. James V. Forrestal, who had served as Secretary of the Navy under Roosevelt and Truman, became the first Secretary of Defense.

Russian Expansionism. Even before the Potsdam Conference in July 1945, there had been signs that Allied unity displayed at Yalta was superficial. Before his death, for example, Roosevelt had warned Stalin that the Yalta agreements concerning Poland must not be ignored. Stalin's initial refusal to send Molotov to the UN conference in April 1945 also aroused Western suspicions of Russian intentions. Then came Potsdam, with Stalin insisting on having his way with Poland and with German reparations. During the last half of 1945 and most of 1946 at meetings of the United Nations and of the Council of Foreign Ministers to draw up peace treaties with the lesser enemy states, the Russians were both demanding and uncooperative.

Especially ominous for the peace of the postwar world was the Soviet Union's refusal to withdraw its troops from Iran stationed there during the war in joint occupation with the British. Only vigorous protests by the United States and the United Nations impelled a Russian withdrawal in late May 1946. Two months later, in early August, the Soviets demanded slices of Turkish territory and a share in the control of the Dardanelles. To many Western observers the Soviet behavior announced a resurgence of historic tsarist expansionism.

Actually, Soviet conquests already far exceeded any dreams of the tsars; Russian armies stood as far west as Germany, and all of eastern Europe lay under their control. Yugoslavia, it is true, was unoccupied by a Russian army, but it was firmly Communist under the regime of Marshal Tito. Indeed, in 1946 Tito was even more truculent in his dealings with the West than was Stalin himself. The same month that the Soviets served their demands upon Turkey, Tito's planes, on two different occasions, shot down unarmed American transport planes which accidentally crossed the Yugoslav frontier.

Churchill, now out of office because of a Labour party victory, gave voice to the concern of the Western nations. At Fulton, Missouri, on March 5, 1946, with President Truman sitting conspicuously on the platform, Churchill called attention to the "iron curtain" which "has descended across the continent" from "Stettin in the Baltic to Trieste in the Adriatic." Moreover, he went on, "Nobody knows what Soviet Russia and its Communist international organization intends to do in the immediate future, or what are the limits, if any, to their expansive and proselytising tendencies." Meanwhile, the Soviets in the UN turned down the American plan for international control of nuclear energy. Since under the plan the United States would have voluntarily surrendered its monopoly of nuclear power, Americans took the Soviet rejection as another sign that the Soviets were not interested in peace and order in the world.

The Problem of Germany. The major European dispute between East and West concerned the future of Germany. In the view of the Western powers, particularly the United States, the revival of a united Germany had been agreed upon at Yalta and reaffirmed at Potsdam. But Russian insistence upon large German reparations could only mean that Stalin intended to keep Germany weak and without hope of recovery for the foreseeable future. As a result the Russians obtained very little in the way of reparations from the Western occupation zones, though in their own zone they carted eastward everything they could.

By the fall of 1946 Secretary of State James F. Byrnes became convinced that the Russians did not really want a reunited and independent Germany. Moreover, he was sure that they were using the continued division of Germany as a means of impeding German recovery. Hence he convinced the British to merge their zone with that of the Americans. (The French, as skeptical of German unification as the Russians, did not join the other Western allies until 1949.) However, in merging the Western zones, Byrnes was helping to divide Germany ever more permanently between East and West. Thus, in Germany as in the United Nations, the Cold War was obviously in being by the end of 1946. Increasingly in the years to come, West Germany (which became independent in 1954) would be viewed by the West as the chief bulwark against Russian expansion into western Europe, while the Soviet Union would see the German Federal Republic as the chief threat to its hegemony in eastern Europe.

The Containment Policy. For a time after World War II it seemed that the Russians might well fulfill their most ambitious plan: the complete Communist domination of war-torn Europe. Economically and militarily prostrate from their struggles, the nations of western Europe were in poor position to defend themselves against Soviet military force and subversion. In France and Italy strong Communist parties seemed on the verge of taking power either through the ballot box or by force. In Greece Communist-led guerrillas fought pro-Western government forces for control of the country. Even Great Britain, presumably one of the principal victors of the war, lay on the verge of bankruptcy. Economically bled, Britain could no longer sustain its traditional role as guardian of Greece's independence; in February 1947 the British announced the imminent withdrawal of aid. In Turkey, too, an unstable government was being pressured by the Soviets for territorial grants and administrative concessions in the Dardanelles.

In Asia and Africa the steady drive for independence had already begun. Independent states had already established themselves in the Middle East when India and Pakistan achieved freedom in 1947. And the movement was obviously growing across the Asian land mass. With their lack of experience in democratic procedures and their difficulties of maintaining stability in the midst of poverty and strife, the new nations were a ripe target for Soviet threats and subversion.

The American response to this global Communist threat was the formation and gradual implementation of the policy of "containment." As publicly announced in July 1947 in an article by State Department aide George F. Kennan, "The main element of any U.S. policy toward the Soviet Union must be that of a long-term, patient but firm and vigilant containment of Russian expansive tendencies." While accepting—though not entirely—the accomplished fact of Soviet control over eastern Europe, the policy of containment did seek to hold the line against the further extension of Soviet imperialism.

The Truman Doctrine. Even before

the containment policy was officially enunciated, the Truman administration had taken steps to stem the Communist advance. After much soul-searching and consultation with congressional leaders of both parties, President Truman urged the United States to take up the burden of aid to Greece and Turkey. In a historic address to Congress and the nation on March 12, 1947, he called for $400 million in economic and military aid for the two beleaguered countries to save them from "aggressive movements that seek to impose upon them totalitarian regimes." His proposal was opposed by conservatives who protested the cost and by liberals and left-wingers who denounced it as warmongering. However, all recognized that this "Truman Doctrine," pledging aid to nations resisting aggression or subversion, signaled a sharp departure from the whole previous practice of American foreign policy. For the first time in peace, the United States was being asked to commit its military might (though that part of the proposal was underplayed by the President) and economic power to the defense of countries outside the Western Hemisphere. By a vote of 67 to 23 in the Senate in April and 287 to 107 in the House in May the Republican Congress sanctioned the new turn in foreign policy by voting the funds.

The Marshall Plan. An immediate Soviet military invasion was not the greatest threat to western Europe in the first postwar years. It was the legacy of war—Europe's persistent poverty, widespread misery and mass unemployment—in which Communism found its greatest ally, especially in countries like Italy and France, where economic and political instability was an open invitation to subversion. Therefore, to stimulate European recovery, the Truman administration began plans for extending massive economic assistance. The idea —first suggested in a speech by Under Secretary of State Dean Acheson—was brought to the attention of the world, and Europe in particular, in a Harvard commencement address delivered by Secretary of State George C. Marshall on June 5, 1947.

Marshall's speech offered American economic aid to any European nation seriously interested in restoring the shattered economy of Europe, including those nations closely associated with Soviet Russia. The nations of western Europe accepted the suggestion with enthusiasm, but Soviet Russia, after some preliminary exploration, compelled its satellites to stay out of the scheme, on the excuse that the Marshall Plan was a cover-up for American imperialistic designs. The proposal also evoked widespread opposition in the United States, from both the right and the left, but leading Republicans, notably Senator Arthur H. Vandenberg, championed it from the outset. Calling the idea a "calculated risk" to "help stop World War III before it starts," Vandenberg countered assertions that it was a gigantic "international WPA" or a "Socialist blueprint." As presented to Congress in December, the measure envisioned the expenditure of $17 billion over a four-year period, with $6.8 billion to be spent in the fifteen months following April 1, 1948.

During the fall and winter of 1947 the continued decline of the European economy and the many stories of starvation and misery in western Europe gave substance to the argument for United States assistance. But equally influential were the continued signs of Soviet pressure. For example, in February 1948 a Communist workers' coup thrust democratic Czechoslovakia behind the Iron Curtain, and in March reports of a Russian advance to the West circulated within government circles. Furthermore, a Communist victory appeared to be a real possibility in the Italian elections coming up in April. Responding to these pressures and to others from an anxious administration, Congress on April 2, 1948, passed the European Recovery Act or Marshall Plan, granting to the President about 90 per cent of the funds he had requested for the first year. Though Congress refused to commit the United States to anything thereafter, subsequent grants were made on an annual basis.

The full four-year plan was never carried out because the Korean War intervened, but the $12.5 billion extended to sixteen western European countries achieved the purpose of reviving the European economy. Between 1948 and 1951 production of all of the countries rose about 37 per cent. With a more prosperous economy and the resultant political stability, the internal threat of Communism receded noticeably. Moreover, the international cooperation fostered by the plan afforded the European nations a new insight into the advantages of closer economic union. That insight bore fruit in the 1950's with the formation of the European Coal and Steel Community and, later, the Common Market or European Economic Community.

Point Four. In his inaugural message of January 1949 President Truman added another dimension to America's commitment to the improvement of the world's economy. As "Point Four" of his foreign policy statement, he announced that the United States was undertaking "a bold new program for making the benefits of our scientific and industrial progress available for the improvement and growth of under-developed areas." In subsequent years American technicians traveled around the globe helping primitive farmers become less so, installing better means of disease prevention and cure, and in general helping to bring the labor-saving and life-saving technology of the West to Asia, Africa, and Latin America.

NATO. Soon after the European Recovery Program went into effect, the East-West conflict over Germany reached its most dangerous stage. In July 1948 the Soviets, vexed by the frictions arising from joint administration of Germany and hoping to force Western evacuation of Berlin, ordered a blockade of all ground communication with the city, which lay deep in the Soviet zone. Faced with the prospect of war if they forced their way to Berlin, the Western Allies instead instituted a gigantic airlift to fly in supplies and food. Although the Russians did not molest the airlift, they did not agree to ending the blockade until May 1949. Meanwhile the airlift had proved its ability to sustain the West Berliners and the Western right of access to Berlin.

The Berlin blockade reinforced the American belief in the need for closer military cooperation among the western European nations. The Brussels Pact of March 1948 had already created a defensive alliance among Great Britain, France, Belgium, Luxembourg, and the Netherlands. Toward the end of 1948 the United States encouraged widening the Brussels Pact alliance to include other nations rimming the North Atlantic. In the spring of 1949, twelve countries, including Canada and the United States in the New World, joined the North Atlantic Treaty Organization, which in 1952 expanded to include Italy and Greece and in 1954 West Germany.

With the signing of the treaty in April 1949, the United States, for the first time in peace, obligated itself to come to the assistance of European nations. This was the strongest commitment yet assumed in the course of the diplomatic revolution which had begun only four years earlier with the ratification of the United Nations Charter. The NATO treaty encountered only slight opposition in the Senate, which ratified it on July 21, 1949. In early 1951 General Dwight D. Eisenhower was appointed Supreme Commander of the new integrated defense force to be fashioned out of the national armies of the twelve signatories.

CHAPTER 23

THE AGE OF COLD WAR, 1948-

THE ASIAN REVOLUTION

The Overthrow of Colonialism. If the results of the war in Europe dropped unexpected problems into the laps of Americans, the consequences of the war in western Asia constituted a revolution. The great colonial powers, though victors in the war, lost virtually all their Asian possessions within five years after the defeat of the Japanese. When the British returned to Malaya and Burma, the Dutch to the East Indies, and the French to Indochina, they were greeted with demands for independence and sometimes by open military rebellion.

One by one the European nations made the only possible response; they got out of Asia. The United States, acting on a prewar promise, led the movement by granting final independence to the Philippines on July 4, 1946. The British followed next, freeing India and Pakistan on August 15, 1947, and Ceylon and Burma less than six months later. Then in 1948, in the face of Zionist and other terrorist activities, the British ended their mandate over Palestine, whose Jewish population successfully fought off the Arabs and proclaimed the new state of Israel. Of the once vast British Empire in Asia only a few pinpoints on the map, like Hong Kong and Singapore, continued to fly the Union Jack. (Malaya gained complete independence in 1957.)

Not all the European powers recognized the shape of the future as clearly as Britain. The Dutch in the East Indies, though faced with armed rebellion, refused to relinquish control; only in 1949, after years of warfare, did the Dutch transfer power to the new nationalist government of the United States of Indonesia. Although in western Asia the French as early as 1946 had evacuated their troops from Lebanon and Syria, in eastern Asia they were, like the Dutch, reluctant to accede to nationalist demands for independence. For almost a decade after 1945 the French sacrificed the flower of their officer corps and thousands of young men in a futile struggle to suppress the nationalist movement in Indochina. French sovereignty ceased in the summer of 1954. The rapid liquidation of colonialism was the first part of the Asian revolution.

The Transformation of Japan. The second part of the revolution in Asia was the American occupation of Japan. Although ostensibly representing all the Allied powers, General Douglas MacArthur, the American occupation commander, in reality was the supreme authority in that country, and his policy was dictated by the United States. Aside from stripping Japan of all its colonies, including Formosa and Korea, the United States deliberately undertook to destroy the old Japan. Thoroughgoing

THE COLONIAL WORLD, 1939

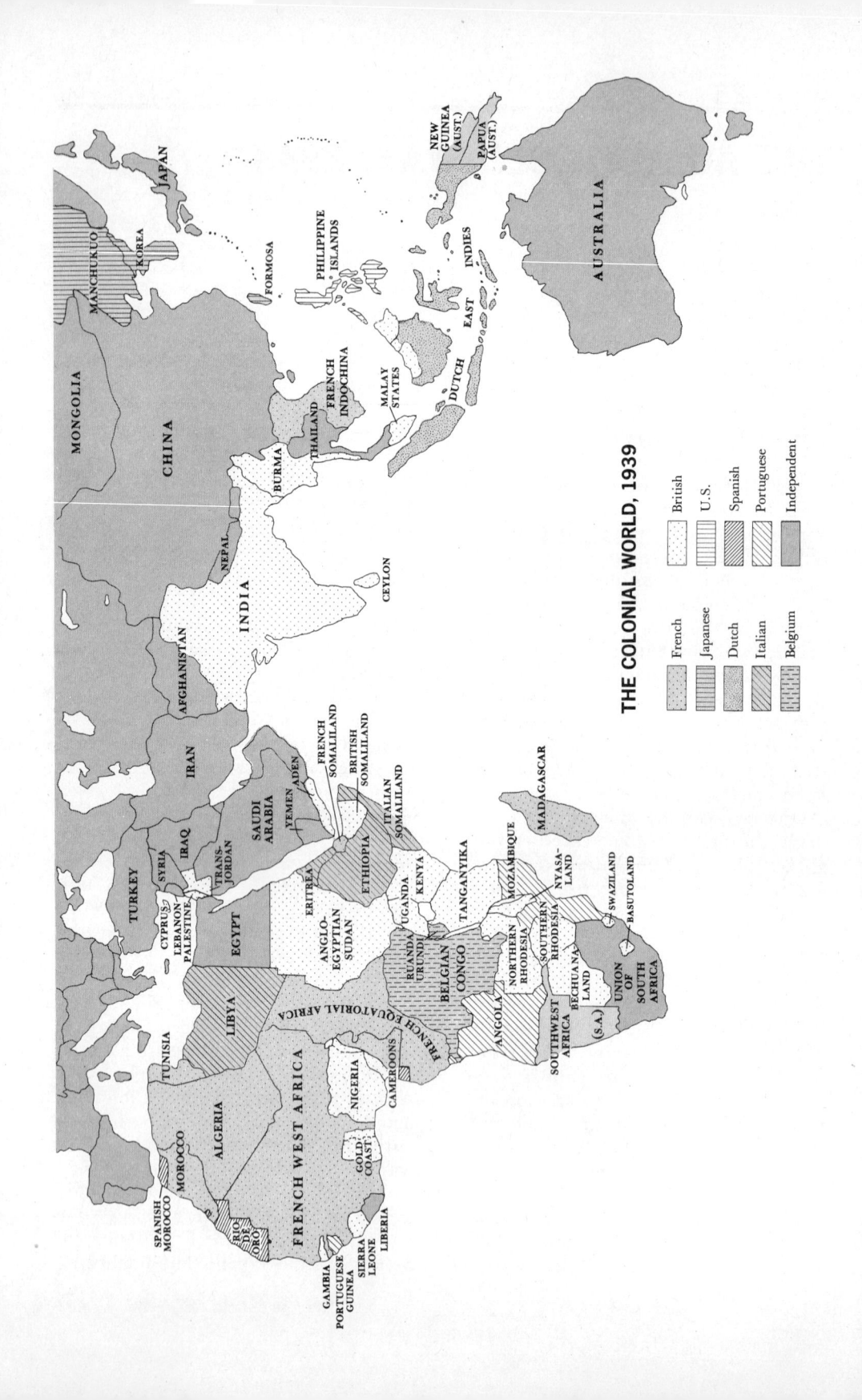

land reform, which spread land ownership more widely than ever before, improved the lot of the peasantry. A new democratic constitution, in which the emperor was reduced from a god to a mere symbol of national unity, also removed the army from politics. Women were enfranchised for the first time and given greater freedom in society and within the family. As Edwin O. Reischauer, an authority on Japanese history and ambassador to Japan under the Kennedy administration, once wrote: "During the early post-war years in Japan, MacArthur played the role not only of the most radical American revolutionary of modern times but also of the most successful."

When the Korean War broke out in 1950 (see pp. 436-39), the United States and its noncommunist allies in the war against Japan hastened to conclude peace with the Japanese, despite the objections of the Soviet Union. The peace treaty was signed in September 1951, and in a separate agreement the United States was permitted to retain military bases in Japan. As with Germany, the United States also encouraged its former enemy in Asia to rebuild its dismantled military machine as a defense against Communism.

The Rise of Chinese Communism. The third prong of the Asian revolution was the Communist conquest of China. When World War II ended, China was accorded the status of a great power, receiving, for example, a permanent seat on the Security Council of the United Nations. With the Japanese defeat, most people assumed that Generalissimo Chiang Kai-shek's Nationalists would reinforce their rule over all China. Even Stalin at the close of the war recognized Chiang's Nationalist government, not Communist leader Mao Tse-tung's, as the rightful regime. But the Chinese Communists had a sizable army and a government in northwestern China and were stronger than many observers thought.

At first the United States helped Chiang in his effort to spread his military authority over all of China. When that failed, the United States attempted through most of 1946 and 1947 to find a basis for agreement between Chiang and Mao Tse-tung, the Communist leader; in December 1945 President Truman had dispatched General George C. Marshall to China, where he worked for over a year on such a mission, but without success. Chiang, long an outspoken opponent of Communism, would have no Communists in his government; and the Reds, scenting success in the wind, would not disband their army as a prerequisite to a coalition government. By the end of 1947 the two sides were fighting it out in open civil war, during which Chiang's lack of support from the masses of the Chinese people became increasingly evident.

In the course of 1948 and early 1949 the Communists advanced steadily, taking Manchuria and most of northern China. By the close of 1949 the principal cities of southern China were in Mao's hands, and Chiang Kai-shek with the remnants of his Nationalist army had fled to the island of Formosa, some one hundred miles off the coast. In October 1949 the Soviet Union extended diplomatic recognition to the communist People's Republic of China, followed in February 1950 by the signing of a Sino-Soviet mutual assistance agreement and pact of alliance. Thus, just as the end of the Berlin blockade and the creation of NATO marked the ebbing of the Communist danger in western Europe, the Cold War came to Asia.

THE DEMOCRATS STAY IN

The Miracle of 1948. By 1948 Harry Truman had warmed up well to the role of the presidency, which had been thrust upon him so suddenly three years be-

THE NEWLY INDEPENDENT NATIONS, 1964

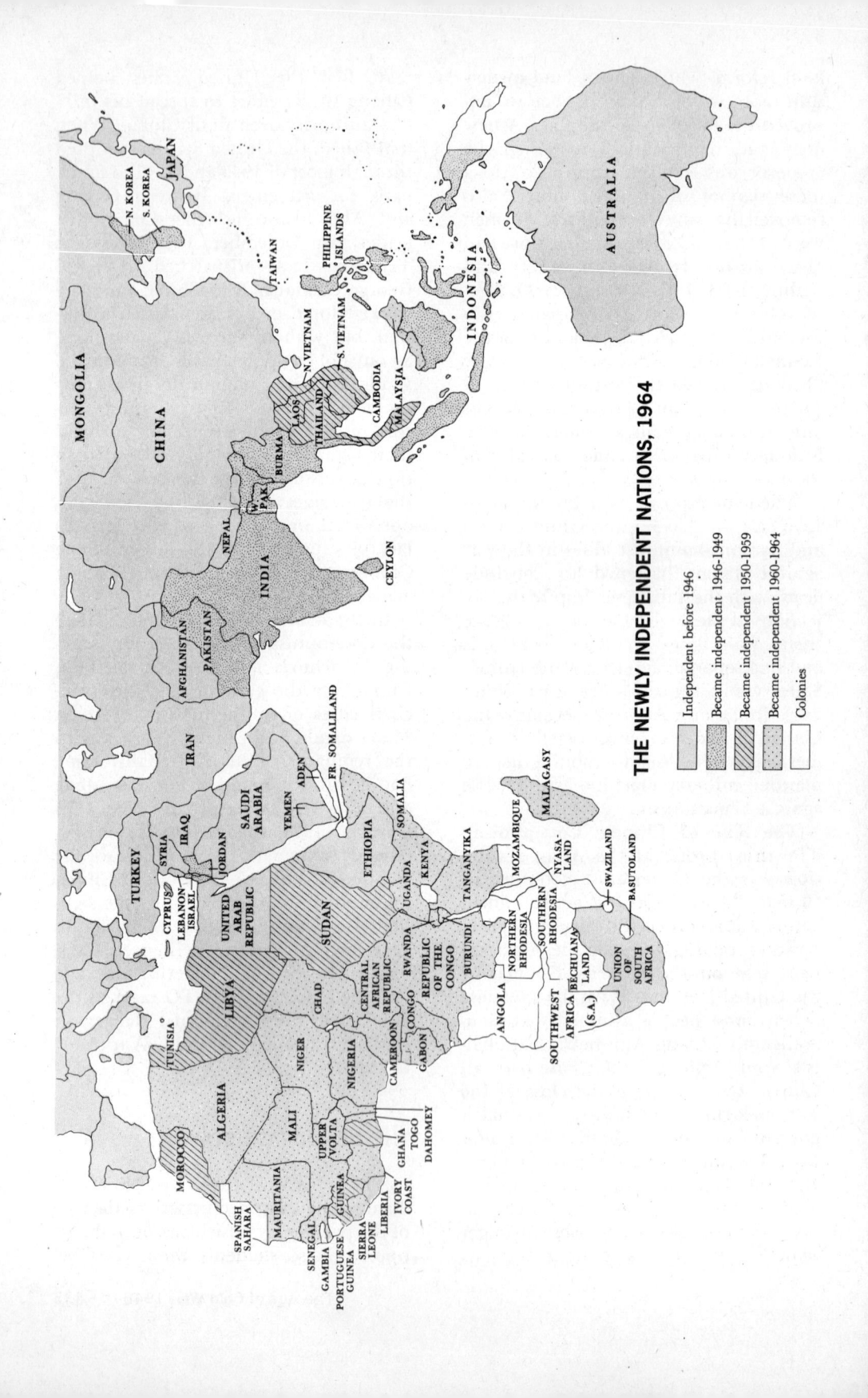

Independent before 1946
Became independent 1946-1949
Became independent 1950-1959
Became independent 1960-1964
Colonies

fore, and he was eager to try himself before the electorate. Although opposed by many Democrats who thought he lacked popular appeal, the President controlled the July Democratic convention, which dutifully renominated him on the first ballot, naming Senator Alben W. Barkley of Kentucky as his running mate. When the Republican Congress was called into special session by Truman that summer and refused to enact his liberal program, Truman went into the campaign talking about the "do-nothing" Eightieth Congress.

In the election Truman faced a serious loss of votes from both the right and left wings of his party. Because the Democratic convention adopted a strong civil rights plank, several southern states bolted Truman and put forth their own States' Rights party candidate, Governor J. Strom Thurmond of South Carolina. Thurmond, it was expected, would cut deeply into Truman's support in the Deep South. The candidacy of Henry A. Wallace on the newly formed Progressive party ticket promised to draw away left-wing and liberal votes, for Wallace campaigned vigorously against the administration's containment policy, contending that it was anti-Russian and would lead to war instead of peace.

The Republicans, more confident of victory than at any time since the Great Depression, nominated for President their 1944 standard bearer, Governor Thomas E. Dewey of New York, pairing him with Governor Earl Warren of California as the vice-presidential nominee. Dewey's campaign was a model of caution; sure of victory, he preached unity and the need for efficiency. Accepting all of the New Deal reforms, even though they were also Truman's stock in trade, Dewey simply said he would administer them better. Even commentators opposed to Dewey conceded, along with the public opinion polls, that a Republican victory was foreordained. Harry Truman, though,

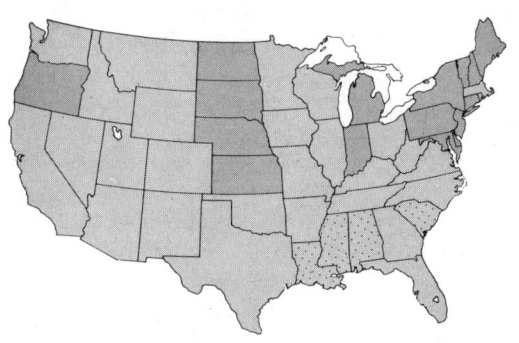

ELECTION OF 1948: ELECTORAL VOTE
Truman: 303
Dewey: 189   Thurmond: 39

was not convinced. He barnstormed around the country, attacking the Republican Congress for being against the people's interests. Republicans, he said, were "old moss backs . . . , gluttons of privilege . . . , all set to do a hatchet job on the New Deal." He traveled some 32,000 miles and made 356 speeches, far exceeding the campaign effort of Dewey, his overly confident and much younger opponent.

Election night brought the big surprise: Truman never lost the slight lead he gained in the early returns. The next morning the miracle had occurred; Harry Truman was elected by two million votes. Truman's vigorous appeals to popular memories of the Great Depression and his uncompromising defense of the New Deal had apparently struck fire in millions of voters. Moreover, by emphasizing the decline in farm prices under Republican farm legislation, Truman actually recaptured the farm vote, which Roosevelt had lost in 1940 and 1944. Although Truman lost four southern states (39 electoral votes) to Thurmond, these were more than balanced by a gain of urban Negro votes in the important industrial states of the North. Wallace's candidacy, as it turned out, hardly affected Truman's chances.

The Fair Deal. In his inaugural speech in January 1949, Truman spoke of his program as the "Fair Deal"; in effect, it was a continuation and extension of the New Deal. It called for civil rights legislation, a national health program, aid for public education, and support for low-income housing. Truman also asked for repeal of the Taft-Hartley Act and the enactment of a new farm subsidy program (the Brannan Plan), but the Congress, despite its Democratic complexion, would agree to neither. A coalition of Republicans and conservative Southern Democrats killed off not only civil rights legislation but most of the other measures of the Fair Deal. On the other hand, in 1949 Truman did succeed in obtaining a housing act and a minimum-wage increase to 75 cents an hour. In 1950 Congress also agreed to broadening the Social Security coverage, placing some ten million more persons under the benefits of the system.

After 1949 Truman was increasingly plagued by revelations of corruption in his administration. Although none of the disclosures compared with the Teapot Dome scandals of the twenties, many officials, especially in the Internal Revenue Service, were proved in court to be corrupt. Moreover, some White House officials turned out to be rather casual in their standards of proper behavior for government officers. In short, the Republican charge that the Democrats had been too long in control of the executive branch of government seemed to have some validity. But an issue of foreign policy was to supersede corruption as a Republican weapon against the administration.

The Outbreak of the Korean War. When in 1945 the United States and the Soviet Union occupied the former Japanese colony of Korea, they arbitrarily divided the country between them along the 38th line of latitude. Originally intended to be temporary, the line, in the suspicious atmosphere of the Cold War, hardened into a border between two Korean regimes—the North under Russian tutelage and the South under American. Because each of the Korean regimes strongly desired unification of the peninsula, border clashes were frequent. When the Americans withdrew their troops from South Korea in 1949, they carefully refrained from leaving behind any offensive weapons like tanks or heavy artillery for fear that the strongly nationalist president of South Korea, Syngman Rhee, would attempt to conquer North Korea by force of arms.

However, the Russians, withdrawing at about the same time, left a well-trained and heavily equipped North Korean army behind and may even have encouraged the North Koreans to attempt unification by force. In any event, on June 25, 1950, the North Korean army stormed across the 38th parallel, quickly overwhelming the thin South Korean defenses. The next day, before the rapidly advancing invaders, Rhee's government fled the capital of Seoul. Thereupon, the Truman administration, faced with a naked act of military aggression, decided to commit the United States to South Korea's defense, even though the American army then comprised no more than ten and one half infantry divisions and one armored division. On June 30, when it became evident that American air and naval support alone could not save the South Koreans, the first U.S. ground troops landed in Korea. Prodded by the United States, the United Nations on June 27 branded the North Koreans as aggressors and called upon all member states to "furnish such assistance to the Republic of Korea as may be necessary to repel the armed attack and to restore international peace and security to the area." On July 7 General Douglas MacArthur was designated United Nations commander in chief. Although all during the fight-

THE KOREAN WAR

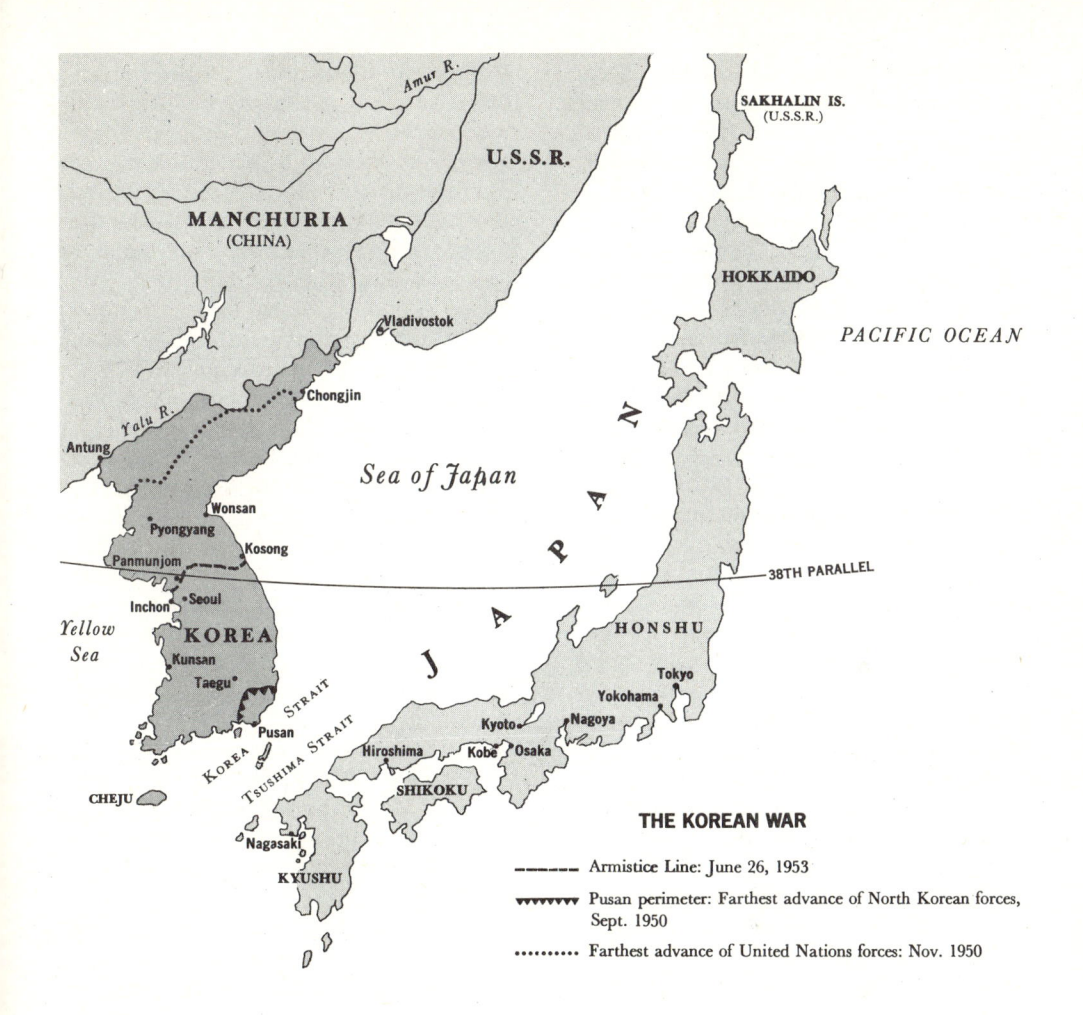

——— Armistice Line: June 26, 1953
vvvvvv Pusan perimeter: Farthest advance of North Korean forces, Sept. 1950
.... Farthest advance of United Nations forces: Nov. 1950

ing in Korea, American and South Korean troops made up the great preponderance of UN forces, by the end of 1950 some twenty nations had sent some kind of support. Because the Russians had been boycotting the Security Council in protest against the West's refusal to admit Communist China to the UN, their representative was not present to veto the resolution which propelled the United Nations into the war.

For over two months the American and South Korean forces suffered uninterrupted defeats as the powerful North Korean armies pushed the United Nations forces down the peninsula into a small pocket around the port city of Pusan. Then on September 15, 1950, in a surprise maneuver, General MacArthur led a successful amphibious landing at Inchon on the west coast, far behind the North Korean lines. A simultaneous drive from the Pusan area caught the Communists in a giant pincer movement. By October 1 the United Nations were on the verge of crossing the 38th parallel into North Korea. When they did, a new phase of the war in Asia opened.

On November 26, as units of the United Nations forces approached the

The Age of Cold War, 1948–

Yalu River (the border between Korea and Communist China), large contingents of Chinese "volunteers" ambushed them, compelling the UN troops to retreat. Thereafter, increasing numbers of Chinese troops poured across the Yalu, once again pushing the United Nations far south of the 38th parallel. Thus deprived of total victory, General MacArthur asked for permission to bomb the Chinese in what he called their "sanctuary" across the Yalu. The Truman administration, however, turned down his request on the ground that such action might well invoke the Sino-Soviet mutual assistance pact and thus bring on a war with the two chief Communist powers.

But if the nation was spared a world war, a limited war far from American shores produced frustrations making the Korean struggle immensely unpopular. Public opinion polls indicated that after January 1951 Truman never again received the support of a majority of the American people. People spoke bitterly of "Truman's War." A draft board in Montana went so far as to refuse to draft any more men until General MacArthur was authorized to bomb as he saw fit in China.

As the leading advocate of striking directly against China, MacArthur inevitably came into fatal clash with the administration. When a letter written to House Republican minority leader Joseph W. Martin was released to the press—a letter in which MacArthur charged administration "diplomats" with fighting the Asian war "with words" rather than "with arms" and declared that "There is no substitute for victory"—President Truman on April 11, 1951, summarily removed the general from his commands in Korea and Japan. The nation was surprised and shocked. The President was widely attacked and MacArthur accorded a hero's welcome when he returned to the United States. After an address by the dismissed general before Congress, a Senate investigation exhaustively inquired into the removal. At the end of several weeks of hearings, during which the pitch of emotionalism gradually declined, the Senate committee agreed with General Omar Bradley when he said that MacArthur's policy would have extended the fighting to the mainland of Asia, which would "involve us in the wrong war, at the wrong place, at the wrong time, and with the wrong enemy."

The Effects of the Korean War. The Korean War demonstrated that aggression could be halted if the nations of the world were determined to do so. Thereby it stimulated the expansion of American armed forces and put life into the recently created NATO. By June 1952 some 2.2 million men and women had been added to the American armed forces, and the air force no longer languished for lack of funds. Domestically the Korean "police action," as Truman once called the war, forced the administration to institute economic controls, but not to the extent of World War II. Although both income and excise taxes went up in 1950 and a new excess profits tax became law in 1951, the end of 1952 was witnessing sufficient military production to permit the easing of many of the economic controls. Indeed, the war had pushed the nation into a new boom, quickly ending the recession of 1948-1949. Thus, conditions of life in the United States were such that many Americans, if they had no relatives in Korea, hardly knew there was a war at all. That such was the case only made the war more unpopular among those who did have sons fighting overseas.

The End of the Korean Fighting. Once the Chinese intervention demonstrated that the whole peninsula could not be united under Syngman Rhee, the Truman administration sought to end the fighting as soon as possible. By the end of 1952, strengthened UN forces had pushed the Chinese northward to the region of the 38th parallel. Although the United States was prepared to strike a truce at that point, the Communists held off. An armistice was not signed in Korea until the middle of 1953 under the Eisenhower administration.

The Great Fear. Between 1949 and 1954 the nation was gripped by a pervasive fear that Communism was about to subvert the Republic. Any program or any idea traceable to Communist ideology became suspect; mere accusation of having been a Communist was sometimes enough to condemn a man to loss of job or friends. A veritable witch hunt of suspected traitors and disloyal citizens was carried out by government and by private groups. Actually, throughout the whole period the number of disloyal people discovered in positions of trust was insignificant.

The Great Fear grew out of the deteriorating international situation of 1946 and 1947, when American Communists showed that regardless of their formal citizenship they owed first loyalty to the Soviet Union. In 1947 the federal government instituted a program to check on the loyalty of government employees, and many public educational institutions, like the University of California, demanded oaths of loyalty from their faculties. Congressional investigations in 1947 and 1948 revealed evidence of spying in government by Communists during the 1930's. The most notable instance was the case of Alger Hiss, a former high-ranking member of the State Department, who was accused of heading an espionage ring in the 1930's that passed on classified documents to the Soviets; his two trials in 1949-1950 for perjury (the statute of limitations prevented indictment for espionage) aroused wide public concern over Communist influence in government.

Hiss' trial and conviction, like other revelations about Communists in government, concerned espionage prior to 1945, but in 1950 the FBI revealed that American spies had transmitted secret A-bomb data to the Russians in 1945 and 1946. Several Americans, including Julius and Ethel Rosenberg, were tried and convicted for espionage. The Rosenbergs, whose cause the Communists tried vainly to make into a new Sacco-Vanzetti case, were executed in 1953.

To these and other sensational revelations of Communist influence in American life, the Congress responded with the Internal Security (or McCarran) Act of 1951, passing it over Truman's veto. The new law required Communist and Communist-front organizations to register with the government and to identify as Communist all their mail and literature; it also forbade employment of Communists in defense work and barred the immigration from abroad of anyone who had belonged to a Communist or fascist organization. The most drastic of all provisions and the one which measured the extremity of congressional concern was the authorization for the government to place Communists, citizens and aliens alike, in concentration camps whenever a national emergency occurred.

The Rise and Fall of McCarthy. The person who more than any other perpetuated the Great Fear during these years was Joseph McCarthy, a Republican senator from Wisconsin. McCarthy first came into national prominence in February 1950 when he charged in a speech at Wheeling, West Virginia, that fifty-seven or more Communists were then working in the State Department. "In my opinion," he said, "the State Department, which is one of the most important government departments, is thoroughly infested with Communists," and it was all the blame of Secretary of State Dean Acheson, that "pompous diplomat in striped pants, with a phony British accent." A Senate investigating committee later exonerated the department, but McCarthy continued to brandish similar unsubstantiated charges of Communists in government, naming names by the score. In the context of the Great Fear, his spectacular, headline-making accusations often gained credence. Occasionally he was courageously repudiated and criticized, but the bulk of government officials, including his fellow senators, feared to gainsay him; to do so laid his accusers open to charges of being "soft" on Communism.

McCarthy's attacks on the State Department and other agencies of the executive branch continued even under Eisenhower's Republican administration. Indeed, during the 1952 campaign Eisenhower hesitated to criticize the senator publicly even though it was widely known that Eisenhower deeply resented the scurrilous attacks that McCarthy had made upon General George C. Marshall, Acheson's predecessor as Secretary of State. As late as January 1954 a Gallup public opinion poll showed that 50 per cent of the American people favored McCarthy's activities and only 29 per cent opposed him, although by then the senator had driven from the State Department almost all of the experts on China on the grounds that they had "lost" China to the Communists.

However, McCarthy's power to frighten came to an abrupt end in 1954 when he obliquely attacked President Eisenhower and directly assailed Secretary of the Army Robert Stevens as an "awful dupe" of the Communists. McCarthy's now-apparent demagoguery caused his popularity to plummet. Coming under senatorial investigation himself for his unmannerly conduct, McCarthy was "condemned" for his behavior by sixty-seven senators in December 1954, although a mere twelve months before only one senator had been willing to stand out against an appropriation for McCarthy's Committee on Government Operations. The senator's influence abruptly collapsed. Soon thereafter he went into a physical decline, dying in May 1957.

McCarthy's fall marked the end of the Great Fear. A symptom of that fear and not a cause of it, McCarthyism could last only so long as Americans believed that the internal menace of Communism was greater than the external threat. By 1954 they no longer thought so.

THE REPUBLICAN INTERLUDE

The Election of 1952. As early as 1950, leading Republicans, especially those of an internationalist persuasion like Thomas E. Dewey, had been talking of Dwight D. Eisenhower as the ideal candidate for the party in 1952. Still incredibly popular because of his war record, Eisenhower also possessed political appeal because his rise from poor boy in Kansas to international renown seemed to epitomize the American dream. When his name was first suggested for the nomination, Eisenhower announced he was not interested, but in July 1952, after much public and private pressure, he resigned his command of the NATO forces and agreed to try for the nomination.

His most formidable opponent for the nomination was Senator Robert A. Taft of Ohio, conservative in domestic affairs and neo-isolationist. Twice Taft's nomination had been turned down in favor of Dewey; now the senator's supporters, who were legion, felt Taft's chance had come. But Eisenhower's backers proved to be the more adroit politicians at the Republican national convention in July; even before the balloting began it was evident that Taft lacked the necessary votes for nomination. The convention nominated Eisenhower on the first ballot, with Senator Richard M. Nixon of California as his running mate. As a congressman a few years earlier, Nixon had gained national renown as a member of the House Un-American Activities Committee which unmasked Alger Hiss.

Since Harry Truman took himself out of the race early in 1952, the Democrats centered their attention upon new prospects, notably Adlai E. Stevenson, governor of Illinois. Although Stevenson was not sure he wanted to run, the July convention "drafted" him on the third ballot. In an effort to heal the wounds from the party split over civil rights in 1948, the convention nominated a liberal Southerner, Senator John J. Sparkman of Alabama, for Vice-President.

From the outset Eisenhower was the favorite. While Stevenson was compelled to defend the Truman Administration, the Republicans fiercely attacked it for its alleged corruption and coddling of Communists in government and, above all, for the Korean War. Late in the campaign Stevenson's manager, referring to the Republican barrage of criticism, remarked: "We are suffering from a new kind of KKK—Korea, Communism, and corruption." However, Stevenson proved to be an admirable candidate. His speeches were undoubtedly the most sophisticated addresses heard from a presidential candidate since the days of Woodrow Wilson. His ratings on the public opinion polls steadily rose during the campaign, but never to the level of Eisenhower's.

Toward the end of October Eisenhower capitalized on the pervasive discontent over Korea by promising that, if he were elected, he would personally make a trip to the battlefront in an effort to bring the fighting to an end. Even Democrats found this appealing. As one Southern Democrat put it: "If the war is settled by November, I'll be

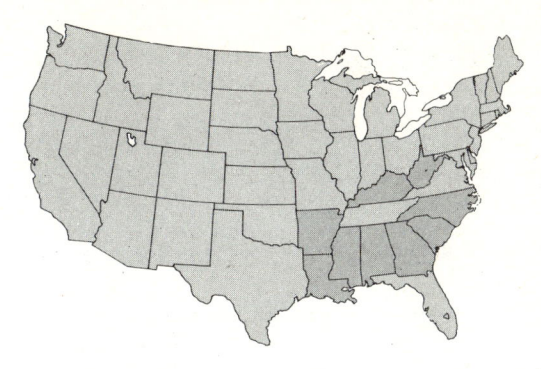

ELECTION OF 1952: ELECTORAL VOTE

Eisenhower: 442   Stevenson: 89

for Stevenson. If not, it's Ike. If we can't get a truce I figure we'll need a military man around to clean things up." Even the prosperous times, which ordinarily would have worked to the advantage of the incumbent party, could not overcome the force of the Korean issue.

Eisenhower scored a sweeping personal victory with 442 electoral votes to Stevenson's 89 and almost 34 million popular votes to Stevenson's 27 million. Eisenhower's popular vote ran 15 per cent ahead of his party's vote for Congress, for the Republicans captured both houses by only slim majorities (and, in fact, lost their control to the Democrats in the mid-term elections two years later). Another measure of Eisenhower's victory was that he broke into the Democratic South, capturing not only the border states and Tennessee and Virginia, but Texas and Florida as well. Even in the traditionally isolationist Middle West and despite his record as an internationalist, Eisenhower won easily. Negroes, rural Southerners, and the big city voters in the North remained loyal to the Democrats.

The First Eisenhower Administration. Many Americans, knowing Eisenhower's long record as a military man, anticipated a stern and exacting leader of Congress and the nation. In fact, Eisenhower turned out quite the opposite. Basically he conceived the President's functions to be quite distinct from those of Congress; generally he refused even to comment upon legislation while it was passing through the legislative mill. The first cabinet was made up largely of successful businessmen; a quip of the day described it as a cabinet of eight millionaires and a plumber, the last a reference to Martin Durkin, Secretary of Labor and former president of the plumbers' union.

The first administration thus was intended to be a businessman's government in the best sense of the phrase—that is, it would not be subservient to business, but it would do its best to encourage business. Thus all economic controls left over from the Korean war were abolished early in February 1953. Similarly, government enterprises which competed with private business were dropped. A balanced budget became the guiding aim of the administration under the leadership of Secretary of the Treasury George C. Humphrey. When he took office, Eisenhower cut over a billion dollars from Truman's foreign aid budget, but in the main he would not let the drive for economy endanger the national security. On the other hand, if there were any choice, the administration generally gave preference to business over government. Thus it awarded an electric power contract to a private utility instead of to the Tennessee Valley Authority; in 1956 the Atomic Energy Commission authorized the private development of electric power through nuclear energy.

In at least two respects the Republicans carried on New Deal–Fair Deal policies without question. One was in showing a willingness to use federal authority to counteract the recession of 1954 and the other was in expanding the coverage of the Social Security system in 1953. Eisenhower also tried to overcome the isolationism which still persisted among many Republicans; indeed, to advance the cause of internationalism, Eisenhower had run in the first place. But it required all of Eisenhower's prestige to prevent the passage in 1954 of the so-called Bricker Amendment, which would have limited the treaty-making power of the government and enlarged congressional control over foreign relations. Although advanced as a means of preventing the treaty-making power from being abused, this proposed amendment to the Constitution would have seriously handicapped the President's handling of foreign affairs.

The Election of 1956. Normally, in view of the President's immense popularity, his renomination in 1956 would have been unquestioned. But in September 1955 the President suffered a severe heart attack which incapacitated him for two months. Although his steady and remarkable recovery emboldened the party leaders to call once again for his nomination, the President himself held off until February 1956 before giving his consent. That summer he was renominated along with Richard M. Nixon. The Democrats also renominated their candidate of 1952, Adlai Stevenson, who this time had eagerly sought the nomination.

Eisenhower won again. The Republican campaign slogan capitalized on "peace and prosperity," but the victory is better explained by the character of a man who could inspire millions of voters to display campaign buttons reading "I like Ike." Eisenhower's personal popularity won him 457 electoral votes to Stevenson's 73. That it was a personal victory was attested by the fact that Eisenhower failed to bring a Republican Congress into office with him. The Democrats controlled the Senate 50-46 and the House 233-202. Not since 1848 had a President failed to carry with him at least one house;

for a popular President such a failure was unprecedented.

Working with Democrats. Throughout his second term Eisenhower was confronted with Democratic majorities in both houses. (In the mid-term elections of 1958, Democratic majorities reached proportions not seen since the mid-1930's.) Conceiving his presidential role to be one of resisting a "wasteful" Democratic Congress, Eisenhower consistently vetoed salary increases for government employees and demands for tax cuts during the 1958 recession. Despite the large Democratic majorities, all save one of Eisenhower's vetoes of Democratic antirecession measures were sustained.

The principal piece of legislation of Eisenhower's second term was the Labor-Management Reporting and Disclosure Act (1959), which grew out of Senate committee hearings on racketeering, corruption, and extortion among labor unions. In a sense, the bill continued the philosophy of the Taft-Hartley Act of 1947: it assumed a divergence of interest between the membership of unions and their leaders. Since Senator John L. McClellan, whose committee held the hearings, and Representative Philip M. Landrum, who sponsored the bill in the House, were Southern Democrats, the bill also symbolized the Republican–Southern Democratic alliance which usually supported the President on labor and financial measures. The Landrum-Griffin Act, as it was also called, (1) set up a "bill of rights" to protect union members against assessments and coercion by labor leaders; (2) required unions to make public, largely for the benefit of their members, all expenditures and all payments made to officers; (3) provided that unions must hold regular elections of officers; and (4) forbade unions to charge employers extraordinary fees for ordinary work—a restriction suggested by the extensive testimony before the McClellan committee on "shake-downs" of employers by unions.

THE SECOND RECONSTRUCTION

The 1954 Decision. On May 17, 1954, in handing down a decision in *Brown* v. *Board of Education of Topeka,* the Supreme Court of the United States unanimously concluded "that in the field of public education the doctrine of 'separate but equal' has no place." In the middle of the twentieth century, "separate education facilities are inherently unequal," the Court concluded. In thus overturning the decision in *Plessy* v. *Ferguson* (1896), on which all southern states rested the validity of their segregated public facilities, the court opened a new chapter in the history of the Negro in America.

Although for over a decade the Supreme Court had been invalidating state laws which discriminated on grounds of race, the school decision shocked the South. Although a few border-state communities like Baltimore and Washington, D.C., began desegregation of schools in 1954, in most of the South the decision met stiff and determined resistance. In September 1956, for example, an angry white mob in the little east Tennessee town of Clinton temporarily halted attempts to desegregate the local high school. By the middle of 1956 only some 350 school districts out of 6300 were desegregated in the South, and none of these desegregated districts was located in the middle or Deep South.

Southern Resistance. In 1957 Southern opposition to school desegregation reached the point of clashes with federal military power. Under a plan of gradual desegregation worked out by the local school board and the federal district court, nine Negro students were scheduled to enter Central High School in Little Rock, Arkansas, in the fall of 1957. However, with the use of state troops, Arkansas' Governor Orville Faubus barred their entrance. Faced with state defiance of federal authority, President Eisenhower, after an inconclusive conference with Governor Faubus, sent in United States paratroopers to enforce the orders of the federal court. For several weeks soldiers with fixed bayonets escorted the Negro students to classes, and federalized Arkansas troops later remained to patrol the school grounds for the entire school year.

If the breakdown of orderly processes of law in Arkansas shocked the nation and the world, in the South the use of federal troops temporarily stiffened resistance. "Massive resistance" statutes, as they were called, were hastily enacted in a number of states, resulting in the closing of schools in Little Rock and in three communities in Virginia. By 1959, though, the more moderate people in Arkansas and Virginia accepted at least token desegregation in preference to no public schools at all. And in 1960 and 1961 token desegregation came to the deep southern states of Louisiana and Georgia, particularly in the big cities of New Orleans and Atlanta.

However, the determined opposition of segregationist leaders and White Citizens Councils in the Deep South was not to be broken so easily. In September and October 1962, a transfixed nation watched as the state of Mississippi, through its elected officials, defied a federal court order requiring the University of Mississippi to permit a Negro, James Meredith, to enroll as a student. The federal authorities tried their best to avoid the use of armed force by working behind the scenes to secure compliance with the court. But Governor Ross Barnett's public statements of defiance encouraged thousands of segregationists, including many students, to attack physically the U.S. marshals assigned to protect Meredith upon his arrival at the university. As a result of the vehemence of the attack the federal government dispatched thousands of federalized Mississippi national guardsmen and regular army troops to the university town of Oxford to restore order and to insure the execution of the court's orders. Meredith did enter the university as its first known Negro student.

Prior to the riots desegregation at the state college and university level had been proceeding almost without incident in all southern states with the exception of Alabama and South Carolina. Although the vast majority of school districts in the South still remained segregated at the close of 1962, Southern acceptance of at least "token" desegregation seemed to be growing.

A New Negro Rights Movement. While the white South was strongly resisting desegregation of schools, Southern Negroes, with a militancy not seen before, made evident their opposition to segregation in a number of ways. On December 5, 1955, the fifty thousand Negro residents of Montgomery, Alabama, began a boycott of local buses in protest against segregated facilities. The boycott, though visiting hardship upon the Negroes who ordinarily depended upon public transportation to get to work, was sustained for almost a year. One of the leaders of the movement, the Reverend Martin Luther King, Jr., a young Southern Negro, became nationally known because of his advocacy of nonviolence in the achievement of equality for Negroes. In November 1956 the United States Supreme Court upheld a lower court in invalidating the segregation of buses in Montgomery.

The slow pace of desegregation also provoked the federal government to take action against discrimination. In August 1957 Congress, after much debate, passed the first Civil Rights Act since the days of Reconstruction. Its purpose was to protect Negro voting rights, and, though the provisions were weaker than those originally advocated by the Eisenhower administration, they empowered federal judges to jail for contempt anyone—including state officials—who prevented a qualified person from voting. The law also created a temporary Civil Rights Commission to investigate violations of civil rights and to make recommendations for new legislation. After a nine-day filibuster by Southern senators, Congress in 1960 passed a second Civil Rights Act to strengthen further the power of the federal government to protect Negro voting in the South. Despite the new laws, though, Negro voting in the South remained far below that of whites.

From 1960 on, Negroes themselves undertook new methods of attacking segregation in the South: there were "sit-ins" at segregated lunch counters and bus depots, "wade-ins" at segregated beaches, "pray-ins" at segregated churches, and the like, all aimed at nonviolent achievement of integration.

Simultaneously with the antisegregation movement in the South, Northern Negroes campaigned against segregated public schools in cities like New York and Chicago. Although unrecognized in law, school segregation in the North often existed in fact because of residential patterns. Negroes demanded, and with some success, that their children be accepted in white schools outside their local districts, where schools were often crowded and run-down.

THE NEW ACTIVIST SUPREME COURT

If in the 1930's the Supreme Court was the center of controversy because of its conservatism, in the 1950's and 1960's it was the object of both criticism and praise because of its willingness to innovate. In at least two different fields the Court exceeded even its customary importance as the final arbiter of American law.

Renewed Interest in Individual Rights. One of these fields was that of civil rights and individual liberties. The most striking instance, of course, was the 1954 decision in which the Court struck down segregated education. But there were other examples, too.

During the 1950's the Court spoke out clearly in defense of individual rights even when the accused were Communists. In the case of *Yates* v. *U.S.* (1957) the Court seriously modified the *Dennis* v. *U.S.* decision of 1951, which had upheld the conviction of eleven Communist leaders for conspiring to overthrow the government by force in violation of the Smith Act; Chief Justice Vinson had stated that the government could act if only "a highly organized conspiracy" to overthrow in the future were evidenced. The Yates decision, however, distinguished between "advocacy of forcible overthrow as mere abstract doctrine" (which is within the free speech protection of the First Amendment) and "advocacy which incites to illegal action" (proscribed by the Smith Act). Thus mere advocacy of a theoretical desirability of violence, as the *Dennis* decision had seemed to accept, was now not sufficient for conviction. Moreover, "mere membership or the holding of office in the Communist party" was held not to be sufficient proof of specific intent to "incite" persons to overthrow the government.

In the same year, in *Watkins* v. *U.S.*, which concerned a defendant who had admitted past Communist activities but had refused to disclose names of communist associates, the Court, in effect, warned congressional investigating committees that not every kind of question asked of a witness was constitutionally permissible. A citizen possessed the right to be fully informed of the purpose of an inquiry before being obliged to supply information; Congress is not a "law enforcement or trial agency" authorized "to expose the private affairs of individuals without justification."

Congress, the Court held, must respect the constitutional rights of witnesses, which include self-protection against incrimination and freedom of speech, of political belief, and of association. Here the Court was boldly protecting the rights of the individual citizen against one of the oldest and most treasured powers of Congress: the necessary right of a legislature to secure facts for the writing of legislation.

The Tennessee Reapportionment Case. The Court's decision in *Baker* v. *Carr*, handed down in March 1962, was freighted with almost as much significance for the future as the one on desegregation. The Baker case concerned the refusal of Tennessee to reapportion its legislative seats in accordance with changes in the distribution of population. The Court held that districts of markedly unequal populations constituted an inequity for which the courts could rightly be expected to provide a remedy. For a number of years, as population flowed from the rural areas to the cities, urban dwellers had smarted under the failure of their growing population to be reflected in increased representation in the state legislatures. It was well known that rural-dominated legislatures simply refused, as in the case of Tennessee, to reapportion seats, for to do so might mean loss of rural control. Until the *Baker* decision the courts had always held that such inequity was a "political" question beyond their jurisdiction. That decision now opened up the possibility that with equitable apportionment of representation the cities would be able to get a better hearing for their problems in the state legislatures.

Already in 1962 the effects of the decision were apparent. Several states undertook to reapportion their legislative seats in accordance with the new rule. In Georgia, where rural dominance in politics had long depended upon underweighting urban populations, the impact of the decision was immediately evident in the new political strength of cities like Atlanta. For a number of years to come the decision promised to upset the politics of many other states where rural control had been maintained only through outmoded apportionment.

A NEW ERA IN FOREIGN AFFAIRS

The Death of Stalin. In early 1953, foreign affairs took a new turn, for by coincidence in January a new Republican administration took office in Washington, and on March 5 Joseph Stalin died in Moscow. The two events, coming so close together, marked a new era in the Cold War. Although no single Soviet leader emerged to inherit Stalin's enormous personal power, the new group of men demonstrated more flexibility and resourcefulness in foreign policy than Stalin had. Notable in this regard was Nikita Khrushchev, who became head of the Communist party in 1953 and premier in 1958. Unlike Stalin, the new Soviet leaders traveled widely outside Russia, selling Communism energetically and even, in the case of Khrushchev in 1959, visiting the United States.

The Eisenhower administration also sought to alter foreign policy by taking a new approach. Despite his overall commitment to the major policies of the Truman administration, John Foster Dulles, the new Secretary of State, hoped to do more than merely contain Communism. Toward the end of 1953, for example, he tried to badger the European nations into a new defense community which would include a rearmed Germany, but he was unsuccessful. A looser grouping, agreed upon in 1954, did provide for a revived German army to be included in NATO.

On the other side of the world in Asia, soon after Communist-led Vietnamese guerrillas drove the French from Indochina in 1954, Secretary Dulles moved to counter further Communist expansion by the formation of the Southeast Asia Treaty Organization (SEATO). It was modeled after NATO but was conspicuously weaker on at least two counts. The signatories were required only to consult, not to take action, in the event of attack. Furthermore, the organization failed to include the chief powers of the region. Composed of Thailand, Australia, New Zealand, the Philippines, Pakistan, Britain, France, and the United States, SEATO did not include India, Indonesia, Ceylon, and Burma, all of which refused invitations to join.

Dulles also hoped to use the threat of American nuclear capability as a means of countering the superior manpower of the Communist bloc. But his threat of "massive retaliation" in the event of aggression was weakened by the fact that the Soviet Union also possessed the new weapons of war. In 1949 the Soviet Union exploded successfully a nuclear bomb of its own and in 1953 added a thermonuclear (hydrogen) bomb to its arsenal. (The United States detonated its first thermonuclear device in 1952.) Hence any use of nuclear weapons against the Soviet Union or its allies would presumably set off a war of catastrophic proportions.

The acquisition of nuclear weapons by the Soviet Union spurred arrangements for a meeting of the heads of government of the United States, Great Britain, France, and the Soviet Union. A meeting at the summit, as Winston Churchill called it, took place in the summer of 1955 at Geneva, Switzerland. Little was achieved concretely, but Eisenhower's suggestion that the United States and the U.S.S.R. exchange plans of their military establishments and permit aerial photography of each others' bases seemed, for a while, like a promising idea. Even though the Russians saw little merit in Eisenhower's "open skies" proposal, the suggestion made evident the American President's sincere and anxious search for a way out of the terrible nuclear impasse between the two giant powers.

Crisis in the Middle East; The Hungarian Revolt. The foreign policies of both the United States and Russia were tested more severely in November 1956. Early that month Israeli, French, and British military forces invaded Egypt. All three countries had deep grievances against Colonel Gamal Nasser's nationalistic regime. Nasser had long been a champion of Arab opposition to Israel, refusing to recognize that new country and constantly threatening invasion. Britain and France thought him a menace because earlier in 1956 he had seized the Suez Canal, contrary to Egypt's treaty obligations. Without informing their ally the United States, Britain and France, ten days after Israel invaded Egypt, dropped paratroopers on the Suez area, quickly overwhelming the inefficient Egyptian army. At almost the same time, the Soviet Union ruthlessly suppressed a widespread and heroic revolt of the Hungarians against Communist rule.

Both the Suez and Hungarian invasions took the United States by surprise. The administration opposed both invasions, but its power over the Soviets was nil; the Hungarian uprising was savagely suppressed with much bloodshed. The opposition of the United States to the Suez adventure, though, was more successful, both because the United States was an ally of Britain and France and because world opinion and the United Nations vehemently condemned it. Piously, the Soviet Union added its voice to that of the United States. Britain, France, and Israel, heeding the United Nations resolution for a cease-fire, withdrew their troops.

The immediate consequence of the Suez crisis was that Egypt drew closer to the Soviet Union, and Communist penetration of the Middle East seemed imminent. Reacting to this development and in response to a request from the President, Congress in March 1957 passed a resolution affirming America's intention to aid any country in the Middle East which seemed to be threatened by a Communist coup, internal or external. The first test of what came to be called the Eisenhower Doctrine occurred in July 1958, when American marines landed in the little country of Lebanon to forestall a possible invasion from neighboring Syria, then a satellite of Nasser's and judged to be overly friendly toward the Soviet Union. The pro-Western regime in Lebanon was not overthrown, and by the end of October 1958 all American troops had withdrawn.

The Middle East crisis of 1956-1958 brought the Eisenhower administration full circle. Once hopeful of avoiding "brush-fire wars," it found itself dispatching troops to trouble spots much as Truman had done in Korea. It was also evident after 1956 that Moscow was not the only source of instability in the world. Rising nationalism in Asia, Africa, and even the Americas presented new problems and dangers. Khrushchev was adept at winning friends in the new regions, and he consciously identified his country with the fierce opposition of the former colonial peoples to their old rulers. In part to offset Khrushchev's successful international salesmanship, the President in December 1959 and through the first half of 1960 embarked upon extensive good-will tours of the Middle East and Southeast Asia, Latin America, and eastern Asia. Although the first two tours were eminently successful, the last, to Asia, proved much less successful, since in Japan anti-American riots prevented the President from visiting that country at all.

The U-2 Incident. Even before the Tokyo riots of June 1960, other events seriously tarnished the American image abroad and impaired still further Soviet-American relations. Early in 1960 the President, still hopeful of being able to arrange some kind of disarmament agreement with Khrushchev, had agreed to another summit meeting in Paris in May. But just before the conference opened the Russians announced the shooting down of a high-flying American espionage plane deep inside the Soviet Union. At first the American officials denied the accusation, but after the Russians triumphantly produced the plane and its pilot, who was still alive, the United States shamefacedly admitted undertaking this and other flights over the Soviet Union. Outraged, Khrushchev called off the summit meeting, deliberately insulting Eisenhower in the process. In their propaganda around the world the Russians made the most of the American admission. The incident of the U-2, as the special plane was called, dealt a heavy blow to American prestige and honor. The flight was not only contrary to standard usages under international law, but the United States had been caught in an official lie which undermined its credibility before the world.

Troubles with Castro. American relations with Cuba also deteriorated seriously in 1960. On January 1, 1959, a young revolutionary, Fidel Castro, succeeded in overthrowing the corrupt dictatorship of General Fulgencio Batista. At first the new government enjoyed the support of the American people, who welcomed Castro when he visited the United States soon after assuming power. But when it became evident that the social revolution which Castro proclaimed also included the confiscation of American property and the wholesale execution of the "enemies of the revolution," the attitude of the American people and their government cooled noticeably. By early 1960 over a billion dollars worth of American property had been confiscated without compensation, and a steady stream of refugees from Cuba entered Miami. Furthermore, Castro made no secret of his friendship with the Soviet Union, with which he concluded trade agreements. In retaliation, late in May 1960 the United States ended all economic aid to Cuba, and in July, at the recommendation of an angry Congress, the President cut the imports of Cuban sugar by 95 per cent. Since the United States was Cuba's principal customer and sugar the island's chief export, this action hurt. The Castro regime became increasingly anti-American.

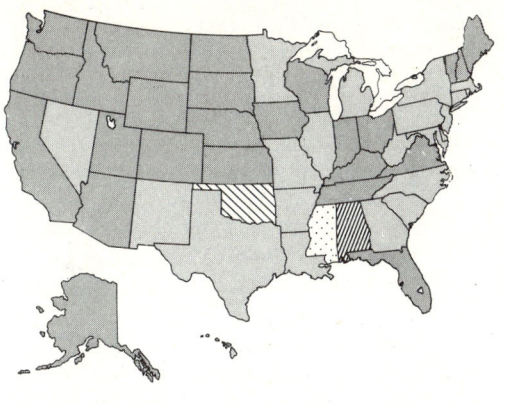

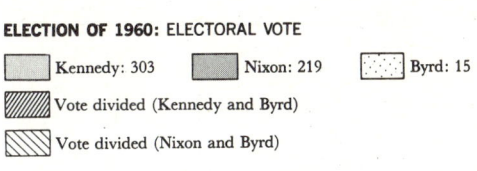

The Election of 1960. Because of the Twenty-second Amendment, which upon ratification in 1952 had limited Presidents to two terms, the Republicans in 1960 did not have to wait to learn if Eisenhower would run for a third term. Nevertheless, the Republican candidate was pretty well known even before the convention met in July, for Vice-President Richard M. Nixon was the choice of most party leaders, including the President. Nixon was nominated on the first ballot, and Henry Cabot Lodge, the United States ambassador to the United Nations, was nominated as his running mate.

The front-runner at the Democratic Convention was Massachusetts Senator John F. Kennedy, who had shown strength in a number of state primaries. Thanks to a well-prepared campaign and a highly organized staff, Kennedy was nominated on the first ballot. Astutely, he urged the nomination of his erstwhile opponent, Senator Lyndon Johnson of Texas, for second place on the ticket. The Democrats wore a deliberately liberal platform, including support of the Supreme Court decision on desegregation.

Since both candidates were in their youthful forties, the campaigning was strenuous, despite extensive use of television and jet travel. Nixon personally visited all fifty states and Kennedy appeared in forty-four. The candidates also inaugurated a series of four joint appearances on television, which probably helped Kennedy, since he had enjoyed less national recognition than Nixon.

Kennedy also ran under the handicap of being a Roman Catholic. Although the Republicans officially did not allude to his religion or use it against him, a number of private persons and organizations did question the fitness of a Catholic in the presidency. Kennedy met the prejudice head-on, candidly and without rancor. His frank answers to questions on the issue quieted the fears of many that he would not support the traditional American doctrine of separation of church and state.

The election turned out to be one of the closest in American history, with Kennedy winning by fewer than 113,000 votes out of a record 68.8 million votes cast. His religion worked both for and against him. In the Northeast, where Catholics were strong, he won easily; in the Southeast, normally a heavily Democratic region, he scored less

ELECTION OF 1960: ELECTORAL VOTE
Kennedy: 303   Nixon: 219   Byrd: 15
Vote divided (Kennedy and Byrd)
Vote divided (Nixon and Byrd)

well than he might have expected. Apparently, many Catholics who had voted for Eisenhower in 1952 and 1956 returned to the Democrats to vote for Kennedy, while many Southern Protestants who were normally Democratic voted their anti-Catholicism. Kennedy's election as the first Roman Catholic President disproved the political platitude that a Catholic could not be elected President, the Constitution notwithstanding.

In Congress, despite the closeness of the presidential race, the Democrats won heavy majorities in both houses, demonstrating that the country was still overwhelmingly Democratic in sentiment.

THE KENNEDY ADMINISTRATION

Limited Success with Congress. In keeping with the kind of youthful, vigorous image he had tried to project during the campaign, John Fitzgerald Kennedy called his program "The New Frontier." More eloquent than any President since Woodrow Wilson, more concerned with elevating and educating the people than any President since Theodore Roosevelt, Kennedy entered office surrounded by driving intellectuals and men of high purpose. But he soon found that the conservative Congress was decidedly cool, if not hostile, to his program. Twice during 1961 and 1962 Congress rejected his bills for medical care for the aged and federal aid to education. Congress also voted down his recommendation for a new cabinet post of urban affairs. In the first two years of his administration, Congress gave the President only a part of his requests for tax reforms; in 1963 it refused to act on his request for an income tax cut of $11 billion, which Kennedy had strongly urged as a necessary stimulus to the economy.

Like Roosevelt and Truman before him, Kennedy discovered that a heavily Democratic Congress was no guarantee that a Democratic President would be able to enact his program. Most of the slowness or hostility of Congress centered in the House of Representatives, which was dominated by conservative Southern Democrats and Republicans, often working in bipartisan coalition. In the congressional elections of 1962 the President vigorously campaigned for a Democratic Congress and, contrary to the usual results of mid-term elections, the Democrats lost very few seats in the House and actually gained some in the Senate. Yet the result for the President's program was largely negative. At the time of the President's death on November 22, 1963, Congress had failed to pass a single major piece of the legislative program he had enunciated the previous January.

The administration's principal legislative success had come in the previous year. The Trade Expansion Act of 1962 was truly epoch-making, for it marked an even more significant departure from protectionism than the Reciprocal Trade Act of 1934. It gave the President new and unprecedentedly wide powers to cut tariff rates, although for decades Congress had jealously guarded its prerogatives in this field. The act also provided for federal aid to business firms and workers adversely affected by the resulting increased competition from abroad. Kennedy correctly hailed the act because it provided means for increasing the rate of American economic growth through the expansion of American exports. By permitting the importation of certain foreign goods, especially those from the booming European Common Market (composed of France, Italy, West Germany, and the Benelux countries) and from Japan, the administration hoped to secure important and wider markets for American goods abroad, while increasing, through competition, the efficiency of industry at home.

Several times Kennedy publicly denied that his administration harbored any of that hostility toward business usually associated with the Democratic regimes of Roosevelt and Truman. But, until his death, the business community clearly felt uneasy about Kennedy's leadership. Businessmen, for example, could not forget the events of the spring of 1962, when the President, incensed over an unexpected rise in steel prices, forced United States Steel, by threats of government intervention and harassment, to rescind its price increases.

Losses and Gains in Foreign Affairs. The Kennedy administration's foreign policy record was mixed. At his death the long-term problems of the Cold War, which Kennedy himself had inherited from Eisenhower, were in turn passed on to his successor. Germany and Berlin were still divided, and the several thousand advisers and support troops that Kennedy had sent to South Vietnam to help its anti-Communist government fight Communist rebels seemed, in December 1963, no closer to success than earlier.

During the early days of his administration, Kennedy launched the Alliance for Progress in Latin America, a long-range economic aid program designed to combat the conditions of poverty that contributed to the spread of Communism and denied a decent living to millions. Through technical advice, loans, and grants, the Alliance endeavored to help Latin Americans help themselves in effecting land reform, improving farming techniques, and accelerating industrial development.

The Alliance's laudable aim of not permitting United States funds to be used to bolster undemocratic or unpopular regimes was not easily put into practice. Military juntas in Argentina, Brazil, and Peru in 1962 and in the Dominican Republic in 1963 interfered with or actually overthrew constitutional governments, thereby bringing into serious question the political stability and commitment to constitutional and democratic procedures of those nations. Nevertheless, by the end of 1963 the Alliance, both in theory and in its limited practice, had at least reversed the short-sighted neglect of a region whose leaders and intellectuals had long resented the indifference of the United States even as they distrusted U.S. intentions and feared U.S. power.

During the Kennedy administration the storm center of Latin American affairs proved to be Cuba. In April 1961, Kennedy ill-advisedly lent token U.S. naval support to an invasion of Cuba by a small group of anti-Castro Cuban refugees. But the effort to overthrow Castro's avowedly Communist regime ended in fiasco when the 1500-man invasion force was easily defeated and its members killed or captured. The United States suffered grievously in prestige because it had once again, as in the U-2 incident, contravened the normal procedures of international law and had broken its own agreements under the inter-American security system. The immediate result was the strengthening of the Castro regime and the tightening of Cuba's connection with the Soviet Union.

The closeness of the Russo-Cuban tie became painfully clear in the summer and fall of 1962, when the Soviet Union began supplying the island nation with large amounts of economic and military aid. Then, in early October, U.S. reconnaissance planes discovered Soviet medium-range missile sites under construction on Cuban soil. Alarmed at what he termed the upsetting of the "nuclear status quo" in the world, Kennedy on October 22, 1962, declared a naval quarantine of Cuba, broadcasting to the world and particularly to the Soviet Union the American intention to risk war rather than to permit a buildup of Soviet missile power in Cuba, only ninety miles from the U.S.

The carefully considered confrontation brought the world to the very brink of nuclear war; within two days, however, the Russians backed down, withdrawing their missiles. Although some 17,000 Soviet technicians and support troops remained on the island, the extension of Soviet nuclear capability to the Western Hemisphere had been stopped.

Despite the Russian thrust into Cuba in October 1962, Kennedy continued to seek ways of breaking the circle of mutual suspicion that perpetuated the Cold War. His most concrete contribution was the working out of a limited test ban treaty with the Russians in the summer of 1963. The treaty, which was ratified overwhelmingly by the Senate in October 1963, prohibited any testing of nuclear weapons in the atmosphere, in outer space, and under water. Although the stockpiles of nuclear weapons continued to grow on both sides, the test ban treaty promised to reduce the contamination of the atmosphere and showed that careful and limited negotiations with the Russians could bear fruit.

On November 22, 1963, in Dallas, Texas, to the horror of a stunned nation and a shocked world on both sides of the Iron Curtain, an assassin's bullet turned to ashes the shining but unfulfilled promise of John Fitzgerald Kennedy.

THE JOHNSON ADMINISTRATION

The Transfer of Power. Within 98 minutes after Kennedy's death, Lyndon B. Johnson was sworn in as President of the United States. Johnson, who had been a rival of Kennedy for the Democratic presidential nomination in 1960, was ready for his new and awesome job. Not only did he pledge himself to fight for his predecessor's uncompleted program, but he quickly moved to assert his authority as a political leader. By the force of personal persuasion for which he had been renowned in his senatorial days, Johnson induced the dilatory Congress to pass Kennedy's long-delayed education bill, granting $1.2 billion for college construction, the most important educational measure enacted since 1958.

Johnson's Philosophy. Johnson, in his terse State of the Union message in January 1964, asserted the liberal philosophy that he had first acquired from Franklin Roosevelt's New Deal while a young Texas congressman. Although he pleasantly surprised wary conservatives by announcing a cut in the $100-billion Kennedy budget, Johnson remained faithful to liberal principles. The President challenged the nation to wage war upon the poverty that still bedeviled the lives of one fifth of the American people. Once again the southern-bred President eloquently affirmed his determination to fight for equality of opportunity for Negroes and for a cut in income taxes to accelerate economic growth. Following up Kennedy's efforts to break the nuclear impasse and to reduce the threat of world destruction, Johnson announced a cutback in the production of nuclear materials and challenged the Russians to follow the American example. His own convictions and his continuation of the Kennedy policies were clearly reflected in his words that the U.S. should support the late President's goals, not out of "our sorrow or sympathy . . . but because they are right." Although he was personally very different from his young, urban-bred, and polished predecessor, Johnson strongly resembled Kennedy in the humanitarianism of his program, in the strength of his leadership, and in the national scope of his outlook.

CHAPTER 24

TOWARD 2000: THEMES OF CONCERN

THE PROBLEMS OF PROSPERITY

The Affluent Society. The massive unemployment of the Great Depression—which the New Deal as late as 1939 was unable to reduce below 17 per cent of the total labor force—evaporated in the war boom. Although some unemployment ensued during the several postwar recessions, the percentage of jobless workers never again reached 8 per cent. After 1940 high productivity and prosperity were the dominant social facts. Goods spilled out of American factories and farms in ever increasing volume and variety. Between 1940 and 1960 the gross national product, even after price changes are taken into account, rose 114 per cent, though the population grew less than 36 per cent. The productivity of agriculture was especially noteworthy. The number of farmers actually declined by 3.5 million during the twenty years, yet total farm production increased. Improved methods and extensive use of machinery, tractors, and trucks accounted for the miracle in production. For the farmer, as for the rest of society, the rise in productivity also spelled prosperity.

Other periods in American history—the 1920's, for example—have been notable for their prosperity, but the novelty of the years after the Second World War was that the lower-income groups, as well as the upper-income levels, shared in it. Millions of American families moved up the income ladder. The movement toward an equality of income distribution was far from complete, of course, but it represented a reversal of the trend of the 1920's. Upon such an improvement in income distribution rested the mass purchasing power which maintained the remarkable prosperity of the two decades since the Great Depression.

A regrettable paradox of the "Affluent Society," as economist John Kenneth Galbraith called it in a book by that name in 1958, was that the public sector of the economy—schools, hospitals, roads, sanitation, and so forth—was not participating in the new prosperity. Although expenditures for schools and highways were way up over 1940, schools were still crowded, the number of beds in mental hospitals was insufficient, and the roads were jammed with cars. Because Americans in the postwar free-enterprise economy found all kinds of luxury commodities, from electrically driven toothbrushes to elaborate mechanical toys, attracting their increased dollars, not much more money than before was left in the citizen's pocket for taxes to finance the public sector. Despite their prosperity, Americans were still finding taxes too high and social welfare too expensive.

Various means of siphoning funds into the public sector were proposed; Galbraith, for example, suggested a sales tax, even though such taxes hit low-income families the hardest. Because local real estate taxes already were heavy, other observers suggested increased federal expenditures for the public sector, and under the Eisenhower administration a multibillion-dollar road program was begun. Although President Kennedy's efforts to provide federal aid to the schools were frustrated twice in Congress, the federal government still seemed the most likely source from which Americans in the future would derive increased expenditures for the public sector.

The Decline of the City. Since 1920 a majority of Americans have lived in towns or cities of 2500 population or greater. By 1960 almost 70 per cent lived in urban areas and the trend appeared irreversible, with each census reporting a decline in the population living on farms. Between 1940 and 1960, however, Americans began to change the kinds of urban areas in which they lived. Central metropolitan districts were not keeping up with the general urban growth: between 1950 and 1960 the aggregate total population of cities over 100,000 increased merely 9.3 per cent, and four out of five of the giant cities of over one million people actually *decreased* in population. The overall increase in urbanization was attributable to the populating of areas ringing these metropolitan centers; for the movement to the suburbs, which had begun in the 1920's, had grown into a mass exodus by the 1950's. In 1953 the editors of *Fortune* compared the suburban migration to the great immigration from Europe in the early years of the twentieth century. About as many people—1.2 million—moved to the suburbs that year as entered the United States in 1907.

This spreading urbanization, however, challenged Americans with new problems. Because the central city was still the place in which the suburbanite earned his living, millions of Americans traveled as much as fifty miles a day from home to work and back again, and an urgent need for safe and efficient means of commuter transportation was created. Because large numbers of commuters preferred automobile travel over train or bus service, expensive highways built to speed travel were often choked with slow-moving cars, many of them occupied by a single person. The consequent demand for parking facilities alone—not to mention the multiplying demands for new expressways and freeways—ate significantly into the prime real estate of the great cities. Moreover, commuter trains, forced to compete with the automobile, found it more and more difficult to make a profit or even to survive, and some were forced to reduce or discontinue their service. Despite the popularity of the automobile, however, much of the metropolitan labor force still depended on the commuter lines for daily transportation, and as a consequence a number of state and local governments faced pressures to subsidize the commuter lines in one fashion or another.

The flight to the suburbs was both a symptom and a cause of the decline of the city as a place of human habitation. Insofar as the city became the home of the poor—it was the middle-class families who fled the overcrowded schools, substandard housing, and polluted air—metropolitan residential areas deteriorated still more. High land prices, caused in part by land speculation and by rapid, unplanned growth, provided a big obstacle to the construction of adequate low- and middle-income housing. Nonexistent or poorly enforced building and housing codes, haphazard zoning laws, and the profits to be made from slum real estate further contributed to the continual rotting of the core cities in America's metropolitan areas. The 1960 census revealed that one fifth of America's housing—11.5 to 16.5 million units—was in a dilapidated or deteriorating condition. Added to the problems of housing were those of overcrowded, understaffed urban schools and the fact that large areas of modern cities were generating increasing rates of crime, including juvenile delinquency.

These perplexing urban problems generated attempts to restore the nation's cities to economic and social health. Under the generic term "urban renewal," many cities attempted to rehabilitate run-down neighborhoods by land clearance and new construction or by renovation of existing structures and to bring such areas into conformity with zoning, housing, health, and safety standards. Cities used their power of condemnation and subsidies from the federal government to clear substantial areas, and rising in many of these areas was low-cost public housing for people meeting certain standards of need; by 1962, in fact, 1200 local authorities operated half a million dwelling units.

But despite the obvious success of urban renewal projects in several of America's metropolitan areas, progress was slow. Land clearance ran into vexing legal delays; the relocation of former tenants was a continuing source of irritation; and renewal critics attacked everything from spiraling costs to the esthetic and social drawbacks of the new construction. They charged that several billions already spent to rejuvenate America's cities had helped only to destroy their individuality; they called the new middle-income housing "a marvel of dullness and regimentation"; and in 1962 some critics predicted that the new low-income projects would themselves be slums by 1975.

Moreover, the very size of the urban renewal task was staggering: in 1962 the American Council to Improve Our Neighborhoods (ACTION) estimated that it would cost $100 billion, spread over a 10-year period, to wipe out slums; but during the decade of the 1960's the federal government was expected to put only about $6 billion into the renewal program and local governments another $2 billion, and according to government statistics urban blight was being overcome at the rate of only 1 per cent a year. Obviously, government expenditures were not doing the whole job, and private investment had not yet found sufficient incentive to provide the enormous funds required.

Perhaps the major obstacle to an effective attack on the problems of urban blight arose from the absence of an overall federal policy with respect to urban land use and urban development. Federal aid programs to cities provided for housing, urban renewal, urban highways, airports, water filtration, eradication of smog and water pollution, industrial development, recreation, and civil defense—but the difficulties of coordinating such programs gave rise to a growing wave of agitation for the establishment of a federal department of urban affairs to coordinate federal aid to urban areas.

The Dominance of White Collars. During most of America's history the majority of workers have been farmers, miners, fishermen, and factory workers —that is, blue-collar workers. But ever since the opening of the twentieth century an increasing proportion of the labor force has comprised white-collar workers—that is, managers, clerks, professionals, government employees, and self-employed proprietors. In 1960 white-collar workers constituted 46.6 per cent of the nonagricultural labor force, blue collars 39.7 per cent, and service workers (policemen, counter salesmen, domestics, etc.) 13.6 per cent. The growth of a white-collar class, a measure of the maturity of an economy, meant that an increasing number of people were being supplied with goods and food by an ever smaller proportion of agricultural and manufacturing employees. Only a highly mechanized and skilled economy could achieve such a division of labor.

White-collar predominance also testified to the consumer nature of the economy. Whereas in previous history most paid labor was employed in making new goods, by the end of the 1950's most working people were consuming goods, helping others to consume goods, or performing a service.

In a society of consumers and white-collar workers the emphasis was on personal relations; people, not things, were the objects of work. As David Riesman pointed out in his book *The Lonely Crowd* (1950), sometimes this emphasis on people ended in outright psychological manipulation, as occurred in certain types of selling and advertising. But even when persuaders were not at work, there was still a tendency for Americans to conform to their neighbors' tastes and opinions.

[Modern man, said Riesman] is taught, vaguely, to do the "best possible" in any given situation. As soon as he can play with other children, he is made sensitive to the judgments of this play group, looking to it for approval and direction as to what is best. . . . The adult never loses this dependence. . . . This new need for approval goes well beyond the human and opportunistic reasons that lead people in any age to care very much what others think of them. People in general want and need to be liked, but it is only the other-directed character type that makes others its chief source of direction and its chief area of sensitivity and concern.[1]

In examining the upper end of the white-collar class in his book *The Organization Man* (1956), William H. Whyte found young executives and corporate salesmen to be less venturesome and more conformist than the traditional conception of the rugged American businessman. They seemed to be as much concerned with job security as were labor union members. As one anthropologist put it:

The individualistic frontiersman, even the aggressive "go-getter" of a generation ago, would throw out of kilter the nicely coordinated gears of the modern corporation. What the modern organization needs is men who are smooth, "cool," who know how to get along, who can go forward without pushing or shoving, who can use "psychology" in dealing with others, who don't arouse hostility with others, or envy by being too smart or too ambitious. . . . Far from finding this prospect [of being "organization men"] distasteful, most college men wish to work for large corporations.[2]

Traditionally, white-collar workers have resisted joining unions, even though white-collar pay was often inferior to industrial wages. In 1958, for example, only 12 per cent of all unionized workers were employed in nonmanual occupations. The growth in the white-collar class thus seemed to explain, at least partly, the stagnation in labor organizing in the 1950's. Despite its organizing drives and power, organized labor, as it entered the 1960's, was not keeping up with the growing size of the working force.

Moreover, a large part of the white-collar class was composed of women, who after 1940 entered the labor force in ever increasing numbers. Indeed, between 1940 and 1960, 9.4 million women joined the working force as compared with only 7.5 million men. And among these working women were increasing numbers of wives and mothers; by 1960 about one third of all married women were employed in paying jobs. In short, women now constituted the largest source of new workers.

Wives and mothers entering employment, however, were frequently compelled to accept jobs less well paid or otherwise less rewarding than their education or training warranted. This was especially true of college-educated women, who, proportionately, returned to work in larger numbers than their non-college sisters. Furthermore, the needs of the economy apparently did not encourage women to develop their powers. In the 1950's women made up

---

1. David Riesman, "The Saving Remnant: A Study of Character," in John W. Chase (ed.), *Years of the Modern: An American Appraisal* (New York: Longmans, Green, 1949), p. 124.

2. Ruth Bunzel, "The Individual and the Patterns of Life Today," in *Contemporary Civilization*, No. 1 (Chicago: Scott, Foresman, 1959), p. 156.

a smaller proportion of all college students than they had in the 1920's; and fewer women, proportionately, were entering graduate schools. In short, in an age when brain power was at a premium, feminine intellect was not being sufficiently employed.

Automation and Technological Unemployment. Automation, which was introduced into an increasing number of industrial processes during the postwar years, promised to displace human labor faster and more widely than any mechanical process ever known before. Automation differed from ordinary mass production in that men were no longer necessary for the continual operation of the machines. Instead, the machines were self-regulating through electronic devices, much as a thermostat turns the heat on and off in a room as the temperature changes. The most advanced form of automated machine was the computer, which performed thousands of tasks, such as mathematical calculations, within a matter of seconds. Although the machine appeared to have the capacity to "think" —that is, to make decisions—actually it had already been "instructed" in the possible answers to any question it might be asked as well as with the reasons why, in a given circumstance, one answer should have been selected over another. Its "thinking," therefore, was really an incredibly rapid electronic canvassing of all the alternatives from which the best answer was selected.

Labor unions estimated that in the six years prior to 1961, 1.5 million blue-collar workers were dropped from manufacturing chiefly because of automation. The widespread introduction of a rather simple mechanical device like the self-service elevator displaced 40,000 operators in New York City alone. Many jobs, especially those involving personal service, would never be automated, but in the 1960's industries like chemicals were already highly automated.

Already by 1960 labor unions were attempting to work out arrangements whereby the introduction of automation would not result in wholesale dismissals. Usually these arrangements took the form of creating funds, to which employers contributed, for retraining workers for new jobs. Although some labor unions feared the effects of automation, on the whole the labor movement seemed ready to make adjustments to the prospect, while expecting employers and the government to assist in the transition. In the long perspective, the diffusion of automation promised to relieve men of hard labor and drudgery, but it would also require social and economic adjustment which could be extremely painful for the millions who would be displaced by machines and for the society which would have to adjust to a sharp decline in the need for human work.

The New Economic System. In an age of automation, mass production, and white-collar predominance, the economy of postwar America was dominated more than ever before by big corporations—those with more than $100 million in assets. Businessmen still talked of a competitive economy sustained by private initiative and private property, but in truth the great corporations bore little resemblance to the individual entrepreneur as depicted in the standard descriptions of capitalism. For one thing, corporations were run not by owners but by managers; the owners usually were thousands of small stockholders who were unversed and often uninterested in the intricacies of the business. In a sense, the managers were bureaucrats in a giant corporation, quite removed from any direct involvement in maximizing profits, as the individual entrepreneur would have been. Even in a bad year, the executive's salary went on as usual.

Because these corporations constituted great aggregations of capital, labor, plant, and research facilities, they could and did by-pass some of the usual restraints of the market. Most giant corporations, for example, obtained capital for expansion from their own surpluses rather than from the public or from banks. For all their concentration of economic power, though, the great corporations were not masters of their own destiny. Labor unions, government regulations and commissions, and public opinion, to which the corporations were especially sensitive, limited their freedom of action. Indeed, as far as organized labor was concerned, the giant corporation was the best to deal with; from it, labor obtained its greatest gains, like escalator clauses, welfare funds, and aid in adjusting to automation.

Government itself had become more than a mere regulator of business practices; it had also become a new kind of partner. The Cold War with its demands for armaments forged a close link between big business and government and, in so doing, not only limited the independence of business but also signified a new industrial-governmental concentration of power in American society. President Eisenhower, in his farewell address to the American people in 1961, observed the dangers:

> . . . This conjunction of an immense military establishment and a large arms industry is new in the American experience. . . . We recognize the imperative need for this development. Yet we must not fail to comprehend its grave implications. . . . In the councils of government, we must guard against the acquisition of unwarranted influence, whether sought or unsought, by the military-industrial complex. The potential for the disastrous rise of misplaced power exists and will persist.

ARTS AND EDUCATION IN AN AFFLUENT AGE

Mass Culture. In the years between 1940 and 1960 literature, the arts, and culture in general became increasingly oriented to the many. In an economy of high productivity, deluging millions of people daily with movies, magazines, books, and television programs, American culture achieved a degree of homogeneity never dreamed of before. However, if such cultural homogeneity spelled loss of individuality—which it undoubtedly did—and if mass culture was often produced primarily for profit and only secondarily for esthetic reasons, nevertheless mass production of "art" made available to millions of people what in previous times had been the privilege only of the aristocratic few. Good radio and phonograph music was available where there had been no music before; there were more symphony orchestras and chamber music groups than ever; and in recent years more Americans purchased tickets to classical concerts than to baseball games. Paintings and items of sculpture—ranging from Greek athletes and Rembrandt's "Aristotle Contemplating the Bust of Homer" to Van Gogh's sunflowers and Rodin's "The Kiss"—were being turned out *en masse* in moderately good reproductions. The world's literature was being distributed in inexpensive paperback editions in every bookshop, drugstore, and transportation terminal. Although much that was being produced was trashy, showy art, and although the sale of comic books and sentimental, cacophonous juke-box favorites ran into the millions, on balance it seemed that mass production, while it might not raise mass culture, would not destroy the growth of genuine taste either.

As a means of distributing tasteful art, mass production was good, but it was largely feeding on the accomplishments of the past. The crucial consideration was what was currently being created in the world of American literature, music, and art. Here the record was uneven.

Theater Trends. Drama, as a form of literature, was particularly blighted by the need for massive success. To be moneymakers, new Broadway productions had to be smash hits, heralded by critical praise and by lines at the box offices. Faced with the steeply rising costs of labor, scenery, costumes, theater rental, and the other ingredients of play production, producers tended to favor lavish musical comedies, whose long runs denoted mass appeal. When *My Fair Lady,* a musical adaptation of George Bernard Shaw's *Pygmalion,* closed on Broadway in September 1962 after a 6½-year run, its world-wide performances had grossed $65.5 million, a figure which did not include subsidiary items like a $5.5 million fee for movie rights and some $25 million from music album sales. Although *My Fair Lady* set a record for financial success, other musicals were also reaping handsome profits.

Serious play writing received little financial encouragement. According to a *New York Times* survey, of the 636 Broadway shows in the twelve seasons prior to 1960-1961, 74 per cent were financial failures; investors received no return on their money.[3] Experimentation in drama was thus hazardous, and only two playwrights of stature emerged, neither of whom approached the genius and inventiveness of Eugene O'Neill of a previous generation. Arthur Miller—whose powerful indictment of a materialistic society in *Death of a Salesman* (1949) carried on the tradition of social criticism prevalent in the 1930's—failed in his later works to cut a high place in literature. Tennessee Williams' *The Glass Menagerie* (1944) and *A Streetcar Named Desire* (1947) portrayed violence and sexuality but with a sensitive understanding of human needs and aspirations. However, Williams' later plays, usually concentrating on weak individuals frustrated by the circumstances of a decaying Southern society, were sometimes more notable for their violence and perversion than for their depth of perception.

Live theater, of course, enjoyed vitality in about twenty "off-Broadway" playhouses scattered in small, often improvised theaters around lower Manhattan. Their costs were lower, their audiences smaller. They offered young, new playwrights, introduced young performers, and often took a chance on novel ideas. And similar theaters were to be found in many other cities. But even their strenuous and commendable efforts did not seem to evoke great talent or enduring significance in American dramatic art.

Literature. The Second World War and the uneasy peace that ensued sharply distinguished the style and outlook of postwar writers from those of the 1930's. The war itself provided the setting for a number of best-selling novels, the most outstanding of which were Norman Mailer's *The Naked and the Dead* (1949), James Gould Cozzens' *Guard of Honor* (1949), James Jones' *From Here to Eternity* (1951), and John Hersey's *The War Lover* (1959).

Whatever the final judgment of the quality of post-World War II writing, the era indeed did not lack literary output, and it is probable that the best work of young writers like J. D. Salinger, Philip Roth, John Cheever, Bernard Malamud, and Truman Capote will be remembered even when measured against the exacting standards of subsequent years.

The themes and settings of postwar novels varied greatly, but most of them had at least one common characteristic: unlike the novelists of the 1920's and 1930's, who were often preoccupied with criticizing social institutions or social types, these new writers turned to a realistic and often profound examination of the individual's search for identity and integrity. In an age of material abundance, imminent nuclear war, and uncertain personal values, these novel-

---

[3]. *The New York Times,* June 5, 1961, p. 1 *et seq.*

ists reflected in their work the individual American's quest for meaning in his personal life, and they projected a kind of private ethic or philosophy which suited one individual but perhaps no other. Thus in *Rabbit Run* (1960), John Updike, one of the most brilliant of the new young men, described "Rabbit" Angstrom's search for identity by flight from responsibility; James Gould Cozzens in *By Love Possessed* (1956) explored the variations in the forms of love; and Saul Bellow in *Henderson the Rain King* (1959) delineated, in a kind of African fantasy, a millionaire's efforts to find himself and his place in the world. Because these new writers abjured social criticism in favor of an investigation of the ways in which the free individual might find his own private adjustment in an admittedly alien and defective world, they were more in the tradition of the nineteenth-century Melville, Twain, and James than of their immediate predecessors like John Dos Passos, John Steinbeck, or Sinclair Lewis.

Although dozens of new writers competed for attention in the postwar years, the great novelists of the 1920's and 1930's—men like William Faulkner and Ernest Hemingway—remained the giants of American fiction. Faulkner's fundamental concern with morality and individual guilt now struck responses in many readers; his sense of the tragedy of the human condition fitted the anguish of the nuclear age. In *The Hamlet* (1940), *Go Down, Moses* (1942), *Intruder in the Dust* (1948), and *The Town* (1957), he continued his exploration of the slow degradation of the people of his mythical Yoknapatawpha County by the corroding influence of racism, money, and industrialism. While Faulkner's stature as a writer burgeoned after the war, Hemingway's reputation fed largely on his accomplishments of the past, with the notable exception of the allegorical novella *The Old Man and the Sea* (1952).

But while Faulkner had only a few imitators among American writers, Hemingway's tense, "tough," laconic style continued to influence writers both in America and in Europe.

Also in the course of the 1950's a group of younger poets—talented, experimental, and reflecting the increasing preoccupation with self instead of society—began to capture attention. Although deeply influenced by the revolution led by T. S. Eliot and Ezra Pound a generation or two earlier, they did not, as Pound himself did, go off into unintelligibility and private language. Among this young group were Elizabeth Bishop, Robert Lowell, Theodore Roethke, and Richard Wilbur, all of whom received Pulitzer Prizes as well as recognition from critics and fellow poets. As far as the general public was concerned, most contemporary poetry was too intellectual and difficult for widespread interest. Good poetry, as always in America, attained only a small, if discriminating, readership.

Music. Unlike a few of the "Beat Generation" writers, who tended to be somewhat flamboyant and self-promoting, the postwar composers were apt to be reticent about their work and their personal lives. Only recently had composers like Aaron Copland, Roy Harris, Walter Piston, Leonard Bernstein, Samuel Barber, Virgil Thomson, Roger Sessions, Howard Hanson, William Schuman, and others begun to attract widespread publicity in the United States and abroad. It was not that the field of serious musical composition lacked activity—throughout the postwar years concert halls, chamber groups, soloists and symphonic orchestras, music schools, libraries, and recording and publishing companies were enjoying phenomenal expansion—but, rather, that the publicity seemed to have no single musical trend upon which to focus its attention. The public did not seem to be able to find emotional or intellectual rapport with the new music simply because most composers themselves were still seeking a definition or synthesis of all the various musical styles arising during the twentieth century. The new "abstract," experimental music was still often difficult for the general public to understand.

The three most influential styles or methods of composition during this century have been (1) *neoclassicism,* which began as a revolt against Romantic lyricism and grandiloquence and called for order, grace, clarity of form, economy of orchestration, and precision of counterpoint and harmony; (2) *atonality,* or the "twelve-tone system," which emphasized dissonance, unconventional chords, and unconventional measures of time; and (3) forms derived from *folk themes*—in America, from songs of the early pioneers, Negro spirituals, and jazz. Contemporary composers have attempted to fuse these various styles, once considered incompatible and mutually contradictory, and to achieve order out of such musical diversity. No longer, as was the case largely in the 1920's and 1930's in both Europe and America, did most American composers commit themselves to single styles.

Painting. During the 1940's and 1950's American art was brimming with vitality. Americans might be buying art reproductions, but they were also buying original works of art. Hundreds of art galleries in major cities were selling paintings and giving shows; every American community had its art center, and every summer resort its painting school and little galleries. And an increasing number of important artists were working in a variety of media and following a diversity of philosophies.

In painting and sculpture the flight from objective representation, only barely noticeable in the 1930's, became almost headlong in the 1940's. Artists like Jackson Pollock and I. Rice Pereira in painting and Alexander Calder in sculpture became so interested in experimenting with abstract form and space that they totally abandoned those conventional forms which alone permit the artist to make his meaning clear to others. Pollock's work, which was perhaps the most extreme in the abstract or nonrepresentational field, abandoned plan completely. He developed his pictures by dribbling paint from a brush or directly from a can onto a large, horizontally placed canvas. Pereira, on the other hand, whose work was no less abstract, experimented painstakingly with new materials like glass, mica, gold leaf, and powdered marble to produce works of brilliant color.

Not all prominent artists were abstractionists. Ben Shahn, for example, who had also been an important artist in the 1930's, continued his concern with social problems and refused to abandon representation. Some of the younger artists, like Andrew Wyeth, showed that they could equal the skill and detail of the nineteenth-century realists and yet manage to convey a sense of underlying dread and mystery. In short, the art of the fifties was vigorous, various, and seemingly headed in several directions. As one symposium of critics agreed in 1950, "American art in its vitality and originality compared very well with that of any European country" if the work of the masters of an earlier generation, like Picasso and Bracque, were not included.[4] Jackson Pollock's canvases, for example, hung in art museums in both Amsterdam and Rome.

Architecture. If American painting was only beginning to achieve European recognition and respect, American architects were among the leaders of the Atlantic artistic community. "For the young European architect," wrote one English architectural critic in 1959, "an American Grand Tour is becoming as important as the Italian was to the eighteenth century English gentle-

---

[4]. Quoted in John I. H. Baur, *Revolution and Tradition on Modern American Art* (Cambridge, Mass.: Harvard University Press, 1951), p. 146.

man."[5] During the 1940's the "international style" of the 1930's became more rectangular, more severe, and colder than ever. The most influential figure was Ludwig Mies van der Rohe, who came from Germany to the United States in 1938. For Mies the low building as well as the skyscraper had to be composed of angles and straight lines, devoid of embellishment, eminently functional, and constructed from contemporary materials like steel and glass. Mies' influence was best seen in Lever House (1952) in New York and the Secretariat building of the United Nations (1950), neither of which he designed, but both of which were duplicates of his style. The classic example of his own work was the austerely rectangular, rational, and eminently functional campus of the Illinois Institute of Technology in Chicago.

A contrary tendency in American architecture was contained in the work of Frank Lloyd Wright. Like Mies van der Rohe, Wright planned a college campus—that of Florida Southern College in the early 1940's. On Wright's campus the buildings comprised a variety of shapes, often with curved walls, usually close to the ground, nestling snugly within orange groves, and interspersed with ponds, lakes, and winding paths. The contrast between Mies and Wright was also evident in New York's Guggenheim Museum (1958), which Wright designed, and Mies' Seagram building (1958) farther downtown. Wright's low-lying structure was developed almost entirely in curves, the dominant part an enormous concrete spiral almost entirely devoid of glass. In stark contrast, the Seagram building was a slender, clean-lined pinnacle thrusting defiantly into the sky, its metallic and glass sheath gleaming like a new and beautiful piece of machinery.

By the mid-1950's the harsh, geometrical forms of Mies were being modified in the direction of embellishment and of beauty for its own sake. Edward Stone's desire to break with the austerity of the Meisian style was evident in the American Embassy building in New Delhi, India, which was one among several United States buildings in foreign countries designed by Stone. He introduced concrete screening, courts, ponds, and ornamentation on the façades of his structures. Another revisionist, Eero Saarinen, son of the famous Eliel Saarinen (see p. 401), displayed in his TWA terminal at New York's Idlewild Airport and his earlier hockey rink at Yale University a genius for radically new roof designs. The roof of the air terminal was a gigantic steel and concrete reproduction of bird's wings, symbolizing the purpose of the structure. In joining Wright's concrete and curvilinear shapes with Mies' lavish expanses of glass, Saarinen accomplished a conciliation of the extremes in modern American architecture.

New Trends in Education. The postwar prosperity was the fundamental inspiration for new styles in architecture, for the boom called for new building all across the nation. Domestic prosperity similarly encouraged more and better schools, a sharp rise in undergraduate and graduate training, and improved curricula, especially in the sciences, where money for new equipment was important.

Americans were seemingly goaded into undertaking educational reform, however, by events in foreign affairs. The orbiting of the first Russian sputnik in the fall of 1957 resulted in a critical reappraisal of American public education to meet what seemed to be a Soviet challenge to the technological leadership of America. Heavy intellectual demands upon students and rigorous standards became the cry of government officials and the public alike. The federal government responded to the new national mood in September 1958 by enacting the Na-

---

5. Ian R. M. McCallum, *Architecture, USA* (New York: Reinhold, 1959), p. 9.

tional Defense Education Act, linking in its very title the national defense and a superior educational system. The new law authorized the spending of $887 million over a period of four years to encourage instruction in science, mathematics, and modern foreign languages.

However, despite the new interest in a more demanding primary and secondary education and despite increasing expenditures for schools by federal, state, and local governments, many school districts still reported overcrowded classrooms, too few teachers, and inadequate equipment.

Although the colleges would not begin to feel the full impact of the postwar increase in the birth rate until 1965, a burgeoning interest in college training already was putting pressure upon colleges and universities to expand enrollments. By 1962 about half of America's high-school graduates were applying for college admission. Never before had a college education seemed so essential to the average American. (In itself this was a sign both of the affluence of American society and of the need for a highly trained working population.)

Although some observers feared that the rising demand for college education must result in lowered academic standards, most colleges apparently did not think so, for they were already in the early 1960's expanding plant and facilities to accommodate the increase in applications. Indeed, it seemed possible that with many more students to choose from, especially after 1965, many colleges would be in a position to be more selective than before. In certain academic fields, particularly in the sciences, where the demand from industry and government was great and salaries were commensurately high, the colleges often had serious difficulties in maintaining or improving the quality of their faculties. By and large, though, the pressure of students, the widespread public demand for tougher courses, and stiffer standards in general were working a revolution in higher education, promising a new age of educational experimentation.

THE UNITED STATES IN A CHANGING WORLD

Despite the demonstrated power of American arms in vanquishing Nazi Germany and Japan, the postwar mood of the American people seemed less secure than it had in 1940. Even graver than Hitler's menace was the new threat of Communist expansionism and nuclear annihilation. Because of the enormous destructive power of the new missiles and nuclear weapons, men began to talk of war itself as being rendered obsolete. At the same time, however, the United States and the Soviet Union continued to add to their nuclear and missile arsenals, and countries like France and Communist China were doing their best to become full-fledged members of the awesome nuclear club. In every generation since the great scientific and technological revolution of the seventeenth century some men have wondered whether human beings could control the machines their genius had created. Heretofore such doubts had always been confined to a tiny minority, but in the age of the intercontinental ballistics missile and the hydrogen bomb, the doubts seemed more pervasive than ever before. The human race has always lived in the shadow of disaster, and everyone's crisis seems to him the worst. But there are sober reasons for believing that the modern nuclear crisis *is* the worst.

Even if there were no war, no Cold War, no conflict of interests among nations, and no weapons capable of destroying civilization, the world would still be endangered by problems of the first magnitude. One of the direst results of the industrial-scientific revolution of the past few centuries has been the dramatic upsurge in the rate of population growth throughout the world. From an estimated 545 million persons in 1650, world population soared to 906 million in 1800 and to 1.6 billion in 1900. In 1960 the numbers of the human race were edging three billion. If population were to continue to grow steadily at the present rate, it would double in a period of about seventy years. With the lowering of death rates through medical and scientific progress, the birth rates that once merely balanced death rates had become an explosive force in many areas of the world.

How to produce sufficient food for all these people was the great social conundrum of the twentieth century. The pessimistic prediction of the late eighteenth-century English economist Thomas Malthus that the population increase would outrun the food supply did not prove correct for the industrialized nations of the West. But in the new nations, still without tools and techniques of modern agriculture, the increase in population pressed hard upon the food supply, resulting in either insufficient diet or mass starvation. In the Far East, for example, the average annual population increase between 1948 and 1951 was 1.3 per cent, while the increase in the food supply was less than one tenth of 1 per cent. Some areas of the world, such as North America and Europe, managed to keep their rate of food production equal to or even in excess of their rate of population growth; but the surpluses of these more fortunate regions were not readily available to the less fortunate, who were often too poor to pay for the food they needed but could not raise themselves.

Some countries of Asia, worried about the disastrous effects uncontrolled population growth could have upon their hopes for economic advancement, had begun programs for family limitation. India and Japan were attempting to popularize contraceptive techniques; Japan, in its concern over the problem, went to the extreme of legalizing abortions. The Japanese effort was the most successful, for the population growth rate was now lower than that of the United States and only slightly higher than that of Belgium, a country which had no population explosion at all. But in spite of the obstacles that uncontrolled population growth presented to economic advancement, few of the new countries were dealing effectively with a problem which would become more pressing as time went on and for which the solution became no easier.

The population explosion was the most pervasive example of a broader problem that the entire world faced in the last decades of the twentieth century—the need for coming to terms with the scientific revolution of our times. The great strides in medicine had created a population explosion; the new electronics had raised the specter of millions of Americans rendered workless by their own marvelous machines; and the wonders of rocketry and nuclear physics had for the first time made it technically possible for man to kill off his own species and to render his planet lifeless.

Obviously, man's scientific and technical capabilities had far outrun the social, economic, and political institutions that he had developed over the centuries for governing the relations among men. Fundamentally, of course, the advances in science promised, for the first time in human history, an age of peace and material well-being for all mankind. The unanswered question was whether men had the wit and wisdom to devise those social institutions which would make it possible to realize that promise. That question was certainly the greatest challenge that Americans, as the acknowledged leaders of Western civilization, had ever confronted in the course of their now quite long and challenging history.

BIBLIOGRAPHY

The classic account of the coming of the war is the very full William L. Langer and S. Everett Gleason, *The Undeclared War, 1940-1941* (New York: Harper, 1953); more readable but as reliable for the Pacific side is Samuel E. Morison, *The Rising Sun in the Pacific* (Boston: Little, Brown, 1948). A popular, but painstaking and fascinating reconstruction of the attack on Pearl Harbor is Walter Lord, *Day of Infamy* (New York: Holt, 1957). There is no readable history of the war on the home front, but Donald M. Nelson, *Arsenal of Democracy* (New York: Harcourt, Brace, 1946) has the virtue as well as the defect of being written by an important figure in the battle for production.

Herbert Feis has devoted himself in several volumes to detailing authoritatively the diplomatic history of the war and immediate postwar years. A central volume in his series is *Churchill, Roosevelt, Stalin* (Princeton: Princeton University Press, 1957). Robert Sherwood, *Roosevelt and Hopkins* (New York: Harper, 1948) is less objective but more interesting and filled with fascinating selections from the sources. Fletcher Pratt, *War for the World* (New Haven: Yale University Press, 1950) is a convenient, short history of military operations; more substantial and dealing with diplomacy to some extent is Louis L. Snyder, *The War: A Concise History, 1939-1945* (New York: Julian Messner, 1960). Chester Wilmot, *The Struggle for Europe* (New York: Harper, 1952) is highly interpretive, but soundly based on the sources and very critical of American policy in the war and as it affected the postwar settlement. The story of the creation of the nuclear bomb is told in dramatic and understandable fashion in William L. Laurence, *Dawn Over Zero* (New York: Knopf, 1946).

Eric Goldman, *The Crucial Decade—and After* (New York: Vintage, 1960), sums up in lively and lucid prose the major events between 1945 and 1960. Although pedestrian in presentation, the *Memoirs* of Harry S. Truman, 2 vols. (Garden City, N. Y.: Doubleday and Company, 1955, 1956) are a must for the years immediately after the war. The best biography of Truman is Jonathan Daniels, *The Man of Independence* (Philadelphia: Lippincott, 1950). One of the most important as well as highly readable studies of politics since the war is Samuel Lubell, *The Future of American Politics*, 2nd ed. (Garden City: Anchor Books, 1956). Alan Barth, *The Loyalty of Free Men* (New York: Viking, 1951) is a highly indignant but effective contemporary critique of the Great Fear. Richard H. Rovere, *Senator Joe McCarthy* (New York: Meridian, 1960) is the best, albeit hostile, study of the Wisconsin senator.

Three handy world-wide surveys of the postwar period are H. S. Commager et al., *Contemporary Civilization* (Chicago: Scott, Foresman, 1961); H. Gatzke, *The Present in Perspective* (Chicago: Rand McNally, 1961); and J. H. Jackson, *The World in the Postwar Decade, 1945-1955* (Boston: Houghton Mifflin, 1957).

Two books on European and world developments are worth noticing: Theodore H. White, *Fire in the Ashes* (New York: William A. Sloan, 1953) on Europe in the early fifties, and Hugh Seton-Watson, *Neither War Nor Peace* (New York: Praeger, 1960) on the state of the world in the late 1950's. Good overall views of the problems facing the underdeveloped countries are Vera M. Dean, *The Nature of the Non-Western World* (New York: Mentor, 1957) and Eugene Staley, *The Future of Underdeveloped Countries: Political Implications of Economic Development* (New York: Harper, 1954). Indispensable sources for the revolution in foreign policy in the postwar years are *The Forrestal Diaries* edited by Walter Millis (New York: Viking Press, 1951) and *The Private Papers of Senator Vandenberg*, edited by Arthur H. Vandenberg, Jr. (Boston: Houghton Mifflin, 1952). In somewhat shrill tones, Norman A Graebner, *The New Isolationism* (New York: Ronald, 1956) tells the story of the fight for internationalism after 1950.

The only critical biography of Eisenhower is Marquis Childs, *Eisenhower: Captive Hero* (New York: Harcourt, Brace, 1958), but it is thin and somewhat partisan. Full of accurate and important private information on the administration is Robert J. Donovan's friendly report *Eisenhower: The Inside Story* (New York: Harper, 1956). The campaign of 1960 is gone into with insight, loving care, and dramatic prose in Theodore White, *The Making of the President, 1960* (New York: Atheneum, 1961).

Bernard Rosenberg and David M. White have edited *Mass Culture* (Glencoe, Ill.: Free Press, 1957) which contains many articles on modern American culture, most of which are hostile. Paul Woodring, *A Fourth of a Nation* (New York: McGraw-Hill, 1957) is a sound, yet essentially idealistic appraisal of American public education. As a critique of the modern economy J. K. Galbraith's trenchant, if somewhat overly iconoclastic *Affluent Society* (Boston: Houghton Mifflin, 1958) cannot be surpassed. David Riesman, *The Lonely Crowd* (Garden City: Anchor Books, 1953) is another contemporary work which has become a classic critique of modern American society. A sophisticated, but somewhat pessimistic, forecast of present trends is R. L. Heilbroner, *The Future as History* (New York: Harper, 1960).

APPENDICES

THE DECLARATION OF INDEPENDENCE
In Congress, July 4, 1776.

The unanimous Declaration of the thirteen united States of America,

When in the Course of human events, it becomes necessary for one people to dissolve the political bands which have connected them with another, and to assume among the Powers of the earth, the separate and equal station to which the Laws of Nature and of Nature's God entitle them, a decent respect to the opinions of mankind requires that they should declare the causes which impel them to the separation.

We hold these truths to be self-evident, that all men are created equal, that they are endowed by their Creator with certain unalienable Rights, that among these are Life, Liberty and the pursuit of Happiness. That to secure these rights, Governments are instituted among Men, deriving their just powers from the consent of the governed, That whenever any Form of Government becomes destructive of these ends, it is the Right of the People to alter or to abolish it, and to institute new Government, laying its foundation on such principles and organizing its powers in such form, as to them shall seem most likely to effect their Safety and Happiness. Prudence, indeed, will dictate that Governments long established should not be changed for light and transient causes; and accordingly all experience hath shown, that mankind are more disposed to suffer, while evils are sufferable, than to right themselves by abolishing the forms to which they are accustomed. But when a long train of abuses and usurpations, pursuing invariably the same Object evinces a design to reduce them under absolute Despotism, it is their right, it is their duty, to throw off such Government, and to provide new Guards for their future security.— Such has been the patient sufferance of these Colonies; and such is now the necessity which constrains them to alter their former Systems of Government. The history of the present King of Great Britain is a history of repeated injuries and usurpations, all having in direct object the establishment of an absolute Tyranny over these States. To prove this, let Facts be submitted to a candid world.

He has refused his Assent to Laws, the most wholesome and necessary for the public good.

He has forbidden his Governors to pass Laws of immediate and pressing importance, unless suspended in their operation till his Assent should be obtained; and when so suspended, he has utterly neglected to attend to them.

He has refused to pass other Laws for the accommodation of large districts of people, unless those people would relinquish the right of Representation in the Legislature, a right inestimable to them and formidable to tyrants only.

He has called together legislative bodies at places unusual, uncomfortable, and distant from the depository of their Public Records, for the sole purpose of fatiguing them into compliance with his measures.

He has dissolved Representative Houses repeatedly, for opposing with manly firmness his invasions on the rights of the people.

He has refused for a long time, after such dissolutions, to cause others to be elected; whereby the Legislative Powers, incapable of Annihilation, have returned to the People at large for their exercise; the State remaining in the mean time exposed to all the dangers of invasion from without, and convulsions within.

He has endeavoured to prevent the population of these States; for that purpose obstructing the Laws for Naturalization of Foreigners; refusing to pass others to encourage their migrations hither, and raising the conditions of new Appropriations of Lands.

He has obstructed the Administration of Justice, by refusing his Assent to Laws for establishing Judiciary Powers.

He has made Judges dependent on his Will alone, for the tenure of their offices, and the amount and payment of their salaries.

He has erected a multitude of New Offices, and sent hither swarms of Officers to harass our people, and eat out their substance.

He has kept among us, in times of peace, Standing Armies without the Consent of our legislatures.

He has affected to render the Military independent of and superior to the Civil Power.

He has combined with others to subject us to a jurisdiction foreign to our constitution, and unacknowledged by our laws; giving his Assent to their acts of pretended Legislation:

For quartering large bodies of armed troops among us:

For protecting them, by a mock Trial, from Punishment for any Murders which they should commit on the Inhabitants of these States:

For cutting off our Trade with all parts of the world:

For imposing taxes on us without our Consent:

For depriving us in many cases, of the benefits of Trial by Jury:

For transporting us beyond Seas to be tried for pretended offences:

For abolishing the free System of English Laws in a neighbouring Province, establishing therein an Arbitrary government, and enlarging its Boundaries so as to render it at once an example and fit instrument for introducing the same absolute rule into these Colonies:

For taking away our Charters, abolishing our most valuable Laws, and altering fundamentally the Forms of our Governments:

For suspending our own Legislatures, and declaring themselves invested with Power to legislate for us in all cases whatsoever.

He has abdicated Government here, by declaring us out of his Protection and waging War against us.

He has plundered our seas, ravaged our Coasts, burnt our towns, and destroyed the lives of our people.

He is at this time transporting large armies of foreign mercenaries to compleat the works of death, desolation and tyranny, already begun with circumstances of Cruelty & perfidy scarcely paralleled in the most barbarous ages, and totally unworthy the Head of a civilized nation.

He has constrained our fellow Citizens taken Captive on the high Seas to bear Arms against their Country, to become the executioners of their friends and Brethren, or to fall themselves by their Hands.

He has excited domestic insurrections amongst us, and has endeavoured to bring on the inhabitants of our frontiers, the merciless Indian Savages, whose known rule of warfare, is an undistinguished destruction of all ages, sexes and conditions.

In every stage of these Oppressions We have Petitioned for Redress in the most humble terms: Our repeated Petitions have been answered only by repeated injury. A Prince, whose character is thus marked by every act which may define a Tyrant, is unfit to be the ruler of a free people.

Nor have We been wanting in attentions to our Brittish brethren. We have warned them from time to time of attempts by their legislature to extend an unwarrantable jurisdiction over us. We have reminded them of the circumstances of our emigration and settlement here. We have appealed to their native justice and magnanimity, and we have conjured them by the ties of our common kindred to disavow these usurpations which, would inevitably interrupt our connections and correspondence. They too have been deaf to the voice of justice and of consanguinity. We must, therefore, acquiesce in the necessity, which denounces our Separation, and hold them, as we hold the rest of mankind, Enemies in War, in Peace Friends.

We, therefore, the Representatives of the united States of America, in General Congress, Assembled, appealing to the Supreme Judge of the world for the rectitude of our intentions, do, in the Name, and by authority of the good People of these Colonies, solemnly publish and declare, That these United Colonies are, and of Right ought to be Free and Independent States; that they are Absolved from all Allegiance to the British Crown, and that all political connection between them and the State of Great Britain, is and ought to be totally dissolved; and that as Free and Independent States, they have full power to levy War, conclude Peace, contract Alliances, establish Commerce, and to do all other Acts and Things which Independent States may of right do. And for the support of this Declaration, with a firm reliance on the Protection of Divine Providence, we mutually pledge to each other our Lives, our Fortunes and our sacred Honor.

JOHN HANCOCK
BUTTON GWINNETT
LYMAN HALL
GEO. WALTON
WM. HOOPER
JOSEPH HEWES
JOHN PENN
EDWARD RUTLEDGE
THOS. HEYWARD, Junr.
THOMAS LYNCH, Junr.
ARTHUR MIDDLETON
SAMUEL CHASE
WM. PACA
THOS. STONE
CHARLES CARROLL
  OF CARROLLTON
GEORGE WYTHE
RICHARD HENRY LEE
TH. JEFFERSON
BENJ. HARRISON
THOS. NELSON, JR.
FRANCIS LIGHTFOOT LEE
CARTER BRAXTON
ROBT. MORRIS
BENJAMIN RUSH
BENJA. FRANKLIN
JOHN MORTON
GEO. CLYMER
JAS. SMITH

GEO. TAYLOR
JAMES WILSON
GEO. ROSS
CAESAR RODNEY
GEO. READ
THO. M'KEAN
WM. FLOYD
PHIL. LIVINGSTON
FRANS. LEWIS
LEWIS MORRIS
RICHD. STOCKTON
JNO. WITHERSPOON
FRAS. HOPKINSON
JOHN HART
ABRA. CLARK
JOSIAH BARTLETT
WM. WHIPPLE
SAML. ADAMS
JOHN ADAMS
ROBT. TREAT PAINE
ELBRIDGE GERRY
STEP. HOPKINS
WILLIAM ELLERY
ROGER SHERMAN
SAM'EL. HUNTINGTON
WM. WILLIAMS
OLIVER WOLCOTT
MATTHEW THORNTON

THE CONSTITUTION OF THE UNITED STATES OF AMERICA

We the People of the United States, in Order to form a more perfect Union, establish Justice, insure domestic Tranquility, provide for the common defence, promote the general Welfare, and secure the Blessings of Liberty to ourselves and our Posterity, do ordain and establish this Constitution for the United States of America.

ARTICLE I.

Section 1.

All legislative Powers herein granted shall be vested in a Congress of the United States, which shall consist of a Senate and House of Representatives.

Section 2.

The House of Representatives shall be composed of Members chosen every second Year by the People of the several States, and the Electors in each State shall have the Qualifications requisite for Electors of the most numerous Branch of the State Legislature.

No Person shall be a Representative who shall not have attained to the Age of twenty five Years, and been seven Years a Citizen of the United States, and who shall not, when elected, be an Inhabitant of that State in which he shall be chosen.

Representatives and direct Taxes shall be apportioned among the several States which may be included within this Union, according to their respective Numbers, which shall be determined by adding to the whole Number of free Persons, including those bound to Service for a Term of Years, and excluding Indians not taxed, three fifths of all other Persons.[1] The actual Enumeration shall be made within three Years after the first Meeting of the Congress of the United States, and within every subsequent Term of ten Years, in such Manner as they shall by Law direct. The Number of Representatives shall not exceed one for every thirty Thousand, but each State shall have at Least one Representative; and until such enumeration shall be made, the State of New Hampshire shall be entitled to chuse three, Massachusetts eight, Rhode-Island and Providence Plantations one, Connecticut five, New-York six, New Jersey four, Pennsylvania eight, Delaware one, Maryland six, Virginia ten, North Carolina five, South Carolina five, and Georgia three.

When vacancies happen in the Representation from any State, the Executive Authority thereof shall issue Writs of Election to fill such Vacancies.

The House of Representatives shall chuse their Speaker and other Officers; and shall have the sole Power of Impeachment.

Section 3.

The Senate of the United States shall be composed of two Senators from each State, chosen by the Legislature thereof, for six Years; and each Senator shall have one Vote.

Immediately after they shall be assembled in Consequence of the first Election, they shall be divided as equally as may be into three Classes. The Seats of the Senators of the first Class shall be vacated at the Expiration of the second Year, of the second Class at the Expiration of the fourth Year, and of the third Class at the Expiration of the sixth Year, so that one third may be chosen every second Year; and if Vacancies happen by Resignation, or otherwise, during the Recess of the Legislature of any State, the Executive thereof may make temporary Appointments until the next Meeting of the Legislature, which shall then fill such Vacancies.[2]

No Person shall be a Senator who shall not have attained to the Age of thirty Years, and been nine Years a Citizen of the United States, and who shall not, when elected, be an Inhabitant of that State for which he shall be chosen.

The Vice President of the United States shall be President of the Senate, but shall have no Vote, unless they be equally divided.

The Senate shall chuse their other Officers, and also a President pro tempore, in the Absence of the Vice President, or when he shall exercise the Office of President of the United States.

The Senate shall have the sole Power to try all Impeachments. When sitting for that Purpose, they shall be on Oath or Affirmation. When the President of the United States is tried the Chief Justice shall preside: And no Person shall be convicted without the Concurrence of two thirds of the Members present.

Judgment in Cases of Impeachment shall not extend further than to removal from Office, and disqualification to hold and enjoy any Office of honor, Trust or Profit under the United States: but the Party convicted shall nevertheless be liable and subject to Indictment, Trial, Judg-

---

1. "Other Persons" being Negro slaves. Modified by Amendment XIV, Section 2.

2. Provisions changed by Amendment XVII.

ment and Punishment, according to Law.

Section 4.

The Times, Places and Manner of holding Elections for Senators and Representatives, shall be prescribed in each State by the Legislature thereof; but the Congress may at any time by Law make or alter such Regulations, except as to the Places of chusing Senators.

The Congress shall assemble at least once in every Year, and such Meeting shall be on the first Monday in December, unless they shall by Law appoint a different Day.[3]

Section 5.

Each House shall be the Judge of the Elections, Returns and Qualifications of its own Members, and a Majority of each shall constitute a Quorum to do Business; but a smaller Number may adjourn from day to day, and may be authorized to compel the Attendance of absent Members, in such Manner, and under such Penalties as each House may provide.

Each House may determine the Rules of its Proceedings, punish its Members for disorderly Behaviour, and, with the Concurrence of two thirds, expel a Member.

Each House shall keep a Journal of its Proceedings, and from time to time publish the same, excepting such Parts as may in their Judgment require Secrecy; and the Yeas and Nays of the Members of either House on any question shall, at the Desire of one fifth of those Present, be entered on the Journal.

Neither House, during the Session of Congress, shall, without the Consent of the other, adjourn for more than three days, nor to any other Place than that in which the two Houses shall be sitting.

Section 6.

The Senators and Representatives shall receive a Compensation for their Services, to be ascertained by Law, and paid out of the Treasury of the United States. They shall in all Cases, except Treason, Felony and Breach of the Peace, be privileged from Arrest during their Attendance at the Session of their respective Houses, and in going to and returning from the same; and for any Speech or Debate in either House, they shall not be questioned in any other Place.

No Senator or Representative shall, during the Time for which he was elected, be appointed to any civil Office under the Authority of the United States, which shall have been created, or the Emoluments whereof shall have been encreased during such time; and no Person holding any Office under the United States, shall be a Member of either House during his Continuance in Office.

Section 7.

All Bills for raising Revenue shall originate in the House of Representatives; but the Senate may propose or concur with Amendments as on other Bills.

Every Bill which shall have passed the House of Representatives and the Senate, shall, before it become a Law, be presented to the President of the United States; If he approve he shall sign it, but if not he shall return it, with his Objections to that House in which it shall have originated, who shall enter the Objections at large on their Journal, and proceed to reconsider it. If after such Reconsideration two thirds of that House shall agree to pass the Bill, it shall be sent, together with the Objections, to the other House, by which it shall likewise be reconsidered, and if approved by two thirds of that House, it shall become a Law. But in all such Cases the Votes of both Houses shall be determined by yeas and Nays, and the Names of the Persons voting for and against the Bill shall be entered on the Journal of each House respectively. If any Bill shall not be returned by the President within ten Days (Sundays excepted) after it shall have been presented to him, the Same shall be a Law, in like Manner as if he had signed it, unless the Congress by their Adjournment prevent its Return, in which Case it shall not be a Law.

Every Order, Resolution, or Vote to which the Concurrence of the Senate and House of Representatives may be necessary (except on a question of Adjournment) shall be presented to the President of the United States; and before the Same shall take Effect, shall be approved by him, or being disapproved by him, shall be repassed by two thirds of the Senate and House of Representatives, according to the Rules and Limitations prescribed in the Case of a Bill.

Section 8.

The Congress shall have Power To lay and collect Taxes, Duties, Imposts and Excises, to pay the Debts and provide for the common Defence and general Welfare of the United States; but all Duties, Imposts and Excises shall be uniform throughout the United States;

To borrow Money on the credit of the United States;

To regulate Commerce with foreign Nations, and among the several States, and with the Indian Tribes;

To establish an uniform Rule of Naturalization, and uniform Laws on the subject of Bankruptcies throughout the United States;

To coin Money, regulate the Value thereof,

---

3. Provision changed by Amendment XX, Section 2.

and of foreign Coin, and fix the Standard of Weights and Measures;

To provide for the Punishment of counterfeiting the Securities and current Coin of the United States;

To establish Post Offices and post Roads;

To promote the Progress of Science and useful Arts, by securing for limited Times to Authors and Inventors the exclusive Right to their respective Writings and Discoveries;

To constitute Tribunals inferior to the supreme Court;

To define and punish Piracies and Felonies committed on the high Seas, and Offences against the Law of Nations;

To declare War, grant Letters of Marque and Reprisal, and make Rules concerning Captures on Land and Water;

To raise and support Armies, but no Appropriation of Money to that Use shall be for a longer Term than two Years;

To provide and maintain a Navy;

To make Rules for the Government and Regulation of the land and naval Forces;

To provide for calling forth the Militia to execute the Laws of the Union, suppress Insurrections and repel Invasions;

To provide for organizing, arming, and disciplining, the Militia, and for governing such Part of them as may be employed in the Service of the United States, reserving to the States respectively, the Appointment of the Officers, and the Authority of training the Militia according to the discipline prescribed by Congress;

To exercise exclusive Legislation in all Cases whatsoever, over such District (not exceeding ten Miles square) as may, by Cession of particular States, and the Acceptance of Congress, become the Seat of the Government of the United States, and to exercise like Authority over all Places purchased by the Consent of the Legislature of the State in which the Same shall be, for the Erection of Forts, Magazines, Arsenals, dock-Yards, and other needful Buildings;—And

To make all Laws which shall be necessary and proper for carrying into Execution the foregoing Powers, and all other Powers vested by this Constitution in the Government of the United States, or in any Department or Officer thereof.

Section 9.

The Migration or Importation of such Persons as any of the States now existing shall think proper to admit, shall not be prohibited by the Congress prior to the Year one thousand eight hundred and eight, but a Tax or duty may be imposed on such Importation, not exceeding ten dollars for each Person.

The Privilege of the Writ of Habeas Corpus shall not be suspended, unless when in Cases of Rebellion or Invasion the public Safety may require it.

No Bill of Attainder or ex post facto Law shall be passed.

No Capitation, or other direct, Tax shall be laid, unless in Proportion to the Census or Enumeration herein before directed to be taken.

No Tax or Duty shall be laid on Articles exported from any State.

No Preference shall be given by any Regulation of Commerce or Revenue to the Ports of one State over those of another: nor shall Vessels bound to, or from, one State, be obliged to enter, clear, or pay Duties in another.

No Money shall be drawn from the Treasury, but in Consequence of Appropriations made by Law; and a regular Statement and Account of the Receipts and Expenditures of all public Money shall be published from time to time.

No Title of Nobility shall be granted by the United States: And no Person holding any Office of Profit or Trust under them, shall, without the Consent of the Congress, accept of any present, Emolument, Office, or Title, of any kind whatever, from any King, Prince, or foreign State.

Section 10.

No State shall enter into any Treaty, Alliance, or Confederation; grant Letters of Marque and Reprisal; coin Money; emit Bills of Credit; make any Thing but gold and silver Coin a Tender in Payment of Debts; pass any Bill of Attainder, ex post facto Law, or Law impairing the Obligation of Contracts, or grant any Title of Nobility.

No State shall, without the Consent of the Congress, lay any Imposts or Duties on Imports or Exports, except what may be absolutely necessary for executing it's inspection Laws: and the net Produce of all Duties and Imposts, laid by any State on Imports or Exports, shall be for the Use of the Treasury of the United States; and all such Laws shall be subject to the Revision and Controul of the Congress.

No State shall, without the Consent of Congress, lay any Duty of Tonnage, keep Troops, or Ships of War in time of Peace, enter into any Agreement or Compact with another State, or with a foreign Power, or engage in War, unless actually invaded, or in such imminent Danger as will not admit of delay.

ARTICLE II.

Section 1.

The executive Power shall be vested in a President of the United States of America. He shall hold his Office during the Term of four Years. and, together with the Vice President, chosen for the same Term, be elected, as follows:

Each State shall appoint, in such Manner as the Legislature thereof may direct, a Number of Electors, equal to the whole Number of Senators and Representatives to which the State may be entitled in the Congress: but no Senator or Representative, or Person holding an Office of Trust or Profit under the United States, shall be appointed an Elector.

The Electors shall meet in their respective States, and vote by Ballot for two Persons, of whom one at least shall not be an Inhabitant of the same State with themselves. And they shall make a List of all the Persons voted for, and of the Number of Votes for each; which List they shall sign and certify, and transmit sealed to the Seat of the Government of the United States, directed to the President of the Senate. The President of the Senate shall, in the Presence of the Senate and House of Representatives, open all the Certificates, and the Votes shall then be counted. The Person having the greatest Number of Votes shall be the President, if such Number be a Majority of the whole Number of Electors appointed; and if there be more than one who have such Majority, and have an equal Number of Votes, then the House of Representatives shall immediately chuse by Ballot one of them for President; and if no Person have a Majority, then from the five highest on the List the said House shall in like Manner chuse the President. But in chusing the President, the Votes shall be taken by States, the Representation from each State having one Vote; A quorum for this Purpose shall consist of a Member or Members from two thirds of the States, and a Majority of all the States shall be necessary to a Choice. In every Case, after the Choice of the President, the Person having the greatest Number of Votes of the Electors shall be the Vice President. But if there should remain two or more who have equal Votes, the Senate shall chuse from them by Ballot the Vice President.[4]

The Congress may determine the Time of chusing the Electors, and the Day on which they shall give their Votes; which Day shall be the same throughout the United States.

No Person except a natural born Citizen, or a Citizen of the United States, at the time of the Adoption of this Constitution, shall be eligible to the Office of President; neither shall any Person be eligible to that Office who shall not have attained to the Age of thirty five Years, and been fourteen Years a Resident within the United States.

In Case of the Removal of the President from Office, or of his Death, Resignation, or Inability to discharge the Powers and Duties of the said Office, the Same shall devolve on the Vice President, and the Congress may by Law provide for the Case of Removal, Death, Resignation or Inability, both of the President and Vice President, declaring what Officer shall then act as President, and such Officer shall act accordingly, until the Disability be removed, or a President shall be elected.

The President shall, at stated Times, receive for his Services, a Compensation, which shall neither be encreased nor diminished during the Period for which he shall have been elected, and he shall not receive within that Period any other Emolument from the United States, or any of them.

Before he enter on the Execution of his Office, he shall take the following Oath or Affirmation:—"I do solemnly swear (or affirm) that I will faithfully execute the Office of President of the United States, and will to the best of my Ability, preserve, protect and defend the Constitution of the United States."

Section 2.

The President shall be Commander in Chief of the Army and Navy of the United States, and of the Militia of the several States, when called into the actual Service of the United States; he may require the Opinion, in writing, of the principal Officer in each of the executive Departments, upon any Subject relating to the Duties of their respective Offices, and he shall have Power to grant Reprieves and Pardons for Offences against the United States, except in Cases of Impeachment.

He shall have Power, by and with the Advice and Consent of the Senate, to make Treaties, provided two thirds of the Senators present concur; and he shall nominate, and by and with the Advice and Consent of the Senate, shall appoint Ambassadors, other public Ministers and Consuls, Judges of the supreme Court, and all other Officers of the United States, whose Appointments are not herein otherwise provided for, and which shall be established by Law: but the Congress may by Law vest the Appointment of such inferior Officers, as they think proper in the President alone, in the Courts of Law, or in the Heads of Departments.

The President shall have Power to fill up all Vacancies that may happen during the Recess of the Senate, by granting Commissions which shall expire at the End of their next Session.

Section 3

He shall from time to time give to the Congress Information of the State of the Union, and recommend to their Consideration such Measures as he shall judge necessary and expedient;

---

4. Provisions superseded by Amendment XII.

he may, on extraordinary Occasions, convene both Houses, or either of them, and in Case of Disagreement between them, with Respect to the Time of Adjournment, he may adjourn them to such Time as he shall think proper; he shall receive Ambassadors and other public Ministers; he shall take Care that the Laws be faithfully executed, and shall Commission all the Officers of the United States.

Section 4.

The President, Vice President and all civil Officers of the United States, shall be removed from Office on Impeachment for, and Conviction of, Treason, Bribery, or other high Crimes and Misdemeanors.

such Place or Places as the Congress may by Law have directed.

Section 3.

Treason against the United States, shall consist only in levying War against them, or in adhering to their Enemies, giving them Aid and Comfort. No person shall be convicted of Treason unless on the Testimony of two Witnesses to the same overt Act, or on Confession in open Court.

The Congress shall have Power to declare the Punishment of Treason, but no Attainder of Treason shall work Corruption of Blood, or Forfeiture except during the Life of the Person attainted.

ARTICLE III.

Section 1.

The judicial Power of the United States, shall be vested in one supreme Court, and in such inferior Courts as the Congress may from time to time ordain and establish. The Judges, both of the supreme and inferior Courts, shall hold their Offices during good Behaviour, and shall, at stated Times, receive for their Services, a Compensation, which shall not be diminished during their Continuance in Office.

Section 2.

The judicial Power shall extend to all Cases, in Law and Equity, arising under this Constitution, the Laws of the United States, and Treaties made, or which shall be made, under their Authority;—to all Cases affecting Ambassadors, other public Ministers and Consuls;—to all Cases of admiralty and maritime Jurisdiction;—to Controversies to which the United States shall be a Party;—to Controversies between two or more States;—between a State and Citizens of another State;—between Citizens of different States,—between Citizens of the same State claiming Lands under Grants of different States, and between a State, or the Citizens thereof, and foreign States, Citizens or Subjects.[5]

In all Cases affecting Ambassadors, other public Ministers and Consuls, and those in which a State shall be Party, the supreme Court shall have original Jurisdiction. In all the other Cases before mentioned, the supreme Court shall have appellate Jurisdiction, both as to Law and Fact, with such Exceptions, and under such Regulations as the Congress shall make.

The Trial of all Crimes, except in Cases of Impeachment, shall be by Jury; and such Trial shall be held in the State where the said Crimes shall have been committed, but when not committed within any State, the Trial shall be at

ARTICLE IV.

Section 1.

Full Faith and Credit shall be given in each State to the public Acts, Records, and judicial Proceedings of every other State. And the Congress may by general Laws prescribe the Manner in which such Acts, Records and Proceedings shall be proved, and the Effect thereof.

Section 2.

The Citizens of each State shall be entitled to all Privileges and Immunities of Citizens in the several States.

A Person charged in any State with Treason, Felony, or other Crime, who shall flee from Justice, and be found in another State, shall on Demand of the executive Authority of the State from which he fled, be delivered up, to be removed to the State having Jurisdiction of the Crime.

No Person held to Service or Labour in one State, under the Laws thereof, escaping into another, shall, in Consequence of any Law or Regulation therein, be discharged from such Service or Labour, but shall be delivered up on Claim of the Party to whom such Service or Labour may be due.

Section 3.

New States may be admitted by the Congress into this Union; but no new State shall be formed or erected within the Jurisdiction of any other State; nor any State be formed by the Junction of two or more States, or Parts of States, without the Consent of the Legislatures of the States concerned as well as of the Congress.

The Congress shall have Power to dispose of and make all needful Rules and Regulations respecting the Territory or other Property belonging to the United States; and nothing in this Constitution shall be so construed as to Prejudice any Claims of the United States, or of any particular State.

---

5. Clause changed by Amendment XI.

Section 4.

The United States shall guarantee to every State in this Union a Republican Form of Government, and shall protect each of them against Invasion; and on Application of the Legislature, or of the Executive (when the Legislature cannot be convened) against domestic Violence.

Article V.

The Congress, whenever two thirds of both Houses shall deem it necessary, shall propose Amendments to this Constitution, or, on the Application of the Legislatures of two thirds of the several States, shall call a Convention for proposing Amendments, which, in either Case, shall be valid to all Intents and Purposes, as Part of this Constitution, when ratified by the Legislatures of three fourths of the several States, or by Conventions in three fourths thereof, as the one or the other Mode of Ratification may be proposed by the Congress; Provided that no Amendment which may be made prior to the Year One thousand eight hundred and eight shall in any Manner affect the first and fourth Clauses in the Ninth Section of the first Article; and that no State, without its Consent, shall be deprived of its equal Suffrage in the Senate.

Article VI.

All Debts contracted and Engagements entered into, before the Adoption of this Constitution, shall be as valid against the United States under this Constitution, as under the Confederation.

This Constitution, and the Laws of the United States which shall be made in Pursuance thereof; and all Treaties made, or which shall be made, under the Authority of the United States, shall be the supreme Law of the Land; and the Judges in every State shall be bound thereby, any Thing in the Constitution or Laws of any State to the Contrary notwithstanding.

The Senators and Representatives before mentioned, and the Members of the several State Legislatures, and all executive and judicial Officers, both of the United States and of the several States, shall be bound by Oath or Affirmation, to support this Constitution; but no religious Test shall ever be required as a Qualification to any Office or public Trust under the United States.

Article VII.

The Ratification of the Conventions of nine States, shall be sufficient for the Establishment of this Constitution between the States so ratifying the Same.

done in Convention by the Unanimous Consent of the States present the Seventeenth Day of September in the Year of our Lord one thousand seven hundred and Eighty seven and of the Independence of the United States of America the Twelfth[6] IN WITNESS whereof We have hereunto subscribed our Names,

G̊: WASHINGTON—Presid:
and deputy from Virginia

New Hampshire	John Langdon Nicholas Gilman
Massachusetts	Nathaniel Gorham Rufus King
Connecticut	W̊: Sam̊: Johnson Roger Sherman
New York	Alexander Hamilton
New Jersey	Wil: Livingston David Brearley. W̊: Paterson. Jona: Dayton
Pensylvania	B Franklin Thomas Mifflin Rob̊: Morris Geo. Clymer Tho̊: FitzSimons Jared Ingersoll James Wilson Gouv Morris
Delaware	Geo: Read Gunning Bedford jun John Dickinson Richard Bassett Jaco: Broom
Maryland	James McHenry Dan of S̊: Tho̊: Jenifer Dan̊: Carroll
Virginia	John Blair— James Madison Jr.
North Carolina	W̊: Blount Rich̊: Dobbs Spaight. Hu Williamson
South Carolina	J. Rutledge Charles Cotesworth Pinckney Charles Pinckney Pierce Butler.
Georgia	William Few Abr Baldwin

AMENDMENTS TO THE CONSTITUTION

[AMENDMENT I]

Congress shall make no law respecting an es-

---

6. The Constitution was submitted on September 17, 1787, by the Constitutional Convention, was ratified by the conventions of several states at various dates up to May 29, 1790, and became effective on March 4, 1789.

tablishment of religion, or prohibiting the free exercise thereof; or abridging the freedom of speech, or of the press; or the right of the people peaceably to assemble, and to petition the Government for a redress of grievances.

[AMENDMENT II]

A well regulated Militia being necessary to the security of a free State, the right of the people to keep and bear Arms, shall not be infringed.

[AMENDMENT III]

No Soldier shall, in time of peace be quartered in any house, without the consent of the Owner, nor in time of war, but in a manner to be prescribed by law.

[AMENDMENT IV]

The right of the people to be secure in their persons, houses, papers, and effects, against unreasonable searches and seizures, shall not be violated, and no Warrants shall issue, but upon probable cause, supported by Oath or affirmation, and particularly describing the place to be searched, and the persons or things to be seized.

[AMENDMENT V]

No person shall be held to answer for a capital, or otherwise infamous crime, unless on a presentment or indictment of a Grand Jury, except in cases arising in the land or naval forces, or in the Militia, when in actual service in time of War or public danger; nor shall any person be subject for the same offense to be twice put in jeopardy of life or limb; nor shall be compelled in any criminal case to be a witness against himself, nor be deprived of life, liberty, or property, without due process of law; nor shall private property be taken for public use, without just compensation.

[AMENDMENT VI]

In all criminal prosecutions, the accused shall enjoy the right to a speedy and public trial, by an impartial jury of the State and district wherein the crime shall have been committed, which district shall have been previously ascertained by law, and to be informed of the nature and cause of the accusation; to be confronted with the witnesses against him; to have compulsory process for obtaining witnesses in his favor, and to have the Assistance of Counsel for his defence.

[AMENDMENT VII]

In Suits at common law, where the value in controversy shall exceed twenty dollars, the right of trial by jury shall be preserved, and no fact tried by a jury, shall be otherwise re-examined in any Court of the United States, than according to the rules of the common law.

[AMENDMENT VIII]

Excessive bail shall not be required, nor excessive fines imposed, nor cruel and unusual punishments inflicted.

[AMENDMENT IX]

The enumeration in the Constitution, of certain rights, shall not be construed to deny or disparage others retained by the people.

[AMENDMENT X]

The powers not delegated to the United States by the Constitution, nor prohibited by it to the States, are reserved to the States respectively, or to the people.[7]

[AMENDMENT XI]

The Judicial power of the United States shall not be construed to extend to any suit in law or equity, commenced or prosecuted against one of the United States by Citizens of another State, or by Citizens or Subjects of any Foreign State.[8]

[AMENDMENT XII]

The Electors shall meet in their respective states, and vote by ballot for President and Vice-President, one of whom, at least, shall not be an inhabitant of the same state with themselves; they shall name in their ballots the person voted for as President, and in distinct ballots the person voted for as Vice-President, and they shall make distinct lists of all persons voted for as President, and of all persons voted for as Vice-President, and of the number of votes for each, which lists they shall sign and certify, and transmit sealed to the seat of the government of the United States, directed to the President of the Senate;—The President of the Senate shall, in the presence of the Senate and House of Representatives, open all the certificates and the votes shall then be counted;—The person having the greatest number of votes for President, shall be the President, if such number be a majority of the whole number of Electors appointed; and if no person have such majority, then from the persons having the highest

---

7. The first ten amendments were all proposed by Congress on September 25, 1789, and were ratified and adoption certified on December 15, 1791.

8. Proposed by Congress on March 4, 1794, and declared ratified on January 8, 1798.

numbers not exceeding three on the list of those voted for as President, the House of Representatives shall choose immediately, by ballot, the President. But in choosing the President, the votes shall be taken by states, the representation from each state having one vote; a quorum for this purpose shall consist of a member or members from two-thirds of the states, and a majority of all the states shall be necessary to a choice. And if the House of Representatives shall not choose a President whenever the right of choice shall devolve upon them, before the fourth day of March next following, then the Vice-President shall act as President, as in the case of the death or other constitutional disability of the President.—The person having the greatest number of votes as Vice-President, shall be the Vice-President, if such number be a majority of the whole number of Electors appointed, and if no person have a majority, then from the two highest numbers on the list, the Senate shall choose the Vice-President; a quorum for the purpose shall consist of two-thirds of the whole number of Senators, and a majority of the whole number shall be necessary to a choice. But no person constitutionally ineligible to the office of President shall be eligible to that of Vice-President of the United States.[9]

[AMENDMENT XIII]

Section 1.

Neither slavery nor involuntary servitude, except as a punishment for crime whereof the party shall have been duly convicted, shall exist within the United States, or any place subject to their jurisdiction.

Section 2.

Congress shall have power to enforce this article by appropriate legislation.[10]

[AMENDMENT XIV]

Section 1.

All persons born or naturalized in the United States, and subject to the jurisdiction thereof, are citizens of the United States and of the State wherein they reside. No State shall make or enforce any law which shall abridge the privileges or immunities of citizens of the United States; nor shall any State deprive any person of life, liberty, or property, without due process of law; nor deny to any person within its jurisdiction the equal protection of the laws.

---

9. Proposed by Congress on December 9, 1803; declared ratified on September 25, 1804; supplemented by Amendments XX and XXIII.

10. Proposed by Congress on January 31, 1865; declared ratified on December 18, 1865.

Section 2.

Representatives shall be apportioned among the several States according to their respective numbers, counting the whole number of persons in each State, excluding Indians not taxed. But when the right to vote at any election for the choice of electors for President and Vice-President of the United States, Representatives in Congress, the Executive and Judicial officers of a State, or the members of the Legislature thereof, is denied to any of the male inhabitants of such State, being twenty-one years of age, and citizens of the United States, or in any way abridged, except for participation in rebellion, or other crime, the basis of representation therein shall be reduced in the proportion which the number of such male citizens shall bear to the whole number of male citizens twenty-one years of age in such State.

Section 3.

No person shall be a Senator or Representative in Congress, or elector of President and Vice President, or hold any office, civil or military, under the United States, or under any State, who, having previously taken an oath, as a member of Congress, or as an officer of the United States, or as a member of any State legislature, or as an executive or judicial officer of any State, to support the Constitution of the United States, shall have engaged in insurrection or rebellion against the same, or given aid or comfort to the enemies thereof. But Congress may by a vote of two-thirds of each House, remove such disability.

Section 4.

The validity of the public debt of the United States, authorized by law, including debts incurred for payment of pensions and bounties for services in suppressing insurrection or rebellion, shall not be questioned. But neither the United States nor any State shall assume or pay any debt or obligation incurred in aid of insurrection or rebellion against the United States, or any claim for the loss or emancipation of any slave; but all such debts, obligations and claims shall be held illegal and void.

Section 5.

The Congress shall have power to enforce, by appropriate legislation, the provisions of this article.[11]

[AMENDMENT XV]

Section 1.

The right of citizens of the United States to vote shall not be denied or abridged by the United States or by any State on account of

---

11. Proposed by Congress on June 13, 1866; declared ratified on July 28, 1868.

race, color, or previous condition of servitude.

Section 2.
The Congress shall have power to enforce this article by appropriate legislation.[12]

[AMENDMENT XVI]
The Congress shall have power to lay and collect taxes on incomes, from whatever source derived, without apportionment among the several States, and without regard to any census or enumeration.[13]

[AMENDMENT XVII]
The Senate of the United States shall be composed of two Senators from each State, elected by the people thereof, for six years; and each Senator shall have one vote. The electors in each State shall have the qualifications requisite for electors of the most numerous branch of the State legislatures.

When vacancies happen in the representation of any State in the Senate, the executive authority of such State shall issue writs of election to fill such vacancies: *Provided,* That the legislature of any State may empower the executive thereof to make temporary appointments until the people fill the vacancies by election as the legislature may direct.

This amendment shall not be so construed as to affect the election or term of any Senator chosen before it becomes valid as part of the Constitution.[14]

[AMENDMENT XVIII]
Section 1.
After one year from the ratification of this article the manufacture, sale, or transportation of intoxicating liquors within, the importation thereof into, or the exportation thereof from the United States and all territory subject to the jurisdiction thereof for beverage purposes is hereby prohibited.

Section 2.
The Congress and the several States shall have concurrent power to enforce this article by appropriate legislation.

Section 3.
This article shall be inoperative unless it shall have been ratified as an amendment to the Constitution by the legislatures of the several States, as provided in the Constitution, within seven years from the date of the submission hereof to the States by the Congress.[15]

[AMENDMENT XIX]
The right of citizens of the United States to vote shall not be denied or abridged by the United States or by any State on account of sex.

Congress shall have power to enforce this article by appropriate legislation.[16]

[AMENDMENT XX]
Section 1.
The terms of the President and Vice President shall end at noon on the 20th day of January, and the terms of Senators and Representatives at noon on the 3d day of January, of the years in which such terms would have ended if this article had not been ratified; and the terms of their successors shall then begin.

Section 2.
The Congress shall assemble at least once in every year, and such meeting shall begin at noon on the 3d day of January, unless they shall by law appoint a different day.

Section 3.
If, at the time fixed for the beginning of the term of the President, the President elect shall have died, the Vice President elect shall become President. If a President shall not have been chosen before the time fixed for the beginning of his term, or if the President elect shall have failed to qualify, then the Vice President elect shall act as President until a President shall have qualified; and the Congress may by law provide for the case wherein neither a President elect nor a Vice President elect shall have qualified, declaring who shall then act as President, or the manner in which one who is to act shall be selected, and such person shall act accordingly until a President or Vice President shall have qualified.

Section 4.
The Congress may by law provide for the case of the death of any of the persons from whom the House of Representatives may choose a President whenever the right of choice shall have devolved upon them, and for the case of the death of any of the persons from whom the Senate may choose a Vice President when-

---

12. Proposed by Congress on February 26, 1869; declared ratified on March 30, 1870.

13. Proposed by Congress on July 12, 1909; declared ratified on February 25, 1913.

14. Proposed by Congress on May 13, 1912; declared ratified on May 31, 1913.

15. Proposed by Congress on December 18, 1917; declared ratified on January 29, 1919; repealed by Amendment XXI.

16. Proposed by Congress on June 4, 1919; declared ratified on August 26, 1920.

ever the right of choice shall have devolved upon them.

Section 5.
Sections 1 and 2 shall take effect on the 15th day of October following the ratification of this article.

Section 6.
This article shall be inoperative unless it shall have been ratified as an amendment to the Constitution by the legislatures of three-fourths of the several States within seven years from the date of its submission.[17]

[AMENDMENT XXI]

Section 1.
The eighteenth article of amendment to the Constitution of the United States is hereby repealed.

Section 2.
The transportation or importation into any States, Territory, or possession of the United States for delivery or use therein of intoxicating liquors, in violation of the laws thereof, is hereby prohibited.

Section 3.
This article shall be inoperative unless it shall have been ratified as an amendment to the Constitution by conventions in the several States, as provided in the Constitution, within seven years from the date of the submission hereof to the States by the Congress.[18]

[AMENDMENT XXII]

Section 1.
No person shall be elected to the office of the President more than twice, and no person who has held the office of President, or acted as President, for more than two years of a term to which some other person was elected President shall be elected to the office of the President more than once. But this Article shall not apply to any person holding the office of President when this Article was proposed by the Congress, and shall not prevent any person who may be holding the office of President, or acting as President, during the term within which this Article becomes operative from holding the office of President or acting as President during the remainder of such term.

Section 2.
This article shall be inoperative unless it shall have been ratified as an amendment to the Constitution by the legislatures of three-fourths of the several States within seven years from the date of its submission to the States by the Congress.[19]

[AMENDMENT XXIII]

Section 1.
The District constituting the seat of Government of the United States shall appoint in such manner as the Congress shall direct:

A number of electors of President and Vice President equal to the whole number of Senators and Representatives in Congress to which the District would be entitled if it were a State, but in no event more than the least populous State; they shall be in addition to those appointed by the States, but they shall be considered, for the purposes of the election of President and Vice President, to be electors appointed by a State; and they shall meet in the District and perform such duties as provided by the twelfth article of amendment.

Section 2.
The Congress shall have power to enforce this article by appropriate legislation.[20]

[AMENDMENT XXIV]

Section 1.
The right of citizens of the United States to vote in any primary or other election for President or Vice President, for electors for President or Vice President, or for Senator or Representative in Congress, shall not be denied or abridged by the United States or any state by reason of failure to pay any poll tax or other tax.

Section 2.
The Congress shall have the power to enforce this article by appropriate legislation.[21]

---

17. Proposed by Congress on March 2, 1932; declared ratified on February 6, 1933.

18. Proposed by Congress on February 20, 1933; declared ratified on December 5, 1933.

19. Proposed by Congress on March 24, 1947; declared ratified on March 1, 1951.

20. Proposed by Congress on June 16, 1960; declared ratified on April 3, 1961.

21. Proposed by Congress on August 27, 1962; declared ratified on January 23, 1963.

PRESIDENTS, VICE-PRESIDENTS, AND CABINET MEMBERS

President and Vice-President	Secretary of State	Secretary of the Treasury	Secretary of War
George Washington (F) .... 1789 J. Adams .... '89	T. Jefferson .... '89 E. Randolph .... '94 T. Pickering .... '95	A. Hamilton .... '89 O. Wolcott .... '95	H. Knox .... '89 T. Pickering .... '95 J. McHenry .... '96
John Adams (F) .... 1797 T. Jefferson (R^J) .... '97	T. Pickering .... '97 J. Marshall .... '00	O. Wolcott .... '97 S. Dexter .... '01	J. McHenry .... '97 J. Marshall .... '00 S. Dexter .... '00 R. Griswold .... '01
Thomas Jefferson (R^J) .... 1801 A. Burr (R^J) .... '01 G. Clinton (R^J) .... '05	J. Madison .... '01	S. Dexter .... '01 A. Gallatin .... '01	H. Dearborn .... '01
James Madison (R^J) .... 1809 G. Clinton (R^J) .... '09 E. Gerry (R^J) .... '13	R. Smith .... '09 J. Monroe .... '11	A. Gallatin .... '09 G. Campbell .... '14 A. Dallas .... '14 W. Crawford ...... '16	W. Eustis .... '09 J. Armstrong .... '13 J. Monroe .... '14 W. Crawford ...... '15
James Monroe (R^J) .... 1817 D. Tompkins (R^J) .... '17	J. Q. Adams .... '17	W. Crawford ...... '17	I. Shelby .... '17 G. Graham .... '17 J. Calhoun .... '17
John Quincy Adams (NR) .... 1825 J. Calhoun (R^J) .... '25	H. Clay .... '25	R. Rush .... '25	J. Barbour .... '25 P. Porter .... '28
Andrew Jackson (D) .... 1829 J. Calhoun (D) .... '29 M. Van Buren (D) .... '33	M. Van Buren ...... '29 E. Livingston ...... '31 L. McLane .... '33 J. Forsyth .... '34	S. Ingham .... '29 L. McLane .... '31 W. Duane .... '33 R. Taney .... '33 L. Woodbury ...... '34	J. Eaton .... '29 L. Cass .... '31 B. Butler .... '37
Martin Van Buren (D) .... 1837 R. Johnson (D) .... '37	J. Forsyth .... '37	L. Woodbury ...... '37	J. Poinsett .... '37
William H. Harrison (W) .... 1841 J. Tyler (W) .... '41	D. Webster .... '41	T. Ewing .... '41	J. Bell .... '41
John Tyler (W and D) 1841	D. Webster .... '41 H. Legare .... '43 A. Upshur .... '43 J. Calhoun .... '44	T. Ewing .... '41 W. Forward .... '41 J. Spencer .... '43 G. Bibb .... '44	J. Bell .... '41 J. McLean .... '41 J. Spencer .... '41 J. Porter .... '43 W. Wilkins .... '44
James K. Polk (D) .... 1845 G. Dallas (D) .... '45	J. Buchanan .... '45	R. Walker .... '45	W. Marcy .... '45
Zachary Taylor (W) .... 1849 M. Fillmore (W) .... '49	J. Clayton .... '49	W. Meredith ...... '49	G. Crawford .... '49
Millard Fillmore (W) 1850	D. Webster .... '50 E. Everett .... '52	T. Corwin .... '50	C. Conrad .... '50
Franklin Pierce (D) .... 1853 W. King (D) .... '53	W. Marcy .... '53	J. Guthrie .... '53	J. Davis .... '53
James Buchanan (D) .... 1857 J. Breckinridge (D) .... '57	L. Cass .... '57 J. Black .... '60	H. Cobb .... '57 P. Thomas .... '60 J. Dix .... '61	J. Floyd .... '57 J. Holt .... '61
Abraham Lincoln (R) .... 1861 H. Hamlin (R) .... '61 A. Johnson (U) .... '65	W. Seward .... '61	S. Chase .... '61 W. Fessenden ...... '64 H. McCulloch ...... '65	S. Cameron .... '61 E. Stanton .... '62
Andrew Johnson (U) 1865	W. Seward .... '65	H. McCulloch ...... '65	E. Stanton .... '65 U. Grant .... '67 L. Thomas .... '68 J. Schofield .... '68
Ulysses S. Grant (R) .... 1869 S. Colfax (R) .... '69 H. Wilson (R) .... '73	E. Washburne ...... '69 H. Fish .... '69	G. Boutwell .... '69 W. Richardson ..... '73 B. Bristow .... '74 L. Morrill .... '76	J. Rawlins .... '69 W. Sherman .... '69 W. Belknap .... '69 A. Taft .... '76 J. Cameron .... '76
Rutherford B. Hayes (R) .... 1877 W. Wheeler (R) .... '77	W. Evarts .... '77	J. Sherman .... '77	G. McCrary .... '77 A. Ramsey .... '79

Party affiliations: D, Democratic; F, Federalist; NR, National Republican; R, Republican; R^J, Republican (Jeffersonian); U, Unionist; W, Whig.

xxii

Secretary of the Navy	Attorney General	Postmaster General	Secretary of the Interior
Established April 30, 1798	E. Randolph.........'89		
B. Stoddert............'98	W. Bradford..........'94		
	C. Lee................'95		
	C. Lee................'97		
	T. Parsons............'01		
B. Stoddert............'01	L. Lincoln............'01		
R. Smith..............'01	R. Smith..............'05		
J. Crowninshield......'05	J. Breckinridge.......'05		
	C. Rodney.............'07		
P. Hamilton...........'09	C. Rodney.............'09		
W. Jones..............'13	W. Pinkney............'11		
B. Crowninshield......'14	R. Rush...............'14		
B. Crowninshield......'17	R. Rush...............'17		
S. Thompson...........'18	W. Wirt...............'17		
S. Southard...........'23		**Cabinet status since March 9, 1829**	
S. Southard...........'25	W. Wirt...............'25		
J. Branch.............'29	J. Berrien............'29	W. Barry.............'29	
L. Woodbury...........'31	R. Taney..............'31	A. Kendall...........'35	
M. Dickerson..........'34	B. Butler.............'33		
M. Dickerson..........'37	B. Butler.............'37	A. Kendall...........'37	
J. Paulding...........'38	F. Grundy.............'38	J. Niles.............'40	
	H. Gilpin.............'40		
G. Badger.............'41	J. Crittenden.........'41	F. Granger...........'41	
G. Badger.............'41	J. Crittenden.........'41	F. Granger...........'41	
A. Upshur.............'41	H. Legare.............'41	C. Wickliffe.........'41	
D. Henshaw............'43	J. Nelson.............'43		
T. Gilmer.............'44			
J. Mason..............'44			**Established March 3, 1849**
G. Bancroft...........'45	J. Mason..............'45	C. Johnson...........'45	
J. Mason..............'46	N. Clifford...........'46		
	I. Toucey.............'48		
W. Preston............'49	R. Johnson............'49	J. Collamer..........'49	Thomas Ewing........'49
W. Graham.............'50	J. Crittenden.........'50	N. Hall..............'50	A. Stuart............'50
J. Kennedy............'52		S. Hubbard...........'52	
J. Dobbin.............'53	C. Cushing............'53	J. Campbell..........'53	R. McClelland........'53
I. Toucey.............'57	J. Black..............'57	A. Brown.............'57	J. Thompson..........'57
	E. Stanton............'60	J. Holt..............'59	
G. Welles.............'61	E. Bates..............'61	H. King..............'61	C. Smith.............'61
	T. Coffey.............'63	M. Blair.............'61	J. Usher.............'63
	J. Speed..............'64	W. Dennison..........'64	
G. Welles.............'65	J. Speed..............'65	W. Dennison..........'65	J. Usher.............'65
	H. Stanbery...........'66	A. Randall...........'66	J. Harlan............'65
	W. Evarts.............'68		O. Browning..........'66
A. Borie..............'69	E. Hoar...............'69	J. Creswell..........'69	J. Cox...............'69
G. Robeson............'69	A. Ackerman...........'70	J. Marshall..........'74	C. Delano............'70
	G. Williams...........'71	M. Jewell............'74	Z. Chandler..........'75
	E. Pierrepont.........'75	J. Tyner.............'76	
	A. Taft...............'76		
R. Thompson...........'77	C. Devens.............'77	D. Key...............'77	C. Schurz............'77
N. Goff...............'81		H. Maynard...........'80	

xxiii

PRESIDENTS, VICE-PRESIDENTS, AND CABINET MEMBERS

President and Vice-President	Secretary of State	Secretary of the Treasury	Secretary of War	Secretary of the Navy	Attorney General
James A. Garfield (R)...1881 C. Arthur (R).........'81	J. Blaine...'81	W. Windom..'81	R. Lincoln...'81	W. Hunt....'81	W. Mac- Veagh.....'81
Chester A. Arthur (R)...1881	F. Frelinghuysen...'81	C. Folger....'81 W. Gresham..'84 H. McCulloch'84	R. Lincoln...'81	W. Chandler.'81	B. Brewster...'81
Grover Cleveland (D)....1885 T. Hendricks (D).....'85	T. Bayard..'85	D. Manning..'85 C. Fairchild..'87	W. Endicott..'85	W. Whitney..'85	A. Garland..'85
Benjamin Harrison (R)..1889 L. Morton (R)........'89	J. Blaine....'89 J. Foster....'92	W. Windom..'89 C. Foster....'91	R. Proctor...'89 S. Elkins....'91	B. Tracy.....'89	W. Miller....'89
Grover Cleveland (D)....1893 A. Stevenson (D).......'93	W. Gresham'93 R. Olney...'95	J. Carlisle.....'93	D. Lamont...'93	H. Herbert..'93	R. Olney....'93 J. Harmon...'95
William McKinley (R)...1897 G. Hobart (R)........'97 T. Roosevelt (R).....'01	J. Sherman.'97 W. Day.....'97 J. Hay.....'98	L. Gage......'97	R. Alger.....'97 E. Root.....'99	J. Long......'97	J. McKenna..'97 J. Griggs.....'97 P. Knox.....'01
Theodore Roosevelt (R)..1901 C. Fairbanks (R).......'05	J. Hay......'01 E. Root....'05 R. Bacon...'09	L. Gage......'01 L. Shaw......'02 G. Cortelyou..'07	E. Root......'01 W. Taft......'04 L. Wright...'08	J. Long......'01 W. Moody...'02 P. Morton...'04 C. Bonaparte '05 V. Metcalf...'07 T. Newberry.'08	P. Knox.....'01 W. Moody...'04 C. Bonaparte.'07
William Howard Taft (R) 1909 J. Sherman (R).......'09	P. Knox....'09	F. MacVeagh '09	J. Dickinson..'09 H. Stimson..'11	G. Meyer....'09	G. Wickersham......'09
Woodrow Wilson (D)....1913 T. Marshall (D).......'13	W. Bryan...'13 R. Lansing..'15 B. Colby...'20	W. McAdoo..'13 C. Glass.....'18 D. Houston..'20	L. Garrison..'13 N. Baker......'16	J. Daniels....'13	J. McReynolds......'13 T. Gregory...'14 A. Palmer...'19
Warren G. Harding (R)..1921 C. Coolidge (R).......'21	C. Hughes..'21	A. Mellon....'21	J. Weeks.....'21	E. Denby....'21	H. Daugherty'21
Calvin Coolidge (R).....1923 C. Dawes (R).........'25	C. Hughes..'23 F. Kellogg..'25	A. Mellon....'23	J. Weeks.....'23 D. Davis.....'25	E. Denby....'23 C. Wilbur...'24	H. Daugherty'23 H. Stone.....'24 J. Sargent....'25
Herbert Hoover (R).....1929 C. Curtis (R).........'29	H. Stimson.'29	A. Mellon....'29 O. Mills.....'32	J. Good.....'29 P. Hurley....'29	C. Adams....'29	W. Mitchell..'29
Franklin D. Roosevelt (D) 1933 J. Garner (D)........'33 H. Wallace (D).......'41 H. Truman (D).......'45	C. Hull....'33 E. Stettinius'44	W. Woodin..'33 H. Morgenthau......'34	G. Dern.....'33 H. Woodring '36 H. Stimson..'40	C. Swanson..'33 C. Edison....'40 F. Knox.....'40 J. Forrestal...'44	H. Cummings'33 F. Murphy...'39 R. Jackson...'40 F. Biddle.....'41
Harry S. Truman (D)...1945 A. Barkley (D)........'49	J. Byrnes...'45 G. Marshall '47 D. Acheson.'49	F. Vinson....'45 J. Snyder....'46	R. Patterson.'45 K. Royall....'47	J. Forrestal..'45	T. Clark.....'45 J. McGrath..'49 J. McGranery'52
			Secretary of Defense **Established July 26, 1947** J. Forrestal........'47 L. Johnson........'49 G. Marshall.......'50 R. Lovett..........'51		
Dwight D. Eisenhower (R)..............1953 R. Nixon (R).........'53	J. Dulles...'53 C. Herter...'59	G. Humphrey'53 R. Anderson..'57	C. Wilson.....'53 N. McElroy.....'57		H. Brownell..'53 W. Rogers...'57
John F. Kennedy (D)....1961 L. Johnson (D).......'61	D. Rusk....'61	D. Dillon....'61	R. McNamara.....'61		R. Kennedy..'61
Lyndon B. Johnson (D)..1963	D. Rusk...'63	D. Dillon....'63	R. McNamara.....'63		R. Kennedy..'63

Party affiliations: D, Democratic; R, Republican.

Postmaster General	Secretary of the Interior	Secretary of Agriculture	Secretary of Commerce and Labor		Secretary of Health, Education, and Welfare
T. James......'81	S. Kirkwood...'81				
T. Howe......'81 W. Gresham...'83 F. Hatton.....'84	H. Teller......'81	**Cabinet status since Feb. 9, 1889**			
W. Vilas......'85 D. Dickinson..'88	L. Lamar......'85 W. Vilas......'88	N. Colman....'89			
J. Wanamaker.'89	J. Noble......'89	J. Rusk........'89			
W. Bissell.....'93 W. Wilson....'95	H. Smith......'93 D. Francis....'96	J. Morton......'93			
J. Gary.......'97 C. Smith......'98	C. Bliss.......'97 E. Hitchcock..'99	J. Wilson.....'97	**Established Feb. 14, 1903**		
C. Smith......'01 H. Payne......'02 R. Wynne.....'04 G. Cortelyou..'05 G. Meyer.....'07	E. Hitchcock...'01 J. Garfield....'07	J. Wilson.....'01	G. Cortelyou....'03 V. Metcalf......'04 O. Straus.......'07		
F. Hitchcock..'09	R. Ballinger...'09 W. Fisher.....'11	J. Wilson.....'09	C. Nagel........'09		
A. Burleson...'13	F. Lane.......'13 J. Payne......'20	D. Houston...'13 E. Meredith...'20	**Secretary of Commerce**	**Secretary of Labor**	
			Established March 4, 1913	**Established March 4, 1913**	
			W. Redfield...'13 J. Alexander...'19	Wm. Wilson...'13	
W. Hays......'21 H. Work......'22 H. New.......'23	A. Fall.......'21 H. Work......'23	H. C. Wallace.'21	H. Hoover.....'21	J. Davis......'21	
H. New.......'23	H. Work......'23 R. West......'28	H. C. Wallace.'23 H. Gore......'24 W. Jardine....'25	H. Hoover.....'23 W. Whiting...'28	J. Davis......'23	
W. Brown.....'29	R. Wilbur.....'29	A. Hyde......'29	R. Lamont....'29 R. Chapin....'32	J. Davis......'29 W. Doak......'30	
J. Farley......'33 F. Walker.....'40	H. Ickes......'33	H. A. Wallace.'33 C. Wickard...'40	D. Roper.....'33 H. Hopkins...'39 J. Jones.......'40 H. A. Wallace.'45	F. Perkins.....'33	
R. Hannegan..'45 J. Donaldson..'47	H. Ickes......'45 J. Krug.......'46 O. Chapman..'49	C. Anderson...'45 C. Brannan...'48	H. A. Wallace..'45 W. A. Harriman'46 C. Sawyer.....'48	L. Schwellen- bach......'45 M. Tobin.....'48	
					Established April 1, 1953
A. Summer- field.......'53	D. McKay....'53 F. Seaton.....'56	E. Benson.....'53	S. Weeks......'53 L. Strauss.....'58 F. Mueller.....'59	M. Durkin....'53 J. Mitchell....'53	O. Hobby.......'53 M. Folsom......'55 A. Flemming....'58
J. Day.......'61 J. Gronouski...'63	S. Udall.......'61	O. Freeman...'61	L. Hodges.....'61	A. Goldberg...'61 W. Wirtz......'62	A. Ribicoff......'61 A. Celebrezze....'62
J. Gronouski...'63	S. Udall......'63	O. Freeman...'63	L. Hodges.....'63	W. Wirtz......'63	A. Celebrezze....'63

XXV

PARTY DISTRIBUTION IN CONGRESS

CONGRESS	YEAR	PRESIDENT	SENATE Majority Party	SENATE Minority Party	Others	HOUSE Majority Party	HOUSE Minority Party	Others
1	1789–91	F (Washington)	Ad 17	Op 9	0	Ad 38	Op 26	0
2	1791–93	F (Washington)	F 16	R^J 13	0	F 37	R^J 33	0
3	1793–95	F (Washington)	F 17	R^J 13	0	R^J 57	F 48	0
4	1795–97	F (Washington)	F 19	R^J 13	0	F 54	R^J 52	0
5	1797–99	F (J. Adams)	F 20	R^J 12	0	F 58	R^J 48	0
6	1799–01	F (J. Adams)	F 19	R^J 13	0	F 64	R^J 42	0
7	1801–03	R^J (Jefferson)	R^J 18	F 14	0	R^J 69	F 36	0
8	1803–05	R^J (Jefferson)	R^J 25	F 9	0	R^J 102	F 39	0
9	1805–07	R^J (Jefferson)	R^J 27	F 7	0	R^J 116	F 25	0
10	1807–09	R^J (Jefferson)	R^J 28	F 6	0	R^J 118	F 24	0
11	1809–11	R^J (Madison)	R^J 28	F 6	0	R^J 94	F 48	0
12	1811–13	R^J (Madison)	R^J 30	F 6	0	R^J 108	F 36	0
13	1813–15	R^J (Madison)	R^J 27	F 9	0	R^J 112	F 68	0
14	1815–17	R^J (Madison)	R^J 25	F 11	0	R^J 117	F 65	0
15	1817–19	R^J (Monroe)	R^J 34	F 10	0	R^J 141	F 42	0
16	1819–21	R^J (Monroe)	R^J 35	F 7	0	R^J 156	F 27	0
17	1821–23	R^J (Monroe)	R^J 44	F 4	0	R^J 158	F 25	0
18	1823–25	R^J (Monroe)	R^J 44	F 4	0	R^J 187	F 26	0
19	1825–27	C (J. Q. Adams)	Ad 26	J 20	0	Ad 105	J 97	0
20	1827–29	C (J. Q. Adams)	J 28	Ad 20	0	J 119	Ad 94	0
21	1829–31	D (Jackson)	D 26	NR 22	0	D 139	NR 74	0
22	1831–33	D (Jackson)	D 25	NR 21	2	D 141	NR 58	14
23	1833–35	D (Jackson)	D 20	NR 20	8	D 147	AM 53	60
24	1835–37	D (Jackson)	D 27	W 25	0	D 145	W 98	0
25	1837–39	D (Van Buren)	D 30	W 18	4	D 108	W 107	24
26	1839–41	D (Van Buren)	D 28	W 22	0	D 124	W 118	0
27	1841–43	W (W. Harrison)						
		W (Tyler)	W 28	D 22	2	W 133	D 102	6
28	1843–45	W (Tyler)	W 28	D 25	1	D 142	W 79	1
29	1845–47	D (Polk)	D 31	W 25	0	D 143	W 77	6
30	1847–49	D (Polk)	D 36	W 21	1	W 115	D 108	4
31	1849–51	W (Taylor)						
		W (Fillmore)	D 35	W 25	2	D 112	W 109	9
32	1851–53	W (Fillmore)	D 35	W 24	3	D 140	W 88	5
33	1853–55	D (Pierce)	D 38	W 22	2	D 159	W 71	4
34	1855–57	D (Pierce)	D 40	R 15	5	R 108	D 83	43
35	1857–59	D (Buchanan)	D 36	R 20	8	D 118	R 92	26
36	1859–61	D (Buchanan)	D 36	R 26	4	R 114	D 92	31
37	1861–63	R (Lincoln)	R 31	D 10	8	R 105	D 43	30
38	1863–65	R (Lincoln)	R 36	D 9	5	R 102	D 75	9
39	1865–67	R (Lincoln)						
		R (Johnson)	U 42	D 10	0	U 149	D 42	0
40	1867–69	R (Johnson)	R 42	D 11	0	R 143	D 49	0
41	1869–71	R (Grant)	R 56	D 11	0	R 149	D 63	0
42	1871–73	R (Grant)	R 52	D 17	5	D 134	R 104	5
43	1873–75	R (Grant)	R 49	D 19	5	R 194	D 92	14
44	1875–77	R (Grant)	R 45	D 29	2	D 169	R 109	14
45	1877–79	R (Hayes)	R 39	D 36	1	D 153	R 140	0
46	1879–81	R (Hayes)	D 42	R 33	1	D 149	R 130	14
47	1881–83	R (Garfield)						
		R (Arthur)	R 37	D 37	1	R 147	D 135	11
48	1883–85	R (Arthur)	R 38	D 36	2	D 197	R 118	10
49	1885–87	D (Cleveland)	R 43	D 34	0	D 183	R 140	2
50	1887–89	D (Cleveland)	R 39	D 37	0	D 169	R 152	4
51	1889–91	R (B. Harrison)	R 39	D 37	0	R 166	D 159	0
52	1891–93	R (B. Harrison)	R 47	D 39	2	D 235	R 88	9
53	1893–95	D (Cleveland)	D 44	R 38	3	D 218	R 127	11
54	1895–97	D (Cleveland)	R 43	D 39	6	R 244	D 105	7
55	1897–99	R (McKinley)	R 47	D 34	7	R 204	D 113	40

xxvi

| CONGRESS | YEAR | PRESIDENT | SENATE ||| HOUSE |||
			Majority Party	Minority Party	Others	Majority Party	Minority Party	Others
56	1899–01	R (McKinley)	R 53	D 26	8	R 185	D 163	9
57	1901–03	R (McKinley)						
		R (T. Roosevelt)	R 55	D 31	4	R 197	D 151	9
58	1903–05	R (T. Roosevelt)	R 57	D 33	0	R 208	D 178	0
59	1905–07	R (T. Roosevelt)	R 57	D 33	0	R 250	D 136	0
60	1907–09	R (T. Roosevelt)	R 61	D 31	0	R 222	D 164	0
61	1909–11	R (Taft)	R 61	D 32	0	R 219	D 172	0
62	1911–13	R (Taft)	R 51	D 41	0	D 228	R 161	1
63	1913–15	D (Wilson)	D 51	R 44	1	D 291	R 127	17
64	1915–17	D (Wilson)	D 56	R 40	0	D 230	R 196	9
65	1917–19	D (Wilson)	D 53	R 42	0	D 216	R 210	6
66	1919–21	D (Wilson)	R 49	D 47	0	R 240	D 190	3
67	1921–23	R (Harding)	R 59	D 37	0	R 303	D 131	1
68	1923–25	R (Coolidge)	R 51	D 43	2	R 225	D 205	5
69	1925–27	R (Coolidge)	R 56	D 39	1	R 247	D 183	4
70	1927–29	R (Coolidge)	R 49	D 46	1	R 237	D 195	3
71	1929–31	R (Hoover)	R 56	D 39	1	R 267	D 167	1
72	1931–33	R (Hoover)	R 48	D 47	1	D 220	R 214	1
73	1933–35	D (F. Roosevelt)	D 60	R 35	1	D 310	R 117	5
74	1935–37	D (F. Roosevelt)	D 69	R 25	2	D 319	R 103	10
75	1937–39	D (F. Roosevelt)	D 76	R 16	4	D 331	R 89	13
76	1939–41	D (F. Roosevelt)	D 69	R 23	4	D 261	R 164	4
77	1941–43	D (F. Roosevelt)	D 66	R 28	2	D 268	R 162	5
78	1943–45	D (F. Roosevelt)	D 58	R 37	1	D 218	R 208	4
79	1945–47	D (F. Roosevelt)						
		D (Truman)	D 56	R 38	1	D 242	R 190	2
80	1947–49	D (Truman)	R 51	D 45	0	R 246	D 188	1
81	1949–51	D (Truman)	D 54	R 42	0	D 263	R 171	1
82	1951–53	D (Truman)	D 49	R 47	0	D 235	R 199	1
83	1953–55	R (Eisenhower)	R 48	D 47	1	R 221	D 212	1
84	1955–57	R (Eisenhower)	D 48	R 47	1	D 232	R 203	0
85	1957–59	R (Eisenhower)	D 49	R 47	0	D 232	R 199	0
86	1959–61	R (Eisenhower)	D 62	R 34	0	D 280	R 152	0
87	1961–63	D (Kennedy)	D 65	R 35	0	D 261	R 176	0
88	1963–65	D (Kennedy)						
		D (Johnson)	D 68	R 32	0	D 258	R 177	0

Ad: Administration; AM: Anti-Masonic; C: Coalition; D: Democratic; F: Federalist; J: Jacksonian; NR: National Republican; Op: Opposition; R: Republican; R^J: Republican (Jeffersonian); U: Unionist; W: Whig.

xxvii

JUSTICES OF THE UNITED STATES SUPREME COURT

NAME *Chief Justices in Capital Letters*	Terms of Service[1]	Appointed By	NAME *Chief Justices in Capital Letters*	Terms of Service[1]	Appointed By
JOHN JAY, N.Y.	1789–1795	Washington	Lucius Q. C. Lamar, Miss.	1888–1893	Cleveland
James Wilson, Pa.	1789–1798	Washington	MELVILLE W. FULLER, Ill.	1888–1910	Cleveland
John Rutledge, S.C.	1790–1791	Washington	David J. Brewer, Kan.	1890–1910	B. Harrison
William Cushing, Mass.	1790–1810	Washington	Henry B. Brown, Mich.	1891–1906	B. Harrison
John Blair, Va.	1790–1796	Washington	George Shiras, Jr., Pa.	1892–1903	B. Harrison
James Iredell, N.C.	1790–1799	Washington	Howell E. Jackson, Tenn.	1893–1895	B. Harrison
Thomas Johnson, Md.	1792–1793	Washington	Edward D. White, La.	1894–1910	Cleveland
William Paterson, N.J.	1793–1806	Washington	Rufus W. Peckham, N.Y.	1896–1909	Cleveland
JOHN RUTLEDGE, S.C.[2]	1795	Washington	Joseph McKenna, Cal.	1898–1925	McKinley
Samuel Chase, Md.	1796–1811	Washington	Oliver W. Holmes, Mass.	1902–1932	T. Roosevelt
OLIVER ELLSWORTH, Conn.	1796–1800	Washington	William R. Day, Ohio	1903–1922	T. Roosevelt
Bushrod Washington, Va.	1799–1829	J. Adams	William H. Moody, Mass.	1906–1910	T. Roosevelt
Alfred Moore, N.C.	1800–1804	J. Adams	Horace H. Lurton, Tenn.	1910–1914	Taft
JOHN MARSHALL, Va.	1801–1835	J. Adams	Charles E. Hughes, N.Y.	1910–1916	Taft
William Johnson, S.C.	1804–1834	Jefferson	Willis Van Devanter, Wy.	1911–1937	Taft
Brockholst Livingston, N.Y.	1807–1823	Jefferson	Joseph R. Lamar, Ga.	1911–1916	Taft
Thomas Todd, Ky.	1807–1826	Jefferson	EDWARD D. WHITE, La.	1910–1921	Taft
Gabriel Duvall, Md.	1811–1835	Madison	Mahlon Pitney, N.J.	1912–1922	Taft
Joseph Story, Mass.	1812–1845	Madison	James C. McReynolds, Tenn.	1914–1941	Wilson
Smith Thompson, N.Y.	1823–1843	Monroe	Louis D. Brandeis, Mass.	1916–1939	Wilson
Robert Trimble, Ky.	1826–1828	J. Q. Adams	John H. Clarke, Ohio	1916–1922	Wilson
John McLean, Ohio	1830–1861	Jackson	WILLIAM H. TAFT, Conn.	1921–1930	Harding
Henry Baldwin, Pa.	1830–1844	Jackson	George Sutherland, Utah	1922–1938	Harding
James M. Wayne, Ga.	1835–1867	Jackson	Pierce Butler, Minn.	1923–1939	Harding
ROGER B. TANEY, Md.	1836–1864	Jackson	Edward T. Sanford, Tenn.	1923–1930	Harding
Philip P. Barbour, Va.	1836–1841	Jackson	Harlan F. Stone, N.Y.	1925–1941	Coolidge
John Catron, Tenn.	1837–1865	Van Buren	CHARLES E. HUGHES, N.Y.	1930–1941	Hoover
John McKinley, Ala.	1838–1852	Van Buren	Owen J. Roberts, Penn.	1930–1945	Hoover
Peter V. Daniel, Va.	1842–1860	Van Buren	Benjamin N. Cardozo, N.Y.	1932–1938	Hoover
Samuel Nelson, N.Y.	1845–1872	Tyler	Hugo L. Black, Ala.	1937–	F. Roosevelt
Levi Woodbury, N.H.	1845–1851	Polk	Stanley F. Reed, Ky.	1938–1957	F. Roosevelt
Robert C. Grier, Pa.	1846–1870	Polk	Felix Frankfurter, Mass.	1939–1962	F. Roosevelt
Benjamin R. Curtis, Mass.	1851–1857	Fillmore	William O. Douglas, Conn.	1939–	F. Roosevelt
John A. Campbell, Ala.	1853–1861	Pierce	Frank Murphy, Mich.	1940–1949	F. Roosevelt
Nathan Clifford, Me.	1858–1881	Buchanan	HARLAN F. STONE, N.Y.	1941–1946	F. Roosevelt
Noah H. Swayne, Ohio	1862–1881	Lincoln	James F. Byrnes, S.C.	1941–1942	F. Roosevelt
Samuel F. Miller, Iowa	1862–1890	Lincoln	Robert H. Jackson, N.Y.	1941–1954	F. Roosevelt
David Davis, Ill.	1862–1877	Lincoln	Wiley B. Rutledge, Iowa	1943–1949	F. Roosevelt
Stephen J. Field, Cal.	1863–1897	Lincoln	Harold H. Burton, Ohio	1945–1958	Truman
SALMON P. CHASE, Ohio	1864–1873	Lincoln	FREDERICK M. VINSON, Ky.	1946–1953	Truman
William Strong, Pa.	1870–1880	Grant	Tom C. Clark, Texas	1949–	Truman
Joseph P. Bradley, N.J.	1870–1892	Grant	Sherman Minton, Ind.	1949–1956	Truman
Ward Hunt, N.Y.	1873–1882	Grant	EARL WARREN, Cal.	1953–	Eisenhower
MORRISON R. WAITE, Ohio	1874–1888	Grant	John Marshall Harlan, N.Y.	1955–	Eisenhower
John M. Harlan, Ky.	1877–1911	Hayes	William J. Brennan, Jr., N.J.	1956–	Eisenhower
William B. Woods, Ga.	1881–1887	Hayes	Charles E. Whittaker, Mo.	1957–1962	Eisenhower
Stanley Matthews, Ohio	1881–1889	Garfield	Potter Stewart, Ohio	1958–	Eisenhower
Horace Gray, Mass.	1882–1902	Arthur	Byron R. White, Colo.	1962–	Kennedy
Samuel Blatchford, N.Y.	1882–1893	Arthur	Arthur J. Goldberg, Ill.	1962–	Kennedy

[1] The date on which the justice took his judicial oath is here used as the date of the beginning of his service, for until that oath is taken he is not vested with the prerogatives of his office. Justices, however, receive their commissions ("letters patent") before taking their oath—in some instances, in the preceding year.

[2] Acting Chief Justice; Senate refused to confirm appointment.

SOVEREIGNS OF ENGLAND AND GREAT BRITAIN, 1485-1820:
Some Historical Notes

Tudor Dynasty: 1485-1603

Henry VII: 1485-1509
The dynastic Wars of the Roses in England ended with the accession of Henry VII, first of the Tudor line that established strong central government in England.

Henry VIII: 1509-1547
In 1534 Henry VIII broke with the Roman Catholic Church and became head of the new Church of England (Anglican Church). The succeeding three English sovereigns were issue of three of his six marriages.

Edward VI: 1547-1553
Protestantism in England accelerated during the brief reign of the boy-king Edward.

Mary I: 1553-1558
An official return to Catholicism followed Catholic Mary's marriage to Philip II of Spain in 1554. Persecution of Protestants earned her the name of "Bloody Mary."

Elizabeth I: 1558-1603
The "Elizabethan Age" was marked by the reëstablishment of Protestant Anglicanism, the repulse of the Spanish invading fleet called the "Spanish Armada" (1588), the great expansion of trade, and the renaissance of English literature.

Stuart Dynasty: 1603-1649

James I: 1603-1625
James Stuart, a descendant of Henry VII, was king of Scotland when the English crown succeeded to him upon the death of Elizabeth; he and his successors were thus rulers of both England and Scotland. Under him Englishmen planted their first permanent colonies in America—at Jamestown and Plymouth.

Charles I: 1625-1649
Both James I and Charles I believed in the "divine right of kings" to rule absolutely without interference and thus were at odds with Parliament. During the reign of Charles I, his adviser William Laud, Archbishop of Canterbury, waged a campaign of persecution against Puritans, thus forcing many of these religionists to flee to America, particularly to New England (thus the "Great Migration" of 1630-1640). In 1642 the English Civil Wars commenced between the Royalists (supporters of Charles I) and the Puritans (representing Parliament) and ended with the capture and beheading of Charles in 1649. The pretender Charles II (son of Charles I) went into exile.

Puritan Commonwealth: 1649-1660

From 1649 to 1660 England was ruled under a republican form of government comprising several Puritan factions. (The passage of the first Navigation Act—of 1651—in part reflected this Puritan-mercantile dominance.) Oliver Cromwell was head of state until his death in 1658, when he was succeeded by his son Richard Cromwell, who in turn resigned in 1659, making way for the restoration of the Stuarts.

Stuart Dynasty (Restoration): 1660-1714

Charles II: 1660-1685
With the "restoration" of the Stuart King Charles II, the Anglican Church was reëstablished in England; and the new Parliament, overwhelmingly royalist, attempted to suppress both Nonconformists (Puritans, Quakers, and other dissenters from the Church of England) and Catholics.

James II: 1685-1688
James II, the Catholic brother of Charles II, tactlessly sought to secure freedom of worship for his fellow Catholics and thus united Parliament against him. To save England from "Catholic tyranny," a group of parliamentary leaders invited Protestant Holland's William of Orange to come to England and depose James II, who fled into exile. Upon completion of this "Bloodless" or "Glorious Revolution" of 1688-1689, William and his queen, Mary (Protestant daughter of James II), became joint sovereigns of England.

William III and Mary II: 1689-1702
Upon the accession of William and Mary, parliamentary supremacy was firmly established in England. The enactment of the English Bill of Rights (1689) and other legislation guaranteed certain fundamental rights to all Englishmen.

Anne: 1702-1714
Under Anne, younger daughter of James II, England and Scotland were formally united under the name of Great Britain (1707).

Hanover Dynasty: 1714-1901

George I: 1714-1727
The accession of George I, who came from the German state of Hanover, stimulated the growth of cabinet government and the power of the House of Commons in Great Britain, for the first two Georges—ineffectual kings who were only marginally interested in English affairs—left much of the affairs of state to the ministers chosen by Parliament.

George II: 1727-1760

George III: 1760-1820
After the conclusion of the Seven Years' War (the "Great War for Empire" or "French and Indian War") in 1763 and the elimination of the French from North America, Parliament and the king's ministers sought to tighten their control over the American colonies. The issue resulted in the Revolutionary War and the independence of the United States. In Britain itself the Industrial Revolution was in full swing with the introduction of steam power in manufacturing in the 1780's.

PRESIDENTIAL ELECTIONS*: ELECTORAL AND POPULAR VOTE

Presidential Candidate[1]	Electoral Vote	Popular Vote
1789[2]: 11 States		
GEORGE WASHINGTON	69	
John Adams	34	
John Jay	9	
R. H. Harrison	6	
John Rutledge	6	
John Hancock	4	
George Clinton	3	
Samuel Huntington	2	
John Milton	2	
James Armstrong	1	
Benjamin Lincoln	1	
Edward Telfair	1	
(Not voted)	12	
1792[2]: 15 States		
GEORGE WASHINGTON *Federalist*	132	
John Adams *Federalist*	77	
George Clinton *Republican*	50	
Thomas Jefferson	4	
Aaron Burr	1	
1796[2]: 16 States		
JOHN ADAMS *Federalist*	71	
Thomas Jefferson *Republican*	68	
Thomas Pinckney *Federalist*	59	
Aaron Burr *Anti-Federalist*	30	
Samuel Adams *Republican*	15	
Oliver Ellsworth *Federalist*	11	
George Clinton *Republican*	7	
John Jay *Independent-Federalist*	5	
James Iredell *Federalist*	3	
George Washington *Federalist*	2	
John Henry *Independent*	2	
S. Johnston *Independent-Federalist*	2	
C. C. Pinckney *Independent-Federalist*	1	
1800[2]: 16 States		
THOMAS JEFFERSON *Republican*	73	
Aaron Burr *Republican*	73	
John Adams *Federalist*	65	

Presidential Candidate[1]	Electoral Vote	Popular Vote
C. C. Pinckney *Federalist*	64	
John Jay *Federalist*	1	
1804: 17 States		
THOMAS JEFFERSON *Republican*	162	
C. C. Pinckney *Federalist*	14	
1808: 17 States		
JAMES MADISON *Republican*	122	
C. C. Pinckney *Federalist*	47	
George Clinton *Independent-Republican*	6	
(Not voted)	1	
1812: 18 States		
JAMES MADISON *Republican*	128	
DeWitt Clinton *Fusion*	89	
(Not voted)	1	
1816: 19 States		
JAMES MONROE *Republican*	183	
Rufus King *Federalist*	34	
(Not voted)	4	
1820: 24 States		
JAMES MONROE *Republican*	231	
John Quincy Adams *Independent-Republican*	1	
(Not voted)	3	
1824: 24 States		
JOHN QUINCY ADAMS	84[3]	108,740
Andrew Jackson	99[3]	153,544
Henry Clay	37	47,136
W. H. Crawford	41	46,618
1828: 24 States		
ANDREW JACKSON *Democratic*	178	647,286
John Quincy Adams *National Republican*	83	508,064
1832: 24 States		
ANDREW JACKSON *Democratic*	219	687,502

*Source: U.S. Bureau of the Census, *Historical Statistics of the United States, Colonial Times to 1957* (Washington, D.C., 1960).

[1] Excludes unpledged tickets and minor candidates polling under 10,000 votes; various party labels may have been used by a candidate in different states; the more important of these are listed.

[2] Prior to the election of 1804, each elector voted for two candidates for President; the one receiving the highest number of votes, if a majority, was declared elected President, the next highest, Vice-President. This provision was modified by adoption of the Twelfth Amendment which was proposed by the Eighth Congress, December 12, 1803, and declared ratified by the legislatures of three fourths of the states in a proclamation of the Secretary of State, September 25, 1804.

[3] No candidate having a majority in the electoral college, the election was decided in the House of Representatives.

Presidential Candidate[1]	Electoral Vote	Popular Vote
Henry Clay	49	530,189
National Republican		
William Wirt	7	
Anti-Masonic		
John Floyd	11	
Nullifiers		
(Not voted)	2	
1836: 26 States		
MARTIN VAN BUREN		765,483
Democratic		
William Henry Harrison	73	
Whig		
Hugh L. White	26	739,795[4]
Whig		
Daniel Webster	14	
Whig		
W. P. Mangum	11	
Anti-Jackson		
1840: 26 States		
WILLIAM HENRY HARRISON	234	1,274,624
Whig		
Martin Van Buren	60	1,127,781
Democratic		
1844: 26 States		
JAMES K. POLK	170	1,338,464
Democratic		
Henry Clay	105	1,300,097
Whig		
James G. Birney		62,300
Liberty		
1848: 30 States		
ZACHARY TAYLOR	163	1,360,967
Whig		
Lewis Cass	127	1,222,342
Democratic		
Martin Van Buren		291,263
Free Soil		
1852: 31 States		
FRANKLIN PIERCE	254	1,601,117
Democratic		
Winfield Scott	42	1,385,453
Whig		
John P. Hale		155,825
Free Soil		
1856: 31 States		
JAMES BUCHANAN	174	1,832,955
Democratic		
John C. Frémont	114	1,339,932
Republican		
Millard Fillmore	8	871,731
American		
1860: 33 States		
ABRAHAM LINCOLN	180	1,865,593
Republican		
John C. Breckinridge	72	848,356
Democratic (South)		
Stephen A. Douglas	12	1,382,713
Democratic		
John Bell	39	592,906
Constitutional Union		

Presidential Candidate[1]	Electoral Vote	Popular Vote
1864: 36 States		
ABRAHAM LINCOLN	212	2,206,938
Republican		
George B. McClellan	21	1,803,787
Democratic		
(Not voted)	81	
1868: 37 States		
ULYSSES S. GRANT	214	3,013,421
Republican		
Horatio Seymour	80	2,706,829
Democratic		
(Not voted)	23	
1872: 37 States		
ULYSSES S. GRANT	286	3,596,745
Republican		
Horace Greeley	[5]	2,843,446
Democratic		
Charles O'Conor		29,489
Straight Democratic		
Thomas A. Hendricks	42	
Independent-Democratic		
B. Gratz Brown	18	
Democratic		
Charles J. Jenkins	2	
Democratic		
David Davis	1	
Democratic		
(Not voted)	17	
1876: 38 States		
RUTHERFORD B. HAYES	185	4,036,572
Republican		
Samuel J. Tilden	184	4,284,020
Democratic		
Peter Cooper		81,737
Greenback		
1880: 38 States		
JAMES A. GARFIELD	214	4,453,295
Republican		
Winfield S. Hancock	155	4,414,082
Democratic		
James B. Weaver		308,578
Greenback-Labor		
Neal Dow		10,305
Prohibition		
1884: 38 States		
GROVER CLEVELAND	219	4,879,507
Democratic		
James G. Blaine	182	4,850,293
Republican		
Benjamin F. Butler		175,370
Greenback-Labor		
John P. St. John		150,369
Prohibition		
1888: 38 States		
BENJAMIN HARRISON	233	5,447,129
Republican		
Grover Cleveland	168	5,537,857
Democratic		
Clinton B. Fisk		249,506
Prohibition		
Anson J. Streeter		146,935
Union Labor		

[4] Whig tickets were pledged to various candidates in various states.

[5] Greeley died shortly after the election and presidential electors supporting him cast their votes as indicated, including three for Greeley, which were not counted.

xxxi

PRESIDENTIAL ELECTIONS: ELECTORAL AND POPULAR VOTE

Presidential Candidate[1]	Electoral Vote	Popular Vote
1892: 44 States		
GROVER CLEVELAND *Democratic*	277	5,555,426
Benjamin Harrison *Republican*	145	5,182,690
James B. Weaver *People's*	22	1,029,846
John Bidwell *Prohibition*		264,133
Simon Wing *Socialist Labor*		21,164
1896: 45 States		
WILLIAM MCKINLEY *Republican*	271	7,102,246
William Jennings Bryan *Democratic*[6]	176	6,492,559
John M. Palmer *National Democratic*		133,148
Joshua Levering *Prohibition*		132,007
Charles M. Matchett *Socialist Labor*		36,274
Charles E. Bentley *Nationalist*		13,969
1900: 45 States		
WILLIAM MCKINLEY *Republican*	292	7,218,491
William Jennings Bryan *Democratic*[6]	155	6,356,734
John C. Wooley *Prohibition*		208,914
Eugene V. Debs *Socialist*		87,814
Wharton Barker *People's*		50,373
Joseph F. Malloney *Socialist Labor*		39,739
1904: 45 States		
THEODORE ROOSEVELT *Republican*	336	7,628,461
Alton B. Parker *Democratic*	140	5,084,223
Eugene V. Debs *Socialist*		402,283
Silas C. Swallow *Prohibition*		258,536
Thomas E. Watson *People's*		117,183
Charles H. Corregan *Socialist Labor*		31,249
1908: 46 States		
WILLIAM HOWARD TAFT *Republican*	321	7,675,320
William Jennings Bryan *Democratic*	162	6,412,294
Eugene V. Debs *Socialist*		420,793
Eugene W. Chafin *Prohibition*		253,840
Thomas L. Hisgen *Independence*		82,872
Thomas E. Watson *People's*		29,100

Presidential Candidate[1]	Electoral Vote	Popular Vote
August Gillhaus *Socialist Labor*		14,021
1912: 48 States		
WOODROW WILSON *Democratic*	435	6,296,547
Theodore Roosevelt *Progressive*	88	4,118,571
William Howard Taft *Republican*	8	3,486,720
Eugene V. Debs *Socialist*		900,672
Eugene W. Chafin *Prohibition*		206,275
Arthur E. Reimer *Socialist Labor*		28,750
1916: 48 States		
WOODROW WILSON *Democratic*	277	9,127,695
Charles Evans Hughes *Republican*	254	8,533,507
A. L. Benson *Socialist*		585,113
J. Frank Hanly *Prohibition*		220,506
Arthur E. Reimer *Socialist Labor*		13,403
1920: 48 States		
WARREN G. HARDING *Republican*	404	16,143,407
James M. Cox *Democratic*	127	9,130,328
Eugene V. Debs *Socialist*		919,799
P. P. Christensen *Farmer-Labor*		265,411
Aaron S. Watkins *Prohibition*		189,408
James E. Ferguson *American*		48,000
W. W. Cox *Socialist Labor*		31,715
1924: 48 States		
CALVIN COOLIDGE *Republican*	382	15,718,211
John W. Davis *Democratic*	136	8,385,283
Robert M. La Follette *Progressive*	13	4,831,289
Herman P. Faris *Prohibition*		57,520
Frank T. Johns *Socialist Labor*		36,428
William Z. Foster *Workers*		36,386
Gilbert O. Nations *American*		23,967
1928: 48 States		
HERBERT HOOVER *Republican*	444	21,391,993
Alfred E. Smith *Democratic*	87	15,016,196

[6]Includes a variety of joint tickets with People's party electors committed to Bryan.

Presidential Candidate[1]	Electoral Vote	Popular Vote
Norman Thomas		267,835
Socialist		
Verne L. Reynolds		21,603
Socialist Labor		
William Z. Foster		21,181
Workers		
William F. Varney		20,106
Prohibition		
1932: 48 States		
FRANKLIN D. ROOSEVELT	472	22,809,638
Democratic		
Herbert Hoover	59	15,758,901
Republican		
Norman Thomas		881,951
Socialist		
William Z. Foster		102,785
Communist		
William D. Upshaw		81,869
Prohibition		
William H. Harvey		53,425
Liberty		
Verne L. Reynolds		33,276
Socialist Labor		
1936: 48 States		
FRANKLIN D. ROOSEVELT	523	27,752,869
Democratic		
Alfred M. Landon	8	16,674,665
Republican		
William Lemke		882,479
Union		
Norman Thomas		187,720
Socialist		
Earl Browder		80,159
Communist		
D. Leigh Colvin		37,847
Prohibition		
John W. Aiken		12,777
Socialist Labor		
1940: 48 States		
FRANKLIN D. ROOSEVELT	449	27,307,819
Democratic		
Wendell L. Willkie	82	22,321,018
Republican		
Norman Thomas		99,557
Socialist		
Roger Q. Babson		57,812
Prohibition		
Earl Browder		46,251
Communist		
John W. Aiken		14,892
Socialist Labor		
1944: 48 States		
FRANKLIN D. ROOSEVELT	432	25,606,585
Democratic		
Thomas E. Dewey	99	22,014,745
Republican		
Norman Thomas		80,518
Socialist		
Claude A. Watson		74,758
Prohibition		
Edward A. Teichert		45,336
Socialist Labor		

Presidential Candidate[1]	Electoral Vote	Popular Vote
1948: 48 States		
HARRY S. TRUMAN	303	24,105,812
Democratic		
Thomas E. Dewey	189	21,970,065
Republican		
J. Strom Thurmond	39	1,169,063
States' Rights		
Henry Wallace		1,157,172
Progressive		
Norman Thomas		139,414
Socialist		
Claude A. Watson		103,224
Prohibition		
Edward A. Teichert		29,244
Socialist Labor		
Farrell Dobbs		13,613
Socialist Workers		
1952: 48 States		
DWIGHT D. EISENHOWER	442	33,936,234
Republican		
Adlai E. Stevenson	89	27,314,992
Democratic		
Vincent Hallinan		140,023
Progressive		
Stuart Hamblen		72,949
Prohibition		
Eric Haas		30,267
Socialist Labor		
Darlington Hoopes		20,203
Socialist		
Douglas A. MacArthur		17,205
Constitution		
Farrell Dobbs		10,312
Socialist Workers		
1956: 48 States		
DWIGHT D. EISENHOWER	457	35,590,472
Republican		
Adlai E. Stevenson	73[7]	26,022,752
Democratic		
T. Coleman Andrews		107,929
States' Rights		
Eric Haas		44,300
Socialist Labor		
Enoch A. Holtwick		41,937
Prohibition		
1960: 50 States		
JOHN F. KENNEDY	303	34,227,096
Democratic; Liberal		
Richard M. Nixon	219	34,108,546
Republican		
Harry F. Byrd	15[8]	116,248
Independent		
Orville Faubus		214,549
States' Rights		
Eric Haas		46,560
Socialist Labor		
Rutherford B. Decker		46,203
Prohibition		
Farrell Dobbs		39,541
Socialist Workers		
Charles L. Sullivan		19,570
Constitution		
J. Bracken Lee		12,912
Conservative		

[7]One Democratic elector voted for Walter Jones.
[8]Byrd's electoral count includes the votes of fourteen unpledged electors from Mississippi and Alabama, in addition to one vote pledged to Nixon but cast for Byrd by an Oklahoma elector.

POPULATION OF THE UNITED STATES: 1790–1870

Division and State	1790	1800	1810	1820	1830	1840	1850	1860	1870
UNITED STATES	3,929,214	5,308,483	7,239,881	9,638,453	12,866,020	17,069,453	23,191,876	31,443,321	39,818,449
NEW ENGLAND	1,009,408	1,233,011	1,471,973	1,660,071	1,954,717	2,234,822	2,728,116	3,135,283	3,487,924
Maine	96,540	151,719	228,705	298,335	399,455	501,793	583,169	628,279	626,915
New Hampshire	141,885	183,858	214,460	244,161	269,328	284,574	317,976	326,073	318,300
Vermont	85,425	154,465	217,895	235,981	280,652	291,948	314,120	315,098	330,551
Massachusetts	378,787	422,845	472,040	523,287	610,408	737,699	994,514	1,231,066	1,457,351
Rhode Island	68,825	69,122	76,931	83,059	97,199	108,830	147,545	174,620	217,353
Connecticut	237,946	251,002	261,942	275,248	297,675	309,978	370,792	460,147	537,454
MIDDLE ATLANTIC	958,632	1,402,565	2,014,702	2,669,845	3,587,664	4,526,260	5,898,735	7,458,985	8,810,806
New York	340,120	589,051	959,049	1,372,812	1,918,608	2,428,921	3,097,394	3,880,735	4,382,759
New Jersey	184,139	211,149	245,562	277,575	320,823	373,306	489,555	672,035	906,096
Pennsylvania	434,373	602,365	810,091	1,049,458	1,348,233	1,724,033	2,311,786	2,906,215	3,521,951
SOUTH ATLANTIC	1,851,806	2,286,494	2,674,891	3,061,063	3,645,752	3,925,299	4,679,090	5,364,703	5,853,610
Delaware	59,096	64,273	72,674	72,749	76,748	78,085	91,532	112,216	125,015
Maryland	319,728	341,548	380,546	407,350	447,040	470,019	583,034	687,049	780,894
Dist. of Columbia	....	8,144	15,471	23,336	30,261	33,745	51,687	75,080	131,700
Virginia	747,610	886,149	983,152	1,075,069	1,220,978	1,249,764	1,421,661	1,596,318	1,225,163
West Virginia	....	....	....	....	....	....	....	....	442,014
North Carolina	393,751	478,103	555,500	638,829	737,987	753,419	869,039	992,622	1,071,361
South Carolina	249,073	345,591	415,115	502,741	581,185	594,398	668,507	703,708	705,606
Georgia	82,548	162,686	252,433	340,989	516,823	691,392	906,185	1,057,286	1,184,109
Florida	....	....	....	....	34,730	54,477	87,445	140,424	187,748
EAST SOUTH CENTRAL	109,368	335,407	708,590	1,190,489	1,815,969	2,575,445	3,363,271	4,020,991	4,404,445
Kentucky	73,677	220,955	406,511	564,317	687,917	779,828	982,405	1,155,684	1,321,011
Tennessee	35,691	105,602	261,727	422,823	681,904	829,210	1,002,717	1,109,801	1,258,520
Alabama	....	1,250	9,046	127,901	309,527	590,756	771,623	964,201	996,992
Mississippi	....	7,600	31,306	75,448	136,621	375,651	606,526	791,305	827,922
WEST SOUTH CENTRAL	....	....	77,618	167,680	246,127	449,985	940,251	1,747,667	2,029,965
Arkansas	....	....	1,062	14,273	30,388	97,574	209,897	435,450	484,471
Louisiana	....	....	76,556	153,407	215,739	352,411	517,762	708,002	726,915
Oklahoma	....	....	....	....	....	....	....	....	....
Texas	....	....	....	....	....	....	212,592	604,215	818,579
EAST NORTH CENTRAL	....	51,006	272,324	792,719	1,470,018	2,924,728	4,523,260	6,926,884	9,124,517
Ohio	....	45,365	230,760	581,434	937,903	1,519,467	1,980,329	2,339,511	2,665,260
Indiana	....	5,641	24,520	147,178	343,031	685,866	988,416	1,350,428	1,680,637
Illinois	....	....	12,282	55,211	157,445	476,183	851,470	1,711,951	2,539,891
Michigan	....	....	4,762	8,896	31,639	212,267	397,654	749,113	1,184,059
Wisconsin	....	....	....	....	....	30,945	305,391	775,881	1,054,670
WEST NORTH CENTRAL	....	....	19,783	66,586	140,455	426,814	880,335	2,169,832	3,856,594
Minnesota	....	....	....	....	....	....	6,077	172,023	439,706
Iowa	....	....	....	....	....	43,112	192,214	674,913	1,194,020
Missouri	....	....	19,783	66,586	140,455	383,702	682,044	1,182,012	1,721,295
North Dakota	....	....	....	....	....	....	....	4,837	2,405
South Dakota	....	....	....	....	....	....	....	....	11,776
Nebraska	....	....	....	....	....	....	....	28,841	122,993
Kansas	....	....	....	....	....	....	....	107,206	364,399
MOUNTAIN	....	....	....	....	....	....	72,927	174,923	315,385
Montana	....	....	....	....	....	....	....	....	20,595
Idaho	....	....	....	....	....	....	....	....	14,999
Wyoming	....	....	....	....	....	....	....	....	9,118
Colorado	....	....	....	....	....	....	....	34,277	39,864
New Mexico	....	....	....	....	....	....	61,547	93,516	91,874
Arizona	....	....	....	....	....	....	....	....	9,658
Utah	....	....	....	....	....	....	11,380	40,273	86,786
Nevada	....	....	....	....	....	....	....	6,857	42,491
PACIFIC	....	....	....	....	....	....	105,871	444,053	675,125
Washington	....	....	....	....	....	....	1,201	11,594	23,955
Oregon	....	....	....	....	....	....	12,093	52,465	90,923
California	....	....	....	....	....	....	92,597	379,994	560,247
Alaska	....	....	....	....	....	....	....	....	....
Hawaii	....	....	....	....	....	....	....	....	....

POPULATION OF THE UNITED STATES: 1880–1960

Division and State	1880	1890	1900	1910	1920	1930	1940	1950	1960
UNITED STATES	50,189,209	62,979,766	76,212,168	92,228,622	106,021,568	123,202,660	132,165,129	151,325,798	179,323,175
NEW ENGLAND	4,010,529	4,700,749	5,592,017	6,552,681	7,400,909	8,166,341	8,437,290	9,314,453	10,509,367
Maine	648,936	661,086	694,466	742,371	768,014	797,423	847,226	913,774	969,265
New Hampshire	346,991	376,530	411,588	430,572	443,083	465,293	491,524	533,242	606,921
Vermont	332,286	332,422	343,641	355,956	352,428	359,611	359,231	377,747	389,881
Massachusetts	1,783,085	2,238,947	2,805,346	3,366,416	3,852,356	4,249,614	4,316,721	4,690,514	5,148,578
Rhode Island	276,531	345,506	428,556	542,610	604,397	687,497	713,346	791,896	859,488
Connecticut	622,700	746,258	908,420	1,114,756	1,380,631	1,606,903	1,709,242	2,007,280	2,535,234
MIDDLE ATLANTIC	10,496,878	12,706,220	15,454,678	19,315,892	22,261,144	26,260,750	27,539,487	30,163,533	34,168,452
New York	5,082,871	6,003,174	7,268,894	9,113,614	10,385,227	12,588,066	13,479,142	14,830,192	16,782,304
New Jersey	1,131,116	1,444,933	1,883,669	2,537,167	3,155,900	4,041,334	4,160,165	4,835,329	6,066,782
Pennsylvania	4,282,891	5,258,113	6,302,115	7,665,111	8,720,017	9,631,350	9,900,180	10,498,012	11,319,366
SOUTH ATLANTIC	7,597,197	8,857,922	10,443,480	12,194,895	13,990,272	15,793,589	17,823,151	21,182,335	25,971,732
Delaware	146,608	168,493	184,735	202,322	223,003	238,380	266,505	318,085	446,292
Maryland	934,943	1,042,390	1,188,044	1,295,346	1,449,661	1,631,526	1,821,244	2,343,001	3,100,689
Dist. of Columbia	177,624	230,392	278,718	331,069	437,571	486,869	663,091	802,178	763,956
Virginia	1,512,565	1,655,980	1,854,184	2,061,612	2,309,187	2,421,851	2,677,773	3,318,680	3,966,949
West Virginia	618,457	762,794	958,800	1,221,119	1,463,701	1,729,205	1,901,974	2,005,552	1,860,421
North Carolina	1,399,750	1,617,949	1,893,810	2,206,287	2,559,123	3,170,276	3,571,623	4,061,929	4,556,155
South Carolina	995,577	1,151,149	1,340,316	1,515,400	1,683,724	1,738,765	1,899,804	2,117,027	2,382,594
Georgia	1,542,180	1,837,353	2,216,331	2,609,121	2,895,832	2,908,506	3,123,723	3,444,578	3,943,116
Florida	269,493	391,422	528,542	752,619	968,470	1,468,211	1,897,414	2,771,305	4,951,560
EAST SOUTH CENTRAL	5,585,151	6,429,154	7,547,757	8,409,901	8,893,307	9,887,214	10,778,225	11,477,181	12,050,126
Kentucky	1,648,690	1,858,635	2,147,174	2,289,905	2,416,630	2,614,589	2,845,627	2,944,806	3,038,156
Tennessee	1,542,359	1,767,518	2,020,616	2,184,789	2,337,885	2,616,556	2,915,841	3,291,718	3,567,089
Alabama	1,262,505	1,513,401	1,828,697	2,138,093	2,348,174	2,646,248	2,832,961	3,061,743	3,266,740
Mississippi	1,131,597	1,289,600	1,551,270	1,797,114	1,790,618	2,009,821	2,183,796	2,178,914	2,178,141
WEST SOUTH CENTRAL	3,334,220	4,740,983	6,532,290	8,784,534	10,242,224	12,176,830	13,064,525	14,537,572	16,951,255
Arkansas	802,525	1,128,211	1,311,564	1,574,449	1,752,204	1,854,482	1,949,387	1,909,511	1,786,272
Louisiana	939,946	1,118,588	1,381,625	1,656,388	1,798,509	2,101,593	2,363,880	2,683,516	3,257,022
Oklahoma	....	258,657	790,391	1,657,155	2,028,283	2,396,040	2,336,434	2,233,351	2,328,284
Texas	1,591,749	2,235,527	3,048,710	3,896,542	4,663,228	5,824,715	6,414,824	7,711,194	9,579,677
EAST NORTH CENTRAL	11,206,668	13,478,305	15,985,581	18,250,621	21,475,543	25,297,185	26,626,342	30,399,368	36,225,024
Ohio	3,198,062	3,672,329	4,157,545	4,767,121	5,759,394	6,646,697	6,907,612	7,946,627	9,706,397
Indiana	1,978,301	2,192,404	2,516,462	2,700,876	2,930,390	3,238,503	3,427,796	3,934,224	4,662,498
Illinois	3,077,871	3,826,352	4,821,550	5,638,591	6,485,280	7,630,654	7,897,241	8,712,176	10,081,158
Michigan	1,636,937	2,093,890	2,420,982	2,810,173	3,668,412	4,842,325	5,256,106	6,371,766	7,823,194
Wisconsin	1,315,497	1,693,330	2,069,042	2,333,860	2,632,067	2,939,006	3,137,587	3,434,575	3,951,777
WEST NORTH CENTRAL	6,157,443	8,932,112	10,347,423	11,637,921	12,544,249	13,296,915	13,516,990	14,061,394	15,394,115
Minnesota	780,773	1,310,283	1,751,394	2,075,708	2,387,125	2,563,953	2,792,300	2,982,483	3,413,864
Iowa	1,624,615	1,912,297	2,231,853	2,224,771	2,404,021	2,470,939	2,538,268	2,621,073	2,757,537
Missouri	2,168,380	2,679,185	3,106,665	3,293,335	3,404,055	3,629,367	3,784,664	3,954,653	4,319,813
North Dakota	36,909	190,983	319,146	577,056	646,872	680,845	641,935	619,636	632,446
South Dakota	98,268	348,600	401,570	583,888	636,547	692,849	642,961	652,740	680,514
Nebraska	452,402	1,062,656	1,066,300	1,192,214	1,296,372	1,377,963	1,315,834	1,325,510	1,411,330
Kansas	996,096	1,428,108	1,470,495	1,690,949	1,769,257	1,880,999	1,801,028	1,905,299	2,178,611
MOUNTAIN	653,119	1,213,935	1,674,657	2,633,517	3,336,101	3,701,789	4,150,003	5,074,998	6,855,060
Montana	39,159	142,924	243,329	376,053	548,889	537,606	559,456	591,024	674,767
Idaho	32,610	88,548	161,772	325,594	431,866	445,032	524,873	588,637	667,191
Wyoming	20,789	62,555	92,531	145,965	194,402	225,565	250,742	290,529	330,066
Colorado	194,327	413,249	539,700	799,024	939,629	1,035,791	1,123,296	1,325,089	1,753,947
New Mexico	119,565	160,282	195,310	327,301	360,350	423,317	531,818	681,187	951,023
Arizona	40,440	88,243	122,931	204,354	334,162	435,573	499,261	749,587	1,302,161
Utah	143,963	210,779	276,749	373,351	449,396	507,847	550,310	688,862	890,627
Nevada	62,266	47,355	42,335	81,875	77,407	91,058	110,247	160,083	285,278
PACIFIC	1,148,004	1,920,386	2,634,285	4,448,660	5,877,819	8,622,047	10,229,116	15,114,964	21,198,044
Washington	75,116	357,232	518,103	1,141,990	1,356,621	1,563,396	1,736,191	2,378,963	2,853,214
Oregon	174,768	317,704	413,536	672,765	783,389	953,786	1,089,684	1,521,341	1,768,687
California	864,694	1,213,398	1,485,053	2,377,549	3,426,861	5,677,251	6,907,387	10,586,223	15,717,204
Alaska	33,426	32,052	63,592	64,356	55,036	59,278	72,524	128,643	226,167
Hawaii	....	....	154,001	192,000	255,912	368,336	423,330	499,794	632,772

XXXV

INDEX

Aachen, Treaty of (1748), 23
ABC Powers, 321
Abercromby, James, 24
Abolition party, 171
Abolitionism, 180-181, 230
Acheson, Dean, 429, 439
Act of Supremacy (1534), 9
Adams, Charles Francis, Jr., 258
Adams, Henry, 256, 264, 272
Adams, John, 34, 35, 49, 70, 73, 83, 84, 85, 86, as peace commissioner, 41; as President, 85-87, 88, 89, 92, 93; as Vice-President, 79, 83
Adams, John Quincy, 115, 132, 171: domestic program of, 125-126; and election of 1824, 124-125; and election of 1828, 127-128; and foreign affairs, 126-127, 134; as Secretary of State, 101, 104-106
Adams-Onís Treaty (1819), 104
Adams, Samuel, 32, 34, 72
Adams, Samuel Hopkins, 299
Adamson bill (1916), 309
Addams, Jane, 294
Administration of Justice Act (1774), 33
Adventists, 165
Age of Faith, 49, 53, 55
Age of Reason. See Enlightenment.
Agricultural Adjustment Acts: (1933) 376, 379, 381; (1938) 385
Agricultural Appropriations Act (1906), 299
Agricultural Marketing Act (1929), 361
Agriculture, 19, 71, 77, 160, 161, 179, 198, 238-239, 266-268, 453; during Great Depression, 371, 373, 376-377, 385; in 1920's, 354, 357, 366-367
Alabama, 208-209, 219
Alamo, Battle of the, 149
Alaska, 70, 105, 126, 141, 178, 304
Albania, 389
Albany, 13, 38
Albany Congress, 24
Aldrich, Nelson W., 248, 259, 266, 298, 299, 304
Aldrich-Vreeland Act (1908), 301
Alexander I of Russia, 98, 105, 127
Algeria, 415
Alien Acts (1798), 86-87
Allen, Ethan, 34, 115
Allen, William V., 271-272
Alliance for Progress, 451
Allison, William B., 298
Alsace-Lorraine, 328, 329
Amendments to U.S. Constitution: 1st, 445; 10th, 80; 13th, 212; 14th, 215-216, 240, 344; 15th, 219; 16th, 305; 18th, 361, 364-365, 376; 19th, 363; 21st, 365, 376; 22nd, 449
America First Committee, 391
American Association of University Professors, 335

American Council to Improve Our Neighborhoods (ACTION), 455
American Economic Association, 276
American Federation of Labor, 251-252, 302, 308, 327, 360, 367, 383, 384-385
American Fur Company, 144-145
American Plan, 367
American Protective Association, 230
American Railway Union, 251
American Revolution, 15, 16, 21, 26-45, 62, 71, 72; background of, 26-36, 66; effects of, 42-45, 65, 68; finance of, 37; military conduct of, 37-42; principles of, 64
American Rights, 28
American Sugar Refining Company, 247
American System, 180
American Tobacco Company, 247, 301
American Unitarian Association, 115, 164
Ames, Edward Scribner, 337
Amherst, Lord Jeffrey, 24
Anderson, Robert, 196
André, John, 40
Andros, Edmond, 16
Anglican Church: in America, 8, 12, 19, 48, 51, 53-54, 56, 57, 113; in England, 8, 49, 52
Anglo-Japanese Alliance, 359
Antietam, Battle of, 202-203, 212
Antifederalists, 72, 77-78, 83
Anti-Masonic party, 131-132, 139
"Appeal of the Independent Democrats," 189
Appomattox Court House, 207
Arabs, 431, 447
Architecture, 117-118, 171, 282, 284, 337-338, 401, 461-462
Argentina, 321, 387, 451
Arista, Mariano, 152
Armory Exhibition of Modern Art, 338, 343
Armour, Philip D., 247
Armstrong, John, 96
Arnold, Benedict, 34, 35, 40
Aroostook War, 138
Art (painting and sculpture), 170-171, 284, 331, 338-340, 401-402, 461
Arthur, Chester A., 261, 263-264
Articles of Confederation, 44, 45, 66-68, 70-72, 74, 77, 78
Ash-Can school, 338, 402
Ashley, William Henry, 145
Astor, John Jacob, 144-145
Atlantic Charter (1941), 410
Atomic Energy Commission, 442
Attlee, Clement, 424
Austerlitz, Battle of, 93
Austin, Moses, 142
Austin, Stephen F., 142, 148
Australia, 385, 414, 447
Austria, 23, 104, 358, 389

Austria-Hungary, 322, 326, 328, 329
Automation, 457
Automobiles, 358, 362-363, 365, 366-367, 384, 397, 404, 454

Bacon, Francis, 54
Bad Axe, Battle of, 142
Badoglio, Pietro, 415
Baker, Ray Stannard, 298
Baker v. Carr, 446
Ballinger, Richard A., 304
Baltimore and Ohio Railroad, 157, 241, 262
Bancroft, George, 162
Bank holiday, 375, 376
Bank of Augusta v. *Earle*, 134
Bank of England, 80
Bank of North America, 37
Bank of the United States: first, 80, 83; second, 99, 100-102, 127, 131-133, 135, 136, 138, 140, 158, 178, 211
Banking: during Great Depression, 372, 375, 376, 377, 379; under New Freedom, 306-307
Banking Act (1933), 379
Baptists, 14, 57, 114, 193, 336, 337
Barbary corsairs, 88
Barkley, Alben W., 435
Barlow, Joel, 65, 108, 115, 117
Barnett, Ross, 444
Bartram, John, 58
Baruch, Bernard, 327
Batista, Fulgencio, 448
Beard, Charles A., 341-344, 404
Bear Flag Revolt, 153
Beauregard, Pierre, 202
Becknell, William, 145
Beecher, Henry Ward, 280-281
Belgium, 322, 328, 358, 390, 422, 430, 464
Bell, John, 194
Bellamy, Edward, 247, 260, 277, 283, 294
Bellow, Saul, 460
Belmont, August, 249
Benelux countries, 450. See also Belgium, Netherlands.
Benton, Thomas Hart, 130, 133, 402
Berkeley, Lord John, 14
Berlin, 423, 424, 430, 433, 451
Beveridge, Albert J., 299, 310, 313
Beverley, Robert, 54
Biddle, Nicholas, 131, 133
Bill of Rights: of state constitutions, 114; of U.S. Constitution, 76-78, 87, 114, 162
Birney, James G., 139
Black Codes, 214
Black Hawk War, 142
Black, Hugo L., 383
Blaine, James G., 258, 260, 262-264
Bland-Allison Act (1878), 262, 271
Bland, Richard P., 271

xxxvi

Board of Customs Commissioners, 32
Board of Indian Commissioners, 255
Board of Trade, 16
Bonaparte, Napoleon, 86, 88, 89, 92-94, 95, 97, 98, 99, 110
Booth, John Wilkes, 214
Border Ruffians, 190
Border slaves states, 199, 212
Boston, 11, 13, 29, 32, 33, 34, 37, 71, 72, 117, 118, 187
Boston Brahmins, 166-167
Boston Massacre, 32
Boston police strike, 354
Boston Port Act (1774), 33
Boston Tea Party, 32-33
Bourbon powers, 41, 42
Bowdoin, James, 71
Bowie, Jim, 149
Boxer Rebellion, 316
Braddock, Edward, 24
Bradford, William, 10, 52
Bradley, Omar, 438
Bradstreet, Anne, 52
Brandeis, Louis D., 307, 308, 343, 383
Brannan Plan, 436
Brazil, 321, 387, 451
Breckinridge, John C., 194
Brewster, William, 10
Bricker Amendment, 442
Bricker, John A., 419
Bridger, Jim, 145, 146
Briscoe v. *Bank of Kentucky*, 134
British East India Company, 7, 33
British Guiana, 311
British West Indies, 22, 83, 126
Brook Farm, 165, 167, 223
Brooks, Preston, 191
Broun, Heywood, 398
Brown, Charles Brockden, 112, 115, 116
Brown, John, 190, 193, 195
Brown v. *Board of Education of Topeka*, 443
Brussels Pact (1948), 430
Bryan, William Jennings, 271-272, 291, 296, 298, 303, 307, 311, 315, 319, 323, 324, 397
Bryant, William Cullen, 116, 260, 283
Bryce, James, 256, 259
Buchanan, James, 191-192, 194
Buena Vista, Battle of, 152
Bulfinch, Charles, 117
Bulge, Battle of the, 422
Bull Moose party. *See* Progressive party.
Bull Run: first Battle of, 154, 202; second Battle of, 203
Bunau-Varilla, Philippe, 318
Bureau of Corporations, 249, 298, 301
Bureau of Forestry, 300
Burgoyne, Sir John, 38
Burke Act (1906), 255
Burlingame Treaty (1868), 262
Burma, 414, 431, 447
Burnside, Ambrose E., 203
Burr, Aaron, 84, 85, 87, 91-92
Business: in Gilded Age, 257-258;

during Great Depression, 372, 375, 380, 385; in 1920's, 368-370
Butler, Andrew P., 190
Butler, Pierce, 381
Byrd, William, II, 54, 58
Byrnes, James F., 417, 419, 428

Cabot, John, 7
Cairo Conference, 416
Calhoun, John C., 95, 101, 124, 126, 127; and nullification, 129-130; and slavery, 172, 183, 184; as Vice-President, 128-129
California, 141, 153-54, 182-84, 186
California Trail, 154
Calvert, Cecilius, 12
Calvert, Sir George, 12, 56
Calvin, John, 49
Calvinism, 57, 110, 113, 114, 115, 163, 164, 168
Cameron, Simon, 243
Canada, 13, 18, 21, 29, 34, 38, 42, 95, 96, 97, 136, 138, 141, 187, 304, 311
Cannon, Joseph G., 304, 305
Cape Breton Island, 23, 24-25
Capone, Al, 364
Cardozo, Benjamin N., 383
Caribbean, 390; diplomacy in, 318-320, 360
Carnegie, Andrew, 244, 246, 249, 293
Carnegie Steel Company, 246, 249
Carolinas, 12, 14, 29, 40, 44, 109
Caroline affair, 136, 138
Carpetbaggers, 216
Carranza, Venustiano, 321-322
Carson, Kit, 146
Carteret, Sir George, 14
Cass, Lewis, 183
Castlereagh, Lord, 98
Castro, Fidel, 448-449, 451-452
Catesby, Mark, 58
Cather, Willa, 339
Central Pacific Railroad Company, 210, 241-242
Chamber of Commerce of U.S., 298, 378
Chamberlain, Neville, 389
Channing, William Ellery, 115, 163-164, 171
Chapultepec, Battle of, 152
Charles I of England, 12, xxix
Charles II of England, 12, 13, 14, xxix
Charles River Bridge v. *Warren Bridge*, 134
Charleston, S.C., 40, 118
Charter colony, 17
Chase, Salmon P., 213
Chase, Samuel, 90
Chesapeake, 93, 97
Chesapeake colonies, 19, 20, 40, 48, 54. *See also* Maryland, Virginia.
Chiang Kai-shek, 386, 411, 416, 423, 433
Child Labor Act (1916), 344
Child labor laws, 297, 307, 309, 344, 378, 386
Children's Bureau, 305
Chile, 321, 387

China, 141, 358, 386. 433; Communist, 437-438, 463; Open Door in, 316-317; in World War II, 388, 423
Christian Socialism, 337
Church and state, separation of, 11, 56, 114, 449
Church of England. *See* Anglican Church.
Churchill, Winston (novelist), 339
Churchill, Winston (statesman), 392, 410, 413, 416, 423, 427, 447
Churubusco, Battle of, 152
Civil rights, 68, 86, 328, 333, 418-419, 436, 441, 443-445, 452
Civil Rights Acts: (1886) 215; (1957) 444-445; (1960) 445
Civil Rights Commission, 445
Civil service, 84, 260, 263, 265, 277
Civil Service Commission, 264
Civil Service Reform Act (1883), 259
Civil War, 99, 161, 200-201, 209, 239; causes of, 176, 197-198; military action in, 201-207; results of, 177, 211-213
Civilian Conservation Corps, 376
Clark, George Rogers, 39, 91
Clark, William, 91
Clarke, Edward Y., 353
Clay, Henry, 95, 101, 124-125, 126, 132, 134, 136-137, 138-139; and Bank of U.S., 100, 131, 133; and internal improvements, 101, 131, 180; omnibus bill of, 184-185, 195
Clayton Antitrust Act (1914), 308
Clemenceau, Georges, 329
Cleveland, Grover, 251, 264-265, 269-271, 311-312
Clinton, De Witt, 96
Clinton, George, 72, 77, 84, 92
Clinton, Sir Henry, 39, 40, 41
Coercive Acts (1774), 29, 32-34
Cold Harbor, Battle of, 154, 206
Colombia, 318
Colonies: administration of, 15-18; economy of, 18-22, 27; of France, 22, 23, 26; governors of, 17, 28, 44, 67; legislatures in, 15, 17; Middle Atlantic, 9-10, 12, 13-14, 20-21; New England, 10-12, 18-19; political life in, 16-18; self-government in, 11, 16-18, 27, 28, 33; social structure of, 47-49; Southern, 14-15, 19-20; of Spain, 22, 26, 27, 41
Columbia Fur Company, 145
Columbian Exposition, 337-338
Columbus, Christopher, 6, 7, 256
Combined Chiefs of Staff, 413, 422
Commerce Department, 357, 366
Commission on National Origins, 356
Committee for Industrial Organization, 384
Committee of Correspondence, 32
Committee on Public Information, 328, 369
Committee on Religious Welfare Activity, 398
Committee to Defend America by Aiding the Allies, 391
Common law, 111, 224, 343
Common Law, 280, 343

xxxvii

Common Market, 430, 450
Common Sense, 35, 62
Commons, John R., 276, 294
Communism, 368, 387; and Communist party, 374, 382, 403, 445; in Europe, 429-430; in U.S., 427, 445; after World War II, 427, 428, 433
Compromise of 1850, 185-189
Compromise Tariff of 1833, 132
Concord, 34, 166
Confederate States of America, 195-196, 207-211
Confederation, 45, 66, 67, 68, 72, 73, 112
Confederation Congress, 66-67, 69-73, 74, 77, 79, 182
Conference for Progressive Political Action, 360
Conference of Liberal Ministers, 115
Congregationalists, 56-57, 113, 114, 336
Congress, 86, 89, 95, 98, 124-125, 151, 210, 220-221, 249; and Bank of U.S., 80, 100; Eightieth, 426, 427, 435; and Kennedy, 450-451; land policies of, 100, 254; and Missouri Compromise, 104, 192; and national debt, 79-80; and Reconstruction, 214-215; and slavery, 181, 183-198, 212; and Wilmot Proviso, 182, 184
Congress of Industrial Organizations, 384-385
Congress of Panama, 126-127
Conkling, Roscoe, 258, 261-263
Connally, Richard B., 259
Connecticut, 11, 12, 16, 29, 44, 45, 67, 78, 92, 101, 114
"Conscience Whigs," 188, 191
Conservatism, 77, 371-372, 374, 379, 380, 381, 397, 398, 429, 445; post-World War I, 352, 357; post-World War II, 426, 450
Considerations on the Authority of Parliament, 35
Considerations on the Propriety of Imposing Taxes in the British Colonies, 31
Constitution, U.S., 68, 72, 79, 80, 162, 171, 181, 183, 290, 303; debate on, 77-78; due process clause of, 240; framing of, 72-78; general welfare clause of, 101, 372; interpretations of, 342-343; and Marshall, 89-91; philosophy of, 73-74; ratification of, 78. *See also* Amendments.
Constitutional Convention, 72-78, 114
Constitutional Unionists, 194
Containment, 428, 435, 446
Continental army, 69
Continental Association, 34
Continental Congress, 34, 35, 36, 37, 41, 42, 44, 66, 68, 72, 79, 114
Contreras, Battle of, 152
Convention of 1818, 104
Conwell, Russell, 337
Coolidge, Calvin, 354-355, 357, 360-361

Cooper, James Fenimore, 116, 117, 169, 170
Cooper, Thomas, 110
Copley, John Singleton, 118
Coral Sea, Battle of the, 414
Cornell, Alonzo B., 261
Cornwallis, Lord, 40
Corporations, 157-159, 240, 253, 280, 281, 305, 369, 457-458
Cotton, 101, 102, 103, 129, 161, 179-180, 181, 207-208
Cotton, John, 53
"Cotton Whigs," 188
Coughlin, Charles Edward, 382
Council of Economic Advisors, 426
Council of Foreign Ministers, 427
"Court-packing" bill, 382-383
Cowpens, Battle of, 40
Cox, James M., 354
Coxey, Jacob S., 270
Cozzens, James Gould, 459, 460
Crane, Stephen, 283, 284
Crawford, Thomas, 170
Crawford, William H., 101, 124-125, 127
Crédit Mobilier, 159, 220, 241
Creel, George, 328, 369
Crittenden, John J., 195
Crocker Company, 241-242
Crockett, Davy, 149, 170
Croly, Herbert, 344-345
Crown colony. *See* Royal colony.
Cuba, 141; under Castro, 448-449, 451-452; and Spanish-American War, 312-316
Cullom Committee, 247
Cullom, Shelby, 249
Currency Act (1764), 28
Curry, John Steuart, 402
Curtis, George William, 260, 264
Custer, George A., 254
Czechoslovakia, 388, 389, 429

Da Gama, Vasco, 7
Daladier, Edouard, 389
Dancing Rabbit, Treaty of (1830), 143
Dardanelles, 328, 427, 428
Darrow, Clarence, 340, 397
Dartmouth College v. Woodward, 90-91
Darwin, Charles, 243, 280, 340, 397
Daugherty, Harry M., 355
Davenport, John, 11
Davis, Jefferson, 141, 195, 209
Davis, John W., 360, 380
Dawes Act (1887), 255, 265
Dawes, Charles G., 359
Dawes Plan (1924), 359, 386
De Lôme, Dupuy, 312
De Tocqueville, Alexis, 65, 112, 113, 172, 230
Debs, Eugene V., 251, 306
Declaration of Independence, 34, 35, 36, 37, 41, 44, 55, 66, 67, 68, 78, 109, 114, 119
Declaratory Act (1776), 31
Deism, 55, 114-115
Delaware, 78, 92, 101

Democracy and Education, 334, 394
Democratic party, 158, 179, 182, 269, 298, 307; and free silver, 270-271; in Gilded Age, 256-261, 265; and gold standard, 270; and New Deal, 404; and popular sovereignty, 190; and Versailles Treaty, 330. *See also* Elections.
Democratic-Republican party. *See* Republican party.
Dennis v. U.S., 445
Dependent Pension Act (1890), 266
Dependent Pension Bill (1887), 265
Depressions, 71, 133, 136, 247, 262, 269-270, 272, 312, 360, 367. *See also* Great Depression, Panics.
Dewey, George, 313
Dewey, John, 279, 334, 336, 343, 344, 352, 394
Dewey, Thomas E., 419, 435, 440
Diaz, Bartholomew, 7
Díaz, Porfirio, 321
Dickinson, Emily, 284
Dickinson, John, 32, 44, 49, 66, 75
Dingley Tariff (1897), 239, 272, 304
Dinwiddie, Governor George, 23, 24
Doenitz, Karl, 423
Doheny, E. L., 355, 360
Dollar diplomacy, 319
Dominican Republic, 319, 320, 360, 451
Dominion of New England, 16
Dooley, Mr., 299, 343
Doolittle, James, 414
Dos Passos, John, 403, 460
Douglas, Stephen A., 185-186, 189, 190, 191, 192, 193, 194
Dred Scott decision, 135, 192-193
Dreiser, Theodore, 339, 403
Drew, Daniel, 241
Du Bois, W. E. Burghardt, 231, 333
Duane, William J., 133
Dulaney, Daniel, 31, 36
Dulles, John Foster, 446-447
Dunkirk, 390
Durkin, Martin, 442
Dutch East India Company, 13
Dutch East Indies, 411, 414, 431
Dutch Reformed Church, 57
Dutch West India Company, 13
Dwight, Timothy, 116, 117

Eakins, Thomas, 284
East India Company (British), 7, 33
Eaton, John H., 128
Eaton, Theophilus, 11
Economic Interpretation of the Constitution, 342-343
Edmunds, George F., 248
Education: federal aid to, 277, 436, 450, 454; in Gilded Age, 282; in mid-1800's, 160, 224-225; in 1920's, 393-395; post-World War II, 462-463; in Progressive Era, 331, 333, 334-336; and Puritanism, 51-52
Edwards, Jonathan, 57
Egypt, 415, 447
1800, Treaty of, 86
Einstein, Albert, 353, 425

xxxviii

Eisenhower Doctrine, 448
Eisenhower, Dwight D.: commander of NATO forces, 430; as President, 440-450, 454; in World War II, 415, 422
El Caney, Battle of, 314
Elections, national: (1789) 78-79; (1792) 83; (1796) 84; (1800) 87, 88; (1804) 92; (1808) 94; (1812) 96; (1816) 101; (1824) 124-125; (1828) 127-128; (1832) 131-132; (1836) 135; (1840) 137; (1844) 138-139, 148; (1848) 183-184; (1852) 187-188; (1854) 189; (1856) 191-192; (1860) 193-194; (1864) 213-214; 1868) 219; (1876) 220-221; (1880) 262-263, 268; (1884) 264; (1888) 265; (1890) 269; (1892) 269; (1896) 270-272; (1900) 315; (1904) 298; (1908) 303; (1912) 305-306; (1916) 324-325; (1920) 330, 354, 366; (1924) 357, 360; (1928) 360; (1932) 373-374; (1934) 380; (1936) 382; (1940) 391; (1944) 419; (1946) 426; (1948) 433-434; (1952) 440-441; (1956) 442-443; (1960) 449-450; (1876-1896) 257
Eliot, Charles W., 225, 282
Eliot, T. S., 340, 460
Elizabeth I of England, 9, xxix
Elkins Act (1903), 298
Emancipation Proclamation, 197, 212
Embargo Act of 1807, 93-94, 95
Embargo of 1794, 82
Emergency Banking Relief Act (1933), 376
Emerson, Ralph Waldo, 164-166, 171, 193, 223, 283
Emigrant Aid Society, 190
Employers Liability Act (1910), 305
Employment Act (1946), 426
England. See Great Britain.
English, William H., 263
Enlightenment, 58-59, 109, 223; in Europe, 54-55, 109, 163; in U.S., 58-59, 108, 114, 180
Enumeration Act (1660), 21
Erie Canal, 156, 157
Erie Railroad, 241
Espionage Act (1917), 328
Essex Junto, 91
Ethiopia, 387
European Coal and Steel Community, 430
European Economic Community. See Common Market.
European Recovery Act. See Marshall Plan.
Eustis, William, 96
Everett, Edward, 194
Evergood, Philip, 402
Exclusion Act (1882), 262
Executive, federal, 67, 73, 74, 84

Fair Deal, 436, 442
Fair Employment Practices Committee, 419
Fair Labor Standards Act (1938), 386

Fall, Albert B., 355
Fallen Timbers, Battle of, 81
Fannin, James Walker, 149
Farewell Address of Washington (1796), 84, 105
Farley, James A., 374
Farm Bureau Federation, 357
Farmer-Labor party, 354
Farmers' Alliances, 268
Farmers' National Alliance and Cooperative Union, 268
Farrell, James T., 403
Fascism, 354, 374, 380, 382, 387-388
Faubus, Orville, 444
Faulkner, William, 403-404, 460
Federal Arts Project, 399-400, 402
Federal Council of Churches of Christ in America, 295, 336, 397, 398
Federal Deposit Insurance Corporation, 379
Federal Emergency Relief Administration, 376
Federal Farm Board, 361, 371
Federal Farm Mortgage Corporation, 377
Federal Home Loan Bank Act (1932), 372
Federal Housing Administration Act (1934), 377
Federal Power Commission, 356
Federal Republic of Germany, 428
Federal Reserve Act (1913), 307, 308
Federal Reserve System, 211, 307, 371
Federal Securities Act (1933), 379-380
Federal Trade Commission, 308, 356, 379
Federal Trade Commission Act (1914), 308
Federalism, 62, 66, 72, 73-74, 77-79
Federalist, 77
Federalist party, 62, 83, 85-86, 88, 91, 92, 96, 98, 101, 124
Ferdinand VII of Spain, 105
Feudal system, 6, 12, 14, 168
Field, James G., 269
Fillmore, Millard, 185, 188, 191-192
First Frame of Government, 14
Fish, Hamilton, 219
Fisk, Jim, 241, 243
Fiske, John, 68, 275
Fitzgerald, F. Scott, 402-403
Fitzhugh, George, 172
Five Forks, Battle of, 154
Fletcher v. Peck, 90
Florida, 14, 42, 70, 89, 104
Floyd, John, 132
Food Administration, 327
Foot Resolution, 129-130
Forbes, Charles R., 355
Force Acts (1865, 1874), 219, 261
Force Bill (1833), 132
Ford, Henry, 294, 366, 384
Fordney-McCumber Tariff (1922), 356
Forest Service, 300, 304
Formosa, 416, 431

Forrestal, James V., 427
Fort Stanwix, Treaty of (1768), 81
Fort Sumter, 154, 195-198, 201
Fort Ticonderoga, 24, 34
Foster, Stephen, 118
Foster, William Z., 374
Four-Power Pact (1922), 359
"Fourteen Points," 328
France, 23, 38, 70, 79, 88, 105, 208, 358-359, 372, 385; and American Revolution, 28, 36, 38-41; colonies of, 26-27; post-World War II, 431, 446-447, 450, 463; and U.S., 1945-1962, 424, 428; in World War I, 322-323, 327-329; in World War II, 387-390, 416, 422
Francis Ferdinand, archduke of Austria, 322
Franklin, Benjamin, 24, 31, 35, 38, 41, 42, 56, 58-59, 72, 77, 109, 115
Fredericksburg, Battle of, 201, 204
Free silver, 269-271
Free-soil resolution, 182, 184
Free-soilers, 183, 191, 192, 218
Freedmen's Bureau, 215
Freeport Doctrine, 193
Frémont, John C., 145, 153, 191
French and Indian War, 23-25, 29
French Revolution, 36, 41, 44, 81-83, 92, 126
Freneau, Philip, 115, 117
Frick, Henry Clay, 246
Frost, Robert, 340
Fuel Administration, 327
Fugitive Slave Act (1850), 186, 188, 193
Fugitive slave law (1793), 102, 154, 186
Fulton, Robert, 156
Fundamental Constitutions, 14
Fundamental Orders, 12
Fundamentalism, 280, 336-337, 397

Gadsden Purchase (1854), 155, 178, 191
Galbraith, John Kenneth, 453-454
Gallatin, Albert, 84, 89, 99
Galloway, Joseph, 34, 36
Gardoqui, Diego de, 70
Garfield, James A., 263, 304
Garner, John Nance, 374
Garrison, William Lloyd, 171, 230
Gas Ring, 259
Gates, Horatio, 38
General Preëmption Act, 138
Geneva Conference (1955), 447
"Gentlemen's Agreement," 317
George, David Lloyd, 329
George, Henry, 247, 260, 277, 282, 294
George III of England, 118, xxix
Georgia, 15, 40, 44, 78, 96, 104, 186, 444, 446
German-Americans, 322-323, 325, 328, 329, 419
Germantown, Battle of, 38
Germany, 310, 311, 319, 321, 358, 359, 372; post-World War II, 428, 430, 446, 450; and U.S., 1945-

xxxix

1962, 424, 433; in World War I, 322-326, 329; in World War II, 387-391, 410-411, 413, 422, 423
Gerry, Elbridge, 73, 75, 76, 77, 86
Gettysburg, Battle of, 202, 203, 204, 263
Ghent, Treaty of (1815), 97-99, 100, 104
Gibbons, James Cardinal, 250, 281
Gibbons v. *Ogden* (1824), 91
Gibraltar, 23, 41
Gilbert Islands, 311, 420-421
Gilded Age: business in, 257-258; culture in, 274-284; politics in, 256-273
Gilman, Daniel Coit, 225, 282
Gladden, Washington, 281, 336, 337
Glass, Carter, 307
Glass-Steagall Act (1932), 372
Glorious Revolution, 16, 35, 55
Godkin, E. L., 260, 274
Gold Rush, 154, 183, 252, 262
Gold standard, 178, 270-271, 272, 372, 374, 379
Gold Standard Act (1900), 272
Goliad, Battle of, 149
Gompers, Samuel, 251, 298, 308
Good Neighbor Policy, 387-388
Gorman, Arthur P., 259, 270
Gould, Jay, 241, 243, 250
Grand Alliance, 422
Grand Army of the Republic, 258, 265, 266
Grange, 267-268
Grant, Ulysses S., 202, 203, 204, 205-207, 219, 257, 262
Grasse, Comte François de, 40
Great Awakening, 55, 57-58, 115
Great Britain, 23, 70, 73, 81-83, 104, 105, 151, 156-157, 181, 310, 311, 317, 319; and American Revolution, 26-42; and Civil War, 208-209; and colonization, 7, 9, 27; and Indians, 81, 83; and Oregon, 147; post-World War II, 431, 447; social structure in, 46-47; and U.S., 1945-1962, 428; in World War I, 322-323, 326, 329; in World War II, 388-391, 410-411, 422, 427
Great Compromise, 75
Great Depression, 277, 357, 365, 366, 370-386, 394, 396-399, 401, 403, 404, 453
Great Lakes, 23, 42, 96, 104, 156
"Great Law," 14
Great Southwestern Strike, 250
Great War for Empire. *See* French and Indian War.
Greece, 428, 429
Greeley, Horace, 220
Greenback Labor party, 263
Greenbacks, 211, 219, 268
Greene, Nathanael, 40
Greenville, Treaty of (1814), 81
Grenville, George, 29-30
Gropper, William, 402
Guadalcanal, 414-415, 420
Guadalupe Hidalgo, Treaty of (1848), 153, 178, 182
Guam, 314, 315, 413

Hague Tribunal, 319
Haiti, 321, 360, 388
Half-Way Covenant, 52-53
Hall, A. Oakey, 259
Hamilton, Alexander, 72, 73, 74, 77, 78, 84, 85, 91-92, 344; as Secretary of the Treasury, 79-80, 81, 83, 84, 99
Hamlin, Hannibal, 194
Hammer v. *Dagenhart*, 309
Hancock, John, 35, 71
Hancock, Winfield Scott, 263
Hanna, Marcus Alonzo, 271-273, 294, 298, 314
Harding, Warren G., 354-356
Harper's Ferry, 193, 203, 204
Harriman, Edward H., 241, 290
Harris, George Washington, 169
Harrison, Benjamin, 265-266, 269
Harrison, William Henry, 95, 96, 100, 135, 137-138, 188
Harte, Bret, 283
Hartford, Conn., 11, 117
Hartford Convention (1814), 98, 101, 130
Hat Act (1732), 22
Havemeyer, Henry O., 243, 247
Hawaii, 70, 141, 178, 316, 317, 413, 419; annexation of, 311, 314
Hawthorne, Nathaniel, 159, 167, 168, 171
Hay–Bunau-Varilla Treaty (1903), 318
Hay, John, 272, 314, 316, 318
Hay-Pauncefote Treaty (1901), 318-319
Hayes, Rutherford B., 220, 260-262
Haymarket Riot, 250-251
Hayne, Robert W., 129-130
Headright, 19, 48
Hearst press, 321, 329
Hearst, William Randolph, 312, 321, 374, 399
Hegel, Georg Wilhelm, 278
Helper, Hinton R., 172
Hemingway, Ernest, 402-403, 460
Henry VIII of England, 8, 9, 49, xxix
Henry, Patrick, 30, 44, 49, 72, 77
Hepburn Act (1906), 298-299
Herrera, José J., 151
Herron, George, 336
Hersey, John, 459
Hill, James J., 241, 281, 290, 293
Hiroshima, 424
Hiss, Alger, 439, 441
History, view of, in Progressive Era, 331, 341-343, 345
Hitler, Adolf, 387-390, 410-411, 414, 421, 423
Hoar, George F., 248, 257
Hobart, Garret A., 271
Holland. *See* Netherlands.
Holmes, Oliver Wendell, I, 166-167, 171, 283
Holmes, Oliver Wendell, II, 280, 343, 344
Holy Alliance, 104-105
Home Owners Loan Corporation, 377

Homer, Winslow, 284
Homestead Act (1862), 253-254
Hooker, Joseph, 204
Hooker, Thomas, 11, 53
Hooper, J. J., 169, 171
Hoover, Herbert, 327, 360, 401; as President, 361-362, 365, 371-372, 374, 387; as Secretary of Commerce, 354, 355, 357
Hopkins, Harry, 391
House of Commons, 17, 28, 31
House of Representatives, 76, 87. *See also* Congress.
House Un-American Activities Committee, 441
Housing Act (1937), 386
Houston, Samuel, 149-150
Howe, Louis M., 374
Howe, Lord Richard, 38
Howe, Sir William, 37, 38, 39, 41
Howells, William Dean, 283
Hudson, Henry, 13
Hudson's Bay Company, 146
Huerta, Victoriano, 321
Hughes, Charles Evans, 325, 354, 357, 358, 359, 381, 383
Huguenots, 14, 20
Hull, Cordell, 412, 416
Humphrey, George C., 442
Hundred Days, 376-377
Hungary, 358, 447
Hutchinson, Thomas, 30, 32

Iceland, 410, 411
Immigration, 8, 15, 20, 331-332; from Asia, 262, 263, 355-356; from Europe, 15, 20, 100, 141, 228-229, 238-239, 292, 355-356; restriction of, 269, 355-356, 360, 363
Impressment, 82, 83, 93, 96, 98
Indentured servitude, 19, 20, 48, 54
Independent Treasury Act (1840), 136, 138
India, 23, 27, 41, 414, 428, 447, 464
Indian Reorganization Act (1934), 255
Indian Springs Treaty (1825), 142
Indians, 23, 24, 28, 38, 44, 96, 116, 145, 150, 169, 254; land of, 11, 14, 44, 45; U.S. policy toward, 81, 254-255; and westward expansion, 81, 95, 141-144, 254-255
Indochina, 411, 414, 431, 447
Indonesia, 431, 447
Industrial Commission, 293
Industrial Revolution: in Europe, 27, 107, 156-157; in U.S., 157-161, 172, 238-252
Industrial Workers of the World, 328
Industrialism, 177, 207, 209-210, 274-275, 404; problems of, 222, 256, 281, 283, 344, 346
Inflation, 133, 418
Influence of Sea Power upon History, 310
Insull, Samuel, 370
Interior Department, 255, 304

xl

Internal improvements, 125-126, 128, 131, 135, 137, 140, 180
Internal Security Act. *See* McCarran Act.
International Workers of the World, 302
Interstate Commerce Act (1887), 248, 265
Interstate Commerce Commission, 248, 299, 305, 356
Intolerable Acts. *See* Coercive Acts.
Ireland, Archbishop John, 281
Irish-Americans, 322, 325, 329
Iron Act (1750), 22
Irving, Washington, 115, 116, 117
Isolationism, 84, 105, 106, 329; and World War I, 324, 325; and World War II, 386, 387, 388, 390, 391, 392, 404, 410, 419, 423; post-World War II, 442
Israel, 431, 447
Italian-Americans, 329, 419
Italy, 358-359, 387; post-World War II, 428, 430, 450; in World War I, 326, 328; in World War II, 388, 390-391, 413-416, 422, 423
Iwo Jima, Battle of, 424

Jackson, Andrew, 88, 96, 97-98, 104, 110, 124-126, 127-128, 132-136, 139, 142, 149, 150, 158; and Bank of U.S., 128, 131, 132-133, 135, 158, 211; foreign policy of, 134, 135; "kitchen cabinet" of, 139-140; and nullification, 130-131, 135; and public land, 134, 135
Jackson, Thomas J., 202-204
James I of England, 9, 10, xxix
James II of England, 13, 16, xxix
James, Henry, 283, 460
James, William, 279, 280, 283, 343
Jamestown, Va., 9, 10
Japan, 318, 358-359, 386, 387, 431-432; and Open Door, 316-318; post-World War II, 448, 450, 464; in World War II, 388, 391, 411-414, 416, 420-421, 425, 431
Jay, John, I, 41, 70, 72, 77, 82-84
Jay, John, II, 261
Jay's Treaty (1794), 82-83, 86, 87
Jefferson, Thomas, 35, 41, 62, 69, 71, 72, 73, 80, 81, 84-87, 93-94, 100, 101, 104, 110, 114, 115, 158, 181; as architect, 117-118, 171; foreign policy of, 92-94; and Louisiana Purchase, 88-89; as President, 88, 91, 92, 150, 273; as Secretary of State, 79, 83
Jews, 114, 325, 353, 398
Johnson, Andrew, 213-214, 218, 257
Johnson, Eastman, 284
Johnson, Hugh S., 357, 378
Johnson, Lyndon B., 449, 452
Johnson, Tom L., 297
Johnston, Albert Sidney, 205
Johnston, Joseph E., 202, 206-207
Joint-stock companies, 7, 10, 12
Jones, James, 459
Judicial Procedure Reform Act (1937), 383
Judiciary, federal, 67, 73, 74, 84
Judiciary Acts: (1789) 79, 90; (1801) 89
Jury trial, right of, 11, 12, 68, 70, 112

Kansas, 189-192
Kansas-Nebraska Act (1854), 189-190, 191, 192
Kearny, Stephen W., 153
Kelley, Oliver Hudson, 267
Kellogg-Briand Pact (1925), 359
Kellogg, Frank B., 359
Kennan, George F., 428
Kennedy, John F., 433, 449; as President, 450-452, 454; assassination of, 452
Kennedy, John P., 168, 171
Kentucky, 43, 86, 96, 102, 112
Keynes, John Maynard, 396-397
Khrushchev, Nikita, 446, 448, 452
"King Caucus," 128, 139
King George's War, 23
King, Martin Luther, Jr., 444
King of England, 27, 28, 34-36, 40
King, Rufus, 77, 92, 101
King's Mountain, Battle of, 40, 162
"Kitchen Cabinet," 139-140
Knights of Labor, 250-251, 268
Know-Nothings, 229-230
Knox, Frank, 391
Knox, Henry, 72, 77, 79
Knox, Philander C., 317
Konoye, Fumimaro, 411, 412
Korea, 317, 431
Korean War, 430, 433, 436-439, 441, 442
Ku Klux Klan, 217-218, 219, 230, 353, 360
Kuhn, Loeb & Co., 249, 290
Kurile Islands, 414, 423
Kurusu, Saburo, 412

La Follette, Robert M., 297, 299, 301, 304, 305, 360
La Follette Seamen's Act (1915), 308
Labor, 8, 77, 160-161, 250-252, 295, 324, 328, 352, 379; organization of, 293, 367-368; in Progressive Era, 301-302, 307-308, 343; during World War II, 417-418; post-World War II, 425-427, 458. *See also* Unions.
Labor-Management Relations Act. *See* Taft-Hartley Act.
Labor-Management Reporting and Disclosure Act. *See* Landrum-Griffin Act.
Labour party, 424, 427
LaFayette, Marquis de, 41
Laissez faire, 158, 227, 239-240, 257, 260, 274-276, 278, 279, 344, 371
Lake Erie, Battle of, 96
Lamar, Mirabeau B., 150
Land, distribution of, 17, 18, 19, 20, 28, 48-49, 51, 68-69, 129, 133-134, 140

Land Ordinance of 1785, 69
Landon, Alfred M., 382
Landrum-Griffin Act (1959), 443
Langer, William E., 404-405
Lansing-Ishii Agreement (1917), 318
Lansing, Robert, 318
"Large Policy," 311, 313, 316
Latrobe, Benjamin, 118, 171
Laurens, Henry, 41
Laws of nature, 35, 55, 58, 59
League of Nations, 325, 328, 329-330, 352, 354, 358, 359, 386-388, 423
Leatherstocking Tales, 169-170
Lebanon, 431, 448
Lecompton Constitution, 192
Lee, Richard Henry, 35, 66, 81
Lee, Robert E., 198, 202-204, 206, 214
Legal theory, 49, 111-112, 280, 331, 343-344
Legislature, federal, 73, 74
Lend-Lease Act (1941), 392, 410, 413
Levant Company, 7
Lewis and Clark expedition, 91, 110, 146, 147
Lewis, John L., 368, 378, 383, 384, 418
Lewis, Meriwether, 91
Lewis, Sinclair, 403, 460
Lexington, Battle of, 34
Leyte Gulf, Battle of, 424
Liberalism, 77, 419, 429
Liberator, 171, 230
Liberty League, 380
Liberty party, 139
Lincoln, Abraham, 142, 177, 188, 193, 194, 199, 202-203, 206-207, 213-214; and Emancipation Proclamation, 197, 212; and Reconstruction, 213-214; and secession, 196-197; and slavery, 212-213
Lincoln-Douglas Debates, 192-193
Lindbergh, Charles A., 366
Lindsay, Vachel, 339
Lippmann, Walter, 344-345, 395, 399
Literary Digest, 382, 399, 400
Literature: in colonies, 51-52; 1783-1830, 115-118; 1824-1848, 164-170; in Gilded Age, 283-284; in Progressive Era, 339-341; 1920-1940, 402-404; 1940-1962, 459-460
Little Big Horn, Battle of, 254
Little Rock, Ark., 443-444
Lloyd, Henry Demarest, 247, 272
Lochner v. *New York*, 303
Locke, John, 14, 35, 108, 109, 113
Lodge, Henry Cabot, 310, 312, 313, 329, 330
Lodge, Henry Cabot (the younger), 449
Logan, James, 58
London Economic Conference (1933), 379
London, Jack, 339
London, Treaty of. *See* Jay's Treaty.
Lonely Crowd, 456
Long, Huey P., 382
Longfellow, Henry Wadsworth, 110, 115, 167, 171, 283

xli

Longstreet, Augustus B., 169, 171
Lord Commissioners for Plantations, 15
Lords of Trade, 15, 16
Louis XVI of France, 82
Louisiana, 23, 25, 102, 444
Louisiana Purchase, 88-89, 91, 92, 94, 103, 104, 141, 150, 162, 182, 189
Louisiana Territory, 88, 91
Lowden, Frank O., 354
Lowell, A. Lawrence, 353
Lowell, Amy, 340
Lowell, James Russell, 167, 171, 283
Loyalists, 36, 37, 38, 40, 42, 107, 112, 114
Lusitania, 323
Lutherans, 14, 114

McAdoo, William, 323, 327, 354, 360, 374
MacArthur, Douglas, 424, 436-438
McCarran Act (1951), 439
McCarthy, Joseph, 439-440
McClellan, George Brinton, 202-203, 206, 213
McClellan, John L., 443
McCormick Harvester Company, 246-247
McCulloch v. Maryland, 90
McCumber, Porter J., 299
McDougall, William, 340
McDowell, Irvin, 202, 203
McKinley bill (1890), 239
McKinley Tariff (1890), 266, 311
McKinley, William, 271-273, 281, 290, 292, 294, 304, 311, 316; and Spanish-American War, 312-315
McLeod, Alexander, 136
McNary-Haugen Bill (1926, 1927), 357, 361
Macon's Bill No. 2 (1810), 94-95
McReynolds, James C., 381
Madero, Francisco, 321
Madison, James, 72, 73, 74, 75, 77, 80, 83, 84, 86, 96, 342; and Louisiana Purchase, 88-89; as President, 94-95, 101; as Secretary of State, 89-90, 93; and War of 1812, 95-98
Magellan, Ferdinand, 7
Mahan, Alfred Thayer, 310
Mailer, Norman, 459
Maine, 11, 12, 42, 104
Maine, sinking of, 312-313
Malaya, 412-413, 431
Malthus, Thomas, 464
Manchuria, 317, 386-387, 416, 425, 433
Mangum, Willie P., 135
Manifest Destiny, 141, 148, 310
Manila, 412, 424
Mann-Elkins Act (1910), 305
Mann, Horace, 224, 393
Mao Tse-tung, 433
Marbury v. Madison, 90
Marbury, William, 90
Marcy, William L., 139
Marin, John, 339, 401

Marshall, George C., 413, 429, 433
Marshall, John, 77, 82, 84, 86, 89, 134, 135, 154, 343
Marshall Plan, 429-430
Martin, Joseph W., 438
Martin v. Hunter's Lessee, 90
Marxism, 342, 396, 404
Maryland, 8, 12, 21, 29, 31, 44, 45, 56, 68, 78, 114
Maryland Toleration Act (1649), 12, 56
Mason, George, 31, 76, 77
Massachusetts, 16, 23, 27, 28, 30, 32, 33, 34, 44, 67, 68, 71, 72, 78, 98, 101, 104, 114
Massachusetts Bay Colony, 7, 8, 10, 11, 12, 50, 51, 52, 53, 55
Massachusetts Bay Company, 11
Massachusetts Government Act (1774), 33
Masters, Edgar Lee, 340
Mather, Cotton, 58, 109
Mayflower, 10
Mayo, Elton, 367
Maysville Road, 131
Meade, George Gordon, 204, 206
Mellon, Andrew, 354, 356, 371
Melville, Herman, 167-168, 171, 460
Mencken, Henry L., 402
Mennonites, 14
Mercantilism, 8
Meredith, James, 444
Merrimac, 203, 208
Methodist Episcopal Church, 295
Methodists, 114, 193, 336
Meuse-Argonne, 327
Mexican War, 140, 148, 151-153, 154, 155, 166, 182, 188
Mexico, 325; and Texas, 134, 148-153; and Wilson, 319-321, 360. See also Mexican War.
Middle Ages, 6, 168
"Midnight Judges," 89
Midway, Battle of, 414
Miles, Nelson A., 313
Miller, Arthur, 459
Minutemen, 34
Missionary Ridge, Battle of, 206
Mississippi River, 39, 42, 69, 70, 83, 180
Missouri, statehood for, 102-104, 144, 182
Missouri Compromise, 103-104, 151, 162, 183, 189, 190, 191, 192, 193, 195
Mitchell, Dr. John, 58, 111
Mitchell, John M., 290
Mitchell, S. Z., 370
Molasses Act (1733), 22
Molino del Rey, Battle of, 152
Molotov, Vyacheslav, 416, 427
Monitor, 203, 208
Monroe Doctrine, 62, 104, 162, 311, 316, 319
Monroe, Harriet, 339
Monroe, James, 72, 84, 96, 98, 354, 382; and Monroe Doctrine, 105; as President, 101, 105, 124, 126, 127, 132
Montcalm, Marquis de, 24

Monterey, Battle of, 152
Montgomery, Bernard L., 415, 423
Montgomery, Richard, 35
Monticello, 94, 104, 118
Morgan, John Pierpont, 241, 243, 249, 270, 293, 301, 323
Morgan, J. P., and Company, 290, 370
Morgan, Lewis Henry, 282
Mormons, 155, 165, 192, 223
Morocco, 88, 415, 416
Morrill Act (1862), 253
Morrill Tariff (1861), 210, 239
Morris, Gouverneur, 73
Morris, Robert, 37, 73
Morton, Levi P., 265
Moscow, 414, 416
Motion pictures, 400-401
Muckrakers, 296, 298, 299, 300
Mugwumps, 260, 264, 291, 296
Mulligan letters, 264
Munich Conference (1938), 389, 390
Munn v. Illinois, 240, 268
Murphy, Frank, 385
Muscle Shoals-Tennessee Valley Development Act (1933), 377
Music, 118, 170, 400
Mussolini, Benito, 387, 389, 415

Nagasaki, 425
Napoleonic Wars, 108
Nasser, Gamal Abdel, 447-448
National Association for the Advancement of Colored People (NAACP), 231, 333
National Association of Manufacturers, 293, 302, 308, 367
National Bank Act (1864), 211
National Board of Trade, 298
National Business League, 298
National Catholic Welfare Conference, 397, 398
National Child Labor Committee, 307
National Civic Federation, 298
National Defense Advisory Commission, 391
National Defense Education Act (1958), 462-463
National Farmers' Alliance and Industrial Union, 268
National Industrial Recovery Act (1933), 378, 381, 383, 386
National Labor Board, 383
National Labor Reform party, 250
National Labor Relations Act. See Wagner Act.
National Labor Relations Board, 381, 383, 384
National Labor Union, 250
National Origins Act (1924), 356
National Recovery Administration, 378, 379, 383
National Reëmployment Agreement (1933), 378
National Road, 126
National Security Act (1947), 427
National Textile Workers' Union, 368

National Trades Union, 160
National Typographical Union, 160
National War Labor Board, 327
Nationalism, 65, 107-108
Natural law, 180
Nature, 164, 165
Navigation Acts, 30, 32; (1651) 21; (1660) 21; (1663) 22; (1673) 22; (1696) 22
Nelson, Donald, 391, 417
Netherlands, 13, 39, 79, 82, 358, 390, 411, 430
Neutrality, 84, 92, 106, 134; in French Revolution, 81, 82, 86; in World War I, 322-323; in World War II, 390, 392
Neutrality Acts: (1794) 82; (1935) 388; (1937) 388; (1940) 390
Nevins, Allan, 404-405
New Amsterdam, 13
New Deal, 300, 397, 398, 404, 426, 435, 442, 453; appraisal of, 404-405; legislation of, 375-386; objectives of, 376; opposition to, 379-381
New France, 13, 27
New Freedom, 306-308
New Guinea, 414, 420
New Hampshire, 12, 16, 78, 90, 114
New Harmony, 165
New Haven, Conn., 11, 12
New Jersey, 13, 14, 16, 20, 28, 29, 38, 78, 91, 112
New Jersey Plan, 74
New Mexico, 141, 153, 184, 186
New Nationalism, 305, 306
New Netherland, 13
New Netherland Company, 13
New Orleans, 70, 83, 88, 205
New Orleans, Battle of, 162
New Republic, 330, 345
New York, 13, 16, 20, 28, 29, 30, 37, 38, 39, 40, 44, 45, 72, 77, 78, 87, 91, 97, 114
New York Central System, 241, 259
New York City, 13, 20, 118
New York Customhouse, 261-263
New York *Journal*, 312
New York, New Haven, & Hartford R.R., 241
New York *Times*, 260, 338
New York *Tribune*, 220, 272, 312
New York *World*, 312
New York Zoning Act (1916), 401
Newfoundland, 9, 104, 390, 410
Newlands Act (1902), 298
Newspapers, 56, 380, 398-399
Newton, Sir Isaac, 47, 54, 109, 110
Nicaragua, 191, 311, 318, 319, 360
Nine-Power Pact (1922), 359
Nixon, Richard M., 441, 442, 449
Nomura, Kichisaburo, 412
Non-Conforming Congregational Separatists, 8, 9, 10, 50
Non-Conforming Congregationalists, 50
Non-Intercourse Act (1809), 94
Non-Partisan League, 354
Nonimportation Acts (1806, 1807), 93

Normandy, 422
Norris, Frank, 339
Norris, George W., 304
Norris-LaGuardia Act (1932), 251
North American Phalanx, 165
North Atlantic Treaty Organization (NATO), 430, 433, 438, 440, 446
North Carolina, 15, 20, 40, 78, 81, 112
Northern Securities Company, 290-291, 293, 294, 301
Northwest Ordinance (1787), 69-70, 91, 102
Northwest Territory, 69-70, 81, 91, 100, 102, 103
Northwestern Alliance, 268
Nuclear energy, 424-425, 427, 442, 447, 463
Nuclear test ban treaty (1963), 452
Nullification Controversy, 129-132, 180
Nullification Proclamation, 132

Ocala platform, 268-269
O'Conor, Charles, 260
Odets, Clifford, 403
Office of Price Administration, 418
Office of Production Management, 392
Office of War Mobilization, 417, 419
Ohio Company, 23
Okinawa, Battle of, 424
Oklahoma, Indians in, 144
Old Guard, 298, 304, 306, 308, 324
O'Neill, Eugene, 403, 459
Onís, Luis de, 104
Open Door policy, 316-318, 359
Ordinance of Secession, 195
Ordinance of 1787, 182
Oregon: claims to, 104, 105, 138, 147-148, 182; joint occupation of, 104, 127, 146-148; settlement of dispute, 140, 141, 178; and slavery, 183
Oregon Trail, 145-146, 154
Oregon Treaty (1846), 148
Organization Man, 456
Oriskany, Battle of, 38
Orlando, Vittorio, 329
O'Sullivan, John L., 141, 162
Otis, James, 49
Overman Act (1918), 327
Over-Soul, 164

Pact of Steel (1939), 389
Paine, Thomas, 35, 62, 115
Pakistan, 428, 431, 447
Palestine, 431
Palmer, A. Mitchell, 352, 353, 354
Palo Alto, Battle of, 151
Pan-American Conference (1933), 388
Pan-American Exposition, 290
Panama, 318, 388
Panama Canal, 318-319
Panics: (1837) 133, 135-136; (1873) 268; (1929) 370, 371
Paris peace conference of 1918, 329
Paris, Treaty of, (1763) 25, 27, 28;

(1783) 42, 81; (1898) 314-315
Parker, Alton B., 298
Parker, Theodore, 164, 171, 187
Parliament, 9, 10, 11, 16, 27, 28, 31, 33, 46-47, 67, 73; acts of, 9, 21-23, 31, 32, 95, 111; authority of, 30, 32, 33, 35
Patrons of Husbandry. *See* Grange.
Pavlov, Ivan, 341
Payne-Aldrich Tariff (1909), 304
Payne's Landing, Treaty of (1832), 143
Peace Convention of 1861, 195
Pearl Harbor, 412-413, 414, 416, 419
Pemberton, John C., 205-206
Pendleton Civil Service Act (1883), 263-264
Penn, William, 14
Pennsylvania, 12, 14, 16, 17, 18, 20, 21, 22, 29, 42, 44, 69, 78, 81, 96
Pennsylvania Railroad, 241, 296
People's party, 268-272, 291-292
Pereira, I. Rice, 461
Permanent Preventatives of Unemployment, conference, 398
Perry, Oliver Hazard, 96
Pershing, John J., 322, 327
Peru, 451
"Pet banks," 133, 136
Philippines, 303, 313-314, 316, 317, 412, 424, 431, 447
Phillips, David Graham, 296
Philosophy, 112-113, 278-280, 343, 395
Pickering, John, 90
Pickering, Timothy, 84, 91
Pierce, Charles S., 279
Pierce, Franklin, 188-192
Pietists, 14, 20, 55, 56, 57
Pilgrims, 10
Pinchot, Gifford, 300, 304-305
Pinckney, Charles, 49, 73, 86, 87, 92, 94
Pinckney, Thomas, 84, 85
Pitt, William, 24
Platt Amendment, 316, 388
Platt, Orville, 248
Platt, Thomas, 259, 263
Plessy v. *Ferguson*, 231, 443
Plymouth colony, 7, 8, 10, 11, 12, 50
Poe, Edgar Allan, 169
Poetry magazine, 339, 340
Point Four, 430
Poland, 328, 329, 388-390, 422, 423, 424, 427
Polk, James K., 138-139, 140, 148, 183, 191; and Texas, 151-153, 182
Pollock, Jackson, 461
Poor Richard's Almanac, 56
Pope Leo XIII, 281, 295
Popular Sovereignty, 183, 189, 192, 193
Population, growth and distribution of, 68, 100, 228, 464
Populism, 268-272, 291-292
Populist party. *See* People's party.
Portugal, 6, 358
Potsdam Conference, 424, 427, 428
Pottawatomie Creek massacre, 190, 193

xliii

Pound, Ezra, 340, 460
Pound, Roscoe, 343, 344
Powderly, Terence V., 250
Preëmption Acts: (1830) 134; (1841) 253
Presbyterian Assembly of 1798, 114
Presbyterians, 14, 49-50, 56, 57, 113, 114, 336
Presidential Succession Law (1886), 265
Privy Council, 15, 28
Progress and Poverty, 247, 277
Progressive Education Association, 334, 394
Progressive party: first, 305, 308-309, 324, 333, 344, 355, 360; second, 435
Progressivism, 290-309, 324-325, 327, 331-346, 352, 357, 373, 380, 394
Prohibition, 223-225, 360, 361, 364-365
Proprietary colony, 12, 13, 17
Protestantism: in colonies, 12, 15; in Europe, 13, 55; in U.S., 114, 179, 198, 222, 229, 278, 280-281, 291, 295, 336-337, 393, 397-398
Providence, R.I., 11, 33
Psychology, 340-341, 344, 363, 393, 395, 403
Public Service Corporation, 296
Public works, 263, 371, 374, 386
Public Works Administration, 378
Puerto Rico, 313-316
Pullman strike, 251, 270
Pure Food and Drug Act (1906), 299
Puritan Commonwealth, 21, xxix
Puritan Revolution, 14
Puritanism, 8, 9, 11, 12, 18, 19, 48-54, 57, 109, 163, 167, 180, 222, 223, 224, 402

Quakers, 14, 51, 167, 180, 284
Quartering Act (1765), 29
Quebec, 25, 29, 35
Quebec Act (1774), 29
Queen Anne's War, 23

Racism, 212-213, 331-333, 334, 419
Radical Republicans, 213, 218, 262
Radio, 362, 366, 398, 399
Railroads, 157, 238, 240-242, 267, 290-291, 293, 296, 309, 368, 370, 379; in Civil War, 200, 209, 239; discriminatory practices of, 292, 298-299; regulation of, 247-248, 297, 298-299, 352; transcontinental, 189, 191, 210, 310
Randolph, Edmund, 74, 76, 77
Randolph, John, 92, 95, 125, 128, 180
Raskob, John J., 361
Rauschenbusch, Walter, 281, 295
Reciprocal Trade Agreements Act (1934), 380, 450
Reconstruction, 213-221, 258, 261-262, 278
Reconstruction Acts (1867-1868), 215-216
Reconstruction Finance Corporation, 372

Red scare: of 1920's, 353-356, 367; of 1950's, 353, 439-440
Redcoats, 29, 32, 33, 34
Reed, Thomas B., 266
Reform, social and economic, 163, 167, 223-227, 260, 275, 277-278, 279-280, 295, 297, 309, 331, 352, 363, 397, 402
Reform Darwinism, 275-276, 294, 296, 332
Reformation, Protestant, 8, 9, 49
Reid, Whitelaw, 260, 269
Reischauer, Edwin O., 433
Reparations: French, 126, 134; World War I, 359, 372, 386-387; World War II, 423, 427-428
Report on Manufactures, 79
Report on the Public Credit, 79
Republican party (Jeffersonian), 83, 100-101
Republican party, 158, 239, 260, 278, 293, 294, 297, 307, 311, 356; ascendancy of, 210-211; in Gilded Age, 256-261, 265; and gold standard, 270; and secession, 197. See also Elections.
Rerum Novarum, 295
Resaca de la Palma, Battle of, 151
Resumption Act (1875), 262
Revenue Acts: (1916) 309; (1921) 356-357; (1935) 381; (1942) 418
Rhee, Syngman, 436, 438
Rhineland, 387
Rhode Island, 11, 16, 29, 55, 56, 67, 78, 98
Richardson, Henry Hobsen, 284
Richmond, Va., 118, 202
Riesman, David, 456
Rights of Englishmen, 28
Roberts, Owen J., 381, 383
Robinson, Edwin Arlington, 339
Robinson, James Harvey, 341-343
Rockefeller, John D., 241, 244, 245, 249, 296
Rockefeller, John D., Jr., 302
Rocky Mountain Fur Company, 145
Rogers, Will, 398
Rolfe, John, 10
Roman Catholic Church, 7, 12, 114, 321, 353, 356, 360, 361, 397-398, 449-450; in England, 8, 49, 55; and social reform, 281, 295
Romanticism, 107-110, 163-171
Roosevelt Corollary, 319
Roosevelt, Franklin Delano: as Assistant Secretary of Navy, 354, 374; first inaugural address of, 375-376, 387; as governor of New York, 373-374; as President, 359, 375-392, 410-423, 427; as vice-presidential candidate, 354, 374; and World War II, 388, 390, 392, 410, 412-413, 416-420, 423-425
Roosevelt, Theodore, 272, 290, 291, 293, 294, 296-307, 310, 318, 319, 322, 323, 329, 339, 343, 344; Far East policies of, 316-317; as President, 297-303; and Spanish-American War, 312-315
Root, Elihu, 304, 313, 322, 330

Root-Takahira Agreement (1908), 317
Rosenberg, Julius and Ethel, 439
Rough Riders, 313-314
Royal colony, 10-13, 15, 17
Royal Proclamation Line, 29
Royce, Josiah, 278
Rush-Bagot Agreement (1817), 104
Russia, 105, 147, 317, 328, 386-389; and Alaska, 126; and Korean War, 433; post-World War II, 439, 447, 462, 463; révolution in, 326, 352; and U.S., 1945-1963, 424, 433, 436, 437, 448, 451-452; in World War II, 410-411, 416, 422, 425
Russo-Japanese War, 317
Ryder, Albert Pinkham, 284

Saarinen, Eero, 462
Saarinen, Eliel, 401
Sacco-Vanzetti case, 353, 439
St. Clair, Arthur, 81
Saipan, 421, 424
Salem, Mass., 11, 167
San Francisco Conference, 423
San Jacinto, Battle of, 150
San Juan Hill, Battle of, 314
San Lorenzo, Treaty of (1795), 83
Sandburg, Carl, 340
Santa Anna, Antonio Lopez de, 149, 150, 152
Santa Clara Co. v. Southern Pacific R.R. Co., 240
Santa Fe Trail, 145-146
Sargent, John Singer, 284
School and Society, 334
Schurz, Carl, 260, 261, 264
Science, 58-59, 110-111, 284, 294-295, 296, 299, 343, 345, 395-396
Scopes, John, trial of, 397
Scott, Sir Walter, 117, 168, 170
Scott, Winfield, 152, 188
Second Report on the Public Credit, 79
Sectionalism, 76, 100, 101-104, 178-198
Securities and Exchange Commission, 380
Securities Exchange Act (1934), 379-380
Sedition Acts: (1798) 86-87, 90; (1918) 328, 352
Segregation, 177, 217, 231, 307, 317, 333, 443-445
Selective service, 326, 391, 410
Self-determination, 328, 389
Seminole Indians, 104, 142, 143-144
Seminole Wars: first, 129; second, 143-144
Separation of powers, 73-74, 306
Serbia, 322, 328
Seven Days Battles, 202
Seven Years' War. See French and Indian War.
Sewall, Arthur, 271
Seward, William H., 194
Seymour, Horatio, 219
Shahn, Ben, 402, 461
Shays, Daniel, 71, 72, 81
Shays' Rebellion, 71, 72, 112

xliv

Clemens), 274, 282, 283, 460
Tweed Ring, 220, 259-260
Tweed, William Marcy, 220, 259-260
Tyler, John, 136, 137-138, 140, 148, 150, 151

Uncle Tom's Cabin, 171-172, 187
Underwood Tariff (1913), 306
Unemployment, 312, 356, 417-418, 426, 429; in Great Depression, 371, 373, 375, 378, 379, 381, 383, 385, 455
Union Labor party, 265
Union Pacific Railroad, 159, 210, 220, 241, 242, 250, 259
Union party, 213
Unions, 160-161, 367-368, 378, 383, 418, 426, 456-457. *See also* Labor.
Unitarianism, 115, 163-164, 171
United Automobile Workers, 384-385
United Labor party, 265
United Mine Workers, 290-291, 302, 308, 368, 383, 418
United Nations, 427, 428, 430, 433, 437; and Korean War, 436-439; organization of, 416, 423; and Suez crisis, 447
United Nations, Declaration of, 413
United States Steel Corp., 249, 293, 301, 384, 450
United Textile Workers, 368
Updike, John, 460
Urbanism, 227, 252, 292, 363, 454-455
Urrea, José, 149
Utah, 153, 155, 182, 186
Utrecht, Peace of (1713), 23, 27

Van Buren, Martin, 127, 128, 129, 132, 136, 137, 138, 150
Van der Rohe, Ludwig Mies, 462
Van Devanter, Willis, 381, 383
Vanderbilt, Arthur H., 429
Vanderbilt, Cornelius, 241, 243
Vanderbilt, William H., 243, 245
Veblen, Thorstein, 276-277, 340-341, 344
Velasco, Treaty of (1836), 150
Venezuela, 311
Vergennes, Count de, 41
Vermont, 96
Versailles Treaty (1919), 329-330, 359, 386, 387
Veterans' Bureau, 355
Vietnam, 446, 451
Villa, Pancho, 321-322
Vinson, Fred M., 445
Virginia, 6-9, 12-14, 20, 21, 24, 28, 29, 31, 33, 35, 43-45, 72, 78, 80, 86, 87, 92, 112, 114, 208
Virginia Company of London, 9, 10
Virginia Plan, 74, 75

Wabash case, 247-248
Wabash Railroad, 250
Wade-Davis bill (1864), 213
Wagner Act (1935), 381, 383, 384
Walden, 166
Walker, William, 191
Wallace, Henry A., 354, 391, 419, 435
War Democrats, 212
War for Independence. *See* American Revolution.
War Industries Board, 327
War Labor Board, 418
War Manpower Commission, 418
War of the Austrian Succession. *See* King George's War.
War of 1812, 93-99, 130, 149; causes of, 95-96; results of, 98-99, 108, 157
War of the Spanish Succession. *See* Queen Anne's War.
War Production Board, 417
Ward, Lester, 275, 276, 282, 294
Warren, Charles Dudley, 274, 283
Warren, Earl, 435
Washington, Booker T., 231, 333
Washington Conference (1922), 358-359
Washington Treaties (1922), 358-359, 386
Washington, George, 23, 24, 35, 70, 71, 82, 84, 87, 94; as commander of army, 34, 36-41; and Constitutional Convention, 72, 77; Farewell Address of, 84, 105-106; as President, 79-82, 84, 88, 92, 93
Watkins v. *U.S.*, 445
Watson, John B., 341
Watson, Thomas E., 271-272
Wealth of Nations, 226, 240
Wealth Tax Act (1935), 381
Weaver, James B., 263, 268, 269
Weaver, Max, 358, 401
Webster-Ashburton Treaty (1842), 136, 138
Webster, Daniel, 101, 129-130, 135, 136, 138, 185, 186
Webster, Noah, 108
Welfare state, 302, 372
West: expansion to, 43, 68, 91, 100, 108, 141-161, 174, 252, 310; land problem in, 29, 33, 44-45, 68
West Indies, 29, 39, 40, 41, 97, 141, 187
West Point, 39, 40
Weyl, Walter, 344-345
Weyler, Valerano, 312
Whigs, 137-138, 158; and free soil, 183; in South, 179; split of, 193. *See also* Elections.
Whiskey Rebellion, 80-81, 87
Whiskey Ring, 220

Whistler, James McNeill, 284
White Citizens Councils, 444
White, Hugh L., 135
White, William Allen, 259, 291, 292, 339, 391
Whitman, Walt, 171, 282, 284
Whitney, Eli, 102
Whittier, John Greenleaf, 171, 283
Whyte, William H., 456
Wickersham Commission, 365
Wickersham, Michael, 52
Wigglesworth, Michael, 52
Wilderness campaign, 206
Wiley, Dr. Harvey W., 299
Wilhelm II, Kaiser, 319
William and Mary, 16, xxix
Williams, Roger, 11, 53, 55-56
Williams, Tennessee, 459
Willkie Wendell L., 391, 419
Wilmot, David, 182
Wilmot Proviso, 182, 184, 185, 186
Wilson-Gorman Tariff (1894), 239, 270, 312
Wilson, James, 35, 73, 74, 75, 77, 108
Wilson, Woodrow, 64, 92, 291, 302, 306, 308, 317-318, 322, 352, 354, 356, 359, 360, and Mexico, 319-322; and Versailles Treaty, 329-330; and World War I, 322-327
Winthrop, John, 11, 51, 52
Wirt, William, 10, 132
Witherspoon, John, 113
"Wobblies" (Industrial Workers of the World), 302, 328
Wolfe, James, 24, 25
Wood, Thomas, 404
Wood, Leonard, 354
Wood, Grant, 402
Woolen Act (1699), 22
Works Progress Administration, 380-381, 400
World Court, 359
World War II, 295, 318, 322-327, 358
World War II, 358, 386-392, 398, 404
Wright, Chauncey, 279
Wright, Frank Lloyd, 337-338, 401, 462

XYZ Affair, 85-86

Yalta Conference, 424, 427, 428
Yancey, William L., 194
Yates v. U.S., 445
Yorktown, Battle of, 40, 41, 162
Youmans, Edward Livingston, 275
Young, Brigham, 155
Young Plan (1929), 359, 386
Yugoslavia, 427

Zimmermann Note, 325

Sherman Antitrust Act (1890), 246, 248-249, 251, 266, 290, 291, 297, 301, 307, 308, 378
Sherman, John, 257, 262-263
Sherman Silver Purchase Act (1890), 266, 269-270, 271
Sherman, William T., 204, 206
Shirley, William, 23
Silver Republican party, 271
Simons, Algie M., 342
Sinclair, Upton, 283, 299
Sino-Soviet alliance, 433, 438
Slaughterhouse Cases (1873), 240
Slavery, 70, 102, 103, 163, 166, 168, 171-172, 179, 181, 197, 212; in colonies, 20; conflict over, 153-154, 180-198, 225; in Texas, 150-151, 153-154
Slidell, John, 151, 208
Smith Act (1940), 445
Smith, Adam, 158, 226, 240, 275
Smith, Alfred E., 360-361, 374, 380
Smith-Connally Act (1943), 418
Smith-Hughes Act (1917), 394
Smith, J. Allen, 342
Smith, Jedediah S., 145
Smith, John, 10
Smith, Joseph, 155
Smoot-Hawley Tariff (1930), 361
Smyth v. Ames, 240
Social Darwinism, 243-244, 274-276, 277, 278, 279, 294
Social Gospel, 281, 295-296, 305, 336
Social Security Act (1935), 381, 383
Social Security system, 381, 442
Socialism, 278, 281, 352, 398, 429
Socialist party, 302, 306, 328, 352-355, 360, 374, 382
Soldiers' bonus bill (1924), 355
Solomon Islands, 310, 414, 420
South: characteristics of, before Civil War, 169, 179; secession of, 161, 191-197
South Carolina, 15, 20, 67, 78, 96, 444; and nullification, 132, 180
"South Carolina Exposition," 129-130
Southeast Asia Treaty Organization (SEATO), 447
Southern Alliance, 268, 269
Soviet Union. See Russia.
Spain, 7, 39, 41, 42, 73, 82-83, 147; colonial system of, 7, 26, 93, 104-105; relations with U.S., 70, 104, and Spanish-American War, 312-315
Spanish-American War, 273, 310, 311-316, 337
Sparkman, John J., 441
Specie Circular, 133, 135, 136
Spencer, Herbert, 243-244, 275, 276, 279, 294
Spoils system, 139, 259, 260, 261, 263
Stalin, Joseph, 413, 421, 423, 427, 428, 433, 446
Stalwarts, 262-263
Stamp Act Congress, 30
Standard Oil Co., 245-247, 301

Stanford, Leland, 242, 259
Staple Act (1663), 22
States' rights, 66, 85, 94, 98, 126, 129-130, 135, 137, 195, 209
States' Rights party, 435
Statute for Religious Freedom (1786), 114
Steffens, Lincoln, 296
Steinbeck, John, 403, 460
Stevenson, Adlai E. (1835-1914), 269
Stevenson, Adlai E. (1900-   ), 441-42
Stieglitz, Alfred, 338
Stimson, Henry L., 391
Stone, Edward, 462
Stone, Harlan F., 383
Stowe, Harriet Beecher, 171-172
Strong, Josiah, 281, 310
Stuart monarchy, 12, 21, 48, 55, xxix
Stuyvesant, Peter, 13
Sudetenland, 389
Suez Crisis, 447-448
Suffrage, requirements for, 17, 53, 68, 139, 214, 215, 221, 363
Suffolk Resolves, 34
Sugar Act (1764), 26, 30, 32
Sullivan, Louis H., 284, 337-338
Sumner, William Graham, 275, 276
Sumner, Charles, 190-191
Sunday, Billy, 337
Supreme Court of U.S., 79, 89, 90, 270, 290, 301, 343-344, 360, 385; and "Court-packing" bill, 382-383; and Dred Scott decision, 192; under Jackson, 134-135; and New Deal legislation, 377, 378, 381; post-World War II, 445-446; and segregation, 231, 443, 449; and Sherman Antitrust Act, 249, 308
Supreme Court Retirement Act (1937), 383
Sutherland, George, 381
Sutter's Mill, 154
Sylvis, William, 250
Syria, 431, 448

Taft-Hartley Act (1947), 426-427, 436, 443
Taft, Robert A., 426, 440
Taft, William Howard, 301, 302-305, 317, 319, 327
Tallmadge, James, Jr., 103-104
Tammany Hall, 220, 259, 296
Taney, Roger B., 133, 134-135, 154, 192
Tarbell, Ida M., 296
Tariff: of 1789, 79; of 1816, 100; of 1824, 126, 129; of 1827, 126; of 1828, 126, 127, 129; of 1832, 132; of 1842, 138
Tariff Commission, 356
Tariff of Abominations (1828), 126, 127, 129
Tariff policies, 99-100, 180, 265, 270, 275, 304, 305, 450; during New Deal, 380; in 1920's, 356, 359.

Taussig, F. W., 341
Taxation, 30, 32; under Articles, 67, 71; in colonies, 18, 30, 33, 67; of income, 268, 269, 270, 271, 297, 305, 324, 327, 426, 438, 450, 452
Taylor, Myron C., 384
Taylor, Zachary, 151-153, 183-185, 188
Tea Act (1773), 33
Teapot Dome Scandal, 355, 356
Technocracy, 374-375
Teheran Conference, 416
Teller Amendment, 313, 314, 315
Teller, Henry M., 271
Temperance movement, 163, 223, 295, 364-365
Tennessee Valley Authority, 300-301, 377, 442
Tenure of Office Act (1867), 218
Texas, 104, 182; annexation of, 140, 141, 148, 150-151, 153-154; Republic of, 142, 147, 148-149; slavery in, 153-154
Texas and Pacific Railroad, 220, 221
Thames, Battle of the, 96
Theater, 57, 170, 403, 458-459
Theory of the Leisure Class, 277, 341
Thomas, Norman, 374
Thoreau, Henry David, 110, 165-166, 171
Thorndike, Edward L., 341
Three-fifths Compromise, 76, 181
Thurman, Allen G., 265
Thurmond, J. Strom, 435
Tilden, Samuel J., 220, 260, 263
Timber and Stone Act (1878), 254
Timber Culture Act (1873), 254
Tippecanoe, Battle of, 95, 96, 137
Tito, Marshal, 427
Tobacco, 18, 20, 21, 42, 102, 179, 180
Tojo, Hideki, 412
Tokyo, 414, 421, 424, 448
Toleration Acts: of 1689, 55, 56; in Maryland, 1649, 12
Townshend Duties, 26, 31, 32
Township system, 18, 69
Trade, 7, 8, 9, 18, 19, 21, 42, 70, 106, 145, 374; with Asia, 141, 310, 314, 316; with Europe, 82, 141, 157; of furs, 13, 23, 144-145, 154; with Indians, 10, 18, 20, 145
Trade Expansion Act (1962), 450, 451
Trading-with-the-Enemy Act (1917), 328
Transcendentalism, 163-165, 223
Transportation, 100, 156-157, 158, 176
Treasury Department, 79, 80
Tripartite Pact (1940), 411
Trist, Nicholas P., 153
Truman Doctrine, 428-429
Truman, Harry S., 419, 423-430, 433-442, 450
Trusts, 244-249, 292, 301, 339, 352
Turkey, 329, 427, 428, 429
Turner, Frederick Jackson, 170, 310, 342
Twain, Mark (Samuel Langhorne